CAMBRIDGE LIBRARY COLLECTION

Books of enduring scholarly value

Classics

From the Renaissance to the nineteenth century, Latin and Greek were
compulsory subjects in almost all European universities, and most early
modern scholars published their research and conducted international
correspondence in Latin. Latin had continued in use in Western Europe long
after the fall of the Roman empire as the lingua franca of the educated classes
and of law, diplomacy, religion and university teaching. The flight of Greek
scholars to the West after the fall of Constantinople in 1453 gave impetus
to the study of ancient Greek literature and the Greek New Testament.
Eventually, just as nineteenth-century reforms of university curricula were
beginning to erode this ascendancy, developments in textual criticism and
linguistic analysis, and new ways of studying ancient societies, especially
archaeology, led to renewed enthusiasm for the Classics. This collection
offers works of criticism, interpretation and synthesis by the outstanding
scholars of the nineteenth century.

Dialogues of Plato

One of the leading scholars and academic administrators of his time,
Benjamin Jowett (1817–93) was Master of Balliol College as well as Regius
Professor of Greek and, for a time, vice-chancellor at Oxford University.
Along with his achievements in the area of academic reform, Jowett
is remembered for this four-volume translation of Plato's dialogues.
Characterising Plato as the 'father of idealism', Jowett reminds readers
that while 'he may be illustrated by the writings of moderns ... he must be
interpreted by his own, and by his place in the history of philosophy'. This
second volume consists of *Timaeus* and *Critias* together with the well-known
Republic; each dialogue is given a separate introduction. Jowett's work
represents a towering achievement in the field of classical and philosophical
studies that had important influence on the subsequent study of Plato.

Cambridge University Press has long been a pioneer in the reissuing of out-of-print titles from its own backlist, producing digital reprints of books that are still sought after by scholars and students but could not be reprinted economically using traditional technology. The Cambridge Library Collection extends this activity to a wider range of books which are still of importance to researchers and professionals, either for the source material they contain, or as landmarks in the history of their academic discipline.

Drawing from the world-renowned collections in the Cambridge University Library, and guided by the advice of experts in each subject area, Cambridge University Press is using state-of-the-art scanning machines in its own Printing House to capture the content of each book selected for inclusion. The files are processed to give a consistently clear, crisp image, and the books finished to the high quality standard for which the Press is recognised around the world. The latest print-on-demand technology ensures that the books will remain available indefinitely, and that orders for single or multiple copies can quickly be supplied.

The Cambridge Library Collection will bring back to life books of enduring scholarly value (including out-of-copyright works originally issued by other publishers) across a wide range of disciplines in the humanities and social sciences and in science and technology.

Dialogues of Plato

Translated into English,
with Analyses and Introduction

VOLUME 2

BENJAMIN JOWETT

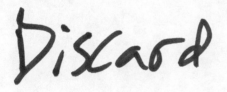

CAMBRIDGE
UNIVERSITY PRESS

CAMBRIDGE UNIVERSITY PRESS

Cambridge, New York, Melbourne, Madrid, Cape Town, Singapore,
São Paolo, Delhi, Dubai, Tokyo

Published in the United States of America by Cambridge University Press, New York

www.cambridge.org
Information on this title: www.cambridge.org/9781108012119

© in this compilation Cambridge University Press 2010

This edition first published 1871
This digitally printed version 2010

ISBN 978-1-108-01211-9 Paperback

THE

DIALOGUES OF PLATO

JOWETT

VOL. II.

a

London

MACMILLAN AND CO.

PUBLISHERS TO THE UNIVERSITY OF

Oxford

THE

DIALOGUES OF PLATO

Translated into English

WITH ANALYSES AND INTRODUCTIONS

BY

B. JOWETT, M.A.

MASTER OF BALLIOL COLLEGE

REGIUS PROFESSOR OF GREEK IN THE UNIVERSITY OF OXFORD

IN FOUR VOLUMES

VOL. II

Oxford

AT THE CLARENDON PRESS

M DCCC LXXI

CONTENTS.

THE REPUBLIC.

INTRODUCTION.

THE Republic of Plato is the longest of his works with the exception of the Laws, and is certainly the greatest of them. There are nearer approaches to modern metaphysics in the Philebus and in the Sophist. The Politicus or Statesman is more ideal; the form and institutions of the State are more clearly drawn out in the Laws; as works of art, the Symposium and the Protagoras are of higher excellence. But no other Dialogue of Plato has the same largeness of view and the same perfection of style; no other contains more graphic descriptions of character, or is richer in humour and imagery. Nor in any other Dialogue is the attempt made to unite the speculative and practical, or to interweave the State with philosophy. Neither must we forget that the Republic is but the third part of a still larger work which was to have included an ideal history of Athens, as well as a political and physical philosophy. Lastly, Plato may be regarded as the 'captain or leader' of a goodly band of followers; in him is to be found the original of Cicero's De Republica, of St. Augustin's City of God, of the Utopia of Sir Thomas More, and of the numerous modern writings which are framed upon the same model. The Republic of Plato is also the first treatise upon education, of which Milton and Locke, Rousseau, Jean Paul, and Goethe are the legitimate descendants. Like Dante or Bunyan, he has a revelation of another world; in the early Church he exercised a real influence on theology, and at the Revival of Literature on politics. And many of the latest thoughts of modern philosophers and statesmen, such as the unity of knowledge, the reign of law, and the equality of the sexes, have been anticipated in a dream by Plato.

The argument of the Republic is the search after Justice, the nature of which is first hinted at by Cephalus—then discussed on the basis of the old proverbial morality by Socrates and Polemarchus—then caricatured by Thrasymachus and partially explained by Socrates—reduced to an abstraction by Glaucon and Adeimantus, and having become invisible in the individual reappears at length in the ideal State which is constructed by Socrates. The·State introduces the subject of education, of which the first outline is drawn after the old Hellenic model, providing only for an improved religion and morality, and more simplicity in music and gymnastic, and greater harmony of the individual and the State. But this leads to the conception of a higher state, in which ' no man calls anything his own,' and in which there is neither ' marrying nor giving in marriage,' and ' kings are philosophers' and ' philosophers are kings;' and there is another and higher education, intellectual as well as moral and religious, of science as well as art, and not of youth only but of the whole of life. Such a State soon begins to degenerate, and is hardly to be realized in this world. The old quarrel of poetry and philosophy which has been lightly touched upon in the earlier books of the Republic is then fought out to the end. Poetry is discovered to be an imitation thrice removed from the truth, and Homer, as well as the dramatic poets, having been condemned as an imitator, is sent into banishment along with them. And the idea of the State is supplemented by the revelation of a future life.

The division into books, like all similar divisions[1], is probably later than the age of Plato. The natural divisions are six in number;—first, book i. and the first half of book ii. down to p. 368, which is introductory; the first book containing a refutation of the popular and sophistical notions of justice, and concluding, like some of the earlier Dialogues, without arriving at a definite conclusion. To this is appended a restatement of the nature of justice according to common opinion, and an answer is demanded to the question—What is justice, stripped of appearances? The second division includes the remainder of the second and the whole of the third and fourth books, which are mainly occupied with the construction of the first State and the first education. The third division consists of the fifth, sixth, and seventh books, in which philosophy rather than justice is the subject of enquiry, and the second State is constructed on principles of communism and ruled by

---

[1] Cp. Sir G. C. Lewis in the Classical Museum, vol. ii. p. 1.

philosophers, and the contemplation of the idea of good takes the place of the social and political virtues. In the eighth and ninth books the perversions of States and the individuals which correspond to them are reviewed in succession; and the nature of pleasure and the principle of tyranny are further analyzed in the individual character. The tenth book is the conclusion of the whole, in which the relations of philosophy to poetry are finally determined, and the happiness of the citizens in this life, which has now been assured, is crowned by the vision of another.

Or a more general division into two parts may be adopted; the first (books i—iv) containing the description of a state framed generally in accordance with Hellenic notions of religion and morality, while in the second (v—x) the Hellenic state is transformed into an ideal kingdom of philosophy, of which all other governments are the perversions. These two points of view are really opposed, and the opposition is only veiled by the genius of Plato. The Republic, like the Phaedrus (see vol. i. p. 551), is an imperfect whole; the higher light of philosophy breaks through the regularity of the Hellenic temple, which at last fades away into the heavens (592 B). Whether this imperfection of structure arises from an enlargement of the plan, or, perhaps, from the composition of the work at different times, is one of those questions, like the similar question about the Iliad and Odyssee, which are worth asking, but which cannot have a distinct answer. In the age of Plato there was no regular mode of publication, and an author would have the less scruple in altering or adding to a work which was known only to a few of his friends. There is no absurdity in supposing that he may have laid his labours aside for a time, or turned from one work to another; and such interruptions would be more likely to occur in the case of a long than of a short writing. In all attempts to determine the chronological order of the Platonic writings on internal evidence, this uncertainty about any single work being composed at one time is a disturbing element, which must be admitted to affect longer works, such as the Republic and the Laws, more than shorter ones. But, on the other hand, the seeming discrepancies of the Republic may only arise out of the discordant elements which the philosopher has attempted to unite in a single whole, perhaps without being himself able to recognize the inconsistency which is obvious to us. For there is a criticism of after ages which few great writers have ever been able to anticipate for themselves. And the supposition that the Republic was written at one time, and without interruption, is confirmed by numerous references from one part of the work to another.

The second title, 'Concerning Justice,' is not the one by which the Republic is generally quoted in antiquity, and may therefore be assumed to be of later date. Morgenstern and others have asked whether the definition of justice, which is the professed aim, or the construction of the State, is the principal argument of the work. The answer is that the two blend in one, and are two faces of the same truth; for justice is the order of the State, and the State is the visible embodiment of justice under the conditions of human society. The one is the soul and the other is the body, and the Greek ideal of the State, as of the individual, is a fair mind in a fair body. In Hegelian language the State is the reality of which justice is the idea. Or, as in Christian theology, the kingdom of God is within, and yet is imagined also as an external kingdom. And when the constitution of the State is completed, the conception of justice is not dismissed, but reappears under the same or different names throughout the work, both as the inner law of the individual soul, and finally as the principle of rewards and punishments in another life. The virtues are based on justice of which common honesty in buying and selling is the shadow, and justice is based on the idea of good, which is the harmony of the world, and is reflected both in the institutions of states and in the motions of the heavenly bodies (cp. Tim. 47).

Neither is it necessary to discuss at length another question which has been raised by Boeckh, respecting the imaginary date at which the conversation was held (the year 411 B.C. which is proposed by him will do as well as any other) ; for a writer of fiction, and especially a writer who, like Plato, is notoriously careless of chronology, only aims at general probability. Whether all the persons mentioned in the Republic could ever have met at any one time is not a difficulty which would have occurred to an Athenian reading the work forty years later, or to Plato himself at the time of writing (any more than to Shakespeare in a parallel case); and need not greatly trouble us now. Yet this may be also one of those questions which are worth asking, because the investigation shows that we cannot argue historically from the dates in Plato, and have therefore no need to waste time in inventing far-fetched reconcilements of them (such, for example, as the conjecture that

Glaucon and Adeimantus are not the brothers but the uncles of Plato)[2], in order to avoid chronological difficulties.

The principal characters in the Republic are Cephalus, Polemarchus, Thrasymachus, Socrates, Glaucon, and Adeimantus. Cephalus appears in the introduction only, Polemarchus drops at the end of the first argument, and Thrasymachus is reduced to silence at the close of the first book. The main discussion is carried on by Socrates, Glaucon, and Adeimantus. Among the audience are Lysias the orator and Euthydemus the sons of Cephalus and brothers of Polemarchus, an unknown Charmantides—these are mute auditors; also there is Cleitophon, who once interrupts (340 A), and there, as in the Dialogue which bears his name, appears as the friend and ally of Thrasymachus.

Cephalus, the father of Polemarchus and his two brothers, is the patriarch of the house who has been appropriately engaged in offering a sacrifice. He is the pattern of an old man who has almost done with life, and is at peace with himself and with all mankind. He seems to linger around the memory of the past, and is not without consolation in the future. He is eager that Socrates should come to visit him, fond of the poetry of the last generation, happy in the consciousness of a well-spent life, glad at having escaped from the tyranny of youthful lusts. His love of conversation, his indifference to money, even his prolixity and repetition, are interesting traits of character. The respectful attention shown to him by Socrates, who must however be asking questions of him as of all men, is also remarkable. The moderation with which old age is pictured by him as a very tolerable portion of existence is characteristic, not only of him, but of Greek feeling generally, and contrasts with the exaggeration of Cicero in his work on old age. The evening of life is described by Plato in the most expressive manner, yet with the fewest possible touches. As Cicero remarks, the aged Cephalus would have been out of place in the discussion which follows, and which he could neither have understood nor taken part in without a violation of dramatic propriety (cp. Melesias in the Laches).

His 'son and heir' Polemarchus has the frankness and impetuousness of youth; he is for detaining Socrates by force in the opening scene, and will not 'let him off' (449 B) on the subject of women and children. Like Cephalus, he is limited in his point of view, and represents the proverbial stage of morality which has rules of life rather than principles; and he quotes Simonides as his father had quoted Pindar. But after appealing to this authority he has no more to say; the inferences which he draws are only elicited from him by the dialectic of Socrates. He has not yet experienced the influence of the Sophists like Glaucon and Adeimantus, nor is he sensible of the necessity of refuting them; he belongs, in short, to the pre-Socratic age. He is bewildered by Socrates to such a degree that he does not know what he is saying. From his brother Lysias (contra Eratos, p. 121) we learn that he fell a victim to the thirty tyrants, but no allusion is made to his fate, nor to the circumstance that Cephalus and his family were of Syracusan origin, and had migrated to Athens.

The 'Chalcedonian giant,' Thrasymachus, of whom we have already heard in the Phaedrus (p. 267), is the personification of the Sophists according to Plato's conception of them, in some of their worst characteristics. He is vain and blustering, refusing to discourse unless he is paid, fond of making an oration, and hoping in that way to escape the inevitable Socrates; but a mere child in argument, and unable to foresee that the next 'move' (to use a Platonic expression) will 'shut him up' (487 B). He has reached the stage of framing general notions, and in this respect may be regarded as in advance of Cephalus and Polemarchus. But he is incapable of defending them in a discussion, and vainly tries to cover his confusion with banter and insolence. He further makes an irrelevant appeal to the experience of daily life. Whether such doctrines as are attributed to him by Plato were really held either by him or by any other Sophist is uncertain:—in the eagerness for generalization such fundamental errors might easily grow up, and are certainly put into the mouths of speakers in Thucydides; but we are concerned at present with Plato's description of him, and not with the historical reality. The inequality of the contest adds greatly to the humour of the scene. He is utterly helpless in the hands of Socrates, who knows how to touch all the springs of vanity and weakness in him. His determination to cram down their throats, or put 'bodily into their souls' his own words, elicits a cry of horror from Socrates. The state of his temper is quite as worthy of remark as the process of the argument. Nothing is more amusing than his complete submission when he has been once thoroughly beaten. At first he seems to carry on the discussion with reluctance, but soon with apparent good-will, and he even testifies his interest at a later stage by one or two occasional remarks (v. 450 A, B). When attacked by Glaucon (in book vi. 498 C, D) he is humorously protected by Socrates 'as one who has never been his enemy and is now his friend.'

When Thrasymachus has been silenced, the two principal respondents, Glaucon and Adeimantus, appear on the scene; here as in Greek tragedy (cp. Introd. to Phaedo, vol. i.) three actors are introduced. At first sight the two sons of Ariston may seem to wear a family likeness, like the two friends Simmias and Cebes in the Phaedo. But on a nearer examination of them the similarity vanishes, and they are seen to be distinct characters. Glaucon is the impetuous youth who can 'just never have enough of fechting' (cp. the character of him in Xen. Mem. iii. 6.); the man of pleasure who is acquainted with the mysteries of love (v. 474 D); the 'juvenis qui gaudet canibus,' and who improves the breed of animals (v. 459 A); the lover of art and music (iii. 398 D, E) who has all the experiences of youthful life. He is full of quickness and penetration, piercing easily below the clumsy platitudes of Thrasymachus to the real difficulty; he turns out to the light the seamy side of human life, and yet does not lose faith in the just and true. It is Glaucon who seizes what may be termed the ludicrous relation of the philosopher or the state of philosophers to the world, to whom a state of simplicity is 'a city of pigs,' who is always prepared with a jest (iii. 398 C, vi. 509 C) when the argument offers him an opportunity, and is ever ready to second the humour of Socrates and to appreciate the ridiculous, whether in the connoisseurs of music (vii. 531 A), or in the lovers of theatricals (v. 475 D), or in the fantastic behaviour of the citizens of democracy (viii. 557 foll.). His weaknesses are several times alluded to by Socrates (iii. 402 E), who, however, will not allow him to be attacked by his brother Adeimantus (viii. 548 D, E). He is a soldier, and, like Adeimantus, has been distinguished at the battle of Megara (ii. 368 A, anno 456?). The character of Adeimantus is deeper and graver, and the profounder objections are commonly put into his mouth. Glaucon is more demonstrative, and generally opens the game; Adeimantus pursues the argument further. Glaucon has more of the liveliness and quick sympathy of youth; Adeimantus has the maturer judgment of a grown-up man of the world. In the second book, when Glaucon insists that justice and injustice shall be considered without regard to their consequences, Adeimantus remarks that they are regarded by mankind in general only for the sake of their consequences. In a similar vein of reflection Adeimantus urges at the beginning of the fourth book that Socrates fails in making his citizens happy, and is answered that happiness is not the direct aim, but the indirect consequence of the good government of a State. It is Adeimantus again who volunteers the criticism of common sense on the Socratic method of argument, and who refuses to let Socrates pass lightly over the question of women and children. It is Adeimantus who is the respondent in the more argumentative, as Glaucon in the lighter and more imaginative portions of the Dialogue. For example, throughout the greater part of the sixth book, the causes of the corruption of philosophy, and the conception of the idea of good are discussed with Adeimantus. At the end of the book, Glaucon resumes his place of principal respondent; but he has a difficulty in apprehending the higher education of Socrates, and makes some false hits in the course of the discussion (526 D, 527 D).

Thus in a succession of characters Plato represents the successive stages of morality, beginning with the Athenian gentleman of the olden time, who is followed by the practical man of that day regulating his life by proverbs and saws; to him succeeds the wild generalization of the Sophists, and lastly come the young disciples of the great teacher, who know the sophistical arguments but will not be convinced by them, and desire to go deeper into the nature of things.

The character of Socrates in the Republic is not wholly consistent. In the first book we appear to have more of the real Socrates, such as he is depicted in the earliest Dialogues of Plato and in the Apology. He is ironical, provoking, questioning, the old enemy of the Sophists, ready to put on the mask of Silenus as well as to argue seriously. But in the sixth book his enmity towards the Sophists abates; he acknowledges that they are the representatives rather than the corruptors of the world (vi. 492 A). He also becomes more dogmatic and constructive, passing beyond the range either of the political or the speculative ideas of the real Socrates. In one passage (vi. 506 C) Plato himself seems to intimate that the time had now come for Socrates, who had passed his whole life in philosophy, to give his own opinion, and not to be always repeating the notions of other men. There is no evidence that either the idea of good or the conception of a perfect state were comprehended in the Socratic teaching, though he certainly dwelt on the nature of the universal and of final causes (cp. Xen. Mem. 1. 4; Phaed. 97); and a deep thinker like him, in his thirty or forty years of public teaching, could hardly have failed to touch on the nature of family relations, for which there is also some positive evidence in the Memorabilia (Mem. 1. 2, 51 foll.). The Socratic method is nominally retained; and every inference is either put into the mouth of the respondent or represented as the common discovery of him and Socrates. But any one can see that this is a mere form, the affectation of which grows wearisome as the work advances. The nature of the process is truly characterized by Glaucon, when he describes himself as a companion who is not good for much in an investigation, but can see what he is shown (iv. 432 C), and may, perhaps, give the answer to a question more aptly than another (v. 474 A).

Neither can we be absolutely certain that Socrates himself taught the immortality of the soul, which is unknown to his disciple Glaucon in the Republic (book x. 608 D); nor is there any reason to suppose that he used myths or revelations of another world as a vehicle of instruction, or that he would have banished poetry or have denounced the Greek mythology. His favourite oath is retained, and a slight mention is made of the daemonium, or internal sign, which is alluded to by Socrates as a phenomenon peculiar to himself (book vi. 496 C). A real element of Socratic teaching, which is more prominent in the Republic than in any of the other Dialogues of Plato, is the use of example and illustration (τὰ φορτικὰ αὐτῷ προσφέροντες, iv. 442 E): 'Let us apply the test of common instances.' 'You,' says Adeimantus, ironically, in the sixth book, 'are so unaccustomed to speak in images.' And this use of examples or images, though truly Socratic in origin, is enlarged by the genius of Plato into the form of an allegory or parable, which embodies in the concrete what has been already described, or is about to be described, in the abstract. Thus the figure of the cave in book vii. is a recapitulation of the divisions of knowledge in book vi. The composite animal in book ix. is an allegory of the parts of the soul. The captain and the ship and the true pilot in book vi. are a figure of the relation of philosophers to the State which is about to be described.

Plato is most true to the character of his master when he describes him as 'not of this world.' And with this the paradox of the ideal state and the other paradoxes of the Republic, though they cannot be shown to have been speculations of Socrates, are in harmony. He is not any nearer the common opinions of mankind when he is constructing than when he is destroying. But it must also be observed that this opposition to the world in the latter part of the work turns to a sort of ironical pity or love. The world is incapable of philosophy, and is therefore at enmity with the philosopher; but this arises from an unavoidable necessity (vi. 494 foll.): for they have never seen him as he truly is in his own proper image; they are only acquainted with artificial systems in which there is no native force of truth—words which admit of another application. They do not know how to measure, and therefore are angry with those who take their measure. They are to be pitied or laughed at, not to be quarrelled with; they mean well with their nostrums, but are unconscious that they are cutting off a Hydra's head (iv. 426 D, E). This moderation towards those who are in error is one of the most characteristic features of Socrates in the Republic. In all the different representations of Socrates, whether of Xenophon or Plato, and amid the differences of the earlier or later Dialogues, he always retains the character of the unwearied and disinterested seeker after truth, without which he would have ceased to be Socrates.

Leaving the characters we may now analyze the contents of the Republic, and then proceed to consider, (1) The general aspects of this Hellenic ideal of the State. (2) The modern lights in which the thoughts of Plato may be read.

BOOK I. The Republic opens with a truly Greek scene—a festival in honour of the goddess Bendis which is held at the Piraeus; to this is added the promise of an equestrian torch-race in the evening. The whole work is supposed to be recited by Socrates on the day after the festival to a small party, consisting of Critias, Timaeus, Hermocrates, and another; this we learn from the first words of the Timaeus.

When the rhetorical advantage of reciting the Dialogue has been gained, the attention is not distracted by any reference to the audience; nor is the reader further reminded of the extraordinary length of the narrative. The incident out of which the conversation had arisen on the preceding day is described as follows:—Socrates and his companion Glaucon are just leaving the festival when they are detained by a message from Polemarchus, who soon arrives accompanied by Adeimantus, the brother of Glaucon, and with playful violence compels them to remain, promising them not only the torch-race, but the pleasure of conversation with the young, which to Socrates is a far greater attraction. They return to the house of Cephalus, Polemarchus' father, who is now in extreme old age, and is found sitting upon a cushioned seat crowned for a sacrifice. 'You should come to me oftener, Socrates, for I am too old to go to you, and at my time of life, having lost other pleasures, I care the more for conversation.' Socrates asks him what he thinks of age, to which the old man replies, that the miseries and discontents of age are to be attributed to the tempers of men, and that age is a time of peace in which the tyranny of the passions is no longer felt. Yes, replies Socrates, but the world will say, Cephalus, that you are happy in old age because you are rich. 'And there is something in that, Socrates, as Themistocles replied to the Seriphian, "Neither you, if you had been an Athenian, nor I if I had been a Seriphian, would ever have been famous," I might reply to you that neither a good poor man can be happy in age, nor yet a bad rich man.' Socrates remarks that Cephalus appears not to care about riches, and would like to know what he considers the chief advantage of them. Cephalus answers that, when you are old the belief in the world below grows upon you, and then to have done justice and never to have been compelled to do injustice through poverty, or to have deceived any one, is felt to be an unspeakable blessing. Socrates, who is evidently preparing for an argument, next asks, What is the meaning of this word justice? To tell the truth and pay your debts? No more than this? Or must we admit exceptions? Ought I, for example, to put back into the hands of my friend, who is a madman, the sword which I borrowed of him when he was in his right mind? 'There must be exceptions.' 'And yet,' said Polemarchus, 'the definition given has the authority of Simonides.' Here Cephalus retires to look after the sacrifices, and bequeaths, as Socrates says, the possession of the argument to his heir, Polemarchus. . . The picture of old age is finished, and Plato, as his manner is, has already lightly touched the key-note of the whole work in asking for the definition of justice, just raising Glaucon's question respecting external goods, and preparing for the concluding mythus of the world below in the slight allusion of Cephalus. The first explanation has been supported by a gnome of Simonides; and now Socrates has a mind to show that the resolution of justice into two unconnected precepts, which have no common principle, fails to satisfy the demands of dialectic.

He proceeds: What did Simonides mean by this saying? Did he mean that I was to give back arms to a madman? 'No, not in that case, not if the parties are friends, and evil would result. He meant that you were to do what was proper, good to friends, and harm to enemies.' Every act does something to somebody; and following this analogy, Socrates asks, What is this due and proper thing which justice does, and to whom? He is answered that justice does good to friends and harm to enemies. But in what way good or harm? 'In making alliances with the one, and going to war with the other.' Then in time of peace what is the good of justice? The answer is that justice is of use in contracts, and contracts are money partnerships. Yes; but how in such partnerships is the just man of more use than any other man? 'When you want to have money safely kept and not used.' Then justice will be useful when money is useless. And there is another difficulty: justice, like war or any other art, must be of opposites, good at attack as well as at defence, at stealing as well as guarding. But then justice is a thief, though a hero notwithstanding, after the fashion of some Homeric heroes, who were 'excellent above all men in theft and perjury'—to such a pass have you and Homer and Simonides brought us; though I do not forget that the thieving must be for the good of friends and the harm of enemies. And still there arises another question: Are friends to be interpreted as real or seeming; enemies as real or seeming? And are our friends to be only the good, and our enemies to be the evil? The answer is that we must do good to our seeming and real good friends, and evil to our seeming and real evil enemies—good to the good, and evil to the evil. But ought we to render evil for evil at all, for this will only make men more evil? Can justice produce injustice any more than heat cold? The final conclusion is, that no sage or poet ever said that the just return evil for evil; this was a maxim of some tyrant, Periander, Perdiccas, or some other tyrant.

. . . . Thus the first stage of aphoristic or unconscious morality is shown to be inadequate to the wants of the age; the authority of the poets is set aside, and through the winding mazes of dialectic we make an approach to the Christian precept of forgiveness of injuries. We may note in passing the antiquity of casuistry, which not only arises out of the conflict of established principles in particular cases, but also out of the effort to attain them, and is prior as well as posterior to our fundamental notions of morality. The 'interrogation' of moral ideas; the appeal to the authority of Homer; the conclusion that the maxim, 'Do good to your friends and harm to your enemies,' being erroneous, could not have been the word of any great man (cp. ii. 380 A, B) are all of them very characteristic of the Platonic Socrates.

Here Thrasymachus, who had made several attempts to interrupt, but had hitherto been kept in order by the company, takes advantage of a pause and rushes into the arena, like a savage animal beginning with a roar. 'Socrates,' he says, 'what folly is this? Why do you agree to be vanquished by one another in a pretended argument?' He then prohibits all the ordinary definitions of justice; to which Socrates replies that he cannot tell how many twelve is, if he is forbidden to say 2×6, or 3×4, or 6×2, or 4×3. At first Thrasymachus is reluctant to argue; but at length, with a promise of payment on the part of the company and of praise from Socrates, he is induced to open the game. 'Listen,' he says; 'my answer is that might is right, justice the interest of the stronger: now praise me.' Let me understand you first. Do you mean that because Polydamas the wrestler, who is stronger than we are, finds the eating of beef for his interest, the eating of beef is also for our interest, who are not so strong? Thrasymachus is indignant at the illustration, and explains his meaning to be that the rulers make laws for their own interests. But suppose, says Socrates, that the ruler or stronger makes a mistake—then the interest of the stronger is not his interest. Thrasymachus escapes this absurdity by introducing the word 'thinks'—not the actual interest of the ruler, but what the ruler thinks his interest, is justice.

This line of argument is not pursued further, and in what follows Thrasymachus does in fact withdraw his admission, that the ruler may make a mistake, by affirming that the ruler as a ruler is infallible. Socrates is quite ready to accept the new position, which he equally turns against Thrasymachus by the help of the analogy of the arts. Every art or science has an interest, but this interest is to be distinguished from the accidental interest of the artist, and is only concerned with the good of the things or persons which come under the art. And justice has an interest which is the interest not of the ruler or judge, but of those who come under his sway.

Thrasymachus is on the brink of the inevitable conclusion, when he makes a bold diversion. 'Tell me, Socrates,' he says, 'have you a nurse?' What a question! Why do you ask? 'Because I should imagine that she never wipes your nose, as she has never taught you what the shepherd does with his sheep. Like the ruler he fattens them for his use. And experience proves that in every relation of life the just man loses and the unjust gains, especially where injustice is on the grand scale, which is quite another thing from the petty rogueries of swindlers and burglars and robbers of temples. The language of men proves this—our gracious and blessed tyrant and the like—all which tends to show (1) that justice is the interest of the stronger; and (2) that injustice is more profitable and also stronger than justice.'

Thrasymachus, who is better at a speech than at a close argument, having deluged the company with words, has a mind to escape. But the others will not let him go, and Socrates adds a humble but earnest request that he would not desert them at such a crisis of their fate. 'And what can I do more for you?' he said; 'would you have me put the words bodily into your souls?' God forbid! replies Socrates; we only want you to be consistent in the use of terms, and not to employ 'physician' in an exact sense, and then again 'shepherd' or 'ruler' in an inexact sense,—whereas the ruler in himself, and the shepherd in himself are looking only to the good of their flocks and not to their own; and yet you will insist that the ruler likes being in office. 'No doubt about that,' replies Thrasymachus. Then why are they paid? Is not the reason that their interest is not comprehended in their art, and is therefore the concern of another art, which is common to the arts in general, and therefore not identical with any one of them; and this is the art of pay. Nor would any man be a ruler unless he were induced by the hope of reward or the fear of punishment; the reward is money or honour, the punishment is the necessity of being ruled by a worse man than himself. And if a State were composed of good men only, there would be as much 'nolo episcopari' as there is at present of the opposite. . . . . This satire on existing governments is heightened by the simple and apparently incidental manner in which the remark is introduced. There is a similar irony in the argument that the governors of mankind are disinterested, because they receive pay. . . . .

Enough of this: the other assertion of Thrasymachus is far more important—that the unjust life is more gainful than the just. Now, as you and I, Glaucon, are not convinced of this, we ought to try and answer him, and as we cannot number the gains of either, we had better proceed by making mutual admissions of the truth to one another.

Thrasymachus had asserted that perfect injustice was more gainful than perfect justice, and after a little hesitation he is induced by Socrates to admit the still greater paradox that injustice is virtue and justice vice. Socrates praises his frankness, and assumes the attitude of one whose only wish is to understand the meaning of his opponents. At the same time he is weaving a net in which Thrasymachus is finally enclosed. The admission is elicited from him that the just man only seeks to gain an advantage over the unjust, but not over the just—while the unjust would gain an advantage over either. Socrates, in order to test this statement, employs once more the favourite analogy of the arts. The musician, doctor, skilled artist of any sort, does not seek to get more than the skilled, but only more than the unskilled (that is to say, he works up to a rule, standard, law, and does not exceed it), whereas the unskilled makes random efforts at excess. Thus the skilled falls on the side of the good, and the unskilled on the side of the evil, and the just is the skilled, and the unjust is the unskilled. . . . .

There was great difficulty in bringing Thrasymachus to this point; the day was hot and he was streaming with perspiration, and for the first time in his life he was seen to blush. But his other thesis that injustice was stronger than justice has not yet been refuted, and Socrates now proceeds to the consideration of this, which, with the assistance of Thrasymachus, he hopes to clear up; the latter is at first churlish, but in the judicious hands of Socrates is soon restored to good humour... Is there not honour among thieves? Is not the strength of injustice only a remnant of justice? Is not absolute injustice absolute weakness also? A house that is divided against itself cannot stand; two men who quarrel detract from one another's strength, and he who is at war with himself is the enemy of himself and the gods. Not wickedness therefore, but semi-wickedness flourishes in states,—a remnant of good is needed in order to make union in action possible,—there is no kingdom of evil in this world.

There is another question to be answered: Is the just or the unjust happier? Has not every art an end, and is there not an excellence or virtue by which every end is accomplished? And is not the end of the soul happiness, and justice the excellence of the soul by which happiness is attained? This is our answer to the question whether the just or the unjust man is the happier?

Thrasymachus replies: 'Let this be your entertainment, Socrates, at the festival of Bendis.' Yes; and a very good entertainment with which your kindness has supplied me, now that you have left off scolding. And yet not a good entertainment—but that was my own fault for tasting of many things. First of all the nature of justice was the subject of our enquiry, and then whether justice is virtue and wisdom, or evil and folly; and then the comparative advantages of just and unjust: and the sum of all is that I know not what justice is; how then shall I know whether the just is happy or not? . . . .

Thus the sophistical fabric has been demolished, chiefly by appealing to the analogy of the arts. 'Justice is like the arts (1) in having no external interest, and (2) in not aiming at excess, and (3) justice is to happiness what the implement of the workman is to his work.' At this the modern reader is apt to stumble, because he forgets that Plato is writing in an age when the arts and the virtues, like the moral and intellectual faculties were still undistinguished. Among early enquirers into the nature of human action the arts helped to fill up the void of speculation; and at first the comparison of the arts and the virtues was not perceived to be fallacious. The contemporaries of Plato had not realized the Aristotelian distinction 'that virtue is concerned with action, art with production.' And yet in the absurdities which follow from some uses of the analogy (cp. 333 E, 334 B), there seems to be an intimation conveyed that virtue is more than art. This is implied in the conclusion that 'justice is a thief,' and in the dissatisfaction which Socrates expresses at the final result. The second of the three arguments, 'that the just does not aim at excess,' has a real meaning, though wrapped up in an enigmatical form. That the good is of the nature of the finite is a peculiarly Hellenic sentiment, which may be compared with the language of those modern writers who speak of virtue as fitness, and of freedom as obedience to law. The mathematical or logical notion of limit easily passes into an ethical one, and even finds a mythological expression in the conception of (φθόνος) envy. Ideas of measure, equality, order, unity, proportion, still linger in the writings of moralists; and the true spirit of the fine arts is better conveyed by such terms than by superlatives.

'When workmen strive to do better than well,'
'They do confound their skill in covetousness.'

In what may be called the epilogue of the discussion with Thrasyma-chus, Plato argues that evil is not a principle of strength, but of discord and dissolution, just touching the question which has been often treated in modern times by theologians and philosophers of the negative nature of evil (cp. on the other hand, x. 610). In the last argument we trace the germ of the Aristotelian doctrine of an end and a virtue directed towards the end, which again is suggested by the arts. The final reconcilement of justice and happiness, and the identity of the individual and the State are also intimated. Nothing is concluded; but the tendency of the dialectical process, here as always, is to enlarge the conception of ideas, and to widen their application to human life.

BOOK II. Thrasymachus is pacified, but the intrepid Glaucon insists on continuing the argument. He begins by dividing goods into three classes:—first, goods desirable in themselves; secondly, goods desirable in themselves and for their results; thirdly, goods desirable for their results only. He then asks Socrates in which of the three classes he would place justice. In the second class, replies Socrates, among goods desirable for themselves and also for their results. 'Then the world in general will be of another mind, for they will say that justice belongs to the troublesome class of goods which are desirable for their results only.' Socrates answers that this is the doctrine of Thrasymachus which he rejects. Glaucon thinks that Thrasymachus was too ready to listen to the voice of the charmer, and proposes to consider the nature of justice and injustice in themselves and apart from the results and rewards which accompany them. He will first of all speak of the nature and origin of justice; secondly, of the manner in which men view justice as a necessity and not a good; and thirdly, he will prove the reasonableness of this view.

'To do injustice is said to be a good; to suffer injustice an evil. As the evil is discovered by experience to be greater than the good, the sufferers, who cannot also be doers, make a compact that they will have neither, and this compact or mean is called justice, but is really the impossibility of doing injustice. No one would observe such a compact if he were not obliged. We may test this by supposing that the just and unjust have two rings, like that of Gyges in the well-known story, which make them invisible, and then no difference would appear in them, for every one would do evil if he could. And he who abstained would be regarded by the world as a fool for his pains. Men might praise him in public out of fear for themselves, but they would laugh at him in their hearts. (Cp. Gorgias, 483 B.)

'And now let us frame an ideal of the just and unjust. Imagine the

unjust man to be master of his craft, seldom making mistakes and easily
correcting them; having gifts of money, speech, strength—the greatest
villain bearing the highest character: and at his side let us place the
just in his nobleness and simplicity—being, not seeming—without name
or reward—clothed in his justice only—the best of men who is thought
to be the worst, and let him die as he has lived. I might add (but I
would rather put the rest into the mouth of the panegyrists of injustice.
They will tell you) that the just man will be scourged, racked, bound,
have his eyes put out, and will at last be crucified [literally impaled]—
and all this because he ought to have preferred seeming to being.
How different is the case of the unjust! who clings to appearance as
the true reality. His high character makes him a ruler; he can marry
where he likes, trade where he likes, help his friends and hurt his
enemies; having got rich by dishonesty he can worship the gods
better, and will therefore be more loved by them than the just.'

I was thinking what to answer, when Adeimantus, like an Homeric
hero, 'brother helping brother,' desired to join in the already unequal
contest. He considered that the most important point of all had been
omitted: 'the grand error has been that men are taught to be just for
the sake of rewards; parents and guardians make reputation the incentive to virtue. And other advantages are promised by them of a
more solid kind; e. g. wealthy marriages, and high offices which depend
upon the good opinion of mankind. There is the picture in Homer
of fat sheep and heavy fleeces, rich corn-fields and trees toppling with
fruit, which the gods provide in this life for the just. And the Orphic
poets add a similar picture of another. Musaeus gets his heroes down
in the world below, and has the saints feasting on couches, with garlands
on their heads, enjoying as the meed of virtue a gross paradise of
immortal drunkenness. Some go further, and speak also of a fair
posterity in the third and fourth generation. But the wicked are
drowned by them in a slough of despond, and are made to carry
water in a sieve. Our description of the infamy and sufferings of the
just is transferred by them to the unjust. This is all that their imagination supplies.

'Take another kind of argument which is found both in poetry and
prose:—"Virtue," as Hesiod says, "is honourable but difficult"—"steep
is the way and narrow is the gate;" but vice is easy and profitable—
"broad is the way and many walk therein." And you may often see

the wicked in great prosperity and the righteous afflicted by the will of heaven. And mendicant prophets knock at rich men's doors, promising to atone for the sins of themselves or their fathers in a pleasant easy manner with festive games, or with charms and invocations to get rid of an enemy good or bad by divine help and at a small charge;— they appeal to a heap of books professing to be written by Musaeus and Orpheus, and carry away the minds of whole cities, and promise to "get souls out of purgatory," and are dangerous if they are refused.

'When a lively-minded ingenuous youth hears all this, what will be his conclusion? "Will he," in the language of Pindar, make justice "his high tower, or fortify himself with crooked deceit?" Justice, he reflects, without the appearance of justice, is misery and ruin; injustice has the promise of a glorious life. Appearance is master of truth and lord of happiness. To appearance then he will turn,—he will put on the show of virtue and trail behind him the fox of Archilochus. And even if there is a danger of being discovered, union and force and rhetoric will do much, and although they cannot prevail over the gods, still how do we know that there are gods? Only from the poets, who acknowledge that they may be appeased by sacrifices. Then why not sin and pay for indulgences out of your sin? For if the righteous are unpunished, the wicked may be unpunished and have the pleasures of sinning too. But is there not a danger of the world below? Nay, my friend, says the argument, there are mysteries and atoning powers who. will set that matter right, as the poets, who are the sons of the gods, tell us, and this is confirmed by the authority of the State.

'On what principle can we resist such arguments in favour of injustice? Add good manners, and, as the wise tell us, we shall fare well both with gods and men; we shall make the best of both worlds. Who that is not a miserable caitiff will refrain from smiling at the praises of justice? Even if a man knows the better part he will not be angry with other men; for he knows also that more than human virtue is needed to save a man, and that he only praises justice who is incapable of injustice.

'And the origin of the evil is that all men from the beginning, heroes, poets, instructors of youth, have always asserted "the temporal dispensation," the honours, glories, profits, expediencies of justice. Had they been taught in early youth the power of justice and injustice immanent in the soul, and unseen by any human or divine eye, they would not have needed others to be their guardians, but every one would have been the guardian of himself. And this is what I want you to show, Socrates;—other men use arguments which rather tend to strengthen the position of Thrasymachus that might is right. But from you I expect better things.'

. . . The thesis, which for the sake of argument is maintained by Glaucon, is the converse of that of Thrasymachus—not right is the interest of the stronger, but right is the necessity of the weaker. Starting from the same premises he carries the analysis of society a step further back;—might is still right, but the might is the weakness of the many combined against the strength of the few.

There have been theories in modern as well as in ancient times which have a family likeness to the speculations of Glaucon: e. g. that power is the foundation of right; or that virtue is self-love or the love of power; or that war is the natural state of man; or that private vices are public benefits. All such theories have a kind of plausibility from their partial agreement with experience. For human nature oscillates between good and evil, and the motives of actions and the origin of institutions may be explained to a certain extent on either hypothesis according to the character or point of view of a particular thinker. But theories of this sort do not represent the real nature of the State, which is based on a vague sense of right gradually corrected and defined by experience (although capable also of perversion), any more than the origin of society, which is to be sought in the family and in the social and religious instincts of man. Nor do they represent the average character of individuals, which cannot be explained simply on a theory of evil, but has always a counteracting element of good. And as men become better such theories appear more and more untruthful to them, because they are more conscious of their own disinterestedness.

The two brothers ask Socrates to prove to them that the just is happy when they have taken from him all that in which happiness is ordinarily supposed to consist. Not that there is (1) any absurdity in the attempt to frame a notion of justice apart from circumstances. For the ideal must always be a paradox when compared with the ordinary conditions of human life. Neither the Stoical ideal nor the Christian ideal is true as a fact, but they may serve as a basis of education, and may exercise an ennobling influence. An ideal is none the worse because 'some one has made the discovery' that no such ideal was ever realized. (Cp. v. 472 D.) And in a few exceptional individuals who are raised above the ordinary level of humanity, the ideal of happiness may be almost, if not altogether, realized in death and misery. This may be the state which the reason deliberately approves, and which the utilitarian as well as every other moralist may be bound in certain cases to prefer.

Nor again, (2) must we forget that Plato, though he agrees generally with the view implied in the argument of the two brothers, is not expressing his own final conclusion, but rather seeking to dramatize one of the aspects of ethical truth. He is developing his idea gradually in a series of positions or situations. He is exhibiting Socrates for the first time undergoing the Socratic interrogation. Lastly, (3) the word 'happiness' involves some degree of confusion because associated in the language of modern philosophy with conscious pleasure or satisfaction, which was not equally present to his mind.

Glaucon has been drawing a picture of the misery of the just and the happiness of the unjust, to which the misery of the tyrant in book ix. is the real counterpart. And still the unjust must appear just; this is 'the homage which vice pays to virtue.' But now Adeimantus proceeds to show that this regard for justice is only for the sake of rewards and reputation, and points out the advantage which is given to such arguments as those of Thrasymachus and Glaucon by the conventional morality of mankind. He seems to feel the difficulty of 'justifying the ways of God to man.' Both of them touch upon the question, how far the morality of actions is determined by their consequences (cp. iv. 420 foll.); and both of them go beyond the position of Socrates, that justice belongs to the class of goods not desirable for themselves only, but desirable for themselves and for their results, to which he recalls them. In their attempt to view justice as an internal principle, and in their condemnation of the poets they anticipate him. The common life of Greece is not enough for them; they must penetrate deeper into the nature of things.

It has been objected that justice is honesty in the sense of Glaucon and Adeimantus, but is taken by Socrates to mean all virtue. May we not more truly say that the old-fashioned notion of justice is enlarged by Socrates, and becomes equivalent to universal order or well-being, first in the State, and secondly in the individual? He has found a new answer to his old question 'whether the virtues are one or many,' viz. that one is the ordering principle of the three others. In seeking to establish the purely internal nature of justice, he is met by the fact that man is a social being, and he tries to harmonize them as well as he can. There is no more inconsistency in this than was inevitable in his age and country; there is no use in turning upon him the cross lights of modern philosophy, which, from some other point of view, would appear equally inconsistent. Plato does not give the final solution of philosophical questions for us; nor can he be judged of by our standard.

The remainder of the Republic is developed out of the question of the sons of Ariston. Three points are deserving of remark in what immediately follows:—First, that the answer of Socrates is altogether indirect. He does not say that happiness consists in the contemplation of the idea of justice, and still less will he be tempted to affirm the Stoical paradox that the just man can be happy on the rack. But first he dwells on the difficulty of the problem and insists on restoring man to his natural condition, before he will answer the question at all. He too will frame an ideal, but his ideal comprehends not only abstract justice, but the whole relations of man. Under the fanciful illustration of the large letters he implies that he will only look for justice in society, and that from the State he will proceed to the individual. His answer in substance amounts to this,—that under favourable conditions, i. e. in the perfect State, justice and happiness will coincide, and that when justice has been once found, happiness may be left to take care of itself. That he falls into some degree of inconsistency, when in the tenth book he claims to have got rid of the rewards and honours of justice, may be admitted; for he has left those which are allowed to exist in the perfect State. Still he preserves the true attitude of moral action. Let a man do his duty towards his country first, without asking whether he will be happy or not, and happiness will be the inseparable accident which attends him. 'Seek first the kingdom of God and his righteousness, and all these things shall be added unto you.'

Secondly, it may be remarked that Plato preserves the true character of Greek thought in beginning with the State and going on to the individual; first ethics then politics is the order of ideas to us; the reverse is the order of history. Only after many struggles of thought does the individual assert his full right and become a perfectly moral agent. Thirdly, we may observe that here begins the confusion or identification of the individual and the State, of ethics and politics, which pervades Greek political speculation, and even in modern times retains a certain degree of influence.

... Socrates praises the sons of Ariston, 'inspired offspring of the renowned hero,' as the elegiac poet terms them; but he is at a loss to understand how they can argue so eloquently on behalf of injustice while their character shows that their own arguments have no influence on them. He does not know how to answer them, although he is afraid of deserting justice in the hour of need. He therefore makes a condition, that having weak eyes he shall be allowed to read the large letters first and then go on to the smaller. He means to say, that he must be allowed to look for justice in the State first, and shall then proceed to the individual. This is agreed, and Socrates constructs the State.

Society arises out of the wants of man. His first want is food; his second a house; his third a coat. The sense of these needs and the possibility of satisfying them by exchange, draw individuals together on the same spot; and this is the beginning of a State, which we take the liberty to invent, although necessity is the real inventor. There must be first a husbandman, secondly, a builder, thirdly, a weaver, to which may be added a cobbler. Four or five citizens at least are required to make a city. Now men have different natures, and one man will do one thing better than many; and business waits for no man. Hence there must be a division of labour into different employments; into wholesale and retail; into workers, and makers of workmen's tools; into shepherds and husbandmen. A city which includes all this will have far exceeded the limit of four or five, and yet not be very large. But then again imports will be required, and imports necessitate exports, and this implies variety of produce in order to attract the taste of purchasers; also merchants and ships. In the city too we must have a market and money and retail trades, otherwise buyers and sellers will never meet, and the valuable time of the producers will be wasted in vain efforts at exchange. If we add hired servants the State will be complete, and we may guess that somewhere in the intercourse of the citizens with one another justice and injustice will appear.

Here follows a rustic picture of their way of life. They build houses, and produce corn and wine, and make coats and shoes. They are lightly clad in summer while at their work, but well shod and clothed in winter. Their principal food is flour and meal, of which they make noble puddings, and these they serve up on wattled reeds or clean leaves. They repose on couches strewn with yew and myrtle, passing their time in pleasant converse with one another, hymning the gods and drinking their wine. 'Yes, Socrates,' said Glaucon, 'but you should give them a relish.' Yes, I replied, and a relish they shall have—salt and olives and cheese and potherbs and chestnuts which they will roast at the fire, indulging in moderate potations. Fed on such a diet they will live in peace and health, and bequeath a similar life to their descendants; and they will be careful not to have too many children. Glaucon said, ''Tis a city of pigs, Socrates.' Why, I replied, what do you want more? 'Only the conveniences of life, which every one has,—sofas to lie upon, tables to eat from, also meats and sweets.' I see that you want not only a State, but a state of luxury; and possibly in the more complex frame we shall sooner find justice and injustice. Then our ideas will have to enlarge themselves; the fine arts must go to work—every instrument and ornament of luxury in furniture and dress and food will be wanted in every form. There will be dancers, painters, sculptors, musicians, cooks, barbers, tire-women, nurses, artists; and we must not forget the swineherds and neatherds too for the animals, and physicians to cure the disorders of which luxury is the source. And then to feed all these superfluous mouths we shall need a part of our neighbours' land, and they will want a part of ours: and this is the origin of war, which may be traced to the same causes as other political evils. Our city will now require the slight addition of a camp, and the citizen will be converted into a soldier. But then our old doctrine of the division of labour must not be forgotten. The art of war cannot be learned in a day, and there must be natural aptitudes for military duties. There will be some warlike natures who have this aptitude—dogs keen of scent and swift of foot to pursue, and strong of limb to fight. And as passion is the foundation of courage, such natures, whether of men or animals, will be full of passion. And here arises a difficulty:—these passionate natures are apt to bite and devour one another; the union of gentleness to friends and fierceness against enemies appears to be an impossibility in nature; and the guardian requires both qualities. Who then can be a guardian? After a pause, Socrates adds that the image of the dog suggests a way of escape. For in dogs too there is a double character of gentleness to friends and enmity to strangers. Your dog is a philosopher and judges by the rule of knowing or not knowing, and philosophy whether in man or beast is the parent of gentleness. And the human watchdogs too must be philosophers or lovers of learning which will make them gentle. And how are they to be learned without education?

But what is education? Is any better than the old-fashioned sort which is comprehended under the names of music and gymnastic? Music includes literature, and literature is of two kinds, true and false. 'What do you mean?' he said. I mean that children hear stories before they learn gymnastics, and that the stories are mostly untrue, or have only one or two grains of truth in a bushel of falsehood. Now early life is very impressible, and children ought not to be allowed to learn what they will have to unlearn when they grow up; and in order to prevent this we must have a censorship of nursery tales, banishing some and keeping some. Some of them are very improper, as we may see in the great instances of Homer and Hesiod, who are really much to blame, for they not only tell lies but bad lies; stories about Uranus and Saturn, which are immoral as well as false, and which should never be spoken of to young persons or indeed at all; or, if at all, then in a mystery after the sacrifice, not of an Eleusinian pig, but of some unprocurable animal. Shall our youth be encouraged to beat their fathers by the example of Zeus, or our citizens be incited to war by seeing the wars of the gods and giants embroidered on the robe of Athene? Shall they hear the narrative of Hephaestus binding his mother, and of Zeus sending him flying for helping her when she was beaten? Even if such tales are capable of a mystical interpretation the interpretation is not obvious to the young at the age when impressions are most powerful. But if any one asks what tales are to be allowed, to that, Adeimantus, you and I answer that we are legislators and not book-makers; we only lay down the principles according to which books are to be written, but to write them is the duty of others.

And our first principle is that God is good, and the author of good, and good only; not that he is the steward of good and evil, or that he has two casks full of destinies, as Homer says; or that Athene and Zeus incited Pandarus to break the treaty; or that God caused the sufferings of Niobe, or of Pelops, or the Trojan war. We maintain, on the contrary, either that these were not the actions of the gods or that God was just, and men were all the better for being punished: but that the deed was evil, and God the author of the deed—this is not to be said or sung in any well-ordered commonwealth by old or young, and is suicidal, immoral, impious. This is our first and great principle,—God is the author of good only.

And the second principle is of the same nature:—With God is no variableness or change of form; he is no Proteus. Reason teaches us this; for if we suppose a change in God, he must be changed either by another or by himself. By another?—but the best works of nature and art and the noblest qualities of mind are least liable to be changed by any external force. By himself?—but he cannot change for the better, and he will hardly change for the worse. He remains for ever fairest and best in his own image. Therefore we refuse to listen to the poets who tell us of the goddess Here begging in the likeness of a priestess, or of other deities who prowl about at night in strange disguises; all that blasphemous nonsense with which mothers fool the manhood out of their children is got at secondhand from the poets and ought to be suppressed. But you will say that God who is himself unchangeable may take a form in relation to us. Why should he do this? For gods as well as men hate the lie in the soul or principle of falsehood; and as for any other form of lying which is used for a purpose and is regarded as innocent in certain exceptional cases—what need have the gods of this? For they are not ignorant of antiquity like the poets, nor are they afraid of their enemies, nor is any madman a friend of theirs. God then is true, he is absolutely true; he changes not, he deceives not, by day or night, by word or sign. This is our second great principle,—God is true. Away with the lying dream of Agamemnon in Homer, and the accusation of Thetis against Apollo in Aeschylus.

. . . In order to give clearness to his conception of the State, Plato prefers to trace the first principles of mutual need and of division of labour in an imaginary community of four or five citizens. Gradually this community increases; the division of labour extends to countries; imports necessitate exports; a medium of exchange is required, and retailers sit in the market-place to save the time of the producers. These are the steps by which Plato constructs the first or primitive state, introducing the elements of political economy by the way. When he makes a transition to a second state, which is framed on the civilized model, this is only a device of style; he indulges in a picture of primitive life, but he does not seriously mean to say that one is better than the other (cp. Politicus, p. 272); nor can any inference be drawn from the description of the first state taken apart from the second, such as Aristotle appears to draw in the Politics, book iv. 4, 12.

The disappointment of Glaucon at the 'city of pigs,' the ludicrous description of the ministers of luxury in the more refined state, and the afterthought of the necessity of doctors, the ironical illustration of the nature of the true guardian taken from the dog, the desirableness of offering some almost unprocurable victim when impure mysteries are to be celebrated, are touches of humour which may be noted in passing. In the education of the young, Plato startles us by affirming that a child must begin by learning falsehood first and truth afterwards. Yet this is not very different from saying that children must be taught through the medium of imagination as well as reason; that their minds can only develope gradually, and that there is much which they must learn without understanding (cp. iii. 402 A.). This is also the substance of Plato's view, though he must also be allowed to have drawn the line somewhat differently from modern ethical writers respecting truth and falsehood. To us economies or accommodations could be only allowable as far as they are required by the human faculties or necessary for the communication of knowledge to the simple and ignorant. But Plato seems to limit the use of them only by requiring that they should have a good moral effect, and that such a dangerous weapon as falsehood should be used by the rulers alone and for great objects.

A singular conception which occurs towards the end of the book is the lie in the soul; this is connected with the Platonic and Socratic doctrine that involuntary ignorance is worse than voluntary. The lie in the soul is the most involuntary of all ignorance, a real deception which he ironically terms a true lie, a false principle hated by gods and men. For example, to represent God as false or immoral, or, according to Plato, as deluding men with appearances, would be a lie of this hateful description. To this is opposed the lie in words, which is only such a deception as may occur in a play or poem, or allegory or figure of speech, or in any sort of accommodation,—which though useless to the gods may be useful to men in certain cases. Reserving for another place the greater questions of religion or education, we may note further, (1) the approval of the old traditional education of Greece; (2) the preparation which Plato is making for the attack on Homer and the poets; (3) the preparation which he is also making for the use of economies in the

State; (4) the familiar use of the allegorical interpretation of the poets in the age of Plato, which here, as in the Phaedrus, is rejected by him; (5) the contemptuous and at the same time euphemistic manner in which here as below (iii. 390) he alludes to the *Chronique Scandaleuse* of the gods.

BOOK III. There is another motive in purifying religion, which is to banish fear; for no man can be courageous who is afraid of death, or who believes the tales which are repeated by the poets concerning the world below. A gentle request should be made to them by the authorities not to abuse hell, accompanied by an intimation that their tales are untrue, and the reverse of inspiring to heroes. The licenser is desired to expunge obnoxious passages, such as the chilling words of Achilles:— 'I would rather be a serving-man than rule over all the dead;' and the verses which tell of the squalid mansions, the meaningless ghosts, the flitting soul mourning over her lost strength and youth, the soul with a gibber going beneath the earth like smoke, the souls of the suitors which flutter about like bats—all this sort of thing Homer and the other poets must not be angry at our erasing. The terrors and horrors of Cocytus and Styx, ghosts and sapless shades, and the rest of their Tartarian nomenclature, must vanish. Such tales may have their use; but they terrify people out of their senses, and are not the proper food for soldiers. As little can we admit the sorrows and sympathies of the Homeric heroes:—Achilles, the son of a goddess, lying first on his back, and then on his face, then starting up and prancing on the sea-shore; or Priam, the cousin of the gods, crying aloud, rolling in the mire. A good man is not altogether prostrated at the loss of children or fortune. Neither is death terrible to him; and therefore lamentations over the dead should not be practised by men of note; they should be the concern of women and of inferior persons only, whether women or men. Still worse is the attribution of such weakness to the gods; as when the goddesses say, 'Alas! my travail!' and worst of all, when the king of heaven himself laments his inability to save Hector, or sorrows over the impending doom of his dear Sarpedon. Such a character of God, if not ridiculed by our young men, is likely to be imitated by them. Nor should our citizens be given to excess of laughter—'Such violent delights have violent ends.' The scene in the Iliad in which the gods are introduced shaking their sides at Hephaestus is unseemly.

Truth should have a high place among the virtues, for falsehood is of no use to the gods and is useful only as a medicine in the case of men. The State physician or ruler may occasionally employ this medicine, but the subject must not in return tell a lie to the ruler; that would be as great an error as for the patient to tell a lie to the physician, or the sailor to his captain. If the ideal State is ever realized, the false word of any common man must be regarded as treason.

In the next place our youth must be temperate, and temperance consists in obedience to the rulers and abstinence from sensual pleasures. That is a lesson which Homer teaches in some places: 'The Achaeans marched breathing prowess in silent awe of their leaders;'—and a very different lesson in other places: 'O heavy with wine, who hast the eyes of a dog, and the heart of a stag.' This is a sort of language not likely to impress the lesson of self-control on the minds of youth. The same may be said of his praises of eating and drinking and of his dread of starvation; also of the verses in which he tells with great circumstance of the rapturous loves of Zeus and Here, which made the former forget his intention of honouring Achilles; or of the tale of the net in which Hephaestus detained Ares and Aphrodite on a similar occasion. There is a nobler strain heard in the words:—'Endure, my soul, thou hast endured worse.' Nor must we allow our citizens to receive bribes, or to say, 'Gifts persuade the gods, gifts reverend kings;' or to applaud the ignoble advice of Phoenix to Achilles that he should get money out of the Greeks before he assisted them; or the meanness of Achilles himself in taking gifts from Agamemnon; or his requiring a ransom for the body of Hector; or his cursing of Apollo; or his insolence to the river-god; or his dedication to the dead Patroclus of his own hair which had been already dedicated to the other river-god Sperchius; or the fit of cruelty which made Cheiron's pupil drag the body of Hector round the walls, and slay the captives at the pyre, especially as he is avaricious as well, which seems to be a contradiction. The amatory exploits of Pirithous and Theseus, Zeus and Poseidon's sons are equally unworthy. Either these sons of gods were not the sons of god, or they were not such as the poets imagine them, any more than the gods themselves are the authors of evil. The youth who believes that such things are done by those who have the blue blood of heaven flowing in their veins will be too ready to imitate their example.

Enough of gods and heroes;—what shall we say about men? what

the poets and story-tellers say?—that the wicked prosper and the
righteous are afflicted, or that justice is another's gain? Not this
at all events, but rather the opposite. Only in raising the question
at all we are anticipating the definition of justice, and had therefore
better defer the enquiry.

Next to subject follows style. Now all style is narrative, and narrative is of three kinds, the simple, imitative, and a composition of
the two. An instance will make my meaning clear. The first scene
in Homer is of the last or mixed kind, being partly description and
partly dialogue. If you throw the dialogue into the 'oratio obliqua'
(I am no poet and therefore I drop the metre), the priest came and (do
not say 'spoke these words,' but) prayed the gods that the Achaeans
might take Troy and have a safe return if Agamemnon would only give
him back his daughter, and the other Greeks assented, but Agamemnon
was wroth, and so on,—then the whole becomes descriptive. Or if
you leave out the intermediate pieces of description and the dialogue
remains, in this case the epic becomes dramatic, and the poet disappears.
Or if you take away the dialogue, then the poet is the only speaker
left, as in dithyrambic poetry. These are the three styles; and I want
to know which of them is to be admitted into our State. 'Do you
ask whether tragedy and comedy are to be admitted?' Nay, perhaps
there is more than this involved; and indeed the question has been
already answered, for we have decided that one man cannot in his
life play many parts. And therefore he cannot both live and act,
or compose both tragedy and comedy, or be a rhapsodist and actor
at once. Human nature is coined into very small pieces, and as our
guardians have their own business already, which is the care of
freedom, they will have enough to do without imitating. But if they
imitate they should not imitate any meanness or baseness, but the
good only, for the mask that the actor wears is apt to become his
face. We cannot allow men to play the parts of women, young or
old, quarrelling or weeping, scolding their husbands, or setting up
their necks against the gods,—least of all when making love or in
labour. They must not represent slaves, or bullies, or cowards, or
drunkards, or madmen, or blacksmiths, or neighing horses, or bellowing
bulls, or sounding rivers, or a raging sea. A good or wise man will
be willing to perform good or wise actions only; and he will prefer
the epic style with as little imitation as possible. The man who has

no self-respect, on the contrary, will imitate any body and anything; sounds of nature, cries of animals; he will whistle like the wind, rattle like hail, growl like thunder, and play on any instrument; also he will bark like a dog, baa like a sheep, and crow like a cock: his whole performance will be imitation of gesture and voice. Now in the descriptive style there are few changes, but in the dramatic there are a great many. Poets and musicians use either, or a compound of both, and this compound is very attractive to youth and their teachers as well as to the vulgar. But our State in which one man plays one part only, and a cobbler is a cobbler, and a ploughman a ploughman, is not adapted for complexity. And when one of these polyphonous pantomimic gentlemen offers to exhibit himself and his poetry we will fall down and worship him as a sweet creature, and a holy and wonderful being; he shall be anointed with myrrh and have a garland of wool set upon his head—but then we shall bid him turn about and go to the next city, for we are patrons of the rough, honest poet, and will not depart from the primitive model. (Cp. Laws, vii. 817.)

Next as to the music. A song or ode has three parts,—the subject, the harmony, and the rhythm; of which the two last are dependent upon the first. As we banished strains of lamentation, so we may now banish the mixed Lydian harmonies, which are the harmonies of lamentation; and as our citizens are to be temperate, we may also banish convivial harmonies, such as the Ionian and pure Lydian. Two remain,—the Dorian and Phrygian, the first for war, the second for peace; the one expressive of courage, the other of obedience, or instruction, or religious feeling. And as we reject varieties of harmony, we shall also reject the queer, many-stringed, variously-shaped instruments which give utterance to them, and in particular the flute, which is more complex than any of them. The lyre and the harp may be permitted in the town, and the Pan's-pipe in the fields. Thus we have made a purgation of music, and will now make a purgation of metres. Metres, like harmonies, should be simple and suitable to the occasion. There are three kinds of them, as there are four notes of the tetrachord, which all have their characters, and there are different characters of feet as well as of rhythms. But about this I must ask Damon, the musical doctor, who speaks, if I remember rightly, of a martial measure as well as of dactylic, trochaic, and iambic rhythms, which he arranges so as to compensate and equalize with one another. We only venture to affirm the general principle that beauty depends upon rhythm, and rhythm upon style, and style upon subject, and subject upon the simplicity and harmony of the soul which is reflected in them. This lesson of simplicity above all things has to be learnt by every one in the days of his youth, and may be gathered anywhere from painting and embroidery, or any other creative and constructive art, as well as from the forms of plants and animals, and is a lesson which runs through nature as well as art, and has a wide kindred in the world.

Other artists as well as poets should be warned against meanness or extravagance or unseemliness in their creations. The same rule applies to sculpture or any other invention. And he who violates the rule must not be allowed to work in our city, and to corrupt the taste of our citizens. For images of deformity are like a hurtful pasture, and day by day, little by little, our guardians gather evil from them, which becomes a festering mass of evil in the soul. Place them only where they may breathe the air of health and beauty, amid fair sights and sounds, and they will quickly drink in from surrounding objects sweet and harmonious influences; and this is the great power of music, which more than any other influence enters into the soul and gives the sense of deformity and beauty. At first the effect is unconscious; but when reason arrives then he who has been thus trained welcomes her as the friend whom he always knew. As in learning to read, first we acquire the elements or letters separately, and afterwards their combinations, and do not recognize the reflections of them in the water until we know the letters themselves;—in like manner we must first attain the elements or essential forms of temperance and courage and liberality and magnificence and the like, and then trace the combinations of them in life and experience. There is a music of the soul which answers to the harmony of the world; and the fairest object of a musical soul is the fair mind in the fair body. Some defect in the latter may be excused, but not in the former. True love is the daughter of temperance, and temperance is utterly opposed to the madness of bodily pleasure. Enough has been said of music, which makes a fair ending with love.

Next we pass on to gymnastics; about which I would remark, that the soul is related to the body as a cause to an effect, and therefore if we educate the mind we may leave the education of the body in her charge, and need only give a general outline of the course to be pursued. In the first place the guardians will abstain from strong drink, for they should be the last persons to lose their wits. Whether the habits of the palaestra are suitable to them is more doubtful, for the ordinary gymnastic is a sleepy, heavy sort of thing, and when left off suddenly is apt to be dangerous. And our warrior athletes must be wide-awake dogs, having all their senses about them, and must also be inured to all changes of food and climate. Hence they will require a finer discipline and a simpler gymnastic, which will be like their music; and for their diet a rule may be found in Homer, who gives his heroes no fish although they were living at the sea-side, nor boiled meats which involve an apparatus of pots and pans. Sweets and Sicilian cookery, and Attic confections, and Corinthian courtezans, must be forbidden them; these are to gymnastic what Lydian and Ionian melodies are to music. Gluttony and intemperance fill the town with doctors and pleaders, who open their halls for practice; and law and medicine give themselves airs as soon as the freemen of a State go out and buy them. But what can show a more disgraceful state of education than the importation of justice from abroad because you have none of your own at home? And yet there *is* something more disgraceful still in the further stage of the same disease, when men have learned to take a pleasure and pride in the twists and turns of the law; not considering how much better it would be for them so to order their lives as to have no need of a nodding justice. And there is a similar disgrace in employing a physician, not for the cure of wounds or epidemic disorders, but because a man has blown himself out like a bladder, and has got more diseases than he knows the names of, or than ever existed in the days of Asclepius. For observe how simple is the Homeric practice of medicine. Eurypylus after he has been wounded drinks a posset of Pramnian wine, which is of a heating nature; and yet the sons of Asclepius blame neither the damsel who gives him the drink, nor Patroclus who is attending on him. The truth is that this modern system of nursing diseases was introduced by Herodicus the trainer; who, being of a sickly constitution, by a compound of training and medicine, tortured first himself and then a good many other people, and died a long time after he ought to have died. Now Asclepius was a statesman, and refused to practise this art, which he knew well enough; but he would not have men wasting time in being ill, and therefore he adopted the rough 'kill or cure' method, which artisans and labourers employ. 'They must be at their business,' they say, 'and have no time for

swathing and dieting: if they recover, well; and if they don't, there is
an end of them.' There is a maxim of Phocylides, that 'when a man
begins to be rich' (or, perhaps, a little before) 'he should practise
virtue.' But how can excessive care of health be inconsistent with an
ordinary occupation, and yet consistent with this maxim? A man ought
to be thinking of something, and he says that philosophy gives him the
headache, and never does anything because he is always unwell. And this
was the reason why Asclepius and his sons practised no such art. They
were in the interest of the public, and did not wish to preserve useless
lives, or raise up a puny offspring to wretched sires. Honest diseases
they honestly cured; and if a man was wounded he might drink a sack
posset,—that did not hinder his recovery. But they would have nothing
to do with persons whose lives were of no use either to themselves or to
others, even though they might have made large fortunes out of them.
And as to the story of Pindar, that Asclepius was slain by a thunderbolt
for restoring a rich man to life, that is a lie; following our old rule we
must say either that he did not take bribes, or that he was not the son
of a god.

Glaucon then asks Socrates whether the best physicians and judges
will not be those who have had the greatest experience of diseases and
of crimes. Socrates is disinclined to place them in the same category.
The physician should have experience of disease in his own body, for
he cures with his mind and not with his body. But with the lawyer this
is otherwise: he controls mind by mind; and therefore he should have
no experience of evil in his own mind. Where then is he to gain experience? How is he to be wise and also innocent? A good man when
he is young is apt to be deceived by evil-doers, because he has no
pattern of evil in himself; and therefore the judge should be advanced
in years; his youth should have been innocent, and he should have
acquired experience of evil late in life by extended observation. This
is the ideal of a judge; your mere detective is wonderful at suspicion
and discovery, but when he has to do with good men he is at fault,
foolishly imagining that every one is as bad as himself. Vice may be
known of virtue, but cannot know virtue. Medicine and law will be
healing arts to better natures; but the evil body will be left to die by
the one, and the evil soul will be put to death by the other. And the
necessity for either will be greatly diminished by good music and good
gymnastic. The former will give harmony to the soul; the latter health

to the body. Not that this division of music and gymnastic really corresponds to soul and body, for both are equally concerned with the soul, which is tamed by the one and aroused and sustained by the other. The mere lover of gymnastic becomes a savage; the musician grows effeminate; but the two together supply our guardians with their twofold nature. The passionate disposition which has too much of gymnastic is hardened and brutalized, the gentle temper of philosophy which has too much music becomes enervated. While a man is singing and twittering and pouring music like water through the funnel of his ears, the edge of his soul gradually wears away, and the passionate or spirited element is dissolved and liquefied. In the spiritless nature this is soon effected, and passion is converted into nervous irritability. In like manner the athlete is at first courageous, but soon degenerates into dulness; his senses are never purged, and like a wild beast he is ready to do everything by blows and nothing by counsel or policy. These are the two principles in man, and the gods have given two arts corresponding to them, and not to the soul and body, as some vainly talk—music and gymnastic; the unity of which makes a harmony higher far than the concord of musical notes. And the true musician is he who attempers them—he shall be the presiding genius of our State.

The next question is, Who are to be our rulers? First, the elder must rule the younger; and the best of the elders will be the best guardians. He who guards best is he who loves best, and he who loves others has an interest in them Those then must be selected who have always been devoted to the interest of their country. And a watch must be put over them to discover whether at every epoch of life they have retained the same opinions and held out against force and enchantment. For time and persuasion and the love of pleasure may seduce a man into a change of purpose, and force may compel him. And therefore we must choose for our guardians men of known firmness, who have been tried by many tests, like gold in the refiner's fire, and who at every age have come out of such trials victorious and without stain in full command of themselves and their principles; having all their faculties in harmonious exercise for their country's good. Those who attain this degree of virtue are worthy of the highest honours both in life and death. It would perhaps be better to speak of those whom we before called guardians as auxiliaries or allies, and to reserve the higher title for the more select class.

And now for one noble, useful lie, a lie upon a grand scale, to be the
corner-stone of our State,—in the belief of which, O that we could train
our rulers! and at any rate let us make the attempt with the rest of the
world.   I know not how to give utterance to my ideas, and yet what I
am going to tell is only a republication of the Phoenician story of Cadmus
and his earthborn men—which has often happened in past times, but
not in our own, for the age of miracles has ceased, and the world is an
unbelieving world.   I am ashamed to look you in the face as I repeat
the audacious tale, which I would have you impart in regular gradation,
first to the rulers, then to the soldiers, and lastly to the people.   The lie
is as follows:—The citizens shall be told that their youth was a dream,
and that during all that time in which they seemed to be undergoing a
process of education they were really being fashioned in the bowels of
the earth, their alma mater and true parent; they are her children, and
therefore brothers and sisters to one another.   'I do not wonder at your
being ashamed to propound such a fiction.'   There is more behind.
These brothers and sisters have different natures, and some of them
God made to rule; these he fashioned of gold, others of silver to be
helps; others again to be husbandmen and craftsmen, and these he
made of brass and iron.   But sometimes a golden parent may have a
silver son, or a silver parent a golden son, and then nature orders a
transposition of ranks; the eye of the ruler must not be pitiful towards
his offspring if he has to descend in the social scale; for an oracle says
'that the State will come to an end if governed by a man of brass.'   Is
there any possibility of making our citizens believe all this?   'Not in the
present generation, but in the next, perhaps yes.'

Now let the earthborn men go forth under the command of their
rulers, and look about and pitch their camp in a high place, which will
be safe against enemies descending upon the fold, and also against
insurrections from within.   There let them sacrifice and set up their
tents; for soldiers they are to be and not shopkeepers, the watchdogs
and guardians of the sheep; and luxury and avarice will turn them into
wolves and tyrants.   Their habits and their dwellings should correspond
to their education.   They should have no property; their pay should
only meet their expenses; and they should have common meals.   Gold
and silver we will tell them that they have from God, and this divine
gift in their souls they must not alloy with that earthly dross which
passes under the name of gold.   They only of the citizens may not

touch it, or be under the same roof with it, or drink from it; it is the accursed thing. Should they ever acquire houses or lands or money of their own, they will become householders and tradesmen instead of guardians, enemies and tyrants instead of helpers, and our society will be a world of ruin and confusion.

The religious and ethical aspect of Plato's education will hereafter be considered under a separate head. Some lesser points may be more conveniently noticed in this place.

1. The constant appeal to the authority of Homer, whom, with a sort of grave irony, Plato, after the manner of his age, summons as a witness about ethics and psychology, as well as about diet and medicine; attempting to distinguish the better lesson from the worse (p. 390), some-times altering the text from design (p. 388), and perhaps (389), more than once quoting or alluding to Homer inaccurately (pp. 391, 406), like the early logographers, turning Homer into prose (p. 393), and delighting to draw far-fetched inferences from his words, or to make ludicrous applications of them. These fanciful and humorous allusions add a charm to Plato's style, and at the same time they have the effect of a satire on the follies of Homeric interpretation. The real, like the Platonic Socrates, as we gather from the Memorabilia of Xenophon, was fond of making similar adaptations. (i. 2, 58; ii. 6, 11.)

2. In the third book of the Republic a nearer approach is made to a theory of art than anywhere else in Plato. His views may be summed up as follows:—True art is not fanciful and imitative, but simple and ideal,—the expression of the highest moral energy, whether in action or repose. To live among works of plastic art which are of this noble and simple character, or to listen to such strains, is the best of influences,— the true Greek atmosphere, in which youth should be brought up. That is the way to create in them a natural good taste, which will have a feeling of truth and beauty everywhere. For though the poets are to be expelled, still art is recognized as another aspect of reason—like love in the Symposium, extending over the same sphere, but confined to the preliminary education; and this conception of art is not limited to strains of music or the forms of plastic art, but pervades all nature. Plato seems rather to desire to reconcile art and nature than to make an opposition between them. The ideal Republic of Plato, like the Athens of Pericles, has an artistic as well as a political side.

3. Plato makes the subtle remark that the physician had better not be in robust health; and should have known what illness is in his own person. On the other hand, the judge ought to have had no similar experience of evil; this should only be attained by him as the result of observation in after life; and therefore, according to Plato, a young man is not fit to be a judge, as, according to Aristotle, he is not fit to be a hearer of moral philosophy. But it may be doubted whether this latter view is justified by experience. The union of gentleness and courage in book ii. at first seemed to be a paradox, yet was afterwards ascertained to be a truth. And had Plato pursued this question in a similar spirit, he might also have found that the intuitive perception of evil may be consistent with the abhorrence of it. There is a directness of aim in virtue which gives an insight into vice. And the knowledge of character is in some degree a natural sense independent of any special experience of good or evil.

4. One of the most remarkable conceptions of the Republic, because un-Greek in character and also unlike anything that existed at all in that age of the world, is that of the transposition of ranks. In the Spartan state there had been indeed enfranchisement of Helots and degradation of citizens under special circumstances, but nothing like that 'open career' which Plato promises to his citizens. Two principles are indicated by him: first, that there is a distinction of ranks dependent on circumstances prior to the individual; second, that this distinction is and ought to be broken through by personal qualities. Here again, as in the Phaedrus, Plato shows a true sense of the nature of mythology, as capable of creation and adaptation to the wants of a State. Every Greek state had a myth respecting its own origin; the Platonic republic may also have a tale of earthborn men. The gravity and verisimilitude with which the tale is told, and the analogy of Greek tradition, are a sufficient verification of the 'monstrous falsehood.' Ancient poetry had spoken of a gold and silver, and brass and iron age succeeding one another, but Plato supposes these differences in the natures of men to exist together in a single state. Mythology supplies abundance of figures under which the world may be conceived (as Protagoras says, 'the mythus is more interesting'), and also enables Plato to touch lightly on new principles without going into detail. He shadows forth a general truth, but he does not tell us by what steps the transposition of ranks is to be effected. Indeed throughout the Republic he allows the lower ranks to fade into the dis-

tance. Nor is there any use in arguing strictly either from this or from other passages of the Republic, or in drawing inferences which were beyond the vision of Plato. Aristotle, in his criticism on the position of the lower classes, does not perceive that the poetical creation is 'like the air, invulnerable,' and cannot be divided by the shafts of his logic. (2, 5, 18 fol.)

5. Lesser matters of style may also be remarked. (1) The affected ignorance of music, which is Plato's way of expressing that he is passing lightly over the subject. (2) The tentative manner in which here, as in the second book, he proceeds with the construction of the State. (3) The description of the State sometimes as a reality, and then again as a work of imagination only; these are the arts by which he sustains the reader's interest. (4) The two companion pictures of the lover of litigation and the valetudinarian (p. 405), the satirical jest about the maxim of Phocylides, the manner in which the image of the gold and silver citizens is taken up into the subject, and the grave argument from the practice of Asclepius, should not escape notice.

BOOK IV. Adeimantus said : ' Suppose a person to argue, Socrates, that you make your citizens miserable, and this by their own free-will; they are the lords of the city, and yet instead of having lands, and houses, and furniture, and gold, and silver, and sacrifices, and hospitalities of their own, like other men, they live as mercenaries and are always mounting guard.' You may add, I replied, that they are on board wages, and have no money to spend on a journey or a lady of pleasure, which, as the world goes, is thought to be happiness. ' Well, suppose all this, what answer do you give?' My answer is, that our guardians may or may not be the happiest of men,—I should not be surprised to find in the long-run that they were,—but this is not the aim of our constitution, which was designed for the good of the whole and not of any one part. If I went to a sculptor and blamed him for having painted the eye, which is the noblest feature of the face, not purple but black, he would reply: 'The eye must be an eye, but you ought to look at the statue as a whole.' Now I can well imagine a fool's paradise, in which everybody is eating and drinking, clothed in purple and fine linen, and potters lie on sofas and have their wheel at hand, that they may work a little when they please; and cobblers and all the other classes of a State lose their distinctive character. And a State may get on without cobblers; but when the guardians degenerate into boon companions, then the ruin is complete. This would be very unlike our State, in which every man is expected to be doing his duty and receiving his share of happiness with the rest. I have another remark to make:—A middle condition is best for artisans; they should have money enough to buy tools, and not money enough to be independent of their business;—the guardians should look to this. And will not the same condition be best for our citizens? They should have neither poverty nor riches, for the one is the parent of meanness and the other of luxury, and both of discontent. 'But then, Socrates, how will our city go to war, not having the sinews of war, especially against a rich enemy?' There may be a difficulty in fighting against one enemy, but there is no difficulty in fighting against two of them. In the first place, remember that the contest will be carried on by trained warriors against well-to-do citizens: and might not a regular boxer upset more than one stout gentleman, stepping lightly back himself and making a sudden turn upon them—in hot weather especially? 'Yes, many a one.' But suppose again, that before engaging we send ambassadors to one of the two cities, saying, 'Silver and gold we neither have nor can have, do you help us and take our share;'—who in such a case would choose to fight with the lean, wiry dogs, instead of joining with them against the fatted sheep? 'But if the wealth of many states coalesce in one, shall we not be in danger?' I am amused to hear you use the word 'state' of any but our own State. They are 'states,' but not 'a state,' many in one;—a game of states at which men play [1]. For every state, however small, has two nations struggling within her, which you may set one against the other. But our State, while at unity with herself and fixed in her principles, will be the mightiest of Hellenic states, and will always have numerous allies and few enemies.

To the size of the state there is no limit but the necessity of unity; it must be neither too large nor too small to be one. This is a matter of secondary importance, like the principle of transposition which was intimated in the parable of the men dug out of the earth. The meaning was that every man should do that for which he was fitted, and be at one with himself, and then the whole city would be united. But all these things are secondary, if education, which is the great matter, be duly regarded. When the wheel has once been set in motion, the speed is always increasing; and each generation improves upon the preceding, both in physical and moral qualities. The care of the governors should

[1] In allusion to a game called cities or states (πόλεις.)

be directed to preserve music and gymnastic from innovation; alter the songs of a country, and you will soon end by altering the laws. When Homer praises new songs, he must not be supposed to praise new kinds of song. Damon assures me that new chants cannot be introduced without danger to the whole political system. The change appears innocent at first, and begins in play; but the evil soon becomes serious, working secretly upon the characters of individuals, then upon social and commercial relations, and lastly upon the institutions of a state; and there is ruin and confusion everywhere. But if education remains in the established form, then the reverse follows; there is a restorative process always going on; nor will any rules be needed for the lesser matters of life —such as when to sit down and when to stand, when to speak and when to be silent, and what mode of tonsure is the true pattern. Education will correct deficiencies and supply the power of self-government. Regulations about the appointment of judges and the order of causes, harbour and market duties, may be left; let them take care of education, and education will take care of all other things.

But without education they may mend and cobble and doctor as they please, they will make no progress, any more than a patient who asks the physician to cure him and will not give up his luxurious mode of living. If such persons are told that they will never improve unless they alter their habits, then they grow angry; their way of going on is charming. 'Charming,—nay, the reverse of charming.' I see that these gentlemen are not in your good graces, nor the state which is like them. And such states there are which first make solemn ordinances that no one under penalty of death shall alter the constitution, and then suffer themselves to be flattered into and out of anything, and they flatter in return, and their rulers, under the influence of flattery, begin to add cubits to their stature, and imagine themselves to be eight feet high at least. When all the world is telling a man this and he has no measure, how can he believe otherwise? 'I am more inclined to pity the deceived than the deceivers.' Don't get into a passion : to see our statesmen trying their nostrums, and fancying that they can cut off at a blow the Hydra-like rogueries of mankind, is as good as a play. Minute enactments are superfluous in good states, and are useless in bad ones.

And now what remains of the work of legislation? Nothing for us; but to Apollo the god of Delphi we leave the ordering of the greatest of all—that is to say, religion. Only our ancestral deity sitting upon the centre and navel of the earth will be trusted by us if we have any sense in an affair of such magnitude. No foreign god shall be supreme in our realms.

. . . Here, as Socrates would say, let us 'reflect' (σκοπῶμεν) on what has preceded: thus far we have not spoken of the happiness of the citizens, but only of the well-being of the State. They may be the happiest of men, but this is not our principal aim in founding the State. Ancient philosophy thus lightly touches on the modern question of the relation of duty to happiness, of right to utility.

First duty, then happiness, is the natural order of our moral ideas. The utilitarian principle is of value as a corrective of long-standing error, and presents a side of ethics which is apt to be neglected. It may be admitted further that right and utility are co-extensive, and that he who makes the happiness of mankind his object has one of the highest and noblest motives of human action. But utility is not the historical basis of morality; nor the aspect in which moral and religious ideas commonly occur to the mind. The greatest happiness of the greatest number may be the far-off result of the divine government of the universe. The greatest happiness of the individual may be the indirect consequence of a life of virtue and goodness. But the first principle is an insufficient interpreter of the appearances of the world around us; the second presents virtue in a form which is hardly natural. The question reappears in the sphere of politics; and all the more ideal systems of politics, as of ethics, agree either in denying the supremacy of utility or happiness, or in explaining the term in some other sense than that of material comfort or prosperity. This is the order of thought in Plato; first, he expects his citizens to do their duty, and then under favourable circumstances, that is to say, in a well-ordered State, their happiness is assured. That he was far from excluding the modern principle of utility in politics, is sufficiently evident from other passages, in which the most beneficial is affirmed to be the most honourable (457 B), and also the most sacred (458 E).

We may note (1) The manner in which the objection of Adeimantus here, as at the commencement of book vi, is designed to draw out and deepen the argument of Socrates. (2) The conception of a whole as lying at the foundation both of politics and of art, in the latter supplying the only principle of criticism, which, under the various names of harmony, symmetry, measure, proportion, unity, the Greek seems to have applied to works of art. (3) The requirement that the State should be limited in size, after the traditional model of a Greek state. (4) The humorous pictures of the lean dogs and the fatted sheep, of the light active boxer upsetting two stout gentlemen at least, of the 'charming' patients who are always making themselves worse; or again, the playful assumption that there is no State but our own; or the grave irony with which the statesman is excused who believes because he is told that he is eight feet high, and having nothing to measure with is happy in his ignorance. (5) The light and superficial manner in which religion is passed over when provision has been made for two great principles,— first, that religion should be based on the highest conception of the gods; secondly, that the true national or Hellenic type shall be maintained.

Socrates proceeds: But where amid all this is justice? Son of Ariston, tell me where. Light a candle and search the city, and get your brother and the rest of our friends to help in seeking for her. 'Nonsense,' replied Glaucon, 'what were you saying about the impiety of deserting justice in the hour of need?' Well, I said, as you remind me of this, I will lead the way, but do you follow. My notion is, that our State being perfect will contain all the four virtues—wisdom, courage, temperance, justice. If we eliminate the three first, the unknown remainder will be justice.

First then, of wisdom: the State which we have called into being will be wise because politic. And policy is one among many kinds of skill, —not the skill of the carpenter, or of the worker in metal, or of the husbandman, but the skill of him who regards the interests of the whole State. And that is the skill of the guardians, who are a small class in number, far smaller than the blacksmiths, but if this small ruling class have wisdom, then the whole State will be wise; in other words, wisdom is the virtue of the guardians.

Our second virtue is courage, which we have no difficulty in finding in another class—that of soldiers. Courage may be defined as a sort of salvation—salvation of the opinions which law and education have pre-scribed concerning dangers. You know the way in which dyers first prepare the white ground and then lay on the dye of purple or of any other colour. The colours which are dyed in this way become fixed, and no soap or lye will ever wash them out. And laughable is the shabby washed-out look of any colour which has not been dyed in this way. Now the ground is education, and the laws are the colours; and if the ground is properly laid, neither the soapiness of pleasure nor the lye of pain or fear will wash them out. The power which preserves right opinion about danger I would ask you to call 'courage,' adding the epithet 'political' or 'civilized' in order to distinguish it from the brute courage of barbarians and from a higher courage which may hereafter be discussed.

Two virtues remain; shall we skip one and go to the other? 'Let us rather take them in their order; first temperance, then justice.' More than the preceding virtues temperance suggests the idea of harmony. Some light is thrown upon the nature of this virtue by the amusing description of a man as master of himself—the absurdity of which is that the master is also the servant. The expression is really a term of praise, meaning that the better principle in a man masters the worse. There are in cities whole classes—of women, slaves and the like—who correspond to the worse, and a few only to the better; and in our State the former class are held under control by the latter. Now to which of these classes does temperance belong? 'To both of them.' And if in any state temperance dwells, that must be ours; and we were right in describing temperance as a harmony which is diffused through the whole, making the dwellers in the city to be of one mind, and uniting the upper and middle and lower classes like the strings of an instrument, whether you suppose them to differ in wisdom, strength or money. This unity, in whatever way acquired, is called temperance.

And now we are near the spot; let us draw in and surround the cover and watch with all our eyes, lest justice should slip away and escape. Tell me if you see the thicket move first. 'Nay, I would have you lead.' Well then, offer up a prayer and follow. There is no path and the way is dark; we must push on. I begin to see a track. 'Good news.' It is there and will not escape. Why, Glaucon, our dulness of scent is quite disgraceful! Shall we not be laughed at? While we are straining our eyes at the distance, justice is tumbling out at our feet. We are as bad as the people who sweep the house to look for a thing which they have in their hands. Have you forgotten our old principle of the division of labour, or of every man doing his own business, concerning which we spoke at the foundation of the State—what but this was justice? Such a notion of justice may fairly compete with wisdom and temperance and courage in the scale of political virtue. For is not every one having his own the great object of our courts of law? and the great object of trade is that every man should do his own business. Not that there is much harm in a carpenter trying to be a cobbler, or a cobbler transforming himself into a carpenter; but great evil may arise from the cobbler leaving his last and turning into a guardian or legislator, or when a single individual is trainer, warrior, legislator, all in one. And this evil is injustice, or every man doing another's business. I do not say that at this point we are in a condition to arrive at a final conclusion. For the definition which we believe to hold good in states has yet to be tested by the individual. Having read the large letters we will now come back to the small. From the two together a brilliant light may be struck out.

. . . Socrates proceeds to discover the nature of justice by a method of residues. Each of the three first virtues corresponds to one of the three parts of the soul, and one of the three classes in the State, although the third, temperance, has more of the nature of a harmony than the two first. If there be a fourth virtue, that can only be sought for in the relation of the three parts in the soul or classes in the State to one another. It is the most obvious and simple of all things, and for that very reason has not been found out. The definition here given of justice is verbally the same as one of the definitions given of temperance in the Charmides (162 A), which however is only provisional, and is afterwards rejected. The temperance and justice of the Republic may be distinguished as follows:—temperance is the virtue of a part only, justice of the whole soul. Temperance is one of three virtues, justice is universal virtue : temperance is the harmony of discordant elements; justice is the perfect order by which all natures and classes do their own business, the right man in the right place, the division and co-operation of all the citizens. Justice, again, is a more abstract notion than the other virtues, and therefore, from Plato's point of view, the foundation of them, to which they are referred and which in idea precedes them. The proposal to omit temperance is a mere trick of style intended to avoid monotony. (Cp. vii. 528.)

There is a famous question in the earlier Dialogues of Plato (cp. Protagoras 329, 330; Ar. Nic. Ethics, vi. 13. 6), 'Whether the virtues are one or many?' This receives an answer which is to the effect that there are four cardinal virtues (now for the first time brought together in ethical philosophy), and one supreme over the rest, which is not like Aristotle's conception of universal justice, virtue relative to others, but the whole of virtue relative to the parts. To this universal conception of justice or order in the first education and in the moral nature of man, the still more universal conception of the good in the second education, and in the speculative division, seems to succeed. Both might be equally described by the terms 'law,' 'order,' 'harmony;' but while the idea of good embraces all time and all existence, the conception of justice is not extended beyond man.

. . . Socrates is now going to identify the individual and the State. But first he must prove that there are three parts of the individual soul. His argument is as follows:—Quantity makes no difference in quality. The word 'just,' whether applied to the individual or the State, has the same meaning. And the term 'justice' implied that the same three principles in the State and in the individual were doing their own business. But are they really three or one? There is a small matter for consideration. 'A very small matter,' is the ironical reply. Nay, the reverse of small; I should rather think one which will never be brought to a conclusion by the methods which we are now employing; there is a surer, but that is also a longer way, which would take up too much time. 'The shorter will satisfy me.' Well then, you would admit that the qualities of states mean the qualities of the individuals who compose them? Ask the question why the Scythians and Thracians are passionate, or our own race intellectual, or the Egyptians and Phoenicians covetous,—there is no difficulty in replying that individuals are of such or such a character, but there is great difficulty in determining whether the several principles are one or three; whether, that is to say, we reason with one part of our nature, desire with another, are angry with another, or whether the whole soul comes into play in each sort of action. This enquiry, however, requires a very exact definition of terms. The same thing in the same relation cannot be affected in two opposite ways. But there will be no impossibility in a man standing still, yet moving his arms, or in a top which is fixed on one spot going round upon its axis. There is no necessity to mention all the possible exceptions; let us provisionally assume that opposites cannot do or be or suffer opposites in the same relation. And to the class of opposites belong assent and dissent, desire and avoidance. And one form of desire is thirst and hunger: and here arises a new point,—thirst is thirst of drink, hunger is hunger of food; not of warm drink or of a particular kind of food, with the single exception of course that the very fact of our desiring anything implies that it is good. When relative terms have no attributes, their correlatives have no attributes; when they have attributes, their correlatives also have them. For example, the term ' greater' is simply relative to 'less,' and knowledge refers to a subject of knowledge. But on the other hand, a particular knowledge is of a particular subject. Again, every science has a distinct character, which is defined by an object; medicine, for example, is the science of health, although not to be confounded with health. Having cleared our ideas thus far, let us return to the original instance of thirst, which has a definite object—drink. Now the thirsty soul may feel two distinct impulses; the animal one saying, Drink; the rational one, which says, Do not drink, and is in direct contradiction to the former. Here are two contradictory acts of the soul; the one derived from reason, the other from desire; these two then are proved to be distinct principles in the soul. Is passion a third principle or, as our first impression may lead us to suppose, akin to desire? There is a story of a certain Leontius which throws some light on this question. He was coming up from the Piraeus by the way beneath the wall, and he passed a spot where there were dead bodies lying by the executioner. He felt a longing desire to see them and also an abhorrence of them; at first he turned away and shut his eyes, then, suddenly tearing them open, he said,— ' Take your fill, ye wretches, of the fair sight.' Now is there not here a third principle which is often found to come to the assistance of reason against desire, but never of desire against reason? This is passion or spirit, of the separate existence of which we may further convince ourselves by putting the following case:—When a man suffers justly, if he be of a generous nature he cannot chafe or boil or get into a state of righteous indignation at the hardships which he undergoes; but when he suffers unjustly, his indignation is his great support; hunger and thirst cannot tame him; the spirit within him must do or die, until the voice of the shepherd, that is, of reason, bidding his dog bark no more, is heard within. This shows that passion is the ally of reason. Is passion then the same as reason? No, for the former exists in children and brutes; and Homer affords a proof of the distinction between them when he says, ' He smote his breast, and thus rebuked his soul.'

And now, after much tossing in the argument, we have reached land, and are able to infer that the virtues of the state and of the individual are the same. For wisdom and courage and justice in the State are severally the wisdom and courage and justice in the individuals who form the State. Each of the three classes will do the work of his own class in the State, and each part in the individual soul; reason, the superior, and passion, the inferior, will be harmonized by the influence of music and gymnastic. The counsellor and the warrior, the head and the arm, will act together in the town of Mansoul, and music and gymnastic will put them in commission over the desires. The courage of the warrior is that quality which preserves a right opinion about dangers in spite of pleasures and pains. The wisdom of the counsellor presides in that small part of the soul which has authority and reason. The virtue of temperance is the friendship of this ruling and the subject-principle, both in the state and in the individual. Of justice we have already spoken; and the notion before given may be further confirmed by common instances. Will the just state or the just individual steal, lie, commit adultery, or be guilty of impiety to gods and men? 'No.' And is not the reason of this that the several principles in either do their own business? And justice is the quality which makes just men and just states. Moreover, our old division of labour, which required that there should be one man for one use, was a sort of dream or anticipation of this;—that dream has now been realized in justice, which begins by binding together the three chords of the soul, and then acts harmoniously in every relation of life. And injustice, which is the habit of being a busybody and of doing another man's business, and which tries to rule and ought to serve, is the opposite of justice, and is inharmonious and unnatural, being to the soul what disease is to the body; for in the soul as well as in the body, good or bad actions produce good or bad habits. And virtue is the health and beauty and wellbeing of the soul, and vice is the disease and weakness and deformity of the soul.

Again the old question returns upon us: Is justice or injustice the more profitable? The question has become ridiculous. For injustice, like mortal disease, is suicidal. Come up with me to the hill which overhangs the city and look down upon the single form of virtue, and the infinite forms of vice or decline in states and individuals. Their name is legion; but there are four special forms of them, corresponding to the four forms of perversion in the State. And there is one form of the true state in which reason rules under one of two names,—monarchy and aristocracy.

. . . In attempting to prove that the soul has three separate faculties, Plato takes occasion to discuss what makes difference of faculties. And the criterion which he proposes is difference in the working of the faculties. The same faculty cannot produce contradictory effects. But the path of early reasoners is beset by thorny entanglements, and he cannot proceed a step without first clearing the ground. This leads him into a tiresome digression, which is intended to explain the nature of contradiction. First, the contradiction must be at the same time and in the same relation. Secondly, no extraneous word must be introduced into either of the terms in which the contradictory proposition is expressed: for example, thirst is of drink, not of warm drink. He is going to argue that if, by the advice of reason, or by the impulse of anger, a man is restrained from drinking, this proves that thirst, or desire under which thirst is included, is distinct from anger and reason. But suppose that we allow the term 'thirst' or 'desire' to be modified, and say an angry thirst, or bloody and revengeful desire, then the two spheres of desire and anger overlap and become confused. This case therefore has to be excluded. And still there remains an exception to the exception in the use of the term 'good,' which is always implied in the object of desire. These are the discussions of an age before logic; and any one who is wearied by them should remember that they are necessary to the clearing up of ideas in the first development of human faculties. Whether there is any higher or ideal sense in which two contradictions may be true, is a question which is not determined by Plato, though in the Parmenides and the Sophist he is not far from the solution.

At the commencement of the discussion he speaks with contempt of the methods which are now in use, and seems to intimate some metaphysic of the future by which these and similar questions might be more surely resolved. In the sixth and seventh books he has given us a sketch of such a metaphysic; but when Glaucon asks for the final revelation of the idea of good, he is put off with the declaration that he has not yet studied the preliminary sciences. How he would have filled up the sketch, or argued about such questions from a higher point of view, we can only conjecture. Perhaps he hoped to find some *a priori* method of developing the parts out of the whole; or he might have asked which of the ideas contains the other ideas, and possibly have stumbled on the Hegelian identity of the 'ego' and the 'universal.' The most certain and necessary truth was to Plato the universal; and to this he was always seeking to refer all knowledge or opinion, just as in modern times we are always seeking to rest them on the opposite pole of experience.

BOOK V. I was going to enumerate the four forms of vice or decline in states, when Polemarchus—he was sitting a little farther from me than Adeimantus—taking him by the coat and leaning towards him, said something in an undertone, of which I only caught the words, 'Shall we let him off?' 'Certainly not,' said Adeimantus, raising his voice. What or whom, I said, are you not going to let off? 'You,' he said. Why? I again asked. 'Why, because we think that you are not dealing fairly with us in omitting women and children, of whom you slily dispose under the general formula that friends have all things in common.' And am I not right in saying that? 'Yes,' he replied, 'but there are many sorts of communism or community, and we want to know which of them is right. The company, as you have just heard, are resolved not to let you off without a further explanation of this matter.' Thrasymachus said, 'Do you think that we have come hither to dig for gold, or to hear you discourse?' Yes, I said; but the discourse should be of a reasonable length. Glaucon added, 'Yes, Socrates, and there is reason in spending the whole of life in listening to such discussions; but without further consideration of us proceed in your own manner, and tell us how this community is to be carried out, and how the interval between birth and education is to be filled up.' Well, I said, the subject has several difficulties—What is possible? is the first question. What is desirable? is the second. 'Fear not,' he replied, 'for you are speaking among friends, who will put a fair and liberal construction on what is said by you.' That, I said, is anything but a consolation; I shall destroy my friends as well as myself. Not that I mind a little innocent laughter; but he who kills the truth is a murderer. 'Then,' said Glaucon, laughing, 'in case you should murder us we will acquit you beforehand, and just as in a criminal cause he who is acquitted is not guilty, you shall be acquitted and not guilty.'

Socrates proceeds: The guardians of our State are to be watch-dogs, and their properties and families must be ordered with a view to this. Dogs are not divided into hes and shes, nor do we take the masculine gender out to hunt and leave the females at home to look after their puppies. They have the same employments—the only difference between them is that the one are stronger and the other weaker. But if women are to have the same employments as men, they must have the same education—they must be taught music and gymnastics, and the art of war. I know that a great joke will be made of their riding on horseback and carrying weapons; the sight of the naked old wrinkled women showing their agility in the palestra, will certainly not be a vision of beauty, and may be expected to become a famous jest. But we must not mind the wits; there was a time when they might have laughed at our present gymnastics. All is habit: people have at last found out that the exposure is better than the concealment of the person, and now they laugh no more. Evil only should be the object of ridicule; 'Honi soi qui mal y pense.'

The first question is, whether women are able either wholly or partially to share in the employments of men. And here we may be charged with inconsistency in making the proposal at all. For we started originally with the division of labour; and the diversity of employments was based on the difference of natures. But is there no difference between men and women? Nay, are they not wholly different? *There* was the difficulty, Glaucon, which made me unwilling to speak of family relations. However, when a man is out of his depth, whether in a pool or in an ocean, he can only swim for his life, and may hope to be saved by Arion's dolphin, or some other miracle. Let us try then and find a way out, if we can.

The argument is, that different natures have different uses, and the natures of men and women are said to differ. 'Exactly.' But observe, Glaucon, that this is only a verbal opposition. We courageously repeat, different natures for different uses, never considering that the difference may be purely nominal and accidental; for example, a bald man and a hairy man are opposed in a single point of view, but you cannot infer that because a bald man is a cobbler a hairy man ought not to be a cobbler. Now why should such an inference be erroneous? Simply because the opposition between them is partial only, like the difference between a male physician and a female physician; but not like the difference between a physician and a carpenter. And if the difference of the sexes is only that the one beget and the other bear children, this does not prove that they ought to have distinct educations. Admitting that women differ from men in capacity, do not men equally differ from one another? Has not nature scattered all the qualities which our citizens require, whether as philosophers or physicians or weavers or makers of cakes, indifferently up and down among the two sexes? and even in the peculiar pursuits of women, are they not often ridiculously enough surpassed by men, though in some cases superior? Women are the same in kind, and have the same aptitude or want of aptitude for gymnastic and war, but in a less degree. One woman will be a good guardian, another not; and the good must be chosen to be help-meets to our guardians. If however their natures are the same, the inference is that their education must also be the same; there is no longer anything unnatural or impossible in a woman learning music and gymnastic. And this education will be the very best, far better than that of cobblers, and will train up the very best women, and nothing can be better for the State than this. Therefore let them strip, clothed in their chastity, and share in the toils of war and in the defence of their country; he who laughs at them is a fool for his pains.

The first wave is past, and the argument is compelled to admit that men and women have common duties and pursuits. A second and greater wave is rolling in—community of wives and children; is this expedient? is this possible? The expediency I do not doubt, but I am not so sure of the possibility. 'Nay, I think that a considerable doubt will be entertained on both subjects.' I meant to have escaped the trouble of proving the first, but as you have detected the little stratagem I must even submit. Only allow me to feed my fancy like the solitary in his walks, with a dream of what might be, and then I will return to the question of what can be.

In the first place our rulers will enforce the laws and make new ones where they are wanted, and their allies or ministers will obey. You, as legislator, have already selected the men; and now you shall select the women. After the selection has been made, they will live in common houses and have their meals in common, and will be brought together by a necessity more certain than that of mathematics. But they cannot be allowed to live in licentiousness; that is an unholy and unlawful thing, which the rulers are determined to prevent. For the avoidance of this, holy marriage festivals will be instituted, and their holiness will be in proportion to their usefulness. And here, Glaucon, I should like to ask (as I know that you are a breeder of birds and animals), Do you not take the greatest care in the mating? 'Certainly.' And there is no reason to suppose that less care is required in the marriage of human beings. But then, our rulers must be physicians, and use many medicines in their treatment of the body corporate; some falsehoods too, which are allowed by us in the practice of medicine. The good must be paired with the good as often as possible, and the bad with the bad as seldom as possible, and the offspring of the one must be reared, and the other destroyed; this will be the only way of preserving the flock in prime condition. But how can this be accomplished? The hymeneal festivals will be celebrated at times fixed with an eye to population, and then the brides and bridegrooms will meet, but not too often; and by an ingenious system of lots the rulers will contrive that the brave only deserve the fair, and that those of inferior breed are paired with inferiors; the latter will ascribe to chance what is really the invention of the rulers. And when children are born, the offspring of the brave and fair will be carried to an enclosure in a certain part of the city, and there attended by suitable nurses; the rest will be hurried away to places unknown. The mothers will be brought to the fold and will suckle the children; care however must be taken that none of them recognise her own offspring; and if necessary other nurses may also be hired. The trouble of watching and getting up at night will be transferred to attendants. ' Then the wives of our guardians will have a fine easy time when they are in the family way.' And quite right too, I said, that they should.

The parents ought to be in the prime of life, which for a man may be fixed at thirty years—from twenty-five, when he has ' passed the point at which the speed of life is greatest,' to fifty-five; and at twenty years for a woman—from twenty to forty. Any one above or below those ages who partakes in the hymeneals shall be guilty of impiety; also every one who forms a marriage connexion at other times. This applies to those who are within the specified ages, after which they may range at will, provided they avoid the prohibited degrees of parents and children, or of brothers and sisters; the latter, however, are not absolutely prohibited, if a dispensation from the oracle be procured. ' But how shall we know the degrees of affinity, when all things are common? The answer is, that brothers and sisters are such as are born seven and ten months after the espousals, and their parents are those who are then espoused, and every one will have many children and every child many parents.

Socrates proceeds: I have now to prove that this scheme is advantageous and also consistent with our entire polity. The greatest good of a State is unity; the greatest evil, discord and distraction. And there will be unity where there are no private pleasures or pains or interests; where if one member suffer all the members suffer, if one citizen is touched all are quickly sensitive—and the least hurt to the little finger of the State runs through the whole body and vibrates to the soul. For the true State has the feelings of an individual, and is injured as a whole when any part is affected. Every State has subjects and rulers, who in a democracy are called rulers, and in other States masters: but in our State they are called saviours and allies; and the subjects who in other States are termed slaves, are by us termed nurturers and paymasters, and those who are termed comrades and colleagues in other places, are by us called fathers and brothers. And whereas in other States members of the same government regard one of their colleagues as a friend and another as an enemy, in our State no man is a stranger to another; for everybody whom he meets is bound to him by ties of blood, and these names and this way of speaking will have a corresponding reality—brother, father, repeated from infancy in the ears of children, will not be mere words. Then again the citizens will have all things in common, and having common property they will have common pleasures and pains.

Can there be strife and contention among those who are of one mind; or lawsuits about property when men have nothing but their bodies which they call their own; or suits about violence and insult when they are all bound to defend one another?—for young men will take the law into their own hands; if they are angry they will fight, and this will be an antidote against the gathering of conspiracies. The old will correct the young, but no young man will strike an elder; two sentinels will hold him back, reverence and fear,—reverence which will prevent him from laying hands on his kindred, and fear that the rest of the family may retaliate. Moreover, they will be rid of the lesser evils of life; there will be no flattering of rich men for the sake of a dinner, or heaping up of money for the support of their families, or borrowing and not paying. But I need not enter further into particulars. Let me say in conclusion, that when compared with the citizens of other States, ours will be Olympic victors, and crowned with blessings greater still,—they and their children having a better maintenance during life, and after death an honourable burial. Nor has the happiness of the individual been sacrificed to the happiness of the State (cp. iv. 419 E); our Olympic victor has not been turned into a cobbler, but he has a happiness beyond that of any cobbler. At the same time, if any conceited youth begins to dream of appropriating the State to himself, we shall do well to read him the lesson out of Hesiod, that ' half is better than the whole.' ' If he were to consult me, I should say to him, Stay where you are, having such a brave life.'

But is such a community possible?—as among other animals, so also among men; and if possible, in what way possible? About war there is no difficulty; the principle of communism is adapted to that. Parents will train their children to the spectacle of war, as potters' boys are trained to the business by looking on at the wheel. And to the parents themselves, as to other animals, the sight of their young ones will prove a great incentive to bravery. Young warriors must learn, but they must not run into danger, although a certain degree of risk is worth incurring when the benefit is great. The young creatures should be under the care of experienced veterans, and they should have wings — that is to say, swift and tractable steeds on which they will fly away and escape. One of the first things to be done is to teach a youth to ride.

Cowards and deserters shall be degraded to the class of husbandmen; gentlemen who allow themselves to be taken prisoners, may be presented to the enemy. But what shall be done to the hero? First of all he shall be crowned by all the youths in the army; secondly, he shall receive the right hand of fellowship; and thirdly, do you think that there is any harm in his being kissed? for the brave should possess the fair, whether male or female. Have we not the authority of Homer for honouring brave men with 'perpetual chines,' which is an appropriate compliment, because meat is a very strengthening thing. Fill the bowl then, and give the best seats and meats to the brave—may they do them good! And he who dies in battle will be at once declared to be of golden race, and shall become one of Hesiod's guardian angels. He shall be worshipped in the manner prescribed by the oracle after death; and not only he, but all other benefactors of the State who die in any other way, shall be admitted to the same honours.

The next question is, How we shall treat our enemies? Shall Hellenes be enslaved? No; for there is too great a risk of the whole race passing under the yoke of the barbarians. Or, Shall the dead be despoiled? Certainly not; for that sort of thing is an excuse for skulking, and has been the ruin of many an army. There is meanness and feminine malice in making an enemy of the dead body, when the soul which was the owner has fled—like a dog who cannot reach his assailants, and quarrels with the stones which are thrown at him instead. Thirdly, arms should not be offered up in the temples, for they are a pollution when they are taken from brethren. And for similar reasons there should be a limit to the devastation of Hellenic territory—the houses should not be burnt, nor more than the annual produce carried off. For war is of two kinds, civil and foreign; the first of which is properly termed 'strife,' and only the second ' war;' and war between Hellenes is in reality civil war—a quarrel in a family, which is ever to be regarded as unpatriotic and unnatural, and ought to be prosecuted with a view to reconciliation in a true phil-Hellenic spirit, as of those who would chasten but not utterly enslave. The war is not against a whole nation who are a friendly multitude of men, women, and children, but only against a few guilty persons; and when they are punished peace will be restored. That is the way in which Hellenes should war against one another—and against barbarians, as they war against one another now.

' But, my dear Socrates, in all this you are only getting away from the main question: Is such a State possible? I grant all and more than you say about the blessedness of being one family—fathers, brothers, mothers, daughters, going out to war together; but I want to ascertain the possibility of this ideal State.' If I loiter for a moment, I said, you make a descent upon me. The first wave and the second wave I have hardly escaped, and now you will certainly drown me with the third. When you see the mountain crest of the wave, I expect you to take pity. ' Not a whit.'

Then let me begin by reminding you that we were led to form our ideal polity in the search after justice, and the just man answered to the just State. Is this ideal at all the worse for being impracticable? Would the picture of a perfectly beautiful man be any the worse because no such man ever lived? Can any reality come up to the idea? Nature will not allow words to be fully realized; but if I am to try and realize the ideal of the State in a measure, I think that an approach may be made to the attainment of this by one or two, I do not say slight, but possible changes in the present constitution of States. I would reduce them to a single one—the great wave, as I call it, at which I expect your laughter to be as the letting out of water. *Until then kings are philosophers, or philosophers are kings, cities will never cease from ill : no, nor the human race ; nor will our ideal polity ever come into being.* I know that this is a hard saying, which few will be able to receive. ' Socrates, all the world will take off his coat and rush upon you with sticks and stones, and therefore I would advise you to prepare an answer to them.'

You got me into the scrape, I said. 'And I was right,' he replied; 'however, I will stand by you as a sort of do-nothing, well-meaning ally.' Having the help of such a champion, I will do my best to maintain my position. And first, I must explain whom I mean and what sort of natures these are who are to be philosophers and rulers. As you are a man of pleasure, I dare say that you have not forgotten how indiscriminate lovers are in their attachments; they love all, and turn blemishes into beauties. The snub-nosed youth is said by you to have a winning grace; the beak of another has a royal look; the featureless are faultless; the dark are manly, and the fair are angels; the sickly have a new term of endearment invented expressly for them, which is 'honey-pale.' Lovers of wine and lovers of ambition also desire their objects in every form. Now here comes the point:—The philosopher too is a lover of knowledge in every form; he has an insatiable curiosity. 'But will curiosity make a philosopher? Are they to be called philosophers who let out their eyes and ears at every Dionysiac festival in country as well as town?' Those are not true philosophers, I said, but only an imitation. 'Then how are we to describe the true?'

You would acknowledge the existence of abstract ideas, such as justice, beauty, good, evil, which are severally one, yet in their various combinations appear to be many. Those who recognize these realities are philosophers; whereas the other class hear sounds and see colours, and understand their use in the arts, but cannot attain to the true or waking vision of absolute justice or beauty or truth; they have not the light of knowledge, but of opinion only, which is a dream. Perhaps he of whom we say the last will be angry with us; can we offer him any consolation without revealing the fact that he is not in his right mind? Come, then, and let us reason with him; if he has knowledge we rejoice to hear it, but knowledge must be of something which is, and not of something which is and is not. The latter is the object-matter of opinion, as being is of knowledge, and not-being of ignorance. Having distinct objects, opinion and knowledge must also have distinct faculties. And by faculties I mean powers unseen and distinguishable only by the difference in their objects, and opinion and knowledge differ in their objects, as the one is liable to err and the other is not, but is the mightiest of all faculties. If being is the object of knowledge, and not-being of ignorance, and these are the extremes, opinion must lie between them, and may be called darker than the one and brighter than the

other. This intermediate or contingent matter is and is not at the same
time, and partakes both of existence and of non-existence. Now I would
ask my good friend, who denies abstract beauty and justice, and affirms
a many beautiful and a many just, whether everything he sees is not
in some point of view different—the beautiful ugly, the pious impious,
the just unjust? Is not the double also the half, and are not heavy and
light relative terms which pass into one another? Everything is and is
not, as in the old riddle—' A man and not a man shot and did not shoot
a bird and not a bird with a stone and not a stone.' The mind cannot
be fixed on either alternative, and these ambiguous, intermediate, erring,
half-lighted objects, which have a disorderly movement in the region
between being and not-being, are the proper matter of opinion, as the
immutable objects are the proper matter of knowledge. And he who
has only this uncertain perception of them grovelling in the world of
sense is not a philosopher, but a lover of opinion only.

... The fifth book is the new beginning of the Republic, in which the
community of property and family are first maintained, and the transition
is made to the kingdom of philosophers. For both of these Plato, after
his manner, has been preparing in some chance words of book iv. (424 A),
which fall unperceived on the reader's mind, as they are supposed at first
to have fallen unperceived on the ear of Glaucon and Adeimantus. The
' paradoxes' of this book of the Republic will be reserved for another
place; a few remarks on the style, and some explanations of difficulties,
may be briefly added.

First, there is the image of the waves, which serves for a sort of
scheme or plan of the book. The first wave, the second wave, the third
and greatest wave come rolling in, and we hear the roar of them. All
that can be said of the extravagance of Plato's proposals is anticipated
by himself. Nothing is more admirable than the hesitation with which
he proposes the solemn text, ' Until kings are philosophers,' &c.; or the
reaction from the sublime to the ridiculous, when Glaucon describes the
manner in which the new truth will be received by mankind.

Some critical and metaphysical difficulties may also be noted. Among
these may be reckoned the imperfect execution of the communistic plan
—nothing is told us of the application of communism to the lower
classes; nor is the table of prohibited degrees capable of being made
out. Plato is afraid of incestuous unions, but at the same time he

does not wish to bring before us the fact that the city would be divided into families of those born seven and nine months after each hymeneal festival. The singular expression which is employed to describe the age of five-and-twenty may, perhaps, be taken from some poet.

In the delineation of the philosopher, the illustrations of the nature of philosophy derived from love are more suited to the apprehension of Glaucon, the Athenian man of pleasure, than to modern tastes or feelings. They are partly facetious, but also contain a germ of truth. That science is a whole remains a true principle of inductive as well as of metaphysical philosophy; and the love of universal knowledge is still the characteristic of the philosopher in modern as well as in ancient times.

At the end of the fifth book Plato introduces the figment of contingent matter, which occurs here for the first time in the history of philosophy. He did not remark that the degrees of knowledge in the subject have nothing corresponding to them in the object. With him, a word must answer to an idea; he could not conceive of an opinion which was an opinion about nothing. On the other hand, the conception of not-being was dark and mysterious to the mind of early thinkers (Sophist, 254 A); they could not see that this terrible apparition which threatened destruction to all knowledge was only a logical determination. In the attempt to introduce order into the first chaos of human thought, Plato seems to have confused perception and opinion, and to have failed to distinguish the contingent from the relative. In the Theaetetus the first of these difficulties begins to clear up; in the Sophist the second; and for this, as well as for other reasons, both these dialogues are probably to be regarded as later than the Republic.

BOOK VI. Having determined that the many have no knowledge of true being, and have no clear patterns in their minds of justice, beauty, truth, and that philosophers have such patterns, we have now to ask which of them shall be rulers in our State: who can doubt that philosophers should be chosen, if they have the other qualities which are required in a ruler? And we may begin by observing, that they are lovers of the knowledge of the eternal and of all being; they are lovers of truth and haters of falsehood; their desires are absorbed in the interests of knowledge; there is no meanness in them, for they are spectators of all time and all existence; and in the magnificence of their contemplation the life of man is as nothing to them, nor is death fearful.

Moreover, they are of a social, gracious disposition, equally free from
cowardice and arrogance. They learn easily; they remember and do
not forget; they are harmonious, well-regulated minds; truth flows to
them sweetly by nature. Can the god of Jealousy himself find any fault
with such an assemblage of good qualities?

Here Adeimantus interposes an objection. 'No man,' he says, 'can
answer you, Socrates; but every man feels that this is owing to his own
deficiency in the power of arguing. He is carried away little by little,
until at last the discrepancy between the premises and the conclusion is
enormous. The argument is like a game of draughts in which the unskilful player is reduced to his last move by his more skilful antagonist.
And in this new game, of which words are the counters, the disputant
is out-argued, and yet he may be in the right. He may know, in this
very instance, that those who make philosophy the business of their
lives, generally turn out rogues if they are bad men, and fools if they
are good. What do you say to this?' I should say that he is quite
right. 'Then how is that admission reconcileable with the doctrine that
philosophers should be kings?'

I shall answer you in a figure which will give you an opportunity of
judging how poor a hand I am at the invention of allegories. The
relation of good men to their governments is so peculiar, that in order
to defend them I must take an illustration from that world of fiction
in which painters find their winged dragons, camel-leopards, and the
like. Conceive the captain, whether of a ship or of a fleet, taller by a
head and shoulders than all his sailors, yet a little deaf, a little blind, and
rather ignorant of the seaman's art. The sailors are wanting to steer,
although they know nothing and have learnt nothing of the art of steering; and they have a theory, which no one is allowed to doubt under pain
of death, that the art cannot be learned. If the care of the helm is
refused them, they drug the captain's posset and bind him hand and
foot; having got rid of him, they take possession of the ship, and make
themselves at home with the stores. He who joins in the mutiny is
termed an able seaman, a good pilot, and what not; they are not aware
that the true pilot is another sort of man, who must observe the wind
and the stars, and who must and will have authority—but such an one
is called by them a fool, prater, star-gazer. And now, I said, do you
interpret the parable to those who ask why the philosopher has such an
evil name, and make them understand that not he, but those who refuse

to use him, are to blame for his uselessness. The philosopher should not blow a trumpet before him, or beg of mankind to be put in authority over them. The wise man is not to seek the rich man, but every man, whether rich or poor, must knock at the door of the physician when he has need of him. Now the philosopher is the pilot—he whom in the parable they call star-gazer, and the sailors are the mob of politicians by whom he is rendered useless. Not that these are the worst enemies of philosophy, who is far more dishonoured by her own professing sons when they are corrupted by the world. Need I recall the original image of the philosopher? Did we not say of him just now, that he loved truth and hated falsehood, and that he could not rest in the multiplicity of phenomena, but was led by a sympathy in his own nature to the contemplation of the absolute? All the virtues as well as truth, who is the leader of them, took up their abode in his soul. But as you were observing, if we turned aside from this ideal to view the reality, we saw that the persons who are thus described, with the exception of a small and useless class, are utter rogues.

The point which has to be considered, is the origin of this corruption in nature. Every one will admit that the philosopher, in our description of him, is a rare being. And what numberless causes tend to destroy these rare beings! There is no good thing which may not be a cause of evil—not only health, wealth, strength and rank, but the virtues themselves, when placed under unfavourable circumstances. For as in the animal or vegetable world the strongest seeds most need the accompaniments of air and soil, so the best of human characters turn out the worst when they fall upon an unsuitable soil; whereas weak natures hardly ever do any considerable good or harm; they are not the stuff out of which either great criminals or great heroes are made. The philosopher follows the same analogy: if he have suitable training he is the best of all men; when surrounded by evil influences he becomes, if left to himself, the worst of all. Some persons say that the Sophists are the corrupters of youth, but do they really corrupt them in any appreciable degree? Is not public opinion the real Sophist who is everywhere present in those very persons, in the assembly, in the courts, in the camp, in the applauses and hisses of the theatre re-echoed by the surrounding hills? Will not a young man's heart leap within him when he hears these sounds?—will any education save him from being carried away in the torrent? And this is not all. For if he will not yield to opinion, there follows the gentle compulsion of exile or death. What principle of rival Sophists or anybody else can overcome in such an unequal contest? Characters there may be more than human, who are exceptions. God may save a man, but not his own strength. Further, I would have you consider that the hireling Sophist only gives back to the world their own opinions; he is the keeper of the monster, who knows how to flatter or anger him, and observes the meaning of his inarticulate grunts. Good is pronounced to be what pleases him, and evil is what he dislikes, and truth and beauty have no other standard but the taste of the brute, and the rules which embody this are the Sophist's wisdom. This is no exaggeration of the case of those who make public opinion the test of truth, whether in art or in morals. The curse is laid upon them of being and doing what they approve, and when such men attempt first principles the failure is ludicrous. Think of all this, and ask yourself whether the world is likely to be a believer in the unity of the idea or in the multiplicity of phenomena. And the world if not a believer in the idea cannot be a philosopher, and cannot help, therefore, being a persecutor of philosophers. There is another evil:—the world does not like to lose the gifted nature, and their way is to flatter the young [Alcibiades] into a magnificent opinion of his own capacity; the tall, proper youth begins to expand, and is dreaming of kingdoms and empires. If at this instant a friend whispers to him, 'Now the gods lighten thee; thou art a great fool and must be educated;' do you think that he will listen? Or suppose a better nature, who is attracted towards philosophy, will they not make Herculean efforts to spoil and corrupt him? Are we not right in saying that philosophical parts, no less than riches, may divert a man from philosophy? Men of this class often become politicians—they are the authors of great mischief in states, and sometimes also of great good. And thus philosophy is deserted by those who are her natural protectors, and others enter in and dishonour her; and this is the reason why she has such an evil name. Vulgar little minds see the land open and rush from the prisons of the arts to get a place in her temple; a clever mechanic, having a soul coarse as his body, thinks that he will gain caste by making a profession of philosophy. For philosophy, even in her fallen estate, has a dignity of her own. He is like a bald little blacksmith's apprentice, who having just got out of durance and made a little money, washes and decks himself out as a bridegroom, and marries his master's daughter; and will not the offspring of such marriages be vile and bastard, devoid of truth and nature? 'They will.' Small, then, is the remnant of genuine philosophers; there may be a few who are citizens of small states, in which politics are not worth thinking of, or who have been detained by Theages' bridle of ill health; for my own case of the oracular sign is almost singular, and too rare to be worth mentioning. And these few, when they have tasted the pleasures of philosophy, and taken a look at that den of thieves and place of wild beasts, which is human life, will go out of the world and stand aside from the storm under the shelter of a wall, and try to preserve their own innocence and to depart in peace. 'A great work, too, will have been accomplished by them.' Great, yes, but not the greatest; for man is a social being, and can only attain the highest development in the society which is best suited to him.

Enough, then, of the causes why philosophy has such an evil name. Another question is, Which of existing states is suited to her? There is none; for at present she has no abiding-place on earth, and may be compared to the exotic seed which degenerates in a strange soil. Only in her proper state will she be shown to be of heavenly growth. 'And is her proper state ours or some other?' Ours in all points but one, which was left undetermined. It was said, indeed, that some living mind or witness of the legislator was needed in states. But we were afraid to enter upon a subject of such difficulty, and now the question recurs and has not grown easier:—How may philosophy be safely studied? Let us bring her to the light of day, and make an end of the inquiry.

In the first place, nothing can be worse than the present mode of study. The fashion is, that for a few years in the days of youth, and in the intervals of household matters and business, persons get a smattering of philosophy, but are off as soon as they approach the real difficulty, which is dialectic. Later, they perhaps accompany a dilettante friend at his request to a lecture on philosophy. Years advance, and the sun of philosophy like that of Heracleitus sets, unlike that of Heracleitus never to rise again. Now this order ought to be entirely reversed; education should never finish—beginning with gymnastics in youth, which will minister to philosophy in after life; but as the man strengthens increasing the gymnastics of the soul. Then, when nature begins to decay and active life is over, he should return to philosophy again and for ever. 'You are in profound earnest, Socrates, and I think that the world will be equally earnest in withstanding you—no one more likely than our friend Thrasymachus.' Do not make a quarrel between Thrasymachus and me, who were never enemies and are now very good friends. And I shall do my best to persuade him and all mankind, and if I cannot, I will at any rate lay a foundation for another life, when after coming to the birth again we hold similar discourses. 'That is a long time hence.' Not long, I said, in comparison with eternity. I do not wonder that the many will not believe, for they have never seen natural unities of ideas, but only ingenious juxtapositions; not free and generous thoughts, but tricks of controversy and quips of law;—a perfect man ruling in a perfect state, even a single one they have not known. And we foresaw that there was no chance of perfection either in states or individuals until a necessity was laid upon that second small class of philosophers—not the rogues, but those whom we called useless—of taking the government; or until the sons of kings were inspired with a true love of philosophy. Whether in the infinity of past time there ever has been, or is in some distant land, or will be hereafter, an ideal such as we have described, we will stoutly maintain that there has been and might be such a state wherever the Muse of philosophy rules. Will you say that the world is of another mind? O, my friend, do not revile the world! They will be of another mind if they are gently entreated, and learn the true nature of the philosopher. Who can hate a man who loves them? or be jealous of one who has no jealousy? A few such natures there may be, but this is not the common temper. Consider, again, that the many hate not the true but the false philosophers—the hirelings who are not the shepherds and who enter in by force, and are always speaking of persons and not of principles, which is the reverse of the philosophical spirit. Whereas the true philosopher has no time to think of the squabbles of men; his eye is fixed on the eternal order in accordance with which he moulds himself into the Divine image (and not himself only, but the characters of other men), and is the creator of the virtues private as well as public. And when mankind see that the happiness of states is only to be found in that image, will they be angry with us for attempting to delineate it? 'Certainly not. But what will be the process of delineation?' The artist will do nothing until he has made a tabula rasa; on this he will draw the constitution of a state, glancing often at the divine truth of nature, and from that deriving the godlike among men, mingling the two elements, rubbing out and painting in, until there is a perfect harmony or fusion of the divine and human. But perhaps the world will doubt the existence of such an artist. What will they doubt? That the philosopher is a lover of truth, having a nature akin to the best?—and if they admit this will they still quarrel with us for making philosophers our kings? 'They will be less disposed to quarrel.' Let us assume then that they make peace. Still, a person may hesitate about the probability of the son of a king being a philosopher. And we do not deny that they are very liable to be corrupted; but yet surely in the course of ages there might be one exception—and one is enough. If one son of a king were a philosopher, and had obedient citizens, he might bring the ideal polity into being, and then the impossible would become possible.

I gained nothing by evading the troublesome questions which arose concerning women and children. I will be wiser now and acknowledge that we must go to the foundation of another question: What is to be the education of our guardians? It was agreed that they were to be lovers of their country, and were to be tested in the refiner's fire of pleasures and pains, and those who came forth pure and remained fixed in their principles were to have honours and rewards in life and after death. That was what we were saying, when, like a coy maiden, the argument put on a veil and turned into another path. There was an unwillingness to make the assertion which I now hazard,—that our guardians must be philosophers. You remember all the contradictory elements, intellectual as well as moral, which met in the philosopher. How difficult to find them all in a single person! The steadfast, immoveable nature which has not the wit to run away in battle is apt to go to sleep at a lecture on philosophy. And yet both elements, as we were saying, are necessary, and therefore both were to be tested in the pleasures and pains of which we spoke; and now we must further add, that they are to be tested in the highest branches of knowledge. You will remember also, that when we spoke of the virtues mention was made of a longer road, which you were satisfied to leave unexplored. 'Enough seemed to us to have been said.' Enough, my friend; but what is enough while anything remains wanting? The watchman, of all men, should not linger in the search after truth; he must be prepared to take the longer road, or he will never reach the summit of perfection. 'What, is there a higher region of truth above the four virtues?' Yes, there is; and of the virtues too he must not only get an outline, but a clear and distinct

vision. (Strange that we should be so precise about trifles, so confused
and inaccurate about the highest truths!) And of this truth you have
heard before a hundred times at least, although you put on that provoking air of unconsciousness—the idea of good, about which we know
so little, and without which though a man gain the world he has no
good of it. Some people imagine that the good is wisdom; but this
involves a circle,—the good is wisdom, wisdom is of the good.
According to another notion the good is pleasure; but this is literally
blasphemous, and involves the absurdity that good is bad, because there
are bad pleasures as well as good. Again, the good must have reality;
a man may desire the appearance of virtue, but he will not desire the
appearance of good. And ought our guardians then to be ignorant of
this supreme principle, of which every man has a presentiment, and
upon which all things depend, and without which no man has any real
knowledge of anything? 'But, Socrates, what is this supreme principle,
knowledge or pleasure, or what other? You may call me a troublesome
fellow, but I say that you have no business to be always repeating the
doctrines of others instead of giving us your own.' Have I any business
to say what I do not know? 'You may offer an opinion.' And will
the crooked way of opinion content you where you ought to require
the clearness of certainty, or will you be satisfied with the cloudiness of
opinion when you might have the light of science? 'I will ask you to
give such an explanation of the good as you did before of "temperance"
and "justice;" that will be enough.' I wish that I could, but the force
that is in me is not sufficient to reach to the height of the knowledge of
the good. To the parent or principal I cannot introduce you, but to the
child begotten in his image, which I may compare with the interest on
the principal, I will. (Audit the account, and do not let me give you a
false statement of the debt.) You remember our old distinction of the
many beautiful and the one beautiful, the particular and the universal,
the objects of sight and the objects of thought? Did you ever consider
that the objects of sight imply a faculty of sight which is the most
complex and costly of our senses, requiring not only objects of sense,
but also a medium, which is light; without which the sight will see
nothing and the colours will remain blank? Which light is the noble
bond between the perceiving faculty and the thing perceived, and the
god who gives us light is the sun, who is the eye of the day, but is not
to be confounded with the eye of man. The sun, or eye of the day, is

what I call the child of the good, standing in the same relation to the visible world as the good to the intellectual. When the sun shines the eye sees, and in the intellectual world where truth is, there is sight and light. Now that which is the sun of intelligible natures, is the idea of good, the cause of knowledge and truth, yet fairer and other than they are, and standing in the same relation to them in which the sun stands to light. O inconceivable height of beauty, which is above knowledge and above truth! ('You cannot surely mean pleasure,' he said. Peace, I replied.) And this idea of good, like the sun, is also the cause of growth and the author not of knowledge only, but of being, and exceeding being in dignity and power. Glaucon said, with a comical air: 'By Heaven! that is a reach of thought more than human.' I must lay the exaggeration to your door, for you made me utter my fancies. 'Nay,' he said, 'go on with the image, for I know that there is more behind.' There is, I said; and bearing in mind our two suns or principles, imagine further their corresponding worlds—one of the visible, the other of the intelligible— you may assist your fancy by figuring the distinction under the image of a line divided into two unequal parts, and may again subdivide each part into two lesser segments representative of the stages of knowledge in either sphere. The lower half of the lower or visible sphere will consist of shadows and reflections, and the upper half of the same sphere will contain real objects in the world of nature or of art. The sphere of the intelligible will also have two divisions,—one of mathematics, in which there is no ascent but all is descent; no inquiring into premises, but only drawing of inferences. In this division the mind works with figures and numbers, the images of which are taken not from the shadows, but from the objects, although the truth of them is seen only with the mind's eye; and they are used without being analysed as hypotheses. Whereas in the other division reason uses the hypotheses as stages or steps in the ascent to the idea of good, to which she fastens them, and then again descends, walking firmly in the region of ideas, and of ideas only, in her ascent as well as descent, and finally resting in them. 'I partly understand your meaning, which is that the ideas of science are superior to the hypothetical, metaphorical conceptions of geometry and the other arts, as with some degree of inaccuracy they may be termed, and the latter conceptions you refuse to make the subject of pure intellect, because they have no first principle, although when resting on a first principle, they pass into the higher sphere.' You understand me very well, I said. And now to those four divisions of knowledge you may assign four corresponding faculties—pure intelligence to the highest sphere; active intelligence to the second; to the third, faith; to the fourth, the perception of likenesses—and the clearness of the several faculties will be in the same ratio as the truth of the objects to which they are related.

. . . . Like Socrates, we may recapitulate the virtues of the philosopher. In language which seems to reach beyond the horizon of that age and country, he is described as 'the spectator of all time and all existence.' He has the noblest gifts of nature, and makes the highest use of them. All his desires are absorbed in the love of wisdom, which is the love of truth. None of the graces of a beautiful soul are wanting in him; neither can he fear death, or think much of human life. The ideal of modern times hardly retains the simplicity of the antique; there is not the same originality either in truth or error which characterized the Greeks. The philosopher is no longer living in the unseen, nor is he sent by an oracle to convict mankind of ignorance; nor does he regard knowledge as a system of ideas leading upwards by regular stages to the idea of good. The eagerness of the pursuit has abated; there is more division of labour and less of comprehensive reflection upon nature and human life as a whole; more of exact observation and less of anticipation and inspiration. Still, in the altered conditions of knowledge, the parallel is not wholly lost; and there may be a use in translating the conception of Plato into the language of our own age. The philosopher in modern times is one who fixes his mind on the laws of nature in their sequence and connexion, not on fragments or pictures of nature; on history, not on controversy; on the truths which are acknowledged by the few, not on the opinions of the many. He is aware of the importance of 'classifying according to nature,' and will try to 'separate the limbs of science without breaking them.' (Phaedr. 265 E.) There is no part of truth, whether great or small, which he will dishonour; and in the least things he will discern the greatest. (Parmen. 130 C.) Like the ancient philosopher, he sees the world pervaded by analogies, but he can also tell 'why in some cases a single instance is sufficient to prove a law,' while in other cases a thousand examples would prove nothing. He inquires into a portion of knowledge only, because the whole has grown too vast to be embraced by a single mind or life. He has a clearer conception of the divisions of science and of their relation to the mind of man than was possible to the ancients. Like Plato, he has a vision of the unity of knowledge, not as the beginning of philosophy to be attained by a study of elementary mathematics, but as the far-off result of the working of many minds in many ages. He is aware that mathematical studies are preliminary to almost every other; at the same time, he will not reduce all varieties of knowledge to the type of mathematics. He too must have a nobility of character, without which genius loses the better half of greatness. Regarding the world as a point in immensity, and each individual as a link in a never-ending chain of existence, he will not think much of human life, or be greatly afraid of death.

Adeimantus objects first of all to the form of the Socratic reasoning, thus showing that Plato is aware of the imperfection of his own method. He brings the accusation against himself which might be brought against him by a modern logician—that he extracts the answer because he knows how to put the question. In a long argument words are apt to change their meaning slightly, or premises may be assumed or conclusions inferred with rather too much certainty or universality; the variation at each step may be unobserved, and yet at last the divergence becomes considerable. Hence the failure of attempts to apply arithmetical or algebraic formulae to logic. The imperfection, or rather the higher and more elastic nature of language, does not allow words to have the precision of numbers or of symbols. And this quality in language impairs the force of an argument which has many steps.

The objection, though fairly met by Socrates in this particular instance, may be regarded as implying a reflection upon the Socratic mode of reasoning. And here, as at p. 506 B, Plato seems to intimate that the time had come when the negative and interrogative method of Socrates must be superseded by a positive and constructive one, of which examples are given in some of the later dialogues. Adeimantus further argues that the ideal is wholly at variance with facts; for experience proves philosophers to be either useless or rogues. Contrary to all expectation (cp. p. 497 for a similar surprise) Socrates has no hesitation in admitting the truth of this, and explains the anomaly in an allegory, first characteristically depreciating his own inventive powers. In this allegory the people are distinguished from the professional politicians, and, as at pp. 499, 500, are spoken of in a tone of pity rather than of censure under the image of 'the noble captain who is not very quick in his perceptions.'

The uselessness of philosophers is explained by the circumstance that mankind will not use them. The world in all ages has been divided between contempt and fear of those who employ the power of ideas and know no other weapons. Concerning the other class, Socrates argues that the best is most liable to corruption; the finer nature is more likely to suffer from alien conditions. There are some kinds of excellence which spring from a peculiar delicacy of constitution; this is evidently true of the poetical and imaginative temperament, which often seems to depend on impressibility, and hence can only live in a certain atmosphere. The man of genius has greater pains and greater pleasures, greater powers and greater weaknesses, and often a greater play of character than is to be found in ordinary men. He can assume the disguise of virtue or disinterestedness without having them, or veil personal enmity in the language of patriotism and philosophy,—he can say the word which all men are thinking, and is ever ready to take various forms as the situation changes. An Alcibiades, a Mirabeau, or a Napoleon the First, are born either to be the authors of great evils in states, or ' of great good when they are drawn in that direction.' Yet the thesis, ' corruptio optimi pessima,' cannot be maintained generally or without regard to the kind of excellence which is corrupted. For the alien conditions which are corrupting influences to one nature, may be the elements of culture to another.

Plato would have us consider how easily the best natures are overpowered by public opinion, and what efforts the rest of mankind will make to get possession of them. The world, the church, their own professions, any political or party organization, are always carrying them off their legs and teaching them to apply high and holy names to their own prejudices and interests. The 'monster' corporation to which they belong judges right and truth to be the pleasure of the community. The individual becomes one with his order; or, if he resists, the world is too much for him, and will sooner or later be revenged on him. This is, perhaps, a one-sided but not wholly untrue picture of the maxims and practice of mankind when they 'sit down together at an assembly,' either in ancient or modern times.

When the higher natures are corrupted by politics, the lower take possession of the vacant place of philosophy. This is described in one of those continuous images in which the argument, to use a Platonic expression, ' veils herself,' and which is dropped and reappears at intervals. Then arises the question,—Why the citizens of states are inimical to philosophy? The answer is, that they do not know her. And yet there is also a better mind of the many; they would believe if they were taught. But hitherto they have only known a conventional imitation of philosophy, words without thoughts, systems which have no life in them; a [divine] person uttering the words of beauty and freedom, the friend of man holding communion with the Eternal, and seeking to frame the state in that image, they have never known. The same double feeling respecting the mass of mankind has always existed among men. The first thought is that the people are the enemies of truth and right; the second, that this only arises out of an accidental error and confusion, and that they do not really hate those who love them, if they could be educated to know them.

In the latter part of the sixth book, three questions have to be considered : 1st, the nature of the longer and more circuitous way, which is contrasted with the shorter and more imperfect method of book iv.; 2nd, the heavenly pattern or idea of the state; 3rd, the relation of the divisions of knowledge to one another and to the corresponding faculties of the soul.

1. Of the higher method of knowledge in Plato we have only a glimpse. Neither here nor in the Symposium, nor yet in the Philebus, does he give any clear explanation of his meaning. He would probably have described his method as proceeding by regular steps to a system of universal knowledge, which inferred the parts from the whole rather than the whole from the parts. This ideal logic is not the method which was pursued by him in the search after justice; there, like Aristotle in the N. Ethics, he is arguing from experience and the common use of language. But at the end of the sixth book he conceives of a higher method, in which all ideas are only steps or grades or moments of thought, forming a connected whole or intellectual world, which is self-supporting, and in which consistency is the test of truth. In modern times, indeed, we hardly need to be reminded that the process of acquiring knowledge is here confused with the contemplation of absolute knowledge. In all science *a priori* and *a posteriori* truths mingle in various proportions. But Plato erroneously imagines that the synthesis is separable from the analysis, and that the method of science

can anticipate science. In entertaining such a vision of *a priori* knowledge he is sufficiently justified, or at least his meaning may be sufficiently explained by the similar attempts of Descartes, Kant, Hegel, and even of Bacon himself, in Modern Philosophy. Nor can we deny that in ancient times knowledge must have stood still, and the human mind been deprived of the very instruments of thought, if philosophy had been strictly confined to the results of experience.

2. Plato supposes that when the tablet has been made blank the artist will fill in the lineaments of the ideal state. Is this a pattern laid up in heaven, or mere vacancy on which he is supposed to gaze with wondering eye? The answer is, that such ideals are framed partly by the omission of particulars, partly by imagination perfecting the form which experience supplies. (Phaedo, 74.) Plato represents these ideals in a figure as belonging to another world; and in modern times the idea will sometimes seem to precede, at other times to co-operate with the hand of the artist. As in science, so also in creative art, there is a synthetical as well as an analytical method. One man will have the whole in his mind before he begins; to another the processes of mind and hand will be simultaneous.

3. There is no difficulty in seeing that Plato's divisions of knowledge are based, first, on the fundamental antithesis of sensible and intellectual which pervades the whole pre-Socratic philosophy; in which is implied also the opposition of the permanent and transient, of the universal and particular. But the age of philosophy in which he lived seemed to require a further distinction;—numbers and figures were beginning to separate from ideas. The world could no longer regard justice as a cube, and was learning to see, though imperfectly, that the abstractions of sense were distinct from the abstractions of mind. Between the Eleatic being or essence and the shadows of phenomena, the Pythagorean philosophy of number found a place, and was, as Aristotle remarks, a conducting medium from one to the other. (Metaph. 1, 6, 4.) Yet the passage from one to the other is really imaginary. Moral philosophy has no connexion with mathematics; number and figure are the abstractions of time and space, not the expressions of purely intellectual conceptions. When divested of metaphor, a straight line or a square has no more to do with right and justice than a crooked line with vice. The figurative association was mistaken for a real one; and thus the three latter divisions of the Platonic scheme were constructed.

There is more difficulty in comprehending how he arrived at the first term of the series, which is nowhere else mentioned, and has no reference to anything else in his system. Nor indeed does the relation of shadows to objects correspond to the relation of numbers to ideas. Probably Plato has been led by the love of analogy (cp. Timaeus, p. 32 B) to make four terms instead of three, although the objects perceived in both divisions of the lower sphere are equally objects of sense. He is also preparing the way, as his manner is, for the shadows of images at the beginning of the seventh book, and the imitation of an imitation in the tenth. The line may be regarded as reaching from unity to infinity, and is divided into two unequal parts, and subdivided into two more; each lower sphere is the multiplication of the preceding. Of the four faculties, faith in the lower division has an intermediate position, contrasting equally with the vagueness of the perception of shadows (εἰκασία) and the higher certainty of understanding (διάνοια) and reason (νοῦς).

The difference between understanding and mind or reason (νοῦς) is analogous to the difference between acquiring knowledge in the parts and the contemplation of the whole. True knowledge is a whole, and is at rest; consistency and universality are the tests of truth. To this self-evidencing knowledge of the whole the faculty of mind is supposed to correspond. But there is a knowledge which is incomplete and in motion always, because unable to rest in the subordinate ideas. Those ideas are called both images and hypotheses—images because they are clothed in forms of sense, hypotheses because they are assumptions only, until they are brought into (a fancied) connexion with the idea of good.

The method of Socrates is hesitating and tentative, awaiting the fuller explanation of the idea of good, and of the nature of dialectic in the seventh book. The imperfect intelligence of Glaucon, and the reluctance of Socrates to make a beginning, mark the difficulty of the subject. The allusion to Theages' bridle and to the oracular sign, which here, as always in Plato, is only prohibitory; the reference to another state of existence which is unknown to Glaucon in the tenth book; the surprise in the answers at pp. 487 and 497; the fanciful irony of Socrates, where he pretends that he can only describe the strange position of the philosopher in a figure of speech; the original remark that the Sophists, after all, are only the representatives and not the leaders of public opinion; the picture of the philosopher standing aside in the shower of sleet under a wall; the 'right noble thought' that the highest truths demand the greatest exactness; the hesitation of Socrates in returning once more to his well-worn theme of the idea of good; the ludicrous earnestness of Glaucon—are characteristic and interesting features.

BOOK VII. After this I took up my parable, and said: Imagine human beings living in a sort of underground den which has a mouth wide open towards the light, and behind them a breastwork such as marionette players might use for a screen; and there is a way beyond the breastwork along which passengers are moving, holding in their hands various works of art, and among them images of men and animals, wood and stone, and some of the passers are talking and others silent. 'A strange parable,' he said, 'and strange captives.' They are ourselves, I replied; and they see nothing but the shadows which the fire throws on the wall of the cave; to these they give names, and if we add an echo which returns from the wall, the voices of the passengers will seem to proceed from the shadows. Suppose now that you suddenly turn them round and make them look with pain and grief to themselves at the real images; will they believe them to be real? Will not their eyes be dazzled, and will they not try to get away from the fire to something which they are able to behold without blinking? And suppose further, that they are dragged up a steep and rugged ascent into the presence of the sun himself, will not their eyes be darkened with the excess of light? Some time will pass before they get the habit of perceiving at all; and at first they will be able to perceive only shadows and reflections in the water; then they will recognize the moon and the stars, and will at length behold the sun in his own proper place as he is. Last of all they will conclude:—This is he who gives us the year and the seasons, and is the author of all that we see. How will they rejoice in passing from darkness to light! How worthless to them will seem the honours and glories of the den or cave out of which they came! As Homer says: 'Better to be the servant of a poor master than a prince over all the dead.' And now imagine further, that they descend into their old habitations;—in that darkness visible they will not see as well as their fellows, and will not be able to compete with them in the measurement of the shadows on the wall; there will be many jokes about the man who went on a visit to the sun and lost his eyes—men should not do such things—and if they find anybody trying to set free and enlighten one of their number, they will put him to death, if they can catch him. Which things are an allegory: The cave or den is the world of sight, the fire is the sun, the way upwards is the way to knowledge, and in the world of knowledge the idea of good is last seen and with difficulty, but when seen is inferred to be the author of good and right—parent of the lord of light in this world and of truth and understanding in the other. And those who attain to the beatific vision are always going upwards, and are unwilling to descend into political assemblies and courts of law. Their eyes are apt to blink at the images or shadows of images which they behold in them. They cannot enter into the ideas of those who have never in their lives understood the relation of the shadow to the substance. Now blindness is of two kinds, and may be caused either by passing out of darkness into light or out of light into darkness, and a man of sense will distinguish between them—he will not laugh equally at both of them, but the blindness which arises from fulness of light he will deem blessed, and pity the other; or if he laugh at the blinking idiot looking up at the sun, he will have more reason to laugh than the inhabitants of the den. There is a further lesson taught by this parable of ours. Some persons fancy that instruction is like giving eyes to the blind, but we say that the faculty of sight was always there, and that the soul only requires to be turned round towards the light. And this is conversion; other virtues are almost like bodily habits, and may be acquired in the same manner, but intelligence has a diviner life, and is indestructible, turning either to good or evil according to the direction given. Did you never observe how the soul of a clever rogue peers out of his eyes, and the more clearly he sees, the more evil he does? Now if you take such an one and circumcise his passions, and cut away from him the leaden weights which drag him down and keep the eye of his soul fixed upon the ground, the same faculty in him will be turned round, and he will behold the truth as clearly as he now discerns his meaner ends. And have we not decided that our rulers must neither be so uneducated as to have no fixed rule of life, nor so over-educated as to be unwilling to leave their paradise for the business of the world? And we must choose out the natures who are most likely to ascend to the light and knowledge of the good, and not allow them to do as they do now. I mean to say that they must not be allowed to remain in the region of light, but must be forced down again among the captives in the den to partake of their labours and honours. 'Is not this hard? and what if they had rather not?' You should remember, my friend, that our purpose in framing the State was not that our citizens should do what they like, but that they should serve the State for the common good of all. May we not fairly say to our philosopher,—Friend, we do you no wrong; for in other States philosophy grows wild, and a wild plant owes nothing to the gardener, but you we have trained to be the rulers and kings of our hive, and therefore we must insist on your descending into the darkness of the den? You must, each of you, take your turn, and become able to use your eyes in the dark, and with a little practice you will see ten thousand times as well as those who quarrel about the shadows, whose knowledge is a dream only, whilst yours is a waking reality. It may be that the saint or philosopher who is best fitted, may also be the least inclined to rule, but necessity is laid upon him, and he must no longer live in the heaven of ideas. And this will be the salvation of the State. For those who rule must not be those who are desirous to rule; and if you can offer to our citizens a better life than that of rulers there will be a chance that the rich, not only in this world's goods, but in virtue and wisdom, may bear rule. And the only life which is better than the life of political ambition is that of philosophy, which is also the best preparation for the government of a State.

Then now comes the question,—How shall we create our rulers; what way is there from darkness to light? How like departed spirits may they be raised from the world below into the upper air? The change is effected by philosophy, which is not the spinning round of an oyster, but the conversion of a soul from night to day, from becoming to being. And what sort of training will draw the soul upwards? Our former education had two branches,—gymnastic, which was occupied with the body, and music, the sister art, which infused a sort of harmony into mind and literature; but neither of these sciences gave any promise of doing what we want. What have we left? All that remains to us is that universal science which is the primary element of all the rest. 'What is that?' A small matter—one, two, three—or in other words, number, of which I say that all arts and sciences are partakers. 'Very true.' Including the art of war? 'Yes, certainly.' Then there is something very ludicrous about Palamedes in the tragedy, coming in and saying that he had invented number, and counted the ranks and set in order the ships. For if Agamemnon could not count his feet (and without number how could he?) he must have been a pretty sort of general indeed. No man should be a soldier who cannot count, and indeed he is hardly to be called a man. But I am not speaking of these practical applications of arithmetic, for number, in my view, is rather to be regarded as a conductor to thought and being. I will explain what I mean by the last expression:—Things sensible are of two kinds; the one class irritate the mind, while in the other the mind acquiesces. Now the irritating class are the things which suggest contrast and relation. For example, suppose that I hold up to the eyes three fingers—a fore finger, a middle finger, a little finger—the sight equally recognizes all three fingers, but cannot distinguish which is first, second, or third. Or again, suppose two objects to be relatively great and small, these ideas of greatness and smallness are supplied not by the sense, but by the mind. And the perception of their contrast or relation quickens and sets in motion the mind, which is puzzled by the confused intimations of sense, and has recourse to number in order to find out whether the things indicated are one or more than one. Number replies that they are two and not one, and are to be distinguished from one another. Again, the sight beholds great and small, but only in a confused chaos, and not until they are distinguished does the question arise of their respective natures, leading on to the distinction between the visible and intellectual. And that was what I meant when I spoke of irritants to the intellect; I was thinking of the contradictions which arise in perception. The idea of unity, for example, like that of a finger, does not arouse thought unless involving some conception of plurality; but when the one is also the opposite of one, the contradiction gives rise to reflection. An example of this is afforded by any object of sight; and what is true of one is true of all number. It raises the mind out of the foam and flux of generation to the contemplation of being, having lesser military and retail uses also. The retail use is not required by us; but as our guardian is to be a soldier as well as a philosopher, the military one may be retained. No science can be more suitable for our higher purpose, when pursued for the sake of knowledge only, and not in the spirit of a shopkeeper. Great is the power of arithmetic in giving abstraction; for numbers are pure abstractions, and the true arithmetician indignantly denies that his unit is capable of division. You may divide, but he insists that you are only multiplying; his one is not material or divisible into parts, but an unvarying and absolute equality; and this shows the purely intellectual character of his study. Note also the great

power which arithmetic has of sharpening the wits; no other discipline
is equally severe, or an equal test of ability in general, or equally improving to a stupid man.

Let our second branch of education be geometry. 'I can easily see,'
replied Glaucon, 'that in manœuvring an army or taking up a position,
the skill of the general will be more than doubled by his knowledge of
geometry.' Not much will be required for this purpose; the use of
geometry, to which I should rather refer, is the assistance given by it in
the contemplation of the idea of good, compelling the mind to look at
true being, and not at generation only. Any one who is the least of a
mathematician is aware that the present mode of pursuing these studies
is mean and ridiculous; they are made to look downwards to the arts,
and not upwards to eternal existence. The geometer is always talking
of squaring, subtending, apposing, as if he had in view action rather
than knowledge; whereas the knowledge of the eternal is the real
object of geometry. The study tends to elevate the soul; to draw
upwards what is tending downwards; and may also have lesser uses in
war and military tactics, and in improving the reasoning faculties.

Shall we propose as a third branch of our education—astronomy?
'Very good,' replied Glaucon; 'the knowledge of the heavens is good
at once for husbandry, navigation, military tactics.' I like your way of
giving useful reasons for everything in order to conciliate the world.
Nor do I deny that there is a difficulty in proving to mankind that
education is not only useful information but an illumination and purification of the soul, better than ten thousand eyes, for by that alone is
truth seen. Now, will you appeal to mankind in general or to the philosopher? or would you prefer to look to yourself only? 'Every man
is his own best friend.' Then take a step backward, for we are out of
order, and insert the third dimension which is of solids, after the second
which is of planes, and then you may proceed to solids in motion. But
the properties of the third dimension can hardly be said to be as yet
discovered. The study is not popular and has not the patronage of the
State, nor is the use of it fully recognized; the difficulty is great, and
the votaries of the study are full of conceit and impatient of direction.
Still the charm of the pursuit wins upon men, and, if the State would
lend a little assistance, there might be great progress made. 'Very true,'
replied Glaucon, 'I admit the charm; and I understand you now to
begin with plane geometry, and to place next solid geometry, which you

omitted as being a pursuit likely to raise a smile; thirdly, astronomy, or
the motion of solids.' Yes, I found the more haste the less speed.
'Very good,' he said; 'and, now that the missing link is supplied, let us
proceed to astronomy.'

'About astronomy I am willing to speak in your lofty strain. No one
can fail to see that the contemplation of the heavens draws the soul
upwards.' I am an exception, then; astronomy as studied at present
appears to me to draw the soul not upwards, but downwards. Star-
gazing is just looking up at the ceiling—no better; a man may float on
his back by land or by water—he may look up or look down, but
there is no science in that. The vision of knowledge of which I speak
is seen not with the eyes, but with the mind. All the magnificence of
the heavens is but the embroidery of a copy which falls far short of the
divine Original, and teaches nothing about the absolute harmonies or
motions of things. They are like mathematical diagrams, drawn by the
hand of Dædalus or any other great artist, which may be used for illustration, but no mathematician would seek to obtain from them true conceptions of equality or numerical relations. How ridiculous then to look for
these in the map of the heavens, in which the imperfection of matter
comes in everywhere as a disturbing element, marring the symmetry of
day and night, of months and years, of the sun and stars in their courses.
Only by problems can we place astronomy on a truly scientific basis.
Let the heavens alone, and exert the intellect.

Still, mathematics admit of other applications, as the Pythagoreans
say, and we agree. There is a sister science of harmonical motion
adapted to the ear as astronomy is to the eye, and there may be other
applications also. Let us inquire of the Pythagoreans about them, not
forgetting that we have a higher aim, which is the relation of these
sciences to the idea of good. The error which pervades astronomy
also pervades harmonics. The musicians put their ears in the place
of their minds. 'Yes,' replied Glaucon, I like to see them laying their
ears alongside of their neighbours' faces—some saying, "that's a new
note," others declaring that the two notes are the same.' Yes, I said;
but you mean the gentlemen who are always twisting and torturing the
strings of the lyre, and who quarrel about the tempers of the strings, as
though they were human beings. These empirics are not the people of
whom I am speaking; I refer rather to the Pythagorean harmonists, whom
we were about to consult. Their error is, that they investigate only the

numbers of the consonances which are heard, and ascend no higher,—
of the true numerical harmony which is unheard, and is only to be
found in problems, they have not even a conception. 'That last,' he
said, 'must be a marvellous thing.' A thing of value, I replied, if pursued
with a view to the good—if pursued in any other spirit, useless.

All these sciences are the prelude of the strain, and are profitable if
they are regarded in their natural relations to one another. 'I dare
say, Socrates,' said Glaucon; 'but such a study will be an endless business.' What study do you mean—of the prelude, or what? For all these
things are only the prelude, and you surely do not suppose that a mere
mathematician is also a dialectician? 'Certainly not. In all my experience I have hardly ever known a mathematician who could reason.'
And yet, Glaucon, is not true reasoning that hymn of dialectic which is
the music of the intellectual world, and which was by us compared to
the effort of sight, when from beholding the shadows on the wall we
arrived at last at the images which gave the shadows? Even so the dialectical faculty withdrawing from sense arrives by the pure intellect at
the contemplation of the idea of good, and never rests but at the very
end of the intellectual world. And the royal road out of the cave into
the light, and the blinking of the eyes at the sun and turning to contemplate the shadows of reality—not the shadows of an image only;
this progress and gradual acquisition of a new faculty of sight by the
help of the mathematical sciences, is the elevation of the soul to the
contemplation of the highest ideal of being. 'I agree in what you say,
though I do not fully understand you.'

And now, leaving the prelude, let us proceed to the hymn. 'What,
then, is the nature of dialectic, and what are the paths which lead
thither?' Dear Glaucon, you cannot follow me here. There can be
no revelation of the absolute truth to one who has not been disciplined
in the previous sciences. But that there is a science of absolute truth,
which is attained in some way very different from those now practised,
I am confident. For all other arts or sciences are relative to the wants
and opinions of men, and are designed for generation and production, or again for the preservation and support of life; and the mathematical sciences are but a dream and hypothesis, never attaining to the
dignity of true knowledge, because never analysing their own principles.
Dialectic only does away with hypotheses, and rises to the principle which
is above them, converting and gently leading the eye of the soul out

of the barbarous slough of ignorance into the light of the upper world, with the help of the arts which we have been describing—arts, as they may indeed be termed, although they require some other name implying greater clearness than opinion and less clearness than science, which may be called understanding. And thus we get four names—two for intellect and two for opinion,—reason or mind, understanding, faith, perception of likenesses, which make a proportion—being : generation : : intellect : opinion—and knowledge : faith : : opinion : perception of likenesses. Dialectic may be further described as that science which defines and explains the essence or being of each nature, which distinguishes and abstracts the good, and is ready to do battle against all opponents in the cause of good. This is that knowledge without which life is but a sleepy dream; and many a man is in his grave before he is well waked up. And would you have the children of your ideal State, who are to be your governors, intelligent beings, or stupid as posts? ' Certainly not the latter.' Then you must train them in dialectic. This is the highest knowledge and the coping-stone of all other knowledge.

I dare say that you have not forgotten the selection of the rulers; the process of selection may now be carried a step further :—They must be not only firm and valiant, and, as far as possible, good-looking, and of manners noble and grand, but must also have the qualities which will be likely to profit by education; that is to say, they must have keenness and be quick at learning, for the soul soon gets tired of mental gymnastics in which the toil is not shared by the body. And they must be retentive, solid, diligent, laborious natures, who combine intellectual with moral virtues,—not lame and one-sided, diligent in bodily exercise and indolent in mind, or conversely ;—not a maimed soul, which hates falsehood and yet unintentionally is always losing the pearl of truth in the mire of ignorance; not a bastard or feeble person, but sound in wind and limb, and in perfect condition for the great gymnastic trial of the mind. Justice herself can find no fault with natures such as these, who will be the saviours of our State; disciples of another sort would only make philosophy more ridiculous than she is at present. Forgive my enthusiasm; I had forgotten that we were not in earnest and became excited; when I see philosophy trampled under foot, I am angry at the authors of her disgrace. ' I did not notice that you were more excited than you ought to have been.' But I felt that I was. Now do not let us forget another point in the selection of our disciples—that they must be young and not old. For Solon is mistaken in saying that old men can be always learning— no more than they can be always running. Youth is the time of study, and here we must remember that the mind is free and dainty, and, unlike the body, must not be made to work against the grain. Learning in youth should be a sort of play, in which the natural bent is detected. As in training them for war the young dogs should only taste blood, but when the necessary gymnastics are over which divide life between sleep and bodily exercise, then the education of the soul will become a more serious matter. At twenty years of age, after various trials in which 'muscular philosophy' is not to be neglected, a selection must be made of the more promising disciples, with whom a new epoch of education will begin. The sciences which they have hitherto learned in fragments will now be viewed in a more comprehensive way, and brought into relation with each other and with true·being; the faculty of combining them is the test of real speculative and dialectical ability. And afterwards there shall be trials for still higher honours; and at thirty a further selection shall be made of those who are able to withdraw from the world of sense into the abstraction of ideas. And here, according to present experience, there is great danger that a negative dialectic may fill them with iniquity. The danger may be illustrated by a parallel case:—Imagine a person who has been brought up in wealth and luxury amid a crowd of flatterers, and who is suddenly informed that he is a supposititious son. He has hitherto honoured his supposed parents and disregarded the flatterers, and now he does the reverse;— this is just what happens with a man's principles. There are certain doctrines which he learnt at home and which had a sort of parental authority over him. Presently he finds that imputations are cast upon them; a troublesome querist comes and asks, 'What is the just and good?' or proves that virtue is vice and vice virtue, and his mind becomes unsettled, and he ceases to love, honour and obey them as he had hitherto done. He is seduced into the life of pleasure, and becomes a lawless person and a rogue. The case of such speculators is very pitiable, and, in order that our thirty years' old pupils may not deserve this pity, let us take every possible care that young persons do not study philosophy too early; a man should have some ballast in his composition before he begins. For a young man is a sort of puppy who only plays with an argument, and is reasoned into and out of his opinions every day; they set upon their neighbours tossing and goring them, and bring themselves into discredit and philosophy with them. A man of thirty has too much sense to run on in this way; he will argue and not merely contradict, and will give a degree of weight and dignity to the pursuit of philosophy. This is a caution which, like all the previous ones, is intended to impress harmony and steadiness of character on our disciples. What time shall we allow for this second gymnastic training of the soul?—say, twice the time required for the gymnastics of the body; six, or perhaps five years, to commence at thirty, and then for fifteen years let the student go down into the den, and command armies, and gain experience of life. At fifty let him return to the end of all things, and have his eyes uplifted to the idea of good, and order his life after that pattern; if necessary, taking his turn at the helm of State, and training up others to be his successors. When his time comes he shall depart in peace to the islands of the blest. He shall be honoured with sacrifices, and be worshipped as a god if the Pythian oracle approves; and at any rate, he shall be revered as a man.

And now the statues of our rulers are finished, and you have only to add that the women will share in all things with the men. And you will admit that our State is not a mere aspiration, and may really come into being in the way which we have described, when there shall arise philosopher-kings, one or more, who will despise the pomps and vanities of this present world, and will be the servants of justice only in the administration of the State. 'And how will they commence their administration?' The first step will be to send away into the country all those who are more than ten years of age, and begin on those who are left. 'That will be a very great saving of time.'

. . . At the commencement of the sixth book, Plato anticipated his explanations of the relation of the philosopher to the world in an allegory; in this, as in other passages, following the order which he prescribes in education, and proceeding from the concrete to the abstract. At the commencement of book vii., under the figure of a cave having an opening towards a fire and a way upwards to the true light, he returns to view the divisions of knowledge, exhibiting familiarly, as in a picture, the result which had been hardly won by a great effort of thought in the previous discussion; at the same time casting a glance onward at the dialectical process, which is represented by the way leading from darkness to light. The shadows, the images, the reflection of the sun and stars in the water, the stars and sun themselves, severally correspond,—the first, to the realm of fancy and poetry,—the second, to the world of sense,—the third, to the abstractions or universals of sense, of which the mathematical sciences furnish the type,—the fourth and last to the same abstractions, imagined to be seen in the unity of the idea, from which they derive a new meaning and power. The true dialectical process begins with the contemplation of the real stars, and not mere reflections of them, and ends with the recognition of the sun, or idea of good, as the parent not only of light but of warmth and growth. To the divisions of knowledge the stages of education partly answer;—first, there is the early education of childhood and youth in the fancies of the poets, and in the laws and customs of the State;—then there is the training of the body to be a warrior athlete, and a good servant of the mind;—and thirdly, after an interval follows the education of later life, which begins with mathematics and proceeds to philosophy in general.

There seem to be two great aims in the philosophy of Plato,—first, to realize abstractions; secondly, to connect them. According to him, the true education is that which draws men from becoming to being and to a comprehensive survey of all being. He desires to develop in the human mind the faculty of seeing the universal in all things; until at last the particulars of sense drop away and the universal alone remains. He never understood that abstractions, as Hegel says, are 'mere abstractions'—of use when employed in the arrangement of facts, but adding nothing to the sum of knowledge when pursued apart from them, or with reference to an imaginary idea of good. Still the exercise of the faculty of abstraction has enlarged the powers of the human mind, and played a great part in the education of the human race. Plato appreciated the value of this, and saw that the faculty might be quickened by the study of number and relation. All things in which there is opposition or proportion are suggestive of reflection. The dull impression of sense evokes no power of thought or of mind, but when objects of sense ask to be compared and distinguished, then philosophy begins. The science of arithmetic first suggests such distinctions. There follow in order the other sciences of plain and solid geometry, and of solids in motion, one branch of which is astronomy or the harmony of the spheres,—to this is appended the sister science of the harmony of sounds. Plato seems also to hint at the possibility of other applications of arithmetical or mathematical proportions.

The modern mathematician will readily sympathise with Plato's delight in the properties of pure mathematics. He will not be disinclined to say with him:—Let alone the heavens, and study the beauties of number and figure in themselves. He, too, will be apt to depreciate their application to the arts. He will observe that Plato has a conception of geometry, in which figures are to be dispensed with; thus in a distant and shadowy way seeming to anticipate the possibility of working geometrical problems by a more general mode of analysis. He will remark with interest on the backward state of solid geometry, which, alas! was not encouraged by the aid of the State in the age of Plato;. and he will recognize the grasp of Plato's mind in his ability to conceive of one science of solids in motion including the earth as well as the heavens,—not forgetting to notice the intimation to which allusion has been already made, that besides astronomy and harmonics the science of solids in motion may have other applications. Still more will he be struck with the comprehensiveness of view which led Plato, at a time when these sciences hardly existed, to say that they must be studied in relation to one another, and to the idea of good, or common principle of truth and being. But he will also see (and perhaps without surprise) that in that stage of physical and mathematical knowledge, Plato has fallen into the error of supposing that he can construct the heavens *a priori* by mathematical problems, and determine the principles of harmony irrespective of their adaptation to the human ear. The illusion was a natural one in that age and country. The simplicity and certainty of astronomy and harmonics seemed to contrast with the variation and complexity of the world of sense;—hence the circumstance that there was some elementary basis of fact, some measurement of distance or time on which they must ultimately rest, was overlooked by him. The modern predecessors of Newton fell into errors at least equally great; and Plato can hardly be said to have been very far wrong, or may even claim a sort of prophetic insight into the subject, when we consider that the greater part of astronomy at the present day consists of abstract dynamics, by the help of which most astronomical discoveries have been made.

The metaphysical philosopher from his point of view recognizes mathematics as an instrument of education,—which strengthens the power of attention, developes the sense of order and the faculty of construction, and enables the mind to grasp under simple formulæ the quantitative differences of physical phenomena. But while acknowledging their value in education, he sees also that they have no connexion with our higher moral and intellectual ideas. In the attempt which Plato makes to connect them, we easily trace the influences of the old Pythagorean notions. There is no reason to suppose that he is speaking of the ideal numbers at p. 525 E; but he is describing numbers which are pure abstractions, to which he assigns a real and separate existence, which, 'as the teachers of the art' (meaning probably the Pythagoreans) would have affirmed, repel all attempts at subdivision, and in which unity and every other number are conceived of as absolute. The truth and certainty of numbers, when thus disengaged from phenomena, gave them a kind of sacredness in the eyes of an ancient philosopher. Nor is it easy to say how far ideas of order and fixedness may have had a moral and elevating influence on the minds of men, ' who,' in the words of the Timaeus, ' might learn to regulate their erring lives according to them.' It is worthy of remark that the old Pythagorean ethical symbols still exist as figures of speech among ourselves. And those who see in modern times the world pervaded by universal law, may also see a faint anticipation of this last word of modern philosophy in the Platonic idea of good, which is the source and measure of all things, and yet only an abstraction. (Cp. Phileb. sub fin.)

Two passages seem to require more particular explanations. First, that which relates to the analysis of vision. The difficulty in this passage may be explained, like many others, from differences in the modes of conception prevailing among ancient and modern thinkers. To us, the perceptions of sense are inseparable from the act of the mind which accompanies them. The consciousness of form, colour, distance, is indistinguishable from the simple sensation, which is the medium of them. Whereas to Plato sense is the Heraclitean flux of sense, not the vision of objects in the order in which they actually present themselves to the experienced sight, but as they may be imagined to appear confused and blurred to the half-awakened eye of the infant. The first action of the mind is aroused by the attempt to set in order this chaos, and the reason is required to frame distinct conceptions under which the confused impressions of sense may be arranged. Hence arises the question, ' What is great, what is small?' and thus begins the distinction of the visible and the intelligible.

The second difficulty relates to Plato's conception of harmonics. Three classes of harmonists are distinguished by him :—first, the Pythagoreans, whom he proposes to consult (as in the previous discussion on music he will consult Damon) and who are acknowledged to be masters in the art, but are nevertheless deficient in the knowledge of its higher import and relation to the good; secondly, the mere empirics, whom Glaucon appears to confuse with them, and whom both he and Socrates ludicrously describe as experimenting by mere auscultation on the intervals of sounds. Both of these fall short in different degrees of the Platonic idea of harmony, which must be studied in a purely abstract way, first by the method of problems, and secondly as a part of universal knowledge in relation to the idea of good.

The allegory has a political as well as a philosophical meaning. The den or cave represents the narrow sphere of politics or law (cp. the description of the philosopher and lawyer in the Theaetetus, 172–176), and the light of the eternal ideas is supposed to exercise a disturbing influence on the minds of those who return to this lower world. In other words, their principles are too wide for practical application; they are looking far away into the past and future, when their business is with the present. The ideal is not easily reduced to the conditions of actual life, and may often seem to be at variance with them. And at first, those who return are unable to compete with the inhabitants of the den in the measurement of the shadows, and are derided and persecuted by them; but after a while they see the things below in far truer proportions than those who have never ascended into the upper world. The difference between the politician turned into a philosopher and the philosopher turned into a politician, is symbolized by the two kinds of disordered eyesight, the one which is experienced by the captive who is transferred from darkness to day, the other, of the heavenly messenger who voluntarily for the good of his fellow-men descends into the den. In what way the brighter light is to dawn on the inhabitants of the lower world, or how the idea of good is to become the guiding principle of politics, is left unexplained by Plato. Like the nature and divisions of dialectic, of which Glaucon impatiently demands to be informed, perhaps he would have said that this could not be revealed except to a disciple of the previous sciences. (Compare Symposium, 210 A.)

Some modern elements of thought may be noted in this part of the Republic. We seem to hear the echo of our own times in the complaints which Plato utters respecting the dangers of speculation in youth. The minds of young men become unsettled, and their extravagance brings discredit on philosophy and on themselves. They argue about the laws and opinions in which they have been brought up, and soon begin to think that one thing is as good as another. Their position is ingeniously compared to that of an illegitimate son, who has made the discovery that his supposed parents are not his real ones, and, in consequence, they have lost their authority over him. The distinction between the mathematician and the dialectician is also noticeable. Plato is very well aware that the faculty of the mathematician is quite distinct from the higher philosophical sense which recognizes and combines first principles (531 E). The contempt which he expresses at p. 533 for distinctions of words, the danger of involuntary falsehood, the apology which Socrates makes for his earnestness of speech, are highly characteristic of the Platonic style and mode of thought. The quaint notion that if Palamedes was the inventor of number Agamemnon could not have counted his feet; the art by which we are made to believe that this State of ours is not a dream only; the gravity with which the first step is taken in the actual creation of the State, namely, the sending out of the city all who had arrived at ten years of age, in order to expedite the business of education by a generation, are also truly Platonic. (For the last, compare the passage at the end of the third book, in which he expects the lie about the earthborn men to be believed in the second generation.)

BOOK VIII. And so we have arrived at the conclusion, that in the perfect State wives and children are to be in common; and their education and pursuits, both in war and peace, are also to be common, and their kings are to be philosophers and warriors. And a further conclusion is, that our soldiers are to live in common houses and to have all things in common; they are to be warrior athletes receiving no pay, but only their food, from the other citizens. Now let us return to the point at which we digressed, and recover the track. ' That is easily done,' he replied; ' You were speaking before we entered on the subject of women and children, of the State which you had constructed, and of the individual who answered to this, both of whom you affirmed to be good, although of both you were able to show still more excellent things; and you said that of inferior States there were four forms and four individuals corresponding to them, which although deficient in various degrees, were all of them worth inspecting with a view to determining the relative happiness or misery of the best or worst man. Then Polemarchus and Adeimantus interrupted you, and this led to another argument,—and so here we are.' Suppose that we put ourselves again in the same position, and do you repeat your question. 'I want to know what are the constitutions of which you spoke?' There are only four of any note:—first, the famous Lacedæmonian or Cretan commonwealth; secondly, oligarchy, which is a State full of evils; thirdly, democracy, which is next in order; fourthly, tyranny, which is the disease or death of all governments; and there are other intermediate forms which exist among barbarians as well as among Hellenes. Now, States are not made of 'rock and oak, but of flesh and blood;' and therefore as there are five states there must be five human natures in individuals, which correspond to them. And first, there is the ambitious nature, which answers to the Lacedæmonian State; secondly, the oligarchical nature; thirdly, the democratical; and fourthly, the tyrannical. This last will have to be compared with the perfectly just, that we may know which is the happier, and then we shall be able to determine whether the argument of Thrasymachus or our own is the more convincing. And as before we began with the State and went on to the individual, so let us do now; beginning with timocracy, let us go on to the timocratical man, and then proceed to the other forms of goverment, and the individuals who answer to them.

But how did timocracy arise out of the perfect State? Plainly, like all changes of government, from division in the rulers; for a government which is united cannot be moved. But whence came division? 'Sing, heavenly Muses,' as Homer says; may we not suppose them to speak to us as to children, putting on a solemn face in jest? 'And what will they say?' They will say that human things are fated to decay, and the immutable city will not escape—when the wheel comes full circle in a period short or long; plants or animals have their times of fertility and sterility, which the intelligence of the rulers alloyed by sense will not enable them to ascertain, and children will be born when they ought not. For whereas divine creations are in a perfect cycle or number, the human creation is in a number which declines from perfection, and has four terms and three intervals of numbers, increasing, waning, assimilating, dissimilating, and yet perfectly commensurate with each other. The base of the number with a fourth added (or which is 3 : 4), multiplied by five and cubed, gives two harmonies:—The first a square number, which is a hundred times the base (or a hundred times a hundred); the second, an oblong, being a hundred squares of the rational diameter of a figure the side of which is five, subtracting one from each square or two perfect squares from all, and adding a hundred cubes of three. This entire number is geometrical and contains the rule or law of generation. And when this law is neglected marriages will be unpropitious; the inferior offspring who are then born will in time become the rulers, and the State will decline, and education will fall into decay, and gymnastic be preferred to music, and the gold and silver and brass and iron will form a chaotic mass, and thus will division arise. Such is the Muses' answer to our question. 'And a true answer; for how can the answer of the Muses be other than true?—What more have the Muses to say?' They say that the two races, the iron and brass, and the silver and gold, will draw the State different ways;—the one to trade and moneymaking, and the others having the true riches and needing no other, will resist them—there will be a contest, which will end in a compromise; they will have private property, and will enslave their fellow-citizens who were once their friends and nurturers. But they will retain their warlike character, and their chief occupation will be to make war, and to control their subjects. This is the origin of that middle state which is intermediate between aristocracy and oligarchy.

The new form of government resembles the ideal in obedience to rulers and contempt for trades and handicrafts, and devotion to warlike and gymnastic exercises. But corruption has crept into philosophy, and simplicity of character which was once her note, is now looked for only in the military class. Arts of war begin to prevail over arts of peace; the ruler is no longer a philosopher; as in oligarchies, there springs up among them an extravagant love of gain—get another man's and save your own, is their principle; and they have dark places in which they hoard their gold and silver, for the use of their women and others; they take their pleasures stealthily, like boys who are running away from their father, the law; and their education is not inspired by the muse, but imposed by the strong arm of power. The leading characteristic of the State is party spirit and ambition. But I have said enough of this, for time would fail me if I attempted to describe all the varieties of States and individuals.

And what manner of man answers to such a State as this? 'In love of contention,' replied Adeimantus, 'he will be like our friend Glaucon.' Perhaps, yes, he may be like him in that, but not in other ways; for he is self-asserting and ill-educated, yet fond of literature and of hearing recitations, although himself not a speaker,—fierce with slaves, but not truly above them—obedient to rulers, and a lover of power and honour, which he hopes to gain by deeds of arms—fond, too, of gymnastics and of hunting. As he advances in years he grows more and more avaricious, having never known a saviour or guardian—that is to say, reason and music—which are the only saviours of men. His origin is as follows:—His father may probably have been a good man dwelling in an ill-ordered State, who has retired from public life that he may be at peace. His mother is angry at her loss of precedence among other women; she is disgusted at the selfishness of her husband, and her woman's tongue expatiates to her son on the unmanliness and indolence of his father. 'Yes,' said Adeimantus, 'that is the way with all women.' Yes, I said, and you may observe also that the old family servant takes up the tale, and says to the youth:—'When you are grown up you must be more of a man than your father, and proceed against debtors and avenge insults.' All the world are agreed that the man who minds his own business is an idiot, while a busybody is highly honoured and esteemed. The young man hears and sees this, and he also hears his father's words and sees his ways, and as he is naturally well disposed, although liable to be perverted by evil influences, he rests at a middle point and becomes ambitious and a lover of honour.

And now, as Æschylus says, 'Set another man over against another city;' or rather, let the city come first. The next form of government is oligarchy, in which the rule is of the rich only. No eyes are needed to see how this form of government springs out of the last. 'How is that?' The private treasury is the beginning of the decline; the possession of gold and silver leads to new fashions of expense, and the citizens and their wives break the law. One draws another on, and the multitude are infected; riches are thrown into the scale, and virtue kicks the beam;—lovers of money take the place of lovers of honour; misers of politicians; and, in time, political privileges are confined to the rich. The latter change is commonly effected by fear and violence.

Thus much of the origin,—let us next consider the evils of oligarchy. Would a man who wanted to be safe on a voyage take a bad pilot

because he was rich, or refuse a good one because he was poor? And
does not the analogy apply still more to the helm of State? And there
are yet greater evils : two nations are struggling together in one State—
the rich and the poor; and the rich dare not put arms into the hands
of the poor, and are unwilling to pay for defenders out of their own
money. And have we not already condemned that State in which the
same persons are warriors as well as shopkeepers? The greatest evil of
all is that a man may sell his property and have no place in the State;
while there is one class which has enormous wealth, the other is entirely
destitute. But observe that these destitutes had not really any more of
the governing nature in them when they were rich than now that they
are poor; they were miserable spendthrifts always. They are the drones
of the hive; only whereas the actual drone is unprovided by nature with
a sting, the 'unfeathered, two-legged things,' which we call drones, do
not all agree in this respect, for some of them are without stings and
some of them have dreadful stings; in other words, there are paupers
and there are rogues. In the cellars and underground places of an
oligarchical city you will always find this scum of the earth, which includes nearly everybody but the governing classes. And this state of
things originates in bad education and in bad government.

Like State, like man,—the change in the latter begins with the timocratic man; he walks at first in the ways of his father, who may have
been a statesman, or general, perhaps; and presently he sees him 'fallen
from his high estate,' the victim of informers, dying in prison or exile,
or by the hand of the executioner. The lesson which he learns from
this is one of caution; he leaves the dangerous arena of politics, and
makes money; hoping to retrieve his father's losses, he represses his
pride and saves pence. Avarice is enthroned as his bosom's lord, and
assumes the style of the Great King, and the newest Persian fashions.
The rational and spirited elements sit humbly on the ground, and the
only speculation in which they are allowed to indulge is how to get
rich. The love of honour turns to love of money; the conversion is
instantaneous. And the man goes through the same process as the
State; he is mean, saving, toiling, the slave of one passion which is the
master of the rest, a skinflint, a hoarder, who chooses a life which the
vulgar approve: Is he not the very image of the State? He has had
no education, or he would never have allowed the blind god of riches
to lead the dance within him. And being uneducated he will have

many slavish desires, some beggarly, some knavish, breeding in his soul. Shall I tell you where you may detect him? If he is the trustee of an orphan, and has the power to defraud, he will show that he is not without the will, and that his passions are only restrained by fear and not by reason. He will be respectable in his dealings generally, but when he has to spend another man's money, he will show that he has the desires of a drone. Hence he leads a divided existence; in which the better desires mostly prevail. But when he is contending for prizes and other distinctions, he is afraid to incur a loss which is to be repaid only by barren honour; he represses his desires, and is small and saving in his expenditure; in time of war he fights with a small part of his resources, and usually saves his money and loses the battle.

Next comes democracy and the democratic man, out of oligarchy and the oligarchical man. Insatiable avarice is the ruling passion of an oligarchy; they allow vice and extravagance among the citizens in order that they may be enriched by the sale of a spendthrift's property; and no man can serve two masters, wealth and virtue. In this disorderly condition of things men of family often lose their property or rights of citizenship, and there they are, not only poor and in debt, but a fixture in the State, with their stings out and arms in their hands—ready for any desperate enterprise against the new owners of their property and against the State. The usurer with stooping walk pretends not to see them; he passes by on the other side, and leaves his sting—that is, his money—in any one else who will be his victim; and many a man is reduced into the state of dronage by him, and has to pay the parent or principal multiplied into a family of children. The only way of diminishing this evil is either to limit a man's use of his property, or to insist that the lender shall lend at his own risk, and have no protection from the law. But in an oligarchy the ruling class do not want to apply a remedy; they are careful only of money, and as careless of virtue as the poorest of the citizens. Now there are occasions on which the governors and the governed meet together,—at festivals, on a journey, voyaging or fighting. The wiry, sunburnt pauper finds that in the hour of danger he is not despised; he sees the rich man under an umbrella puffing and panting, and draws the conclusion which he privately imparts to his companions, —'that our people are not good for much;' and as a sickly frame is made ill by a mere touch from without, or sometimes without external impulse is ready to fall to pieces of itself, so from the least cause, perhaps from some offer of aristocratic or democratic help, or with no cause at all, the city, like the sick man, falls ill and fights a battle for life or death. And democracy comes into existence when the poor are the victors, killing some and exiling some, and giving equal shares in the government to all the rest.

The manner of life in such a State is that of democrats; there is freedom and plainness of speech, and every man does what is right in his own eyes, and has his own way of life. Hence arise the most various developments of character; the State is like a piece of embroidery of which the colours and figures are the manners of men, and there are many who, like women and children, prefer this variety to real beauty and excellence. The State is not one but many, like a bazaar at which you can buy anything which you want. The great charm is, that you may do as you like; you may govern if you like, let it alone if you like; go to war and make peace if you feel disposed, and all quite irrespective of anybody else. When you put men to death they come to life again; a gentleman is desired to go into exile, and he stalks about the city like a hero, and nobody sees him or cares for him. Take another look at the free and lordly nature of democracy, how grandly she sets her foot upon all our fine theories of education,—how little does she care for the training of her statesmen! The only qualification which is demanded by her is the profession of patriotism. Such is democracy;—a pleasing, lawless, various sort of government, distributing equality to equals and unequals alike.

Let us now inspect the individual democrat; and first, as in the case of the State, we will trace his antecedents. He is the son of a miserly oligarch, and has been taught by him to restrain the love of unnecessary pleasures. Perhaps for the sake of clearness I ought to explain the meaning of this latter term; necessary pleasures are those which are good, and which we cannot do without; unnecessary pleasures are those which do no good, and of which the desire might be eradicated by early training. For example, the pleasures of eating and drinking are necessary and healthy, up to a certain point; beyond that point they are alike hurtful to body and mind, and the excess may be avoided. When in excess, they may be rightly called expensive pleasures, in opposition to the useful ones. And the drone, as we called him, was the slave of these unnecessary pleasures, while the miserly oligarch is under the dominion of the others.

The oligarch changes into the democrat in the following manner:—
The youth who had a mean and miserly bringing up, gets a taste of the
drone's honey; he meets with wild reckless companions, who introduce
him to every new pleasure. Thus the change begins; and, as in the
State, there are allies on both sides, temptations from without and
passions from within; there is reason also and external influences of
parents and friends in alliance with the better nature; and these two
factions or armies are in violent conflict with one another. Sometimes
the party of order prevails, but then again new desires and new disorders arise, and a whole mob of passions get possession of the Acropolis, that is to say, the head, which they find unguarded—void of
acquirements and virtues, best sentinels over the lives of men dear to
the gods. Falsehoods and illusions ascend to take their place; the
prodigal goes back into the country of the Lotophagi or drones, and
openly dwells there. And if any offer of alliance or parley of individual elders comes from home, the false spirits shut the gates of the
castle and permit no one to enter,—there is a battle, and the victory is
with them; and then they banish modesty, which they call folly, and thrust
away temperance; and all law and order are quickly despatched over the
border by them and the rabble who are at their heels. And when the
house is clean swept and garnished, their favourite is initiated by them;
—they dress up the exiled vices in bright array, and bring them back
again crowned with garlands, and give them new names. Insolence
they call gentility, anarchy freedom, waste magnificence, impudence
courage. Such is the change from the use of the necessary pleasures
to the unnecessary ones; after this the youth is divided impartially between them; and if he be fortunate and not too far gone in his badness,
when he gets older and the turbulence of his passions begins to pass
away, he receives back some of the exiles and lives in a sort of equilibrium; he indulges first one pleasure and then another, as they offer;
and if reason comes and tells him that some pleasures are good and
honourable, and others bad and vile, she is not admitted into the
citadel—he shakes his head and says that they are all alike, and
he will have no invidious distinctions between them. Thus he lives
in the fancy of the hour; sometimes he is drunken and lapped in
wine and song; then he will drink water only and get thin; he takes
to the gymnasium, or he does nothing at all; then again he would
be a philosopher or a politician, and he jumps up and says anything

that comes into his head; or again, he would be a warrior and get a fortune:—

> 'A man so various that he seemed to be
> Not one but all mankind's epitome.'

There remains still the finest and fairest of all men and all States—tyranny and the tyrant. Tyranny springs from democracy much in the same way that democracy springs from oligarchy. 'How do you mean?' Both arise from excess; the one from excess of wealth, the other from excess of freedom. 'The great natural good which makes life worth having,' says the democrat, 'is freedom.' And this exclusive love of freedom and regardlessness of everything else, is the cause of the change from democracy to tyranny. The State is athirst for freedom, and being served by evil cupbearers, swills the strong wine of freedom, and presently in a fit of drunken patriotism breaks out and beats her rulers; those who are loyal to them are called good for nothing, hereditary bondsmen and the like; equality and fraternity of governors and governed, is the approved principle. Anarchy is the law, not of the State only but of private houses, and is diffused over all. Father and son, citizen and foreigner, teacher and pupil, old and young, are all on a level, and fathers and teachers fear their sons and pupils, and the wisdom of the young man is a match for the elder, and the old imitate the jaunty manners of the young because they are afraid of being thought morose. Slaves whom you have bought with money are on a level with their masters and mistresses, and there is no difference between men and women. And why, as Æschylus says, should I not utter the word which comes to my lips? The very animals in a democratic State have a freedom which is unknown in other places. The she-dogs are as good as their she-mistresses, and horses and asses march along with dignity and run their noses into anybody who comes in their way;—such exuberance is there and superabundance of freedom. 'I have often remarked that, and in my country walks have experienced the same.' The end is, that the skins of the citizens become so sensitive that they cannot endure the yoke of laws, written or unwritten; they would have no man call himself their master. Such is the fair, glorious beginning of things out of which tyranny springs. 'Glorious, indeed; and what is to follow?' The ruin of oligarchy is the ruin of democracy; there is a law of contraries; the greatness of anything goes before a fall. The excess of freedom passes into the excess of slavery, and the greater the freedom the greater the slavery. You will remember that in the oligarchy were found two classes, one of poor and the other of idle men; the one were the leaders, the others the followers—rogues and paupers, who were compared by us to drones with and without stings. These two classes are to the State what phlegm and bile are to the human body; and the duty of the State physician, or legislator, is to purge them away in the same manner that a bee-keeper would cut out the cells of drones. Now in a democracy, too, there are drones, but of a much more dangerous sort than in the oligarchy; there they are inert and unpractised, here they are full of life and animation; and the keener sort speak and act, while the others buzz about the bema and prevent their opponents from being heard. And there is another class in democratic States, of trading, thriving individuals,—these are like a sponge, to be squeezed when the drones have need of their possessions; there is moreover a third class, who are the labourers and artizans, and they make up the mass of the people. When the people meet, they are omnipotent, but there is a difficulty in bringing them together unless they are attracted by a little honey; and the rich supply the honey, of which the demagogues keep the greater part for themselves and give the others a taste only. The possessions of the rich begin to be taken, and they are compelled to protect themselves; when they see the demagogues urging on their followers to do what they would not do of themselves, they are driven mad by the stings of the drones, and become downright oligarchs in self-defence. Then follow informations and convictions for treason. The people have some protector whom they nurse into greatness, and from this root the tree of tyranny springs. The nature of the change is indicated in the old fable of the temple of Zeus Lycaeus: the story is, that he who tastes human flesh mixed up with the flesh of other victims, will be turned into a wolf. Even so the protector, who in his hour of popularity tastes human blood, and slays some and exiles others with and without pretence of law, and proclaims abolition of debts and division of lands, must either perish or become a wolf—that is, a tyrant. Perhaps he is driven out, but he soon comes back from exile in full power; and then if his enemies cannot get rid of him by legal means, they plot his assassination. Thereupon the friend of the people makes his famous request for a body-guard, which they readily grant, thinking only of his danger and not of their own. When he hears of this, let the rich man make to himself wings, and not turn back to take anything

in the house, for he will never run away again if he does not do so
then.   And the Great Protector, instead of his vast bulk lying upon the
earth, overstrides others, and stands like a colossus in the chariot of
State, a full-blown tyrant now.   Let us enquire into the nature of his
happiness.

In the early days of his tyranny he has a smile and 'Peace be with
you' for everybody; he is not a 'dominus,' no, not he: he has only
come to put an end to debt and the monopoly of land.   He is soon
reconciled to the enemies of his power abroad, and then he makes himself necessary to the State by always going to war.   War-taxes depress
the poor; this has the incidental advantage of keeping them from conspiring against him; and he can only get rid of bolder spirits by handing
them over to the enemy,—hence he must always be stirring up war.
Then comes unpopularity; some of those who assisted in setting him
up have the courage to tell him a piece of their minds.   The consequence is, that he must put them out of the way; he will always be
keeping a sharp look-out on the high spirited, the wise, the wealthy; and
such is his blessed condition of life, that he is obliged to make a purgation of them.   'And what a purgation!'   Yes, he purges away the good
as the physician purges away the bad; he has to choose between death
and a hateful and shameful life.   And the more hated he is, the more he
will require trusty guards; but whom will he trust, and where will he get
them?   'They will come flocking like birds, for pay.'   You mean that he
will hire drones out of foreign parts; would he not rather obtain them
on the spot?   'But how is that possible?'   He will take the slaves from
their owners and make them his body-guards; these are his trusted
friends, from whom alone he receives the tribute of love and admiration.
Verily the tragedians are wise, and Euripides wiser than any of them,
who says,—

> ' Tyrants are wise by converse with the wise;'

meaning to say, that they are the wise who consort with tyrants.   Moreover, he magnifies tyranny as a state of superhuman glory; and this is an
excellent reason, as he will allow if he has any wit, why we should refuse
to admit him into our State.   'I think that he may have wit enough for
that.'   He will go to other cities, and gather the mob about him with
grand and plausible words, and change commonwealths into tyrannies
and democracies,—receiving honours and rewards for this; first of all

from tyrants, secondly from democracies, but the higher he and his friends ascend constitution hill, the more their honour will fail and become 'too asthmatic to mount.' But to return to the tyrant;—how will he support that rare army of his? First, by confiscation, which will lighten the taxes; then he will take all his father's property, and spend this on his companions, male or female. Now his father is the demus, and if the demus gets angry, and says that a great hulking son ought not to be a burden on his parents, and tells him to depart and take his riotous crew with him, then will the parent know what a monster he has been fostering in his bosom, and that the son whom he would fain expel is too strong for him. 'You do not mean to say that he will beat his father?' Yes, he will, after having first taken away his arms. 'Then he is a parricide, and a cruel, unnatural son to a parent whom he is bound to cherish and maintain.' And the people have jumped from the fear of slavery into slavery, out of the smoke into the fire. Thus liberty, when out of all order and reason, passes into the worst form of slavery.

... In the previous books Plato has described the ideal State; now he returns to the perverted or declining forms, on which he had lightly touched at the end of book iv. These he describes in a succession of parallels between the individual and the State, tracing the origin of either in the State or individual which has preceded them. He begins by asking the point at which he digressed; and is thus led shortly to recapitulate the substance of the three former books, which also contain a parallel of the philosopher and the State.

Of the first decline he gives no intelligible account; he would not have liked to admit the most probable causes of the fall of his ideal State, which to us would appear to be the impracticability of communism or the natural antagonism of the ruling and subject classes. Hence he throws a veil of mystery over the origin of the decline, which he attributes to ignorance of the law of population. Of this law the famous geometrical figure or number is the expression. Like the ancients in general, he had no idea of the perfectibility of man or of the education of the human race. His ideal was not to be attained in the course of ages, but was to spring in full armour from the head of the legislator. When good laws had been given, he thought only of the manner in which they were likely to be corrupted, or of how they might be filled up in detail or restored in accordance with their original spirit.

He appears not to have reflected upon the full meaning of his own words, 'in the brief space of human life, nothing great can be accomplished' (book x. 608 B); or again, as he afterwards says in the Laws, iii. 676, 'infinite time is the maker of cities.' The order of constitutions which is adopted by him represents an order of thought rather than a succession of time, and may be considered as the first attempt to frame a philosophy of history.

The first of these declining States is timocracy, or the government of soldiers, and lovers of honour, which answers to the Spartan State; this is a government of force, in which education is not inspired by the Muses, but imposed by the law, and in which all the finer elements of organization have disappeared. The philosopher himself has lost the love of truth, and the soldier, who is of a simpler and honester nature, rules in his stead. The individual who answers to timocracy has some noticeable qualities. He is described as ill educated, but, like the Spartan, a lover of literature; and although he is a harsh master to his servants he has no natural superiority over them. His character is based upon a reaction against the circumstances of his father, who in a troubled city has retired from politics, and his mother, who is dissatisfied at her own position, is always urging him towards the life of political ambition. Such a character may have had this origin, and indeed Livy attributes the Licinian laws to a feminine jealousy of a similar kind (vii. 34). But there is obviously no connection between the manner in which the timocratic State springs out of the ideal, and the mere accident by which the timocratic man is the son of a retired statesman.

The two next stages in the decline of constitutions have even less historical foundation. For there is no trace in Greek history of a polity like the Spartan or Cretan passing into an oligarchy of wealth, or of the oligarchy of wealth passing into a democracy. The order of history appears to be different; first, in the Homeric times there is the royal or patriarchal form of government, which a century or two later was succeeded by an oligarchy of birth rather than of wealth, and in which wealth was only the accident of the hereditary possession of land and power. Sometimes this oligarchical government gave way to a government based upon a qualification of property, which, according to Aristotle's mode of using words, would have been called a timocracy; and this in some cities, as at Athens, became the conducting medium to democracy. But such was not the necessary order of succession in

States; nor, indeed, can any order be discerned in the endless fluc-
tuation of Greek history (like the tides in the Euripus), except, perhaps,
in the almost uniform tendency from monarchy to aristocracy in the
earliest times. At first sight there appears to be a similar inversion in
the last step of the Platonic succession, for tyranny instead of being the
natural end of democracy, in early Greek history appears rather as a
stage leading to democracy; the reign of Peisistratus and his sons is an
episode which comes in between the legislation of Solon and the constitution of Cleisthenes; and some secret cause common to them all
seems to have led the greater part of Hellas at her first appearance in
the dawn of history, e. g. Athens, Argos, Corinth, Sicyon, and nearly
every State with the exception of Sparta, through a similar stage of
tyranny, which ended either in oligarchy or democracy. But then we
must remember that Plato is describing rather the contemporary history
of the Sicilian States, which was an alternation between democracy and
tyranny, than the ancient history of Athens or Corinth.

The portrait of the tyrant himself is just such as the later Greek
delighted to draw of Phalaris and Dionysius, in which, as in the lives of
mediaeval saints or mythic heroes, the conduct and actions of one were
attributed to another in order to fill up the outline. There was no
enormity which the Greek was not ready to believe of them; the tyrant
was the negation of government and law; his assassination was glorious;
there was no crime, however unnatural, which might not with probability
be attributed to him. In this, Plato was only following the common
thought of his countrymen, which he embellished and exaggerated with
all the power of his genius. There is no need to suppose that he drew
from life; or that his knowledge of tyrants is derived from a personal
acquaintance with Dionysius. The manner in which he speaks of them
would rather tend to render doubtful his ever having 'consorted' with
them, or entertained the schemes which are attributed to him in the
Epistles, of regenerating Sicily by their help.

Plato describes with a sort of amusement the follies of democracy, of
which the political condition is reflected in social life. He conceives
democracy as a state of individualism or dissolution; in which every
one is doing what is right in his own eyes. Of a people animated by
a common spirit of liberty, rising as one man to repel the Persian host,
which is the leading idea of democracy in Herodotus and Thucydides,
he never seems to think. But if he is not a believer in liberty, still less

is he a lover of tyranny. His deeper and more serious condemnation is reserved for the tyrant, who is the ideal of wickedness and also of weakness, and who in his utter helplessness and suspiciousness is leading an almost impossible existence, without that remnant of good which, in Plato's opinion, was required to give power to evil (book i. p. 352). This ideal of wickedness living in helpless misery, is the reverse of that other portrait of perfect injustice ruling in happiness and splendour, which first of all Thrasymachus, and afterwards the sons of Ariston had drawn, and is also the reverse of the king whose rule of life is the good of his subjects.

Each of these governments and individuals has a corresponding ethical gradation: the ideal State is under the rule of reason, not extinguishing but harmonising the passions, and training them in virtue; in the timocracy and the timocratic man one virtue still remains, but has superseded all the rest: the constitution, whether of the State or of the individual, is based, first, upon courage, and secondly, upon the love of honour, which is hardly a virtue. In the second stage of decline the virtues have altogether disappeared, and the love of gain has succeeded to them; in the third stage, or democracy, the various passions are allowed to have free play, and the virtues and vices are impartially cultivated. But this freedom, which leads to many curious extravagances of character, is in reality only a state of weakness and dissipation. At last, one monster passion takes possession of the whole nature of man—this is tyranny. In all of them excess—the excess first of wealth and then of freedom, is the element of decay.

The eighth book of the Republic abounds in pictures of life and fanciful allusions; the use of metaphorical language is carried to a greater extent than anywhere else in Plato. We may remark, first, the description of the two nations in one, which become more and more divided, as in the feudal ages, and perhaps in our own times, so also among the Greeks; the notion of democracy expressed in a sort of Pythagorean formula as equality among unequals; the free and easy ways of men and animals, which are characteristic of liberty, as foreign mercenaries and universal mistrust are of the tyrant. The proposal that mere debts should not be recoverable by law is a speculation which has often been entertained by reformers of the law in modern times, and is in harmony with the tendencies of modern legislation. Debt and land were the two great difficulties of the ancient lawgiver; and we may be said to have almost, if not quite, solved the one of these difficulties but hardly the other.

Still more remarkable are the corresponding portraits of individuals: there is the family picture of the father and mother and the old servant of the timocratical man, and the outward respectability and inherent meanness of the oligarchical; the uncontrolled licence and freedom of the democrat, in which the young Alcibiades seems to be depicted, doing right or wrong as he pleases, and who at last, like the prodigal, goes into a far country (note here the play of language by which the democratic man is himself represented under the image of a State having a citadel and receiving embassies); and there is the wild-beast nature, which breaks loose in his successor. The hit about the tyrant being a parricide; the representation of the tyrant's life as an obscene dream; the rhetorical surprise of the more miserable than the most miserable of men in book ix.; the requirement that the poets will have the good sense to see that if they are the friends of tyrants they ought to be excluded from the State; the continuous image of the drones who are of two kinds, swelling at last into the monster drone having wings (see infra, book ix.), are among Plato's happiest touches.

There remains to be considered the great difficulty of this book of the Republic, the so-called number of the State. This is a puzzle almost as great as the Number of the Beast in the Book of Revelation, and though apparently known to Aristotle, is referred to by Cicero as a proverb of obscurity (Ep. ad Att. vii. 13, 5). And some have imagined that there is no answer to the puzzle, and that Plato has been practising upon his readers. But such a deception as this is inconsistent with the manner in which Aristotle speaks of the number (Pol. v. 12. 7), and would have been ridiculous to any reader of the Republic who was acquainted with Greek mathematics. As little reason is there for supposing that Plato intentionally used obscure expressions; the obscurity only arises from our want of familiarity with the subject. On the other hand, Plato himself indicates that he is not altogether serious, and in describing his number as a solemn jest of the Muses, he appears to imply some degree of satire on the symbolical use of number.

Our hope of understanding the passage depends principally on an accurate study of the words themselves; on which a faint light is thrown by the parallel passage in the ninth book. Another help is the allusion in Aristotle, who makes the important remark that the latter part of the

passage (from ὧν ἐπίτριτος πυθμὴν, κ.τ.λ.) describes a solid figure[1]. Some
further clue may be gathered from the appearance of the Pythagorean
triangle, which is denoted by the numbers 3, 4, 5, and in which, as in
every right-angled triangle, the squares of the two lesser sides equal the
square of the hypothenuse ($3^2 + 4^2 = 5^2$ or $9 + 16 = 25$).

Plato begins by speaking of a perfect or cyclical number (cp. Tim.
39 D; i.e. a number in which the sum of the divisors equals the whole);
this is the divine or perfect number in which all lesser cycles or revolutions are complete; he also speaks of a human or imperfect number,
having four terms and three intervals of numbers which are related to
one another as roots to powers, and which he describes as assimilating
and dissimilating, waxing and waning; in the latter half of the passage
he finds certain proportions, which give two harmonies, the one square
the other oblong; but he does not say that the square number answers
to the divine, or the oblong number to the human cycle.

Nor is there any trace in the passage that this second number either
has reference to a period of time, or is the number of the population of
the State. Plato is only thinking of some progression of number with
which he chooses to connect the regulation of births. There would be
less confusion if, instead of being termed the number of the world and
of the State (of which nothing is said in Plato), the two numbers were
called respectively the divine and human number of marriage or generation. For Plato does not suppose their influence to extend to anything but births. They preside over these in the same mysterious
manner in which the stars preside over them, or in which, according
to the Pythagoreans, opportunity, justice, marriage, are represented by
some number or figure.

I need not repeat the translation and explanations of terms given in
the text (p. 546), in which I have supposed the number to be 8000.
This interpretation derives a certain degree of plausibility,—first, from
the circumstance that the numbers suggested in the first half of the
passage coincide with the series of numbers which denote the interval
between royal and tyrannical pleasure; secondly, the number 8000
is the ancient number of the Spartan citizens (Herod. vii. 34), and would

[1] Pol. v. 12, 8 :—'He says that the cause (of the change in the perfect state) is the
instability of all things, and their changing in a certain period; and that this is dependent
on certain progressions of number, when a root in the ratio of 3 : 4 joined with the number
5 gives two harmonies, meaning when the number of the diagram becomes solid.'

be what Plato might have called 'a number befitting the population of a city;'—the mysterious disappearance of the Spartan population may possibly have suggested to him the first cause of his decline of States; thirdly, the lesser or square harmony of 400 might be a symbol of the guardians—the larger or oblong harmony, of the people, and the numbers 3, 4, 5 might refer to the three orders in the State or parts of the soul, the four virtues, the five forms of government. But in this explanation no clear connection is shown between the first and second half of the passage, nor are the words of Aristotle (ὅταν γένηται στέρεος) sufficiently explained. And the phrase ἐπίτριτος πυθμὴν seems to mean, not the number 3 with a third added (4), but the ratio of 4 : 3. For there would be no meaning in thus describing the number 4. And the connection with the Pythagorean triangle, the sides of which are represented by 3, 4, 5, would be lost.

More may be urged in defence of the number 216, which is adopted by Schleiermacher and ably supported by Dr. Donaldson (Proc. of the Philolog. Society, vol. i. p. 81 foll.). According to the latter, the θεῖον γεννητὸν is the world (?); the ἀνθρώπειον either man or the State (?); αὐξήσεις δυνάμεναί τε καὶ δυναστευόμεναι multiplications of the square by its square root (?); similar numbers are those whose factors, or the sides of the figures represented by them, are in the same ratio, e. g. 3 and 27 (?); increasing numbers are those which are less than the sum of their parts, e. g. 12 and 18 (?); προσήγορα is used of numbers which are expressible in the same terms, e. g. 8, 12, 18, 27 ($\frac{3}{2}$), ῥητὰ when expressible at all in terms of one another; ἐπίτριτος πυθμὴν is the fundamental number $\frac{4}{3}$; ἁρμονίαν ἴσην, κ.τ.λ. a square number multiplied by 100,—this is the first harmony. The second harmony is a cube of the same number, and is also described as 100 (ἰσομήκη μὲν τῇ), multiplied by the three following terms:—(1) the square of the rational diameter of 5, less 1, = 48; (2) two incommensurable diameters, i. e. the two first irrationals, 2 and 3; (3) the cube of 3, = 27. The first series of numbers is 8 : 12 :: 18 : 27, or the cubes of 2 and 3 with their mean proportionals. The first harmony is $(\frac{4}{3} \times 5)^2 = 100 \times \frac{2^2}{3^2} = \frac{400}{9}$. The second harmony is $(48 + 5 + 27) \times 10^2 \times \frac{1}{3^3} = 1000 \times \frac{2^3}{3^3} = \frac{8000}{27}$. The period of the world is defined by the first perfect number 6, that of the State by the cube of $6 = 216 = 5^3 + 4^3 + 3^3$; this, taking the roots instead of the cubes (5, 4, 3), represents the sides of the Pythagorean triangle, and has various other numerical and harmonic properties, e. g. $216 = 2^3 \times 3^3$ (cp. the first series); again, $\frac{4}{3} \times 5^3 = \frac{3}{2} \times 10^3$ and $\frac{4}{3} \times \frac{3}{2} = 2$. The number 216 also includes the three musical numbers, 3, 4, 5, and is the period of Pythagorean metempsychosis.

Other interpreters have suggested the number 5040, which is the number of citizens in the Laws; or 17500, which is the addition of the square of 100 (10,000) + 4800 + 2700, making a series 10,000 : 7500 : 4800 : 2700, of which the first is supposed to be the perfect or square number, and the three last stand to one another in the ratios of $5^2 : 4^2 : 3^2$. The number has also been supposed to be 50, apparently because the number 50 is equivalent to the squares of the three sides of the sacred triangle, and this is the opinion of Philo; or 10, which multiplied to the fourth power gives 10,000, and is supposed to be the perfect number, as 5 is the imperfect number: or again, the number is said to be made up of the two progressions of the Pythagorean tetractys 1 : 2 : 4 : 8 and 1 : 3 : 9 : 27. All these explanations show curious coincidences of number, which may put us on our guard against accepting other coincidences, but none of them is self-proving. A later explanation—that of Weber—deserves more notice.

He argues rightly for the substantial genuineness of the text; and supposes that the first division of the passage contains a general description of the proportions which are to be found in the second half; and explains 'assimilating and dissimilating' and 'waxing and waning' numbers respectively as numbers which form squares or which form oblongs. The increments of number which give these proportions are said to 'equal' and be 'equalled in power' (δυνάμεναι καὶ δυναστευόμεναι), because they are obtained by multiplying powers of 3, 4, 5—the numbers of the Pythagorean triangle, of which the hypothenuse is said to 'equal in power' the two lesser sides. The numbers themselves are 6400, 4800, 3600, and 2700, which are then gained afresh by multiplying the numbers 4×5 and 3×5 (ἐπίτριτος πυθμὴν πεμπάδι συζυγεὶς) with the sides of the Pythagorean triangle :—

First Series.	Second Series.
i. e. $3 \times 4 \times 5 = 60$	$3 \times 3 \times 5 = 45$
$4 \times 4 \times 5 = 80$	$4 \times 3 \times 5 = 60$
$5 \times 4 \times 5 = 100.$	$5 \times 3 \times 5 = 75.$

The former series squared, and multiplied with the second, gives the following results :—

$60^2 = 3,600$	$60 \times 45 = 2,700$
$80^2 = 6,400$	$80 \times 60 = 4,800$
$100^2 = 10,000.$	$100 \times 75 = 7,500.$

Thus two convenient series of numbers are obtained which agree with the description already given in the first part of the passage, and with the explanation of assimilating and dissimilating numbers as square and oblong. But there is no proof that this was the manner in which Plato intended the roots 3 : 5 and 4 : 5 to be multiplied. Nor is it likely that he would have used the term τρὶς αὐξηθεὶς to mean, not the raising of them to the third power, but the multiplication of them by 3, 4, 5. Nor is there any reason to suppose with Weber, that the words, 'this whole number is geometrical' refer only to the second of the two harmonies, or that the word τέλειος would be applied in such a passage as this (in which periods of revolution are spoken of) to any but a cyclical number; or that the first harmony answers to the perfect number.

And here we take leave of the difficulty, without attempting a further solution. The meaning of many words in the passage is so uncertain that there is little probability of our finding the answer to the riddle. Among uncertain expressions may be reckoned, δυνάμεναι, δυναστευόμεναι, ὁμοιούντων, ἀνομοιούντων, αὐξόντων, φθινόντων, ἐπίτριτος πυθμὴν πεμπάδι συζυγείς; and even the words ἁρμονία, τέλειος, αὐξήσεις, ἐν ᾧ πρώτῳ, γεωμετρικὸς, are variously explained; again, the clause δεομένων ... δυεῖν may be either taken as an explanation of ἀρρήτων or as a further subtraction of 100, so that the entire number becomes either 4900 or 4800. And there is the further uncertainty of the relation of the first to the second half of the passage, and of the two harmonies to one another.

The discovery of the riddle would be useless, and would throw no light on ancient mathematics. The point of interest is that Plato should have used such a symbol, and that so much of the Pythagorean spirit should have existed in his age. His general meaning is, that divine creation is perfect, and represented or presided over by a perfect or cyclical number; human generation is imperfect, and represented or presided over by an imperfect number or series of numbers. The number 5040, which is the number of the State in the Laws, is expressly based by him on utilitarian grounds, namely, the convenience of the number for division; but in this passage he is thinking of Pythagorean symbols and not of utility. The contrast of the perfect and imperfect number may have been easily suggested by the corrections of the cycle, which were made first by Meton and secondly by Callippus; (the latter is said to have been a pupil of Plato). Of the degree of importance or of exactness to be attributed to the problem, the number of the tyrant

in book ix. ($729 = 365 \times 2$), and the slight correction of the error in the
number $5040 \div 12$ (Laws, 771 C) may furnish a criterion.   There is
nothing surprising in the circumstance that those who were seeking for
order in nature and had found order in number, should have imagined
one to give law to the other, or should have held that a mysterious connection existed between them.

BOOK IX. Last of all comes the tyrannical man, about whom we
have to enquire, Whence he is, and how does he live—in happiness or
in misery?   There is, however, a previous question of the nature and
number of the appetites, which I should like to consider first.   Some of
them are unlawful, and yet admit of being chastened and weakened in
various degrees by the power of reason and law.   ' What appetites do
you mean?' I mean those which are awake when the reasoning powers
are asleep, which get up and walk about naked without any self-respect
or shame; and there is no conceivable folly or crime, however cruel or
unnatural, of which, in imagination, they may not be guilty.   ' True,' he
said, ' very true.' But when a man's pulse beats temperately; and he has
supped on a feast of reason and come to a knowledge of himself before
going to rest, and has satisfied his desires just enough to prevent their
perturbing his reason, which remains clear and transparent, and when
he is free from quarrel and heat,—the visions which he has on his bed
are least irregular and abnormal.   I want you to bear in mind, for I
have something more to say about this, that even in good men there is
such an irregular wild-beast nature, which peers out in sleep.

To return:—You remember what was said of the democrat; that he
was the son of a miserly father, and that he encouraged the saving
desires and repressed the ornamental and expensive ones; presently he
got into fine company, and began to entertain a dislike to his father's
narrow ways; and being a better man than the corrupters of his youth,
he came to a mean, and led a life, not of lawless or slavish passion, but
of regular and successive indulgence.   Now imagine a generation to
have passed away.   The youth has become a father, and has a son who
is exposed to the same temptations, and has companions who lead him
into every sort of iniquity, which they call liberty, and he has parents
and friends who try to keep him right.   The counsellors of evil find that
their only chance of success is to implant in his soul a monster drone, or

love; while other desires buzz around him and mystify him with sweet sounds and scents, this monster love takes possession of him and carries him off, and puts an end to every true or modest thought or wish that remains in him.   Love has of old been called a tyranny, and drunkenness is a tyranny, and a madman has in him the spirit of a tyrant, and is fancying that he can rule over gods and men.   And the tyrannical man, whether made by nature or habit, is just a drinking, lusting, infuriated sort of animal.

And how does such an one live?   'That is for you to tell me, not for me to tell you.'   Well then, I fancy that he will live amid revelries and harlotries, and love will dwell in the house, lord and master of all that is therein.   Many desires require much money; he spends all that he has and borrows more, and when he has nothing the young ravens are still in the nest in which they were hatched, crying for food.   Love, whose attendants they are, sets them on; and they must be gratified by force or fraud, or if not, they become painful and troublesome; and as the new pleasures take the place of the old ones, so the son will be for taking the inheritance of his parents; and if they show signs of refusing, he will defraud and deceive them; and if they openly resist, do not you think that he will possibly be guilty of some tyrannical action?   'I can only say, that I should not much like to be in their place.'   But, O heavens, Adeimantus, to think that for some new-fangled love of a harlot or for the waxen beauty of a youth, he will give up his old father and mother, best and dearest of friends, or even enslave them to the fancies of the hour.   A tyrannical son is truly a blessing to his father and mother. He begins by taking their property first; and when that comes to an end, and he finds his lusts still pressing upon him, he turns burglar or pickpocket, or robs a temple.   Love, attended by the enfranchised lusts, gets the better of the thoughts of his youth, and he becomes always in life and reality the monster that he was sometimes in sleep.   Love is his only lord, under the rule of whom he is strong in all violence and lawlessness; ready for any deed of daring that will supply the wants of his rabble-rout, whether coming from without or generated within.   Where there are only a few such in a well-ordered State, in time of war they go out and become the mercenaries of the tyrant.   In time of peace they stay at home and do mischief; they are the thieves, burglars, footpads, cutpurses, man-stealers of the community; and if they are able to speak, they come out in another line as false-witnesses and informers.   'Yes,' said he, 'and a small catalogue of crimes truly, even if the perpetrators of them are not numerous.' Yes, I said, but small and great are relative terms, and the greatest crimes which are done by them do not approach the tyrant; and where there are many of them and they wax strong, they create the tyrant out of their number. They choose out their representative man, and if the State resists, then the old story is repeated —they beat their fatherland and motherland, and place mercenaries over them who are their servants. Such men in their early days live with flatterers, and they themselves flatter others, and are all things to all men, in order to gain their ends; but they soon discard them, when they have no need of them; they are always either masters or servants, never the friends of anybody; no tyrant ever tasted the joys of friendship. And they are utterly treacherous and unjust, if the nature of justice be at all understood by us. In a word, such men are the waking vision of the dream which we described; and he who is the most of a tyrant by nature, and leads the life of a tyrant for the longest time, will be the worst of them, and being the worst of them, will also be the most miserable.

Like man, like State,—the tyrannical man will answer to tyranny, which is the extreme opposite of the royal State; for one is the best and the other the worst. We need not stop to enquire which is which, but may at once proceed to the next question, Which is the happier? And great and terrible as is the outward appearance of the tyrant sitting upon a throne in the midst of his satellites, let us not be afraid to go in and ask; and the answer is, that the monarchical is the happiest, and the tyrannical the most miserable, of States. And may we not ask the same question about the men themselves, requesting some one to look into them who is able to penetrate the inner nature of man, and will not be struck all of a heap like a child by the vain pomp of tyranny. I will suppose that he is one who has lived with him, and has seen him in his undress when he is no longer a hero, and perhaps in the hour of trouble and danger. Let him who has seen all this tell us of his happiness and misery.

In order to elicit the points of comparison in the individual and in the State, I will ask first of all, whether the State is likely to be free or enslaved; will there not be a little freedom and a great deal of slavery? And the freedom is of the bad, and the slavery of the good; and this is true of the man as well as of the State; for his soul is full of meanness

and slavery, and the better part is that which is enslaved, and the
madman and beast have power over him. He cannot do what he would,
and his mind is full of confusion; taking the whole man, he is the reverse of a freeman. And the State will be poor and not rich, and the
man's soul will be poor. And the State will be full of groans and
lamentations and sorrow, and will be the most miserable of States, and
the man will be full of sorrows, and the most miserable of men. No,
not the most miserable, for there is yet a more miserable. 'Who is
that?' The tyrannical man who has the misfortune also to become a
public tyrant. 'There I suspect that you are right.' Suspect, yes, but
how much better to be sure about a matter which is of vital importance
to morals. He is like a wealthy owner of slaves, only he has more of
them than any private individual; and, as you know, the owners are not
generally in any fear of their slaves. And why is this? Because the whole
city is in a league which protects the individual. But suppose that one
of these owners and his household is carried off by a god into a wilderness, where there are no freemen to help him (he is the master say of
about fifty slaves);—will he not be in an agony of terror?—will he not
be compelled to flatter his slaves and to promise them many things
much against his will? And suppose the same god who carried him off
were to surround him with neighbours who declare that no man has any
right to have slaves, and that the owners of them should be punished
with death. 'Still worse and worse! He will be in the midst of his
enemies.' And is not our tyrant such an imprisoned, captive soul, who
is made up of fears and loves, who has a swarm of passions which he is
incapable of indulging; living indoors always like a woman, and being
jealous of those who have the freedom of going about and seeing the
world?

Having so many evils, will not the most miserable of men be still
more miserable in a public station? Master of others when he is not
master of himself, like a sick man who is compelled to be an athlete,—
he is the meanest of slaves and most abject of flatterers; wanting all
things, and having all his desires craving about him; always in fear
and distraction, like the State of which he is the representative. His
jealous, hateful, faithless temper grows 'worse with command; he is more
and more faithless, envious, unrighteous, the most wretched of men, and
the cause of wretchedness to himself and to others. And so let us
have a final trial and proclamation; need we hire the herald, or shall I

proclaim the result? The son of Ariston (the best) is of opinion that the best and justest of men is also the happiest, and that this is he who is the most royal master of himself; and that the unjust man is he who is the greatest tyrant of himself and his State. 'Let the proclamation be made.' And shall I add further—'seen or unseen by gods or men?'

This is our first proof. The second is derived from the three kinds of pleasure, which answer to the three divisions of the soul—reason, passion, desire; under which last may be comprehended avarice as well as sensual appetite, while passion may be said to include ambition, party-feeling, love of reputation. Reason, on the other hand, is solely directed to the attainment of truth, and may be truly described as a lover of knowledge and wisdom, careless of money and reputation. In accordance with the difference of men's natures, one of these three principles is in the ascendant—love of wisdom, love of honour, love of gain, having their several pleasures corresponding to them. Interrogate now the three natures, and each one will be found praising his own pleasures and depreciating those of others. The money-maker will contrast the vanity of knowledge with the solid advantages of gold and silver. The ambitious man will think knowledge which is without honour all smoke and nonsense; whereas the philosopher will regard only the fruition of truth, which is not far from the heaven of pleasure, and will deem all other pleasures to be necessary rather than good. Now, how shall we decide between them? 'I cannot say.' Well, is there any better criterion than experience and knowledge? And which of the three has the truest knowledge and the widest experience? The experience of youth makes the philosopher acquainted with the two kinds of desire, but the avaricious and ambitious man never taste the pleasures of truth and wisdom. Honour he has equally with them; for the wise man is honoured as well as the great and rich; and he is their equal in experience; they are 'judged of him,' but he is 'not judged of them,' for they never attain to the knowledge of true being. And his instrument is reason, whereas their measure is wealth and honour; and if by reason we are to judge, his good will be the truest. And so we arrive at the result that the pleasure of the rational part of the soul, and a life passed in such pleasure, is the pleasantest. He who has a right to judge judges thus. And next comes the life of ambition, and, in the third place, that of money.

Twice has the just man overthrown the unjust—once more, as in an Olympian contest, first offering up a prayer to the saviour Zeus, let him try a fall. A wise man whispers to me that the pleasures of the wise are true and pure; all others are a shadow only. Let us examine this: Is not pleasure opposed to pain, and is there not a mean state of rest between the two? When a man is sick, nothing is more pleasant to him than health. This he never found out while he was well. But in pain he desires only to cease from pain; his wishes reach no further. When he is in an ecstasy of pleasure, on the other hand, rest is painful to him. Thus rest or cessation is both pleasure and pain. But can that which is neither be both? Again, pleasure and pain are motions, but the absence of them is rest: here is another contradiction. Thus we are led to infer that all this is appearance only, and witchery of the senses. And these are not the only pleasures, for there are others which have no preceding pains. Pure pleasure then is not the absence of pain. nor pure pain the absence of pleasure; although most of the pleasures which reach the mind through the body are of this character, and have not only their reactions when they depart, but their anticipations before they come. Shall I find a simile which will help to describe them? There is in nature an upper, lower, and middle region, and he who goes from the lower to the middle imagines that he is going up; but he who ascends from the upper to the middle imagines that he is making the downward descent; and this confusion happens with pleasure and pain, and with many other things. The man who compares grey with black, calls grey white; and the man who compares absence of pain with pain, calls the absence of pain pleasure. Again, hunger and thirst are inanitions of the body, ignorance and folly of the soul; and food is the satisfaction of the one, and knowledge of the other. Now which is the purer satisfaction—that of eating and drinking, or that of knowledge? Consider the matter thus: The satisfaction of that which has more existence is truer than of that which has less. And the invariable and immortal has a more real existence than the variable and mortal, and has a corresponding measure of knowledge and truth. And the soul has more existence and truth and knowledge than the body, and is therefore more really satisfied and has a more natural pleasure. Those who feast only on earthly food, are always going at random up to the middle and down again; but they never pass into the true upper world, or have a taste of true pleasure. Like animals, their heads are always turned towards the ground, and their bodies are on the dining-table; they butt at one another with iron horns and hoofs, and kill one another by reason of their insatiable lust, for they are not filled with true being, and their vessel is leaky. (Cp. Gorgias, 243 A, foll.) Their pleasures are mixed with pain, and are mere shadows of pleasure, infected by their proximity to the opposite, intensified by contrast, and therefore intensely desired; and men go fighting about them, as Stesichorus says that they fought about the shadow of Helen, in ignorance of the truth.

The same may be said of the passionate element, whether the ruling motive be ambitious envy, party violence, or angry discontent. The desires of the ambitious soul, as well as of the covetous, have an inferior satisfaction. Only when under the guidance of reason do either of the other principles attain the true pleasure which is natural to them. When not attaining, they compel the other parts of the soul to pursue a shadow of pleasure which is not theirs. And the more distant they are from law and order, the more illusive will be their pleasures. The desires of love and tyranny are the farthest from this limit, and those of the king are nearest to it. There is one genuine pleasure, and two spurious ones: the tyrant goes beyond these latter, beyond law and reason. Nor can the measure of his inferiority be told, except in a figure. The tyrant is the third removed from the oligarch, and has therefore not a shadow of his pleasure, but the shadow of a shadow only. The oligarch, again, is thrice removed from the king, and thus we get the formula 3×3, which is the number of a surface, representing the shadow which is the tyrant's pleasure, and if you like to cube this number of the beast you will find that the measure of the difference amounts to 729; the king is 729 times more happy than the tyrant. And this extraordinary number is *nearly* equal to the number of days and nights which there are in a year ($365 \times 2 = 730$); and is therefore akin to human life. This is the measure of the interval between a good and bad man in happiness only,—what must be the difference between them in comeliness of life, in beauty and virtue?

Perhaps you may remember some one saying at the beginning of our discussion that the unjust man was profited if he had the reputation of justice? Now that we have determined the nature of justice and injustice, let us make an ideal image of the soul like the fabulous monsters of mythology, which will personify his words. First of all, fashion a multitudinous many-headed beast, having a ring of heads of all manner of animals, tame and wild, and able to produce and change them at pleasure. 'That would be no easy task for a statuary; but as imagination can create anything, I will do as you say.' Suppose now another form of a lion, and another of a man; the second smaller than the first, and the third smaller than the second, and join them together and cover them outside with a human skin, in which you completely conceal all that is within. When this has been done, let us tell the supporter of injustice that he is feeding up the two beasts and starving the man, whom they torment and hate. The maintainer of justice, on the other hand, is aiming at strengthening the man; he is nourishing the gentle part and making an alliance with the lion half, in order that he may be able to keep down the many-headed hydra, and bring all into unity with each other and with themselves. Thus in every point of view, whether in relation to pleasure, honour, or advantage, the just man is right, and the unjust wrong.

Come then, let us reason with the unjust, who is not intentionally in error. 'Sweet sir,' we will say to him, 'is not the noble that which subjects the beast to the man, or rather to the God in man; the ignoble, that which subjects the man to the beast?' He can hardly avoid admitting this. And if so, who would receive gold on condition that he was to degrade the noblest part of himself under the worst?—who would sell his son or daughter into the hands of brutal and evil men, for any amount of money? And will he sell his own fairer and diviner part without any compunction to the most godless and foul? Would he not be a traitor worse than Eriphyle, who sold her husband's life for a necklace? And intemperance is the letting loose of the multiform monster, and pride and sullenness are the growth and tension of the lion and serpent element, and luxury and effeminacy are caused by the too great relaxation of this. Flattery and meanness again arise from the spirited element being subjected to avarice, and the lion metamorphosed into a monkey. And the real disgrace of handicraft arts is, that those who are engaged in them have no control over themselves; they have to flatter, instead of mastering their desires; therefore we say that they should be placed under the control of the better principle in another because they have none of their own; not, as Thrasymachus imagined, to the injury of the subjects, but for their good. And this is the intention of the education of the young,—namely, to give them self-control; the law desires to nurse up in them a higher principle, and when this is attained, they may go their ways.

' What, then, shall a man profit, if he gain the whole world' and become more and more wicked? Or what shall he profit by escaping discovery, if the concealment of evil prevents the cure? Whereas if he had been punished, the brutal part of him would have been silenced, and the gentler element liberated; and he would have begun to add to temperance justice, and to justice wisdom, which is a union fairer far than the combination of beauty and health and strength in the body in the same degree that the soul is fairer than the body. He who has understanding will honour knowledge above all, and to this direct his energies; in the next place he will keep under his body, not only for the sake of health and strength, but for the sake of creating in himself the most perfect harmony of body and soul. In the acquisition of riches, too, he will aim at the same harmonious limit; he will not be led by the admiration of the vulgar to heap up wealth without measure, but he will fear that the increase of wealth will disturb the constitution of his own soul. For the same reason he will only accept such honours as will make him a better man; any others he will decline. ' Then,' said he, ' he will not be a politician if this is his chief care.' By the dog of Egypt, he will, I said, in his own city, but probably not in his native country, unless by some divine accident. ' I understand you,' he said, ' to mean that he will be a citizen of the ideal city, which has no place upon earth.' But, I replied, there is a pattern of such a city, which is laid up in heaven for him who has eyes to see and desires to order his life after that image. Whether such a state is or ever will be, matters not; he will act according to that pattern and no other.

.... The most remarkable points in the 9th Book of the Republic are :—(1) the account of pleasure; (2) the number of the interval which divides the king from the tyrant; (3) the pattern which is in heaven.

1. Plato's account of pleasure is remarkable for moderation, and in this respect contrasts with the later Platonists and the views which are attributed to them by Aristotle. He is not, like the Cynics, opposed to all pleasure, but rather desires that the several parts of the soul shall have their natural satisfaction; he even agrees with the Epicureans in describing pleasure as something more than the absence of pain. This is proved by the circumstance that there are pleasures which have no antecedent pains (as he also remarks in the Philebus), such as the pleasures of smell, and also the pleasures of hope and anticipation. In

the previous book (pp. 558, 559) he had made the distinction between necessary and unnecessary pleasure, which is repeated by Aristotle, and he now observes that there are a further class of 'wild beast' pleasures, corresponding to Aristotle's θηριότης. He dwells upon the relative and unreal character of sensual pleasures and the illusion which arises out of the contrast of pleasure and pain, pointing out the superiority of the pleasures of reason, which are at rest, over the fleeting pleasures of sense and emotion. The pre-eminence of royal pleasure is shown by the fact that reason is able to form a judgment of the lower pleasures, while the two lower parts of the soul are incapable of judging the pleasures of reason. Thus, in his treatment of pleasure, as in many other subjects, the philosophy of Plato is 'sawn up into quantities' by Aristotle; the analysis which was originally made by him became in the next generation the foundation of technical distinctions. Both in Plato and Aristotle we may observe the illusion under which the ancients fell of regarding the transience of pleasure as a proof of its unreality, and of confounding the permanence of the intellectual pleasures with the unchangeableness of the knowledge from which they are derived. All experience shows us that the pleasures of knowledge, though more elevating, are not more lasting than any other pleasures, and are almost equally dependent on the accidents of our bodily state. (Cp. Introd. to Philebus.)

2. The number of the interval which separates the king from the tyrant and royal from tyrannical pleasures is 729 the cube of 9, which Plato characteristically designates as a number suitable to human life, because *nearly* equivalent to the number of days and nights in the year. He is desirous of proclaiming that the interval between them is immeasurable, and invents a formula to give expression to his idea. Those who spoke of justice as a cube, of virtue as an art of measuring (Prot. 357 A), saw no inappropriateness in conceiving the soul under the figure of a line, or the pleasure of the tyrant as separated from the pleasure of the king by the numerical interval of 729. And in modern times we sometimes use metaphorically what Plato employed as a philosophical formula. 'It is not easy to estimate the loss of the tyrant, except perhaps in this way,' says Plato. So we might say, that although the life of a good man is not to be compared to that of a bad man, yet you may measure the difference between them by valuing one minute of the one at an hour of the other ('one day in thy courts is better than a thousand'), or you might say that 'there is an infinite difference.' But

this is not so much as saying, in homely phrase, 'they are a thousand miles asunder.' And accordingly Plato finds the natural vehicle of his thoughts in a progression of numbers; this arithmetical formula he draws out with the utmost seriousness, and both here and in the number of generation seems to find an additional proof of the truth of his specu- lation in forming the number into a geometrical figure. In speaking of the number 729 as proper to human life, he probably intended to inti- mate that one year of the tyrannical = 12 hours of the royal life.

The simple observation that the comparison of two solids is effected by the comparison of the cubes of their sides, is the mathematical groundwork of this fanciful expression. There is some difficulty in explaining the steps by which the number 729 is obtained; the oligarch is removed in the third degree from the royal and aristocratical, and the tyrant in the third degree from the oligarchical, but we have to arrange the terms as the sides of a square and to count the oligarch twice over, thus reckoning them not as = 5 but as = 9. The square of 9 is passed lightly over as only a step towards the cube.

3. Towards the close of the Republic, Plato seems to be more and more convinced of the ideal character of his own speculations. At the end of the 9th Book the pattern which is in heaven takes the place of the city of philosophers on earth. The vision which has received form and substance at his hands, is now discovered to be at a distance. And yet this distant kingdom is also the rule of man's life. (Bk. vii. 540 E.) ('Say not lo! here, or lo! there, for the kingdom of God is within you.') Thus a note is struck which prepares for the revelation of a future life in the following Book. But the future life is present still; the ideal of politics is to be realized in the individual.

BOOK X. Many things pleased me in the order of our State, but there is nothing which I like better than the regulation about poetry. The division of the soul throws a new light on our exclusion of imita- tion. For I do not mind saying to you, what I would rather not have you repeat to the poets and their votaries, that all poetry is an outrage on the understanding of the hearers, if they have not that balm of know- ledge which heals error. I have loved Homer ever since I was a boy, and he appears to me to be the great author and master of tragic poetry. But much as I love the man, I love truth more, and therefore I must speak out: and first of all, will you tell me what is the nature of imitation, for really I do not understand? 'How likely then that I shall understand!' That may very well be, for the duller often sees better than the keener eye. 'That is true, but in your presence I can hardly venture to say what I think.' Then suppose that we begin in the old fashion, with the doctrine of universals;—let us assume the existence of beds and tables. There is one idea of a bed, or of a table, which the maker of each had in his mind when making them; he did not make the ideas of beds and tables, but he made beds and tables according to the ideas. And is there not a maker of the works of all workmen? 'A rare artist that!' Wait a little, and you may have some reason for that exclamation: This is he who makes plants and animals, himself, and all other things; the earth and heaven, and things under the earth; he makes the Gods also. 'He must be a wizard, indeed!' But do you not see that there is a sense in which you could do the same? You have only to take a mirror, and catch the reflection of the sun, and the earth, and plants and animals, and yourself in that,—there you have made them. 'Yes, in appearance, but not in reality.' And that is what I mean; the painter is such a creator as you are with the mirror, and is even more unreal than the carpenter, although the carpenter or any other artist cannot be said to make the absolute bed. 'That is what the wise tell us.' Nor is there any reason for wondering that his bed has but an indistinct relation to the truth. Reflect:—Here are three beds: one in nature, which is made by God; another, which is made by the carpenter; and the third, by the painter; and there are three artists, who preside over them,—God, the maker of the bed, the painter. God only made one, nor could he have made more than one; for if there had been two, there would always have been a third—more absolute and abstract than either, under which they would have been included. We may therefore conceive God as the natural maker of the bed, and in another sense the carpenter is also the maker; but the painter may be more properly described as the imitator of what the other two make; he has to do with a creation which is thrice removed from reality. And the tragic poet is an imitator, and, like every other imitator, is thrice removed from the king and from the truth. The painter imitates not the absolute truth, but the truth of the created object. And this, without being really different, appears to be different, and has many points of view, of which only one is caught by the painter, who represents everything because he represents a piece of everything, and that piece an image. And he

can paint any artist, although he knows nothing of their arts; and this
with sufficient skill to deceive children or simple people. Let us now
imagine that some one comes and tells us of his having met a man who
knows all that everybody knows, and better than anybody. Should we
not infer that he is a simpleton who has no discernment of truth and
falsehood, and has met with a wizard or enchanter, whom he fancied to
be all-wise? And when we hear persons saying that Homer and the
tragedians know all the arts and all the virtues, must we not infer that
the persons who say these things are under a similar delusion? they do
not see that the poets are imitators, and that their creations are only
imitations. 'Very true.' But if a person could create as well as imitate,
he would rather leave some permanent work and not an imitation only;
he would rather be the receiver than the giver of praise. 'Yes, for then
he would have more honour and advantage.' And now let me apply
this to the case of Homer and the poets. Friend Homer, I would say
to him, I am not going to ask you about medicine, or any of the arts to
which your poems incidentally refer, but about their main subjects,—
war, military tactics, politics. If you are not the creator of a shadow
thrice removed from the truth but only twice, please to inform us what
good you have ever done to mankind? Is there any city which professes to have received laws from you, as Sicily and Italy have from
Charondas, Sparta from Lycurgus, Athens from Solon? Or was there
ever any war carried on by your counsels? or any notion or invention
which is attributed to you, as there is to Thales and Anacharsis? Or is
there any Homeric way of life, such as Pythagoras taught, in which you
instructed men, and which is called after you? 'Nothing of the kind is
recorded, and indeed that companion of Homer who had the misfortune
to be called Flesh-child, was more unfortunate in his breeding than he
was in his name, if, as tradition says, Homer in his lifetime was allowed
by him and his other friends to starve.' Yes, that is the tradition; but
could this ever have happened if Homer had really been the educator of
Hellas? Would he not have had many attached followers? Can we
suppose that Protagoras and Prodicus could have persuaded their contemporaries that no one could manage house or State without them, at
which their admirers were so greatly delighted that they were ready to
carry them about on their heads, and that Homer and Hesiod would
have been allowed to go about as beggars—I mean if they had really
been able to do the world any good, would not mankind have sought

after them more than after gold and silver, and have gone about with them in order to get education? But they did not, and therefore we may infer that Homer and all the poets are only imitators, who imitate the appearance of all things; as a painter may paint a cobbler by a knowledge of figure and colour without any practice in cobbling, so the poet can put the colours of language on any art, and give harmony and rhythm to the cobbler and also to the general; for you know that mere narration, when deprived of the ornaments of metre, is like a face which has lost the beauty of youth and never had any other. Once more, the imitator has no knowledge of reality, but only of appearance. The painter paints, and the worker in metal or leather makes a bridle and reins, but neither understands the use of them—the knowledge of this is confined to the horseman; and this is true of other things. Thus we have three arts: one of use, another of invention, a third of imitation; and the user furnishes the rule to the two others. The flute-player will know the good and bad flute, and the maker will put faith in him; but the imitator will neither know nor have faith—neither science nor opinion can be ascribed to him. Imitation, then, is devoid of knowledge, being only a kind of play or sport,—and the tragic and epic poets are in the highest degree imitators.

And now let us enquire, what is the faculty in man which answers to imitation? Allow me to explain my meaning thus:—Objects are differently seen when in the water and when out of the water, when near and when at a distance; and the painter or juggler makes use of this variation to impose upon us. And the art of measuring and weighing and calculating comes in to assist our bewildered minds, and save them from the power of appearance; for, as we were saying, two contrary opinions of the same about the same and at the same time, cannot both of them be true. But which is true is determined by the art of calculation, and this is allied to the better faculty in the soul, as the arts of imitation are to the worse. And there is yet another aspect of poetical imitation, which I will invite you to consider. Men imitate actions voluntary or involuntary, in which there is an expectation of a good or bad result, and present experience of pleasure and pain. But is a man in harmony with himself when he is the subject of these conflicting influences? Is there not rather a contradiction in him? Let me further ask, whether he is more likely to control sorrow when he is alone or when he is in company with others? 'The latter.' And reason and law are the controlling principles, while feeling would lead him to indulge his sorrow. The law tells him to be patient, and that he cannot know whether his affliction is good or evil, and that no human thing is of any great consequence, but that sorrow is the greatest impediment to that which we most need :—and this is good counsel, which will advise what is best under the circumstances. For when we stumble, we should not like children set up a cry, holding the part affected in our hands, but we should be up and doing, not making a lament but finding a cure. The better part is ready to follow the suggestion of reason, while the irrational principle is full of grief and sorrow at the recollection. And in this irrational part are found the chief materials of the imitative arts. For reason is ever in repose and cannot easily be displayed, especially to a mixed multitude who have no experience of her. Thus the poet is like the painter in two ways: first he paints an inferior degree of truth, and secondly, he is concerned with an inferior part of the soul. He indulges the feelings, while he enfeebles the reason; and we refuse to allow him to have authority over the mind of man; for he has no measure of greater and less, and is a maker of images and very far gone from truth.

And we have not yet mentioned the heaviest count in the indictment, the power which poetry has of injuriously exciting the feelings. When we hear Homer, or some tragedian, reciting at length the sorrows of heroes lamenting and beating their breast, you know that we sympathize with them and praise the poet; and yet in our sorrows any such exhibition of feeling is regarded as effeminate and unmanly (cp. Ion, 535 E). Now, ought a man to feel pleasure in seeing another do what he hates and abominates in himself? Remember that he gives way to that which in his own case he would control, whose hunger and thirst after sorrow is then satisfied, and that the better principle in us when only contemplating another's sorrow, is apt to be deceived, and does not feel that any self-restraint is necessary—he may enjoy the luxury of sorrow without disgrace, and will be the gainer by the pleasure. But this self-indulgence has a further effect. For he who begins by weeping at the sorrows of others, will end by weeping at his own. The same is true of comedy,—you may often laugh at buffoonery which you would be ashamed to utter, and the love of coarse merriment on the stage will at last turn you into a buffoon at home. Poetry feeds and waters the passions and desires, and lets them rule instead of ruling them. And therefore, when we hear the encomiasts of Homer affirming that he is the educator of Hellas, and that he supplies a rule of life for human things, we may allow that they have good intentions as far as their light extends, and agree with them that Homer is a great poet and tragedian. At the same time, we will maintain our rule against all poetry which goes beyond hymns to the Gods and praises of famous men. Not pleasure and pain, but law and reason shall rule in our State.

These are our reasons for expelling poetry; and let us also make an apology to her, that she may not charge us with discourtesy. We will say to her that there is an ancient quarrel between poetry and philosophy, and many are the civilities which pass between them, such as the saying of 'the she-dog, yelping against her mistress,' and 'the philosophers who are ready to circumvent Zeus,' and 'the philosophers who are paupers;' and there are numberless other signs of enmity between them. Still we should like to hear her speak in her own defence. For we acknowledge that we are charmed by her; (you would acknowledge, would you not, that you are a lover of Homer?) but if she cannot show that she is useful as well as delightful, we must do violence to ourselves, and like rational lovers renounce our loves, though endeared to us by early associations. Having come to years of discretion, we know that poetry is not truth, and that a man should be careful how he introduces her to that state or constitution which he himself is; for there is a mighty issue at stake—mightier than appears—the good or evil of the human soul. And it is not worth while to forsake justice and virtue for the attractions of poetry, any more than for the sake of honour or wealth. To that he replied, 'I agree.'

And yet the rewards of virtue are greater far than I have described. 'And can we conceive still greater honours?' Why, yes; I said, in the brief span of life there can be no greatness worth mentioning. Shall an immortal being care about anything short of eternity? 'Yes, I think that he should—but what do you mean?' Do you not know that the soul is immortal? 'Good heavens,' he said, looking hard at me, 'you do not mean to say that you can prove that.' Quite easily, I said. 'I should like to hear this argument, of which you make so light.'

You would admit that there is an element of good and evil, which is the salvation and corruption of all things. And all things have their own corrupting element, and that which is undestroyed by this is indestructible. And the soul has her own corrupting principles, which are injustice, intemperance, cowardice, and the like. But none of these destroy the soul in the same sense that disease destroys the body. The soul may be full of all iniquities, but is not by reason of them all brought any nearer to death. For nothing ever perished by external affection of evil, which was not destroyed from within. The body, which is one thing, cannot be destroyed by food, which is another, unless infected from within. Neither can the soul, which is one thing, be corrupted by the body, which is another, unless she herself is corrupted. And as no bodily evil can infect the soul, neither can any bodily evil destroy the soul. Nothing of the nature of fever or any other disease—not even the discerption of the body into the minutest fragments—can kill the soul, unless these things can be shown to render the soul unholy and unjust. But no one will ever prove that the souls of men will become more unjust because of death. And if a person has the audacity to deny this, the answer is — then why do criminals require the hand of the executioner, and not die of themselves? 'Truly,' he said, 'injustice would lose its terrors if it would bring a cessation of evil; but I should rather think that the injustice which may destroy others may greatly quicken and stimulate the life of the unjust.' In that you are right. If the natural inherent evil of the soul be unable to destroy the soul, hardly will anything else destroy her. But the soul which cannot be destroyed either by internal or external evil must last for ever, and if lasting for ever, must be immortal. Now if this be true, souls will always exist in the same number. They cannot diminish, because they cannot be destroyed; nor yet increase, for then all would become immortal. Neither is the soul variable and diverse; for that which is eternal must be of the fairest composition. If the soul is to be conceived truly, she must be viewed in the purity of her nature by the light of reason; then we shall behold justice and injustice far more clearly than now; in her present condition we see her only like the sea-god Glaucus, knocked about and crushed by the waves, overgrown with sea-weed and shells, and anything but what she by nature is. Her true image is to be seen in philosophy, when she is holding converse with the divine and immortal and eternal;—thereby we may conceive what she would be if she were wholly devoted to such pursuits;—now she is bruised and maimed in the sea, which is the world, and has been crushed against the rocks and covered with earth and stones, which adhere to her from the entertainments of earth. Then you might see her true nature and know whether she is simple or diverse,—her state and form in this present world have been sufficiently described.

Thus far I have said nothing of the rewards and honours which

Homer and Hesiod attribute to her. Justice in herself has been shown to be best for the soul in herself, though a man may put on a Gyges' ring and have a helmet of Hades too. And now I may fairly enumerate the rewards of justice in life and after death. I granted, for the sake of argument, as you will remember, that evil might perhaps escape the knowledge of Gods and men, although this was really impossible. And now that I have shown that justice has reality, you must grant me also that she has the palm of appearance. In the first place, the just man is known to the Gods, and he is therefore the friend of the Gods, and therefore the recipient from them of every good, always excepting such evil as is the necessary consequence of former sins. All things therefore may be supposed to end in good to him, either in life or after death, although they may be apparent evils; for the Gods have a care of him who desires to be in their likeness. And what shall we say of men? Is not honesty the best policy? The clever rogue makes a great start at first, but he looks foolish when he appears at the goal with his ears trailing on his shoulders and without a crown; whereas the true runner perseveres to the end, and receives the prize. And you must allow me to repeat all the blessings which you attributed to the fortunate unjust,—they are the rulers, can marry and give their children in marriage to whom they like; and the evils which you attributed to the unfortunate just, do really fall in the end on the unjust, although, as you implied, their sufferings may be more genteelly veiled in silence.

But all the blessings of this present life are as nothing when compared with those which await good men after death. 'I should like to hear about them.' Come, then, and I will tell you a tale not taken from the 'Pilgrim's Progress,' and yet a story of a valiant man, Er, the son of Armenius, who was supposed to have died in battle, and when he had been put on the funeral pyre and lain there twelve days, he came to life again, and told what he had seen in the world below. He said that when his soul left the body, he went with a great company to a wonderful place, in which there were two chasms near together in the earth beneath, and two chasms corresponding to them in the heaven above. And there were judges sitting in the intermediate space, bidding the just ascend by the heavenly way on the right hand, having the seal of their judgment set upon them before; and the unjust, having the seal behind, were bidden to descend in like manner by the way on the left hand. Him they told to look and listen, as he was to be their messenger and to carry to men the tidings of the world below. And he looked and saw the souls departing at either chasm, some coming up from the earth, who were dusty and worn with travel; others, who came from heaven, were clean and bright. They seemed as if they had come a long way, and were delighted to rest in the meadow; and there they discoursed with one another of the things which they had seen in the other world. Those who came from the earth wept at the remembrance of their sorrows, while the spirits from heaven spoke of glorious sights and heavenly bliss. He said that for every evil deed they were punished tenfold, and the journey was of a thousand years' duration, because the life of man was reckoned as a hundred years. All the cruelties and treacheries and impieties which they had done they also suffered—and the rewards of virtue were distributed in the same proportion. I omit something which he said of infants and young children, and of special modes of torture. He was present when one of the spirits asked,—Where is Ardiaeus the great? (Now this Ardiaeus was a horrible wicked tyrant, who had murdered his old father, and his elder brother, a thousand years before.) The answer was, 'He comes not here, and will never come.' And I myself, he said, actually saw this sight of terror. For at the entrance of the chasm, as we were about to re-ascend, Ardiaeus appeared, and some other sinners—most but not all of whom had been tyrants—and just as they fancied that they were returning to life, the chasm gave a roar, and then fiery wild-looking men who knew what this meant, seized him and some others, and bound them hand and foot and threw them down, and dragged them along at the side of the road, lacerating them and carding them, and explaining to the passers-by, that they were going to be cast into hell. The greatest terror of the souls was lest they should hear the voice, and when there was silence they passed up with joy; and to these sufferings there were corresponding delights.

Now when they had rested seven days, on the eighth day the souls of the pilgrims resumed their journey, and in four days came to a spot at which was to be seen a column of light like a rainbow, only brighter and clearer. One day more brought them to the place, and at the ends of the column they saw the chain of light which encompasses heaven and earth, after the manner of the rope which fastens a trireme. At the extremity there was the distaff of Necessity, on which all the heavenly bodies turned;—the hook and spindle were of adamant, and the whorl of a mixed substance. And the form of the whorl was like a number of boxes fitting into one another with their edges turned upwards, making together a single whorl, which was pierced by the spindle. Now the outermost had the edge broadest, and the whorls within were narrower and narrower. The largest (or fixed stars) was diverse—the seventh (or sun) was brightest—the eighth (or moon) shone by the light of the seventh—the second and fifth (Mercury and Saturn) were most like one another—the third (Venus) had the whitest light—the fourth (Mars) was red—the sixth (Jupiter) was in whiteness second. All the seven in their orbs moved gently in the opposite direction to the outer circle, and the others had various degrees of swiftness and slowness. The spindle turned on the knees of Necessity, and a Siren stood hymning upon each circle, while Lachesis, Clotho, and Atropos, the daughters of Necessity, sat on thrones at equal intervals, singing of past, present, and future, responsive to the music of the Sirens; Clotho from time to time guiding the outer circle with a touch of her right hand; Atropos with her left hand touching and guiding the inner circle; Lachesis in turn putting forth her hand to guide both of them from time to time. On their arrival the pilgrims went to Lachesis, and there was an interpreter who arranged them, and taking from her knees lots, and samples of lives, got up into a pulpit and said: ' Mortal souls, hear the words of Lachesis, the daughter of Necessity. A new period of mortal life has begun, and you may choose what divinity you please—the responsibility of choosing is with you—God is blameless.' After speaking thus, he gave them the lots, and then placed on the ground before them the samples of lives. There were tyrannies ending in misery and exile, and lives of men famous for their different qualities; and also mixed lives, made up of wealth and poverty, sickness and health. And here, beloved Glaucon, is the great risk of human life, and therefore the whole of education should be directed to the acquisition of such a knowledge as will teach a man to refuse the evil and choose the good. He should know all the combinations which occur in life—of beauty with poverty or with wealth,— of knowledge with external goods,—and at last choose with reference to the nature of the soul, regarding that only as the better life which makes men better, and leaving the rest. And a man must take with him an iron sense of truth and right into the world below, that there too he may remain undazzled by wealth and determined to avoid the extremes and choose the mean. For this, as the interpreter said, and as the messenger reported, is the true happiness of man ; and any man, as he

proclaimed, may, if he choose with understanding, have a good lot, even
though he come last. 'Let not the first be careless of his choice, nor the
last despair.' He spoke; and when he had spoken, he who had drawn
the first lot chose a tyranny; he did not see that he was fated to devour
his own children—and when he afterwards discovered this, he bewailed
his misfortune, blaming not himself, as the interpreter had bidden him,
but chance and the Gods and anybody rather than himself. He was one
of those who had come from heaven, and in his previous life had been a
citizen of a well-ordered State, but he had only habit and no philosophy.
And this was the reason why he, like many others, made a bad choice,
whereas those who came from earth were not in such a hurry to choose.
Hence there was often an interchange of souls, owing to their inexperience; if a man had a reasonably good lot, and when he came to earth
followed the pursuits of philosophy, he was not only happy here, but his
pilgrimage from this world to the other, and from the other to this, was
smooth and heavenly. Nothing was more curious than the spectacle of the
choice,—sad and laughable and wonderful; most of the souls only seeking to avoid their own condition in a previous life. He saw the soul of
Orpheus changing into a swan because he would not be born of a woman;
there was Thamyris becoming a nightingale; musical birds, like the
swan, choosing to be men; the twentieth soul, which was that of Ajax,
preferring the life of a lion to that of a man, in remembrance of the
injustice which was done to him in the judgment of the arms; and
Agamemnon, from a like enmity, passing into an eagle. About the
middle was the soul of Atalanta choosing the honours of an athlete,
and next to her Epeus going into the nature of a workwoman; among
the last was Thersites, who had been metamorphosed into a monkey.
Thither, the last of all, came Odysseus, and chose the lot of a private
man, which lay neglected and could hardly be found, and when he found
it he went away rejoicing, and said that he was weary of ambition, and
that if he had been first instead of last, he would have made the same
choice. And he saw men passing into animals, and wild and tame
animals passing into one another.

When all the souls had chosen they went to Lachesis, who sent with
each of them their genius or attendant to fulfil their lot. He first of
all brought them under the hand of Clotho, who drew them within the
revolution of the spindle impelled by her hand; from her they were
carried to Atropos, who made the threads irreversible; whence, without

turning round, they passed beneath the throne of Necessity; and when they had all passed, they moved on in scorching heat through the desert to the river Ameles (Negligence), the water of which could not be retained in any vessel; of this they had all to drink a certain quantity—some of them drank more than was required, and he who drank forgot all things. Er himself was prevented from drinking. When they had gone to rest, about the middle of the night there were thunderstorms and earthquakes, and suddenly they were all driven diverse ways, shooting like stars to their birth. Concerning his return to the body, he only knew that awaking suddenly in the morning he saw himself lying on the pyre.

Thus, Glaucon, the tale has been saved, and will be our salvation if we believe that the soul is immortal, and hold fast to the heavenly way of Justice and Knowledge. So shall we pass undefiled over the river of Lethe, and be dear to ourselves and to the Gods, and have a crown of reward and happiness both in this world and also in the millennial pilgrimage of the other.

The Tenth Book of the Republic of Plato falls into two divisions; first, resuming an old thread which has been interrupted, he assails the poets, who, now that the nature of the soul has been analysed, are seen to be very far gone from the truth; and secondly, having shown the reality of the happiness of the just, he demands that appearance shall be restored to him, and then proceeds to prove the immortality of the soul. The argument, as in the Phaedo and Gorgias, is supplemented by the vision of a future life.

Why Plato, who was himself a poet, and whose dialogues are poems and dramas, should have been hostile to the poets as a class, and especially to the dramatic poets; why he should not have seen that truth may be embodied in verse as well as in prose, and that there are some indefinable lights and shadows of human life which can only be expressed in poetry—some elements of imagination which always entwine with reason; why he should have supposed epic verse to be inseparably associated with the impurities of the old Hellenic mythology; why he should try Homer and Hesiod by the unfair and prosaic test of utility,—are questions which have always been debated amongst students of Plato. Though unable to give a complete answer to them,

we may show—first, that his views arose naturally out of the circumstances of his age ; and secondly, we may elicit the truth as well as the
error which is contained in them.

He is the enemy of the poets because poetry was declining in his own
lifetime, and a theatrocracy, as he says in the Laws (Book III. 701 A),
had taken the place of an intellectual aristocracy. Euripides exhibited
the last phase of the drama, and in him Plato saw the friend and apologist
of tyrants, and the Sophist of tragedy. Nor can he have been expected
to look with favour on the licence of Aristophanes, who had begun
by satirizing Socrates in the Clouds, and in a similar spirit forty years
afterwards had satirized the founders of ideal commonwealths in his
Eccleziazusae, or Female Parliament. The old and middle comedy
was almost extinct in the age of Plato, and the new had not yet
arisen.

There were also deeper reasons for the antagonism of Plato to poetry.
The profession of an actor was regarded by him as a degradation of
human nature, for 'one man in his life' cannot 'play many parts;' the
characters which the actor performs seem to destroy his own character,
and to leave nothing which can be truly called himself. Taking this
view, he is more decided in his expulsion of the dramatic than of the
epic poets, though he must have known that the Greek tragedians
afforded noble lessons and examples of virtue and patriotism, to which
nothing in Homer can be compared. But great dramatic or even great
rhetorical power is hardly consistent with firmness or strength of mind,
and dramatic talent is often incidentally associated with a dissolute
character.

In the Tenth Book Plato introduces a new series of objections. First,
he says that the poet or painter is inferior to the maker, and in the third
degree removed from the truth. In modern times we should say that
art is not merely imitation, but rather the expression of the ideal in forms
of sense. Even adopting the humble image of Plato, from which his
argument derives a colour, we should maintain that in painting a bed the
painter may ennoble the bed by the folds of the drapery, or by the feeling
of home which he introduces ; and there have been modern painters who
have been enabled to impart an ideal interest to a blacksmith's or a carpenter's shop. Still more would this apply to the greatest works of art,
which seem to be the visible embodiment of the divine. Had Plato
been asked whether the Zeus of Pheidias was the imitation of an imita-

tion only, would he not have been compelled to admit that something more was to be found there than in the form of any mortal?

Again, Plato objects to the fine arts that they express the emotional rather than the rational part of human nature. He does not admit Aristotle's theory, that tragedy or other serious imitations are a purification of the passions by pity and fear; to him they appear only to afford the opportunity of indulging them. For there may be a gratification of the higher as well as of the lower feelings,—thought, and feelings which are too deep for thought, may find an utterance in works of art. Few persons who have any degree of sensibility would deny that they have been really elevated by strains of music or by the sublimity of architecture. Plato has himself acknowledged, in the earlier part of the Republic, that art might have the effect of harmonizing as well as of enervating the mind; but in the Tenth Book he regards the influences of art through a sort of Stoic or Puritan medium. Like Kant, he would make virtue as abstract as possible, not seeing that human life is necessarily concrete, and has many forms and colours.

He tells us that he rejoices in the banishment of the poets, since he has found by the analysis of the soul that they are concerned with the inferior faculties. The meaning of this is, that the higher part of the soul is discovered to be that which deals in abstractions. The poets are on a level with their own age, but not on a level with Socrates and Plato; and he was well aware that the older poets could not be made a rule of life by any process of legitimate interpretation: his ironical use of them is in fact a denial of their authority; he saw, too, that the poets were not critics—as he says in the Apology, 'any one was a better interpreter of their writings than they were themselves.' He, too, had ceased to be a poet when he became a disciple of Socrates; though, as he tells us of Solon, 'he might have been one of the greatest of them, if he had not been deterred by other pursuits.' (Tim. 21 C.) Thus from many points of view there is an antagonism between Plato and the poets, which he himself thought that he saw foreshadowed in the old quarrel between philosophy and poetry. The poets, as he says in the Protagoras, are the Sophists of their day—new foes under an old face. They are regarded by him chiefly in one point of view, as the enemies of reasoning and abstraction, though in the case of Euripides more with regard to his immoral sentiments about tyrants and the like. For Plato is the prophet who came to convince the world—first of the fallibility of sense and opinion, and secondly of the reality of abstract ideas. Whatever strangeness there may appear to be in modern times in opposing philosophy to poetry, which to us seem to have so many elements in common, the strangeness will disappear if we conceive of poetry as allied to sense, and of philosophy as equivalent to abstraction.

The things that are seen are opposed in Scripture to the things that are unseen—they are equally opposed in Plato to universals and ideas; all particulars, according to Plato, have a taint of error and even of evil. There is no difficulty in seeing that this is an illusion; for there is no more error and evil in an individual man, horse, bed, &c., than in the class man, horse, bed, &c.; nor is the truth which is displayed in individual instances less certain than that which is conveyed through the medium of ideas. But Plato, who is deeply impressed with the real importance of universals as instruments of thought, attributes to them an essential truth which is imaginary and unreal, for universals may be often false and particulars true. Had Plato attained to any clear conception of the individual, which is the synthesis of the universal and the particular, or had he been able to distinguish between opinion and sensation, which the ambiguity of the words δόξα, φαίνεσθαι, εἰκὸς and the like, tended to confuse, he would not have denied truth to the particulars of sense.

A similar answer may be given to the other objection of Plato, that the imitative arts by their very nature tend to call forth the emotions. For the emotions are neither bad nor good in themselves, and are not most likely to be controlled by the attempt to eradicate them, but by the moderate indulgence of them. And the vocation of art is to present thought in the form of feeling, to enlist the feelings on the side of reason, to inspire even for a moment courage or resignation; perhaps to suggest a sense of infinity and eternity in a way which mere language is incapable of attaining. True, the same power which in the purer age of art embodies gods and heroes only, may be made to express the voluptuous image of a Corinthian courtezan. But this only shows that art, like other outward things, may be turned to good and also to evil, and is not more closely connected with the lower than with the higher part of the soul. Something of ideal truth is sacrificed for the sake of the representation; the soul is only partly expressed in the lineaments of the face, and something in the exactness of the representation is sacrificed to the ideal. Still, works of art have a permanent element; they idealize and detain the passing thought, and are the intermediates between sense and ideas.

In our present imperfect state of knowledge, poetry and works of imagination may be regarded as a good. But we can also understand the existence of an age in which scientific fact has taken the place of poetry. At any rate we must admit that poetry holds a different place at different periods of the world's history. In the infancy of mankind poetry, with the exception of proverbs, is the whole of literature, and the only instrument of intellectual culture; in modern times she is the shadow or echo of her former self, and seems to have a precarious existence. At the same time we must remember, that what Plato would have called her charms have been partly transferred to prose; thus there is an ambiguity in the question. Milton doubted whether an epic poem was any longer possible. The illusion of the feelings commonly called love, has been the inspiring influence of modern poetry and romance, and has exercised a humanizing if not a strengthening influence on the world. But whether this influence has been on the whole a benefit or not, whether the stimulus which love has given to fancy is not now exhausted, may fairly be doubted. The philosopher may be excused if he imagines an age when poetry and sentiment have disappeared, and truth has taken the place of imagination, and the feelings of love are understood and estimated at their proper value.

Nor can art ever claim to be on a level with philosophy or religion, and may often corrupt them. It is certainly possible to conceive a state of the human mind in which all artistic or poetical representations are regarded as a false and imperfect expression, either of the religious ideal or of the philosophical ideal. That such a conception is far from being unnatural, is proved by the fact that the Mahommedans, and many sects of Christians, have renounced the use of pictures and images. It is possible also to conceive that they might only be used to express the highest truth and the purest sentiment. Some anticipations of this sort may have floated before the mind of Plato, who seems to waver between these two views, when he insists that youth should be brought up (Book III.) amidst wholesome imagery, and when (in Book X.) he banishes the poets from his Republic.

The same mixture of truth and error appears in other parts of the argument. He is aware of the absurdity of mankind framing their whole lives according to Homer; just as in the Phaedrus he intimates the absurdity of interpreting mythology upon rational principles; both these were the modern tendencies of his own age, which he deservedly ridicules. On the other hand his argument that Homer, if he had been able to teach mankind anything worth knowing, would not have been allowed by them to go about begging as a rhapsodist, is both false and contrary to the spirit of Plato.

The argument for the immortality of the soul seems to rest on the absolute dualism of soul and body. The soul can not be destroyed by her own proper evil, which is vice, and therefore by no other. Yet Plato has admitted that the soul may be so overgrown by vice as to lose her own nature, and in the Republic, and still more in the Timaeus, he recognizes the influence which the body has over the mind; in the latter he denies even the voluntariness of human actions, on the ground that they proceed from physical states, (Tim. 86.) In the Republic, as elsewhere, he wavers between the original soul which has to be restored, and the character which is developed by training and education.

The vision of another world is ascribed to Er, the son of Armenius, who is said by Clement of Alexandria to have been Zoroaster. The tale has certainly an oriental character, and may be compared with the pilgrimages of the soul in the Zend Avesta. But no trace of acquaintance with Zoroaster is found. elsewhere in Plato's writings, and there is no reason for giving him the name of Er, the Pamphylian. There is no real evidence that the philosophy of Heraclitus was derived from Zoroaster and the East, and still less the myths of Plato.

The local arrangement of the vision is less distinct than that of the Phaedrus and Phaedo. Astronomy is mingled with symbolism and mythology; the great sphere of heaven is represented under the symbol of a cylinder or box, containing the orbits of the planets and the fixed stars; this depends upon a spindle which turns on the knees of Necessity; the revolutions of the eight orbits are guided by the fates, and their harmonious motion produces the music of the spheres. Through the innermost or eighth of these, which is the moon, is passed the pole or axis; but it is doubtful whether this is the continuation of the column of light, from which the travellers contemplate the heavens. The words of Plato imply that they are connected, but not the same; the column of light is clearly not of adamant. The cylinder containing the orbits of the stars is almost as much a symbol as the figure of Necessity turning the spindle;—for the outermost rim is the sphere of the fixed stars, and nothing is said about the intervals of space which divide the paths of the stars in the heavens. The description is both a picture and an orrery. The column of light is probably not the milky way, which is neither straight, nor like a rainbow, but the imaginary axis of the earth. This is compared to the rainbow in respect not of form but of colour, and not to the undergirders of a trireme, but to the straight rope running from prow to stern in which the undergirders meet.

There is little trace of any resemblance between the orrery of the Republic, and the circles of the same and of the other in the Timaeus. For although the fixed stars are distinguished from the planets, they are not supposed to exercise any controlling influence over them, as in the Timaeus, and they move in orbits parallel to them, although in an opposite direction; and in the Republic, (as in the Timaeus,) they are all moving round the axis of the earth, though we are not equally certain that they are moving round the earth. Plato probably intended to represent the earth, from which Er and his companions are viewing the heavens, as stationary in place; but whether or not herself revolving, unless this is implied in the revolution of the axis, is uncertain (cp. Tim.) The spectator might be supposed to look at the heavenly bodies, either from above or below. The earth is a sort of earth and heaven in one, like the heaven of the Phaedrus, on the back of which the spectator goes out to take a peep at the stars and is borne round in the revolution. There is no distinction between the equator and the ecliptic, though probably, as in the Timaeus, Plato is led to imagine that Mars, the third swiftest planet, moves in an opposite direction to the others, in order to account for the appearances of the planets which are within the earth's orbit. In the description of the meadow, and the retribution of the good and evil after death, there are traces of Homer.

The description of the axis as a spindle, and of the heavenly bodies as forming a whole, probably arises out of the attempt to connect the motions of the heavenly bodies with the mythological image of the web, or weaving of the Fates. The giving of the lots, the weaving of them and the making of them irreversible, which are ascribed to the three Fates—Lachesis, Clotho, Atropos, are obviously derived from their names. The element of chance in human life is indicated by the order of the lots. But chance, however adverse, might be overcome by the wisdom of man, if he knew how to choose aright; there was a worse enemy to man than chance, and this was himself. He who was moderately fortunate in the number of the lot—even the very last comer—might have a good life if he chose with wisdom. And as Plato does not like to make an assertion which is unproven, he more than confirms this statement a few sentences afterwards by the example of Odysseus, who chose last. But the life of innocence and bliss is not sufficient to enable a man to make a right choice; he must have a touch of philosophy in him if he is to act rightly, when placed under circumstances in which custom is no longer his guide. Plato is amused at seeing men the slaves of custom and habit in another world as in this; and, as Coleridge says, 'Common sense is intolerable which is not based on metaphysics,' so Plato would have said, 'Custom is worthless which is not based upon philosophy.' The moral of the whole is a truly Platonic sentiment:—Men must live not by custom only, but by ideas and principles which will survive custom.

The verisimilitude which is given to the pilgrimage of a thousand years, by the intimation that Ardiaeus had lived a thousand years before; the coincidence of Er coming to life on the twelfth day after he was supposed to have been dead with the seven days which the pilgrims passed in the meadow, and the four days during which they journeyed to the column of light; the precision with which the soul is mentioned who chose the twentieth lot; the passing remarks that there was no definite character among the souls, and that the souls which had chosen ill, blamed any one rather than themselves; or that some of the souls drank more than was necessary of the waters of forgetfulness, while Er himself was hindered from drinking; the desire of Odysseus to rest at last, unlike the conception of him in Dante and Tennyson; the feigned ignorance of how Er returned to the body, when the other souls went shooting like stars to their birth, add greatly to the truthfulness of the narrative. They are such touches of nature as the art of Defoe might have introduced, when he wished to win credibility for marvels and apparitions.

There still remain to be considered some points which have been intentionally reserved to the end: first, the Janus-like character of the Republic, which presents two faces—one, an Hellenic state, the other, a kingdom of philosophers. Connected with the latter of the two aspects are (2) the paradoxes of the Republic, as they have been termed by

Morgenstern: (a) the community of property; (β) of families; (γ) the rule of philosophers; (δ) the analogy of the individual and the State, which, like some other analogies in the Republic, is carried too far. We may then proceed to consider (3) the subject of education as conceived by Plato, bringing together in a general view the education of youth and the education of after life; lastly, (4) some light may be thrown on the Republic of Plato by his imitators; and hence we may take occasion to consider the nature and value of political ideals.

I. Plato expressly says that he is intending to found an Hellenic State (Book V. 470). The germs of many things in the Republic are Spartan, such as the prohibition of money, the military caste of the rulers, the training of youth in military exercises. And in Sparta a nearer approach was made than in any other Greek State to equality of the sexes and community of property. To the Spartan type the ideal State reverts in the first decline; and the character of the individual timocrat is borrowed from the Spartan citizen. The love of Lacedaemon not only affected Plato and Xenophon, but was shared by many undistinguished Athenians; there they seemed to find a principle of order which was wanting in their own democracy. Fascinated by the idea, they would imitate the Lacedaemonians in their dress and manners; they were known to the contemporaries of Plato as 'the persons who had their ears bruised,' like the Roundheads of the Commonwealth. The love of another church or country when seen at a distance only, the longing for an imaginary simplicity in civilized times, the desire of what we are not, are tendencies of the human mind which are often displayed among ourselves. Such feelings would meet with a response in the Republic of Plato.

But there are other features of the Platonic Republic, as, for example, the literary and philosophical education, and the grace and beauty of life, which are the reverse of Spartan. Plato wishes to give his citizens a taste of Athenian freedom as well as of Lacedaemonian discipline. His individual genius is purely Athenian, although in theory he is a lover of Sparta; and he is something more than either—he has also a true Hellenic feeling. He is desirous of humanizing the wars of Hellenes against one another; he acknowledges that the Delphian God is the grand hereditary interpreter of all Hellas. The spirit of harmony and the Dorian mode are to prevail, and the whole State is to have an external beauty which is the reflex of the harmony within. But he has not yet found out the truth which he afterwards enunciated in the Laws—that he was a better legislator who made men to be of one mind, than he who trained them for war.   The citizens, as in other Hellenic States, democratic as well as aristocratic, are really an upper class; for, although no mention is made of slaves, the lower classes are allowed to fade away into the distance, and are represented in the individual by the passions.   Plato has no idea either of a social State in which all classes are harmonised, or of a federation of the world in which different nations have a place.   His city is equipped for war rather than for peace, and this would seem to be justified by the ordinary condition of Hellenic States.   The mythe of the earth-born men is an embodiment of the orthodox tradition of Hellas, and the allusion to the four ages of the world is also sanctioned by the authority of Hesiod and the poets.   Thus we see that the Republic is partly founded on the ideal of the old Greek *polis*, partly on the actual circumstances of Hellenic States.   Plato, like the old painters, retains the traditional form, and like them he has also a vision of a city in the clouds.

But there is another thread of gold or silk which is also interwoven with the work; the Republic is not only a Dorian State, but a Pythagorean order.   The way of life which was connected with the name of Pythagoras, like the modern monastic orders, showed the power which the mind of an individual might exercise over his contemporaries, and might naturally suggest to Plato the possibility of reviving such ' mediaeval institutions.'   Like the Pythagoreans, he would have enforced a rule of life, and a moral and intellectual training.   The influence ascribed to music, which to us seems exaggerated, is also a Pythagorean feature, and is not to be regarded as representing the real influence of music in Hellas.   The unity of the State and the division into castes also contain traces of Pythagoreanism.   And similar traces are found in his mystical number, in his expression of the interval between the king and the tyrant, in the doctrine of transmigration, in the music of the spheres, as well as in the great though secondary importance ascribed to mathematics in education, and in the harmony pervading art and nature.

But as in his philosophy, so also in the form of his State, he goes far beyond the old Pythagoreans.   He attempts a task really impossible, which is to unite the past of Greek history with the future of philosophy, analogous to that other impossibility, which has often been the dream of Christendom, the attempt to unite the past history of Europe with the kingdom of Christ.   Nothing actually existing in the world at all resembles Plato's ideal State; nor does he himself imagine that such a State is possible. This he repeats again and again; first in the Laws (Book V. 739), where, casting a glance back on the Republic, he admits that the perfect state of communism and philosophy is unattainable in the present state of the world, though still to be retained as a pattern. The same doubt is implied in the earnestness with which he argues in the Republic (Book V. 472 D) that ideals are none the worse because they cannot be realized in fact, and in the chorus of laughter, like 'the letting out of water,' which, as he anticipates, will greet the mention of his proposals, though like other writers of fiction, he uses all his art to give reality to his inventions. When asked how the ideal polity can come into being, he answers ironically, when one son of a king becomes a philosopher; he designates the fiction of the earth-born men as 'a noble lie;' and at the end of the Ninth Book, when he has completed the structure, he fairly tells you that his Republic is a vision only which in some sense may have reality, but not in the vulgar one of a reign of philosophers upon earth. It has been said that Plato flies as well as walks, but this hardly expresses the whole truth, for he flies and walks at the same time, and is in the air and on firm ground in successive instants.

Niebuhr has asked a trifling question, which may be briefly noticed in this place—Was Plato a good citizen? If by this is meant, Was he loyal to Athenian institutions? he can hardly be said to be the friend of democracy, but neither is he the friend of existing forms of government; all of them he regarded as 'states of faction' (Laws VIII. 832); none of them came up to his ideal of a voluntary rule over voluntary subjects, which seems indeed more nearly to describe democracy than any other, and the worst of them is tyranny. The truth is, that the question has hardly any meaning when applied to a great philosopher whose writings are not meant for a particular age and country, but for all time and all mankind. The decline of Athenian politics was probably the motive which led Plato to frame an ideal State, and the Republic may be regarded as reflecting the departing glory of Hellas. As well might we complain of St. Augustin, whose great work 'The City of God' originated in a similar motive, for not being loyal to the Roman Empire; or even a nearer parallel might be afforded by the first Christians, who cannot fairly be charged with being bad citizens because, though subject to the higher powers, they were looking forward to a city which is in heaven.

II. The idea of the perfect State is full of paradox when judged of according to the ordinary notions of mankind. The paradoxes of one age often become the commonplaces of the next; but the paradoxes of Plato are at least as paradoxical to us as they were to his contemporaries. The modern world has either ridiculed them as absurd or denounced them as unnatural and immoral; yet as being the thoughts of one of the greatest of human intelligences, and of one who has done most to elevate morality and religion, they seem to deserve a better treatment at our hands. We may have to address the public, as Plato does poetry, and assure them that we mean no harm to existing institutions. But still the consideration of social questions in their most abstract form, may not be without use as a speculation, even if incapable of being reduced to practice.

(*a*) The first paradox is the community of goods, which is mentioned slightly at the end of the Third Book, and seemingly, as Aristotle observes, is confined to the guardians; at least no mention is made of the other classes. But the omission is not of any real significance, and probably arises out of the plan of the work, which prevents the writer from entering into details.

Aristotle censures the community of property much in the spirit of modern political economy, as tending to repress industry, and as doing away with the spirit of benevolence. Modern writers almost refuse to consider the subject, which is supposed to have been long ago settled by the common opinion of mankind. But it must be remembered that the sacredness of property is a notion far more fixed in modern than in ancient times. The world has grown older, and is therefore more conservative. Primitive society offered many examples of land held in common, either by a tribe or by a township, and such may probably have been the original form of landed tenure. Ancient legislators had invented various modes of dividing and preserving the divisions of land among the citizens; according to Aristotle there were nations who held the land in common and divided the produce, and there were others who divided the land and stored the produce in common. The evils of debt and the inequality of property were far greater in ancient than in modern times, and the accidents to which property was subject from war, or revolution, or taxation, or other legislative interference, were also greater. All these circumstances gave property a less fixed and sacred character. The early Christians are believed to have held their property in common, and the principle is sanctioned by the words of Christ himself, and has been maintained as a counsel of perfection in almost all ages of the Church. Nor have there been wanting instances of modern enthusiasts who have made a religion of communism; in every age of religious excitement, notions like Wycliffe's 'inheritance of grace' have tended to prevail.

We can hardly judge what effect Plato's views would have upon his own contemporaries; they would perhaps have seemed to them only an exaggeration of the Spartan commonwealth. Even modern writers would acknowledge that the right of private property is based on expediency, and may be interfered with in a variety of ways for the public good. And if any other mode of vesting property were found to be more advantageous, that would acquire the same basis of right; 'the most useful,' in Plato's language, 'would be the most sacred.' The lawyers and philosophers of former ages would have spoken of property as a sacred institution. But they only meant by such language to oppose the greatest amount of resistance to any invasion of the rights of individuals and of the Church.

When we consider the question, without any fear of immediate application to practice, in the spirit of Plato's Republic, are we quite sure that the received notions of property are the best? Is the distribution of wealth which is customary in civilized countries the most favourable that can be conceived for the education and development of the mass of mankind? Can 'the spectator of all time and all existence' be quite convinced that one or two thousand years hence, great changes will not have taken place in the rights of property, or even that the very notion of property, beyond what is necessary for personal maintenance, may not have disappeared? This was a distinction familiar to Aristotle, though likely to be laughed at among ourselves. Such a change would not be greater than some other changes through which the world has passed in the transition from ancient to modern society; as, for example, the emancipation of the serfs, or the abolition of slavery (a work which has only been completed in our own day), or than is measured by the interval which even now separates the Eastern from the Western World. And to accomplish such a change in the course of centuries, would not imply a greater rate of progress than has actually existed during the last fifty or sixty years. Many opinions and beliefs which have been cherished quite as strongly as the right of property have passed away, and the most untenable propositions respecting the right of bequests or entail have been maintained with as much fervour as the most moderate. The reflection will occur that the state of society can hardly be final in which the interests of thousands are perilled on the life or character of a single person. And many will indulge the hope that the state in which we live will be only transitional, and may conduct to a higher state, in which property, besides ministering to the enjoyment of the few, may also furnish the means of the highest culture to all, and will be a greater benefit to the public generally, and also more under the control of public authority. There may come a time when the saying, 'Have I not a right to do what I will with my own,' may appear to be a barbarous relic of individualism.

Such reflections appear wild and visionary to the eye of the practical statesman, but they are fairly within the range of possibility to the philosopher. He can imagine that in some distant age or clime, and through the influence of some poet or philosopher, the notion of common property may or might have sunk as deep into the heart of a race, and have become as fixed to them, as private property is to us. He is willing to believe that some day men's notions of property in our own country may materially alter, and private interests be much more subservient to public. In our own age even Utopias may affect the spirit of legislation, and the philosopher may be allowed sometimes to feast his imagination with speculations which he never hopes to see realized.

The objections that would be generally urged against Plato's community of property, are the old ones of Aristotle, that motives for exertion would be taken away, and that disputes would arise when each was dependent upon all. Mankind could never become disinterested, or regard the interests of the community as the interests of the individual. But it may be doubted whether our present individualism is not rather an artificial result of the industrial state of modern Europe. Moral and political feelings seem from time to time to rise up and reassert themselves, even in a world bound hand and foot in the chains of economic necessity. And if we cannot expect the mass of mankind to become disinterested, at any rate we seem to observe in them the growth of a spirit of party and a power of organization which fifty years ago would never have been suspected. The same forces which have revolutionized the political system of Europe, may affect a similar change in the social and industrial relations of mankind. And if we suppose the influence of some good as well as neutral motives working in the community, there will be no absurdity in expecting that the mass of mankind having the power in their own hands, and becoming enlightened about the higher possibilities of human life, when they come to see how much more is attainable for all than is at present the possession of a favoured few, may pursue the common interest with an intelligence and persistency which the world has not yet seen.

Neither to the mind of Plato or Aristotle did the doctrine of community of property at all present the same difficulty, or appear the same violation of the common Hellenic sentiment, as the paradox of the community of wives and children. This he prefaces by another proposal, that the pursuits of men and women shall be the same, and that to this end they shall have a common training and education. Male and female animals have the same pursuits—why not also the two sexes of man?

But here we seem to have fallen into a contradiction with our former principle, that different natures should have different pursuits. Men and women differ: are they capable then of the same pursuits? Is not this inconsistent with our notion of the division of labour? The objection is no sooner raised than answered, for there is no organic difference between men and women, but only the accidental difference of the one bearing and the other begetting children. Following the analogy of the other animals, Plato contends that all the natural gifts are scattered about indifferently among men and women, though there may be a superiority of degree on the part of the men. The objection on the score of delicacy to men and women partaking of the same gymnastic exercises, is met by Plato's assertion that the existing feeling is a matter of habit.

In no former age of the world would Plato's ideas on this subject have received so much assent as in our own. That he should have emancipated himself from the customs of his own country and from the example of the East, is a wonderful proof of philosophical insight. He is as much in advance of modern nations as they are in advance of the customs of Greek society. Greek women had certainly noble conceptions of womanhood in the goddesses Athene and Artemis, and in the heroines Antigone and Andromache. But these poetical ideals had no counterpart in actual life. The Athenian woman was in no respect the equal of her husband; she was not the entertainer of his guests or the mistress of his house, but only his housekeeper and the mother of his children. She took no part in military or political matters; nor is there any instance in the later ages of Greece of a woman becoming famous as an authoress. 'Hers is the greatest glory who has the least renown among men,' is the historian's conception of feminine excellence. A very different ideal of womanhood is held up by Plato to the world; she is to be the companion of the man, and to share with him in the toils of war and in the cares of the government. She is to be similarly trained both in bodily and mental exercises. She is to lose as far as possible the incidents of maternity and the characteristics of the female sex.

The modern antagonist of the equality of the sexes would argue that the differences between men and women are not confined to the single point urged by Plato; that sensibility, softness, feeling, are the qualities of women, while energy, strength, higher intelligence, are to be looked for in men. And this is true : the differences affect the whole nature, and are not, as Plato supposes, confined to a single point. But neither can we say how much of this difference is due to education and the opinions of mankind, or physically inherited from the habits and opinions of former generations. Women have been always taught, not exactly that they are slaves, but that they are in an inferior position, which is also supposed to have compensating advantages; and to this position they have conformed. Add to this that the physical form may easily change in the course of generations through the mode of life; and the weakness or delicacy, which was once a matter of opinion, may pass into a physical fact. The difference between the two sexes varies greatly in different countries and ranks of society, and at different ages in the same individuals. And Plato may have been right in denying that there was any ultimate difference in the sexes other than that which exists in animals, because all other differences may be conceived to disappear in other states of society, or under different circumstances of life and training.

(β) The first wave is past, and we proceed to the second—community of wives and children. 'Is it possible ? Is it desirable ?' For as Glaucon intimates, and as we far more strongly assert, 'Great doubts may be entertained about both these points.' Any free discussion of the question is impossible, and mankind are perhaps right in not allowing the ultimate bases of social life to be examined. Still, the manner in which Plato arrived at his conclusions should be considered. For here, as Mr. Grote has remarked, is a wonderful thing, that one of the wisest and best of men should have entertained ideas of morality which are wholly at variance with our own. And if we would do Plato justice, we must examine carefully the character of his proposals. First, we may observe that the relations of the sexes supposed by him are the reverse of licentious; they seem rather to aim at an impossible strictness. There is no sentiment or imagination in the connections which they are supposed to form; human nature is reduced as nearly as possible to the level of the animals, neither exalting to heaven, nor yet abusing and over-indulging the natural instincts. All that world of poetry and fancy which the passion of love has called forth in modern literature and romance would have been banished by Plato. The arrangements of marriage in the Republic of Plato aimed at one object only, the improvement of the race. In successive generations a great development both of bodily and mental qualities might be possible. The experience of animals showed that mankind could within certain limits receive a change of nature. And as in animals we should commonly select the best for breeding, and destroy the others, so there must be a selection made of the human beings whose lives are worthy to be preserved.

We start back horrified from this Platonic ideal, in the belief, first, that the instincts of human nature are far too strong to be crushed out in this way; secondly, that if the plan could be carried out, we should be poorly recompensed by improvements in the breed for the loss of the best things in life. The greatest regard for the least and meanest things of humanity —the deformed infant, the culprit, the insane, the idiot—truly seems to us one of the noblest results of Christianity. Such views are comparatively recent in modern times, and were foreign to the age of Plato, as they have very different degrees of strength in different parts of the world, even among Christians. To the Greek the family was a sort of customary institution binding the members together by a tie far inferior in strength to that of friendship, and having a far less solemn and sacred sound than that of country. That which existed on the lower level of custom, Plato imagined that he was raising to the higher level of nature and reason; while from the modern and Christian point of view we regard him as sanctioning murder and destroying the first principles of morality. And we remark with surprise that, while repudiating all the ordinary feelings of men, he is singularly careful to avoid pollution of blood.

Yet, on the other hand, we cannot deny that Christianity, or any other form of religion and society, has hitherto not been able to cope with this greatest and most difficult of social problems, and that the side from which Plato regarded it is that from which we habitually turn away. For our physical seem in some respects to be at war with our moral interests. The state physician hardly likes to uncover or probe the wound : this is a matter which is beyond his art ; which he cannot safely let alone, but which he dare not touch. The late Dr. Combe is said by his biographer to have resisted the temptation to marriage, because he knew that he was subject to hereditary consumption. This little fact suggests the reflection, that one person in a thousand did from a sense of duty what the other nine hundred and ninety-nine ought to have done, if they had not been regardless of all the misery which they were likely to bring into the world. If we could prevent such marriages without any violation of feeling or propriety, we clearly ought ; and the prohibition in the course of time would be protected by a 'horror naturalis' similar to that which, in all civilized ages and countries, has prevented the marriage of near relations by blood. But a free agent cannot have his fancies regulated by law ; and the execution of the law would be rendered impossible, owing to the uncertainty of the cases in which marriage was to be forbidden. Nor is there any reason to suppose that marriages are to any great extent influenced by considerations of this sort, which seem too distant to be able to make any head against the irresistible impulse of individual attach-ment. Lastly, no one can have observed the first rising flood of the passions in youth, the difficulty of regulating them, and the effects on the whole mind and nature which follow from them, the stimulus which the mere imagination gives to them, without feeling that there is something unsatisfactory in our method of treating them. That the most important influence on human life should be wholly left to chance or shrouded in mystery, and instead of being disciplined or understood, should be required to conform only to an external standard of propriety—cannot be regarded by the philosopher as a safe or satisfactory condition of human things.

Nor is Plato wrong in asserting that family attachments may interfere with higher aims. If there have been those who 'to party gave up what was meant for mankind,' there have certainly been those who to family gave up what was meant for mankind or for their country. The cares of children, the necessity of procuring money for their support, the flat-teries of the rich by the poor, the exclusiveness of caste, the pride of birth or wealth, the tendency of family life to divert men from the pursuit of the ideal or the heroic, are as lowering in our own age as in that of Plato. And if we prefer to look at the gentle influences of home, the development of the affections, the amenities of society, the devotion of one member of a family for the good of the others, which form one side of the picture, we must not quarrel with him, or perhaps ought rather to be grateful to him, for having presented to us the reverse. Without attempting to defend Plato on grounds of morality, we may allow that his conception of the relation of the sexes takes rank among the great original thoughts of mankind.

(γ) But Plato has an equal, or, in his own estimation, even greater paradox in reserve, which is summed up in the famous text, ' Until kings are philosophers or philosophers are kings, cities will never cease from ill.' And by philosophers he explains himself to mean those who are capable of apprehending ideas, especially the idea of good; and to the attainment of this the second education is to be directed. Through a process of training which has already made them good citizens, they are now to be made good legislators. We find with some surprise (not unlike the feeling which Aristotle in a well-known passage describes the hearers of Plato's lectures as experiencing, when they went to a discourse on the idea of good, expecting to be instructed in moral truths, and received instead of them arithmetical and mathematical formulae) that Plato does not propose for his future legislators any study of finance or law or military tactics, but only of abstract mathematics, as a preparation for the still more abstract conception of good. We ask, with Aristotle, what is the use of a man knowing the idea of good, if he does not know and has never understood what is good for this man, this state, this condition of society? We do not understand how Plato's legislators or guardians are to be fitted for their work of statesmen by the bare study of the five mathematical sciences. Nothing can appear to modern ideas more inappropriate or absurd.

The discovery of a great metaphysical conception seems to ravish the mind with a prophetic consciousness of the new power which has been imparted to man. No metaphysical enquirer has ever seen the real value of his own speculations, nor understood that what appeared to him to be absolute truth may reappear in the next generation as a form of logic or an instrument of thought. And posterity have also sometimes equally misunderstood the real value of his speculations. They seem to them to have contributed nothing to the stock of human knowledge. The *idea* of good is apt to be regarded by the modern thinker as an unmeaning abstraction; but he forgets that this abstraction is waiting ready for use, and will hereafter be filled up by the divisions of knowledge. When mankind do not as yet know that the world is subject to law, the introduction of the mere conception of law or design or final cause, or the far-off anticipation of the unity of knowledge, are great steps onward. Even the crude generalization of the unity of all things leads men to view the world with different eyes, under an aspect of harmony which may easily affect their conception of human life and of politics, and even their own conduct and character. We can well imagine how a great mind like that of Pericles might derive a sort of elevation from his intercourse with Anaxagoras. To be struggling towards a higher but unattainable conception is a more favourable condition of mind than to rest satisfied in a narrow portion of ascertained fact. And the earlier, which have sometimes been the greater conceptions of science, are often lost sight of at a later period. Nor is there anything unnatural in the hasty application of these vast metaphysical conceptions to practical and political life. In the first enthusiasm of ideas men see them everywhere, and apply them in the most remote sphere. They do not understand that the experience of ages is required to enable them to fill up ' the intermediate axioms.' Plato himself seems to have imagined that the truths of psychology, like those of astronomy and harmonics, would be arrived at by a process of deduction, and that the method which he has pursued in the Fourth Book, of inferring them from experience and the use of language, was imperfect and only provisional. But when, after having arrived at the idea of good, which is the end of the science of dialectic, he is asked, What is the nature, and what are the divisions of the science? he refuses to answer, and seems to imply that the state of knowledge which then existed in the world was not such as would allow the philosopher to enter into his final rest. The previous sciences must first be studied, and will, we may add, continue to be cultivated till the end of time, although in a sense far other than Plato could have conceived. But we may observe, that while he is aware of the vacancy of his own ideal, he is full of enthusiasm in the contemplation of it. Looking into the orb of light, he sees nothing, but he is warmed and elevated. The Hebrew prophet believed that faith in God was enough to enable him to govern the world; the Greek philosopher imagined that contemplation of the good would make a legislator. There is as much to be filled up in the one case as in the other, and the one mode of conception is to the Israelite what the other is to the Greek. Both find a repose in a divine perfection, which, whether in a more personal or impersonal form, exists without them and independently of them, as well as within them.

The question has been asked, In what relation did Plato suppose the idea of good to stand to the nature of God? Is God above or below the idea of good? Or is the idea of good another mode of conceiving God? The latter seems to be the true answer. To the Greek philosopher the perfection and unity of God was a far higher conception than his personality, which he hardly found a word to express, and which to him would have seemed to be borrowed from mythology. To the Christian, or to the modern thinker in general, it is difficult if not impossible to attach reality to what he terms mere abstraction; whereas to Plato this very abstraction is the truest and most real of all things. Hence, from a difference in forms of thought, Plato appears to be resting on a creation of his own mind only. But if we may be allowed to paraphrase the idea of good by the words 'intelligent principle of law and order in the universe, embracing equally man and nature,' we find a meeting point between him and ourselves.

The question whether the ruler or statesman should be a philosopher is one that has not lost interest in modern times. In most countries of Europe and Asia there has been some one in the course of ages who has truly united the power of command with the power of thought and reflection, as there have been also many false combinations of these qualities. Some kind of speculative power is necessary both in practical and political life; like the rhetorician in the Phaedrus, men require to have a conception of the varieties of human character, and to be raised on great occasions above the commonplaces of ordinary life. Yet the idea of the philosopher-statesman has never been popular with the mass of mankind; partly because he cannot take the world into his confidence or make them understand the motives from which he acts; and also because they are jealous of a power which they do not understand. The revolution which human nature desires to effect step by step in many ages is likely to be precipitated by him in a single year or life. They fear too that in the pursuit of his greater aims he may disregard the common feelings of humanity. He is too apt to be looking into the distant future or back into the remote past, and unable to see actions or events which, to use an expression of Plato's, 'are tumbling out at his feet.' Besides, as Plato would say, there are other corruptions of these philosophical statesmen. Either 'the native hue of resolution is sicklied o'er with the pale cast of thought,' and at the moment when action above all things is required he is undecided, or general principles are enunciated by him in order to cover some change of policy; or his ignorance of the world has made him more easily fall a prey to the arts of others; or in some cases he has been converted into a courtier, enjoying the luxury of liberal opinions and accompanying them with illiberal actions. No wonder that mankind have been in the habit of calling statesmen of this class pedants, sophisters, doctrinaires, visionaries. For, as we may be allowed to say, a little parodying the words of Plato, 'they have seen bad imitations of the philosopher-statesman.' But a man in whom the power of thought and action are perfectly balanced, equal to the present, reaching forward to the future, 'such a one,' ruling in a constitutional state, 'they have not seen.'

But as the philosopher is apt to fail in the routine of political life, so the ordinary statesman is also apt to fail in extraordinary crises. When the face of the world is beginning to alter, he is still guided by his old maxims, and is the slave of his inveterate party prejudices; he cannot perceive the signs of the times: instead of looking forwards he looks back; he learns nothing and forgets nothing; with 'wise saws and modern instances' he would stem the rising tide of revolution. He lives more and more within the circle of his own party, as the world without him becomes stronger. This seems to be the reason why the old order of things makes so poor a figure when confronted with the new, why churches can never reform, why most political changes are made blindly and convulsively. The great crises in the history of nations have often been met by a sort of feminine positiveness, and a more obstinate reassertion of principles which have lost their hold upon a nation. The fixed ideas of a reactionary statesman may be compared to madness; he grows more and more convinced of the truth of his notions as he becomes more isolated, and would rather await the inevitable than in any degree yield to circumstances.

(δ) Plato labouring under what, to modern readers, would appear to be a confusion of ideas, identifies the individual and the state—ethics with politics. He thinks that, most of a state which is most like one man, and in which the citizens have the greatest uniformity of character. He does not see that the analogy of the individual and the state is partly fallacious, and that the will or character of a state or nation is really the balance or rather the surplus of individual wills, which are limited by the condition of having to act in common. The movement of a body of men can never have the pliancy or facility of a single man; the freedom of the individual, which is limited, becomes an imperfect necessity when transferred to a nation. The power of action and feeling is necessarily weaker and more uncertain when they are diffused through a community; hence arises the often discussed question, 'Whether a nation, like an individual, can have a conscience?' We hesitate to say that the characters of nations are nothing more than the sum of the characters of the individuals who compose them; because there may be tendencies in individuals which react upon one another; or a whole nation may be wiser than any one man; or may be animated by some common opinion or feeling which could not equally have affected the mind of a single individual. Plato does not appear to have analysed the complications which arise out of the collective action of mankind. He is capable of discerning many of the illusions of language and logic, but he is not capable of seeing that analogies, though specious as arguments, might often have no foundation in fact, or of distinguishing between what is intelligible or vividly present to the mind, and what is true. In this respect he is far below Aristotle, who is comparatively seldom imposed upon by false analogies. In like manner Plato cannot see the difference between the arts and the virtues—at least he is always arguing from one to the other. His notion of music is transferred from harmony of sounds to harmony of life: in this he is assisted by the ambiguities of language as well as by the prevalence of Pythagorean notions. And having once identified the individual with the state, he imagines that he will find the succession of states paralleled in the lives of individuals.

Still, through this fallacious medium, a real enlargement of ideas is attained. When the virtues as yet presented no distinct conception to the mind, a great advance was made by the comparison of them with the arts; for virtue is partly art, and has an outward form as well as an inward principle. The harmony of music affords a lively image of the harmony of the world and of human life, and may be regarded as a splendid illustration which was naturally mistaken for a real analogy. In the same way the identification of ethics with politics has a tendency to give definiteness to ethics, and also to elevate and ennoble men's notions of the aims of government and of the duties of citizens: for ethics from one point of view may be conceived as an idealized law and politics; and politics, as ethics reduced to the conditions of human society. There have been evils which have arisen out of the attempt to identify them, and this has led to the separation or antagonism of them, which has been introduced by modern political writers. But we may also feel that something has been lost in their separation, and that the ancient philosophers who regarded the moral and intellectual wellbeing of mankind first, and the wealth of nations and individuals second, may have a salutary influence on some of the speculations of modern times. Many political maxims originate in a reaction against the opposite error; and when the errors against which they were directed have passed away, in their turn become errors.

III. Plato's views of education are in several respects remarkable; like the rest of the Republic they are partly Greek and partly ideal, beginning with the ordinary curriculum of the Greek youth, and extending to after life. Plato is the first writer who distinctly expresses the thought that education is to comprehend the whole of life, and to be a preparation for another in which education is to begin again. This is the continuous thread which runs through the whole of the Republic, and which more than any other of his ideas admits of an application to modern life.

He has long given up the notion that virtue cannot be taught; and he is disposed to modify the thesis of the Protagoras, that the virtues are one and not many. Neither is he unwilling to admit the sensible world into his scheme of truth. Nor does he positively assert in the Republic the involuntariness of vice, which reappears, however, in the Timaeus, Sophist, and Laws. Nor do the so-called Platonic ideas recovered from a former state affect his theory of mental improvement. Still we trace in him the remains of the old Socratic doctrine, that true knowledge must be elicited from within, and is to be sought for in ideas, not in particulars of sense. Education will implant a principle of intelligence which is better than ten thousand eyes. There is also a trace of his old doctrine that the virtues are one, and of the Socratic notion that all virtue is knowledge; this is seen in the supremacy given to justice over the rest, and in the tendency to absorb the moral virtues in the intellectual, and to centre all goodness in the contemplation of the idea of good. The world of sense is still depreciated and identified with opinion, though admitted to be a shadow of the true, and to be the source from which the figures of geometry are derived. And in the Republic he has not altogether given up the involuntariness of vice; as is shown in the feeling that evil arises chiefly from ignorance, and the tone in which the multitude is regarded as hardly responsible for what they do. A faint allusion to the doctrine of remininiscence occurs in the Tenth Book (p. 621); but Plato's views of education have no more real connection with a previous state of existence than our own; he only proposes to elicit from the mind that which is there already. His conception of education is represented, not like many modern views, under the image of filling a vessel, but of turning the eye of the soul towards the light.

He begins with music or literature, which he divides into true and false, and then goes on to gymnastics; he takes no notice of infancy in the Republic, though in the Laws he gives sage counsels about the nursing of children and the management of the mothers; and would have an education which is even prior to birth. But in the Republic he begins with the age at which the child is capable of perceiving ideas, and boldly asserts, in language which sounds paradoxical to modern ears, that he must be taught the false before he can learn the true. The modern and ancient philosophical world are not agreed in their conceptions of truth and falsehood; the one identifies truth almost exclusively with fact, the other with ideas. There is a like difference between ourselves and Plato, which is, however, partly a difference of words. For we too should admit that a child must learn many things which he cannot understand; he must be taught some things in a figure only, and some perhaps which he can hardly be expected to believe when he grows older; but we should limit the use of fiction by the necessity of the case. Plato would draw the line somewhat differently; according to him the aim of early education is not truth as a matter of fact, but truth as a matter of principle; the child is to be taught first simple religious truths, and then simple moral truths, and insensibly to learn the lesson of good manners and good taste. He proposes an entire reformation of the old mythology; like Xenophanes and Heracleitus he is sensible of the deep chasm which separates his own age from Homer and Hesiod, whom he quotes, and invests with an imaginary authority, but only for his own purposes. The lusts and treacheries of the gods are to be banished; the terrors of the world below are to be dispelled; the misbehaviour of the

Homeric heroes is not to be a model for youth. But there is another strain heard in Homer which may teach our youth endurance; and something may be learnt in medicine from the simple practice of the Homeric age. The principles on which religion is to be based are two only: first, that God is true; secondly, that he is good. Modern and Christian writers have often fallen short of these; they can hardly be said to have got beyond them.

Education, according to Plato, is to place youth in happy circumstances, in which no sights or sounds of evil, or allurements of passion, can hurt the character or vitiate the taste. They are to live in an atmosphere of health; the breeze is always to be wafting to them the impressions of truth and goodness. Could such an education be realized, or even could religious education be bound up with truth and virtue and good manners and good taste, that would perhaps be the best hope of human improvement. Plato, like ourselves, is looking forward to changes in the moral and religious world, and is preparing for them. He recognizes the danger of unsettling young men's minds, and doing away with the sacredness of one set of ideas before we have anything to put in their place which has an equal hold on the mind. There is to be an absence of excitement in the Platonic Republic, and for this reason dramatic representations are excluded. Plato does not wish to have his children taken to the theatre; he thinks that the effect on the spectators is bad, and on the actors still worse. His idea of education is that of harmonious growth, in which are learnt the lessons of temperance and endurance, and the body and mind develope in equal proportions. The great principle which is to be recognized in all art and nature, and is to hold sway in education, is simplicity.

The next stage of education is gymnastic, which answers to the period of muscular growth and development. The simplicity which is enforced in music is extended to gymnastics; Plato is aware that the training of the body may be inconsistent with the training of the mind, and that bodily exercise may be easily overdone. Men are apt to have a headache or go to sleep at a lecture on philosophy, and this they attribute not to the true cause, which is the excess of bodily training, but to the nature of the subject. Two points are noticeable in Plato's theory of gymnastic:—First, that the time of learning them is entirely separated from the time of literary education. He seems to have thought that two things of an opposite and different nature could not be learnt at the same time. We can hardly agree with him in this, judging by experience of the effect on the mind of spending three years between the ages of fourteen and seventeen in mere bodily exercise. Secondly, he regards gymnastic not primarily as a training of the body, but of the mind, which is to discipline the passionate element, as music restrains the appetitive and calls forth the rational. His whole idea is based upon the notion that the body depends upon the mind, and is to be trained to its service. And doubtless the mind may exercise a very great and almost paramount influence over the body, if exerted not only at a particular moment, but in making preparation for the whole of life. Other writers had seen the error of Spartan discipline. Plato was the first who asserted that music and gymnastic are not, as common opinion affirms, the one intended for the cultivation of the mind, the other of the body; but that they are both equally designed for the improvement of the mind.

The subject of gymnastic leads Plato to the sister subject of medicine, and this he further illustrates by the parallel of law. The modern disbelief in medicine has led in this, as in some other departments of knowledge, to a demand for greater simplicity; physicians are becoming aware that they often make diseases 'greater and more complicated' by their treatment of them. In 2000 years their art has made but slender progress; what they have gained in the analysis of the parts is partly lost by their feebler conception of the human frame as a whole. They have attended more to the cure of diseases than to the conditions of health; and the improvements in medicine have been probably counterbalanced by the disuse of gymnastics. Until lately they have hardly thought of air and water, the importance of which was well understood by the ancients; as Aristotle remarks, 'air, being the element which we most use, has the greatest effect upon us.' For ages physicians have been under the dominion of prejudices which have only recently given way; there are as many opinions in medicine as in theology, and almost as much scepticism about them. Plato has several good notions about medicine;—according to him, 'the eye cannot be cured without the rest of the body, nor the body without the mind.' (Charm. 156 E.) Yet we can hardly praise him when, in obedience to the authority of Homer, he depreciates diet, or approves of the inhuman spirit in which he would get rid of invalid and useless lives by leaving them to die. He does not seem to have considered that the 'bridle of Theages' might be accompanied by qualities which were of far more value to the State than the health or strength of the citizens. The physician himself (this is a delicate and subtle observation) should not be a man in robust health; he should have experience of disease in his own person, because by this his powers of observation are likely to be quickened in the case of others.

The perplexity of medicine is paralleled by the perplexity of law; in which, again, Plato would have men follow the golden rule of simplicity. Greater matters are to be determined by the legislator, but lesser matters are to be left to the temporary regulation of the citizens themselves. Plato is aware that *laissez faire* is an important element of government. The diseases of a State are like the heads of a hydra, which multiply when they are cut off. He raises a curious question whether the judge should have the same experience of crime in his own person, which the physician is supposed to have of disease. But he does not answer the question with equal truth to human nature. He does not seem to have observed that the knowledge of evil, even in youth, may be quite consistent with the abhorrence of it.

When the first education is completed, there follows the first trial of active life. But soon education is to begin again from a new point of view. In the interval between the Fourth and Seventh Books, we have discussed the nature of knowledge, and have thence been led to form a higher conception of education. For true knowledge, according to Plato, is of abstractions, and has to do not with particulars or individuals, but with universals only; not with the beauties of poetry, but with the ideas of philosophy. And the great aim of education is the cultivation of the habit of abstraction. This is to be acquired through the study of the mathematical sciences. They alone are capable of giving ideas of relation, and of arousing the dormant energies of thought.

Mathematics in Plato's age comprehended a very small part of that which is now included in them; but they also bore a much larger proportion to the sum of human knowledge. They were the only organon of thought which the human mind at that time possessed, and the only measure by which the chaos of particulars could be reduced to rule and order. The faculty which they trained was naturally at war with the poetical or imaginative; and hence to Plato the difference between him who knew and who did not know mathematics, is like the difference between an educated and uneducated man. They gave a new sense of power and seemed to have an inexhaustible application, partly because their true limits were not yet understood. These Plato himself is beginning to investigate; though not aware that numbers and figures are the abstractions of sense, he recognized that the figures of geometry borrow their forms from the sensible world. He also seeks to find the ultimate ground of mathematical ideas in the idea of good; though in his conception of the relation of ideas to number, he falls very far short of the definiteness attributed to him by Aristotle (Met. i. 84, ix. 17). But if he failed to recognize the true limits of mathematics, he has also reached a point beyond them; in his view, ideas of number became secondary to a higher conception of knowledge. The one, the self-proving, is the only perfect truth to which all things ascend, and in which they finally repose.

This self-proving unity or idea of good is a mere vision of which no distinct explanation can be given, relative only to a particular stage in Greek philosophy. And yet this vision may have an immense effect. Although the method of science cannot anticipate science, the idea of science in the future may be a great and inspiring principle in the mind. For in the pursuit of knowledge we are always pressing forward to something beyond us; and as a false conception of knowledge may lead men astray during many ages, for example the scholastic philosophy, so the true ideal, though vacant, may draw all their thoughts in a right direction. Whether the general expectation of knowledge, as this indefinite feeling may be termed, conforms truly to the laws of the mind, is of great importance; for a true conception of what knowledge ought to be may be often combined with a slender experience of facts. The correlation of the sciences, the consciousness of the unity of knowledge, the sense of the importance of classification, the unwillingness to stop short of certainty or to confound probability with truth, are important principles of the higher education. Although Plato could tell us nothing, and perhaps knew that he could tell us nothing, of the absolute truth, he has exercised an influence on human thought which even at the present day is not exhausted; and political and social questions may yet arise in which the thoughts of Plato may be read anew and receive a fresh meaning.

This vision of truth or good is represented in the Symposium under the aspect of beauty, and is supposed to be attained there by stages of initiation, as here by regular gradations of knowledge. Viewed from the intellectual side, the vision of good is the process or science of dialectic.

This is the science which, according to the Phaedrus, is the true basis of rhetoric, which alone is able to distinguish the natures and classes of men and things — which divides a whole into the natural parts, and reunites the scattered parts into a natural or organized whole; which defines the abstract essences or universal ideas of all things and connects them; which pierces the veil of hypotheses and reaches the final cause or first principle of all; which regards the sciences in relation to the idea of good. This ideal science resembles the natural process of thought, and may be described as the mind talking to herself, and in another form is the everlasting question and answer—the ceaseless interrogative of Socrates. The dialogues of Plato are themselves the best examples of the nature and method of dialectic.

If now we ask whether this science which Plato only half reveals to us is more akin to logic or to metaphysics, the answer is that they are not as yet distinguished in his mind. Nor has he determined whether this science of dialectic is at rest or in motion, concerned with the contemplation of absolute being, or with the process by which this is to be attained. Modern metaphysics may be described as the science of abstractions, or as the science of the evolution of thought; modern logic, when passing beyond the bounds of mere Aristotelian forms, may be defined as the science of method. The germ of both of them is contained in the Platonic dialectic; all metaphysicians have something in common with the ideas of Plato; all logicians have derived something from the method of Plato. But the nearest approach in modern philosophy to the universal science of Plato, is to be found in the Hegelian ' succession of moments in the unity of the idea.' There is, however, a difference between them: for whereas Hegel is thinking of all the minds of men as one mind, which developes the stages of the idea in different countries or at different times in the same country, with Plato these gradations are regarded only as an order of thought or ideas; the history of the human mind had not yet dawned upon him. The education of Plato is really the ideal life of the philosopher or man of genius, interrupted for a time by the application to practical duties—a life not for the many, but for the few. And he has already told us that the world could not be a philosopher, and that a very few such natures at all existed. Whether the combination of politics and philosophy is possible, is a question which has been much debated, and may perhaps be resolved by saying that the great practical leaders of mankind must have some element of philosophy. But we do Plato injustice when we apply to his theories the test of practicability, for in his conception of education he is really describing his ideal of a philosopher, and in his ideal of a philosopher he is embodying his principles of knowledge. We may read the Republic as a work of art, and measure it by the test of dramatic or poetical consistency, but when regarded as a treatise on philosophy we must endeavour to separate the substance from the form, and sometimes ask ourselves what Plato really meant by all this, and how far we are to regard him as speaking seriously or as only dramatizing a thesis.

IV. Others as well as Plato have chosen an ideal Republic as the form of conveying thoughts which they could not definitely express, or which were beyond the horizon of their own age. The classical writing which approaches most nearly to the Republic is the 'De Republica' of Cicero; but neither in this nor in any other of his dialogues does he rival the art of Plato. He would confine the terms King or State to the rule of reason and justice, and he will not concede that title either to a democracy or to a monarchy. But under the rule of reason and justice he is willing to include the natural superior ruling over the natural inferior, which he compares to the soul ruling over the body. The two images of the just and the unjust are depicted by him and transferred to the state—Philus maintaining against his will the necessity of injustice as a principle of government, while Laelius supports the opposite thesis. His views of language and number are derived from Plato; like him, in the person of Scipio, he denounces the drama, and declares that if his life were to be twice as long he would have no time to read the lyric poets. The picture of democracy is translated by him word for word, though he has hardly shown himself able to 'carry the jest' of Plato. But his most remarkable imitation of Plato is the adaptation of the vision of Er, which is converted by Cicero into the 'Somnium Scipionis;' he has 'romanized' the myth of the Republic, adding an argument for the immortality of the soul taken not from the Republic but from the Phaedrus, and some other touches derived from the Phaedo and the Timaeus. Though a beautiful tale and containing splendid passages, the 'Somnium Scipionis' is very inferior to the vision of Er in dramatic power, and hardly allows the reader to suppose that the writer believes in his own description. Whether, as he says, his dialogues were framed on the model of the lost dialogues of Aristotle, or of Plato, to which they bear so many superficial resemblances, the orator always appears in them; he is not conversing, but making speeches, and is never able to mould the intractable Latin to the grace and ease of the Greek Platonic dialogue.

Plato's Republic has been said to be a church and not a state; and such an ideal of a city in the heavens has always hovered over the Christian world, and is embodied in St. Augustine's 'De Civitate Dei,' which is suggested by the decay and fall of the Roman Empire, much as the Republic of Plato is, by the decline of Greek politics. He stands in much the same relation to cotemporary Rome as Plato did to his cotemporaries in Greece. In all such parallels there is a certain degree of resemblance and also of difference, and the Christian church is even more an ideal than the Republic of Plato and further removed from any existing institution. In many other respects the resemblance between the Republic and the great work of St. Augustine is merely nominal. The 'Civitas Dei' is a controversial treatise which maintains the thesis that the destruction of the Roman Empire is due not to the rise of Christianity but to the corruption of paganism. He has no sympathy with the old Roman life as Plato has with Greek life, nor has he any idea of the ecclesiastical kingdom which was to arise out of the ruins. The work of St. Augustine is a curious repertory of antiquarian learning and quotations, feeble in reasoning and criticism; entering little into the spirit of the ancient Roman life, but deeply penetrated with Christian ethics. He has no power such as Plato possessed of conceiving a different state of the world, or of feeling or understanding anything external to his own theology. Of all the ancient philosophers he is most attracted by Plato, though he is very slightly acquainted with his writings. He is inclined to believe that the idea of creation in the Timaeus is derived from the narrative in Genesis; and he is strangely taken with the coincidence (?) of Plato's saying that 'the philosopher is the lover of God,' and the words of the Book of Exodus in which God reveals himself to Moses. (Ex. iii. 14.)

The 'Utopia' of Sir Thomas More is a surprising monument of his genius, and shows a reach of thought far beyond his cotemporaries. He is possessed of far greater dramatic art than any one who succeeded him, with the exception of Swift. He is as free as Plato from the scruples of his age, and has as exalted a notion of religion. His views of toleration; his dislike of capital punishment, and plans for the reformation of offenders; his evident detestation both of priests and of great men; his remark that 'although every one may hear of ravenous dogs and wolves and cruel man-eaters, it is not easy to find states that are well and wisely governed,' curiously disagree with the notions of his age and with his own life. There are many points in which he shows a modern feeling and a prophetic insight like Plato. He is a sanitary reformer; he maintains that civilized states have a right to the soil of waste countries; he is inclined to the opinion which places happiness in pleasure. His ceremonies before marriage; his *humane* proposal that war should be carried on by assassinating the leaders of the enemy may be compared to some of the paradoxes of Plato. He has a charming fancy worthy of the Timaeus that the Utopians learnt the language of the Greeks with the more readiness because they were originally of the same race with them. In several passages he alludes to Plato and quotes or adapts thoughts both from the Republic and from the Timaeus. He declares himself strongly in favour of the community of property, though aware of the arguments which may be urged on the other side [1]. He is full of satirical reflections on the governments of mankind and on the state of the world. He quotes the words of Plato describing the philosopher 'standing out of the way under a wall until the driving storm of sleet and rain be overpast;' which admit of a singular application to More's own fate; although writing twenty years before (about the year 1514), he can hardly be supposed to have foreseen this. There is no touch of satire which strikes deeper than his quiet remark that the greater part of the precepts of Christ are more at variance with the lives of ordinary Christians than the discourse of Utopia [2]. The 'Utopia' is also very interesting as illustrating

---

[1] 'When, I say, I balance all these things in my thoughts, I grow more favourable to Plato, and do not wonder that he resolved not to make any laws for such as would not submit to a community of all things; for so wise a man as he was could not but foresee that setting all upon a level was the only way to make a nation happy, which cannot be attained so long as there is property.' (Utopia, Phoenix Library, p. 49.)

[2] 'The greatest part of his precepts are more disagreeing to the lives of the men of this age than any part of my discourse has been; but the preachers seemed to have learned that craft to which you advise me; for they, observing that the world would not willingly suit their lives to the rules that Christ has given, have fitted his doctrine as if it had been a leaden rule to their lives, that so, some way or other, they might agree with one another.'

Sir Thomas More's character, which has been deeply affected by the study of Plato.

The 'New Atlantis' is only a fragment, and far inferior in merit to the 'Utopia.' The work is full of ingenuity but wanting in creative fancy, and by no means impresses the reader with a sense of credibility. In some places Lord Bacon is characteristically different from Sir Thomas More, as, for example, in the external state which he attributes to the governor of Solomon's House, whose dress he minutely describes, while to Sir Thomas More such external trappings appear simply ridiculous. Yet, after this programme of dress, Bacon adds the beautiful trait, 'that he had a look as though he pitied men.' Several things are borrowed from the Timaeus; but he has injured the unity of style by adding thoughts and passages which are taken from the Hebrew Scriptures.

Other writings on ideal States, such as the 'De Monarchia' of Dante, which is a dream of another Roman Empire, existing by the side of the Papacy, and like that deriving authority immediately from God;—the divine right of this second power is established in true scholastic form, and by quotations from Scripture and the Classics; the 'Oceana' of Harrington in which the Lord Archon, meaning Cromwell, is described not as he was but as he ought to have been; the 'Argenis' of Barclay, which is a political allegory of his own time, are too unlike Plato to be worth mentioning. The change of government in the time of the Commonwealth set men thinking about first principles, and gave rise to many works of this class. In the 'City of the Sun,' by Campanella, who wrote in the year 1623, a community of women and goods is established, and the principal magistrate, who is called the Sun, is elected after a strict examination in all kinds of science[3]. There are no traces in Swift of an acquaintance with Plato. Nor do I observe any knowledge of Plato in Dante's 'De Monarchia,' which is in many ways the most remarkable of these modern works, though he is well acquainted with the Nicomachean Ethics and with Augustine's 'De Civitate Dei.'

Human life and conduct are affected by ideals in the same way that they are affected by the examples of eminent men. Neither the one nor the other are immediately applicable to practice, but there is a

---

[3] See Hallam's Lit. of Europe, vol. iii. p. 166.

virtue flowing from them which tends to raise individuals above the common routine of society or trade, and to elevate States above the mere interests of commerce or the necessities of self-defence. Like the ideals of art they are partly framed by the omission of particulars; they require to be viewed at a certain distance, and are apt to fade away if we attempt to approach them. They gain an imaginary distinctness when embodied in a State or an individual, but still remain the visions of 'a world unrealized.' Most men live in a corner and see but a little way beyond their own home or place of occupation; they 'do not lift up their eyes to the hills;' they are not awake when the dawn appears. But in Plato as from some 'tower of speculation' we look into the distance and behold the future of the world and of philosophy. The ideal of the State and of the life of the philosopher; the ideal of an education continuing through life and extending equally to both sexes; the ideal of the unity and correlation of knowledge; the faith in good and immortality—are the vacant forms of light on which Plato is seeking to fix the eye of mankind.

THE REPUBLIC.

BOOK I.

PERSONS OF THE DIALOGUE.

SOCRATES, *who is the narrator.*   CEPHALUS.
GLAUCON.   THRASYMACHUS.
ADEIMANTUS.   CLEITOPHON.
POLEMARCHUS.

And others who are mute auditors.

The scene is laid in the house of Cephalus at the Piraeus; and the whole discourse is narrated the day after it actually took place to Timaeus, Hermocrates, Critias, and a nameless person, who all reappear in the Timaeus.

I WENT down to the Piraeus yesterday with Glaucon the son of Ariston, that I might offer up a prayer to the goddess; and also because I wanted to see in what manner they would celebrate the festival of Bendis[1], which was a new thing. I was delighted with the procession of the inhabitants; this, however, was equalled or even exceeded in beauty by that of the Thracians. When we had finished our prayers and the spectacle was over, we turned in the direction of the city; and at that instant, Polemarchus the son of Cephalus, who had caught sight of us at a distance as we were departing homewards, told his servant to run and bid us wait for him. The servant took hold of me by the cloak behind, and said: Polemarchus desires you to wait.

I turned round, and asked him where his master was.

He is coming, said the youth, if you will only wait.

Certainly we will, said Glaucon; and in a few minutes Polemarchus appeared, and with him Adeimantus, Glaucon's brother,

[1] The Thracian Artemis.

Niceratus the son of Nicias, and several others who had been at the procession.

Polemarchus said to me: I perceive, Socrates, that you and your companion are already on your way to the city.

That is a good guess, I said.

But do you see, he said, how many we are?

I do.

And are you stronger than all these? for if not, you will have to remain where you are.

May there not be yet another possibility, I said, that we may persuade you to let us go?

But can you persuade us, if we refuse to listen to you? he said.

No indeed, replied Glaucon.

Then we are not going to listen; of that you may be assured.

Adeimantus added: Has no one told you that there is to be 328 an equestrian torch-race in the evening in honour of the goddess?

Indeed, that is a novelty, I replied. Will the horsemen carry torches and pass them to one another during the race?

Yes, he said; and there will also be a festival at night which is well worth seeing. If we rise from supper in good time we shall see this, and we shall find youths enough there with whom we may discourse. Stay then, and do not be perverse.

Glaucon said: I suppose that we must stay.

Well, as you please, I replied.

Accordingly we went with Polemarchus to his house; and there we found his brothers Lysias and Euthydemus, and with them Thrasymachus the Chalcedonian, Charmantides the Paeanian, and Cleitophon the son of Aristonymus. There too was their father Cephalus, whom I had not seen for a long time, and I thought him very much aged. He was seated on a cushioned chair, and had a garland on his head, for he had been holding a sacrifice in the court; and we sate down by him on other chairs, which were arranged in a circle around him. He welcomed me eagerly, and then he said:—

You don't come to see me, Socrates, as often as you ought. For if I were able to go to you I would not ask you to come to me. But at my age I can hardly get to the city, and therefore you ought to come oftener to the Piraeus. For, indeed, I find that at my time of life, as the pleasures and delights of the body fade away, the love of discourse grows upon me. I only wish therefore that you would come oftener, and be with your young friends here, and make yourself altogether at home with us.

I replied: There is nothing which I like better, Cephalus, than conversing with aged men like yourself; for I regard them as travellers who have gone a journey which I too may have to go, and of whom I ought to enquire, whether the way is smooth and easy, or rugged and difficult. And this is a question which I should like to ask of you who have arrived at that time which the poets call the 'threshold of old age'—Is life harder towards the end, or what report do you give of it?

329   I will tell you, Socrates, he said, what my own feeling is. Old men flock together; they are birds of a feather, as the proverb says; and at our meetings the tale of my acquaintance commonly is—I cannot eat, I cannot drink; the pleasures of youth and love are fled away: there was a good time once, but that is gone, and now life is no longer life. Some of them lament over the slights which are put upon them by their relations, and then they tell you plaintively of how many evils old age is the cause. But I do not believe, Socrates, that the blame is where they say; for if old age were the cause, I too being old, and every other old man would have felt the same. This, however, is not my own experience, nor that of others whom I have known. How well I remember the aged poet Sophocles, when in answer to the question, How does love suit with age, Sophocles,—are you still the man you were? Peace, he replied; most gladly have I escaped that, and I feel as if I had escaped from a mad and furious master. That saying of his has often come into my mind since, and seems to me still as good as at the time when I heard him. For certainly old age has a great sense of calm and freedom; when the passions relax their hold, then, as Sophocles says, you have escaped from the control not of one master only, but of many. And of these regrets, as well as of the complaint about relations, Socrates, the cause is to be sought, not in men's ages, but in their characters and tempers; for he who is of a calm and happy nature will hardly feel the pressure of age, but he who is of an opposite disposition will find youth and age equally a burden.

I was delighted at his words, and wanting to draw him out I went on to say: Yes, Cephalus; but I suspect that people in general do not believe you when you say this; they think that old age sits lightly upon you, not because of your happy disposition, but because you are rich, and wealth is well known to be a great comforter.

That is true, he replied; they do not believe me: and there is something in what they say; not, however, so much as they imagine. I might answer them as Themistocles answered the Seriphian who was abusing him and saying that he was famous, not for his own merits but because he was an Athenian: 'If 330 you had been an Athenian and I a Seriphian, neither of us would have been famous.' And to those who are not rich and are impatient of old age, the same reply may be made; for neither can a good poor man lightly bear age, nor can a bad rich man ever be at peace with himself.

May I ask, Cephalus, whether you inherited or acquired the greater part of your wealth?

How much did I acquire, Socrates? he replied,—is that your question? Well, the property which Cephalus, my grandfather, originally inherited was nearly of the same value as my own is at present; this he doubled and trebled, but my father Lysanias reduced below the original amount; and I, who am neither a spender of money like the one, nor a gainer of money like the other, shall be satisfied if I leave my sons a little more than I received.

That was why I asked you the question, I said, because I saw that you were not fond of money, which is a characteristic rather of those who have inherited their fortunes than of those who have acquired them; for the latter have a second or extraordinary love of money as a creation of their own, resembling the affection of authors for their own poems, or of parents for their children, besides that other love of money for the sake of use and enjoyment which is common to them and all men. And hence they are very bad company, for they talk about nothing but the praises of wealth.

That is true, he said.

Yes, that is very true, I said; but may I ask you one more question? which is this—What do you consider to be the greatest blessing which you have reaped from wealth?

Not one, he said, of which I could easily convince others. For let me tell you, Socrates, that when a man thinks himself to be

near death he has fears and cares which never entered into his mind before ; the tales of a life below and the punishment which is exacted there of deeds done here were a laughing matter to him once, but now he is haunted with the thought that they may be true : either because of the feebleness of age, or from the nearness of the prospect, he seems to have a clearer view of the other world ; suspicions and alarms crowd upon him, and he begins to reckon up in his own mind what wrongs he has done to others.   And when he finds that the sum of his transgressions is great he will many a time like a child start up in his sleep for fear, and he is filled with dark forebodings.   But he who is con-
331 scious of no sin has in age a sweet hope which, as Pindar charmingly says, is a kind nurse to him.

'Hope,' as he says, 'cherishes the soul of him who lives in holiness and righteousness, and is the nurse of his age and the companion of his journey ;— hope which is mightiest to sway the eager soul of man.'

That is an expression of his which wonderfully delights me.   And this is the great blessing of riches, I do not say to every man, but to a good man, that he has had no occasion to deceive another, either intentionally or unintentionally ; and when he departs to the other world he is not in any apprehension about offerings due to the gods or debts which he owes to men.   Now the possession of wealth has a great deal to do with this ; and therefore I say that, setting one thing against another, this, in my opinion, is to a man of sense the greatest of the many advantages which wealth has to give.

That is excellent, Cephalus, I replied ; but then is justice no more than this—to speak the truth and pay your debts ?   And are there not exceptions even to this ?   If I have received arms from a friend when in his right mind and he asks for them when he is not in his right mind, ought I to give them back to him ?   No one would say that I ought, any more than they would say that I ought always to speak the truth to one who is in that condition.

You are quite right, he replied.

But then, I said, speaking the truth and paying your debts is not a correct definition of justice.

And yet, said Polemarchus, that is the definition which has the authority of Simonides.

I fear, said Cephalus, that I must look to the sacrifices; and therefore I now take leave of this argument, which I bequeath to you and Polemarchus.

Is not Polemarchus your heir? I said.

To be sure, he answered, and went away laughing to the sacrifices.

Tell me then, O thou heir of the argument, what did Simonides say, and according to you truly say, about justice?

He said that the return of a debt is just, and in that he appears to me to be right.

I should be sorry to doubt the word of such a wise and inspired man, I said, but I cannot understand his meaning, which though probably clear to you is the reverse of clear to me. For he certainly does not mean, as we were just now saying, that I ought to return a deposit of arms or anything else to one who is not in his right senses; and yet a deposit cannot be denied to be a debt. 33²

True.

Then when the person who asks me is not in his right mind I am not to make the return?

Certainly not.

Then Simonides did not mean to include that case when he said that justice was the payment of a debt?

Certainly not; for he would say that a friend is under an obligation to do good to a friend and not evil.

I understand, I said, that the return of a deposit of gold to the injury of the receiver, if the two parties are friends, is not the return of a debt,—that is what you would imagine him to say?

Yes.

And are enemies also to have their debt or due?

Yes, he said, they are to have what is due to them, and what is really due from an enemy to an enemy is that which is appropriate to him,—that is to say, evil.

Simonides, then, after the manner of poets, would seem to have spoken of the nature of justice in a parable; for he meant to say that justice would give each man what is appropriate to him, and this he termed his debt or due.

That must have been his meaning, he said.

By Zeus! I replied; and if he were asked what due or appropriate thing is given by medicine, and to whom, what answer do you think he would make?

He would surely reply that medicine gives drugs and meat and drink to human bodies.

And what due or appropriate thing is given by cookery, and to whom?

Seasoning to food.

And what is that which justice gives, and to whom?

If, Socrates, we are to be guided at all by the analogy of the preceding instances, then justice is the art which gives good and evil to friends and enemies.

That is his meaning then?

Yes.

And who is best able to do good to his friends and evil to his enemies in time of sickness?

The physician.

Or when they are on a voyage and amid the perils of the sea?

The pilot.

And in what sort of actions is the just man most able to do them good?

In wars and alliances.

But in time of health there is no need of a physician?

No.

And he who is not on a voyage has no need of a pilot?

No.

Then in time of peace justice will be of no use?

I hardly think that.

333   Then you think that justice may be of use in peace as well as war?

Yes.

Like husbandry which acquires corn, or like shoemaking which acquires shoes,—that is what you would say?

Yes.

And what similar use or power of acquisition has justice in time of peace?

In contracts, Socrates, justice is of great use.

And by contracts you mean partnerships?

Exactly.

But is the just man or the skilful player a more useful or better partner at a game of draughts?

The skilful player.

And in the laying of bricks and stones is the just man a more useful or better partner than the builder?

Quite the reverse.

Then in what sort of partnership is the just man a better partner than the harp-player, as the harp-player is certainly a better partner than the just man in playing the harp?

In a money partnership.

But surely not in the use of money, Polemarchus; for you do not want a just man to be your counsellor in the purchase or sale of a horse; a man who is knowing about horses would be better for that, would he not?

Certainly.

And when you want to buy a ship, the shipwright or the pilot would be better?

True.

Then in what common use of silver or gold is the just man to be preferred?

When you want a deposit to be kept safely.

You mean when money is not wanted, but allowed to lie?

Precisely.

That is to say, justice is useful when money is useless?

That is the inference.

And when you want to keep a pruning-hook safe, then justice is useful to the individual and to the state; but when you want to use it, then the art of the vine-dresser?

Clearly.

And when you want to keep a shield or a lyre, and not to use them, you would say that justice is useful; but when you want to use them, then the art of the soldier or of the musician?

Certainly.

And so of all other things;—justice is useful when they are useless, and useless when they are useful?

That is the inference.

Then justice is not of much use. But let us consider this further point: Is not he who can strike any kind of blow also able to ward any kind of blow?

Certainly

And he who can prevent or elude² a disease is best able to create one?

True.

And he is the best guard of a position who is best able to steal 334 a march upon the enemy?

Certainly.

Then he who is a good keeper of anything is also a good thief?

That, I suppose, is to be inferred.

Then if the just man knows how to keep, he knows how to steal money?

That is what the argument implies.

Then after all the just man has turned out to be a thief. And this is a lesson which I suspect you must have learnt out of Homer; for he, speaking of Autolycus, the maternal grandfather of Odysseus, affirms that he was excellent above all men in theft and perjury—this is the way in which he praises one of his favourites. And so, then, you and Homer and Simonides are agreed that justice is a thief; though I must not forget to add 'for the good of friends and for the harm of enemies,'—that was what you were saying?

No, indeed, anything but that; though I really do not know what I did say, but I still stand by the latter words.

Well, there is another question: Are friends to be interpreted as real or seeming, enemies as real or seeming?

Surely, he said, a man may be expected to love those whom he thinks good, and to hate those whom he thinks evil.

Yes, but do not persons often err in their judgment of good and evil?

That is true.

Then to them the good will be enemies and the evil will be their friends?

True.

And still the principle holds, that it is just for men to do good to the evil and evil to the good?

Apparently.

But the good are just and would not do an injustice?

True.

---

² Reading φυλάξασθαι καὶ λαθεῖν.

Then according to your argument it is just to injure those who do no wrong?

Certainly not, Socrates; that would be immoral.

Then I suppose that they ought to do good to the just and harm to the unjust?

I like that better.

But see the consequence:—Many a man who is ignorant of the world has bad friends, and then he ought to do harm to them; and he has good enemies whom he ought to benefit; and thus we arrive at the exact converse of the proposition of Simonides.

That is true, he said; and I think that we had better correct an error into which we have fallen in the use of the words 'friend' and 'enemy.'

What was the error, Polemarchus? I replied.

The error lay in the assumption that he is a friend who seems or is thought good.

And how is the error to be corrected?

We should rather say that he is a friend who is, as well as seems, good; and that he who seems only, and is not good, only seems to be and is not a friend; and of an enemy the same may be said.

You would argue that the good are our friends and the bad our enemies?

Yes.

And instead of saying as we did at first that it is just to do good to your friends and harm to your enemies, you would rather say now, It is just to do good to your friends when they are good and harm to your enemies when they are evil?

Yes, that appears to me to be the truth.

But then ought the just to injure any one at all?

Undoubtedly he ought to injure the wicked who are his enemies.

And when horses or dogs are injured, are they improved or deteriorated?

The latter.

Deteriorated, that is to say, in the good qualities of horses, not of dogs?

Yes, of horses.

And dogs are deteriorated in the good qualities of dogs, and not of horses?

Of course.

And will not men who are injured be deteriorated in their proper human virtue?

Certainly.

And that human virtue is justice?

Yes, certainly.

Then men who are injured cannot but be rendered unjust?

That is the result.

But can the art of the musician make men unmusical?

Certainly not.

Or the art of horsemanship make bad horsemen?

Impossible.

And can the just by justice make men unjust, or the good by virtue make them bad?

Assuredly not.

Nor can heat produce cold?

No.

Nor drought moisture?

Never.

Nor can the good harm, any but only the evil?

Clearly.

And the just is the good?

Certainly.

Then to injure a friend or any one else is not the act of a just man, but of the opposite, who is the unjust?

I think that what you say is quite true, Socrates.

Then if a man says that justice consists in repaying a debt, meaning that a just man ought to do good to his friends and injure his enemies, he is not really wise; for he says what is not true, if, as has been clearly shown, the injuring of another can be in no case just.

I agree with you, said Polemarchus.

Then you and I are prepared to take up arms against any one who attributes such a saying to Simonides or Bias or Pittacus, or any other sage or saint?

I am quite ready to join with you, he said.

336 Shall I whisper in your ear whose I believe the saying to be?

Whose is the saying?

I believe that Periander or Perdiccas or Xerxes or Ismenias

the Theban, or some other rich and mighty man, who had a great opinion of his own power, first said that justice is doing good to your friends and harm to your enemies.

Most true, he said.

Yes, I said; but if this definition of justice also breaks down, what other can be offered?

Several times in the middle of our discourse Thrasymachus had made an attempt to get the argument into his own hands by interrupting us, and had been put down by the rest of the company, who wanted to hear the end. But when I had done speaking and there was a pause, he could no longer hold his peace; and, gathering himself up, he came at us like a wild beast seeking to devour us, and Polemarchus and I quaked with fear.

What folly has possessed you, Socrates? he said, with a roar. Why do you drop down at one another's feet in this silly way? I say that if you want to know what justice really is, you should answer and not ask, and you shouldn't pride yourself in refuting others, but have your own answer; for there is many a one who can ask and cannot answer. And don't tell me that justice is duty or advantage or profit or gain or interest, for that sort of watery stuff won't do for me; I must and will have a precise answer.

I was panic-stricken at these words, and trembled at the very look of him; and I verily believe that if I had not caught his eye first, I should have been deprived of utterance: but now, when I saw his fury rising, I had the presence of mind to keep my eye upon him, and this enabled me to reply to him.

Thrasymachus, I said, with a quiver, have mercy on us. Our error, if we were guilty of any error, was certainly unintentional; and therefore you, in your wisdom, should have pity upon us, and not be angry with us. If we were seeking for gold, you would not imagine that we were pretending only, or dropping down, as you say, out of foolish complaisance, at one another's feet. Do not imagine, then, that we are pretending to seek for justice, which is a treasure far more precious than gold.

How characteristic of Socrates! he replied, with a bitter laugh; 337 —that's your ironical way! Did I not foresee—did I not tell you all, that he would refuse to answer, and try irony or any other shift in order that he might avoid answering?

You are a philosopher, Thrasymachus, I replied, and well know that if you ask what numbers make up twelve, taking care to prohibit the person whom you ask from answering twice six, or three times four, or six times two, or four times three, 'for this sort of nonsense won't do for me,'—then obviously, if that is your way of putting the question to him, neither he nor any one can answer. And suppose he were to say, 'Thrasymachus, what do you mean? And if the true answer to the question is one of these numbers which you interdict, am I to say some other number which is not the right one?—is that your meaning?' How would you answer him?

Yes, said he; but how remarkably parallel the two cases are?

Very likely they are, I replied; but even if they are not, and only appear to be parallel to the person who is asked, can he to whom the question is put avoid saying what he thinks, even though you and I join in forbidding him?

Well, then, I suppose you are going to make one of the interdicted answers?

I dare say that I may, notwithstanding the danger, if upon reflection I approve of any of them.

But what if I give you a new and better answer, he said, than any of these? What do you deserve to have done to you?

Done to me! I can but suffer the penalty of ignorance; and the penalty is to learn from the wise—and that is what I deserve to have done to me.

What, and no payment! that's a pleasant notion!

I will pay when I have the money, I replied.

But you have, Socrates, said Glaucon; and you, Thrasymachus, need be under no anxiety about money, for we will all make a contribution for Socrates.

Yes, he replied, and I know what will happen; Socrates will do as he always does—not answer, but take and pull the argument to pieces.

Why, my good friend, I said, how can any one answer who knows, and says that he knows, just nothing; and who, even if he has some faint notions of his own, is told by a man of authority not to utter them? The natural thing is, that the speaker should 338 be one who knows, like yourself; and I must earnestly request that you will kindly answer for the edification of the company and of myself.

Glaucon and the rest of the company joined in my request, and Thrasymachus, as any one might see, was really eager to speak; for he thought that he had an excellent answer, and would distinguish himself. But at first he affected to insist on my answering; at length he consented to begin. Behold, he said, the wisdom of Socrates; he refuses to teach himself, and goes about learning of others, to whom he never even says Thank you.

That I learn of others, I replied, is quite true; but that I am ungrateful I wholly deny. Money I have none, and therefore I pay in praise, which is all I have; and how ready I am to praise any one who speaks well you will very soon find out when you answer, for I expect that you will answer well.

Listen, then, he said; I proclaim that might is right, justice the interest of the stronger. But why don't you praise me?

Let me first understand you, I replied. Justice, as you say, is the interest of the stronger. Now what, Thrasymachus, is the meaning of this? You cannot mean to say that because Polydamas, the pancratiast, who is stronger than we are, finds the eating of beef for his interest, that this is equally for our interest who are weaker than he is?

That's abominable of you, Socrates; why you are just taking the words in the way which is most damaging to the argument.

Not at all, my good sir, I said; I am trying to understand them; and I wish that you would be a little clearer.

Well, he said, I suppose you know that forms of government differ; there are tyrannies, and there are democracies, and there are aristocracies?

Yes, I know that.

And the government is that which has power in each state?

Certainly.

And the different forms of government make laws democratical, aristocratical, tyrannical, with a view to their several interests; and these laws, which are made by them for their interests, they deliver to their subjects as justice, and punish him who transgresses them as a breaker of the law, and unjust. And that is what I mean when I say that in all states there is the same principle of justice which is neither more nor less than the interest of the government; and as the government must be supposed to 339 have power, the reasonable conclusion is, that everywhere there is one principle of justice which is the interest of the stronger.

Now I understand you, I said; and whether you are right or not I will try to learn. But let me first remark, that you have yourself said ' interest,' although you forbade me to use that word in answer. I do not, however, deny that in your definition the words are added ' of the stronger.'

A slight addition, that you must allow, he said.

Great or small, never mind that; the simple question is, whether what you are saying is the truth. Now we are both agreed that justice is interest of some sort, but we are not agreed as to the additional words ' of the stronger;' and this is the point which I will now examine.

Proceed.

That I will; and first tell me, Do you admit that it is just for subjects to obey their rulers?

I do.

But are the rulers of states absolutely infallible, or are they sometimes liable to err?

To be sure, he replied; they are liable to err.

Then in making their laws they may sometimes make them rightly, but they are not always right?

True.

When they make them rightly, they make them agreeably to their interests; when they are mistaken, contrary to their interests,—that is what you would say?

Yes.

And the laws which they make must be obeyed by their subjects,—and that is what you call justice?

Doubtless.

Then justice, according to your argument, is not only the interest of the stronger but the reverse?

What are you saying? he asked flurriedly.

I am only saying what you were saying, I believe. But let us consider. Have we not admitted that the rulers may be mistaken about their own interest in what they command, and also that to obey them is justice? Has not that been admitted?

Yes.

Then you must also have acknowledged that justice is not the interest of the stronger, when the rulers who are stronger unintentionally command that which is to their own injury. For if, as you say, justice is the obedience which the subject renders to their commands, then in the case supposed, O thou wisest of men, is there any escape from the conclusion that justice is the injury and not the interest of the stronger, which is imposed on the weaker?

Nothing can be clearer, Socrates, said Polemarchus.

Yes, said Cleitophon, interposing, if you are admitted as his 340 witness.

But there is no need of any witness, said Polemarchus, for Thrasymachus himself acknowledges that rulers command what is not for their own interest, and that to obey them is justice.

Yes, Polemarchus,—Thrasymachus said that for subjects to do what was commanded by the rulers was just.

Yes, but he also said that justice was the interest of the stronger, and, while admitting both these propositions, he further admitted that the stronger commands what is not for his own interest; whence follows that justice is the injury quite as much as the interest of the stronger.

But, said Cleitophon, he meant by the interest of the stronger what the stronger thought to be for his interest.

That was not the statement, said Polemarchus.

Never mind, I said; let us accept the new statement, if Thrasymachus has changed his opinion.

Tell me then, I said, Thrasymachus, did you mean by justice what the stronger thought to be his interest, whether really so or not?

Certainly not, he said. Do you suppose that I call him who is mistaken the stronger at the time when he is mistaken?

Yes, I said, that I supposed to be your meaning when you admitted that the ruler was not infallible and might be mistaken.

You are a sharper, Socrates, in argument. Pray do you imagine that he who is mistaken about the sick is a physician in that he is mistaken and at the time that he is mistaken? or that he who errs in arithmetic or grammar is an arithmetician or grammarian in that he is mistaken and at the time that he is mistaken? True, we say that the arithmetician or grammarian or physician has made a mistake, but this is only a way of speaking; for the fact is that neither the grammarian nor any other person of skill ever makes a mistake in as far as he is what his name implies:

they all of them err only when their skill fails them. No craftsman or sage or ruler errs at the time when he is what he is called, though he is commonly said to err; and after this manner I answered you. But the more precise expression, since you will have precision, is that the ruler, as ruler, is unerring, 341 and, being unerring, always commands that which is for his own interest; and the subject is required to execute this: and therefore, as I said at first and now repeat, justice is the interest of the stronger.

Indeed, Thrasymachus, and do you really think that I am a sharper?

Certainly, he replied.

And do you think that I ask these questions with any special design of injuring you?

Nay, he replied, I am quite sure of it; and your dishonesty shall do you no good, for I shall detect you, and in a fair argument you will not be able to overthrow me.

I shall certainly not attempt that; but to avoid anything of the kind occurring between us again, please to say, when you speak of a ruler or stronger whose interest the weaker is required to execute, do you speak of a ruler in the popular or in the strict sense of the term?

The ruler in the strictest of all senses, he said. And now cheat and deceive if you can; I ask no quarter at your hands. But you won't be able.

And do you imagine, I said, that I am such a madman as to try and cheat Thrasymachus? I might as well try to shave a lion.

Why, he said, you made the attempt a minute ago, although you failed, as you will again.

Well, I said, I will not continue these civilities. I would rather ask you a question: Is the physician, in that strict sense of which you are speaking, a healer of the sick or a maker of money? And remember that I am now speaking of the true physician.

A healer of the sick, he replied.

And the pilot—that is to say, the true pilot—is he a captain of sailors or a mere sailor?

A captain of sailors.

The circumstance that he sails in the ship is not to be

reckoned; this is an accident only, and has nothing to do with the name pilot, which is significant of his skill and of his authority.

Very true, he said.

Now, I said, each of these has an interest?

Certainly.

And the art has to find and provide for this interest?

Yes, that is the aim of the art.

And the interest of each of the arts is the perfection of each of them; nothing but that?

What do you mean?

I mean what I may illustrate negatively by the example of the body. Suppose you were to ask me whether the body is self-sufficing or has wants, I should reply: Certainly the body has wants; for the body may be ill and require to be cured, and has therefore interests to which the art of medicine ministers; and this is the origin and intention of medicine, as you will acknowledge. Am I not right in saying that?

Quite right, he replied.

342

But is the art of medicine or any other art faulty or deficient in any quality in the same way that the eye may be deficient in sight or the ear fail of hearing, and, in consequence of this defect, require another art to provide for the interest of seeing and hearing? Has art, I say, any similar liability to fault or defect, and does every art require another supplementary art to provide for its interests, and that another and another without end? Or may the arts be said to look after their own interests? Or have they no need of either?—having no faults or defects, they have no need to correct them, either by the exercise of their own art or of any other—that is not required of them for the preservation of their interests; they have only to consider the interest of their subject-matter, for every art remains pure and faultless while remaining true—that is to say, while perfect and unimpaired? Is not all this clear? And I would have you take the words in your precise manner.

Yes, that is clear.

Then medicine does not consider the interest of medicine, but the interest of the body?

True, he said.

Nor does farriery consider the interests of farriery, but the interests of the horse; neither do any other arts care for themselves, for they have no needs, but they care only for that which is the subject of their art?

True, he said.

But surely, I added, the arts are the superiors and rulers of their own subjects; you will admit that, Thrasymachus?

To this he assented with a good deal of reluctance.

Then, I said, no science or art considers or enjoins the interest of the stronger or superior, but only the interest of the subject and weaker?

He acquiesced in this after a feint of resistance.

Then, I continued, no physician, in as far as he is a physician, considers his own good but the good of the patient; for the true physician is also a ruler having the human body as a subject, and is not a mere money-maker; that has been admitted?

Yes.

And the pilot likewise, in the strict sense of the term, is a ruler of sailors and not a mere sailor?

That has been admitted.

And such a pilot and ruler will provide and prescribe for the interest of the sailor who is under him, and not for his own or the ruler's interest?

He gave a very reluctant 'Yes.'

Then, I said, Thrasymachus, there is no one in any rule who, in as far as he is a ruler, considers or enjoins that which is for his own interest, but always that which is for the interest of his subject and of his art; to that he looks, and that alone he considers in everything which he says and does.

343   When we had got to this point in the argument, and every one saw that the definition of justice had been completely reversed, Thrasymachus, instead of replying to me, said: I want to know, Socrates, whether you have a nurse?

Why do you ask such a question, I said, instead of answering as you ought?

Why, he said, because she lets you go about running at the nose like a drivelling idiot, and has never taught her baby how to know the shepherd from the sheep.

What makes you say that? I replied.

Because you fancy that the shepherd or neatherd fattens or

tends the sheep or oxen with a view to their own good and
not to the good of himself or his master; and you further imagine
that the rulers of states, who are true rulers, never think of their
subjects as sheep, and that they are not studying their own advantage day and night. Oh, no; and so entirely astray are you in
the very rudiments of justice and injustice as not even to know
that justice and the just are in reality another's good; that is to
say, the interest of the ruler and stronger, and the loss of the
subject and servant; whereas the reverse holds in the case of
injustice; for the unjust is lord over the truly simple and just:
he is the stronger, and his subjects do what is for his benefit,
and minister to his happiness, which is very far from being their
own. Consider further, most foolish Socrates, that the just is
always a loser in comparison with the unjust. First of all in
their private dealings: wherever the unjust is the partner of the
just the conclusion of the affair always is that the unjust man
has more and the just less. Next, in their dealings with the
State: when there is an income-tax, the just man will pay more
and the unjust less on the same amount of income; and when
there is anything to be received the one gains nothing and the
other much. Observe also that when they come into office, there
is the just man neglecting his affairs and perhaps suffering other
losses, but he will not compensate himself out of the public purse
because he is just; moreover he is hated by his friends and
relations for refusing to serve them in unlawful ways. Now all
this is reversed in the case of the unjust man. I am speaking of
injustice on a large scale in which the advantage of the unjust is 344
most apparent, and my meaning will be most clearly seen in that
highest form of injustice the perpetrator of which is the happiest
of men, as the sufferers or those who refuse to do injustice are the
most miserable—I mean tyranny, which by fraud and force takes
away the property of others, not retail but wholesale; comprehending in one, things sacred as well as profane, private and
public; for any one of which acts of wrong, if he were detected
perpetrating them singly he would be punished and incur great
dishonour; for they who are guilty of any of these crimes in
single instances are called robbers of temples, and man-stealers
and burglars and swindlers and thieves. But when a man has
taken away the money of the citizens and made slaves of them,

then, instead of these dishonourable names, he is called happy and blessed, not only by the citizens but by all who hear of his having achieved the consummation of injustice. For injustice is censured because the censurers are afraid of suffering, and not from any fear which they have of doing injustice. And thus, as I have shown, Socrates, injustice, when on a sufficient scale, has more strength and freedom and mastery than justice; and, as I said at first, justice is the interest of the stronger, whereas injustice is a man's own profit and interest.

Thrasymachus, when he had thus spoken, having, like a bathman, deluged our ears with his words, had a mind to go away. But the company would not allow this, and they compelled him to remain and defend his position; and I myself added my own humble request that he would not leave us. Thrasymachus, I said to him, ex-cellent man, how suggestive are your words! And are you going away before you have fairly taught or learned whether they are true or not? Is the attempt to determine the way of man's life such a small matter in your eyes—the attempt to determine the way in which life may be passed by each one of us to the greatest advantage?

My reason is that I do not agree with you, he replied.

I should rather think, Thrasymachus, that you have no feeling about us, I said; you don't seem to care whether we live better or worse from not knowing what you say you know. Prithee, friend, be obliging and impart your wisdom to us; any benefit which is conferred on a large party such as this is will not be 345 unrewarded. For my own part I frankly admit that I am not convinced, and that I do not believe injustice to be more gainful than justice, even if uncontrolled and allowed to have free play. For, granting that there may be an unjust man who is able to commit injustice either by fraud or force, still this does not convince me of the superior advantage of injustice, and there may be others who are in the same predicament as myself. Perhaps we may be wrong; if so, you should convince us that we are mistaken in preferring justice to injustice.

And how am I to convince you, he said, if you are not already convinced by what I have just said; what more can I do for you? Would you have me put the proof bodily into your souls?

Heaven forbid! I said; I would only ask you to be consistent;

or, if you change, change openly and let there be no deception. For I must observe, Thrasymachus, if you will look back at what preceded, that you began by defining the true physician in an exact sense, but did not think it necessary to observe the same exactness when speaking of the shepherd, whom you regard as a shepherd, and yet maintain that he tends the sheep not with a view to their own good, but as a mere feaster or diner with a view to the pleasures of the table; or, again, as a trader with a view to the market, not as a shepherd. Yet surely the art of the shepherd is concerned only with the good of his subjects; he has only to provide the best for them, since what is best for his art has been already provided when the duties of the shepherd are adequately fulfilled. And that was what I was saying just now about the ruler. I imagined that the art of the ruler, considered as ruler, could only regard the good of his flock or subjects both in his public and private conduct; whereas you seem to think that the rulers—and those of whom you speak are the true rulers —enjoy being in authority.

Think! Nay, I am sure of that.

Then why in lesser offices of command do they never voluntarily hold office but always demand payment, unless under the idea that they govern for the advantage of others and have 346 no interest of their own? Let me ask you a question: Does not the difference of arts consist in their having different functions? And, my dear illustrious friend, do say what you think, that we may make a little progress.

Yes, that is the difference, he replied.

And each art gives us a particular good and not merely a general one—health, for example, is the good of medicine; safety at sea is the good of navigation?

Yes, he said.

And the art of payment has the special function of giving pay: but we do not confuse these with one another; because the health of the pilot may be improved by a sea voyage, you would not say that navigation is the art of medicine—that is to say, if language is to be used in your exact manner?

Certainly not, he said.

Or because a man is in good health when he receives pay you would not say that medicine is the art of payment?

No, he said.

Nor would you say that medicine is the art of receiving pay because a man takes fees when he is engaged in healing?

Certainly not.

And we have admitted, I said, that the good of each art is specially confined to the art?

Yes.

Then, if there be any good which all artists have in common, that is to be attributed to something of which they all have the common use?

True, he replied.

And when the artist is benefitted by receiving pay the advantage is gained by a use of the additional art of pay, which is not the art which he professes?

He gave a reluctant assent to this.

Then the pay is not derived by the artists from their respective arts. But the truth is, that while the art of medicine gives health, and the art of the builder builds a house, another art attends them which is the art of pay. The various arts may be doing their own business and benefitting that over which they preside, but would the artist receive any benefit from his art unless he were paid?

I suppose not.

But does he therefore confer no benefit when he works for nothing?

I admit that he does.

Then now, Thrasymachus, there is no longer any doubt that neither arts nor governments provide for their own interests; but, as we were before saying, for the interests of their subjects who are the weaker and not the stronger—to those attending and ordering them and not to those of the superior. And that is the reason, my dear Thrasymachus, why, as I was just now saying, no one is willing to govern; because no one likes to take in hand the reformation of evils which are not his concern without 347 an equivalent; for the true artist in proceeding according to his art does not do the best for himself, nor consult his own interest, but that of his subjects; and this is why men must be paid for being willing to govern in one of the three modes of payment, money, or honour, or a penalty for refusing to govern.

How is that, Socrates? said Glaucon. The two first modes of payment are intelligible enough, but what the penalty is I do not understand, or how a penalty can be a payment.

You mean that you do not understand the nature of this payment which to the best men is the great inducement to rule? Of course you know that ambition and avarice are deservedly discredited?

True, he said.

And for this reason money and honour have no attraction for them; they do not wish to be directly paid for governing and so get the name of hirelings, nor by indirectly helping themselves out of the public revenues to get the name of thieves. And not being ambitious they do not care about honour; and therefore necessity must be laid upon them and they must be induced to serve from the fear of punishment. And this, as 1 imagine, is the reason why the forwardness to take office instead of awaiting the call of necessity has been thought disgraceful. Now he who refuses to rule is liable to be ruled by one who is worse than himself, than which no punishment can be greater. And the fear of this, as I conceive, induces the good to take office, not because they would but because they cannot help; nor under the idea that they are going to have any benefit or enjoyment themselves, but as a necessity, and because they are not able to commit the task of ruling to any one who is better than themselves, or indeed as good. For the probability is that if a city were composed entirely of good men, then to avoid office would be as much an object of ambition as to obtain office is at present; then we should have plain proof that the true ruler is not meant by nature to regard his own interest, but that of his subjects; and he who is aware of this will therefore choose rather to receive a benefit from another than to have the trouble of conferring one. So far am I from agreeing with Thrasymachus that justice is the interest of the stronger. That, however, is a question which I will not now further discuss; but when Thrasymachus says that the life of the unjust is more advantageous than that of the just, this new statement of his appears to me to be a far more serious matter. Which of us is right, Glaucon? And which sort of life do you deem the most advantageous?

The life of the just, he answered.

348   Did you hear all the advantages of the unjust which Thrasymachus was rehearsing?

Yes, I heard him, but I was not convinced by him.

And would you desire to convince him, if we can only find a way, that he is saying what is not true?

Most certainly, he replied.

If, I said, he makes a set speech and we make another set speech and tell our friend all the good of being just, and he answers and we rejoin, there must be a numbering and measuring of the goods that are claimed on either side, and the end will be that we shall want judges to decide; but if we proceed in our enquiry as we lately did, by a method of mutual agreement, we shall unite the office of judge and advocate in our own persons.

Very good, he said.

And which method do I understand you to prefer? I said.

That which you propose.

Well then, Thrasymachus, I said, suppose that you begin at the beginning and answer me. Your statement is that perfect injustice is more gainful than justice?

Yes, that is my statement, the grounds of which I have also stated.

And you would call one of them virtue and the other vice?

Certainly.

I suppose that you would call justice virtue and injustice vice?

That is a charming notion and so likely, seeing that I affirm injustice to be profitable and justice not.

What else then?

The opposite, he replied.

And would you call justice vice?

No, I would rather say sublime simplicity.

And would you call injustice malignity?

No; I would rather say discretion.

And do the unjust appear to you to be wise and good?

Yes he said; at any rate this is true of those who are able to be perfectly unjust, and who have the power of subduing states and nations; but I dare say that you imagine me to be talking of cut-purses. Even that, if undetected, has advantages, though they are hardly worth mentioning when compared with the other.

I do not think that I misapprehend your meaning, Thrasymachus, I replied; but still I cannot hear without amazement that you class injustice with wisdom and virtue, and justice with the opposite.

Certainly, that is the way in which I do class them.

Now, I said, you are on more substantial and almost unanswerable ground; for if the injustice which you were maintaining to be profitable had been admitted by you or by other men to be vice and deformity, an answer might have been given to you on received principles; but now I perceive that you will call injustice strong and honourable, and to the unjust you will assign all the qualities which were assigned by us before to the just, seeing 349 that you do not hesitate to place injustice on the side of wisdom and virtue.

That is exactly the truth, he replied.

Now, I said, I see that you are speaking your mind, and therefore I do not shrink from the argument; for I do believe, Thrasymachus, that you are in earnest and are not amusing yourself at our expense.

What is it to you, he said, whether I am in earnest or not? your business is to refute the argument.

Very true, I said; and will you be so good then as to answer another question?—Does the just man try to gain any advantage over the just?

Far otherwise; if he did he would not be the simple amusing creature which he is.

And does he try to gain more than his just share in action?

He does not.

And how would he regard the attempt to gain an advantage over the unjust man or action; would that be considered by him as just or unjust?

He would think that just, and would try to gain the advantage. But he could not.

Whether he could or could not, I said, is not the question. I simply asked whether the just man, while refusing to have more than another just man, would wish and claim to have more than the unjust?

Yes, he would.

And what of the unjust—does he claim more than the just man and more than the just action?

Of course, he said, he claims to have more than all men.

And the unjust man will desire more than the unjust man and action, and will strive to get more than all?

True.

Let us put the matter thus, I said; the just does not desire more than his like but more than his unlike, whereas the unjust desires more than both like and unlike.

Nothing, he said, can be better than that statement.

And the unjust is good and wise, and the just is neither?

Good again, he said.

And is not the unjust like the wise and good and the just unlike them?

Of course, he said, he who is just is like the just, and the unjust is like the unjust.

Each of them, I said, is such as his like is?

Certainly, he replied.

Then now, Thrasymachus, I said, let us try these statements by the analogy of the arts. You would admit that one man is a musician and another not a musician?

Yes.

And the musician is wise, and he who is not a musician is unwise?

True.

And in that he is wise he is good, and in that he is unwise he is bad?

Yes.

And you would say the same sort of thing of the physician?

Yes.

And do you think, my excellent friend, that a musician when he adjusts the lyre would desire or claim to be in excess of a musician in the tightening or loosening the strings?

I do not think that he would.

But he would claim to be in excess of the non-musician?

Of course.

350 And what would you say of the physician? In prescribing

meats and drinks would he wish to go beyond another physician or beyond the art of medicine?

He would not.

But he would wish to exceed the non-physician?

Yes.

And about knowledge and ignorance in general; see whether you think that any man of intelligence whatsoever would wish to have the choice of saying or doing more than another man of intelligence. Would he not rather say or do the same as his like in the same case?

That, I suppose, is not to be denied.

And what would you say of the unintelligent? would he not desire to have more than either intelligent or unintelligent?

That, I suppose, must be as you say.

And the intelligent is wise?

Yes.

And the wise is good?

True.

Then the wise and good will not desire to gain more than his like, but more than his unlike?

That is evident.

Whereas the bad and ignorant will desire to gain more than both?

Yes.

But were you not saying, Thrasymachus, that the unjust exceeds both his like and unlike?

Yes, I did say that.

And you also said that the just will not exceed his like but his unlike?

Yes, he said.

Then the just is like the wise and good, and the unjust like the evil and ignorant?

That is the inference.

And each of them is such as his like is?

That was admitted.

Then the just has turned out to be wise and good and the unjust evil and ignorant.

Thrasymachus made all these admissions, not readily, as I

repeat them, but with infinite pains and effort, and oceans of perspiration, for the weather was hot; and then I saw what I had never seen before, Thrasymachus blushing. As we were agreed that justice was virtue and wisdom, and injustice vice and ignorance, I proceeded to another point. Well, I said, Thrasymachus, that is now settled; but were we not also saying that injustice had strength; do you remember?

Yes, I remember, he said, but do not suppose that I approve of what you are now saying or have no answer; if I do not answer, that is because I know you would accuse me of haranguing; therefore either permit me to have my say out, or if you would rather ask, do so, and I will answer 'Very good' as they say to story-telling old women, and will nod and shake my head.

Surely not, I said, if contrary to your real opinion.

Yes, he said, I will, to please you, since you will not let me speak. What else would you have?

Nothing in the world, I said; and if you are so disposed I will ask and you shall answer.

Proceed.

Then I will repeat the question which I asked before, in order 351 that our examination of the relative nature of justice and injustice may be carried on regularly. A statement was made to the effect that injustice is more powerful than justice, but now I say that justice having been identified with wisdom and virtue is easily shown to be stronger than injustice, if injustice is ignorance; every one must acknowledge that. But I want to view the matter, Thrasymachus, in a new way. You would not deny that a state may be unjust and may unjustly attempt to enslave other states, or may have already enslaved them, and may be holding many of them in subjection.

True, he replied; and I will add that the best and most perfectly unjust state will be most likely to do this.

I know, I said, that such was your notion; but what I would further consider is, whether this power can be exercised with justice only or without justice.

If you are right in your view, and justice is wisdom, then with justice only; but if I am right, then without justice.

I am delighted, Thrasymachus, to see you not only nodding

and shaking your head, but making answers that are quite
excellent.

That is out of courtesy to you, he replied.

And very good of you too, I said; and I wish you would have
the goodness also to inform me whether you think that an army,
or a band of robbers and thieves, or any other gang of evil-doers
could act at all if they injured one another?

No indeed, he said, they could not.

But if they abstained from injuring one another, then they
might act better?

Yes.

And this is because from injustice spring divisions and hatreds
and fighting, as from justice harmony and friendship; is not that
true, Thrasymachus?

I grant that, he said, because I do not wish to quarrel with
you.

Thank you, I said; and I should like to know also, if the effect
of injustice is to cause hatred then will not injustice, whether
existing among slaves or freemen, make them hate one another
and set them at variance and render them incapable of common
action?

Certainly.

And even if injustice be found in two only, will they not quarrel and fight, and become enemies to one another and to the
just?

They will.

And suppose, my brave sir, injustice abiding in a single person,
will the injustice lose or retain her natural power?

Let us say that she retains her power.

Yet is not the power which injustice exercises of such a nature
that the subject in which injustice takes up her abode, whether
city or army or family or any other body, is in the first place
rendered incapable of united action by reason of sedition and 352
distraction and becomes its own enemy and at variance with all
that opposes it, and with the just? Is not this as I say?

Yes, certainly.

And is not injustice equally suicidal when existing in an individual; in the first place rendering him incapable of action
because he is not at unity with himself, and in the second place

making him an enemy to himself and the just? Is not that true, Thrasymachus?

Yes.

And O my friend, I said, surely the gods are just?

Let us say that they are.

Then, as the gods are just, he will also be the enemy of the gods, and the just will be the friend of the gods?

Take your fill of the argument, and be of good cheer; I will not oppose you, lest I should displease the company.

Well then, proceed with your answers, and let me have the rest of my feast. For that the just are clearly wiser and better and abler than the unjust, and that the unjust are incapable of common action—this has been already shown; nay more, when we speak thus confidently of gangs of evil-doers acting together, this is not strictly true, for if they had been perfectly unjust, they would have laid hands upon one another; but there must evidently have been some remnant of justice in them, or they would have injured one another as well as their victims, and then they would have been unable to act together; they were but semi-villainous, for had they been whole villains, wholly unjust, they would have been wholly incapable of action. That, as I believe, is the truth of the matter, and not what you said at first. But whether the just have a better and happier life than the unjust is a further question which we also proposed to consider. I think that they have, and for the reasons which I have given; but still I should like to examine further, for this is no light matter, concerning nothing less than the true rule of life.

Proceed.

I will proceed by asking a question: Would you not think that a horse has some end or use?

I should.

And that would be the end or use of a horse or anything which could not be accomplished, or not so well accomplished, by any other thing?

I do not understand, he said.

Let me explain then. Can you see, except with the eye?

Certainly not.

Or hear, except with the ear?

No.

These then are the uses or ends of these faculties?

They are.

But you can cut off a vine-branch with a carving-knife or with 353 a chisel?

Of course.

And yet not so well as with a pruning-hook made for the purpose?

True.

May we not say, then, that this is the use of the pruning-hook?

We may.

Then now I think you will have no difficulty in understanding my meaning when I said that the end or use of anything was that which could not be accomplished, or not so well accomplished, by any other thing?

I understand your meaning, he said, and assent.

And as all things have ends, have they not also excellences? Need I ask again whether the eye has an end?

It has.

And has not the eye an excellence?

Yes.

And the ear has an end and an excellence also?

True.

And the same is true of all other things; they have each of them an end and a special excellence?

That is so.

Well, and can the eyes fulfil their end if they are wanting in their own proper excellence and have a defect instead?

How can they, he said, if they are blind?

You mean to say, if they have lost their proper excellence, which is sight; but I have not arrived at that point yet. I would rather ask the question more generally, and only enquire whether the things which fulfil their ends fulfil them by their own proper excellence, and fail of fulfilling them by their proper defect?

Yes, I assent to that, he replied.

I might say the same of the ears; when deprived of their own proper excellence they cannot fulfil their end?

True.

And the same may be said of all other things?

I agree.

And has not the soul an end which nothing else can fulfil?
for example, to provide and command and advise and the like.
Are not these peculiar to the soul, and can they rightly be assigned to any other?

To no other.

And is not life to be reckoned among the ends of the soul?

Assuredly, he said.

And has not the soul an excellence also?

Yes.

And can she or can she not fulfil her ends or uses when deprived
of that excellence?

She cannot.

Then an evil soul must necessarily be an evil ruler, and a good
soul a good ruler?

Yes, that must be as you say.

And we have admitted that justice is the excellence of the soul,
and injustice the defect of the soul?

That has been admitted.

Then the just soul and the just man will live well, and the unjust man will live ill?

That is involved in your argument.

354 And he who lives well will be blessed and happy, and he who
lives ill the reverse of happy?

Certainly.

Then the just is happy, and the unjust miserable?

Granted.

But happiness and not misery is profitable. Then, my blessed
Thrasymachus, injustice can never be more profitable than justice.

Let this, Socrates, be your entertainment at the Bendidea.

And for this I am indebted to you, I said, now that you have
grown gentle towards me and have left off scolding. Nevertheless, I have not been well entertained; but that was my own
fault and not yours. I may liken myself to an epicure who
snatches a taste of every dish which is successively brought to
table before he has fairly enjoyed the one before; and this has
been the case with me. For before I discovered the nature of
justice, I left that and proceeded to enquire whether justice was
virtue and wisdom or evil and folly; and then arose a further

question about the comparative advantages of justice and injustice, and I could not refrain from passing on to that. And the result of all is that I know nothing at all. For I know not what justice is, and therefore I am not likely to know whether it is or is not a virtue, nor can I say whether the just is happy or unhappy.

BOOK II.

357   WITH these words I was thinking that I had made an end of the discussion; but the end, in truth, proved to be only a beginning. For Glaucon, who is at all times the boldest of men, was dissatisfied at Thrasymachus' retirement; he wanted to have the battle out. So he said to me: Socrates, do you wish really to persuade us, or only to seem to have persuaded us, that to be just is always better than to be unjust?

I should wish really to persuade you, I replied, if I could.

Then you certainly have not succeeded. And will you tell me, he said, how you would arrange goods; is there not one class of goods which are desirable in themselves, and independently of their results, as, for example, mere innocent pleasures and enjoyments, upon which nothing follows?

I think that there is such a class, I replied.

What would you say to a second class of goods which are desirable not only in themselves, but also for their results, such as knowledge, sight, health?

To that likewise I assent.

Thirdly, would you recognize a class of goods troublesome in themselves, yet profitable to us; such, for example, as gymnastic exercises, or the healing and treatment of disease, and the business of money-making, which no one would choose for their own sakes, but only for the sake of some reward or result of them?

There is, I said, this third class also. But why do you ask?

Because I want to know in which of the three classes you would place justice?

358   In the highest and noblest class, I replied, of goods, which he who is to be happy desires for their own sakes as well as for their results.

Then the many are of another mind; they think that justice is of the troublesome class of goods, which are to be pursued for the sake of rewards and reputation, but in themselves are rather to be avoided.

I know, I said, that this is their doctrine, and this was also the sentiment of Thrasymachus, when originally he blamed justice and praised injustice; but I appear not to understand him.

I wish, he said, that you would hear me as well as him, and then I shall see whether you and I agree. For Thrasymachus seems to me to have been charmed by your voice, like a snake, sooner than he ought to have been; and I am not yet satisfied with the account which has been given of the nature of justice and injustice. Leaving the rewards and results of them, I want to know what they, either of them, are in themselves, and what power they have in the soul. If you please, then, I will revive the argument of Thrasymachus. And first I will speak of the nature and origin of justice according to the common view of them. Secondly, I will show that all men who practise justice do so against their will, and not as a good, but as a necessity. And thirdly, I will maintain that there is reason in this, for in their view, the life of the unjust is better far than the life of the just. That is only what they say, Socrates, for I myself am not of their opinion. But still I acknowledge that I am perplexed when I hear the voices of Thrasymachus and myriads of others dinning in my ears; and, on the other hand, I have never yet heard the thesis that justice is better than injustice maintained in a satisfactory way. If I could hear the praises of justice and injustice considered in themselves, then I should be satisfied, and you are the person from whom I expect to hear this; and therefore I will praise the unjust life to the utmost of my power, and the manner in which I speak will indicate also the manner in which I desire to hear you praising justice and censuring injustice. Will you say whether you approve of this?

Indeed I do; nor can I imagine any theme about which a man of sense would oftener wish to converse.

I am delighted, he replied, to hear you say that, and shall begin by speaking of the nature and origin of justice.

They say that to do injustice is, by nature, good; to suffer injustice, evil; but that the evil is greater than the good. And when men have done and suffered and had experience of both, not being able to avoid the one and obtain the other, they think 359 that they had better agree with one another to have neither, and thence arise laws and covenants among them; and that which is ordained by law they term lawful and just. This, as they affirm, is the origin and nature of justice arising out of a mean or compromise, between the best of all which is to do and not to suffer injustice, and the worst of all which is to suffer without the power of retaliation; and justice, being in a mean between the two, is tolerated not as a good, but as the lesser evil, and honoured by reason of the inability of men to do injustice. For no man who is worthy to be called a man would submit to such an agreement if he were able to resist; he would be mad if he did. This, Socrates, is the received account of the nature and origin of justice.

Now that justice is only the inability to do injustice will best appear if we imagine something of this kind: suppose we give both the just and the unjust entire liberty to do what they will, and let us attend and see whither desire will lead them; then we shall detect the just man in the very act; the just and unjust will be found going the same way—following their interest, which all natures conceive to be their good, and are only diverted into the path of justice by the force of law. The liberty which we are supposing may be most conveniently given to them in the form of such a power as is said to have been possessed by Gyges, the ancestor of Crœsus the Lydian[1]. For Gyges, according to the tradition, was a shepherd and servant of the king of Lydia, and, while he was in the field, there was a storm and earthquake which made an opening in the earth at the place where he was feeding his flock. He was amazed at the sight and descended into the opening where, among other marvels, he beheld a hollow brazen horse, having doors, at which he stooping and looking in saw a dead body of stature, as appeared to him, more than human, and having nothing on but a gold ring; this he took from the finger of the dead and reascended out of the opening. Now the shepherds met together, according to custom, that they might send their monthly report concerning the flock to the king; and into their assembly he came having the ring on his finger, and as he was sitting among them he chanced to turn the collet of the ring towards the inner side

---

[1] Reading Γύγῃ τῷ Κροίσου τοῦ Λυδοῦ προγόνῳ.

of the hand, when instantly he became invisible, and the others began to speak of him as if he were no longer there. He was 360 astonished at this, and again touching the ring he turned the collet outwards and reappeared; thereupon he made trials of the ring, and always with the same result; when he turned the collet inwards he became invisible, when outwards he reappeared. Perceiving this, he immediately contrived to be chosen messenger to the court, where he no sooner arrived than he seduced the queen, and with her help conspired against the king and slew him, and took the kingdom. Suppose now that there were two such magic rings, and the just put on one of them and the unjust the other; no man is of such adamantine temper that he would stand fast in justice—that is what they think. No man would dare to be honest when he could safely take what he liked out of the market, or go into houses and lie with any one at his pleasure, or kill or release from prison whom he would, and in all respects be like a God among men. Then the actions of the just would be as the actions of the unjust; just or unjust would arrive at last at the same goal. And this is surely a great proof that a man is just, not willingly or because he thinks that justice is any good to him individually, but of necessity, for wherever any one thinks that he can safely be unjust, there he is unjust. For all men believe in their hearts that injustice is far more profitable to the individual than justice, and he who takes this line of argument will say that they are right. For if you could imagine any one having such a power and never doing any wrong or touching what was another's, he would be thought by the lookers on to be a most wretched idiot, although they would praise him to one another's faces, and keep up appearances with one another from a fear that they too might be sufferers of injustice. Enough of this.

Now, if we are to form a real judgment of the life of the just and unjust, we must isolate them; there is no other way; and how is the isolation to be effected? I answer: Let the unjust man be entirely unjust, and the just man entirely just; nothing is to be taken away from either of them, and both are to be perfected for the fulfilment of their respective parts. First, let the unjust be like other distinguished masters of crafts;

361 like the skilful pilot or physician, who knows his own powers and attempts only what is within their limits, and who, if he fails at any point, is able to recover himself. So let the unjust make his unjust attempts in the right way, and keep in the dark if he means to be great in his injustice : (he who is detected is nobody :) for the highest reach of injustice is, to be deemed just when you are not. Therefore, I say that to the perfectly unjust man we must attribute the most perfect injustice; there is to be no deduction, and we must allow him, while doing the most unjust acts, to have won for himself the greatest reputation for justice. If he has taken a false step he must be able to retrieve himself, being one who can speak with effect, if any of his deeds come to light, and force his way where force is required, and having gifts of courage and strength, and command of money and friends. And at his side let us place the just man in his nobleness and simplicity, being, as Aeschylus says, and not seeming. There must be no seeming, for if he seem to be just he will be honoured and rewarded, and then we shall not know whether he is just for the sake of justice or for the sake of honours and rewards; therefore, let him be clothed in justice only, and have no other covering; and he must be imagined in a state of life very different from that of the last. Let him be the best of men, and be esteemed to be the worst; then let us see whether his virtue is proof against infamy and its consequences. And let him continue thus to the hour of death; being just, let him seem to be unjust. Then when both have reached the uttermost extreme, the one of justice and the other of injustice, let judgment be given which of them is the happier of the two.

Heavens! my dear Glaucon, I said, how energetically you polish them up for the decision, first one and then the other, as if they were two statues.

I do my best, he said. And now that we know what they are like there is no difficulty in tracing out the sort of life which awaits either of them. But as you may think the description of this a little too coarse, I will ask you to fancy, Socrates, that the words which follow are not mine. Let me put them into the mouths of the eulogists of injustice. They will tell you that in the case described the just man will be scourged, racked, bound —will have his eyes burnt out; and, at last, after suffering every kind of evil, he will be impaled. This will teach him that he ought to seem only, and not to be, just; and that the words of Aeschylus 362 may be more truly spoken of the unjust than of the just. For the unjust, as they will say, is pursuing a reality; at any rate, he does not live with a view to appearances, he wants to be really unjust, and not to seem only:—

> 'His mind is like a deep and fertile soil
> Out of which his prudent counsels spring [2].'

In the first place, he is thought just, and therefore bears rule; he can marry whom he will, and give in marriage to whom he will; also he can trade and deal where he likes, and always to his own advantage, because he has no misgivings about injustice; and in every contest, whether public or private, he gets the better of his antagonists; and has gains, and is rich, and out of his gains he can benefit his friends, and harm his enemies; moreover, he can offer sacrifices, and dedicate gifts to the gods abundantly and magnificently, and can honour the gods and any man whom he wants to honour in far better style than the just, which is a very good reason why he should be dearer to the gods than the just. Thus they make to appear, Socrates, that the life of the unjust is so ordered both by gods and men as to be more blessed than the life of the just.

I was going to say something in answer to Glaucon, when Adeimantus his brother interposed: Socrates, he said, you don't suppose that there is nothing more to be urged?

Why, what else is there? I answered.

The strongest point of all has not been even mentioned, he replied.

Well, then, according to the proverb, 'Let brother help brother;' and if he fails in any part do you assist him; although I must confess that Glaucon has already said quite enough to lay me in the dust, and take from me the power of helping justice.

Nonsense, he replied; I want you to hear the converse of Glaucon's argument, which is equally required in order to bring out what I believe to be his meaning; I mean the argument of those who praise justice and censure injustice, with a view to their consequences only. Parents and tutors are always telling

[2] Seven against Thebes, 574.

their sons and their wards that they are to be just; but why? not
363 for the sake of justice, but for the sake of character and reputation; in the hope of obtaining some of those offices and marriages
and other advantages which Glaucon was enumerating as accruing
to the unjust from a fair reputation. More, however, is made
of appearances by this class than by the others; for they throw
in the good opinion of the gods, and will tell you of a shower
of benefits which the heavens, as they say, rain upon the pious;
and this accords with the testimony of the noble Hesiod and
Homer, the first of whom says, that for the just the gods make—

'The oaks to bear acorns at their summit, and bees in the middle;
Añd the sheep are bowed down with the weight of their own fleeces³,'

and many other blessings of a like kind are provided for them.
And Homer has a very similar strain; for he speaks of one whose
fame is—

'As the fame of some blameless king who, like a god,
Maintains justice; to whom the black earth brings forth
Wheat and barley, whose trees are bowed with fruit,
And his sheep never fail to bear, and the sea gives him fish⁴.'

Still grander are the gifts of heaven which Musaeus and his son
offer the just; they take them down into the world below where
they have the saints feasting on couches with crowns on their
heads, and passing their whole time in drinking; their idea seems
to be that an immortality of drunkenness is the highest meed
of virtue. Some extend their rewards to the third and fourth
generation; the posterity, as they say, of the faithful and just
shall survive them. This is the style in which they praise justice.
But about the wicked there is another strain; they bury them in
a slough, and make them carry water in a sieve; that is their
portion in the world below, and even while living they bring
them to infamy, and inflict upon them the punishments which
Glaucon described as the portion of the just, who are reputed
unjust; nothing else does their invention supply. Such is their
manner of praising the one and censuring the other.

Again, Socrates, let me mention another way of speaking
about justice and injustice, which is not confined to the poets, but
364 is also found in prose writers. The universal voice of mankind
is saying that justice and virtue are honourable, but grievous and

---

³ Hesiod, Works and Days, 230.   ⁴ Homer, Od. xix. 109.

toilsome; and that the pleasures of vice and injustice are easy
of attainment, and are only censured by law and opinion. They
say also that honesty is generally less profitable than dishonesty;
and they are quite ready to call wicked men happy, and to honour
them both in public and private when they are rich or have other
sources of power, while they despise and neglect those who may
be weak and poor, even though acknowledging that these are
better than the others. But the most extraordinary of all their
sayings is about virtue and the gods: they say that the gods
apportion calamity and evil to many good men, and good and
happiness to the evil. And mendicant prophets go to rich men's
doors and persuade them that they have a power committed to
them of making an atonement for their sins or those of their
fathers by sacrifices or charms, with rejoicings and games; and
they promise to harm an enemy, whether just or unjust, at a small
charge; with magic arts and incantations binding the will of
heaven to do their work. And the poets are the authorities to
whom they appeal, some of them dispensing indulgences out
of them, as when the poet sings:—

'Vice may be easily found, and many are they who follow after her; the
way is smooth and not long. But before virtue the gods have set toil[5],'

and a path which they describe as tedious and steep. Others,
again, cite Homer as a witness that the gods may be influenced
by men, as he also says:—

'The gods, too, may be moved by prayers; and men pray to them and
turn away their wrath by sacrifices and entreaties, and by libations and the
odour of fat, when they have sinned and transgressed[6].'

And they produce a host of books written by Musaeus and Orpheus,
who are children of the Moon and the Muses—that is what they say
—according to which they perform their ritual, and persuade not
only individuals, but whole cities, that expiations and atonements
for sin may be made by sacrifices and amusements which fill
a vacant hour, and are equally at the service of the living and the
dead; the latter they call mysteries, and they redeem us from 365
the pains of hell, but if we neglect them no one knows what
awaits us.

He proceeded: And now when the young hear all this said

[5] Hesiod, Works and Days, 287.   [6] Homer, Iliad, ix. 493.

about virtue and vice, and the manner in which gods and men regard them, how are they likely to be affected, my dear Socrates; those of them, I mean, who are quickwitted, and, like bees on the wing, light on everything which they hear, and thence gather inferences as to the character and way of life which are best for them? Probably the youth will say to himself in the words of Pindar—

'Can I by justice or by crooked ways of deceit ascend a loftier tower, which shall be a house of defence to me all my days?'

For what men say is that, if I am really just without being thought just, this is no good, but evident pain and loss. But if, though unjust, I acquire the character of justice, a heavenly life is to be mine. Since then, as philosophers say, appearance is master of truth and lord of bliss, to appearance I must wholly devote myself. Around and about me I will draw the simple garb of virtue, but behind I will trail the subtle and crafty fox, as Archilochus, first of sages, counsels. But I hear some one exclaiming that wickedness is not easily concealed; to which I answer that nothing great is easy. Nevertheless, this is the road to happiness; and the way by which we must go, following in the steps of the argument; and as to concealment, that may be secured by the co-operation of societies and political clubs. And there are professors of rhetoric who teach the philosophy of persuading courts and assemblies; and so, partly by persuasion and partly by force, I shall make unlawful gains and not be punished. Still I hear a voice saying that the gods cannot be deceived, neither can they be compelled. But what if there are no gods? or, suppose that the gods have no care about human things—in either case the result is the same, that we need not trouble ourselves with concealment. And even if there are gods, and they have a care of us, yet we know about them only from the traditions and genealogies of the poets; and these are the very persons who say that they may be influenced by prayers and offerings. Let us be consistent then, and either believe both or neither. And if we believe them, why then we had better be unjust, and offer 366 of the fruits of injustice; for if we are just we shall indeed escape the vengeance of heaven, but we shall lose the gains of injustice; whereas, if we are unjust, we shall keep the gains, and by our sinning and praying, and praying and sinning, the gods will be propitiated, and we shall be forgiven. 'But there is a world below in which either we or our children will suffer for our deeds.' Yes, my friend, will be the reply, but there are mysteries and atoning deities, and these have great power. That is what mighty cities declare; and the children of the gods, who are their poets and prophets, affirm the same.

On what principle, then, shall we choose justice rather than the worst injustice? when, if we only unite the latter with a deceitful regard to appearances, we shall fare to our mind both with gods and men, here as well as hereafter, as say the most numerous and the highest authorities. Knowing all this, Socrates, how can any one who has any advantage of mind or person or rank or wealth, be willing to honour, or indeed refrain from laughing at the praises of justice? For even if there should be any one who is able to disprove my words, and who is satisfied that justice is best, still he is not angry with the unjust; he is very ready to forgive them, knowing as he also does that men are not just of their own free will; unless, peradventure, there be some one whom the divinity within him has inspired with a hatred of injustice, or who abstains because he has found knowledge—but no other man. He only blames injustice who, owing to cowardice or age or some weakness, is incapable of being unjust. And this is proved by the fact that those who are incapable when they have the power, and in as far as they have the power, are the first to be unjust.

Now all this simply arises out of the circumstance which you may remember, Socrates, that my brother and I both mentioned to you at the beginning of the argument. We told you how astonished we were to find that of all the professing panegyrists of justice—beginning with the heroes of old, of whom any memorial has been preserved to us, and ending with the men of our own time—no one has ever blamed injustice or praised justice except with a view to the glories, honours and benefits which flow from them. No one has ever adequately described either in verse or prose the true essential nature of either of these immanent in the soul, and invisible to any human or divine eye; or shown that of all the things of a man's soul which he has within him, justice is the greatest good, and injustice the greatest evil. Had this been the universal strain, had you sought to per- 367 suade us of this from our youth upwards, we should not have been on the watch to keep one another from doing wrong, but every one would have been his own watchman, because afraid, if he did wrong, of having the greatest evil dwelling with him. I dare say that Thrasymachus and others would seriously hold the language which I have been only repeating, and more of the same sort about justice and injustice, grossly, as I conceive, perverting their true nature. But I am speaking with all my might, as I must confess, only because I want to hear you speak on the opposite side; and I would ask you to show not only the superiority of justice over injustice, but what they do to the possessors of them that makes the one to be a good and the other an evil to him. And please, as Glaucon said, to exclude reputation; for unless you clothe the just in the garb of injustice, and the unjust in that of justice, we shall say that you do not praise justice, but the appearance of justice; we shall think that you are only exhorting us to keep injustice dark, and that you really agree with Thrasymachus in thinking that justice is another's good and the interest of the stronger, and that injustice is a man's own profit and interest, though injurious to the weaker. Now as you have admitted that justice is one of that highest class of goods which are desired as well for their results as, in a far greater degree, for their own sakes — just as sight or knowledge or health, or any other real and natural and not merely conventional goods, are desired for their own sakes—I would ask you to direct your praises to that one point only: I mean to the essential good of justice and evil of injustice. Let others praise the rewards and appearances of justice; that is a manner of arguing which, as coming from them, I am ready to tolerate, but from you who have spent your whole life in thinking of this, unless I hear the contrary from your own lips, I expect something better. And therefore, I say, not only prove to us that justice is better than injustice, but show what they either of them do to the possessors of them, which makes the one to be good and the other an evil, whether seen or unseen by gods and men.

I had always admired the genius of Glaucon and Adeimantus, 368 but when I heard this I was quite charmed, and said: That was not a bad beginning of the Elegiacs in which the admirer of Glaucon addressed you as your father's sons after you distinguished yourselves at the battle of Megara :—

'Sons of Ariston, divine offspring of a glorious hero.'

The epithet is very appropriate, for there is something truly divine in being able to argue as you have done for the superiority of injustice and remaining uninfluenced by your own arguments. And I do believe that you are not influenced; this I infer from your general character, for had I judged only from your speeches I should have mistrusted you. But now trusting you I have all the greater mistrust of myself. For I am in a strait between two; on the one hand I feel my own inability to maintain the cause of justice—your unwillingness to accept the answer which I made to Thrasymachus about the superiority of justice over injustice proves to me that I am unequal to the task; and yet on the other hand I cannot refuse to help, for I fear that there may be a sin when justice is evil spoken of in standing by and failing to offer help or succour while breath or speech remain to me. And therefore I must give such help as I can. Glaucon and the rest entreated me by all means not to let the question drop, but to proceed in the investigation. They wanted to arrive at the truth, first, about the nature of justice and injustice, and secondly, about their relative advantages. I told them, what I really thought, that the search would be no easy one, and would require very good eyes. Seeing then, I said, we are no great wits, I think that we had better adopt a method which might be recommended to those who are short-sighted, and are bidden by some one to read small letters a long way off; one of the party recollects that he has seen the very same letters elsewhere written larger and on a larger scale—if they were the same and we could read the larger letters first, and then proceed to the lesser—that would be thought a rare piece of good fortune.

Very true, said Adeimantus; but how does this apply to our present enquiry?

I will tell you, I replied; justice, which is the subject of our enquiry, is, as you know, sometimes spoken of as the virtue of an individual, and sometimes as the virtue of a State.

True, he replied.

And is not a State larger than an individual?

It is.

Then in the larger the quantity of justice will be larger and more easily discernible. I propose therefore that we enquire into the nature of justice and injustice as appearing in the State first,

369 and secondly in the individual, proceeding from the greater to the lesser and comparing them.

That, he said, is an excellent proposal.

And suppose we imagine the State as in a process of creation, and then we shall see the justice and injustice of the State in process of creation also.

Very likely.

When the State is completed there may be a hope that the object of our search will be more easily discovered.

Yes, more easily.

And shall we make the attempt? I said; although I cannot promise you as an inducement that the task will be a light one. Reflect therefore.

I have reflected, said Adeimantus, and am anxious that you should proceed.

A State, I said, arises, as I conceive, out of the needs of mankind; no one is self-sufficing, but all of us have many wants. Can any other origin of a State be imagined?

None, he replied.

Then, as we have many wants, and many persons are needed to supply them, one takes a helper for one purpose and another for another; and when these helpers and partners are gathered together in one habitation the body of inhabitants is termed a State.

True, he said.

And they exchange with one another, and one gives, and another receives, under the idea that the exchange will be for their good.

Very true.

Then, I said, let us begin and create a State; and yet the true creator is necessity, who is the mother of our invention.

True, he replied.

Now the first and greatest of necessities is food, which is the condition of life and existence.

Certainly.

The second is a dwelling, and the third clothing and that sort of thing.

True.

And now let us see how our city will be able to supply this great demand. We may suppose that one man is a husbandman, another a builder, some one else a weaver—shall we add to them a shoemaker, or perhaps some other purveyor to our bodily wants?

Quite right.

The barest notion of a State must include four or five men.

Clearly.

And how then will they proceed? Will each give the result of his labours to all?—the husbandman, for example, producing for four, and labouring in the production of food for himself and others four times as long and as much as he needs to labour; or shall he leave others and not be at the trouble of producing for them, but produce a fourth for himself in a fourth of the time, 370 and in the remaining three fourths of his time be employed in making a house or a coat or a pair of shoes?

Adeimantus thought that the former would be the better way.

I dare say that you are right, I replied, for I am reminded as you speak that we are not all alike; there are diversities of natures among us which are adapted to different occupations.

Very true.

And will you have a work better done when the workman has many occupations, or when he has only one?

When he has only one.

Further, there can be no doubt that a work is spoilt when not done at the right time?

No doubt of that.

For business is not disposed to wait until the doer of the business is at leisure; but the doer must be at command, and make the business his first object.

He must.

Thus then all things are produced more plentifully and easily and of a better quality when one man does one thing which is natural to him and is done at the right time, and leaves other things.

Undoubtedly.

Then more than four citizens will be required, for the husbandman will not make his own plough or mattock, or other implements of agriculture, if they are to be good for anything. Neither will the builder make his tools—and he too, needs many; and the same may be said of the weaver and shoemaker.

True.

Then carpenters, and smiths, and other artisans, will be sharers in our little State, which is already beginning to grow?

True.

Yet even if we add neatherds, shepherds, and other herdsmen, in order that our husbandmen may have oxen to plough with, and builders as well as husbandmen have the use of beasts of burden for their carrying, and weavers and curriers of their fleeces and skins,—still our State will not be very large.

That is true; yet neither will that be a very small State which contains all these.

Further, I said, to place the city on a spot where no imports are required is wellnigh impossible.

Impossible.

Then there must be another class of citizens who will bring the required supply from another city?

There must.

371 But if the trader goes empty-handed, taking nothing which those who are to supply the need want, he will come back empty-handed.

That is certain.

And therefore what they produce at home must be not only enough for themselves, but such both in quantity and quality as to accommodate those from whom their wants are supplied.

That is true.

Then more husbandmen and more artisans will be required?

They will.

Not to mention the importers and exporters, who are called merchants.

Yes.

Then we shall want merchants?

We shall.

And if merchandise is to be carried over the sea, skilful sailors will be needed, and in considerable numbers?

Yes, in considerable numbers.

Then, again, within the city, how will they exchange their productions? and this, as you may remember, was the object of our society.

The way will be, that they will buy and sell.

Then they will need a market-place, and a money-token for purposes of exchange.

Certainly.

Suppose now that a husbandman, or possibly an artisan, brings some production to market, and he comes at a time when there is no one to exchange with him,—is he to leave his work and sit idle in the market-place?

Not at all; he will find people there who, seeing this want, take upon themselves the duty of sale. In well-ordered states they are commonly those who are the weakest in bodily strength, and therefore unable to do anything else; for all they have to do is to be in the market, and take money of those who desire to buy goods, and in exchange for goods to give money to those who desire to sell.

This want, then, will introduce retailers into our State. Is not ' retailer' the term which is applied to those who sit in the market-place buying and selling, while those who wander from one city to another are called merchants?

Yes, he said.

And there is another class of servants, who are intellectually hardly on the level of companionship; still they have plenty of bodily strength for labour, which accordingly they sell, and are called, if I do not mistake, hirelings, hire being the name which is given to the price of their labour.

True.

Then hirelings will help to make our population.

And now, Adeimantus, is our State matured and perfected?

Surely.

Where, then, is justice, and where is injustice, and in which part of the State are they to be found?

Probably in the relations of these citizens with one another. 372 I cannot imagine any other place in which they are more likely to be found.

I dare say that you are right in that suggestion, I said; still, we had better consider the matter further, and not shrink from the task.

First, then, let us consider what will be their way of life, now that we have thus established them. Will they not produce corn, and wine, and clothes, and shoes, and build houses for themselves? And when they are housed, they will work in summer commonly stripped and barefoot, but in winter substantially clothed and shod. They will feed on barley and wheat, baking the wheat and kneading the flour, making noble puddings and loaves; these they will serve up on a mat of reeds or clean leaves, themselves reclining the while upon beds of yew or myrtle boughs. And they and their children will feast, drinking of the wine which they have made, wearing garlands on their heads, and having the praises of the gods on their lips, living in sweet society, and having a care that their families do not exceed their means; for they will have an eye to poverty or war.

But, said Glaucon, interposing, you have not given them a relish to their meal.

True, I replied, I had forgotten that; of course they will have a relish—salt, and olives, and cheese, and onions, and cabbages or other country herbs which are fit for boiling; and we shall give them a dessert of figs, and pulse, and beans, and myrtle-berries, and beech-nuts, which they will roast at the fire, drinking in moderation. And with such a diet they may be expected to live in peace to a good old age, and bequeath a similar life to their children after them.

Yes, Socrates, he said, and if you were making a city of pigs, how else would you feed the beasts?

But what would you have, Glaucon? I replied.

Why, he said, you should give them the proprieties of life. People who are to be comfortable are accustomed to lie on sofas, and dine off tables, and they should have dainties and dessert in the modern fashion.

Yes, said I, now I understand; the question which you would have me consider is, not only how a State, but how a luxurious State is to be created; and possibly there is no harm in this, for in such a State we shall be more likely to see how justice and injustice grow up. I am certainly of opinion that the true State, and that which may be said to be a healthy constitution, is the one which I have described. But if you would like to see the inflamed constitution, there is no objection to this. For I suppose that 373 many will be dissatisfied with the simpler way of life. They will be for adding sofas, and tables, and other furniture; also dainties, and perfumes, and incense, and courtesans, and cakes, not of one sort only, but in profusion and variety; our imagination must not be limited to the necessaries of which I was at first speaking, such as houses, and clothes, and shoes; but the art of the painter and embroiderer will have to be set in motion, and gold and ivory and other materials of art will be required.

True, he said.

Then we must enlarge our borders; for the original healthy State is too small. Now will the city have to fill and swell with a multitude of callings which go beyond what is required by any natural want; such as the whole tribe of hunters and actors, of which one large class have to do with figures and colours, another are musicians; there will be poets and their attendant train of rhapsodists, players, dancers, contractors; also makers of divers kinds of utensils, not forgetting women's ornaments. And we shall want more servants. Will not tutors be also in request, and nurses wet and dry, tirewomen and barbers, as well as confectioners and cooks; and swineherds, too, who were not needed and therefore not included in the former edition of our State, but needed in this? They must not be forgotten: and there will be hosts of animals, if people are to eat them.

Certainly.

And living in this way we shall have much greater need of physicians than before?

Much greater.

And the country which was enough to support the original inhabitants will be too small now, and not enough?

Quite true.

Then a slice of our neighbours' land will be wanted by us for pasture and tillage, and they will want a slice of ours, if, like ourselves, they exceed the limit of necessity, and give themselves up to the unlimited accumulation of wealth?

That, Socrates, will be unavoidable.

And then we shall go to war, Glaucon,—that will be the next thing.

So we shall, he replied.

Then, without determining as yet whether war does good or harm, thus much we may affirm, that now we have discovered war to be derived from causes which are also the causes of almost all the evils in States, private as well as public.

Undoubtedly.

Then our State must once more enlarge; and this time the enlargement will be nothing short of a whole army, which will

374 have to go out and fight with the invaders for all that we have, as well as for the precious souls whom we were describing above.

Why? he said; are they not capable of defending themselves?

No, I said; not if you and all of us were right in the principle which was acknowledged at the first creation of the State: that principle was, as you will remember, that one man could not practise many arts.

Very true, he said.

But is not war an art?

Certainly.

And an art requiring as much attention as shoemaking?

Quite true.

And the shoemaker was not allowed to be a husbandman, or a weaver, or a builder—in order that we might have our shoes well made; but to him and to every other worker one work was assigned by us for which he was fitted by nature, and he was to continue working all his life long at that and at no other, and not to let opportunities slip, and then he would become a good workman. And is there any more important work than to be a good soldier? But is war an art so easily acquired that a man may be a warrior who is also a husbandman, or shoemaker, or other artisan; although no one in the world would be a good dice or draught player who merely took up the game as a recreation, and had not from his earliest years devoted himself to this and nothing else? The mere handling of tools will not make a man a skilled workman, or master of defence, nor be of any use to him who knows not the nature of each, and has never bestowed any attention upon them. How then will he who takes up a shield or other implement of war all in a day become a good fighter, whether with heavy-armed or any other kind of troops?

Yes, he said, the tools which would teach their own use would be of rare value.

And the greater the business of the guardian is, I said, the more time, and art, and skill will be needed by him?

That is what I should suppose, he replied.

Will he not also require natural gifts?

Certainly.

We shall have to select natures which are suited to their task of guarding the city?

That will be our duty.

And anything but an easy duty, I said; but still we must endeavour to do our best as far as we can?

We must.

The dog is a watcher, I said, and the guardian is also a watcher; and regarding them in this point of view only, is not the noble youth very like a well-bred dog? 375

How do you mean?

I mean that both of them ought to be quick to observe, and swift to overtake the enemy; and strong too if, when they have caught him, they have to fight with him.

All these qualities, he replied, will certainly be required.

Well, and your guardian must be brave if he is to fight well?

Certainly.

And is he likely to be brave who has no spirit, whether horse or dog or any other animal? Did you never observe how the presence of spirit makes the soul of any creature absolutely fearless and invincible?

Yes; I have observed that.

Then now we have a clear idea of both the bodily qualities which are required in the guardian.

True.

And also of the mental ones; his soul is to be full of spirit?

Yes.

But then, Glaucon, those spirited natures are apt to be furious with one another, and with everybody else.

That is a difficulty, he replied.

Whereas, I said, they ought to be gentle to their friends, and dangerous to their enemies; or, instead of their enemies destroying them, they will destroy themselves.

True, he said.

What is to be done then, I said; how shall we find a gentle nature which has also a great spirit, for they seem to be inconsistent with one another?

True.

And yet he will not be a good guardian who is wanting in either of these two qualities; and, as the combination of them appears to be impossible, this is equivalent to saying that to be a good guardian is also impossible.

I am afraid that is true, he replied.

Here feeling perplexed I began to think over what preceded. My friend, I said, we deserve to be in a puzzle; for if we had only kept the simile before us, the perplexity in which we are entangled would never have arisen.

What do you mean? he said.

I mean to say that there are natures gifted with those opposite qualities, the combination of which we are denying.

And where do you find them?

Many animals, I replied, furnish examples of them; our friend the dog is a very good one: you know that well-bred dogs are perfectly gentle to their familiars and acquaintances, and the reverse to strangers.

I know that.

Then there is nothing impossible or out of the order of nature in our finding a guardian who has a similar combination of qualities?

Certainly not.

Would you not say that he should combine with the spirited nature the qualities of a philosopher?

I do not apprehend your meaning.

376 The trait of which I am speaking, I replied, may be also seen in the dog, and is very remarkable in an animal.

What trait?

Why a dog, whenever he sees a stranger, is angry; when an acquaintance, he welcomes him, although the one has never done him any harm, nor the other any good. Did this never strike you as curious?

I never before made the observation myself, though I quite recognize the truth of your remark.

And surely this instinct of the dog is very charming;—your dog is a true philosopher.

Why?

Why, because he distinguishes the face of a friend and of an enemy only by the criterion of knowing and not knowing. And must not the creature be fond of learning who determines what is friendly and what is unfriendly by the test of knowledge and ignorance?

Most assuredly.

And is not the love of learning the love of wisdom, which is philosophy?

They are the same, he replied

And may we not say confidently of man also, that he who is likely to be gentle to his friends and acquaintances, must by nature be a lover of wisdom and knowledge?

That we may safely affirm.

Then he who is to be a really good and noble guardian of the State will require to unite in himself philosophy and spirit and swiftness and strength?

Undoubtedly.

Then we have found the desired natures; and now that we have found them, how are they to be reared and educated? Is this an enquiry which may be fairly expected to throw light on the greater enquiry which is our final end—How do justice and injustice grow up in States? for we do not want to admit anything which is superfluous, or leave out anything which is really to the point.

Adeimantus thought that the enquiry would be of use to us.

Then, I said, my dear friend, the task must not be given up, even if somewhat long.

Certainly not.

Come then, and like story-tellers, let us be at leisure, and our story shall be the education of our heroes.

By all means.

And what shall be their education? Can we find a better than the old-fashioned sort?—and this has two divisions, gymnastic for the body, and music for the soul.

True.

Music is taught first, and gymnastic afterwards.

Certainly.

And when you speak of music, do you rank literature under music or not?

I do.

And literature may be either true or false?

Yes.

And the young are trained in both kinds, and in the false 377 before the true?

I do not understand your meaning, he said.

You know, I said, that we begin by telling children stories which, though not wholly destitute of truth, are in the main fictitious; and these stories are told them when they are not of an age to learn gymnastics.

Very true.

That was my meaning in saying that we must teach music before gymnastics.

Quite right, he said.

You know also that the beginning is the chiefest part of any work, especially in a young and tender thing; for that is the time at which the character is formed and most readily receives the desired impression.

Quite true.

And shall we just carelessly allow children to hear any casual tales which may be framed by casual persons, and to receive into their minds notions which are the very opposite of those which are to be held by them when they are grown up?

We cannot allow that.

Then the first thing will be to have a censorship of the writers of fiction, and let the censors receive any tale of fiction which is good, and reject the bad; and we will desire mothers and nurses to tell their children the authorised ones only. Let them fashion the mind with these tales, and not the tender frame with the hands only. At the same time, most of those which are now in use will have to be discarded.

Of what tales are you speaking? he said.

You may find a model of the lesser in the greater, I said; for they are necessarily cast in the same mould, and there is the same spirit in both of them.

That may be very true, he replied; but I don't as yet know what you would term the greater.

Those, I said, which are narrated by Homer and Hesiod, and the rest of the poets, who have ever been the great story-tellers of mankind.

But which are the stories that you mean, he said; and what fault do you find with them?

A fault which is most serious, I said; the fault of telling a lie, and a bad lie.

But when is this fault committed?

Whenever an erroneous representation is made of the nature of gods and heroes,—like the drawing of a limner which has not the shadow of a likeness to the truth.

Yes, he said, that sort of thing is certainly very blameable; but what are the stories which you mean?

First of all, I said, there was that greatest of all lies in high places, which the poet told about Uranus, and which was an immoral lie too,—I mean what Hesiod says that Uranus did, and what Cronus did to him[7]. The fact is, that the doings of Cronus, 378 and the sufferings which his son inflicted upon him, even if they were true, ought not to be lightly told to young and simple persons; if possible, they had better be buried in silence. But if there is an absolute necessity for their mention, a very few might hear them in a mystery, and then let them sacrifice not a common (Eleusinian) pig, but some huge and unprocurable victim; this would have the effect of very greatly reducing the number of the hearers.

Why, yes, said he, those stories are certainly objectionable.

Yes, Adeimantus, they are stories not to be narrated in our State; the young man should not be told that in committing the worst of crimes he is far from doing anything outrageous, and that he may chastise his father when he does wrong in any manner that he likes, and in this will only be following the example of the first and greatest among the gods.

I quite agree with you, he said; in my opinion those stories are not fit to be repeated.

Neither, if we mean our future guardians to regard the habit of quarrelling as dishonourable, should anything be said of the wars in heaven, and of the plots and fightings of the gods against one another, which are quite untrue. Far be it from us to tell them of the battles of the giants, and embroider them on garments; or of all the innumerable other quarrels of Gods and heroes with their friends and relations. If they would only believe us we would tell them that quarrelling is unholy, and that never up to this time has there been any quarrel between citizens; this is what old men and old women should begin by telling children, and the same when they grow up. And these are the sort of fictions

7 Hesiod, Theogony, 154, 459.

which the poets should be required to compose. But the narrative of Hephaestus binding Here his mother, or how on another occasion Zeus sent him flying for taking her part when she was being beaten,—such tales must not be admitted into our State, whether they are supposed to have an allegorical meaning or not For the young man cannot judge what is allegorical and what is literal, and anything that he receives into his mind at that age is apt to become indelible and unalterable; and therefore the tales which they first hear should be models of virtuous thoughts.

There you are right, he replied; that is quite essential: but, then, where are such models to be found? and what are the tales in which they are contained? when that question is asked, what will be our answer?

I said to him, You and I, Adeimantus, are not poets in what 379 we are about just now, but founders of a State: now the founders of a State ought to know the general forms in which poets should cast their tales, and the limits which should be observed by them, but they are not bound themselves to make the tales.

That is true, he said; but what are these forms of theology which you mean?

Something of this kind, I replied:—God is always to be represented as he truly is; that is one form which is equally to be observed in every kind of verse, whether epic, lyric, or tragic.

Right.

And is he not truly good? and must he not be represented as such?

Certainly.

And no good thing is hurtful?

No, indeed.

And that which is not hurtful hurts not?

Certainly not.

And that which hurts not does no evil?

No.

And that which does no evil is the cause of no evil?

Impossible.

And the good is the advantageous?

Yes.

And the good is the cause of well-being?

Yes.

The good is not the cause of all things, but of the good only, and not the cause of evil?

Assuredly.

Then God, if he be good, is not the author of all things, as the many assert, but he is the cause of a few things only, and not of most things that occur to men; for few are the goods of human life, and many are the evils, and the good only is to be attributed to him: of the evil other causes have to be discovered.

That appears to me to be most true, he said.

Then we must not listen to Homer or any other poet who is guilty of the folly of saying that

'At the threshold of Zeus lie two casks full of lots, one of good, the other of evil [8],'

and that he to whom Zeus gives a mixture of the two

'Sometimes meets with good, at other times with evil fortune;'

but that he to whom is given the cup of unmingled ill,

'Him wild hunger drives over the divine earth.'

And again—

'Zeus, who is the dispenser of good and evil to us.'

And if any one asserts that the violation of oaths and treaties of which Pandarus was the real author [9], was brought about by Athene and Zeus, or that the strife and conflict of the gods was instigated by Themis and Zeus, he shall not have our approval [10]; neither will we allow our young men to hear the words of Aeschylus, when he says, that 'God plants guilt among men when 380 he desires utterly to destroy a house.'   And if a poet writes of the sufferings of Niobe, which is the subject of the tragedy in which these iambic verses occur, or of the house of Pelops, or of the Trojan war, or any similar theme, either we must not permit him to say that these are the works of God, or, if they are of God, he must devise some such explanation of them as we are seeking: he must say that God did what was just and right, and they were the better for being punished; but that those who are punished are miserable, and God the author of their misery;—that the poet

---

[8] Iliad, xxiv. 527.   [9] Ib. ii. 69.   [10] Ib. xx.

is not to be permitted to say, though he may say that the wicked are miserable because they require to be punished, and are benefited by receiving punishment from God; but that God being good is the author of evil to any one, that is to be strenuously denied, and not allowed to be sung or said in any well-ordered commonwealth by old or young. Such a fiction is suicidal, ruinous, impious.

I agree with you, he replied, about this law, and am ready to give my assent.

Let this then be one of the rules of recitation and invention,—that God is not the author of evil, but of good only.

That will do, he said.

And what do you think of another principle? Shall I ask you whether God is a magician, that he should appear insidiously now in one shape, and now in another — sometimes himself changing and becoming different in form, sometimes deceiving us with the appearance of such transformations; or is he one and the same immutably fixed in his own proper image?

I cannot answer you without more thought.

Well, I said; but if we suppose a change in God or in anything else, that change must be effected either by another or by himself?

That is most certain.

And things which are at their best are also least liable to be altered or discomposed; for example, when healthiest and strongest the human frame is least liable to be affected by meats, and drinks and labours, and the plant which is in the fullest vigour also suffers least from heat or wind, or other similar accidents.

Of course.

381 And this is true of the soul as well as of the body; the bravest and wisest soul will be least affected by any external influence.

True.

And further, I conceive that this principle applies to all works of art—vessels, houses, garments; and that when well made and in good condition, they are least altered by time and circumstances.

That is true.

Then everything which is well made by art or nature, or both, is liable to receive the least change at the hands of others? and God and his attributes are absolutely perfect?

Of course.

He is therefore least likely to take many forms.

He is.

But suppose again that he changes and transforms himself?

Clearly, he said, that must be the case if he is changed at all.

And will he then change himself for the better, or for the worse?

If he change at all he must change for the worse, for we cannot suppose that he is deficient in virtue or beauty.

Very true, Adeimantus; but then, would any one, whether God or man, desire to change for the worse?

That cannot be.

Then God too cannot be willing to change; being, as is supposed, the fairest and best that is conceivable, he remains absolutely and for ever in his own form.

That necessarily follows, he said, in my judgment.

Then, I said, my dear friend, let none of the poets tell us that

'The gods, in the disguise of strangers, prowl about cities having diverse forms [11];'

and let no one slander Proteus and Thetis, neither let any one, either in tragedy or any other kind of poetry, introduce Here disguised in the likeness of a priestess,

'asking an alms for the life-giving daughters of the river Inachus;'

let us have no more lies of that sort. Neither must we have mothers under the influence of the poets scaring their children with abominable tales

'of certain gods who go about by night in the likeness, as is said, of strangers from every land;'

let them beware lest they blaspheme against the gods, and at the same time make cowards of their children.

That ought certainly to be prohibited, he said.

But still you may say that although God is himself unchangeable, he may take various forms in order to bewitch and deceive us.

Suppose that, he replied.

[11] Hom. Od. xvii. 485.

Well, but can you imagine that God will be willing to lie, whether in word or action, by making a false representation of himself?

382   I cannot say, he replied.

Do you not know, I said, that the true lie, if I may use such an expression, is hated of gods and men?

What do you mean? he said.

I mean this, I said,—that no one is willing to be deceived in that which is the truest and highest part of himself, or about the truest and highest matters; there he is most afraid of a lie having possession of him.

Still, he said, I do not comprehend you.

The reason is, I replied, that you attribute some grand meaning to me; whereas all that I am saying is, that deception, or being deceived or uninformed about true being in the highest faculty, which is the soul, and in that part of them to have and to hold the lie, is what mankind least like;—that, I say, is what they utterly detest.

There is nothing more hateful to them.

And, as I was just now saying, this ignorance in the soul of the lie within may be called the true lie; for the lie in words is only a kind of imitation and shadowy image of a previous affection of the soul, not pure unadulterated falsehood. Am I not right in saying this?

Perfectly right.

The true lie is hated not only by the gods, but also by men.

Yes.

Whereas the lie in words is in certain cases useful and not hateful; in dealing with enemies—that would be an instance; or again, as a cure or preventive of the madness of so-called friends; also in the tales of mythology, of which we were just now speaking—because we do not know the truth about ancient traditions, we make falsehood as much like truth as we can, and there is use in this.

Very true, he said.

But can any of these reasons apply to God. Can we suppose that he is ignorant of antiquity, and therefore has recourse to invention?

That would be ridiculous, he said.

The lying poet then has no place in God?

I should say not.

But peradventure he may tell a lie because he is afraid of enemies?

That is inconceivable.

But he may have friends who are senseless or mad?

But no mad or senseless person can be a friend of God.

Then no motive can be imagined why God should lie?

None.

Then the superhuman and divine is absolutely incapable of falsehood?

Yes.

Then is God perfectly simple and true both in deed and word; he changes not; he deceives not, either by dream or waking vision, by sign or word.

Your words, he answered, are the very expression of my own feelings. 383

You agree with me, I said, that this is the second type or mould in which we are to cast our ideas about divine things; the Gods are not magicians who transform themselves, neither do they deceive mankind in word or deed.

I grant that.

Then, although we are lovers of Homer, we do not love the lying dream which Zeus sends to Agamemnon; neither will we praise the verses of Aeschylus in which Thetis says that Apollo at her nuptials

'Was celebrating in song her fair progeny whose days were to be long, and to know no sickness. And gathering all in one he raised a note of triumph over the blessedness of my lot, and cheered my soul. And I thought that the word of Phoebus being prophetic and divine would not fail. And now he himself who uttered the strain, he who was present at the banquet, and who said this—he was the very one who slew my son.'

These are the kind of sentiments about the Gods which will arouse our anger; and he who utters them shall be refused a chorus; neither shall we allow them to enter into education, meaning, as we do, that our guardians, as far as men can be, should be true worshippers of the Gods and like them.

I entirely agree, he said, in the propriety of these principles, and promise to make them my laws.

BOOK III.

386 Such then, I said, are our principles of theology—some tales are to be told, and others are not to be told to our disciples from their youth upwards, if we mean them to honour the gods and their parents, and to value friendship with one another.

Yes; and I think that our principles are right, he said.

Well, I said, and if they are to be courageous, must they not learn, besides these, other lessons also, such as will have the effect of taking away the fear of death? Can any man be courageous who has the fear of death in him?

Certainly not, he said.

And can he be fearless of death, or will he choose death in battle rather than defeat and slavery, who believes in the reality and the terror of the world below?

Impossible.

Then we must assume a control over this class of tales as well as over the others, and beg the relators of them not simply to revile, but rather to commend the world below, intimating to them that their descriptions are untrue, and will do no good to our future warriors.

That will be our duty, he said.

Then, I said, we shall have to obliterate obnoxious passages, beginning with the verse,—

'I would rather be a serf on the land of a poor portionless man who is not well to do, than rule over all the dead who have come to nought [1].'

We must also expunge the verse,—

'He feared lest the mansions grim and squalid which the Gods abhor should be seen both of mortals and immortals [2].'

Or again:—

'O heavens! is there in the house of Hades soul and ghostly form but no mind [3]?'

[1] Od. xi. 489.   [2] Il. xx. 64.   [3] Ib. xxiii. 103.

Again :—

'To him (Teiresias) alone had the Gods given wisdom; the other souls do
but flit as shadows[4].'

Again :—

'The soul flying from the limbs had gone to Hades, lamenting her fate,
leaving strength and youth[5].'

Again :—

'And the soul, with shrilling cry, passed like smoke beneath the earth[6].'   387

And,—

'As bats in hollow of mystic cavern, whenever any of them dropping out
of the string falls from the rock, fly shrilling and hold to one another, so did
they with shrilling cry hold together as they moved[7].'

And we must beg Homer and the other poets not to be angry if
we strike out these and similar passages, not because they are
unpoetical, or unattractive to the popular ear, but because the
greater the charm of them as poetry, the less are they meet for
the ears of boys and men who are to be sons of freedom, and are
to fear slavery more than death.

Undoubtedly.

Also we shall have to reject all the terrible and appalling
names which describe the world below—Cocytus and Styx, ghosts
under the earth, and sapless shades, and any other words of the
same type, the very mention of which causes a shudder to pass
through the inmost soul of him who hears them. I do not say
that these tales may not have a use of some kind; but there
is a danger that the nerves of our guardians may become affected
by them.

We have reason to fear that, he said.

Then there must be no more of them.

True.

Another and a nobler strain will be ours.

Clearly.

And shall we proceed to get rid of the weepings and wailings
of famous men?

[4] Od. x. 495.   [5] Il. xvi. 856.   [6] Ib. xxiii. 100.   [7] Od. xxiv. 6.

They will go with the others.

But shall we be right in getting rid of them? Reflect: our principle is that the good man will not consider death terrible to a good man.

Yes; that is our principle.

And therefore he will not sorrow for his departed friend as though he had suffered anything terrible?

He will not.

Such an one, as we further maintain, is enough for himself and his own happiness, and therefore is least in need of other men.

True, he said.

And for this reason the loss of a son or brother, or the deprivation of fortune is to him of all men least terrible.

Assuredly.

And therefore he will be least likely to lament, and will bear with the greatest equanimity any misfortune of this sort which may befall him.

Yes, he will feel such a misfortune less than another.

Then we shall be right in getting rid of the lamentations of famous men, and making them over to women (and not even to 388 women who are good for anything), or to men of a baser sort, that those who are being educated by us to be the defenders of their country may scorn to do the like.

We shall be very right.

Then we will once more entreat Homer and the other poets not to depict Achilles[8], who is the son of a goddess, as first lying on his side, then on his back, and then on his face; then starting up again in a frenzy and in full sail upon the shores of the barren sea, nor again taking the dusky ashes in both his hands[9] and pouring them over his head, or bewailing and sorrowing in the various modes which Homer has delineated. Nor should he describe Priam the kinsman of the gods,

'Rolling in the dirt, calling each man loudly by his name[10].'

Still more earnestly will we beg of him not to introduce the gods lamenting and saying,

'Alas! my misery! Alas! that I bore the bravest to my sorrow[11].'

But if he must introduce the gods, at any rate let him not dare

---

[8] Il. xxiv. 10.   [9] Ib. xviii. 23.   [10] Ib. xxii. 414.   [11] Ib. xviii. 45.

to represent the greatest of the gods in words so unlike the truth as these,—

'O heavens! with my eyes I behold a dear friend of mine driven round and round the city, and my heart is sorrowful [12].'

Or again :—

'Woe is me that I am fated to have Sarpedon, dearest of men to me, subdued at the hands of Patroclus the son of Menoetius [13].'

For if, my sweet Adeimantus, our youth seriously believe in such unworthy representations of the gods, instead of laughing at them as they ought, hardly will any of them deem that he himself, being but a man, can be dishonoured by similar actions; neither will he rebuke any inclination that may arise in his mind to say and do the like. And instead of having any shame or self-control, he will be always whining and lamenting on slight occasions.

Yes, he said, that is very certain.

Yes, I replied; but that, as we are arguing, is just what ought not to be: and this will remain our conviction until we find a better.

True.

Neither ought our guardians to be given to laughter. For a fit of laughter which has been indulged to excess almost always occasions an equally violent reaction.

That I believe.

Then persons of worth, even if only mortal, must not be represented as overcome by laughter, and still less must such a representation of the gods be allowed.

Still less of the gods, as you say, he replied.

Then we shall not suffer such expressions to be used about the gods as that in which Homer describes how

389

'Inextinguishable laughter arose among the blessed gods, when they saw Hephaestus bustling about the mansion [14].'

On your views, we must not admit them.

On my views, if you like to father them on me; that we must not admit them is certain.

[12] Il. xxii. 168.   [13] Ib. xvi. 433.   [14] Ib. i. 599.

Again, truth should be highly valued; if, as we were saying, a lie is useless to the gods, and useful only as a medicine
to men, then the use of such medicines will have to be re-
stricted to physicians; private individuals have no business with
them.

Clearly not, he said.

Then the rulers of the State are the only persons who ought to
have the privilege of lying, either at home or abroad; they may be
allowed to lie for the good of the State. But nobody else is to
meddle with anything of the kind; and for a private man to lie
in return to the rulers is to be deemed a more heinous fault
than for a patient or the pupil of a gymnasium not to speak the
truth about his own bodily illnesses to the physician or trainer,
or for a sailor not to tell the captain truly how matters are going
on in a ship.

Most true, he said.

If, then, the ruler catches anybody beside himself lying in the
State,

   ' Any of the craftsmen, whether he be priest or physician or carpenter[15],'

he will punish him for introducing a practice which is equally
subversive of ship or State.

Yes, he said, if our principle is to be consistently carried out.

Next, will not our youth require temperance?

Certainly.

Under temperance, speaking generally, are included obedience
to commanders and command of self in sensual pleasures.

True.

Then would you praise or blame the injunction of Diomede in
Homer,

      ' Friends, sit still and obey my word[16],'

and the verses which follow,

      ' The Greeks marched breathing prowess [17],
        In silent awe of their leaders[18],'

and other sentiments of the same kind?

They are good.

---

[15] Od. xvii. 383 sq.   [16] Il. iv. 412.   [17] Ib. iii. 8.   [18] Ib. iv. 431.

What again of this line,

'O heavy with wine, who hast the eyes of a dog and the heart of a stag[19],'

and of the verses which follow? Would you say that these, or 390 any other impertinent words which private men are supposed to address to their rulers, whether in verse or prose, are well or ill spoken?

They are ill spoken.

They may very possibly afford some amusement, but they do not conduce to temperance. And therefore they are likely to do harm to our young men—you would agree with me in that?

Yes.

And then, again, to make the wisest of men say that nothing in his opinion is more glorious than

'When the tables are full of bread and meat, and the cup-bearer carries round wine which he draws from the bowl and pours into the cups[20];'

is this fit or improving for a young man to hear? Or that other verse which affirms that

'Hunger is the worst way of encountering destiny and death[21]?'

What would you say again to the tale of Zeus, who, while other gods and men were asleep (observe, that he was the only person awake), lay devising plans, but forgot them all in a moment through his lust, and was so completely overcome at the sight of Here that he would not even go into the tent, but wanted to lie with her on the ground, declaring that he had never been in such a state of rapture before, even when they first met one another without the knowledge of their parents[22]; or that other tale of how Hephaestus, in consequence of a similar piece of work, bound Ares and Aphrodite[23]?

Indeed, he said, I am strongly of opinion that they ought not to hear that sort of thing.

But any deeds of endurance which are acted or told by famous men, these they ought to see and hear; as, for example, what is said in the verses,

'He smote his breast, and thus reproached his soul,
Endure, my soul, thou hast endured worse[24].'

[19] Il. i. 225.　　　　[20] Od. ix. 8.　　　　[21] Ib. xi. 342.
[22] Il. xiv. 291.　　　[23] Od. viii. 266.　　　[24] Ib. xx. 17.

Certainly, he said.

In the next place, we must not let them be receivers of gifts or lovers of money.

Certainly not.

Neither must we sing to them of

'Gifts persuading gods, and persuading reverend kings[25].'

Neither is Phoenix, the tutor of Achilles, to be approved or regarded as having given his pupil good counsel when he told him that he should assist the Greeks and take their gifts[26], but that without a gift he should not be reconciled to them. Neither will we allow that Achilles himself was such a lover of money that he took Agamemnon's gifts, or required a price as the ransom of the dead[27].

391 Undoubtedly, he said, these are not sentiments which ought to be approved.

Loving Homer as I do, I hardly like to say what I must say, nevertheless, that in speaking thus of Achilles, or in believing these words when spoken of him by others, there is downright impiety. As little can I credit the narrative of his insolence to Apollo, where he says,

'Thou hast wronged me, O far-darter, most abominable of deities. Verily I would be even with thee, if I had only the power[28];

or his insubordination to the river-god[29], on whose divinity he is ready to lay hands; or the dedication to the dead Patroclus of his own hair[30], which had been previously dedicated to the other river-god Spercheius; or his dragging Hector round the tomb of Patroclus[31], and his slaughter of the captives at the pyre[32]; all this I cannot believe, any more than I can believe that he, Cheiron's pupil, the son of a goddess and of Peleus who was the gentlest of men and third in descent from Zeus, was in such rare perturbation of mind as to be at one time the slave of two seemingly inconsistent passions, meanness, not untainted by avarice, combined with overwhelming contempt of gods and men.

You are quite right, he replied.

---

[25] Quoted by Suidas as attributed to Hesiod.   [26] Il. ix. 515.
[27] Ib. xxiv. 175.   [28] Ib. xxiii. 151.   [29] Ib. xxi. 222.
[30] Ib. xxiii. 151.   [31] Ib. xxii. 394.   [32] Ib. xxiii. 175.

And let us equally refuse to believe, or allow to be repeated, the tale of Theseus son of Poseidon, or of Peirithous son of Zeus, going forth to perpetrate such a horrid rape; or of any other hero or son of a god desiring to do such impious and horrible things as they falsely ascribe to them in our day: and let us compel the poets to declare either that these acts were not done by them, or that they were not the sons of gods;—both in the same breath they shall not be permitted to affirm. We will not have them teaching our youth that the gods are the authors of evil, and that heroes are no better than men; for, as we were saying, these sentiments are neither pious nor true, being at variance with our demonstration that evil cannot come from God. Also they are likely to have a bad effect on those who hear them; for everybody will begin to excuse his own vices when he is convinced that similar wickednesses are always being perpetrated by the kindred of the gods,

'The relatives of Zeus, whose paternal altar is in the heavens and on the mount of Ida,'

and who have

'the blood of deity yet flowing in their veins.'

And therefore let us put an end to such tales, lest they engender laxity of morals among the young.

392

Most certainly, he replied.

And now, is there any class of subjects which still remains to be considered? About gods and demigods and heroes and the world below we have already made regulations.

Very true.

And what shall we say about men? That is clearly the remaining portion of our subject.

True.

But we are not in a condition to settle this at present.

And why not?

Because, if I am not mistaken, we shall have to say that poets and story-tellers make the gravest misstatements about men when they say that many wicked men are happy, and good men miserable; and we shall forbid them to utter these things, and command them to sing and say the opposite.

I am sure that we shall, he replied.

But if you admit that I am right in this, then I shall say that you have admitted the point which we have been all along trying to determine, viz. whether justice is in itself good.

You are right in reminding me of that, he said.

Well then, I said, we must defer coming to final agreement about this subject until we have discovered what justice is, and how naturally advantageous to the possessor, whether seen to be just or not.

Most true, he said.

Enough of the subjects of poetry: let us now speak of the style; and when this has been considered, both matter and manner will have been completely treated.

I don't know what you mean, said Adeimantus.

Then I must endeavour to explain. I suppose you are aware that all mythology and poetry is a narration of events, either past, present, or to come?

Certainly, he replied.

And narration may be either simple narration, or imitation, or a union of the two?

That again, he said, I do not quite understand.

I fear, I said, that I must be a ludicrous teacher not to make myself better understood. Like a bad speaker, therefore, I will not take the whole of the subject, but will break a piece off as an illustration of my meaning. I dare say that you remember the first lines of the Iliad, in which the poet says that Chryses begs
393 Agamemnon to release his daughter, and Agamemnon flies into a passion with Chryses, who invokes the anger of the gods against the Achaeans. As far as these lines,

'And he prayed all the Greeks, but especially the two sons of Atreus, the chiefs of the people,'

the poet is speaking in his own person; he never leads us to suppose that he is any one else. But in what follows he takes the person of Chryses, and then he does all that he can to make us believe that the speaker is not Homer, but the aged priest himself. And this is the general form of the narrative both in the Iliad and the Odyssee.

Yes.

And it is narrative when the poet recounts both the speeches and the passages between?

Quite true.

But when the poet speaks in the person of another, may we not say that he assimilates his style to that of the person who, as he informs you, is going to speak?

Certainly.

And this assimilation of himself to another is the imitation, either by voice or gesture, of the person whose character he assumes?

Of course.

Then in this case the narrative of the poet may be said to proceed by way of imitation?

Very true.

Or, if the poet everywhere appears and never conceals himself, then again the imitation is dropped, and his poetry becomes simple narration. However, in order that I may make my meaning quite clear, I will return to my example. Suppose that Homer had said, 'The priest came, having his daughter's ransom in his hands, the suppliant of the Achaeans, and above all of the kings;' and then, instead of speaking in the person of Chryses, suppose that he had continued in his own person, the imitation would have passed into narration. He would have said (I am no poet and therefore I drop the metre), 'Chryses came and prayed the gods on behalf of the Greeks that they might take Troy and return in peace, if Agamemnon would only give him back his daughter, taking the ransom, and reverencing the gods. Thus he spoke, and the other Greeks respected him and consented. But Agamemnon was wroth, and bade him depart and not come again, lest the sceptre and crown of the god should be of no avail to him—the daughter of Chryses, he said, should not be released until she had first grown old with him in Argos. And then he told him to go away and not to provoke him, if he intended to get home safely. And the old man went away in fear 394 and silence, and, having left the camp, he called upon Apollo by his many names, and said if ever in building his temple or offering sacrifice to him he had done anything grateful to him, his prayer was that this might be returned to him, and that the Achaeans might expiate his tears by the arrows of the god,'— and so on. In this way the whole becomes narrative.

That I understand, he said.

Or you may suppose that the intermediate pieces of narration are omitted, and the dialogue only remains; this is the opposite case.

That again, he said, I understand; you mean, for example, as in tragedy.

That is my meaning; and I believe that you now see clearly what you did not see before, that poetry and mythology are, in some cases, wholly imitative—instances of this are supplied by tragedy and comedy; of the opposite style, in which the poet is the only speaker, the dithyramb is the best example; and the combination of both is found in epic poetry, and in some other styles of poetry. Do I take you with me?

Yes, he said; I now understand what you meant to say.

I will beg you also to recall what I began by saying that we had done with the subject, and might proceed to the style.

Yes, I remember.

In saying this, I meant to imply that we must come to an understanding about the mimetic art,—whether the poets, in narrating their stories, are to be allowed to imitate, and if so, whether in whole or in part, and if the latter, in what parts; or should all imitation be prohibited?

You mean, I suspect, to ask whether tragedy and comedy shall be admitted into our State?

Yes, I said; but there may be more than this in question: I really do not know as yet, but whither the wind carries the argument, thither we go.

And go we will, he replied.

Then, I said, Adeimantus, let me ask you whether our guardians ought to be imitators, or whether in fact this question has not been already answered by our previous recognition of the principle that one man can only do one thing well, and not many; and that if he attempt many, he will altogether fail of gaining much reputation in any?

Certainly.

And this is equally true of imitation; no one man can imitate many things as well as he would imitate a single one?

He cannot.

395 Then the same person will hardly be able to play the serious part of life, and at the same time be an imitator and imitate many other parts as well; for even when two species of imitation

are nearly allied, the same persons cannot succeed in both, as is plain in the case of tragedy and comedy, which are imitations as you were just now terming them?

Yes I did; and you are right in supposing that the same persons cannot succeed in both.

Any more than they can be rhapsodists and actors at once.

True.

Neither are actors the same as comic and tragic poets; yet all these are imitations.

Yes, they are imitations.

And human nature, Adeimantus, appears to have been coined into yet smaller pieces, and to be as incapable of imitating many things well, as of performing well the actions of which the imitations are likenesses.

Quite true, he replied.

If then we would retain the notion with which we began, that our guardians are to be released from every other art, and to be the special artificers of freedom, and to minister to this and no other end, they ought not to practise or imitate anything else; and, if they imitate at all, they should imitate the characters which are suitable to their profession—the temperate, holy, free, courageous, and the like; but they should not depict or be able to imitate any kind of illiberality or other baseness, lest from imitation they should come to be what they imitate. Did you never observe how imitations, beginning in early youth, at last sink into the constitution and become a second nature of body, voice, and mind?

Yes, certainly, he said.

Then, I said, we will not allow those for whom we profess a care and desire that they should be good men, to imitate a woman, whether young or old, quarrelling with her husband, or striving and vaunting against the gods in conceit of her happiness, or when she is in affliction, or sorrow, or weeping; and certainly not one who is in sickness, love, or labour.

Very right, he said.

Neither must they represent slaves, male or female, doing the offices of slaves?

They must not.

And surely not rogues or cowards, or any who do the reverse

of what we have prescribed—jesting, scolding, reviling, in drink
or out of drink; misbehaving either to themselves or others in
396 word or deed, as the manner of such is. Neither should they be
trained to imitate madmen either in word or deed, for madness,
like vice, is to be known only to be avoided.

Very true, he replied.

Any more than they may imitate smiths or other artificers, or
oarsmen, or boatswains, or any similar actions?

Impossible, he said; how can they imitate that of which the
very pursuit is not permitted to them?

And would you have them imitate the neighing of horses, the
bellowing of bulls, the murmur of rivers and roll of the ocean,
thunder, and all that sort of thing?

Nay, he said, if madness is forbidden, then neither may they
copy the behaviour of madmen.

You mean, I said, if I understand you rightly, that there is one
sort of narration which may be used or spoken by a truly good
man, and that there is another sort which will be exclusively
adapted to a man of another character and education.

And which are these two sorts? he asked.

Suppose, I answered, that a just and good man in the course
of narration comes on some saying or action of another good
man,—I should imagine that he will like to impersonate him, and
will not be ashamed of this sort of imitation: he will be most
ready to play the part of the good man when he is acting firmly
and wisely; in a less degree when his steps falter owing to sickness or love, or again from intoxication or any other mishap.
But when he comes to a character which is unworthy of him, he
will not make a study of that; he will disdain to wear the likeness of his inferiors, unless indeed during some brief interval
when they may be doing any good; at other times he will be
ashamed to play a part which he has never practised, nor will he
like to fashion and frame himself after the baser models; he feels
that this would be beneath him, when carried beyond a pastime.

That is what I should expect, he replied.

Then he will adopt a mode of narration such as we have illustrated out of Homer, that is to say, his style will be both imitative
and narrative; but there will be very little of the former, and a
great deal of the latter. Do you agree?

Certainly, he said; that is the model which such a speaker must necessarily take.

But another sort of character will narrate anything, and the worse he is the more unscrupulous he will be; nothing will be 397 beneath him: moreover he will be ready to imitate anything, not as a joke, but in right good earnest, and before a large audience. As I was just now saying, he will attempt to represent the roll of thunder, the rattle of wind and hail, or the various sounds of pulleys, of pipes, of flutes, and all sorts of instruments; also he will bark like a dog, bleat like a sheep, and crow like a cock; his entire art will consist in imitation of voice and gesture, and there will be very little narration.

That, he said, is sure to be his way.

Then these, I said, are the two kinds of style.

Yes, he said.

And you would agree with me in saying that one of them is simple and has but slight changes; and if the harmony and rhythm are also chosen for their simplicity, the result is that the speaker, if he speaks correctly, is always pretty much the same in style, and keeps within the limits of a single harmony (for the changes are not great), and also keeps pretty nearly the same rhythm?

That is quite true, he said.

Whereas the other style requires all sorts of harmonies and all sorts of rhythms, if the music is to be expressive of the variety and complexity of the words?

That is also perfectly true, he replied.

And do not the two styles, or the mixture of the two, comprehend all poetry, and every form of expression in words? No one can say anything except in one or other or both of them?

They include all, he said.

And shall we receive them all, or only one of the two pure styles? or would you include the mixed?

I should prefer only to admit the pure imitator of virtue.

Yes, I said, Adeimantus; but the mixed style is also very charming: and indeed the pantomimic style, which is the opposite of the one which you have chosen, is the most popular with children and their instructors, and with the world in general.

I admit that.

But I suppose you mean to say that such a style is unsuitable to our State, in which human nature is not twofold or manifold, for one man plays one part only?

Yes; quite unsuitable.

And this is the reason why in this State, and in this State only, we shall find a shoemaker to be a shoemaker and not a pilot also, and a husbandman to be a husbandman and not a dicast also, and a soldier a soldier and not a trader also, and the same of all the other citizens?

True, he said.

398 And therefore when any one of these clever multiform gentlemen, who can imitate anything, comes to our State, and proposes to exhibit himself and his poetry, we will fall down and worship him as a sweet and holy and wonderful being; but we must also inform him that there is no place for such as he is in our State,— the law will not allow them. And so when we have anointed him with myrrh, and set a garland of wool upon his head, we shall send him away to another city. For we mean to employ for our souls' health the rougher and severer poet and story-teller, who will imitate the style of the virtuous only, and will follow those models which we prescribed at first when we began to speak of the education of our soldiers.

That, he said, we certainly will do, if we have the power.

Then now, my friend, I said, that part of music or literary education which relates to the story or myth may be considered to be finished, for the matter and manner have both been discussed.

I think so too, he said.

Next in order will follow melody and song.

That is plain.

Every one can say what has to be said about them, now that he has the principle.

I fear, said Glaucon, laughing, that the word 'every one' hardly includes me, for I cannot at the moment say, though I may guess.

At any rate you can tell that a song or ode has three parts,— the words, the melody, and the rhythm—that degree of knowledge I may suppose?

Yes, he said; so much as that you may.

And as for the words, there will be no difference between words that are and are not set to music; both will conform to the same laws, and these have been already determined by us?

Yes.

Also the melody and rhythm will go with the subject?

Certainly.

And we were saying, as you may remember, in speaking of the words, that we had no need of strains of sorrow and lamentation?

True.

And which are the harmonies expressive of sorrow? As you are a musician, I wish that you would tell me.

The harmonies which you mean are the mixed or tenor Lydian, and the full-toned or bass Lydian, and others which are like them.

These then, I said, must be banished; even to women of virtue and character they are of no use, and much less to men.

Certainly.

In the next place, drunkenness and softness and indolence are utterly at variance with the character of our guardian.

Of course.

Then I must ask you again, which are the soft or drinking harmonies?

The Ionian, he replied, and the Lydian; they are termed 399 'solute.'

Well, and are these of any military use?

Quite the reverse, he replied; but then the Dorian and the Phrygian appear to be the only ones which remain.

I answered: Of the harmonies I know nothing, but I want to have one warlike, which will sound the word or note which a brave man utters in the hour of danger and stern resolve, or when his cause is failing and he is going to wounds or death or is overtaken by some other evil, and at every such crisis meets fortune with calmness and endurance; and another which may be used by him in times of peace and freedom of action, when there is no pressure of necessity—expressive of entreaty or persuasion, of prayer to God, or instruction of man, or again, of willingness to listen to persuasion or entreaty and advice; and which represents him when he has accomplished his aim, not carried away by success, but acting moderately and wisely, and acquiescing in the event. These two harmonies I ask you to leave; the strain of necessity and the strain of freedom, the strain of the unfortunate and the strain of the fortunate, the strain of courage, and the strain of temperance; these, I say, leave.

And these, he replied, are the very ones of which I was speaking.

Then, I said, if only the Dorian and Phrygian harmonies are used in our songs and melodies, we shall not want multiplicity of notes or a panharmonic scale?

That is evident.

Then we shall not maintain the artificers of lyres with three corners and complex scales, or of any other many-stringed curiously-harmonized instruments?

Certainly not.

But what do you say to flute-makers and flute-players? Would you admit them, when you reflect that in this composite use of harmony the flute is worse than all the stringed instruments put together, for even the panharmonic music is only an imitation of the flute?

Clearly not.

There remain then, only the lyre and the harp for use in the city, and you may have a pipe in the country.

Yes, that will be quite in accordance with our principles.

That we should prefer Apollo and his instruments to Marsyas and his instruments is not at all strange, I said.

Not at all, he replied.

And so, by the dog of Egypt, I swear that we have been unconsciously purging the State, which not long ago we termed luxurious.

That is very wise of us, he replied.

And now let us finish the purgation, I said. Next in order to harmonies, rhythms will naturally follow, and they should be subject to the same rules, for we ought not to have complex or manifold systems of metre, but rather to discover what rhythms 400 are the expressions of a courageous and harmonious life; and the words should come first, and the rhythms should be adapted to them, not the rhythms first and the words afterwards. To say what rhythms they are will be your business, as you have already taught me the harmonies.

But, indeed, he replied, I cannot tell you. I only know that there are some three principles of rhythm ($\frac{1}{2}$, $\frac{1}{1}$, $\frac{3}{2}$) out of which metrical systems are framed, just as in sounds there are four elements[33] into which the harmonies are resolved; that is an observation which I have made. But what is the character of these metres I am unable to say.

Then, I said, we shall have to take Damon into our counsels; and he will tell us what rhythms are expressive of meanness, or insolence, or fury, or other unworthiness, and what there are remaining for the expression of opposite feelings. And I think that I have an indistinct recollection of his mentioning a complex Cretic rhythm; also a dactylic and heroic, which he arranged, I know not how, so as to compensate in the rise and fall, passing into short and long times; and, unless I am mistaken, he spoke of an iambic, as well as of a trochaic rhythm, and assigned to them short and long quantities[34]. Also in some cases he appeared to praise or censure the movement of the foot quite as much as the rhythm; at any rate, his words were applicable to both, and I cannot be certain which he meant. This, however, as I was saying, had better be referred to him, for the subject is difficult—you would allow that?

Certainly.

But you have no difficulty in discerning that grace or the absence of grace is the effect of good or bad rhythm, accompanying good and bad style, and the same is true of good and bad harmony; as our principle is that rhythm and harmony are regulated by the words, and not the words by them.

Certainly, he said, they should follow the words.

And the words and the character of the style should depend on the temper of the soul?

Yes.

And everything else on the words?

Yes.

Then good language and harmony and grace and rhythm depend on simplicity,—I mean the simplicity of a truly and nobly or-

---

[33] i. e. the four notes of the tetrachord.

[34] It is not possible to explain accurately what Socrates professes not to describe accurately. In the first part of the sentence he appears to be speaking of paeonic rhythms, in the ratio of $\frac{3}{2}$; in the second part of the sentence of dactylic rhythms, which are in the ratio of $\frac{1}{1}$; in the last clause of iambic and trochaic rhythms, which are in the ratio of $\frac{1}{2}$ or $\frac{2}{1}$.

dered mind, not that other simplicity which is only a euphemism for folly?

Very true, he replied.

And if our youth are to do their work in life, must they not make these their perpetual aim?

They must.

401 And all life is full of them, as well as every creative and constructive art; the art of painting, weaving, and embroidery, and building, and the manufacture of vessels, as well as the frames of animals and of plants; in all of them there is grace or the absence of grace. And absence of grace and inharmonious movement and discord are nearly allied to ill words and ill nature, as grace and harmony are the sisters and images of goodness and virtue.

That is quite true, he said.

But is our superintendence to go no further, and are the poets only, to be required by us to impress a good moral on their poems as the condition of writing poetry in our State? Or is the same control to be exercised over other artists, and are they also to be prohibited from exhibiting the opposite forms of vice and intemperance and meanness and indecency in sculpture and building and the other creative arts; and is he who does not conform to this rule of ours to be prohibited from practising his art in our State, lest the taste of our citizens be corrupted by him? We would not have our guardians grow up amid images of moral deformity, as in some noxious pasture, and there browse and feed upon many a baneful herb and flower day by day, little by little, until they silently gather a festering mass of corruption in their own soul. Let our artists rather be those who are gifted to discern the true nature of beauty and grace; then will our youth dwell in a land of health, amid fair sights and sounds; and beauty, the effluence of fair works, will meet the sense like a breeze, and insensibly draw the soul even in childhood into harmony with the beauty of reason.

There can be no nobler training than that, he replied.

Is not this, I said, the reason, Glaucon, why musical training is so powerful, because rhythm and harmony find their way into the secret places of the soul, on which they mightily fasten, bearing grace in their movements, and making the soul graceful of him who is rightly educated, or ungraceful if ill-educated; and also because he who has received this true education of the inner being will most shrewdly perceive omissions or faults in art and nature, and with a true taste, while he praises and rejoices over, and receives into his soul the good, and becomes noble and good, 402 he will justly blame and hate the bad, now in the days of his youth, even before he is able to know the reason of the thing; and when reason comes he will recognize and salute her as a friend with whom his education has made him long familiar.

Yes, he said, I quite agree with you in thinking that these are the reasons why there should be a musical education.

Just as in learning to read, I said, we want to know the various letters in all their recurring sizes and combinations; not slighting them as unimportant whether they be large or small, but everywhere eager to make them out; and are not supposed to be perfect in the art until we recognize them wherever they are found:

True—

Or, as we recognize the reflection of letters in the water, or in a mirror, only when we know the letters themselves; the same art giving us the knowledge of both:

Exactly—

Even so, I have no hesitation in saying that neither we nor our guardians, whom we have to educate, can ever become musical until we know the essential forms of temperance, courage, liberality, magnificence, as well as the cognate and contrary forms, in all their combinations, and can recognize them and their images wherever they are found, not slighting them either in small things or great, but believing them all to be within the sphere of one art and study.

Most assuredly.

And when a beautiful soul harmonizes with a beautiful form, and the two are cast in one mould, that will be the fairest of sights to him who has the eye to contemplate the vision?

The fairest indeed.

And the fairest are also the loveliest?

That may be assumed.

And the man who has music in his soul will be most in love with the loveliest; but if they are inharmonious in soul he will not love them?

That is true, he replied, if the deformity be in the soul, but any merely personal defect he will be willing to regard with complacency.

I perceive, I said, that you have had experiences of that sort, and I agree. But let me ask you another question. Have temperance and the excess of pleasure any affinity?

Nay, he said, for pleasure deprives a man of the use of his faculties as much as pain.

But has pleasure no affinity to any other virtue?

403 None whatever.

Any to wantonness and intemperance?

Yes, the greatest.

And is there any greater or keener pleasure than that of bodily love?

None, certainly; and there is none which is more irrational.

Whereas true love is a love of beauty and order—temperate and harmonious?

Quite true, he said.

Then nothing violent or irrational must be allowed to approach true love?

Nothing.

Then no irrational pleasure must be allowed to approach the lover and his beloved, for they can have no affinity with such pleasure if their mutual love is to be a right love?

No, indeed, Socrates, it must never come near them.

Then I suppose that in the city which we are founding you would make a law that a friend should use no other familiarity to his love than a father would use to his son, and this only for a virtuous end, and he must first have the other's consent; and this rule is to limit him in all his intercourse, and he is never to go further, or, if he exceeds, he is to be deemed guilty of coarseness and bad taste.

I quite agree, he said.

Thus much then is said of music which makes a fair ending, for what should be the end of music if not the love of beauty?

I agree, he said.

After music comes gymnastic, in which our youth are next to be trained.

Certainly.

And gymnastic as well as music should receive careful attention in childhood, and continue through life. Now my belief is,—and this is a matter upon which I should like to have your opinion, but my own belief is,—not that the good body improves the soul, but that the good soul improves the body. What do you say?

Yes, I agree.

Then, if we have educated the mind, the minuter care of the body may properly be committed to the mind, and we need only indicate general principles for brevity's sake.

Very good.

That they must abstain from intoxication has been already remarked by us, for of all persons a guardian should be the last to get drunk and not know where in the world he is.

Yes, he said; that a guardian should require another to guard him is ridiculous indeed.

But next, what shall we say of their food; for the men are athletes in the great contest of all, are they not?

Yes, he said.

And will gymnastic exercises be a suitable training for them?   404

I cannot say.

I am afraid, I said, that such exercise is but a sleepy sort of thing, and rather perilous to health. Do you not observe that athletes sleep away their lives, and are liable to most dangerous illnesses if they depart, in ever so slight a degree, from their customary regimen?

Yes, I observe that.

Then, I said, a finer sort of training will be required for our warrior athletes, who are to be like wakeful dogs, and to see and hear with the utmost keenness; they will have to endure many changes of water and also of food, of summer heat and winter cold, and yet they must not be liable to break down in health.

That is quite my view, he said.

The really excellent gymnastic is twin sister of that simple music which we were just now describing.

How is that?

Why, I conceive that there is a gymnastic also which is simple and good; and that such ought to be the military gymnastic.

What do you mean?

My meaning may be learned from Homer; he, you know, feeds

his heroes when they are campaigning on soldiers' fare; they
have no fish, although they are on the shores of the Hellespont,
and they are allowed nothing but roast meat—which only requires
fire, and is therefore the most convenient diet for soldiers—and not
boiled, as this would involve a carrying about of pots and pans.

True.

And I can hardly be mistaken in saying that sweet sauces are
not even mentioned by him. In this, however, he is not singular, as all professional athletes know that a man who is to be
in good condition should take nothing of that sort.

Yes, he said; and knowing this, they are quite right in not
taking them.

Then you would not approve of Syracusan dinners, and the
refinements of Sicilian cookery?

I think not.

Nor, if a man is to keep his health, would you allow him to
have a Corinthian girl as his fair friend?

Certainly not.

Neither would you approve of the delights, as they are
esteemed, of Athenian confectionary?

I should not.

Such a way of feeding and living may be likened to the composition of melody and song in the panharmonic style, and in all
the rhythms.

Exactly.

There complexity engendered licence, and here disease; whereas
simplicity in music was the parent of temperance in the soul, and
simplicity in gymnastic, of health in the body.

Most true, he said.

405 But when intemperance and diseases multiply in a State, halls
of justice and medicine are always being opened; and the arts of
the doctor and the lawyer begin to give themselves airs, finding
how keen is the interest which the very freemen of a city take
about them.

Most true.

And yet what greater proof can there be of a bad and disgraceful state of education than this, that not only the meaner
classes and the artisans are in need of the high skill of physicians and judges, but also those who would tell us that they have

had a liberal education? Is not this disgraceful, and a great sign
of the want of education, that a man should have to go abroad for
his law and physic because he has none of his own at home, and
must therefore surrender himself into the hands of others?

Nothing, he said, can be more disgraceful.

Would you say that, I replied, when you consider that there
is a further stage of the evil in which a man is not only a life-
long litigant, passing his days always in the courts either as
plaintiff or defendant, but is led by his bad taste even to pride
himself on this; he is ready to fancy that he is a master in
cunning; and he will take every crooked turn and wriggle into
and out of every hole, bending like a withy[35] and getting away,
and all for what? in order that he may gain small points not
worth mentioning, not knowing that so to order his life as to
be able to do without a nodding judge is a far higher and nobler
sort of thing.   Is not that still more disgraceful?

Yes, he said, that is still more disgraceful.

Well, I said, and to require the help of medicine, not when
a wound has to be cured, or on occasion of an epidemic, but just
because, by their lives of indolence and luxury, men fill themselves
like pools with waters and winds, compelling the ingenious sons
of Asclepius to give diseases the names of flatulence and catarrh;
is not this, too, a disgrace?

Yes, he said, those are certainly strange and newfangled names
of diseases.

Yes, I said, and I do not believe that there were such diseases
in the days of Asclepius; and this I infer from the circumstance
that the hero Eurypylus, after he has been wounded in Homer,
drinks a posset of Pramnian wine besprinkled with flour and
cheese, which are certainly rather inflammatory, and yet the sons 406
of Asclepius who were at the Trojan war do not blame the
damsel who gives him the drink, or rebuke Patroclus, who is
treating his case.

Well, he said, there is something strange in a person who
was in his condition having such a drink given to him.

Not strange, I replied, if you bear in mind that in former days,
as is commonly said, before the time of Herodicus, the guild
of Asclepius did not practise our present system of medicine,

---

35 Reading λυγιζόμενος.

which may be said to educate diseases. But Herodicus, being a trainer, and himself of a sickly constitution, by a happy combination of training and doctoring, found out a way of torturing first and principally himself, and secondly the rest of the world.

How was that? he said.

By the invention of lingering death; for he had a mortal disease which he perpetually tended, and as recovery was out of the question, he passed his entire life as a valetudinarian; he could do nothing but attend upon himself, and he was in constant torment whenever he departed in anything from his usual regimen, and so dying hard, by the help of science he struggled on to old age.

What a noble reward of the physician's skill!

Yes, I said; such a reward as a man might fairly expect who knew not the wisdom of Asclepius, and did not consider that, if he failed to instruct his descendants in these arts, this arose not from ignorance or inexperience of such a department of medicine, but because he knew that in all well-ordered states every individual has an occupation to which he must attend, and therefore has no leisure to spend in continually being ill. This we remark in the case of the artisan, but, ludicrously enough, fail to apply the same rule to people of the richer sort.

How is that? he said.

I replied; when a carpenter is ill he asks the physician for a rough and ready remedy; an emetic or a purge or cautery or the knife,—these are his remedies. And if any one tells him that he must go through a course of dietetics, and swathe and swaddle his head, and all that sort of thing, he replies at once that he has no time to be ill, and that he sees no good in a life which is spent in nursing his disease to the neglect of his ordinary calling; and therefore saying good-bye to this sort of physician, he resumes his customary diet, and either gets well and lives and does his business, or, if his constitution fails, he dies and has done with it.

Yes, he said, and a man in his condition of life ought to use this summary art of medicine.

407 Has he not, I said, an occupation; and what profit would there be in his life if he were deprived of his occupation?

Very true, he said.

But the rich man, as we say, is a gentleman who has no work which he ought to do or die?

He is generally supposed to have nothing to do.

Then you never heard of the saying of Phocylides, that as soon as a man has a livelihood he should practise virtue?

Nay, he said, I think that he need not wait for that.

I don't want to raise that question, I replied; I want rather to know whether the practice of virtue is obligatory on the rich, and ought to be a necessity of life to him; and, if so, whether this dieting of disorders, which is an impediment to the application of the mind in carpentering and the mechanical arts, does not equally stand in the way of the maxim of Phocylides?

Of that, he replied, there can be no doubt; such excessive care of the body, when carried beyond the rules of gymnastic, is most inimical to the practice of virtue, and equally incompatible with the management of a house, an army, or an office of state.

Yes, and even more incompatible, I replied, with any kind of study or thought or self-reflection; and this is the worst part of the affair—there is apt to be a suspicion that a headache or swimming has arisen from this cause, and hence a complete stop is put to any such higher cultivation[36] or essay of virtue; for a man is always fancying that he is ill, and has some bodily pain or other.

Yes, likely enough.

And may not this have been the reason why our politic Asclepius exhibited the power of his art only to persons who, being generally of healthy constitution and habits of life, had a definite ailment; such as these he cured by purgations and operations, and bade them live as usual, and in this consulted the interests of the State; but bodies which disease had penetrated through and through he would not have attempted to cure by gradual processes of evacuation and infusion: he did not want to lengthen out useless lives, or to raise up puny offspring to an enfeebled sire;— if a man was not able to live in the ordinary way he had no business to cure him; this was all in the interest of the State.

Then, he said, you regard Asclepius as a statesman.

Clearly, I said; and this is shown also by the example of his sons who, as you may observe, were heroes as well as physicians 408

35 Reading ὥστε ὅπῃ ταύτῃ ἀρετὴ ἀσκεῖται κ.τ.λ.

at the siege of Troy. I dare say that you remember how, when
the arrow of Pandarus wounded Menelaus, they

' Sucked the blood out of the wound, and sprinkled soothing remedies[37],'

but they never prescribed what the patient was afterwards to eat or
drink in the case of Menelaus, any more than in the case of Eurypylus; the remedies, as they conceived, were enough to heal any
man who was healthy and sound; and even though he did chance
to drink a sack posset, he might get well all the same. But they
would have nothing to do with unhealthy and intemperate subjects,
whose lives were of no use either to themselves or others; the
art of medicine was not designed for their good, and though they
were as rich as Midas, the sons of Asclepius would have declined
to attend them.

There was much good sense, he said, in those sons of Asclepius.

Why, yes, I replied; and you would expect to find that in them.
Nevertheless, the tragedians and Pindar, in violation of our
principles, although they say that Asclepius was the son of
Apollo, say also that he was bribed into healing a rich man who
was at the point of death, and this was the reason why he was
struck by lightning. But we, in accordance with our previously-
declared rule, will not believe both;—if he was the son of a
god, we maintain that he was not avaricious; or, if he was
avaricious, he was not the son of a god.

All that, Socrates, he said, is excellent; but I should like to put
a question to you. Ought there not to be good physicians in a
State, and are not the best those who have the greatest experience
of constitutions good and bad, just as good judges are those who
are acquainted with all sorts of moral natures?

Yes, I said, I quite agree about the necessity of having good
judges and good physicians. But do you know whom I think good?

Will you inform me?

Yes, if I can. Let me however note that in the same question
you join two things which are not the same.

How is that? he said.

Why, I said, you join physicians and judges. Now skilful
physicians are those who, besides knowing their art, have from
their youth upwards had the greatest experience of disease; they
had better not be in robust health, and should have had all manner

[37] Iliad, iv. 218.

of diseases in their own persons. For the body, as I conceive, is not the instrument with which they cure the body; in that case we would not allow them ever to be sickly; but they cure the body with the mind, and the mind which is or has become sick can cure nothing.

That is very true, he said.

But with the judge the case is different; he governs mind by mind, and he cannot be allowed therefore to have been reared among vicious minds, and to have associated with them from youth upwards, in order that, having gone through the whole calendar of crime, he may infer the crimes of others like their diseases from the knowledge of himself; but the honourable mind which is to form a healthy judgment ought rather to have had no experience or contamination of evil habits when young. And this is the reason why in youth good men often appear to be simple, and are easily practised upon by the evil, because they have no samples of evil in their own souls. 409

Yes, he said, that very often happens with them.

Therefore, I said, the judge should not be young; he should have learned to know evil, not from his own soul, but from late and long observation of the nature of evil in others: knowledge, and not his own experience, should be his guide.

Yes, he said, that is the ideal of a judge.

Yes, I replied, and he will be good too (and this answers your question); for he is good whose soul is good; now your cunning and suspicious character, who has committed many crimes, when he is among men who are like himself, is wonderful in his precautions against others, because he judges of them by himself: but when he gets into the company of men of virtue, who have the experience of age, he appears to be a fool again, owing to his unseasonable suspicion: he cannot recognize an honest man, because he has nothing in himself at all parallel to judge from; at the same time, as the bad are more numerous than the good, and he meets with them oftener, he thinks himself, and others think him, rather wise than foolish.

Most true, he said.

Then the good and wise judge whom we are seeking is not this man; the other is better suited to us; for vice cannot know virtue, but a virtuous nature, educated by time, will acquire a knowledge both of virtue and vice: the virtuous, and not the vicious man has wisdom; that is my view.

And mine also.

This is the sort of medicine, and this is the sort of law, which you will sanction. They will be healing arts to better natures in their souls and in their bodies; but the worse nature or constitution they will in the case of the body leave to die, and the diseased and incurable soul they will put to death themselves.

That is clearly best for them and for the State.

And thus our youth, having been educated only in that simple music which infuses temperance, will be reluctant to go to law.

That is evident.

And in the same way simple gymnastic will incline him to have as little as possible to do with medicine.

That I quite believe.

The very exercises and toils he will undertake in order to stimulate the spirited element of his nature, rather than with a view of increasing his strength; he will not, like common athletes, use exercise and regimen to develope his muscles.

Very right, he said.

Neither are the two arts of music and gymnastic really designed, the one for the training of the soul, the other for the training of the body.

But what is the real object?

I believe, I said, that the teachers of both have in view chiefly the improvement of the soul.

How is that? he asked.

Did you never observe, I said, the effect on the mind of exclusive devotion to gymnastic, or the opposite effect of an exclusive devotion to music?

In what is that shown? he said.

In producing a temper of hardness and ferocity, or again of softness and effeminacy, I replied.

Yes, he said, I am quite aware that your mere athlete becomes too much of a savage, and that the musician is melted and softened beyond what is good for him.

Moreover, I said, that fierce quality gives spirit, and, if educated rightly, will be valiant, but, if overstrained, is likely to become hard and brutal.

That I quite think.

The philosopher is the type of the gentler character. This, if too much relaxed, will turn to softness, but, if educated, will be gentle and modest.

True.

And our view is that the guardians ought to have both these qualities?

They ought.

They should be harmonized?

Beyond question.

And the harmonious soul is both temperate and valiant?   411

Yes.

And the inharmonious is cowardly and boorish?

Very true.

And, when a man allows music to play and pour over his soul through his ears, which are the funnel, those sweet and soft and melancholy airs of which we were just now speaking, and his whole life is passed in warbling and the delights of song; in the first stage of the process the passion or spirit which is in him is tempered like iron, and made useful, instead of brittle and useless. But, if he carries on the softening process, in the next stage he begins to melt and consume, until the passion of his soul is melted out of him, and what may be called the nerves of his soul are cut away, and he makes but a feeble warrior.

Very true.

If the element of spirit is naturally weak in him this is soon accomplished, but if he have a good deal, then the power of music weakening the spirit renders him excitable;—he soon flames up, and is speedily extinguished; instead of having spirit he becomes irritable and violent and very discontented.

Exactly.

Thus in gymnastics also, if a man works hard and is a great feeder, and the reverse of a great student of music and philosophy, at first the high condition of his body fills him with pride and spirit, until he is twice the man that he was.

Certainly.

But if he do nothing else, and never cultivates the Muses, even that intelligence which there may be in him, having no taste of any sort of learning or enquiry or thought or music, becomes feeble and dull and blind, because never roused or sustained, and because the senses are not purged of their mists.

True, he said.

And he ends by becoming a hater of philosophy, uncultivated, never using the weapon of persuasion,—he is like a wild beast, all violence and fierceness, and knows no other way of dealing; and he lives in all ignorance and evil conditions, and has no sense of propriety and grace.

That is quite true, he said.

And as there are two principles of human nature, one the spirited and the other the philosophical, my belief is that God has given mankind two arts answering to them (and only indirectly to the soul and body), in order that these two principles may be duly 412 attuned and harmonized with one another.

That I am disposed to believe.

And he who mingles music with gymnastic in the fairest proportions, and best attempers them to the soul, may be called the true musician and harmonist in a far higher sense than the tuner of the strings.

I dare say, Socrates.

And such a presiding genius will be always required in our State if the government is to last.

Yes, he will be absolutely necessary.

Such, then, are our principles of nurture and education. There would be no use in going into further details about their dances, their hunting or chasing with dogs, their gymnastic and equestrian contests; for these all follow the general principle, and there will be no longer any difficulty in discovering them.

I dare say that there will be no difficulty.

Very well, I said; and what is the next question? Must we not ask who are to be rulers and who subjects?

Certainly.

There can be no doubt that the elder sort must rule the younger.

Clearly.

And that the best of the elder sort must rule.

That is also clear.

Now, are not the best husbandmen those who are most devoted to husbandry?

Yes.

And as we must have the best guardians for our city, must they not be those who have most the character of guardians?

Yes.

And to this end they ought to be wise and efficient, and to have a special interest about the State?

True.

And a man will be most likely to care about that which he happens to love?

That may be truly inferred.

And he will be most likely to love that which he regards as having the same interests with himself, and anything the good or evil fortune of which he imagines to involve as a result his own good or evil fortune, and to be proportionably careless when he is less concerned?

Very true, he replied.

Then there must be a selection. Let us note among the guardians those who in their whole life show the greatest desire to do what is for the good of their country, and will not do what is against her interests.

Those are the right men.

They will have to be watched at every turn of their lives, in order that we may see whether they preserve this resolution, and never, under the influence either of force or enchantment, forget or let go their duty to the State.

I do not understand, he said, the meaning of the latter words.

I will explain them to you, I replied. A resolution may go out of a man's mind either with his will or against his will; with his will when he gets rid of a falsehood, against his will whenever he 413 is deprived of a truth.

I understand, he said, the willing loss of a resolution; the meaning of the unwilling I have yet to learn.

Why, I said, do you not see that men are unwillingly deprived of good, and willingly of evil? Is not to have lost the truth an evil, and to have the truth a good? and you would allow that to conceive things as they are is to have the truth?

Yes, he replied; I agree with you in thinking that mankind are deprived of truth against their will.

And do they not experience this involuntary effect owing either to theft, or force, or enchantment?

Still, he replied, I do not understand you.

I fear that I must have been talking darkly, like the tragedians. All that I mean is that some men change and others forget; persuasion steals away the hearts of the one class, and time of the other; and this I call theft. Now you understand me?

Yes.

Those again who are forced, are those whom the violence of some pain or grief compels to change their opinion.

That, he said, I understand, and you are quite right.

And you would also acknowledge with me that those are enchanted who change their minds either under the softer influence of pleasure, or the sterner influence of fear?

Yes, he said; everything that deceives may be said to enchant.

Therefore, as I was just now saying, we must enquire who are the best guardians of their own conviction that the interest of the State is to be the rule of all their actions. We must watch them from their youth upwards, and propose deeds for them to perform in which they are most likely to forget or to be deceived, and he who remembers and is not deceived is to be selected, and he who fails in the trial is to be rejected. That will be the way.

Yes.

And there should also be toils and pains and conflicts prescribed for them, in which they will give further proof of the same qualities.

Very right, he replied.

And then, I said, we must try them with enchantments—that is the third sort of test—and see what will be their behaviour: like those who take colts amid noises and cries to see if they are of a timid nature, so must we take our youth amid terrors of some kind, and again pass them into pleasures, and try them more thoroughly than gold is tried in the fire, in order to discover whether they are armed against all enchantments, and of a noble bearing always, good guardians of themselves and of the music which they have learned, and retain under all circumstances a rhythmical and harmonious nature, such as will be most serviceable to the man himself and to the State. And he who at every age, as boy and youth and in mature life, has come out of the trial victorious 414 and pure, shall be appointed a ruler and guardian of the State; he shall be honoured in life and death, and shall receive sepulture and other memorials of honour, the greatest that we have to give. And as he is chosen his opposite is rejected. I am inclined to think that this is the sort of way in which our rulers and guardians should be chosen. I speak generally, and not with any pretension to exactness.

And, speaking generally, I agree with you, he said.

And perhaps the word 'guardian' in the fullest sense ought to be applied to this class only who are our warriors abroad and our peacemakers at home, and who save us from those who might have the will or the power to injure us. The young men whom we before called guardians may be more properly designated auxiliaries and allies of the principles of the rulers.

In that I agree with you, he said.

How then may we devise one of those falsehoods in the hour of need, I said, which we lately spoke of—just one royal lie which may deceive the rulers, if that be possible, and at any rate the rest of the city?

What sort of lie? he said.

Nothing new, I replied; only an old Phoenician tale of what has often occurred before now in other places, (as the poets say, and have made the world believe,) though not in our time, and which is indeed not very likely to occur again, and still more unlikely to be believed.

Your words, he said, seem to hesitate on your lips.

You will not wonder, I replied, at my hesitation when you have heard.

Speak, he said, and fear not.

Well then, I will speak, although I really know not how to look you in the face, or in what words to utter the audacious fiction, which I propose to communicate gradually, first to the rulers, then to the soldiers, and lastly to the people. They are to be informed that their youth was a dream, and the education and training which they received from us an appearance only; in reality during all that time they were in process of formation and nourishment in the womb of the earth, where they themselves and their arms and appurtenances were manufactured; and when they were completed, the earth, their mother, sent them up; and, their country being their mother and also their nurse, they are therefore bound to advise for her good, and to defend her against attacks, and her citizens they are to regard as children of the earth and their own brothers.

I cannot wonder, he said, at your feeling ashamed of uttering the lie.

415   Nay, I replied, there is more yet; I have not told you all. Citizens, we shall say to them in our tale, you are brothers, yet God has framed you differently. Some of you have the power of command, and these he has composed of gold, wherefore also they have the greatest honour; others of silver, to be auxiliaries; others again who are to be husbandmen and craftsmen he has made of brass and iron; and the species will generally be preserved in the children. But as you are of the same original family, a golden parent will sometimes have a silver son, or a silver parent a golden son. And God proclaims to the rulers, as a first principle, that before all they should watch over their offspring, and see what elements mingle in their nature; for if the son of a golden or silver parent has an admixture of brass and iron, then nature orders a transposition of ranks, and the eye of the ruler must not be pitiful towards his child because he has to descend in the scale and become a husbandman or artisan, just as there may be others sprung from the artisan class who are raised to honour, and become guardians and auxiliaries. For an oracle says that when a man of brass or iron guards the State, it will then be destroyed. Such is the tale; is there any possibility of making our citizens believe in it?

Not in the present generation, he replied; I do not see any way of accomplishing this; but their sons may be made to believe, and their sons' sons, and posterity after them.

I see the difficulty, I replied; yet even this amount of belief may make them care more for the city and for one another. Enough, however, of the fiction, which may now be borne on the wings of rumour, while we arm our earth-born heroes, and lead them forth under the command of their rulers. Let them look around and select a spot whence they can best prevent insurrection, if any prove refractory within, and also defend themselves against enemies, who like wolves may come down on the fold from without; there let them encamp, and when they have encamped, let them sacrifice and prepare their dwellings.

And what sort of dwellings are they to have?

Dwellings that will shield them against the cold of winter and the heat of summer.

I suppose that you mean houses, he replied.

Yes, I said; but they must be the houses of soldiers, and not of shop-keepers.

What is the difference? he said.

That I will endeavour to explain, I replied. To keep watch- 416 dogs, who, from want of discipline or hunger, or some evil habit or other, would turn upon the sheep and worry them, and behave not like dogs but wolves, would be a foul and monstrous thing?

Truly monstrous, he said.

And, therefore, every care must be taken lest our auxiliaries, as they are stronger than our citizens, should prevail over them, and become savage tyrants instead of gentle allies to them?

Yes, care should be taken.

And would not education be the best preparation and safeguard of them?

But they are well-educated, he replied; that is a safeguard which they already have.

I cannot be so confident of that, my dear Glaucon, I said; I am much more certain that they ought to be, and that true education, whatever that may be, will greatly tend to civilize and humanize them in their relations to one another, and to those who are under their protection.

True, he replied.

And not only their education, but their habitations, and also their means of subsistence, should be such as will neither impair their virtue as guardians, nor tempt them to prey upon the other citizens. Any man of sense will say that.

He will.

Such is our conception of them; and now let us consider what way of life will correspond with this conception. In the first place, none of them should have any property beyond what is absolutely necessary; neither should they have a private house with bars and bolts closed against any one who has a mind to enter; their provisions should be only such as are required by trained warriors, who are men of temperance and courage; their agreement is to receive from the citizens a fixed rate of pay, enough to meet the expenses of the year and no more, and they will have common meals and live together, like soldiers in a camp. Gold and silver we will tell them that they have from God ; the diviner metal is within them, and they have therefore no need of that earthly dross which passes under the name of gold, and ought not to pollute the divine by earthly admixture, for that 417 commoner metal has been the source of many unholy deeds; but their own is undefiled. And they alone of all the citizens may not touch or handle silver or gold, or be under the same roof with them, or wear them, or drink from them. And this will be their salvation, and the salvation of the State. But should they ever acquire homes or lands or moneys of their own, they will become housekeepers and husbandmen instead of guardians, enemies and tyrants instead of allies of the other citizens; hating and being hated, plotting and being plotted against, they will pass through life in much greater terror of internal than of external enemies, and the hour of ruin, both to themselves and to the rest of the State, will be at hand. For all which reasons may we not say that these are to be the regulations of our guardians respecting houses and all other things, and that such shall be our laws?

Yes, said Glaucon.

BOOK IV.

HERE Adeimantus interposed a question. He said: How would you answer, Socrates, if a person were to say that you make your citizens miserable, and all by their own doing; for they are the actual owners of the city, and yet they reap no advantage from this; whereas other men acquire lands, and build large and handsome houses, and have everything handsome about them; offering sacrifices to the gods on their own account, and practising hospitality; and also, as you were saying only just now, they have gold and silver, and all that is usual among the favourites of fortune, while our poor citizens are no better than mercenaries who are fixed in the city and do nothing but mount guard?

Yes, I said; and you may add that they are only fed, and not 420 paid, in addition to their food, like other men; and therefore they cannot make a journey of pleasure, they have no money to spend on a mistress or any other luxurious fancy, which, as the world goes, is thought to be happiness; and many other accusations of the same nature might be added.

But, said he, let us suppose all that included in the charge.

You mean to ask, I said, what is to be our answer?

Yes, he replied.

If we proceed along the path which we are already going, I said, my belief is that we shall find the answer. Even if our guardians were such as you describe, there would not be anything wonderful in their still being the happiest of men; but let that pass, for our object in the construction of the State is the greatest happiness of the whole, and not that of any one class; and in a State which is ordered with a view to the good of the whole, we think that we are most likely to find justice, and in the ill-ordered State injustice: and, having found them, we shall then be able to decide which of the two is the happier. At present we are constructing the happy State, not piecemeal, or with a view of making a few happy

citizens, but as a whole; and by-and-bye we will proceed to
view the opposite kind of State. If we were painting a statue,
and some one were to come and blame us for not putting the
most beautiful colours on the most beautiful parts of the body—
for the eyes, he would say, ought to be purple, but they are black
—in that case we should seem to excuse ourselves fairly enough
by saying to him, 'Pray, Sir, do not have the strange notion that
we ought to beautify the eyes to such a degree that they are no
longer eyes; but see whether, by giving this and the other features
their due, we make the whole beautiful. And, I say again, in
like manner do not compel us to assign to the guardians a sort of
happiness which will make them anything but guardians; for we
also should have no difficulty in clothing our husbandmen in fine
linen, and setting crowns of gold on their heads, bidding them
till the ground no more than they like. Neither is ignorance the
reason why we do not allow our potters to repose on couches, and
feast by the fireside, passing round the glittering bowl, while their
wheel is conveniently at hand, and working at pottery as much
as they like, and no more; or, why we do not make every class
happy in this way—and then, as you imagine, the whole State
would be happy. But do not suggest this; for, if we listen to
421 you, the husbandman will be no longer a husbandman, the potter
will cease to be a potter, and nobody will have any distinct
character. Now this is not of much importance where the corruption of society, and pretension to be what you are not extends
only to cobblers; but when the guardians of the laws and of the
government are only seemers and not real guardians, that, as
you will observe, is the utter ruin of the State: for they alone
are the authors of happiness and order in a State. If we are
right in depicting our guardians as the saviours and not the
destroyers of the State, and the author of the other picture is
representing peasants at a festival, happy in a life of revelry,
rather than fulfilling the duties of citizens, we mean different
things, and he is speaking of something which is not a State.
And therefore we must consider whether we appoint our guardians
with a view to their greatest happiness, or whether this principle
of happiness does not rather reside in the State as a whole; but
if so, the guardians and auxiliaries, and all others equally with
them, must be compelled or induced to do their own work in the

best way; and then the whole State growing up in a noble order, the several classes will only have to receive the proportion of happiness which nature assigns to them.

I think that you are quite right.

I wonder whether you will agree with another remark which occurs to me.

What may that be?

There seem to be two causes of the deterioration of the arts.

What are they?

Wealth, I said, and poverty.

How do they act?

The process is as follows. When a potter becomes rich he no longer takes the same pains with his art?

Certainly not.

He grows more and more indolent and careless?

Very true.

And the result is that he becomes a worse potter?

Yes; he greatly deteriorates.

But, on the other hand, if he has no money, and is unable to buy tools or instruments, he will not work equally well himself, nor will he teach his sons or apprentices to work equally well.

Certainly not.

Then workmen and also their works are apt to degenerate under the influence both of poverty and of wealth?

That is evident.

Here, then, is a discovery of new evils, I said, which the guardians will have to watch, or they will creep into the city unobserved.

What evils?

Wealth, I said, and poverty; for the one is the parent of luxury 422 and indolence, and the other of meanness and viciousness, and both of discontent.

That is very true, he replied; but still I should like to know, Socrates, how our city will be able to go to war, especially against an enemy who is rich and powerful, if deprived of the sinews of war.

There may possibly be a difficulty, I replied, in going to war with one such enemy; but there is no difficulty where there are two of them.

How is that? he asked.

In the first place, I said, our side will be trained warriors fighting against a number of wealthy individuals.

That is true, he said.

And do you not suppose, Adeimantus, that a single boxer who was perfect in his art would easily be a match for two stout and well-to-do gentlemen who were not boxers?

Hardly, if they came upon him at once.

What, not, I said, if he were able to run away and then turn and strike at the one who first came up? And supposing he were to do this several times under the heat of a scorching sun, do not you think that he might overturn more than one stout personage?

Certainly, he said, there would be nothing wonderful in that.

And yet rich men are probably not so inferior to others in boxing as they are in military qualities.

That is very likely.

Then probably our athletes will be able to fight with three or four times their own number?

I believe that you are right, he said.

And suppose that, before engaging, our citizens send an embassy to one of the two cities, telling them the truth: Silver and gold we neither have nor are permitted to have; in that we are not like you; do you therefore come and help us in war, and take the spoils of the other city. Who, on hearing these words, would choose to fight the lean wiry dogs, rather than, with the dogs on their side, to fight fat and tender sheep?

Very true; but still there might be a danger to the poor State if the wealth of many States were to coalesce in one.

States! I said; why, what simplicity is this, that you should use the term 'state' of any but our own State! Other States may indeed be spoken of more grandiloquently in the plural number, for they are many in one—a game of cities at which men play. Any ordinary city, however small, is in fact two cities, one the city of the poor, the other of the rich, at war with one another; and in 423 either division there are many smaller ones, and you would make a great mistake if you treated them as single States; but if you deal with them as many, and give the money or means or persons of the one to the others, you will always have a great many friends, and not many enemies. And your State, while the wise order which has now been prescribed continues to prevail in her, will be the greatest of States, not in reputation or appearance only, but in deed and truth, though she number not more than a thousand defenders. A State which is her equal you will hardly find, either among Hellenes or barbarians, though many that appear to be as great and many times greater.

That is most true, he said.

And this, I said, will be the best limit for our rulers to fix when they are considering the size of the State and the amount of territory which they are to include, and beyond which they will not go.

What limit?

I think, I said, that the State may increase to any size which is consistent with unity; that is the limit.

Yes, he said; that is excellent.

Here then, I said, is another order which will have to be conveyed to our guardians,—that our city is to be neither large nor small, but of such a size as is consistent with unity.

And surely, said he, this is not a very severe order which we impose upon them.

And this, said I, is lighter still of which we were speaking before,—I mean the duty of degrading the offspring of the guardians when inferior, and of elevating the offspring of the lower classes, when naturally superior, into the rank of guardians. The intention was, that, in the case of the citizens generally, we should put each individual man to that use for which nature designed him, and then every man would do his own business, and be one and not many, and the whole city would be one and not many.

Yes, he said; there will be even less difficulty in that.

These things, my good Adeimantus, are not, as might be supposed, a number of great principles, but trifling all of them, if care be taken, as the saying is, of the one great thing,—a thing, however, which I would rather call not great, but enough for our purpose.

What may that be? he asked.

Education, I said, and nurture. For if they are well educated, and grow into sensible men, they will easily see their way through all this as well as other matters which I do not mention; such, for example, as the possession of women and marriage and the pro-

⁴²⁴ creation of children, which will all follow the general principle that friends have all things in common, as the proverb says.

That will be excellent, he replied.

Also, I said, the State, if once started well, goes on with accumulating force like a wheel. For good nurture and education implant good constitutions, and these good constitutions having their roots in a good education improve more and more, and this improvement affects the breed in man as in other animals.

True, he said.

Then to sum up. This is the point to which, above all, the attention of our rulers should be directed,—that music and gymnastic be preserved in their original form, and no innovation made. They must do all they can to maintain this. And when any one says that mankind most regard

'The song which is the newest that the singers have[1],'

they will be afraid that he may be praising, not new songs, but a new kind of song; and this ought not to be praised, nor is this to be regarded as the meaning of the poet; for any musical innovation is full of danger to the State, and ought to be prevented. This is what Damon tells me, and I can quite believe him;—he says that when modes of music change, the fundamental laws of the State always change with them.

Yes, said Adeimantus; and you may add my suffrage to Damon's and your own.

Then, I said, our guardians must lay the foundations of the fortress in music?

Yes, he said; and licence easily creeps in; there can be no doubt of that.

Yes, I replied, in a kind of play, and at first sight appears harmless.

Why, he said, and there is no harm; but the evil is, that little by little this spirit of licence, finding a home, penetrates into manners and customs; thence, issuing with greater force, invades agreements between man and man, and from agreements proceeds to laws and constitutions, in utter recklessness, and ends by an overthrow of things in general, private as well as public.

Is all that true? I said.

[1] Od. i. 351.

That is my belief, he replied.

Then, as I was saying, our youth should be educated in a stricter rule from the first, for if education becomes lawless, and the youths themselves become lawless, they can never grow up into well- 425 conducted and virtuous citizens.

Very true, he said.

And the education must begin with their plays. The spirit of law must be imparted to them in music, and the spirit of order, instead of disorder, will attend them in all their actions, and make them grow, and if there be any part of the State which has fallen down, will raise that up again.

Very true, he said.

Thus educated, they will have no difficulty in rediscovering any lesser matters which have been neglected by their predecessors.

What do you mean?

I mean such things as these:—when the young are to be silent before their elders; how they are to show respect to them by sitting down and rising up; what honour is due to parents; what garments or shoes are to be worn; what mode of wearing the hair is to be the pattern; and the fashions of the body, and manners in general. You would agree with me in that?

Yes.

You think, as I am disposed to think, that there would be small wisdom in legislating about them; for that is never done, nor are any precise verbal enactments about them likely to be lasting.

Impossible.

We may assume, Adeimantus, that the direction in which education starts a man will determine his future life. Does not like always invite like?

No question.

Ending, as you may say, at last in some one rare and grand result, which may be good, and may be the reverse of good.

That is not to be denied, he answered.

And for this reason, I said, I shall not attempt further to legislate about them.

Naturally enough, he replied.

Well, I said, and about the business of the agora, or about bargains and contracts with artisans; about insult and injury, or the order in which causes are to be tried, and how judges are to be appointed; there may also be questions about impositions and exactions of market and harbour dues, and in general touching the administration of markets or towns or harbours and the like. But, oh heavens! shall we condescend to legislate on any of these particulars?

I think, he said, that there is no need to impose them by law on good men; most of the necessary regulations they will find out soon enough for themselves.

Yes, I said, my friend, if God will only guard the laws that we have given them.

And without divine help, said Adeimantus, they will go on for ever making and mending their laws and their lives in the hope of attaining perfection.

You would compare them, I said, to those invalids who, having no self-restraint, will not leave off their habits of intemperance?

Exactly.

Yes, I said; and how charming those people are! they are always doctoring and increasing and complicating their disorders, fancying they will be cured by some nostrum which somebody advises them to try,—never getting better, but rather growing worse.

426 That is often the case, he said, with invalids such as you describe.

Yes, I replied; they have a charming way of going on, and the charming thing is that they deem him their worst enemy who tells them the truth, which is simply that, unless they give up eating and drinking and lusting and sleeping, neither drug nor cautery nor spell nor amulet nor anything will be of any avail.

Charming! he replied. I see nothing charming in going into a passion with a man who tells you what is good.

These gentlemen, I said, do not seem to be in your good graces?

No, indeed.

Nor would a State which acts like them stand high in your estimation. And are not ill-governed States like them, which begin by proclaiming to their citizens that no one, under penalty of death, shall alter the constitution of the State, while he who conforms to their politics and most sweetly serves them, who indulges them and fawns upon them and has a presentiment of their wishes, and is skilful in gratifying them, he is esteemed as their good man, and the wise and mighty one who is to be held in honour by them?

Yes, he said; the States are as bad as the men; and I am far from approving them.

But do you not admire, I said, the coolness and dexterity of these ready ministers of political corruption?

Yes, he said, that I do; but not of all of them, for there are some whom the applause of the multitude has deluded into the belief that they are really statesmen, and they are not much to be admired.

What do you mean? I said; you should have more feeling for them. When a man cannot measure, and a great many others who cannot measure declare that he is four cubits high, can he help believing them?

He cannot.

Well, then, do not be angry with them; for are they not as good as a play, trying their hand at legislation, and always fancying that by reforming they will make an end of the dishonesties and rascalities of mankind, not knowing that they are in reality cutting away the heads of a hydra?

Yes, he said; that is a very just description of them.   427

I conceive, I said, that the true legislator will not trouble himself with enactments of this sort in an ill-ordered any more than in a well-ordered State; for in the former they are useless, and in the latter there will be no difficulty in inventing them, and many of them will naturally flow out of our institutions.

What, then, he said, is still remaining to us of the work of legislation?

Nothing to us, I replied; but to Apollo, the god of Delphi, there remains the ordering of the greatest and noblest and chiefest of all.

What is that? he said.

The institution of temples and sacrifices, and in general the service of gods, demigods, and heroes; also the ordering of the repositories of the dead, and the rites which have to be observed in order to propitiate the inhabitants of the world below. For these are matters of which we are ignorant, and as founders of a city we should be unwise in trusting to any interpreter but our ancestral deity. He is the god who sits in the centre, on the navel of the earth, and interprets them to all mankind.

You are right, he said; we will do as you propose.

But where, amid all this, is justice? Son of Ariston, tell me

where. Now that our city has been made habitable, light a
candle and search, and get your brother and Polemarchus, and the
rest of our friends, to help, and let us see whether we can discover
the place of justice and injustice, and discern the difference
between them, and find out which of them the man who would
be happy should have as his portion, whether perceived or unperceived by gods and men.

Nonsense, said Glaucon; did you not promise to search yourself, saying that to desert justice in her need would be an impiety?

Very true, I said; and as you remind me, I will be as good as
my word; but you must join.

That we will, he replied.

Well, then, I hope to make the discovery in this way. I mean
to proceed by a method of residues, beginning with the assumption that our State, if rightly ordered, is perfect.

That is most certain.

And being perfect, our State is wise and valiant and temperate and just.

That is also clear.

And of whatever is known, that which is unknown will be the
residue; this is the next step.

428 Very good.

Suppose the number of terms to be four, and we were searching
for one of them, that one might be known to us at first, and there
would be no further trouble; or, if we knew the other three first,
and could eliminate them, then the fourth would clearly be the
remainder.

Very true, he said.

And is not this the method to be pursued about the virtues,
which are also four in number?

Clearly.

First among the virtues found in the State wisdom comes into
view, and in this I detect a certain peculiarity.

What is that?

The State that we have been describing is said to be wise as
being good in counsel: that is true?

Yes.

And good counsel is clearly a kind of knowledge, for not by
ignorance, but by knowledge, do men counsel well?

Clearly.

And the kinds of knowledge in a State are many and diverse?

Of course.

There is the knowledge of the carpenter; but is that the sort of knowledge which gives a city the title of wise and good in counsel?

Certainly not; that would only give a city the reputation of skill in carpentering.

Then a city is not to be called wise because possessed of knowledge which counsels for the best about wooden implements?

Certainly not.

Nor by reason of a knowledge which advises about brazen implements, he said, nor as possessing any other similar knowledge?

Not by reason of any of them, he said.

Nor by reason of agricultural knowledge; that would give the city the name of agricultural?

Yes, that is what I should suppose.

Well, I said, and is there any knowledge in our recently-founded State among any of the citizens which advises, not about any particular thing in the State, but about the whole State, and considers what may be regarded as the best policy, both internal and external?

There certainly is.

And what is this knowledge, and among whom found? I asked.

This is the knowledge of the guardians, he replied, and is found among those whom we were just now describing as perfect guardians.

And is there any name which the city derives from the possession of this sort of knowledge?

The name of good in counsel and truly wise.

And do you suppose that there will be as many of these true guardians as there are blacksmiths in a city?

No, he replied; the blacksmiths will be far more numerous.

Will they not be the smallest of all the classes who receive a name from the profession of some kind of knowledge?

Much the smallest.

And by reason of this smallest part or class of a State, which is the governing and presiding class, and of the knowledge which

resides in them, the whole State, being in the order of nature, will
429 be called wise; and Nature appears to have ordained that this,
which has the only knowledge worthy to be called knowledge,
should be the smallest of all classes.

Most true, he said.

Thus, then, I said, the nature and place in the State of one of
the four virtues has somehow been discovered.

I am sure, he said, that the discovery is to my mind quite
satisfactory.

Again, I said, there is no difficulty in seeing the nature of
courage, and in what part that quality resides which gives the
name of courageous to the State.

How do you mean?

Why, I said, every one who calls any State courageous or
cowardly, will be thinking of that part which fights and goes to
battle on the State's behalf.

No one, he replied, would ever think of any other.

The rest of the citizens may be courageous or may be cowardly,
but that, as I conceive, will not have the effect of making the city
either one or the other.

Certainly not.

The city will be courageous in virtue of a portion of the city
in which there resides a never-failing quality preservative of the
opinion which the legislator inculcated about the right sort of
fear; and this is what you term courage.

I should like to hear what you are saying once more, for I do
not think that I perfectly understand you.

I mean, I said, that courage is a kind of preservation.

What kind of preservation?

The preservation, I said, of the opinion about the nature and
manner of dangers which the law implants through education; and
I mean by the word 'never-failing,' to intimate that in pleasure or
in pain, or under the influence of desire or fear, a man preserves,
and does not lose this opinion. Shall I give you an illustration of
my meaning?

If you will.

You know, I said, that the dyers, when they want to dye wool
for making the true sea-purple, begin by selecting their white
colour first; this they prepare and dress with no slight circum-

stance, in order that the white ground may take the purple hue
in full perfection. The dyeing then proceeds; and whatever is
dyed in this manner becomes a fast colour, and no washing with
lyes or without lyes can take away the bloom of the colour. I
dare say that you know how these, or indeed any colours, look
when the ground has not been duly prepared?

Yes, he said; I know that they have a washed-out and ridiculous appearance.

Then now, I said, you will understand what our object was in
selecting our soldiers, and educating them in music and gymnas- 430
tic; we were contriving influences which would prepare them to
take the dye of the laws in perfection, and the colour of their
opinions about dangers and every other opinion was to be inde-
libly fixed by their nurture and training, and not to be washed
away by any such potent lyes as pleasure—mightier agent far
in washing the soul than any soda or lye; and sorrow, fear,
and desire mightier solvents than any others. And this sort of
universal preserving power of true opinion in conformity with
law about real and false dangers, I call and maintain to be
courage, unless you can suggest another view.

But I have no other to suggest, and I suppose that you mean to
exclude mere uninstructed courage, such as that of a wild beast
or of a slave—this, in your judgment, is not courage in conformity with law, and ought to have another name.

That is as you say.

Then I may infer that this is courage?

Why, yes, said I, that you may infer, and if you add the word
'political,' you will not be far wrong;—hereafter we may pursue
that enquiry further, but at present we are seeking not for courage
but justice, and with a view to this there is nothing more wanted.

You are right, he replied.

Two virtues remain to be discovered in the State—first, temperance, and then justice, which is the great object of our search.

Very true.

Now, can we find justice without troubling ourselves about
temperance?

I do not know how that can be accomplished, he said, nor do I
desire that justice should be brought to light, and temperance lost
sight of; and therefore I wish you would do me the favour of
considering temperance first.

Certainly, I replied, I cannot be wrong in granting you a favour.

Then do as I ask, he said.

Yes, I replied, I will do as you ask, and next consider temperance; this, as far as I can see at present, has more of the nature of symphony and harmony than the preceding.

How is that? he asked.

Temperance, I replied, is, as I conceive, a sort of order and control of certain pleasures and desires; this is implied in the saying of a man being his own master; and there are other traces of the same notion.

No doubt, he said.

431 There is something ridiculous in the expression 'master of himself;' for the master is also the slave and the slave the master; and in all these modes of speaking the same person is predicated.

Certainly.

But the real meaning of the expression, I believe, is that the human soul has a better principle, and has also a worse principle; and when the better principle controls the worse, then a man is said to be master of himself; and this is certainly a term of praise: but when, owing to evil education or association, the better principle, which is less, is overcome by the worse principle, which is greater, this is censured; and he who is in this case is called the slave of self and unprincipled.

Yes, he said, there is reason in that.

And now, I said, look at our newly-created State, and there you will find one of these two conditions realized; for the State, as you will acknowledge, may be justly called master of self, if the words temperance and self-mastery truly express the rule of the better over the worse.

Yes, he said, I have looked, and perceive the truth of what you say.

Moreover, I said, the pleasures and desires and pains, which are many and various, are found in children and women and servants, and in the lower classes of the free citizens.

Certainly, he said.

Whereas the simple and moderate desires which follow reason, and are under the guidance of mind and true opinion, are confined to a few, being those who are the best born and the best educated.

S 2

Very true, he said.

And these also, I said, as you may perceive, have a place in our State, but the meaner desires of the many are held down by the virtuous desires and wisdom of the few.

That I perceive, he said.

Then if there be any city which may be described as master of pleasures and desires, and master of self, ours may claim that designation?

Certainly, he replied.

And also that of temperate, and for the same reasons?

Yes, he said.

And if there be any State in which rulers and subjects will be agreed about the question who are to rule, that again will be our State?

No doubt at all of that.

And the citizens being thus agreed among themselves, in which class will temperance be found,—in the rulers or in the subjects?

In both, as I should imagine, he replied.

Do you observe, I said, that we were pretty right in our anticipation that temperance was a sort of harmony?

Why do you say that?

Why, because temperance is unlike courage and wisdom, each of which resides in a portion of the State only, which the one makes wise and the other valiant; but that is not the way with 432 temperance, which extends to the whole, and runs through the notes of the scale, and produces a harmony of the weaker and the stronger and the middle class, whether you suppose them to be stronger or weaker in wisdom or strength or numbers or wealth, or whatever else may be the measure of them. Most truly, then, do we describe temperance as the natural harmony of master and slave, both in states and individuals, in which the subjects are as willing to obey as the governors are to rule.

I entirely agree with you.

And so, I said, three of the virtues have been discovered in our State, and this is the form in which they appear. There remains the last element of virtue in a State, which must be justice, if we only knew what that was.

That, he said, is obvious.

The time then has arrived, Glaucon, when, like huntsmen, we should surround the cover, and look sharp that justice does not slip away, and pass out of sight, and get lost; for there can be no doubt that we are in the right direction; only try and get a sight of her, and if you come within view first, let me know.

I wish that there were any chance of that, he said; but I believe that you will find in me a follower who has just eyes enough to see what you show him; that is as much as I am good for.

Offer up a prayer, I said, and follow.

I will follow, he said, but you must show me the way.

Here is no path, I said, and the wood is dark and perplexing; still we must push on.

Let us push on then.

Halloo! I said, I begin to perceive indications of a track, and I believe that the quarry will not escape.

That is good news, he said.

Truly, I said, we are very stupid.

Why so?

Why, my good Sir, I said, when we first began, ages ago, there lay justice rolling at our feet, and we, fools that we were, failed to see her, like people who go about looking for what they have in their hands: And that was the way with us; we looked away into the far distance, and I suspect this to have been the reason why we missed her.

What do you mean?

I mean to say that we have already had her on our lips and in our ears, and failed to recognize her.

I get impatient at the length of your exordium.

433 Well, then, say whether I am right or not; you will remember the original principle of which we spoke at the foundation of the State, that every man, as we often insisted, should practise one thing only, that being the thing to which his nature was most perfectly adapted;—now justice is either this or a part of this.

Yes, that was often repeated by us.

Further, we affirmed that justice was doing one's own business, and not being a busybody; that was often said by us, and many others have said the same.

Yes, that was said by us.

Then this doing one's own business in a certain way may be assumed to be justice. Do you know why I say this?

I do not, and should like to be told.

Because I think that this alone remains in the State when the other virtues of temperance and courage and wisdom are abstracted; and this is the ultimate cause and condition of the existence of all of them, and while remaining 'in them is also their preservative; and we were saying that if the three were discovered by us, justice would be the fourth or remaining one.

That follows of necessity.

Still, I said, if a question should arise as to which of these four qualities contributed most by their presence to the excellence of the State, whether the agreement of rulers and subjects, or the preservation in the soldiers of the opinion which the law ordains about the true nature of dangers, or wisdom and watchfulness in the rulers would claim the palm, or whether this which I am about to mention, and which is found in children and women, bond and free, artisan, ruler, subject, is not the one which conduces most to the excellence of the State,—this quality, I mean, of every one doing his own work, and not being a busybody,—the question would not be easily determined.

Certainly, he replied, that would be difficult to determine.

Then the power of each individual in the State to do his own work appears to compete in the scale of political virtue with wisdom, temperance, and courage?

Yes, he said.

And the virtue which enters into this competition is justice?

Exactly.

Look at this in another light. Are not the rulers in a State those to whom you would entrust the office of determining causes?

Certainly.

And they will decide on the principle that individuals are neither to take what is another's, nor to be deprived of what is their own; that will be the principle at which they will aim?

Yes; that will be their principle.

And that is a just principle?

Yes.

Then on this view also justice will be admitted to be the having and doing what is a man's own, and belongs to him?

434   That is true.

Think, now, and say whether you agree with me. Suppose a carpenter to be doing the business of a cobbler, or a cobbler of a carpenter; and suppose them to exchange implements or prerogatives, or the same person to be doing the work of both; do you think that any great harm would happen to the State?

Not at all, he said.

But when the cobbler leaves his last, and he or any other whom nature designed to be a trader and whose heart is lifted up by wealth or strength or numbers, or any like advantage, attempts to force his way into the class of warriors, or a warrior into that of legislators and guardians, for which he is unfitted, or when one man is trader, legislator, and warrior all at once, then I think you will agree with me that this interchange of duties and implements and this meddling of one with another is the ruin of the State.

Most true.

Then, said I, as there are three distinct classes, any meddling of them with one another, or the change of one into another, is the greatest harm to the State, and may be most justly termed evil-doing?

Precisely.

And the greatest degree of evil-doing to one's own city you would characterize as injustice?

Certainly.

This then is injustice; and let us once more repeat the thesis in the opposite form. When the trader, the auxiliary, and the guardian do their own business, that is justice, and will make the city just.

I think that is true, he said.

Let us not, I said, be overpositive as yet; but if, on trial, this conception of justice be verified in the individual as well as in the State, then there will be no longer any room for doubt; but, if not, there must be another enquiry. At present, however, let us finish the old investigation, which we began, as you remember, under the impression that, if we could first examine justice on the larger scale, there would be less difficulty in recognizing her in the individual. That larger example appeared to be the State, and we made the best that we could, knowing well that in the good State justice would be found to exist. Let us now apply what we found there to the individual, and if they agree, well and good; or, if there be a difference in the individual, we will come back to the State and have another trial of the theory. The friction of the two when rubbed together may possibly strike a light in which justice will shine forth, and the 435 vision which is then revealed we will fix in our souls.

That is the right way, he said; let us do as you say.

I proceeded to ask: When two things, a greater and less, are called by the same name, are they like or unlike in so far as they are called the same?

Like, he replied.

The just man then, in being just, and in reference to the mere principle of justice, will be like the just State?

He will.

And a State was thought by us to be just when the three classes in the State did their own business; and also thought to be temperate and valiant and wise by reason of certain other affections and qualities of these same classes?

True, he said.

And so of the individual; we shall be right in arguing that he has these same principles in his own soul, and may fairly receive the same appellations as possessing the affections which correspond to them?

Certainly, he said.

Once more then, O my friend, we have alighted upon an easy question—whether the soul has these three principles or not?

An easy question! Nay, rather, Socrates, the proverb holds that hard is the good.

Very true, I said; and I confess that the method which we are employing, in my judgment, seems to be altogether inadequate to the accurate solution of this question; for the true method is another and a longer one. Still we may arrive at a solution not below the level of the previous enquiry.

May we not be satisfied with that? he said;—under the circumstances, I am quite content.

I too, I replied, shall be extremely well satisfied.

Then faint not in pursuing the speculation, he said.

Can I be wrong, I said, in acknowledging that in the individual there are the same principles and habits which there are in the

State; for if they did not pass from one to the other, whence did they come? Take the quality of spirit or passion;—there would be something ridiculous in thinking that this quality, which is characteristic of the Thracians, Scythians, and in general of the northern nations, when found in States, does not originate in the individuals who compose them; and the same may be said of the love of knowledge, which is the special characteristic of our part of the world, or the love of money, which may, with equal truth,
436 be attributed to the Phoenicians and Egyptians.

Exactly, he said.

There is no difficulty in understanding this.

None whatever.

But the difficulty begins as soon as we raise the question whether these principles are three or one; whether, that is to say, we learn with one part of our nature, are angry with another, and with a third part desire the satisfaction of our natural appetites; or whether the whole soul comes into play in each sort of action—to determine that is the difficulty.

Yes, he said, that is the difficulty.

Then let us now try and determine whether they are the same or different.

How shall we do that? he asked.

I replied as follows: The same thing clearly cannot act or be acted upon in the same part in the same relation, at the same time, in contrary ways; and therefore whenever this occurs in things apparently the same, we shall know that they are not really the same, but different.

Good.

For example, I said, can the same thing be at rest and in motion at the same time and in the same part?

That is impossible.

Still, I said, let us have a more precise understanding, that we may not hereafter have a misunderstanding. Imagine the case of a man who is standing and also moving his hands and his head, and suppose a person to say that one and the same person is in motion and at rest at the same moment—to such a mode of speech we should object, and should rather say that one part of him is in motion while another is at rest.

Very true.

And suppose the objector to refine still further, and draw the nice distinction that not only parts of tops, but whole tops, when they are borne round with their centre fixed on the same spot, are at rest and in motion at the same time (and he may say the same of anything which revolves in the same spot), this would not be admitted by us, because in such cases things are not at rest and in motion in the same parts of themselves; but we should say rather that they have inhering in them a circular and a perpendicular direction, and that they stand in the perpendicular line which admits of no deviation, and move in the circle. But if, while revolving, the axis inclines either to the right or left, forwards or backwards, then in no point of view can they be at rest.

That is the correct mode of describing them, he replied.

Then none of these objections will confuse us, nor incline us to the belief that the same thing at the same time, in the same part or the same relation, can be or act or be acted upon in con- 437 trary ways.

That I shall never believe, he said.

Yet, I said, that we may not be compelled to examine all such objections, and prove at length that they are untrue, let us assume this proposition, and proceed on the understanding that hereafter, if the assumption turn out to be untrue, the consequences which follow shall be withdrawn.

Yes, he said, that will be the best way.

Well, I said, would you not allow that assent and dissent, desire and refusal, attraction and repulsion, are all of them opposites, whether they are regarded as active or passive, (for that makes no difference in the fact of their opposition) ?

Yes, he said, they are opposites.

Well, I said, and hunger and thirst, and the desires in general, including willing and wishing,—all those you would refer to the classes already mentioned. You would say—would you not ?—that the soul of him who desires is seeking after the object of desire; or that he draws to himself the thing which he wishes to possess; or again, when a person wills anything to be given him, his mind longing for the realization of his desire makes a sign of willingness to have the thing, as if in assent to a question?

I should agree to that.

And what would you say of unwillingness and dislike and the

absence of desire; would you not refer these to the opposite class of repulsion and rejection?

Certainly.

Admitting this to be true of desire generally, let us now proceed to single out a particular class of desires,—shall we say those desires which are the most evident to sense, and which are termed hunger and thirst?

Let us take that class, he said.

The object of one is food, and of the other drink?

Yes.

And here comes the point: is not thirst the desire which the soul has of drink, and of drink only; not of drink qualified by anything else; for example, warm or cold, or much or little, or, in a word, drink of any particular sort: but if the thirst be accompanied by heat, then the desire is of cold drink; or, if accompanied by cold, then of warm drink; or, if the thirst be excessive, then the drink which is desired will be excessive; or, if not great, the quantity of drink will also be small: but thirst, regarded as thirst, will only desire drink which is the natural satisfaction of thirst, as hunger too will only desire food?

Yes, he said, in every case the simple desire is of the simple object, and the qualified desire of the qualified object; that is as you say.

438 But here, I said, I should wish to guard against an objection. Some one may argue that no man desires drink only, but good drink, or food only, but good food; for good is the universal object of desire, and therefore thirst will necessarily be thirst after good drink; and this will hold equally of every other desire.

Yes, he said, that objection does appear to raise a difficulty.

Nevertheless, I said, relatives may be correctly divided into compounds which have a quality attached to either term of the relation, and into simples whose correlative is simple.

I do not know what you mean, he said.

Well, I said, you know that the greater is relative to the less?

Yes.

And the much greater to the much less?

Yes.

And the sometimes greater to the sometimes less, and the greater that is to be to the less that is to be?

Certainly, he said.

And this applies generally to the greater and less, and also to other correlative terms, such as the double and the half, or again to the heavier and the lighter, the swifter and the slower, to hot and cold, and any other relatives;—is not this true?

Yes.

And does not the same hold with the sciences? The object of science is knowledge (assuming that to be the true definition), but the object of a particular science is a particular kind of knowledge; I mean, for example, that the building of a house is a kind of knowledge which is defined and distinguished from other kinds of knowledge as house-building.

Certainly.

Because having a particular quality which no other has?

Yes.

And having this particular quality or nature, because having an object of a certain kind; and this is true of the other arts and sciences?

Yes.

Now, then, if I have made myself clear, you will understand my original meaning in what I said about relatives. My meaning was, that if the first term of a relation is taken alone, the second is taken alone; if the first term is qualified, the second is also qualified. I do not say that the two relatives need be 'in pari materiâ,' or that the science of health is healthy, or of disease necessarily diseased, or that the sciences of good and evil are therefore good and evil; but only that, from having health and disease as an object, the science of medicine has come to be of a certain nature, and is hence called not merely science, but medical science.

I understand your meaning, and assent to you.

Would you not say then, I said, that thirst is one of these 439 relative terms, thirst being obviously——

Yes, thirst is relative, and of drink.

And a certain kind of thirst is relative to a certain kind of drink; but thirst taken alone is neither of much nor little, nor of good nor bad, nor of any particular kind of drink, but of drink only?

Certainly.

Then the soul of the thirsty one, in that he thirsts, desires only drink, and feels an impulse towards drink?

That is plain.

And if you suppose something which pulls a thirsty soul away from drink, that must be different from the thirsty principle which draws him like a beast to drink; for, as we were saying, the same thing cannot at the same time with the same part act in contrary ways about the same.

Impossible.

No more than you can say of the archer that his hands push and pull the bow at the same time, but what you say is that one hand pushes and the other pulls.

Exactly, he replied.

And might a man be thirsty, and yet unwilling to drink?

Yes, he said, that often happens.

And in such a case what is one to say? Would you not say that there is one principle in the soul bidding a man to drink, and a second forbidding him, which is other and stronger than that which bids him?

That is my view, he replied.

And the forbidding principle is derived from reason, and the bidding and attracting principles are the effects of passion and disorder?

Clearly.

Then we may fairly infer that they are two, and that they differ from one another; one of them we may call the rational principle of the soul, the other, which accompanies certain pleasures and satisfactions, is that with which a man loves and hungers and thirsts and feels the emotions of desire, and may be rightly termed irrational or appetitive?

Yes, he said, we shall not be far wrong in that.

Then let these be marked out as the two principles which there are existing in the soul.

And what shall we say of passion, or spirit? Is that a third, or akin to one of the preceding?

I should be inclined to say—akin to desire.

Well, I said, there is a story which I remember to have heard, and on which I rely. The story is that Leontius, the son of Aglaion, was coming up from the Piraeus, under the north wall on the outside, and observed some dead bodies lying on the ground by the executioner. He felt a longing desire to see them, and also a disgust and abhorrence of them; for a time he turned away and averted his eyes, and then, suddenly overcome by the impulse, forced them open, and ran up, saying (to his eyes), Take your fill, ye wretches, of the fair sight. 440

I have heard the story myself, he said.

Now this seems to imply that anger differs from the desires, and is sometimes at war with them.

That is implied, he said.

And are there not many other cases in which we observe that, when a man's desires violently prevail over his reason, he reviles himself, and is angry at the violence within him, and that in this struggle, which is like the struggle of factions in a State, his spirit is on the side of his reason;—but that the passionate or spirited element should side with the desires when reason decides that she is not to be opposed[2], this sort of thing, I believe, you will say that you never observed occurring in yourself, nor, as I think, in any one else?

Certainly not, he said.

Suppose, I said, that a man thinks he has done a wrong to another, the nobler he is the less able he is to get into a state of righteous indignation; his anger refuses to be excited at the hunger or cold or other suffering, which he deems that the injured person may justly inflict upon him?

True, he said.

But when he thinks that he is the sufferer of the wrong, then he boils and chafes, and is on the side of what he believes to be justice; and because he suffers hunger or cold or other pain he is only the more determined to persevere and conquer; he must do or die, and will not desist, until he hears the voice of the shepherd, that is, reason, bidding his dog bark no more.

That is a very good illustration, he replied; and in our State, as we were saying, the auxiliaries were to be dogs, and to hear the voice of the rulers, who are their shepherds.

I perceive, I said, that you quite understand me; there is, however, a further point which I would wish you to consider.

---

2 Reading μὴ δεῖν ἀντιπράττειν, without a comma after δεῖν.

What may that be?

You remember that passion or spirit appeared at first sight to be a sort of desire, but now we should say the contrary; for in the conflict of the soul spirit is arrayed on the side of the rational principle.

Most assuredly.

But a further question arises. Is spirit different from reason also, or only a sort of reason; in which case, instead of three principles in the soul, there will be only two, the rational and 441 the concupiscent; or rather, as the State was composed of three classes, traders, auxiliaries, counsellors, so may there not be in the individual soul a third element which is passion or spirit, and which is the auxiliary of reason when not corrupted by education?

Yes, he said, there must be a third.

Yes, I replied, if passion, which has already been shown to be different from desire, turn out also to be different from reason.

But that is obvious, he said, and is proved in the case of young children, who are full of spirit almost as soon as they are born, whereas some of them never seem to attain to the use of reason, and a good many only late in life.

Excellent I said, and the same thing is seen in brute animals, which is a further proof of the truth of what you are saying. And Homer, whose words we have already quoted, may be again summoned as a witness, where he says,

'He smote his breast, and thus rebuked his soul[3];'

for in those lines Homer has clearly supposed the power which reasons about the better and worse to be different from the unreasoning principle which is the subject of the rebuke.

That is true, he said.

And now, after much tossing in the argument, we have reached land, and are fairly agreed that the principles which exist in the State, like those in the individual, are three in number, and the same with them.

Exactly.

And must we not infer that the individual is wise in the same way, and in virtue of the same quality which makes the State wise?

[3] Od. xx. 17.

Certainly.

And the same quality which constitutes bravery in the State constitutes bravery in the individual, and the same is true of all the other virtues?

Assuredly.

And the individual will be acknowledged by us to be just in the same way that the State was just?

That will also follow of course.

And the justice of the State consisted, as we very well remember, in each of the three classes doing the work of that class?

We are not very likely to forget that, he said.

And we must also remember that the individual whose several principles do their own work will be just, and will do his own work?

Yes, he said, we must remember that.

And ought not the rational principle, which is wise, and has the care of the whole soul, to rule, and the passionate or spirited principle to be the subject and ally?

Certainly.

And, as you were saying, the harmonizing influence of music and gymnastic will bring them into accord, nerving and educating the reason with noble words and lessons, and softening and consoling and civilizing the wildness of passion with harmony 442 and rhythm?

Quite true, he said.

And these two, thus nurtured and educated, and having learned truly to know their own functions, will set a rule over the concupiscent part of every man, which is the largest and most insatiable; over this they will set a guard, lest, waxing great with the fulness of bodily pleasures, as they are termed, and no longer confined to her own sphere, the concupiscent soul should attempt to enslave and rule those who are not her natural-born subjects, and overturn the whole life of man?

Very true, he said.

The two will be the defenders of the whole soul and the whole body against attacks from without; the one counselling, and the other fighting under the command of their leader, and courageously executing his counsels.

True.

And he is to be deemed courageous who, having the element of passion working in him, preserves, in the midst of pain and pleasure, the notion of danger which reason prescribes?

Right, he replied.

And he is wise who has in him that little part which rules and gives orders; that part being supposed to have a knowledge of what is for the interest of each and all of the three other parts?

Assuredly.

And would you not say that he is temperate who has these same elements in friendly harmony, in whom the one ruling principle of reason, and the two subject ones of spirit and desire are equally agreed that reason ought to rule, and do not rebel?

Certainly, he said, that is the true account of temperance whether in the State or individual.

And surely, I said, a man will be just in the manner of which we have several times already spoken and no other?

That is very certain.

And is the edge of justice blunted in the individual, or is there any reason why our definition of justice should not apply equally to the individual and to the State?

None in my judgment, he said.

Because, I said, if any doubt is still lingering in our minds, a few commonplace instances will satisfy us of the truth of this.

What sort of instances do you mean?

Why, for example, I said, who would imagine that the just State, or the man who is trained in the principles of such a 443 State, would be more likely than the unjust to make away with a deposit of gold or silver?

No one, as I should suppose, he replied.

Will such an one, I said, ever be guilty of sacrilege or theft, or treachery either to his friends or to his country?

That will be far from him.

Neither will he ever break faith where there have been oaths or agreements?

Impossible.

No one will be less likely to commit adultery, or to dishonour his father and mother, or to fail in his religious duties?

No one.

And the reason of this is that each part of him is doing his own business, whether in ruling or being ruled?

That is the truth.

Are you satisfied then that the quality which makes such men and such states is justice, or do you hope to discover some other?

Not I, indeed.

Then our dream has been realized; and as we were saying at the beginning of our work of construction, some divine power must have conducted us to a sort of first principle or form of justice—that suspicion of ours has been now verified?

Yes, certainly.

And the division of labour which required the carpenter and the shoemaker and the rest of the citizens to be doing each his own business, and not another's, was a kind of shadow of justice, and therefore of use?

Clearly.

And justice was the reality of which this was the semblance; dealing, however, not with the outward man, but with the inward, which is the true self and concernment of a man: for the just man does not permit the several elements within him to meddle with one another, or any of them to do the work of others, but he sets in order his own inner life, and is his own master, and at peace with himself; and when he has bound together the three principles within him, which may be compared to the middle, higher, and lower divisions of the scale, and the intermediate intervals—when he has bound together all these, and is no longer many, but has become one entirely temperate and perfectly adjusted nature, then he will begin to act, if he has to act, whether in a matter of property, or in the treatment of the body, or some affair of politics or private business; in all which cases he will think and call just and good action that which preserves and co-operates with this condition, and the knowledge which presides over this wisdom; and unjust action, that which at any time destroys this, and the opinion which 444 presides over unjust action, ignorance.

That is the precise truth, Socrates.

Very good; and if we were to say that we had discovered the just man and the just State, and the place of justice in each of them, that would not be a very vain boast?

No, indeed.

May we be so bold then as to say this?

Let us be so bold, he replied.

And now, I said, injustice has to be considered.

That is evident

Then, assuming the threefold division of the soul, must not injustice be a kind of quarrel between these three—a meddlesomeness, and interference, and rising up of a part of the soul against the whole soul, an assertion of unlawful authority, which is made by a rebellious subject against a true prince, of whom he is the natural vassal—that is the sort of thing; the confusion and error of these parts or elements is injustice and intemperance and cowardice and ignorance, and in general all vice?

Exactly so, he said.

And if the nature of justice and injustice be known, then the meaning of acting unjustly and being unjust, or, again, of acting justly, will also be perfectly clear?

What do you mean? he said.

Why, I said, they are like disease and health; being in the soul just what disease and health are in the body.

How is that? he said.

Why, I said, that which is healthy causes health, and that which is unhealthy causes disease.

Yes.

And just actions cause justice, and unjust actions cause injustice?

That is certain.

And the creation of health is the creation of a natural order and government of one another in the parts of the body; and the creation of disease is the creation of a state of things in which they are at variance with this natural order?

True.

And is not this equally true of the soul? Is not the creation of justice the creation of a natural order and government of one another in the parts of the soul, and the creation of injustice the opposite?

Exactly, he said.

Then virtue is the health and beauty and well-being of the soul, and vice is the disease and weakness and deformity of the soul?

True.

And good practices lead to virtue, and evil practices to vice?

Assuredly.

Still our old question of the comparative advantage of justice 44 and injustice has not been answered: Which is the more profitable, to be just and do justly, and practise virtue, whether seen or unseen of gods and men, or to be unjust and do unjustly, if only unpunished and unimproved?

In my judgment, Socrates, the question has now become ridiculous. If, when the bodily constitution is gone, life is no longer endurable, though pampered with every sort of meats and drinks, and having all wealth and all power, shall we be told that life is worth having when the very essence of the vital principle is undermined and corrupted, even though a man be allowed to do whatever he pleases, if at the same time he is forbidden to escape from vice and injustice, or attain justice and virtue, seeing that we now know the true nature of each?

Yes, I said, that is ridiculous, as you say. Still, as we are near the spot at which we may see the truth with our own eyes, let us not faint by the way.

Certainly not, he replied.

Come hither then, I said, ascend the hill which overhangs the city, and see the various forms of vice.

I am following you, he replied: proceed.

I said, We seem to have reached a summit of speculation from which you may look down and see the single form of virtue, and the forms of vice innumerable; there being four special ones which are deserving of note.

What do you mean? he said.

I mean, I replied, that there appear to be as many forms of the soul as there are forms of the State.

How many?

There are five of the State, and five of the soul, I said.

What are they?

The first, I said, is that which we have been describing, and which may be said to have two names, monarchy and aristocracy, according as rule is exercised by one or many.

True, he replied.

But I regard this as one form only; for whether the government is in the hands of one or many, if the governors have been trained in the manner which we have described, the fundamental laws of the State will not be subverted.

That is true, he replied.

BOOK V.

Such is the good and true State, and the good and true man is of the same pattern; and if this is right every other is wrong; and the error is one which affects not only the ordering of the State, but also the regulation of the individual soul. There are four forms of this evil.

What are they? he said.

I was proceeding to tell the order in which the four evil forms appeared to me to succeed one another, when Polemarchus began to whisper to his neighbour Adeimantus, who was sitting just beyond him on the further side. He put out his hand, and took him by the coat at the upper part, by the shoulder, and drew him towards him, leaning forward himself and saying something, of which I only caught the words, 'Shall we let him off, or what?'

Certainly not, said Adeimantus, raising his voice.

What is that, I said, which you refuse to let off?

You, he said.

Still I asked for an explanation [1].

Why, he said, we think that you are lazy and mean to cheat us out of the best part of the story; and you have a notion that you will not be detected in passing lightly over an entire and very important division of the subject,—that which relates to women and children,—as if there could be no manner of doubt in this instance also that 'friends will have all things in common.'

And am I not right, Adeimantus?

Yes, he said; but the word 'right,' like everything else, has to be explained; for this community may be of many kinds. Please, therefore, to say which you mean; for we have been expecting that you would tell us something about their family life—how

---

[1] Reading ἔτι ἐγὼ εἶπον.

they would bring children into the world, and rear them when they arrived, and, in general, what is the nature of this community of women and children—as we are of opinion that the right or wrong management of these matters will have a great and paramount influence on the State for good or for evil. And now, as you are taking in hand another State, without having determined these points, we have resolved, as you heard, not to 450 let you go until you give a satisfactory explanation of all this, as of the rest.

In that resolution, said Glaucon, you may regard me as consentient.

And without more ado, you may take that, said Thrasymachus, as the decision of us all.

I said, You do not know what you are doing in thus assailing me. What an argument are you raising! Just as I thought that I had finished, and was only too glad that I had laid this question to sleep, and was reflecting how fortunate I was in your acquiescence in what I then said, you begin again, ignorant of what a hornet's nest of words you are arousing. Now I foresaw this coming trouble, and this was the reason why I made the omission.

What, said Thrasymachus; do you think that we are come to look for the philosopher's stone, or to hear discourse?

Yes, said I, but discourse should have a limit

Yes, Socrates, said Glaucon, and the whole of life is the only limit which wise men assign to the hearing of such discourses. But do not regard that; only in your own way answer the question: What sort of community of women and children is this which is to prevail among the guardians? and how are their children to be brought up in infancy, which is apparently the most difficult part of education? Tell us how these things will be.

Yes, my simple friend, but the answer is the reverse of easy; for many more doubts arise about this than about our previous enquiries. For the practicability of what is said may be doubted; and looked at in another point of view, whether the scheme, if ever so practicable, will be for the best, is also doubtful. Hence there arises a fear, as we draw near, lest our aspiration should be a dream only.

Fear not, he replied, for your audience are not exacting, any more than they are sceptical or hostile.

I said: My good friend, I suppose that you mean to encourage me by these words.

Yes, he said.

Then let me tell you that you are doing just the contrary; the consolation would have been good had I believed myself that I knew what I was talking about: for to know and to declare the truth in matters of high interest which a man loves among wise men who love him is a safe thing and gives confidence; but to carry on an argument when you are yourself only a doubting enquirer, which is my case, that is a dangerous and slippery thing; 451 and the danger is not that I shall be laughed at (the fear of that would be childish), but that I shall miss my footing when I ought to be surest of the truth, and drag my friends after me in my fall. And I pray Nemesis not to visit upon me the words which I am going to utter. For I do indeed believe that to be an involuntary homicide is a less crime than to be a deceiver about the beautiful, the good, and the just in institutions. And that is a risk which I would rather run among enemies than among friends, and there-fore you do well to console me 2.

Glaucon laughed and said: Well then, Socrates, in case you and your argument do us any serious injury you shall be acquitted beforehand, as though you were a homicide, and shall not be held to be a deceiver; take courage then and speak.

Well, I said, the law says that when a man is acquitted he is free from guilt, and if in that case then also in this.

Then why should you mind?

Well, I replied, I suppose that I must retrace my steps and say what I perhaps ought to have said before. The men have played out their part, and now comes the women's turn; of whom I will proceed to speak, and the more so as I am invited by you. For men born and educated like our citizens, the only way, in my opinion, of arriving at a right conclusion about the possession and use of women and children is to follow the principle which has been already laid down about the men; that principle was that they were to be the guardians and watchdogs of the herd.

True.

Let us proceed then to give the women a similar training and education, and see how far that accords with our design.

2 Reading ὥστε εὖ με παραμυθεῖ.

What do you mean? he said.

What I mean may be put into the form of a question, I said: Do we divide dogs into hes and shes, and take the masculine gender out to hunt, or have them to keep watch and ward over the flock, while we leave the females at home, under the idea that the bearing and suckling their puppies hinder them from sharing in the labours of the males?

No, he said, they share alike; the difference between them is only one of strength and weakness.

But can you use different animals for the same purpose, unless they are fed and bred in the same way?

You cannot.

Then, if women are to have the same duties as men, they must
452 have the same education?

Yes.

The education which was assigned to the men was music and gymnastic.

Yes.

Then women must be taught music and gymnastic and also the art of war, which they must practise like the men?

I suppose that is the inference.

I should rather expect, I said, that several of our proposals, if they are carried out, being unusual, may appear ridiculous.

No doubt of that.

Yes, I said, and the most ridiculous thing of all will be the sight of women naked in the palaestra, exercising with the men, especially when they get old; they certainly will not be a vision of beauty any more than the wrinkled old men who have anything but an agreeable appearance when they take to gymnastics; this, however, does not deter them.

Yes, indeed, he said: according to present notions the proposal would appear ridiculous.

But then, I said, as we have determined to speak our minds, we must not fear the jests of the wits which will be directed against this sort of innovation; how they will talk of women's attainments in music as well as in gymnastic, and above all about their wearing armour and riding upon horseback!

Very true, he replied.

Yet having begun we must go on and attack the difficulty;

at the same time begging of these gentlemen for once in their life to be serious. Not long ago, as we shall remind them, the Greeks were of the opinion, which is still generally received among the barbarians, that the sight of a naked man was ridiculous and improper; and when first the Cretans and then the Lacedaemonians introduced naked exercises, the wits of that day might have ridiculed all this equally.

No doubt.

But when experience showed that to let all things be seen was far better than to cover them up, and the ludicrous effect to the outward eye vanished before the approval of reason, that showed the man to be a fool who laughs or directs the shafts of his ridicule at any other sight but that of folly and vice, or seriously inclines to measure the beautiful by any other standard but that of the good.

That is very true, he replied.

First then, whether a man likes to put the question in jest or in earnest, let us ask about the nature of woman: Is she capable 453 of sharing either wholly or partially, or not at all, in the actions of men? And is the art of war one of those arts in which she can or can not share? That will be the best way of commencing the enquiry, and will probably lead to the fairest conclusion.

That will be best.

Suppose that we take the other side and begin by arguing against ourselves, in order that the adversary's position may be fairly defended.

You may as well do that, he said.

Then let us put a speech into the mouths of our opponents. They will say: 'Socrates and Glaucon, no adversary need convict you, for you are self-convicted by the admission which you originally made of the principle that every one was to do his own work according to his nature.' And certainly, if I am not mistaken, there was such an admission made by us. Then he will proceed to say: 'Is there not the greatest difference between the natures of men and women?' And we shall reply: Of course, there is. And he will ask 'whether men and women ought not to have different tasks imposed upon them, such as are agreeable to their different natures?' Certainly they ought. 'Have you not then fallen into a great inconsistency in saying that men and women, who are entirely different, ought to perform the same tacions?'—What defence will you make for us, my good Sir, against any one who offers these objections?

That, he said, is not an easy question to answer on the instant; and I shall and I do beg of you to draw out the case on our side.

There, Glaucon, I said, is just the difficulty which made me hesitate in having anything to do with the law about the condition of women and children; and that is not the only difficulty.

Why yes, he said, there is something of a difficulty.

Yes, I said, but the fact is that when a man is out of his depth, whether he has fallen into a swimming bath, or into a mighty ocean, he has to swim all the same.

Very true.

And must not we swim and make for some haven, in the hope that Arion's dolphin or some other miraculous help may save us?

That must be the way, I suppose, he said.

Well then, let us see if we can discover a way of escape. Our principle was that different natures ought to have different pursuits, and that men's and women's natures are different. And now what are we saying?—that different natures ought to have the same pursuits,—this is the inconsistency which is charged upon us.

Precisely.

454   Verily, Glaucon, I said, glorious is the power of the art of contradiction!

Why do you say that?

Because I think that many a man falls into this practice against his will. When he thinks that he is reasoning he is really disputing, just because he is unable to define and divide that of which he is speaking; and he will pursue a merely verbal opposition in the spirit of contention and not of fair discussion.

Yes, he replied, that is very often the case; but what has that to do with us and our argument?

A great deal; for there is certainly a danger of our getting unintentionally into a verbal opposition.

In what way?

Why we valiantly and pugnaciously insist upon the verbal truth, that the same natures ought to have the same pursuits [3],

---

[3] Reading τὸ τὴν αὐτὴν φύσιν ὅτι τῶν αὐτῶν κ. τ. λ.

but we never considered at all what is the difference of nature implied in the words 'same' and 'other,' or what was our meaning in defining them and assigning different pursuits to different natures.

Why, no, he said, that was never considered by us.

I said: Suppose that by way of illustration we were to ask the question whether there is not an opposition in nature between bald men and hairy men; and if there is, why then, if bald men are cobblers, forbid the hairy men, or if the hairy men are cobblers, then forbid the bald men to be cobblers?

That would be a famous jest, he said.

Yes, I said, a jest; and why? the absurdity only arises from the circumstance that our original idea of differences of nature entering into the construction of the State did not extend in each case to every difference, but only to those differences which affected the pursuit in which the individual is engaged; thus, for example, a man or a woman who has the soul [4] of a physician may be said to be essentially the same.

True.

Whereas the physician and the carpenter are different?

Certainly.

And if, I said, the male and female sex appear to differ in their fitness for any art or pursuit, we should say that such pursuit or art ought to be assigned to one or the other of them; but if the difference consists only in women bearing and men begetting children, this does not amount to a proof that a woman differs from a man in that respect of which we are speaking; and we shall therefore continue to maintain that our guardians and their wives ought to have the same pursuits.

That is true, he said.

The next step will be to desire our opponent to show how, in reference to any of the pursuits or arts of citizens, the nature of 455 a woman differs from that of a man? That will be very fair; and perhaps he, like yourself, will reply that to give an answer on the instant is not easy; a little reflection is needed.

Yes, perhaps.

Suppose then that we invite him to come along with us in the

---

[4] Reading ἰατρικὸν μὲν καὶ ἰατρικὴν τὴν ψυχὴν ὄντας.

argument, and then we may hope to show him that there is no special function which a woman has in the administration of the State.

By all means.

Let us say to him: Come now, and we will ask you a question: —when you say that one man has natural gifts and another not, was this your meaning?—that the former will acquire a thing easily which the latter will have a difficulty in acquiring; a little learning will lead the one to discover a great deal; whereas the other, after a great deal of learning and application, will only forget what he has learned; or again, you may mean, that the one has a body which is a good servant to his mind, while the body of the other is at war with his mind:—these would be the sort of differences which distinguish the man of capacity from the man who is wanting in capacity?

That, he said, will be universally allowed.

Can you mention any pursuit of man in which the male sex has not all these qualities in a far higher degree than the female? Need I waste time in speaking of the art of weaving, and the management of pancakes and preserves, in which woman-kind does really appear to be great, and in which the superiority of the other sex is the most laughable thing in the world?

You are quite right, he replied, in maintaining the general inferiority of the female sex; at the same time many women are in many things superior to many men, though, speaking generally, what you say is true.

And so, I said, my friend, in the administration of a State neither a woman as a woman, nor a man as a man has any special function, but the gifts of nature are equally diffused in both sexes; all the pursuits of men are the pursuits of women also, and in all of them a woman is only a lesser man.

Very true.

Then are we to impose all our enactments on men and none of them on women?

That will never do.

One woman has a gift of healing, another not; one is a musician, and another is not a musician?

Very true.

And one woman has a turn for gymnastic and military exercises, 456 while another is unwarlike and hates gymnastics?

Beyond question.

And one woman is a philosopher, and another is an enemy of philosophy; one has spirit, and another is without spirit?

That is also true.

Then one woman will have the temper of a guardian, and another not; for was not the selection of the male guardians determined by these sort of differences?

That is true.

Then the woman has equally with the man the qualities which make a guardian; she differs only in degrees of strength?

That is obvious.

And those who have such qualities are the women who are to be selected as the companions and colleagues of our guardians, and who will resemble them in ability and character?

Very true.

And being of the same nature with them, ought they not to have the same pursuits?

They ought.

Then, as we were saying before, there is nothing unnatural in assigning music and gymnastic to the wives of the guardians. To that we come round again.

Very good.

The law which enacted this instead of being an impossibility or mere aspiration was agreeable to nature, and the contrary practice, which prevails at present, is in reality a violation of nature.

That appears to be true.

There was, first, the possibility, and secondly, the advantage of such an arrangement, which had to be considered?

Yes.

And the possibility has been allowed?

Yes.

And the advantage has next to be acknowledged?

That is the next question.

You would admit that the same education which makes a man a good guardian will make a woman a good guardian; for their original nature is the same?

Yes.

I should like to ask you a question: Would you say that all men are equal in excellence, or is one man better than another?
The latter.

And in our imaginary commonwealth which do you reckon the better, the guardians who have been brought up on our model system or the cobblers whose education has been cobbling?
What a ridiculous question!

That is your answer, I replied. Well, and may we not further say that these are the best of our citizens?
Far the best.

And will not these be the best women?
Yes, again I say the very best.

And can there be anything better for the interests of the State than that the men and women of a State should be as good as possible?
There can be nothing better.

457 And our course of music and gymnastic will accomplish this?
Certainly.

Then we have made an enactment not only possible but in the highest degree advantageous to the State?
True.

Then let the wives of our guardians strip, having virtue for their robe, and share in the toils of war and the defence of their country; only in the distribution of labour the lighter labours are to be assigned to the women, as being the weaker vessels, but in other respects their duties are to be the same. And as for the man who laughs at naked women exercising in gymnastics for the sake of the highest good, his laughter is,

'A fruit of unripe wisdom,'

which he gathers, and he himself is ignorant of what he is laughing at, or what he is about;—for that is, and ever will be, the best of sayings, that the useful is the noble and the hurtful the base.
Very true.

Here, then, is one difficulty in our law about women which we have escaped; the wave has not swallowed us up alive for enacting that the guardians of either sex should have all their pursuits in common; to the utility and possibility of this the argument is its own witness.

Yes, he said; that was a mighty wave which you have escaped.

Yes, I said, but a much greater is coming; you will not think much of this when you see the next.

Go on, he said; let me see.

The law, I said, which is the sequel of this and of all that has preceded, is to this effect,—'that the wives of these guardians are to be common, and their children also common, and no parent is to know his own child, nor any child his parent.'

Yes, he said, that is a much greater wave than the other; and the utility as well as the possibility of such a law is far more doubtful.

I do not think, I said, that there can be any dispute about the very great utility of having wives and children in common; the possibility is quite another matter, and will be very much disputed.

I think, he said, that a good many doubts may be raised about both questions.

You insist on joining the two questions, I said.   Now I meant that you should admit the utility; and in this way, as I thought, I should escape from one of them, and then there would remain only the possibility.

But that little attempt is detected, and therefore you will please to give a defence of both.

Well, I said, I submit to my fate, yet grant me a little favour: let me feast my mind as day-dreamers are in the habit of feasting 458 themselves with their own dreams when they are walking alone; for before they have discovered any means of effecting their wishes—that is a matter which never troubles them—they would rather not tire themselves by thinking about possibilities; but assuming that what they desire is already theirs, they pursue their plan, and delight in detailing what they are going to do when their wish has come true—that is a way which they have of not doing much good to a capacity which was never good for much.   And I too am beginning to lose heart, and would wish to reserve the question of possibility; and assuming this, for the present only, if you will allow me I will proceed to enquire what measures the rulers will take for the execution of the plan, which, if executed, I will prove to be of the greatest use to the State and to the guardians.   I will ask you, if you have no objection, to assist me, first of all, in considering the advantages of this, and then I will return to the question of possibility.

I have no objection; proceed.

First, I think that if our rulers and their auxiliaries are to be worthy of the name which they bear, there must be willingness to obey in the one and the power of command in the other; the guardians must themselves obey the laws and imitate their spirit in the details which are entrusted to them.

That is right, he said.

You, I said, in the capacity of their legislator, having selected the men, will now select the women who are most akin to them and give them to them, and they will live in common houses and meet at common meals. None of them will have anything specially his or her own; and they will be together and associate at gymnastic exercises, and be brought up together. And so they will be drawn by a necessity of their natures to have intercourse with each other: necessity is not too strong a word I think?

Yes, he said;—necessity, not geometrical, but another sort of necessity which lovers know, and which is far more convincing and constraining to the mass of mankind.

True, I said; and this, Glaucon, like all the rest, must proceed after an orderly fashion,—in a city of the blessed, licentiousness is an unholy thing which the rulers will forbid.

Yes, he said, and so they ought.

Then clearly our plan will be to make matrimony as holy as possible, and the most beneficial marriages will be the most holy?

459 Exactly.

And how can marriages be made most beneficial?—that is a question which I put to you, because I observe in your house hunting dogs and of the nobler sort of birds not a few. Now, do tell me, did you ever attend to their pairing and breeding?

In what respect?

Why, in the first place, although they are all of a good sort, are not some better than others?

True.

And do you breed from them all indifferently, or do you take care to breed from the best only?

From the best.

And do you take the oldest or the youngest, or only those that are of ripe age?

I choose only those of ripe age.

And if none of this care was taken in the breeding, your dogs and birds would deteriorate?

Certainly.

And the same principle holds of horses and of animals in general?

Undoubtedly.

Good heavens! my dear friend, I said, what consummate skill will our rulers need if the same principle holds of the human species!

Certainly, the same principle holds; but why does this involve such a high requirement?

Because, I said, our rulers will have to practise upon the body corporate with medicines. Now you know that when patients do not require medicines, but have only to be put under a regimen, the inferior sort of practitioner is deemed to be good enough; but when medicine has to be given, then the doctor should be more of a man.

That is quite true, he said; but what do you mean?

I mean, I replied, that our rulers will find a considerable dose of falsehood and deceit necessary for the good of their subjects: we were saying that they might be used with advantage as medicines.

True, he said.

And this lawful use of them seems likely to be often needed in the regulations of marriages and births.

How will that be?

Why, I said, the principle has been already laid down that the best of either sex should be united with the best as often as possible, and the inferior with the inferior; and they are to rear the offspring of the one sort of union, but not of the other; for this is the only way of keeping the flock in prime condition. Now these goings on must be a secret which the rulers only know, or there will be a further danger of our herd, as the guardians may be termed, breaking out into rebellion.

Very true, he said.

Had we not better appoint certain festivals at which the brides and bridegrooms will meet, and there will be sacrifices offered

460 and suitable hymeneal songs composed by our poets: the number of weddings is a matter which must be left to the discretion of the rulers, whose aim will be to preserve the average of population; and there are many things which they will have to consider, such as the effects of wars and diseases and any similar agencies, in order to prevent the State becoming either too large or too small.

Very true, he replied.

We shall have to invent some ingenious kind of lots which the less worthy may draw on each occasion of meeting, and then he will accuse his own ill-luck and not the rulers.

To be sure, he said.

And I think that our braver and better youth, besides their other honours and rewards, might have greater facilities of inter-course with women given them; their bravery is a good pretext, and such fathers ought to have as many sons as possible.

True.

And the proper officers, whether male or female or both, for offices are to be held by women as well as by men—

Yes.

The proper officers will take the offspring of the good parents to the pen or fold, and there they will deposit them with certain nurses who dwell in a separate quarter; but the offspring of the inferior, or of the better when they chance to be deformed, they will conceal in some mysterious, unknown place. Decency will be respected.

Yes, he said, that will require to be done if the breed of the guardians is to be kept pure.

They will provide for their nurture, and will bring the mothers to the fold when they are full of milk, taking the greatest possible care that no mother recognizes her own child; and other wet-nurses may be had if any more are required. Care will also be taken that the process of suckling shall not be tedious to them; and they will have no trouble or getting up at night, but will hand over all this to the nurses and attendants.

You suppose the wives of our guardians to have a fine easy time of it when they are having children.

Why, said I, and so they ought. Let us, however, proceed with our scheme. As we were saying, the parents should be in the prime of life.

Very true.

And what is the prime of life? May not that be defined as a period of about twenty years in a woman's life, and thirty in a man's?

Which years do you mean to include?

A woman, I said, may begin to bear children to the State at twenty years of age, and continue to bear until forty; a man may begin at five-and-twenty, when he has passed the point at which the speed of life is greatest, and continue to beget children until he be fifty-five.

Certainly, he said, both in men and women that is the prime 461 of physical as well as of intellectual vigour.

Any one above or below those ages who takes part in the public hymeneals shall be said to have done an unholy and unrighteous thing; he is the father of a child who, if he steals into life, will have been conceived under other auspices than those of sacrifice and prayers, which at each hymeneal priestesses and priests and the whole city will offer, that the new generation may be better and more useful than their good and useful parents: instead of this his child will be the offspring of darkness and strange lust.

Very true, he replied.

And the same law will apply to any one of those within the prescribed age who forms a connection with any woman in the prime of life without the sanction of the rulers; for we shall say that he is raising up a bastard to the State, uncertified and unconsecrated.

Very true, he replied.

This applies, however, only to those who are within the specified age: after that we allow them to range at will, except that a man may not marry his daughter or his daughter's daughter, or his mother or his mother's mother; and women, on the other hand, are prohibited from marrying their sons or fathers, or son's son or father's father, and so on in either direction. And we grant all this, accompanying the permission with strict orders to them to do all they can to prevent any embryo which may come into being from seeing the light; and if any force a way to the birth, they must understand that the offspring of such an union cannot be maintained, and make their arrangements accordingly.

That also, he said, is a reasonable proposition. But how will they know who are fathers and daughters, and so on?

They will never know. The way will be this:—dating from the day of the hymeneal, the bridegroom who was then married will call all the male children who are born ten and seven months afterwards his sons, and the female children his daughters, and they will call him father, and he will call their children's children his grandchildren, and they will call the elder generation grandfathers and grandmothers. And those who were born at the same time with them they will term brothers and sisters, and they are not to intermarry. This, however, is not to be understood as an absolute prohibition of such marriages; if the lot favours them, and they have the sanction of the Pythian oracle, the law will still allow them.

Quite right, he replied.

Such is the scheme according to which the guardians of our State are to have their wives and families in common. I must now make the argument prove that this community is consistent with the rest of our polity, and also that nothing can be better—that is what you want?

462 Yes, certainly.

And shall we begin by asking ourselves what we conceive to be the greatest good, and what ought to be the chief aim of the legislator in the organization of a State, and what is the greatest evil, and then consider whether our previous description has the mark and stamp of the good or of the evil?

By all means.

And can there be any greater evil than discord and distraction and plurality where unity ought to reign? or any greater good than the bond of unity?

There cannot.

And there is unity where there is community of pleasures and pains—where all the citizens are glad or sorry on the same occasions?

No doubt.

Yes; and where there is no common but only private feeling, that disorganizes a State—when you have one half of the world triumphing and the other sorrowing at the same events happening to the city and the citizens?

Certainly.

Such differences commonly originate in a disagreement about the use of the terms 'meum' and 'tuum,' mine and his.

Exactly.

And is not that the best-ordered State in which the greatest number of persons apply the terms 'mine' and 'not mine' in the same way to the same thing?

True, very true.

Or that again which most nearly approaches to the condition of the individual—as in the body, when but a finger is hurt, the whole frame, drawn towards the soul and forming one realm under the ruling power therein, feels the hurt and sympathizes all together with the part affected, and then we say that the man has a pain in his finger; or again, in any other part, when there is a sensation of pain or pleasure at suffering or alleviation of suffering, the same expression is used?

Yes, he replied, that is as you say; and I agree with you that in the best-ordered State there is the nearest approach to this common feeling which you describe.

Then when any one of the citizens experiences any good or evil, the whole State will make his case their own, and either rejoice or sorrow with him?

Yes, he said, that will be true in a well-ordered State.

It will now be time, I said, for us to return to our State and see whether this or any other form is most in accordance with these principles.

Very good.

Our State like every other has rulers and subjects.   463

That is true.

All of whom will call one another citizens?

Of course.

But is there not another name which people give to their rulers in other States?

Generally they call them masters, but in democratic States they simply call them rulers.

And what name besides that of citizens do the people give the rulers in our State?

The name of preservers and auxiliaries, he replied.

And what do the rulers call the people?

Their maintainers and foster-fathers.

And what do they call them in other States?

Slaves.

And what do the rulers call one another in other States?

Fellow-rulers.

And what in ours?

Fellow-guardians.

Did you ever know an example in other States of a ruler who would speak of one of his colleagues as a friend and of another as alien to him?

Yes, that is very common.

And the friend he describes and regards as one in whom he has an interest, and the other as one in whom he has no interest.

Exactly.

But would any of your guardians speak of one of their fellows as a friend and of another as alien to him?

Certainly not; for every one whom they meet will be regarded by them either as a brother or sister, or father or mother, or son or daughter, or as the child or parent of those who are thus connected with him.

That is an admirable answer, I said; but let me ask you one small question: Will you give them the names of family ties only, or are they in all their actions to conform to these names? For example, in the use of the word 'father', would the care of a father be implied and the filial reverence and duty and obedience to him which the law commands? and is the violator of these duties to be regarded as an impious and unrighteous person who is not likely to receive much good either from the hands of God or man? Are these to be the strains which the children will hear repeated in their ears by all the citizens about their parents and kindred when they are pointed out to them?

These, he said, and none other; for what can be more ridiculous than for them to utter the names of family ties with the lips only and not to act upon them?

Then in our city the language of harmony and concord will be more often heard than in any other. As I was describing before, when any one is well or ill, the universal word will be 'mine is well' or 'mine is ill.'

464   Most true.

And were we not saying also that they would have their pleasures and pains in common, and that their mode of thinking or speaking would coincide with the fact?

Yes, and that is true.

And they will have a common interest in the same which they will call 'my own,' and having this common interest they will have a common feeling of pleasure and pain?

Yes, they will have a far greater community of feeling.

And the reason of this, over and above the general constitution of the State, will be that the guardians have a community of women and children?

That will be the chief reason.

And that this unity of feeling will be the greatest good was implied in our own comparison of a well-ordered State to the relation of the body and the members, when affected by pleasure or pain?

That was acknowledged, and very rightly.

Then the community of wives and children is clearly the source of the greatest good to the State?

Certainly.

And this agrees with the other principle which we were affirming,—that the guardians were not to have houses or lands or any other property; their pay was to be their food, which they were to receive from the other citizens, and they were only to spend in common: that was all designed to preserve their true character of guardians.

Right, he replied.

Both the community of property and the community of families, as I am saying, tend to make them more truly guardians; they will not tear the city in pieces by differing about 'meum' and 'tuum;' the one dragging any acquisition which he has made into a private house which is his, and which has a separate wife and separate children and private pleasures and pains; but all are affected as far as may be by all the same pleasures and pains because they are all of one opinion about what is near and dear to them, and therefore all tend towards a common end.

Certainly, he replied.

And as they have nothing but their persons which they can call their own, suits and complaints will have no existence among them; they will be free from all those quarrels of which money or children or relations are the occasion.

That of course follows.

Neither can trials for assault or insult ever be expected to occur among them. For that equals should defend themselves against equals we shall surely maintain to be fair and right; and in this way we shall oblige them to keep themselves in condition.

465   That is good, he said.

Yes; and there is this further good in the law—that if a man has cause of offence against another he will satisfy his resentment and be less likely to make a commotion in the State.

Certainly.

To the elder shall be assigned the duty of ruling and chastising the younger.

Clearly.

Nor can there be a doubt that the younger will not strike or do any other violence to an elder, unless the magistrates command him; nor is he likely to be disrespectful to him in any way. For there are two guardians, shame and fear, mighty to prevent him: shame, which makes men refrain from laying hands on those who are to them in the relation of parents; fear, that the injured one will be succoured by the others who are his brothers, sons, fathers.

That is true, he replied.

Then in every way the laws will help the citizens to keep peace with one another.

Yes, there will be a certainty of peace.

And as the guardians will never quarrel among themselves there will be no danger of the rest of the city being divided either against them or against one another.

None whatever.

I hardly like to speak of the little meannesses of which they will be rid, for they are beneath mention. Such, for example, as the flattery of the rich by the poor, and all the pains and pangs of bringing up a family, finding the money to buy the necessaries of their household, borrowing and then repudiating, getting how they can, and giving the money into the hands of women and slaves to keep: what people suffer in this way is mean enough and obvious enough, and not worth speaking of.

Yes, he said, a man has no need of eyes in order to perceive that.

And from all that they will be delivered, and their life will be blessed as the life of Olympic victors and yet more blessed.

How can that be?

Why, I said, they are counted happy in receiving a part only of the happiness which is the lot of our citizens, who have won a more glorious victory and have a more complete maintenance at the public cost. For the victory which they have won is the salvation of the whole State; and the crown with which they and their children are crowned is the fullness of all that life needs; they receive rewards from the hands of their country while living and after death have an honourable burial.

Yes, he said, they are indeed glorious rewards.

Do you remember, I said, how in the course of the previous discussion [5] some one who shall be nameless accused us of making 466 our guardians unhappy—they had nothing and might have possessed all things—to whom we replied that on some future occasion we might perhaps consider the question, but that, as at present advised, we would make our guardians truly guardians, and that we were not fashioning any particular class with a view to their happiness, but in order that the whole State might be the happiest possible?

Yes, I remember.

And what do you say now that the life of our protectors is made out to be far better and nobler than that of Olympic victors; will you compare such a life with that of shoemakers, or any other artisans, or of husbandmen?

Certainly not.

At the same time I ought to repeat what I was then saying, that if any of our guardians shall get into his head the youthful conceit, that he being a guardian ought to have a happiness which would make him no longer a guardian, and is not content with this safe and harmonious life, than which, in our judgment, there never was a better, but shall proceed to monopolize the State, then he will have to learn out of Hesiod, that he verily was a wise man who said 'half is better than the whole.'

If he were to consult me, I should say to him: Stay where you are, having the promise of such a life.

And you agree then, I said, that men and women are to have a common way of life such as we have described—common education, common children; and they are to watch over the citizens in common whether abiding in the city or going out to war; they are to guard together, and to hunt together like dogs; and always and in all things women are to share with the men? And this will be for the best, and in doing this they will not violate the natural relation?

I agree with you, he replied.

The enquiry, I said, has yet to be made, whether such a community will be found possible—as among other animals so also among men—and if possible, in what way possible?

That, he said, is just the question which I was going to ask.

As to war, I said, there is no difficulty in seeing how that will be managed.

How will that be? he asked.

Why, of course they will go on expeditions together; and will take with them any of their children who are strong enough, that, like the children of artisans in general, they may look on at the work, which they will have to do when they are grown 467 up; and besides looking on they will be able to help and be of use in war, and to wait upon their fathers and mothers. Did you never observe in the arts how the potters' boys look on and help, long before they touch the wheel?

Certainly.

And shall potters be more careful than our guardians in educating their children and giving them the opportunity of seeing and practising their duties?

That would be ridiculous, he said.

There is another thing; which is the effect on the parents, with whom, as with other animals, the presence of their cubs will be the greatest incentive to valour.

That is quite true, Socrates; and yet if they are defeated, which may often happen in war, how great the danger is! the children will be lost as well as their parents, and the State will never recover.

True, I said; but would you never allow them to run any risk?

I am far from saying that.

Well, but if they are ever to run a risk should they not run the risk when there is a chance of their improvement?

Clearly.

Whether the future soldiers do or do not see war in the days of their youth is a very important matter, for the sake of which some risk may fairly be incurred.

Yes, that is very important.

Then, in the first place, we must provide that the children should see war, and then contrive a way of safety for them; thus all will be well.

True.

Their parents may be supposed to have ordinary common sense and understanding of the risks of war; they will know what expeditions are safe and what dangerous?

That may be supposed.

And they will take them on the safe expeditions and be cautious about the dangerous ones?

True.

And they will give them as commanders experienced veterans who will be their leaders and teachers?

Yes, that is very proper.

Still, the dangers of war cannot always be foreseen; there is a good deal of chance about them?

True.

Then against such chances the children must be at once furnished with wings, in order that in the hour of need they may fly away and escape.

What do you mean? he said.

I mean that we must mount them on horses in their earliest youth and take them on horseback to see war, in order that they may learn to ride [6]; the horses must not be spirited and warlike, but the most tractable and yet the swiftest that can be had. In this way they will get an excellent view of what is hereafter to be their business; and if there is danger they have only to 468 follow their elder leaders and escape.

I believe that you are right, he said.

Next, as to war; what are to be the relations of your soldiers to one another and to their enemies? I should be inclined to propose that the soldier who leaves his rank or throws away

---

[6] Reading διδαξομένους.

his arms, or is guilty of any other act of cowardice, should be degraded into the rank of a husbandman or artisan. What do you think?

By all means, I should say.

And he who allows himself to be taken prisoner may even be made a present of to his enemies; he is their prey and they may do as they like with him.

Certainly.

But the hero who has distinguished himself, what shall be done to him? In the first place, he shall receive honour in the army from his youthful comrades; every one of them in succession shall crown him. What do you say to that?

I approve.

And what do you say to his receiving the right hand of fellowship?

To that too, I agree.

But I suspect that you will hardly agree to my next proposal.

What is that?

That he should kiss and be kissed by them.

That I entirely approve, and should be disposed to add another clause: Let no one whom he has a mind to kiss refuse to be kissed by him while the expedition lasts. So that if there be a lover in the army, whether his love be youth or maiden, he may be more eager to win the prize of valour.

That is good, I said. That the brave man is to have more wives than others has been already determined; and he is to have first choices in such matters more than others, in order that he may have as many children as possible.

That was agreed.

And the propriety of thus honouring brave youths may be proved out of Homer; who tells how Ajax [7], after he had distinguished himself in battle, was rewarded with long chines, which seems to be a complement appropriate to a hero in the flower of his age, being not only a tribute of honour but also a very strengthening thing.

Very true, he said.

Then in this, I said, Homer will be our teacher; and we too, at

---

sacrifices and on the like occasions, will honour the brave with hymns

> 'and seats of precedence, and meats and flowing goblets[8];'

not only honouring them, but also exercising them in virtue.

That, he replied, is excellent.

Good, I said; and when a man dies gloriously in war shall we not say, in the first place, that he is of the golden race?

To be sure.

Nay, have we not the authority of Hesiod for affirming that when they are dead

> 'They are holy angels upon the earth, authors of good, averters of ill, the 469 guardians of speaking men[9]?'

And we shall believe him.

And suppose that we enquire of the god how we are to order the sepulture of divine and heroic personages, and do as he bids?

By all means.

In ages to come we will do service to them and worship at their shrines as heroes. And not only they but all other benefactors who die from age, or in any other way, shall be admitted to the same honours.

That is very right, he said.

Next, how shall our soldiers treat their enemies? What do you say about this?

In what respect do you mean?

I mean, shall they be made slaves? Do you think that Hellenes ought to enslave Hellenes, or allow others to enslave them, as far as they can help? Should not their custom be to spare them, considering the danger which there is that the whole race may one day fall under the yoke of the barbarians?

To spare them is infinitely better.

Then no Hellene should be owned by them as a slave; that is a rule which they will observe and advise the other Hellenes to observe.

Certainly, he said; that is the way to unite them against the barbarians and make them keep their hands off one another.

Next as to the slain; ought the conquerors, I said, to take anything but their armour? Does not the practice of despoiling an enemy afford an excuse for not facing the battle? They skulk

---

[8] Iliad, viii. 162.   [9] Works and Days, 110.

about the dead, pretending to be executing a duty, and many an army before now has been lost from this love of plunder.

Very true.

And is there not illiberality and avarice, and a degree of meanness and womanishness, in robbing a corpse and making the dead body an enemy when the real enemy has walked away and left only his fighting gear behind him,—is not this rather like a dog who cannot get at his assailant, quarrelling with the stones which strike him instead?

That is exactly parallel, he said.

Then we must abstain from spoiling the dead or hindering their burial?

Yes, he replied, that we must.

470 Neither, as our object is to preserve good feeling among the Hellenes, shall we offer up the arms of Hellenes at any rate, at the temples of the gods; nay, we have some reason to be afraid that such an offering may be a pollution unless commanded by the god himself.

Very true.

Again, as to the devastation of an Hellenic territory or the burning of houses, what is to be the practice?

Will you let me have the pleasure, he said, of hearing your opinion upon this?

Both should be forbidden, in my judgment; I would take the annual produce and no more. Would you wish to know why I say this?

Very much.

Why, I imagine that as there is a difference in the names 'discord' and 'war,' there is also a difference in their natures; the one is expressive of what is internal and domestic, the other of what is external and foreign; and the first of these is properly termed discord, and only the second, war.

That is a very just distinction, he replied.

Shall I further add that the Hellenic race is all united by ties of blood and friendship and alien and strange to the barbarians?

Very good, he said.

And therefore when Hellenes fight with barbarians and barbarians with Hellenes, they will be described by us as being at war when they fight, and by nature in a state of war, and this kind of antagonism is to be called war; but when Hellenes fight with one another we shall say that they are by nature friends, and at such a time Hellas is in a state of disorder and distraction, and enmity of that sort is to be called discord.

In that view, I agree.

Consider then, I said, when that which is now acknowledged by us to be discord occurs, and a city is divided, if both parties destroy the lands and burn the houses of one another, how wicked does the strife appear—how can either of them be a lover of his country? for no true lover of his country would tear in pieces his nurse and mother: there might be reason in the conqueror depriving the conquered of their harvest, but still they would have the idea of peace in their hearts and not of everlasting war.

Yes, he said, that is a better temper than the other.

And when you found a state, are you not intending to found an Hellenic state?

Of course, he replied.

Then will not the citizens be good and civilized?

To be sure.

And will they not be lovers of Hellas, and think of Hellas as their own land, and share in the common temples?

Most certainly.

And any difference that arises among Hellenes will be regarded by them as discord only—a quarrel among friends, which is not 471 to be called a war?

Certainly not.

Then they will quarrel as those who intend some day to make up their quarrel?

Certainly.

Correcting them in love, not punishing them with a view to enslaving or destroying them; as correctors, not as enemies?

That is very true.

And as they are Hellenes themselves they will not devastate Hellas, nor will they burn houses, nor ever suppose that the whole population of a city—men, women, and children—are equally their enemies, for they know that the guilt of war is always confined to a few persons and that the many are their friends. And for all these reasons they will be unwilling to waste their lands and rase their houses; their enmity to them will only last until the many innocent sufferers have compelled the guilty few to give satisfaction?

I agree, he said, in thinking that these are the sort of rules which our citizens ought to observe towards their (Hellenic) adversaries; in their wars with barbarians the present practice of the Hellenes to one another will afford a sufficient rule.

Let this then be enacted for the observance of our guardians:— that they are neither to devastate the ground or to burn houses.

Yes, let that be enacted; and we may safely maintain that this and all our previous enactments are excellent.

But still, Socrates, I must say, that if you are allowed to go on in this way you will entirely forget the other question which in entering on this discussion you put aside, viz. the enquiry as to whether such an order of things is possible, and if possible, in what way possible? For, admitting the possibility, I am quite ready to acknowledge that the plan has every sort of advantage. I will add, what you have omitted, that they will be the bravest of warriors, ever exhorting one another by the names of fathers, brothers, and sons, and therefore never leaving their ranks; and if you suppose the women to join their armies, whether in the same rank or in the rear, either as a terror to the enemy, or as auxiliaries in case of need, I know that this will make them altogether invincible; and there are many domestic advantages which might be mentioned as well, and these also I fully acknowledge. But, as I admit all these advantages and as many more as you please, if this State of yours were to come into being, say no more of that; and let us now come to the question of possibility and ways and means—all the rest may be left.

472   If I loiter[10] for a moment, you instantly make a raid upon me, I said, and have no mercy; I have hardly escaped the first and second waves, and you don't seem to be aware that you are now bringing upon me the third, which is the greatest. When you have seen this, and heard the roar, I think you will acknowledge that some fear and hesitation was natural, considering the marvellous nature of the proposal which I have to offer for consideration.

The more appeals of this sort which you make, he said, the more determined are we that you should tell us how such a State is possible: speak out and at once.

[10] Reading στραγγευομένῳ.

Let me begin by reminding you that we found our way hither in the search after justice and injustice.

True, he replied; but what makes you say this?

I was only going to ask whether, if we have discovered them, we are to require that the just man should in nothing fail of absolute justice; or may we be satisfied with an approximation, and the attainment of a higher degree of justice than is to be found in other men?

The approximation will be enough.

Then the nature of justice and the perfectly just man, and of injustice and the perfectly unjust, was only an ideal? We were to look at them in order that we might judge of our own happiness and unhappiness according to the standard which they exhibited and the degree in which we resembled them, not with any view of demonstrating the possibility of their existence?

That is true, he said.

How would a painter be the worse painter because, after having minutely painted an ideal of a perfectly beautiful man, he was unable to show that any such man could ever have existed?

He would not.

Well, and were we not creating an ideal of a perfect State?

To be sure.

And is our theory a worse theory because we are unable to prove the possibility of a city being ordered in the manner described?

Surely not, he replied.

That must be acknowledged, I said. But if, at your request, I am to try and show how and under what condition the possibility is highest, I must ask you, having this in view, to repeat your former admissions.

What admissions?

I want to know whether words do not surpass realities; and 473 whether the actual, whatever a man may think, does not fall short of the truth? What do you say?

I admit that.

Then you must not insist on my proving that the actual State will in every respect agree with the description of the ideal: if we are only able to discover how a city may be governed nearly in the way that we propose, you will admit that we have discovered the possibility which you demand; and that will content you. I am sure that I should be contented with that—will not you ?

Yes, I will.

Then let me next endeavour to show what is that fault in States which is the cause of their present maladministration, and what is the least change which will enable a State to pass into the truer form; and let the change, if possible, be of one thing only, or, if not, of two; at any rate, let the changes be as few and slight as possible.

Certainly, he replied.

I think then, I said, that there might be a revolution if there were just one change, which is not a slight or easy though still a possible one.

What is that ? he said.

Now then, I said, I go to meet that which I liken to the greatest of waves, yet shall the word be spoken, even though the running over of the laughter of the wave shall just sink me beneath the waters of laughter and dishonour; and do you attend to me.

Proceed, he said.

I said: Until, then, philosophers are kings, or the kings and princes of this world have the spirit and power of philosophy, and political greatness and wisdom meet in one, and those commoner natures who follow either to the exclusion of the other are compelled to stand aside, cities will never cease from ill—no, nor the human race, as I believe—and then only will this our State have a possibility of life and behold the light of day: this was what I wanted but was afraid to say, my dear Glaucon; for to see that there is no other way either of private or public happiness is indeed a hard thing.

Socrates, he said, what a speech is this! I would have you consider that the word which you have uttered is one at which numerous persons, and very respectable persons too, will in a moment pull off their coats, as I may in a figure say, and in light 474 array, taking up any weapon that comes to hand, they will run at you might and main, intending to do heaven knows what; and if you don't prepare an answer, and put yourself in motion, you will be ' pared by their fine wits,' and no mistake.

You got me into the scrape, I said.

And I was quite right, he said; however, I will do all I can to get you out; but I can only give you wishes and exhortations, and also, perhaps, I may be able to fit answers into your questions better than another—that is all. And now, having such an auxiliary, you must do your best to show the unbelievers that you are right.

I ought to try, I said, as I have an offer of such valuable assistance. And I think that, if there is to be a chance of our escaping, we must define who these philosophers are who, as we say, are to rule in the State; then we shall be able to defend ourselves: there will be discovered to be some natures who ought to rule and to study philosophy; and others who are not born to be philosophers, and are meant to be followers rather than leaders.

Then now for a definition, he said.

Follow me, I said, and I hope that I may somehow or other be able to give you a satisfactory explanation.

Proceed, he replied.

I daresay that you remember, and therefore I need not remind you, that a lover, if he is worthy of the name, ought to show his love, not to one part of a class rather than another, but to the whole.

I believe that I must ask you to explain, for I really do not understand.

I do not think, I replied, that you should say that; a man of pleasure like you ought to know that all who are in the flower of their youth do in a manner raise a pang or emotion in a lover's breast, and seem to be worthy of his affectionate regards. Is not this a way which you have with the fair: one, because he has a snub nose, has the epithet 'naïve' used in his praise; another's beak, as you say, has a royal look; while he who is neither snub nor hooked has the grace of regularity: the dark visage is manly, and the white are angels; and as to the sweet, 'honey pale,' as they are called, what is the very name but the invention of a lover who uses these pet names, and is not averse to paleness on the cheek of youth? In a word, there is no excuse which you will not make, and nothing which you will not say, in order to pre- 475 serve for your use every flower that has the bloom of youth.

If you are determined to make me play the part of a lover, I am ready to be your illustration, if I can be of any service to the argument.

And what do you say of lovers of wine? Do you not see them doing the same? They are glad of any pretext of drinking any wine.

Very good.

And the same is true of ambitious men; if they cannot be generals, they are willing to be captains; and if they cannot be honoured by really great and important persons, they are glad to be honoured by inferior people,—but honour of some kind they must have?

Exactly.

Once more let me ask: Does he who desires any class of goods, desire the whole class or a part only?

The whole.

And may we not say of the philosopher that he is a lover, not of a part of wisdom only, but of the whole?

True.

Then he who dislikes knowledge, especially in youth, when he has no power of judging what is good and what is not good, such an one we maintain not to be a philosopher or a lover of knowledge, just as he who refuses his food is not hungry, and may be said to have a bad appetite and not a good one?

And in that we are right, he said.

Whereas he who has a taste for every sort of knowledge and who is curious to learn and is never satisfied, may be justly termed a philosopher? Is not that true?

Glaucon said: If curiosity makes a philosopher, you will find many a strange being claiming the name. For all the lovers of sights have a delight in learning, and will therefore have to be included. Musical amateurs, too, are a folk wonderfully out of place among philosophers, as they are the last persons in the world who would come to anything like a philosophical discussion, if they could help, while they run about at the Dionysiac festivals as if their ears were under an engagement to hear every chorus; whether the performance is in town or country—that makes no difference—they are there. Now are we to maintain that all these and any who have similar tastes, as well as the professors of minor arts, are philosophers?

Certainly not, I replied, they are only an imitation.

He said: But who are the true philosophers?

Those, I said, who are lovers of the sight of truth.

That is also good, he said; but I should like to know what you mean?

To another, I replied, I might have a difficulty in explaining; but I am sure that you will admit a proposition which I am about to state.

What is that?

That beauty is the reverse of ugliness; they are two and not one?

Certainly.

And as they are two, each of them is one?   476

True again.

And the same holds of every class—just and unjust, good and evil: taken singly, each of them is one; but in all the various combinations of them with things and persons and with one another, they are seen in various lights and appear many?

That is true.

And this is the distinction which I draw between the sight-loving, art-loving, practical class and those of whom I am speaking, and who are alone worthy of the name of philosophers.

How do you distinguish them? he said.

The lovers of sounds and sights, I replied, are, as I conceive, fond of fine tones and colours and forms and all the artificial products that are made out of them, but their mind is incapable of seeing or loving absolute beauty.

That is true, he replied.

Few are they who are able to attain the sight of absolute beauty.

Very true.

And he who, having a sense of beautiful things has no sense of absolute beauty, or who, if another lead him to a knowledge of that beauty is unable to follow—of such an one I ask, Is he awake or in a dream only? Reflect: is not the dreamer, either awake or asleep, one who puts the resemblance in the place of the real object?

I should certainly say that such an one was dreaming.

But take the case of the other, who recognizes the existence of absolute beauty and is able to distinguish the idea from the objects which participate in the idea, neither putting the objects in the place of the idea nor the idea in the place of the objects— is he a dreamer, or is he awake?

He is the reverse of a dreamer, he replied.

And may we not say that the mind of the one has knowledge and that the mind of the other has opinion only?

Certainly.

But suppose that the latter quarrels with us and disputes our statement, can we administer any soothing cordial or advice to him, without revealing to him that there is sad disorder in his wits?

That is what is wanted, he replied.

Come, then, and let us think of something to tell him. Suppose we begin by assuring him that he is welcome to any knowledge he may have, and that we rejoice to see him in possession of such a blessing. But we should like to ask him a question: Does he who has knowledge know something or nothing? (You must answer for him.)

I answer that he knows something.

Something that is or is not?

Something that is; for how can that which is not ever be known?

477 And are we assured, after looking at the matter in every point of view, that perfect existence is or may be perfectly known, but that the absolutely non-existent is utterly unknown and unknowable?

Nothing can be more certain.

Good. But if there be anything which is of such a nature as to be and not to be, that will have a place intermediate between pure being and the absolute negation of being?

Yes, between them.

And, as knowledge corresponded to being and ignorance to not being, for that intermediate between being and not being there has to be discovered a corresponding intermediate between ignorance and knowledge, if there be such?

Certainly.

Do we admit the existence of opinion?

Undoubtedly.

As being the same with knowledge, or another faculty?

Another faculty.

Then opinion and knowledge have to do with different kinds of matter corresponding to this difference of faculties?

Yes.

And knowledge is relative to existence and knows existence: but I will first make a division.

What division?

I will begin by placing faculties in a class by themselves: they are powers in us and in all things by which we do as we do. Sight and hearing, for example, I should call faculties. Have I clearly explained the class which I mean?

Yes, I quite understand.

Then let me tell you my view about them. I do not see them, and therefore the distinctions of figure, colour, and the like, which enable me to discern the differences of some things, do not apply to them. In speaking of a faculty I think only of the end and working; and that which has the same end and the same operation I call the same faculty, but that which has another end and another operation I call different. Would that be your way of speaking?

Yes.

To return. Would you place knowledge among faculties, or in some other class?

Certainly knowledge is a faculty and the most powerful of all faculties.

And is opinion also a faculty?

Certainly, he said; for opinion is that with which we are able to form an opinion.

And yet you were surely admitting a little while ago that knowledge is not the same as opinion?

Why, yes, said he: for how can any reasonable being ever 478 identify that which is infallible with that which errs?

That is very good, I said, and clearly shows that there is a distinction between them which is admitted by us?

Yes.

Then knowledge and opinion having distinct powers have also distinct ends or subject-matters?

That is certain.

Being is the end or subject-matter of knowledge, and knowledge is the knowledge of being?

Yes.

And opinion is to have an opinion?

Yes.

And is the subject-matter of opinion the same as the subject-matter of knowledge?

Nay, he replied, that is already disproven; if difference in faculty implies difference in the end or subject-matter, and opinion and knowledge are equally faculties and also distinct faculties, the subject-matter of knowledge cannot be the same as the subject-matter of opinion.

Then if being is the subject-matter of knowledge, something else must be the subject-matter of opinion?

Yes, something else.

Well then, is not-being the subject-matter of opinion? or, rather, how can there be an opinion at all about not-being? Reflect: when a man has an opinion, has he not an opinion about something? Can he have an opinion which is an opinion about nothing?

Impossible.

He who has an opinion has an opinion about some one thing?

Yes.

And not-being is not one thing but, properly speaking, nothing?

True.

Of not-being, ignorance was assumed to be the necessary correlative; of being, knowledge?

True, he said.

Then opinion is not concerned either with being or with not-being?

Not with either.

And can therefore neither be ignorance nor knowledge?

That seems to be true.

Then is opinion to be sought without and beyond either of them in a greater clearness than knowledge, or in a greater darkness than ignorance?

Neither.

Then I suppose that opinion appears to you darker than knowledge, but lighter than ignorance?

Both; and in no small degree.

And also to be within and between them?

Yes.

Then you would infer that opinion is intermediate?

No question.

But were we not saying before, that if anything appeared to be of a sort which is and is not at the same time, that sort of thing would appear also to lie in the interval between pure being and absolute not-being; and that the corresponding faculty is neither knowledge nor ignorance, but will also be discovered in the interval between them?

True.

And in that interval there has now been discovered a thing which we call opinion?

There has.

Then what remains to be discovered is the object which partakes equally of the nature of being and not-being, and cannot rightly be termed the pure form of either; this unknown term, when discovered, we may justly hail as the subject of opinion, and assign to each their due—to the extremes the faculty of the extreme, and to the mean the faculty of the mean.

True.

This being premised, I would ask the gentleman who is of 479 opinion that there is no absolute or unchangeable idea of beauty —in whose opinion the beautiful is diverse—he, I say, your lover of beautiful sights, who cannot bear to be told that the just is one, or the beautiful is one, or that anything is one—to him I would appeal, saying, Best of men, of all these beautiful things is there one which will not also appear ugly; or of the just, which will not appear to be unjust; or of the holy, which will not also be unholy?

No, he replied; they must in some way appear both beautiful and ugly: and the same is true of the rest.

And may not the many which are doubles be also halves?— doubles, that is, of one thing, and halves of another?

Yes.

And things great and small, heavy and light, may equally be termed either in different points of view?

Yes; either name will always attach to all of them.

And can anything which is called by a particular name be said to be this rather than not to be this?

He replied: They are like the punning riddles which are asked at feasts and the children's puzzle about the eunuch aiming at the bat, with what he hit him, as they say in the puzzle, and what the bat was sitting upon; for these things are a riddle also, and have a double sense: nor can you fix them in your mind, either as being or not-being, or both or neither.

Then what do you do with them? I said. Can they have a better place than between being and not-being? For they are clearly not in greater darkness or negation than not-being, or more full of light and existence than being.

That is quite true, he said.

Thus then we seem to have discovered that the diverse principles of beauty and the like, which are held by divers men, are tossing about in some region which is intermediate between pure existence and pure non-existence?

That has now been discovered by us.

Yes; and we have before agreed that anything of this kind which we might find was to be described as matter of opinion, and not as matter of knowledge; being the intermediate flux which is caught and detained by the intermediate faculty.

That was admitted.

Then those who see the many beautiful, and who yet neither see, nor can be taught to see, absolute beauty; who see the many just, and not absolute justice, and the like,—such persons may be said to have opinion but not knowledge?

That is certain.

But those who see the absolute and eternal and immutable may be said to know, and not to have opinion only?

Neither can that be denied.

The one love and embrace the subjects of knowledge, the other those of opinion? The latter are the same, as I dare say you will 480 remember, who listened to sweet sounds and gazed upon fair colours, but would not tolerate the existence of absolute beauty.

Yes, I remember.

Shall we then be guilty of any impropriety in calling them lovers of opinion rather than lovers of wisdom, and will they be very angry with us for thus describing them?

I shall tell them that they ought not to be angry at a description of themselves which is true.

But those who embrace the absolute are to be called lovers of wisdom and not lovers of opinion.

Assuredly.

BOOK VI.

And thus, Glaucon, after the argument has gone a weary way, the true and the false philosophers have at length appeared in view.

I do not think, he said, that the way could have been shortened.

I suppose not, I said; and yet I believe that the contrast might be made still more striking if there were not many other questions awaiting us, which he who desires to see in what the life of the just differs from that of the unjust must consider.

And what question is next in order? he asked.

Surely, I said, there can be no doubt about that. Inasmuch as philosophers only are able to grasp the eternal and unchangeable, and those who wander in the region of the many and variable are not philosophers, I must· ask you which of the two kinds should be the rulers of our State?

And what would be a fair answer to that question? he said.

Ask yourself, I replied, which of the two are better able to guard the laws and institutions of our State; and let them be our guardians.

Very good, he said.

Neither, I said, can there be any question that the guardian who is to keep anything should have eyes rather than no eyes?

There can be no question of that.

And are not those who are deprived of the knowledge of the true being of each thing, and have in their souls no clear pattern, and are unable as with a painter's eye to look at the very truth and to that original to repair, and having perfect vision of the other world to order the laws about beauty, goodness, justice in this, and to guard and preserve the order of them—are they not, I say, simply blind?

Indeed, he replied, they are much in that condition.

And shall these be our guardians when there are others who, besides being their equals in experience and not inferior to them in any particular of virtue, have also the knowledge of the true being of everything?

485 There can be no reason, he said, for rejecting those who have this great and pre-eminent quality, if they do not fail in any other respect.

Suppose then, I said, that we determine how far they can unite this and the other excellences.

By all means.

First of all, as we began by observing, their nature will have to be ascertained; and if we are agreed about that, then, if I am not mistaken, we shall also be agreed that such an union of qualities is possible, and that those in whom they are united, and those only, should be rulers in the State. Let us begin by assuming that philosophical minds always love that sort of knowledge which shows them the eternal nature in which is no variableness from generation and corruption.

Let that be acknowledged.

And further, I said, let us admit that they are lovers of all being; there is no part whether greater or less, or more or less honourable, which they are willing to renounce; that has been already illustrated by the example of the lover and the man of ambition.

True.

There is another quality which they will also need if they are to be what we were saying.

What quality is that?

Truthfulness: they will never intentionally receive falsehood, which is their detestation, and they will love the truth.

Yes, he said, that may be affirmed.

'May be,' my friend, I replied, that is not the word; say rather, 'must be affirmed:' for he whose nature is amorous of anything cannot help loving all that belongs or is akin to the object of his affections.

Right, he said.

And is there anything more akin to wisdom than truth?

Impossible, he said.

Or can the same nature be a lover of wisdom and a lover of falsehood?

Never.

The true lover of learning then must from his earliest youth, as far as in him lies, desire all truth?

Assuredly.

But then again, he whose desires are strong in one direction will have them weaker in others; they will be like a stream which has been drawn off into another channel.

True.

He whose desires are drawn towards knowledge in every form will be absorbed in the pleasures of the soul, and will hardly feel bodily pleasure—I mean, if he be a true philosopher and not a sham one.

That is most certain.

Such an one is sure to be temperate and the reverse of covetous; for the motives which make another man covetous and also profuse in expenditure, are no part of his character. There is another criterion of the philosophical nature which has also to 486 be considered.

What is that?

There should be no secret corner of meanness; for meanness is entirely opposed to a soul that is always longing after the whole of things both divine and human.

Most true, he replied.

Can the soul then, which has magnificence of conception and is the spectator of all time and all existence, think much of human life?

Impossible, he replied.

Or can such an one account death fearful?

No indeed.

Then the cowardly and mean nature has no part in true philosophy?

I should say not.

Or again: can he who is harmoniously constituted, who is not covetous or mean, or a boaster, or a coward—can he, I say, ever be unjust or hard in his dealings?

Impossible.

You will note also whether a man is righteous and gentle,

or rude and unsociable; these are the signs which distinguish even in youth the philosophical nature from the unphilosophical.

True.

And there is another point which should be remarked.

What is that?

Whether he has or has not a pleasure in learning; for no one will love that which gives him pain, and in which after much toil he makes little progress.

Certainly not.

And again, if he is forgetful and retains nothing of what he learns, will he not be an empty vessel?

That is certain.

Labouring in vain, he must end in hating himself and his fruitless occupation?

Yes.

Then the forgetful soul cannot be ranked among philosophers; a philosopher ought to have a good memory?

Certainly.

But the inharmonious and unseemly nature can only tend to disproportion?

No doubt of that.

And do you consider truth to be akin to proportion or disproportion?

To proportion.

Then, besides other qualities, let us seek for a well-proportioned and gracious mind whose own nature will of herself be drawn to the true being of everything.

Certainly.

Well, and do not all these qualities go together, and are they not necessary to a soul, which is to have a full and perfect participation of being?

487 They are absolutely necessary, he replied.

And must not that be a blameless study which he only can pursue who has a good memory, and is quick to learn, noble, gracious, the friend of truth, justice, courage, temperance, who are his kindred?

The god of jealousy himself, he said, could find no fault with such a study.

And to these, I said, when perfected by years and education, and to these only you will entrust the State.

Here Adeimantus interposed and said: To this, Socrates, no one can offer a reply; but there is a feeling which those who hear you talk as you are now doing often experience, and which I may describe in this way: they fancy that they are led astray a little at each step in the argument, owing to their own want of skill in asking and answering questions; these littles accumulate, and at the end of the discussion they are found to have sustained a dire reverse and to be at the antipodes of their former selves. And as unskilful players of draughts are at last shut up by their skilled adversaries and have no piece to move, so they find themselves at last shut up and have no word to say in this new game of which words are the counters; and yet all the time they are in the right. This observation is suggested to me by what is now occurring. For at this instant any one will say, that although in words he is not able to meet you at each step in the argument, as a fact he sees that the votaries of philosophy who carry on the study, not only in youth with a view to education, but as the pursuit of their maturer years —that these men, I say, for the most part grow into very strange beings, not to say utter rogues, and that the result with those who may be considered the best of them is, that they are made useless to the world by the very study which you extol.

Well, I said; and do you think that they are wrong?

I cannot tell, he replied; but I should like to know what is your opinion.

Let me tell you then that I think they are quite right.

Then how can you be justified in saying that cities will not cease from evil until philosophers rule in them, when philosophers are acknowledged by us to be of no use to them?

You ask a question, I said, which I can only answer in a parable.

Yes, said he; and that is a way of speaking to which you are not accustomed, I suppose.

I perceive, I said, that you are vastly amused at having got me to speak on such an impossible theme; and now you shall hear the parable in order that you may judge better of the meagreness 488 of my imagination: for the treatment which the best men experience from their States is so grievous that no single thing on earth can be compared with them; and therefore in defending them I must have recourse to fiction, and make a compound of many things, like the fabulous unions of goats and stags which are found in pictures. Imagine then a fleet or a ship in which there is a captain who is taller and stronger than any of the crew, but he is a little deaf and has a similar infirmity in sight, and his knowledge of navigation is not much better. Now the sailors are quarrelling with one another about the steering; every one is of opinion that he ought to steer, though he has never learned and cannot tell who taught him or when he learned, and will even assert that the art of navigation cannot be taught, and is ready to cut in pieces him who says the contrary. They throng about the captain, and do all that they can to make him commit the helm to them; and then, if they fail on some occasion and others prevail, they kill the others or throw them overboard, and having first chained up the noble captain's senses with drink or some narcotic drug, they mutiny and take possession of the ship and make themselves at home with the stores; and thus, eating and drinking, they continue their voyage with such success as might be expected of them. Him who is their partisan and zealous in the design of getting the ship out of the captain's hands into their own, whether by force or persuasion, they compliment with the name of sailor, pilot, able seaman, and abuse the other sort of man and call him a good-for-nothing; but they have not even a notion that the true pilot must pay attention to the year and seasons and sky and stars and winds, and whatever else belongs to his art, if he intends to be really qualified for the command of a ship; at the same time that he must and will be the steerer, whether people like him to steer or not; and they think that the combination of this with the art of navigation is impossible[1]. Now in vessels and among sailors, whose condition is such 489 as this, how will the true pilot be regarded? Will he not be called by the mutineers useless, prater, star-gazer?

Of course, said Adeimantus.

[1] Or, applying ὅπως δὲ κυβερνήσει to the mutineers, 'But determined to rule in spite of other people, and not believing that the practice of this can be combined with the pilot's art.'

I do not suppose, I said, that you would care to hear the interpretation of the figure, which is an allegory of the true philosopher in his relation to the State; for you understand already.

Certainly.

Then suppose you now take the parable to the gentleman who is surprised at finding that philosophers have no honour in their cities, and explain to him and try to convince him that their having honour would be far more extraordinary.

I will.

Say to him, that, in deeming the best of the votaries of philosophy to be useless to the rest of the world, he is right; but he ought to attribute their uselessness to the fault of those who will not use them, and not to themselves. The pilot should not humbly beg the sailors to be commanded by him—that is not the order of nature; neither are the wise to go to the doors of the rich (the ingenious author of this told a lie), for the truth is, that, when a man is ill, whether he be rich or poor, he must go to the physician's door—the physician will not come to him, and he who is asking to be governed, to the door of him who is able to govern. No ruler who is good for anything ought to ask his subjects to obey him; he is not like the present governors of mankind who may be compared to the mutinous sailors, and the true helmsman to those whom they call useless and star-gazers.

Precisely, he said.

For these reasons, and among men like these, the noblest pursuit of all is not likely to be much esteemed by those who are of the opposite persuasion; not that the greatest and most lasting injury is done to philosophy by them, but by her own professing followers, the same of whom you suppose the accuser to say, that the greater number of them are arrant rogues, and the best are useless; in which opinion I agreed.

Yes.

And the reason why the good are useless has been now explained?

True.

Then shall we now endeavour to show that the corruption of the greater number is also unavoidable, and that this is not to be laid to the charge of philosophy any more than the other?

By all means.

And let us ask and answer in turn, first going back to the

490 description of the gentle and noble nature. Truth, as you will remember, was his captain, whom he followed always and in all things; failing in this, he was an impostor, and had no part or lot in true philosophy.

Yes, that was said.

Well, and is not this quality alone greatly at variance with our present notions of him?

Certainly, he said.

And have we not a right to say, in his defence, that the true lover of knowledge is always striving after being—that is his nature; he will not rest in the fanciful multiplicity of individuals, but will go on—the keen edge will not be blunted, neither the force of his desire abate until he have attained the knowledge of the true nature of every essence by a kindred power in the soul, and by that power drawing near and mingling incorporate with very being, having begotten mind and truth, he will know and live and grow truly, and then, and not till then, will he cease from his travail.

Nothing, he said, can be more just than such a description of him.

And will the love of a lie be any part of a philosopher's nature? Will he not utterly hate a lie?

That he will.

And when truth is the captain, we cannot suspect any evil of the band which he leads?

Impossible.

Justice and health will be of the company, and temperance will follow after.

True, he replied.

Neither is there any reason why I should again set in array the philosopher's virtues, as you will doubtless remember that courage, magnanimity, apprehension, memory, were his natural gifts. And you objected that, although no one could deny what I then said, still, if you leave words and look at facts, the persons who are thus described are some of them useless, and the greater number wholly depraved; and this led us to enquire into the grounds of these accusations, and we had arrived at the point of asking why are the many bad, which question of necessity brought us back to the examination and definition of the true philosopher.

Exactly.

And now we have to consider the corruptions of this nature, why so many are spoiled and so few escape spoiling — those, I mean, whom you call useless but not wicked; and after that we will consider the imitators who turn into philosophers, what 491 manner of natures are they who aspire after a profession which is above them and of which they are unworthy, and then, by their manifold inconsistencies, bring upon philosophy, and upon all philosophers, that universal reprobation of which we speak.

But what, he said, is the nature of these corruptions?

That I will try to explain to you, I said, if I can. Every one will admit that a nature thus gifted, and having all the supposed conditions of the philosophic nature perfect, is a plant that rarely grows among men—there are not many of them.

They are very rare.

And what numberless causes may tend utterly to destroy these rare natures!

What causes?

In the first place there are their own virtues, their courage, temperance, and the rest of them, every one of which praiseworthy qualities (and this is a most singular circumstance) destroys and distracts from philosophy the soul which is the possessor of them.

That is very singular, he replied.

Then there are all the ordinary goods of life—beauty, wealth, strength, rank, and great connections in the State — on which I need not enlarge, having given you a general outline of them; these also have the effect of corrupting and distracting them.

I know the goods which you mean, and I should like to know what you mean about them.

Grasp the truth, then, as a whole, I said, and in the right way, and you will have no difficulty in understanding the preceding remarks, and they will not appear strange to you.

And how am I to do that? he asked.

Why, I said, we know that when any seed or plant, whether vegetable or animal, fails to meet with proper nutriment or climate or soil, the greater the vigour, the greater the need also of suitable conditions, because, as I imagine, evil is a greater enemy to good than to the not-good.

Very true.

There is reason in supposing that the finest natures, when under alien conditions, receive more injury than the inferior, because the contrast is greater.

That is true.

And may we not say, Adeimantus, that the most gifted minds, when they are ill-educated, become the worst? Do not great crimes and the spirit of pure evil spring out of a fullness of nature ruined by education rather than from any inferiority, whereas weak natures are scarcely capable of any very great good or very great evil?

There I think that you are right.

492 And our philosopher follows the same analogy—he is like a plant which, having proper nurture, grows and matures into all virtue, but, if sown and planted in an alien soil, becomes the most noxious of all weeds, unless saved by some divine help. Do you really think, as people are fond of saying, that our youth are corrupted by the Sophists, or that individual Sophisters corrupt them in any degree worth speaking of? Are not the public who say these things the greatest of all Sophists? And do they not educate to perfection alike young and old, men and women, and fashion them after their own hearts?

When is this accomplished? he said.

When they meet together, and the world sits down at an assembly, or in a court of law, or a theatre, or a camp, or at some other place of resort, and there is a great uproar, and they praise some things which are being said or done, and blame other things, equally exaggerating in both, shouting and clapping their hands, and the echo of the rocks and the place in which they are assembled redoubles the sound of the praise or blame—at such a time will not a young man's heart leap within him? Will the influences of education stem the tide of praise or blame, and not rather be carried away in the stream? And will he not have the notions of good and evil which the public in general have— he will do as they do, and as they are, such will he be?

Yes, Socrates; necessity will compel him.

And yet, I said, there is a still greater necessity, which has not been mentioned.

What is that?

The 'gentle force' of attainder or exile or death, which, as you are aware, these new Sophists and educators, who are the public, apply when their words are powerless.

Indeed they do, and no mistake.

Now what opinion of any other Sophist, or of any private man, can be expected to overcome in such an unequal contest?

None, he replied.

No, indeed, I said, even to make the attempt is a piece of folly; for there neither is, has been, nor ever can be, as I think, another type of character, trained to virtue independently of them—I speak, my friend, of man only; what is more than man, as the proverb says, is not included: for I would not have you ignorant that, in the present evil state of governments, whatever is saved and comes to good is saved by the power of God, as you may truly say. 493

To that I quite assent, he replied.

Then let me beg your assent also to a further observation.

What is that?

Why, that all those mercenary adventurers, whom the world calls Sophists and rivals, do but teach the collective opinion of the many, which are the opinions of their assemblies; and this is their wisdom. I might compare them to a man who should study the tempers and desires of a mighty strong beast who is fed by him— he would learn how to approach and handle him, also at what times and from what causes he is dangerous or the reverse, and what is the meaning of his several cries, and by what sounds, when another utters them, he is soothed or infuriated; and you may suppose further that when, by constantly living with him, he has become perfect in all this which he calls wisdom, he makes a system or art, which he proceeds to teach, not that he has any real notion of what he is teaching, but he names this honourable and that dishonourable, or good or evil, or just or unjust, all in accordance with the tastes and tempers of the great brute, when he has learnt the meaning of his inarticulate grunts. Good he pronounces to be what pleases him and evil what he dislikes; and he can give no other account of them except that the just and noble are the necessary, having never himself seen, and having no power of explaining to others, the nature of either, or the immense difference between them. Would not he be a rare educator?

Indeed, I think that he would.

And in what respect does he differ from him who thinks that
wisdom is the discernment of the tastes and pleasures of the
assembled multitude, whether in painting or music, or, finally, in
politics? For I suppose you will agree that he who associates
with the many, and exhibits to them his poem or other work
of art or political service, making them his judges, except under
protest[2], will also experience the fatal necessity of producing whatever they praise. And yet the reasons are utterly ludicrous which
they give in confirmation of their notions about the honourable
and good. Did you ever hear any of them which were not?

No, nor am I likely to hear.

You recognize the truth of what has been said? Then let me
ask you to consider further whether the world will ever be induced
to believe in the existence of absolute beauty rather than of the
494 many beautiful, or of the absolute in each kind rather than of the
many in each kind?

Certainly not.

Then the world cannot possibly be a philosopher?

Impossible.

And therefore philosophers must inevitably fall under the
censure of the world?

They must.

And of individuals who consort with the mob and seek to
please them?

That is evident.

Then, do you see any way in which the philosopher can be
preserved in his calling to the end? and remember what we were
saying of him, that he was to have knowledge and memory and
courage and magnanimity—these were admitted by us to be the
true philosopher's gifts.

Yes.

Now, will not such an one be, from the first, in all things first
among all, especially if his bodily endowments are like his mental
ones?

Certainly, he said.

And his friends and fellow-citizens will want to use them as
he gets older for their own purposes?

No question.

[2] Putting a comma after τῶν ἀναγκαίων.

Falling at his feet, they will make requests to him and do him honour and flatter him, because they want to get into their hands the power which he will one day possess.

That is often the way, he said.

And what will he do under such circumstances, especially if he be a citizen of a great city, rich and noble, and a tall proper youth? Will he not be full of boundless aspirations, and fancy himself able to manage the affairs of Hellenes and of barbarians, and in the thought of this he will dilate and elevate himself in the fullness of vain pomp and senseless pride?

Very true, he said.

Now, when he is in this state of mind, if some one gently comes to him and tells him that he is without sense, which he must have, and that the missing sense is not to be had without serving an apprenticeship, do you think that, under such adverse circumstances, he will be easily induced to listen to him?

That would be very unlikely.

But suppose further that there is one person who has feeling, and who, either from some excellence of disposition or natural affinity, is inclined or drawn towards philosophy, and his friends think that they are likely to lose the advantages which they were going to reap from his friendship, what will be the effect upon them? Will they not do and say anything to prevent his learning and to render the teacher powerless, using to this end private intrigues as well as public prosecutions?

There can be no doubt of that.   495

And how can one who is thus circumstanced ever become a philosopher?

Impossible.

Then, were we not right in saying that even the very qualities which make a man a philosopher may, if he be ill-educated, serve to divert him from philosophy, no less than riches and their accompaniments and the other so-called goods of life?

That was quite true.

Thus, my excellent friend, is brought about the ruin and failure of the natures best adapted to the best of all pursuits, who, as we assert, are rare at any time; and this is the class out of whom come those who are the authors of the greatest evil to States and individuals; and also of the greatest good when the tide carries them in the direction of good; but a small man never was the doer of any great thing either to individuals or States.

That is most true, he said.

They fall away, and philosophy is left desolate, with her marriage-rite incomplete : for her own have forsaken her, and while they are leading a false and unbecoming life, she, like an orphan bereft of her kindred, is dishonoured by other unworthy persons, who enter in and fasten upon her the reproaches which her reprovers utter; by whom, as you say, her votaries are affirmed, some of them to be good for nothing, and the greater number deserving of everything that is bad.

That is certainly what is said.

Yes; and what else would you expect, I said, when you think of the puny creatures who, seeing this land open to them—a land well stocked with fair names and showy titles—like prisoners who run away out of prison into a sanctuary, take a leap out of the arts into philosophy; those who do so being probably the cleverest hands at their own miserable crafts? for, although philosophy be in this evil case, still there remains a dignity about her which is not found in the other arts. And many are thus attracted by her whose natures are imperfect and whose souls are marred and enervated by their meannesses, as their bodies also are disfigured by their arts and crafts. Is not that true?

Yes.

Are they not exactly like a bald little tinker who has just got out of durance and come into a fortune; he washes the dirt off him and has a new coat, and is decked out as a bridegroom going to marry his master's daughter, who is left poor and desolate?

496 The figure is exact.

And what will be the issue of such marriages? Will they not be vile and bastard?

There can be no question of that.

And when persons who are unworthy of education approach philosophy and make an alliance with her who is in a rank above them, what sort of ideas and opinions are likely to be generated? Will they not be sophisms captivating to the ear, yet having nothing in them genuine or worthy of or akin to true wisdom?

No doubt, he said.

Then there is a very small remnant, Adeimantus, I said, of worthy disciples of philosophy : perchance some noble nature, brought up under good influences, and in the absence of temptation, who is detained by exile in her service, which he refuses to quit; or some lofty soul born in a mean city, the politics of which he contemns or neglects; and perhaps there may be a few who, having a gift for philosophy, leave other arts, which they justly despise, and come to her;—and peradventure there are some who are restrained by our friend Theages' bridle (for Theages, you know, had everything to divert him from philosophy; but his ill-health kept him from politics). My own case of the internal sign is indeed hardly worth mentioning, as very rarely, if ever, has such a monitor been vouchsafed to any one else. Those who belong to this small class have tasted how sweet and blessed a possession philosophy is, and have also seen and been satisfied of the madness of the multitude, and known that there is no one who ever acts honestly in the administration of States, nor any helper who will save any one who maintains the cause of the just. Such a saviour would be like a man who has fallen among wild beasts—unable to join in the wickedness of his fellows, neither would he be able alone to resist all their fierce natures, and therefore he would be of no use to the State or to his friends, and would have to throw away his life before he had done any good to himself or others. And he reflects upon all this, and holds his peace, and does his own business. He is like one who retires under the shelter of a wall in the storm of dust and sleet which the driving wind hurries along; and when he sees the rest of mankind full of wickedness, he is content if only he can live his own life and be pure from evil or unrighteousness, and depart in peace and good will, with bright hopes.

And he who does this, he said, will have done a great work before he departs.

Yes, I said, a great work, but not the greatest, unless he find a State suitable to him; for in a State which is suitable to him, 497 he will have a larger growth and be the saviour of his country, as well as of himself.

Enough, then, of the causes why philosophy is in such an evil name; how unjustly, has been explained: and now is there anything more which you wish to say?

Nothing more of that, he replied; but I should like to know which of the existing governments you deem suitable to philosophy.

Not any of them, I said; and that is the very accusation which I bring against them: not one of them is worthy of the philosophic nature; and hence that nature is warped and alienated from them;—as the exotic seed which is sown in a foreign land becomes denaturalized, and assimilates to the character of the soil, which gets the better, even so this growth of philosophy, instead of persisting, receives another character. But if philosophy ever finds that perfection in the State which she herself is, then will be seen that she is in truth divine, and that all other things, whether natures of men or institutions, are but human;—and now, I know, that you are going to ask what that State is.

No, he said; there you are wrong, for I was going to ask another question—whether this is the State of which we are the founders and inventors, or another?

Yes, I replied, ours in most respects; but you may remember our saying before that some living authority would always be required in the State whose idea of the constitution would be the same which guided you originally when laying down the laws.

That was said, he replied.

Yes, but imperfectly said; you frightened us with objections, which certainly showed that the discussion would be long and difficult; and even what remains is the reverse of easy.

What is that?

The question how the study of philosophy may be so ordered as to be consistent with the preservation of the State; for all great things are attended with risk; as the saying is, 'hard is the good.'

Still, he said, let us clear that point up and the enquiry will then be complete.

I shall not be hindered, I said, by any want of will, but, if at all, by a want of power: of my zeal you shall have ocular demonstration; and please to remark how bold I am just now in venturing to assert that a State ought not to have philosophy studied after the present fashion.

How do you mean?

498   At present, I said, even those who study philosophy in early youth, and in the intervals of money-making and house-keeping, do but make an approach to the most difficult branch of the study,

and then take themselves off—(I am speaking of those who have
the most training, and by the most difficult branch I mean dialectic); and in after-life they perhaps go to a discussion which is
held by others, and to which they are invited, and this they deem
a great matter, as the study of philosophy is not regarded by them
as their proper business: then, as years advance, in most cases
their light is quenched more truly than Heracleitus' sun, for they
never rise again[3].

But what ought to be their course?

Just the opposite. In childhood and youth their study, and
what philosophy they learn, should be suited to their tender
age: let them take care of their bodies during the period of
growth, and thus philosophy will have her instruments ready; as
the man advances to mature intelligence, increasing the gymnastics of the soul; but when their strength fails and is past civil and
military duties, then let them range at will and have no other
serious employment, as we intend them to live happily here, and,
this life ended, to have a similar happy destiny in another.

How truly in earnest you are, Socrates! he said; I am sure of
that; and yet I believe that most of your hearers are likely to be
still more earnest in their opposition to you, and will never be
converted; Thrasymachus least of all.

Don't raise a quarrel, I said, between Thrasymachus and me,
who have just become friends, although, indeed, we were never
enemies; for I shall go on using every effort until I either con-
vert him and other men, or do something which avails against
the day when they live again, and hold the like discourse in
another existence.

That will be a long time hence.

Say rather, I replied, a time which is not to be reckoned in
comparison with eternity. That the world will not believe my
words is quite natural; for they never saw that of which we are
now speaking realized; what they saw was a conventional imitation
of philosophy, which consisted of words artificially brought together, not like these agreeing of their own accord, but a human
being who in word and work is perfectly moulded, as far as he can
be, into the proportion and likeness of virtue; such an one ruling

[3] Heracleitus said the sun was extinguished every evening and new every
morning.

499 in a city which bears the same image they have never yet seen, in the case of one any more than of many—do you think they ever did?

No, indeed.

No, my friend, nor have they often heard the words of beauty and freedom; such words as those, which men use when they are earnestly and in every way seeking after truth, for the sake of knowledge, while they look coldly on the subtleties of controversy, the end of which is opinion and strife, whether they meet with them in the courts of law or in society.

They are strangers, he said, to the words of which you speak.

And this was what we foresaw, and this was the reason why truth forced us to admit that there is no chance of perfection, either in cities or governments or individuals, until a necessity was laid upon the second small class of philosophers (not the rogues, but those whom we termed useless), of taking care of the State and obeying the call of the State; or until kings themselves, or the sons of kings or potentates, were inspired with a true love of philosophy. Now I maintain that there is no reason in saying that either of these alternatives, or both of them, is impossible; if they were, we might indeed be justly ridiculed as dreamers and visionaries. Am I not right?

Quite right.

If then, in the countless ages of the past, or at the present hour in some foreign clime which is far away and beyond our ken, the perfected philosopher is or has been or shall be hereafter compelled by a superior power to have the charge of the State, we are ready to assert to the death, that this our constitution has been, is, yea, and will be at any time, when the Muse of Philosophy is queen. Neither is there any impossibility in this; the difficulty is not denied by us.

I agree with you, he said.

But you will say that mankind in general are not agreed?

That is what I should say, he replied.

O my friend, I said, do not have such a bad opinion of mankind: they will surely be of another mind, if gently and with the view of soothing them and removing the evil name of too much learning, you show them the philosopher as just now described,

500 according to his true character and profession, and then they will see that you are not speaking of those whom they supposed; if

they view him in this light, they will surely change their mind, and answer in another strain[4]. Who can be at enmity with one who loves them, who that is himself gentle and free from envy will be jealous of one in whom there is no jealousy? Nay, let me answer for you, that a few such there may be, but not many who have so harsh a temper.

I entirely agree with you, he said.

And do you not agree with me also as to the cause of the harsh feeling which the many have towards philosophy? This originates in the pretenders, who enter in, like a band of revellers, where they have no business, and are always abusing and quarrelling with them, who make persons instead of things the theme of their conversation; and this is most unbecoming in philosophers.

Most unbecoming.

For he, Adeimantus, whose mind is fixed upon true being has no time to look down upon the affairs of men, or to be filled with jealousy and enmity in the struggle against them; his eye is ever directed towards fixed and immutable principles, which he sees neither injuring nor injured by one another, but all in order moving according to reason; these he imitates, and to these he would, as far as he can, conform himself. Can a man help imitating that with which he holds reverential converse?

Impossible.

And the philosopher also, conversing with the divine and immutable, becomes a part of that divine and immutable order, as far as nature allows; but all things are liable to detraction.

Certainly.

And if a necessity be laid upon him of fashioning, not only himself, but human nature generally, whether in States or individuals, into that which he there beholds, think you that he will be an unskilful artificer of justice, temperance, and every civil virtue?

Anything but unskilful.

And if the world perceives that we are speaking the truth about him, will they be angry with philosophy? Will they disbelieve us, when we tell them that the State can only be happy which is planned by artists who make use of the heavenly pattern?

---

[4] Reading ἢ καὶ ἐὰν οὕτω θεῶνται with a question. Or, taking ἀλλοίαν δόξαν in a new sense: 'Do you mean to say, that, even viewing him in this light, they will be of another mind from yours, and answer in another strain?'

They will not be angry if they only understand, he replied. But what do you mean about the plan?

I mean, I replied, that they will take a State and human nature for their tablet and begin by making a clean surface. Now this is not an easy thing to do; and this is the mark which at once distinguishes them from every other legislator,—they will have nothing to do, either with individual or State, and will inscribe no laws, until they have either found, or themselves made, a clean surface.

They will be very right, he said.

Having effected this, they will proceed to make an outline of the constitution.

No doubt.

And in the course of the work, as I conceive, they will often turn their eyes first towards one, then towards the other. I mean that they will look at justice and beauty and temperance as they are in nature, and again at the corresponding quality in mankind, and they will inlay the true human image, moulding and selecting out of the various forms of life; and this they will conceive according to that other image, which, when existing among men, Homer calls the form and likeness of God.

That is true, he said.

And one feature they will erase, and another they will inscribe, until they have made the ways of men, as far as possible, agreeable to the ways of God?

Indeed, he said, in no other way could they make a fairer picture.

And now, I said, do you think that we are beginning to persuade those whom you said were rushing at us with might and main, that the painter of constitutions is such an one as we were praising,—he, I mean, at whom they were so much infuriated, because into his hands we committed the State, or are they growing calmer at what they hear?

Much calmer, if there is any sense in them.

Why, where can they still find any ground for objection? Will they doubt that the philosopher is a lover of truth and being?

That would be monstrous.

Or that his nature, being such as we have delineated, is akin to the highest good?

Neither can they doubt that.

But again, will they tell us that such a nature, if properly trained, will not be perfectly good and wise as much as any that ever was? Or will they prefer those whom we have set aside?

Surely not.

Then will they still be angry at our saying, that, until philosophers bear rule in States, the evils of States and individuals will never cease, nor will this our imaginary State ever be realized?

I think that they will be less angry.

Shall we assume that they are not only less angry but quite gentle, and that they have been converted and for very shame 502 cannot refuse to come to terms?

Certainly, he said.

Then now we may assume that they have been converted. And will any one deny the other point, that there may be sons of kings who are philosophers?

No one will doubt that, he said.

And when they have come into being will any one say that they must of necessity be destroyed; for that they can hardly be saved is not denied even by us, but all will allow that, in the whole course of ages, peradventure a single one may be saved?

Surely.

But, said I, one is enough; let there be one man who has a city obedient to his will, and he might bring the ideal polity into being.

Yes, one is enough.

When the ruler has framed these laws and institutions, the citizens may possibly be willing to obey them?

Certainly.

And that others should approve, of what we approve, is no miracle or impossibility?

I think not.

But we have sufficiently shown, in what has preceded, that all this, if only possible, is assuredly for the best.

Yes, that has been proved.

The conclusion is then, that our laws are best, and, though difficult of attainment, are not wholly unattainable.

Very good.

And now that this difficulty is ended another arises; how and by what studies and pursuits, will saviours of the constitution be formed, and at what ages are they to apply themselves to their several studies?—that has now to be discussed.

Yes, certainly.

I omitted the troublesome business of the possession of women, and the procreation of children, and the appointment of the rulers, because I knew that the perfect State would be eyed with jealousy and was difficult of attainment; but that piece of cleverness was not of much use to me, for I had to discuss them all the same. And now, having done with the women and children, I must pursue the other question of the rulers, beginning at the beginning. We were saying, as you will remember, that they 503 were to be lovers of their country, tried amid the influences of pleasures and pains, and neither in labours, nor fears, nor any other change of circumstances were to lose their patriotism; he who failed in this was to be rejected, but he who always came forth pure, like gold tried in the refiners' fire, was to be made a ruler, and to receive honours and rewards in life and after death. That was the sort of thing which was being said, and then the argument turned aside and veiled her face; not liking to stir the question which has now arisen.

I perfectly remember that, he said.

Yes, my friend, I said, and I then shrank from hazarding the bold word; but now let me dare to say—that the perfect guardian must be a philosopher.

Yes, he said, let that be proclaimed.

And consider, I said, that there will not be many of them— that is not to be expected; for the gifts which we said were essential rarely grow together; they are mostly found in shreds and patches.

What do you mean? he said.

You are aware, I replied, that persons who have quick intelligence, memory, sagacity, shrewdness, and all that sort of thing, are not often of a nature which is willing at the same time to live orderly and in a peaceful and settled manner; and this is equally true of the high-spirited and magnanimous; they are driven any way by their impetuosity, and all their solid principle goes out of them.

That is true, he said.

On the other hand, those steadfast, immovable natures upon which you can rely, and which have not the wit to run away in a battle, are equally immovable when there is anything to be learned; they seem to be in a torpid state, and are apt to yawn and go to sleep over any intellectual toil.

That is true.

And yet we were saying that both qualities were necessary in those to whom the higher education is to be imparted, and who are to share in any office or command.

True, he said.

And will they be a class which is rarely found?

Yes, indeed.

Then the aspirant must be tested in those labours and dangers and pleasures which we mentioned before; and there is another kind of probation which we did not mention—they must be exercised also in many kinds of knowledge, to see whether the soul will be able to endure the highest of all, or will faint under them, as many do amid the toils of the games.   504

Yes, he said, that is the way in which we ought to regard them. But what do you mean by the highest of all knowledge?

You may remember, I said, that we divided the soul into three parts; and the several natures of justice, temperance, courage, and wisdom were compared and defined by us?

Indeed, he said, if I had forgotten that, I should not deserve to hear more.

And do you remember, I said, what preceded the discussion of them?

What was that?

We spoke, if I am not mistaken, of a perfect way, which was longer and more circuitous, at the end of which they were to appear in full view; this however, as we said, need not prevent our offering an exposition of a popular sort, in character like what had preceded. And you replied that such an exposition would be enough for you, and so the enquiry was continued in what appeared to me to be a very imperfect manner; but whether you were satisfied or not is for you to say.

Yes, he said, I thought and the others thought that you gave us a fair measure of truth.

But, my friend, I said, a measure of such things which in any degree falls short of the truth is not fair measure; for nothing imperfect is the measure of anything, although persons are too apt to be contented and think that they need search no further.

Yes, that is not uncommon when people are indolent.

Yes, I said; and there cannot be any worse fault in the guardian of a State and the laws.

True.

The guardian then, I said, must be required to take the longer route, and toil at learning as well as at gymnastics, or he will never reach the height of that knowledge which is his proper calling.

What, he said, is there a knowledge still higher than these—higher than justice and the other virtues?

Yes, I said, there is. And of these too we must behold not the outline merely, as at present—nothing short of the most perfect representation should satisfy us. When little things are elaborated with an infinity of pains, in order that they may appear in full clearness and precision, how ridiculous that the highest truths should not be held worthy of the greatest exactness!

Yes, said he, and that is a right noble thought; but do you suppose that we shall refrain from asking you which are the highest?

Nay, I said, ask if you will; but I am certain that you have often heard the answer, and now you either do not understand or you are disposed to be troublesome; I incline to think the 505 latter, for you have been often told that the idea of good is the highest knowledge, and that all other things become useful and advantageous only by their use of this. And you must be quite aware that of this I am about to speak, concerning which, as I shall say, we know so little; and, wanting which, any other knowledge or possession of any kind will profit us nothing. Do you think that the possession of the whole world is of any value without the good? or of all wisdom, without the beautiful and good?

No, indeed, he said.

You are doubtless aware that most people call pleasure good, and the finer sort of wits say wisdom? And you are aware that the latter cannot explain the nature of wisdom, but are obliged after all to say that wisdom is of the good?

That is very ridiculous, he said.

Yes, I said, that they should begin by reproaching us with our ignorance, and then presume our knowledge of good—for wisdom, as they say, is of the good, which implies that we understand them when they use the term 'good'—is certainly ridiculous.

Most true, he said.

And those who make pleasure their good are in equal perplexity; for they are compelled to admit that there are bad pleasures as well as good.

Certainly.

And therefore to acknowledge that bad and good are the same?

True.

There can be no doubt about the numerous difficulties in which this question is involved.

There can be none.

Well, and is not this an obvious fact, that many are willing to possess, or to do, or to wear the appearance of the just and honourable without the reality; but no one is satisfied to possess the appearance of good—the reality is what they seek; the appearance in the case of the good is despised by every one.

Very true, he said.

This then, which every man pursues and makes his end, having a presentiment that there is such an end, and yet hesitating because neither knowing the nature nor having the same sure proof of this as of other things, and therefore having no profit in other 506 things,—is this, I would ask, a principle about which those who are called the best men in the State, and to whom everything is to be entrusted, ought to be in such darkness?

Certainly not, he said.

I am sure, I said, that he who does not know how the beautiful and the just are likewise good will not be worth much as a guardian of them: and I suspect that no one will have a true knowledge of them without this knowledge.

That, he said, is a shrewd suspicion of yours.

And if we only have a guardian who has this knowledge our State will be perfectly ordered?

Of course, he replied; but I wish you would tell me whether you conceive this supreme principle of the good to be knowledge or pleasure, or different from either?

Aye, I said, I knew quite well that a fine gentleman [5] like you would not be contented with the thoughts of other men.

True, Socrates; and I must say that you have no right to be always repeating the opinions of others, and never to tell your own, and this after having passed a lifetime in the study of philosophy.

Well, but has any one a right to say, positively, what he does not know?

Not, he said, with the positiveness of knowledge; he has no right to do that: but he ought to say what he thinks, as a matter of opinion.

But do you not know, I said, that opinions are bad all, and the best of them blind? You would not deny that those who have any true notion without intelligence are only like blind men finding their way along a straight road?

Very true.

And do you wish to behold what is blind and crooked and base, when brightness and beauty are within your reach?

Still, I must implore you, Socrates, said Glaucon, not to turn away just as you are reaching the goal—if you will only give such an explanation of the good as you have already given about justice and temperance and the other virtues, that will satisfy us.

Yes, my friend, I said, and that will satisfy me too extremely well, but I cannot help fearing that I shall fail, and that in my zeal I shall make a fool of myself. No, sweet sirs, let us not at present ask what is the actual nature of the good, for to reach what is in my thoughts now is too much for me in my present mood. But of the child of the good who is likest him, I would fain speak, if I could be sure that you wished to hear—otherwise, not.

Nay, he said, speak; the child shall be the interest [6], and you shall remain in our debt for an account of the parent or principal.

507 I do indeed wish, I replied, that I could pay, and you receive, the parent or principal account, and not, as now, the interest or child only; take, however, the child, which is the interest, and at the same time have a care that I do not render a false account, although I have no intention of deceiving you.

---

[5] Reading ἀνὴρ καλός.   [6] τόκος.

Yes, we will take all the care that we can: proceed.

Yes, I said, but I must first come to an understanding with you, and remind you of what I have mentioned in the course of this discussion, and at many other times.

What is that? he said.

The old story, that there is a many beautiful and a many good, and so of other things which we describe and define; to all of them the term 'many' is applied.

True, he said.

And there is an absolute beauty and an absolute good, and so of other things to which the term 'many' is applied; they may be brought under a single idea, which is called the essence of each.

That is true.

The many, as we say, are seen but not known, and the ideas are known but not seen.

Exactly.

And what is the organ with which we see the visible things?

The sight, he said.

And with the hearing, I said, we hear, and with the other senses perceive the other objects of sense?

True.

But have you remarked that sight is by far the most costly and complex piece of workmanship which the artificer of the senses ever contrived?

No, I never have, he said.

Then reflect: does the ear hear, and is the voice heard by virtue of some other nature which is required as a third condition before they can meet?

Nothing of the sort.

No, indeed, I replied; and the same is true of most, if not all, the other senses: you would not regard any of them as requiring such an addition?

Indeed not.

But you see that without such an addition there is no seeing or being seen?

How do you mean?

Sight being, as I conceive, in the eyes, and the possessor making use of his vision, and colour being also present in them, unless there is a third nature at hand designed for this special purpose, you know that the sight will see nothing and the colours will be invisible?

And of what nature are you speaking?

Of that which you term light, I replied.

True, he said.

508   Noble, then, is the bond which links together sight and visibility, and great beyond other bonds by no small difference of nature; for light is their bond, and light is no ignoble thing.

Nay, he said, the reverse of ignoble.

And which, I said, of the gods in heaven would you say was the lord of this element? Whose is that light which makes the eye to see perfectly and the visible to appear?

You mean the sun, as you and all mankind say.

May not the relation of sight to this deity be described as follows?

How?

Neither sight nor the eye in which sight resides is the sun?

No.

Yet of all the organs of sense the eye is likest the sun?

Far the likest.

And the power which the eye possesses is a sort of effluence which is dispensed from the sun?

Exactly.

Then the sun is not sight, but the author of sight who is recognized by sight?

True, he said.

And this is he whom I call the child of the good, whom the good begat in his own likeness, to be in the visible world, in relation to sight and the things of sight, what the good is in the intellectual world in relation to mind and the things of mind?

Will you be a little more explicit? he said.

Why, you know, I said, that the eyes, when a person no longer directs them towards those objects on the colours of which the light of day is shining, but the moon and stars only, see dimly, and are nearly blind; they seem to have no clearness of vision in them?

Very true.

But when they are directed towards objects on which the sun shines, they see clearly and there is sight in them?

Certainly.

And the soul is like the eye: when resting upon that on which truth and being shine, the soul perceives and understands, and is radiant with intelligence; but when turning towards the twilight of generation and destruction, then she has opinion only, and goes blinking about, and is first of one opinion and then of another, and seems to have no intelligence?

Yes.

Now, that which imparts truth to the object and knowledge to the subject is what I would have you term the idea of good, and that you will regard as the cause of science[7] and of truth, as known by us; beautiful too, as are both truth and knowledge, you will be right in esteeming this other nature as more beautiful than either; and, as in the previous instance, light and sight may 509 be truly said to be like the sun, and yet not to be the sun, so in this other sphere, science and truth may be deemed like the good, but not the good: the good has a place of honour yet higher.

What a wonder of beauty that must be, he said, which is the author of science and truth, and yet surpasses them in beauty; for you surely cannot mean to say that the good is pleasure?

Speak not of that, I said; but please to consider the image in another point of view.

What is that?

Why, you would say that the sun is not only the author of visibility in all visible things, but of generation and nourishment and growth, though not himself a generation?

Certainly.

In like manner the good may be said to be not only the author of knowledge in all things known, but of their being and essence, and yet the good is not essence, but far exceeds essence in dignity and power.

Glaucon said, with a ludicrous earnestness: By the light of heaven, how amazing!

Yes, I said, and that all comes of you, for you made me utter my fancies.

Nay, he said, but do not leave off; at any rate let us hear if there is anything more to be said about the similitude of the sun.

7 Reading διανοοῦ.

Yes, I said, there is a great deal more.

Then omit nothing, however slight.

I will do my best; but I fancy, I said, that a great deal will have
to be omitted.

I hope not, he said.

You have to imagine, then, that there are two ruling powers,
and that one of them is set over the intellectual world, the
other over the visible. I do not say heaven, lest you should fancy
that I was refining about the name (οὐρανός, ὁρατός). May I suppose that you have this distinction of the visible and intelligible
fixed in your mind?

I have.

Now take a line which has been cut into two unequal[8] parts,
and divide each of them again in the same proportion, and suppose
the two main divisions to answer, one to the visible and the other
to the intelligible, and then compare the subdivisions as to their
relative clearness and want of clearness, and you will find that
the first section in the sphere of the visible consists of images.
510 And by images I mean, in the first place, shadows, and in the
second place, reflections in water and in solid, smooth and polished
bodies, and all that sort of thing, as you understand.

Yes, I understand.

Imagine, now, the other section, of which this is only the
resemblance, to include ourselves and the animals, and everything
in nature and everything in art.

Very good.

Would you not admit that this latter section has a different
degree of truth, and that the copy is to the object which is copied
as the sphere of opinion is to the sphere of knowledge?

Most undoubtedly.

Next proceed to consider the manner in which the sphere of
the intellectual is to be divided.

In what manner?

As thus:—There are two subdivisions, in the lower of which
the soul uses the figures given by the former division as images;
the enquiry can only be hypothetical, and instead of going upwards to a principle descends to the other end; in the higher of

[8] Reading ἄνισα.

the two, the soul passes out of hypotheses, and goes up to a principle which is above hypotheses, making no use of images [9] as in the former case, but proceeding only in and by the ideas themselves.

I do not quite understand your meaning, he said.

I will try again, I said; for you will understand me better now that I have made these preliminary remarks. You are aware that students of geometry, arithmetic, and the kindred sciences assume the odd and the even and the figures and three kinds of angles and the like in their several branches of science; these are their hypotheses, which everybody is supposed to know, and of which therefore they do not deign to give any account either to themselves or others; but they begin with these, and go on until they arrive at last, and in a consistent manner, at their conclusion?

Yes, he said, I know that.

And do you not know also that although they use and reason about the visible forms, they are thinking not of these, but of the ideals which they resemble; not of the figures which they draw, but of the absolute square and the absolute diameter, and so on: and, while using as images these very forms which they draw or make, and which in turn have their shadows and reflections in the water, they are really seeking for the things themselves, which can only be seen with the eye of the mind?

That is true.

And of this kind I still spoke as intelligible, although in enquiries of this sort the soul is compelled to use hypotheses; not proceeding to a first principle because unable to ascend above hypotheses, but using as images the objects of which the shadows are resemblances in a still lower sphere, they having in relation to the shadows a higher value and distinctness [10].

I understand, he said, that you are speaking of geometry and the sister arts.

And when I speak of the other division of the intellectual, you will also understand me to speak of that knowledge which reason herself attains by the power of dialectic, using the hypotheses not as first principles, but only as hypotheses—that is to say, as

---

[9] Reading ὥνπερ ἐκεῖνο εἰκόνων.
[10] Or, 'they, in relation to the ideas, being valued and esteemed for their distinctness.'

steps and points of departure into a region which is above
hypotheses, in order that she may soar beyond them to the first
principle of the whole; and clinging to this and then to that
which depends on this, by successive steps she descends again
without the aid of any sensible object, beginning and ending in
ideas.

I understand you, he replied; not perfectly, for the matter of
which you speak is too great for that; but, at any rate, I understand you to say that knowledge and being, which the science of
dialectic contemplates, are clearer than the notions of the arts, as
they are termed, which proceed from hypotheses only: these are
also contemplated by the understanding, and not by the senses:
yet, because they start from hypotheses and do not ascend to a
principle, those who contemplate them appear to you not to
exercise the higher reason upon them, although when a first
principle is added to them they are cognizable by the higher
reason. And the habit which is concerned with geometry and
the cognate sciences I suppose that you would term understanding
and not reason, as being intermediate between opinion and
reason.

You have quite conceived me, I said; and now, corresponding
to these four sections, let there be four faculties in the soul—
reason answering to the highest, understanding to the second,
faith or persuasion to the third, and knowledge of shadows to the
last—and let there be a scale of them, and let us suppose that the
several faculties have clearness in the same degree that their
objects have truth.

I understand, he replied, and give my assent, and will arrange
them as you say.

BOOK VII.

AFTER this, I said, imagine the enlightenment or ignorance of our nature in a figure :—Behold! human beings living in a sort of underground den, which has a mouth open towards the light and reaching all across the den; they have been here from their childhood, and have their legs and necks chained so that they cannot move, and can only see before them; for the chains are arranged in such a manner as to prevent them from turning round their heads. At a distance above and behind them the light of a fire is blazing, and between the fire and the prisoners there is a raised way; and you will see, if you look, a low wall built along the way, like the screen which marionette players have before them, over which they show the puppets.

I see, he said.

And do you see, I said, men passing along the wall carrying vessels, which appear over the wall; also figures of men and animals, made of wood and stone and various materials; and some of the passengers, as you would expect, are talking, and 515 some of them are silent?

That is a strange image, he said, and they are strange prisoners.

Like ourselves, I replied; and they see only their own shadows, or the shadows of one another, which the fire throws on the opposite wall of the cave?

True, he said; how could they see anything but the shadows if they were never allowed to move their heads?

And of the objects which are being carried in like manner they would only see the shadows?

Yes, he said.

And if they were able to talk with one another, would they not suppose that they were naming what was actually before them [1]?

Very true.

[1] Reading παρόντα.

And suppose further that the prison had an echo which came from the other side, would they not be sure to fancy that the voice which they heard was that of a passing shadow?

No question, he replied.

There can be no question, I said, that the truth would be to them just nothing but the shadows of the images.

That is certain.

And now look again, and see how they are released and cured of their folly. At first, when any one of them is liberated and compelled suddenly to go up and turn his neck round and walk and look at the light, he will suffer sharp pains; the glare will distress him, and he will be unable to see the realities of which in his former state he had seen the shadows; and then imagine some one saying to him, that what he saw before was an illusion, but that now he is approaching real being and has a truer sight and vision of more real things,—what will be his reply? And you may further imagine that his instructor is pointing to the objects as they pass and requiring him to name them,—will he not be in a difficulty? Will he not fancy that the shadows which he formerly saw are truer than the objects which are now shown to him?

Far truer.

And if he is compelled to look at the light, will he not have a pain in his eyes which will make him turn away to take refuge in the objects of vision which he can see, and which he will conceive to be clearer than the things which are now being shown to him?

True, he said.

And suppose once more, that he is reluctantly dragged up a steep and rugged ascent, and held fast and forced into the presence of the sun himself, do you not think that he will be 516 pained and irritated, and when he approaches the light he will have his eyes dazzled, and will not be able to see any of the realities which are now affirmed to be the truth?

Not all in a moment, he said.

He will require to get accustomed to the sight of the upper world. And first he will see the shadows best, next the re-flections of men and other objects in the water, and then the objects themselves; next he will gaze upon the light of the moon and the stars; and he will see the sky and the stars by night, better than the sun, or the light of the sun, by day?

Certainly.

And at last he will be able to see the sun, and not mere reflections of him in the water, but he will see him as he is in his own proper place, and not in another; and he will contemplate his nature.

Certainly.

And after this he will reason that the sun is he who gives the seasons and the years, and is the guardian of all that is in the visible world, and in a certain way the cause of all things which he and his fellows have been accustomed to behold?

Clearly, he said, he would come to the other first and to this afterwards.

And when he remembered his old habitation, and the wisdom of the den and his fellow-prisoners, do you not suppose that he would felicitate himself on the change, and pity them?

Certainly, he would.

And if they were in the habit of conferring honours on those who were quickest to observe and remember and foretell which of the shadows went before, and which followed after, and which were together, do you think that he would care for such honours and glories, or envy the possessors of them? Would he not say with Homer,

'Better to be a poor man, and have a poor master,'

and endure anything, rather than to think and live after their manner?

Yes, he said, I think that he would rather suffer anything than live after their manner.

Imagine once more, I said, that such an one coming suddenly out of the sun were to be replaced in his old situation, is he not certain to have his eyes full of darkness?

Very true, he said.

And if there were a contest, and he had to compete in measuring the shadows with the prisoners who have never moved out of the den, during the time that his sight is weak, and before 517 his eyes are steady (and the time which would be needed to acquire this new habit of sight might be very considerable), would he not be ridiculous? Men would say of him that up he went and down he comes without his eyes; and that there was no use in even thinking of ascending : and if any one tried to loose another and lead him up to the light, let them only catch the offender in the act, and they would put him to death.

No question, he said.

This allegory, I said, you may now append to the previous argument; the prison is the world of sight, the light of the fire is the sun, the ascent and vision of the things above you may truly regard as the upward progress of the soul into the intellectual world; that is my poor belief, to which, at your desire, I have given expression. Whether I am right or not God only knows; but, whether true or false, my opinion is that in the world of knowledge the idea of good appears last of all, and is seen only with an effort; and, when seen, is also inferred to be the universal author of all things beautiful and right, parent of light and the lord of light in this world, and the source of truth and reason in the other: this is the first great cause which he who would act rationally either in public or private life must behold.

I agree, he said, as far as I am able to understand you.

I should like to have your agreement in another matter, I said. For I would not have you marvel that those who attain to this beatific vision are unwilling to descend to human affairs; but their souls are ever hastening into the upper world in which they desire to dwell; and this is very natural, if our allegory may be trusted.

Certainly, that is quite natural.

And is there anything surprising in one who passes from divine contemplations to human things, misbehaving himself in a ridiculous manner; if, while his eyes are blinking and before he has become accustomed to the darkness visible, he is compelled to fight in courts of law, or in other places, about the images or shadows of images of justice, and is endeavouring to meet the conceptions of those who have never yet seen the absolute justice?

There is nothing surprising in that, he replied.

518 Any one who has common sense will remember that the bewilderments of the eyes are of two kinds, and arise from two causes, either from coming out of the light or from going into the light, which is true of the mind's eye, quite as much as of the bodily eye; and he who remembers this when he sees the

soul of any one whose vision is perplexed and weak, will not be too ready to laugh; he will first ask whether that soul has come out of the brighter life, and is unable to see because unaccustomed to the dark, or having turned from darkness to the day is dazzled by excess of light. And then he will count the one happy in his condition and state of being, and he will pity the other; or, if he have a mind to laugh at the soul which comes from below into the light, there will be more reason in this than in the laugh which greets the other from the den.

That, he said, is a very just remark.

But if this is true, then certain professors of education must be mistaken in saying that they can put a knowledge into the soul which was not there before, like giving eyes to the blind.

Yes, that is what they say, he replied.

Whereas, I said, our argument shows that the power is already in the soul; and that as the eye cannot turn from darkness to light without the whole body, so too, when the eye of the soul is turned round, the whole soul must be turned from the world of generation into that of being, and become able to endure the sight of being, and of the brightest and best of being—that is to say, of the good.

Very true.

And this is conversion; and the art will be how to accomplish this as easily and completely as possible; not implanting eyes, for they exist already, but giving them a right direction, which they have not.

Yes, he said, that may be assumed.

And hence while the other qualities seem to be akin to the body, being infused by habit and exercise and not originally innate, the virtue of wisdom is part of a divine essence, and has a power which is everlasting, and by this conversion is rendered useful and profitable, and is also capable of becoming hurtful and useless. Did you never observe the narrow intel- 519 ligence flashing from the keen eye of a clever rogue—how eager he is, how clearly his paltry soul sees the way to his end; he is the reverse of blind, but his keen eye-sight is taken into the service of evil, and he is dangerous in proportion to his intelligence?

Very true, he said.

But what if there had been a circumcision of such natures in the days of their youth; and they had been severed from the leaden weights, as I may call them, with which they are born into the world, which hang on to sensual pleasures, such as those of eating and drinking, and drag them down and turn the vision of their souls about the things that are below—if, I say, they had been released from them and turned round to the truth, the very same faculty in these very same persons would have seen the other as keenly as they now see that on which their eye is fixed.

That is very likely.

Yes, I said; and there is another thing which is likely, or rather a necessary inference from what has preceded, that neither the uneducated and uninformed of the truth, nor yet those who never make an end of their education, will be able ministers of State: not the former, because they have no single aim of duty which is the rule of their actions, private as well as public; nor the latter, because they will not act at all except upon compulsion, fancying that they are already in the islands of the blest.

Very true, he replied.

Then, I said, the business of us who are the founders of the State will be to compel the best minds to attain that knowledge which has been already declared by us to be the greatest of all— to that eminence they must ascend and arrive at the good, and when they have ascended and seen enough we must not allow them to do as they do now.

What do you mean?

I mean that they remain in the upper world: but this must not be allowed; they must be made to descend again among the prisoners in the den, and partake of their labours and honours, whether they are worth having or not.

But is not this unjust? he said; ought we to give them an inferior life, when they might have a superior one?

You have again forgotten, my friend, I said, the intention of the legislator; he did not aim at making any one class in the State happy above the rest; the happiness was to be in the whole State, and he held the citizens together by persuasion and necessity, making them benefactors of the State, and therefore 520 benefactors of one another; to this end he created them, not that they should please themselves, but they were to be his instruments in binding up the State.

True, he said, I had forgotten that.

Observe then, I said, Glaucon, that there will be no injustice in compelling our philosophers to have a care and providence of others; we shall explain to them that in other States, men of their class are not obliged to share in the toils of politics: and this is reasonable, for they grow up at their own sweet will, and the government would rather not have them. Now the wild plant which owes culture to nobody, has nothing to pay for culture; but we have brought you into the world expressly for this end, that you may be rulers of the hive, kings of yourselves and of the other citizens. And you have been educated far better and more perfectly than they have, and are better able to share in the double duty. And therefore each of you, when his turn comes, must go down to the general underground abode, and get the habit of seeing in the dark; for all is habit; and when you are accustomed you will see ten thousand times better than those in the den, and you will know what the images are, and of what they are images, because you have seen the beautiful and just and good in their truth. And thus the order of our State will be a waking reality, and not a dream, as is commonly the manner of States; in most of them men are fighting with one another about shadows and are distracted in the struggle for power, which in their eyes is a great good. But the truth is, that the State in which the rulers are most reluctant to govern is best and most quietly governed, and that in which they are most willing, the worst.

Quite true, he replied.

And will our pupils, when they hear this, refuse to share in turn the toils of State, when they are allowed to spend the greater part of their time with one another in the heaven of ideas?

Impossible, he answered; for they are just men, and the commands which we impose upon them are just; there can be no doubt that every one of them will take office as a stern necessity, and not like our present ministers of state.

Yes, my friend, I said; and that is just the truth of the case. If you contrive for your future rulers another and a better life than 521 that of a ruler, then you may have a well-ordered State; for only in

the State which offers this will they rule who are truly rich, not
in silver and gold, but in virtue and wisdom, which are the true
blessings of life. Whereas if they go to the administration of
public affairs, poor and hungering after their own private advantage, thinking that hence they are to snatch the good of life, order
there can never be; for they will be fighting about office, and the
civil and domestic broils which thus arise will be the ruin of the
rulers themselves and of the whole State.

Most true, he replied.

And the only life which looks down upon the life of political
ambition is that of true philosophy? Do you know of any other?

No, indeed, he said.

And those who govern ought not to be lovers of the task? If
they are there will be rival lovers, and they will fight.

No question.

Whom then would you choose rather than those who are wisest
about affairs of State, and who at the same time have other
honours and another and a better life?

They are the men, and I will choose them, he replied.

Would you like us then to consider in what way such guardians
may be called into existence, and how they are to be brought
from darkness to light,—as some are said to have ascended from
the world below to the gods?

Certainly I should, he replied.

The process, I said, is not the spinning round of an oyster-shell,
but the conversion of a soul out of darkness visible to the real
ascent of true being[2], which is true philosophy. Now what sort
of knowledge has the power of effecting this? that is a question
which has to be considered.

Certainly.

Then what sort of knowledge is there which would draw the
soul from becoming to being? At the same time there is another
thing which occurs to me. You will remember that our young
men are to be warrior athletes?

Yes, that was said.

Then this new kind of knowledge must have another quality?

What quality?

---

[2] Reading οὖσαν ἐπάνοδον.

Usefulness in war.

Yes, if possible.

There were two parts in our former scheme of education, were there not?

True.

There was gymnastic which presided over the growth and decay of the body, and may therefore be regarded as having to do with generation and corruption?

True.

Then that is not the knowledge which we are seeking to 522 discover?

No.

But what do you say of music, as far as that entered into our scheme?

That, he said, as you will remember, was the counterpart of gymnastic, and trained the guardians by the influences of habit, giving them, not science, but a sort of harmonical composition, and a kind of rhythmical movement; and the words, whether true or false, had kindred elements of rhythm and harmony in them; but musical knowledge was not of a kind which tended to that good which you are now seeking.

You are most accurate, I said, in your recollection; for there certainly was nothing of that kind in our previous education. But then what branch of knowledge is there, my dear friend, which is of the desired nature? For the useful arts were rejected by us as mean.

Undoubtedly; and yet if music and gymnastic are excluded, and the arts are also excluded, what remains?

Well, I said, there may be nothing left; and then we shall have to take something which is of universal application.

What is that?

A something which all arts and sciences and intelligences use in common, and which every one ought to learn among the elements of education.

What is that?

The little matter of distinguishing one, two, and three, which I may sum up under the name of number and calculation,—of that all arts and sciences are necessarily partakers.

Very true.

Then the art of war partakes of them?

To be sure.

Then Palamedes, when he appears in the play, proves Agamemnon ridiculously unfit to be a general. Did you never remark how he declares that he had invented number, and had numbered and set in array the ranks of the army at Troy; which implies that they had never been numbered before, and Agamemnon must be supposed literally to have been incapable of counting his own feet—how could he if he was ignorant of number? And if that is true, what sort of general must he have been?

I should say a very strange one, certainly.

Must not a warrior then, I said, in addition to his military skill have a knowledge of arithmetic?

Certainly he must, if he is to have the slightest knowledge of military tactics, or indeed, I should rather say, if he is to be a man at all.

I should like to know whether you have the same notion which I have of this study?

What is that?

523 I am of opinion that this is a study of the kind which we are seeking, and which leads naturally to reflection, but one which has never been rightly used as simply conducting towards being.

Will you explain your meaning? he said.

I will try, I said; and I wish you would consider and help me, and say 'yes' or 'no' when I attempt to distinguish in my own mind what branches of knowledge have this conducting power, in order that we may have clearer proof that this is one of them.

Explain, he said.

I mean to say that objects of sense are of two kinds; some of them do not excite thought because the sense is an adequate judge of them; while in the case of other objects there is a mistrust of the senses which only stimulates enquiry.

You must be referring, he said, to the manner in which the senses are imposed upon by distance, and by painting in light and shade.

No, I said, that is not my meaning.

Then what is your meaning?

When speaking of unexciting objects, I mean those which do not pass out of one sensation into an opposite one; exciting objects are those which give opposite sensations; as when the sense coming upon the object, and this not only at a distance but near, gives no more vivid idea of any particular object than of its opposite. An illustration will make my meaning clearer:— here are three fingers—a little finger, a second finger, and a middle finger.

Very good.

You may suppose that they are seen quite close. And here comes the point.

What is that?

Each of them equally appears a finger, whether seen in the middle or at the extremity, whether white or black, or thick or thin—that makes no difference; a finger is a finger all the same. And in all these cases the question what is a finger? is not presented to the ordinary mind; for the sight never intimates to the soul that a finger is other than a finger.

That is true.

And therefore, I said, there is nothing here which excites or quickens intelligence.

There is not, he said.

But is this equally true of the greatness and smallness of the fingers? Can sight adequately perceive them? and is no difference made by the circumstance that one of the fingers is in the middle and another at the extremity? And in like manner does the touch adequately perceive the qualities of thickness or thinness, or softness or hardness? And so of the other senses; do they give perfect intimations of such matters? Is not their mode of operation rather on this wise—the sense which is concerned 524 with the quality of hardness is necessarily concerned also with the quality of softness, and only intimates to the soul that the same thing is felt to be hard and soft?

Very true, he said.

And must not the soul be perplexed at this intimation of a hard which is also soft? What again, is the meaning of light and heavy, if that which is light is also heavy, and that which is heavy, light?

Yes, he said, these intimations are very curious and have to be explained.

Yes, I said, and in these perplexities the soul naturally sum-

mons to her aid calculation and intelligence, that she may see
whether the several objects announced are one or two.

True.

And if they turn out to be two, is not each of them one, and
different?

Certainly.

And if each is one, and both are two, she will conceive the
two as in a state of division, for if they were undivided they
could only be conceived of as one?

True.

Moreover the eye beheld both small and great, but only in an
indistinct, confused fashion.

Yes.

But the thinking mind, intending to introduce clearness into
this chaos of sense, was compelled to reverse the process, and
look at small and great as separate and not confused. And this
was the beginning of the enquiry 'What is great?' and 'What
is small?'

Very true.

And thus arose the distinction of the visible and the intelligible.

Most true.

And that is an illustration of my meaning in describing impressions as stimulating to the intellect, or the reverse—the
stimulating impressions are simultaneous with opposite impressions.

I understand, he said, and agree with you.

And to which class do unity and number belong?

I do not know, he replied.

Think a little and you will see that what has preceded will
supply the answer; for if absolute unity be perceived by the sight
or any other sense, then, as we were saying in the case of the
fingers, their will be nothing to attract towards being; but when
there is some contradiction always present, and one is the reverse
of one and involves the conception of plurality, then thought
begins to be aroused within, and the soul perplexed and wanting
to arrive at a decision asks 'What is absolute unity?' And this
525 is the way in which the study of the one has a power of drawing
and converting the mind to the contemplation of true being.

And surely, he said, this occurs notably when we look at one, for the same thing is seen by us as one and as infinite in multitude?

Yes, I said; and this being true of one must be equally true of all number?

Certainly.

And all arithmetic and calculation have to do with number?

Yes.

And they are conductors to truth?

Yes, in an eminent degree.

Then this is the sort of knowledge of which we are in search, having a double use, military and philosophical; for the man of war must learn the art of number that he may know how to array his troops, and the philosopher also, because he has to rise out of the sea of change and lay hold of true being, if he would be an arithmetician.

That is true.

And our guardian is both warrior and philosopher?

Certainly.

Then this is a kind of knowledge which legislation may fitly prescribe; and we must endeavour to persuade the principal men of our State to go and learn arithmetic, not as amateurs, but they must carry on the study until they see the nature of numbers in the mind only; nor again, in the spirit of merchants or traders, with a view to buying or selling, but for the sake of their military use, and of the soul herself; and because this will be the easiest way for her to pass from generation to truth and being.

That is excellent, he said.

Yes, I said, and how ingenious the science is! the very mention of it suggests that: and how conducive, in many ways, to our desired end, if pursued in the spirit of a philosopher, and not of a shop-keeper!

How do you mean?

I mean, as I was saying, that arithmetic has a very great and elevating effect, compelling the soul to reason about abstract number, and if visible or tangible objects are obtruding upon the argument, refusing to be satisfied. You know how steadily the masters of the art repel and ridicule any one who attempts to divide absolute unity when he is calculating, and if you divide, they multiply[3], taking care that the unit shall not cease to be a unit and become lost in fractions.

That is very true.

526   Now, suppose a person were to say to them: O my friends, what are these wonderful numbers about which you are reasoning, in which, as you say, there is a unity such as you require, and each unit is equal, invariable, indivisible, what would they answer?

They would answer, as I suppose, that they are speaking of those numbers which are only realized in thought.

Then you see that this knowledge may be truly called necessary, as necessitating the use of the pure intelligence in the attainment of pure truth?

Yes; that is a marked characteristic.

And have you further remarked, that those who have a natural talent for calculation are generally quick at every other kind of knowledge; and even the dull, if they have had an arithmetical training, gain in quickness, if not in any other way?

That is true, he said.

And indeed, you will not easily find a more difficult study, and not many as difficult.

You will not.

And, for all these reasons, arithmetic must not be given up; and this is a kind of knowledge in which the best natures should be trained.

I agree.

Let this then be made one of our subjects of education. And next, shall we enquire whether the kindred science also concerns us?

You mean geometry?

Yes.

Certainly, he said; that part of geometry which relates to war is clearly our concern; for in pitching a camp, or taking up a position, or closing or extending the lines of an army, or any other military manœuvre, whether in actual battle or on a march, there will be a great difference in a general, according as he is or is not a geometrician.

---

[3] Meaning either (1) that they integrate the number because they deny the possibility of fractions; or (2) that division is regarded by them as a process of multiplication, and thus the unity and indivisibility of one is still maintained.

Yes, I said, but for that purpose a very little of either geometry or calculation will be enough; the question is rather of the higher and greater part of geometry, whether that tends towards the great end—I mean towards the vision of the idea of good; and thither, as I was saying, all things tend which compel the soul to turn her gaze towards that place, where is the full perfection of being, of which she ought, by all means, to attain the vision.

True, he said.

Then if geometry compels us to view essence, it concerns us; if generation only, it does not concern us?

Yes, that is what we assert.

Yet, at present, I said, the science is in flat contradiction to the 527 language which geometricians use, as will hardly be denied by those who have any acquaintance with their study: for they speak of finding the side of a square, and applying and adding as though they were doing something and had a practical end in view; their 'necessity' is 'il faut vivre,' which is ridiculous; whereas knowledge is the real object of the whole science.

Certainly, he said.

Then must not a further admission be made?

What admission?

The admission that this knowledge at which geometry aims is of the eternal, and not of the perishing and transient.

That, he replied, may be readily allowed, and is true.

Then, my noble friend, geometry will draw the soul towards truth, and create the mind of philosophy, and raise up that which is now unhappily allowed to fall down.

Nothing will be more effectual.

Then nothing should be more effectually enacted, than that the inhabitants of your fair city should learn geometry. Moreover the science has indirect effects, which are not small.

Of what kind are they? he said.

There are the military advantages of which you spoke, I said; and in all departments of study, as experience proves, any one who has studied geometry is infinitely quicker of apprehension.

Yes, he said, the difference between a geometrician and one who is not a geometrician is very great indeed.

Then shall we propose this as a second branch of knowledge which our youth will study?

Let us make the proposal, he replied.

And suppose we make astronomy the third—what do you say?

I am strongly inclined to that, he said; the observation of the seasons and of months and years is quite essential to husbandry and navigation, and not less essential to military tactics.

I am amused, I said, at your fear of the world, which makes you guard against the appearance of insisting upon useless studies; and I quite admit the difficulty of convincing men that in every soul there is an organ which is purified and illumined by these studies, when by other pursuits lost and dimmed; and this eye of the soul is more precious far than ten thousand bodily ones, for this alone beholds the vision of truth. Now there are two classes of persons: one class who will agree in this and will take your words as a revelation; another class who have no perception of the thing meant, to whom they will naturally seem to be idle and unprofitable tales. And you had better decide at once with which of the two you are arguing, or whether without regard to either you would not prefer to carry on the argument chiefly for your own sake; not that you have any jealousy of others, who may benefit if they please.

I think that I should prefer to carry on the argument on my own behalf.

Then take a step backward, for we have gone wrong in the order of the sciences.

What was the mistake? he said.

After plane geometry, I said, we took solids in revolution, instead of taking solids in themselves; whereas after the second dimension the third, which is concerned with cubes and dimensions of depth, ought to have followed.

That is true, Socrates; but these subjects seem to be as yet hardly explored.

Why, yes, I said, and for two reasons:—in the first place, no government patronises them, which leads to a want of energy in the study of them, and they are difficult; in the second place, students cannot learn them unless they have a teacher. But then a teacher is hardly to be found, and even if one could be found, as matters now stand, the students of these subjects, who are very conceited, would not mind him. That, however, would be otherwise if the whole State patronised and honoured them; then they would listen, and there would be continuous and earnest search, and discoveries would be made; since even now, disregarded as they are by the world, and maimed of their fair proportions, and although none of their votaries can tell the use of them, still these studies force their way by their natural charm, and very likely they may emerge into light.

Yes, he said, there is a remarkable charm in them. But I do not clearly understand the change in the order. First you began with a geometry of plane surfaces?

Yes, I said.

And you placed astronomy next, and then you made a step backward?

Yes, I said, the more haste the less speed; the ludicrous state of solid geometry made me pass over this branch and go on to astronomy, or motion of solids.

True, he said.

Then regarding the science now omitted as supplied, if only encouraged by the State, let us go on to astronomy.

That is the natural order, he said. And now, Socrates, as you rebuked the vulgar manner in which I praised astronomy before, my praises shall accord with the method of your enquiry. For 529 every one, as I think, must feel that astronomy compels the soul to look upwards and leads us from this world to another.

I am an exception then, for I should rather say that those who elevate astronomy into philosophy make us look downwards and not upwards.

Why, how is that? he asked.

You, I replied, have evidently a sublime conception of the knowledge of the things above. And I dare say that if a person were to throw his head back and study the fretted ceiling, you would still think that his mind was the percipient, and not his eyes. And you are very likely right, and I may be a simpleton: for, in my opinion, only that knowledge which is of being and the unseen can make the soul look upwards, and whether a man gapes at the heavens or blinks on the ground, seeking to learn some particular of sense, I would deny that he can learn, for nothing of that sort is matter of science; his soul is looking, not upwards, but downwards, whether his way to knowledge is by water or by land, and he may float on his back in either element.

I acknowledge, he said, the justice of your rebuke. Still, I should like to know how astronomy can be learned in any other way more conducive to that knowledge of which we speak?

In this way, I answered: the embroidery of heaven is wrought upon a visible ground, and therefore, although the fairest and most perfect of visible things, must necessarily be deemed inferior far to the true motions of absolute swiftness and absolute slowness, which are relative to each other, and carry with them that which is contained in them, in the true number and in every true figure. Now, these are to be apprehended by reason and intelligence, but not by sight.

True, he replied.

The starry heavens are to be used as the patterns of that higher knowledge; their beauty is like the beauty of figures or pictures wrought by the hand of Daedalus, or some other great artist, which we may chance to behold; any geometrician who saw them would appreciate the exquisiteness of their workmanship, but he would never dream of thinking that in them he could find the 530 true equal or the true double, or the truth of any other proportion.

No, he said, that would be ridiculous.

And will not a true astronomer have the same feeling when he looks at the movements of the stars? Will he not think that heaven and the things in heaven are framed by the Creator in the most perfect manner? But when he reflects that the proportions of night and day, or of both to the month, or of the month to the year, or of the other stars to these and to one another, are but visible and material, he will never fall into the error of supposing that they are eternal and liable to no deviation—that would be monstrous; he will rather seek in every possible way to discover the truth of them.

I quite agree when I hear you say this.

Then, I said, astronomy, like geometry, should be pursued by the method of problems—let alone the heavens—if astronomy is to become a real part of education improving the natural use of reason.

That, he said, is a work infinitely beyond our present astronomers.

Yes, I said; and there are many other things which must also have a similar extension given to them, if our legislation is to be of any use.

Can you tell me of any other suitable study?

No, he said, not without thinking.

Motion, I said, has many forms, and not one only; two of them are obvious enough; and there are others, as I imagine, which may be left to wiser heads than ours.

But where are the two?

There is a second, I said, which is the counterpart of the one already named.

And what may that be?

It would seem, I said, that one is to the ears what the other is to the eyes; for I conceive that as the eyes are appointed to look up at the stars, so are the ears to hear harmonious motions, and these are sister sciences? that is what the Pythagoreans say, and we, Glaucon, assent to them?

Yes, he replied.

But this, I said, is a laborious study, and therefore we had better go and learn of them; and they will tell us whether there are any other applications of these sciences. At the same time, we must not lose sight of our own higher object.

What is that?

There is a perfection which all knowledge ought to reach, and which our pupils ought also to attain, and not to fall short of this, as I was saying that they did in astronomy. For in the science of harmony, as I dare say you know, they are equally empirical. The sounds and consonances which they compare are those which are 531 heard only, and their labour, like that of the astronomers, is in vain.

Yes, by heaven! he said; and 'tis as good as a play to hear them talking about a sort of condensed notes, as they call them; they put their ears alongside of their neighbours as if to get a sound out of them—one set of them declaring that they catch an intermediate note and have found the least interval which should be the unit of measurement; the others maintaining the opposite theory that the two sounds have passed into the same—either party setting their ears before their understanding.

You mean, I said, those gentlemen who tease and torture the strings and rack them on the pegs of the instrument: I might carry on the metaphor and speak after their manner of the blows which the plectrum gives, and the accusations against the strings, both of backwardness and forwardness to sound; but this would be tedious, and therefore I will only say that these are not the men, but that I am speaking of the Pythagoreans, of whom I was just now proposing to enquire about harmony. For they too are in error, like the astronomers; they investigate the numbers of the harmonies which are heard, but they never attain to problems—that is to say, they never reach the natural harmonies of number, or reflect why some numbers are harmonious and others not.

That he said, is a thing of more than mortal knowledge.

A thing, I replied, which I would rather call useful; that is, if pursued with a view to the beautiful and good; but if pursued in any other spirit, useless.

There is reason in that, he said.

Now, when all these studies reach the point of intercommunion and connection with one another, and come to be considered in their mutual affinities, then, I think, but not till then, will the pursuit of them have a value for our objects; otherwise they are useless.

That, Socrates, is also my own notion; but it is a vast work of which you speak.

What do you mean? I said: the prelude or what? Are we not advised that this is but the prelude of the actual strain which we have to learn? For I imagine that you would not regard the skilled mathematician as a dialectician?

No, indeed, he said; very few mathematicians whom I have ever known are reasoners in that sense.

But do you imagine that men who are unable to give and take
532 a reason will have the knowledge which we require of them?

Neither can this be said any more than the other.

Thus, Glaucon, I said, we have arrived at the end; and this is the strain of which dialectic is the performer—the intellectual strain which the faculty of sight did but imitate: that, as you may remember, was finally imagined by us to behold real animals and the stars, and last of all the sun himself; and, in like manner, when a person begins dialectics, and starts on the discovery of the absolute by the light of reason only, and without any assistance of sense, and does not rest until by pure intelligence he attains pure good, he finds himself at the end of the intellectual world, as in the other case at the end of the visible.

Exactly, he said.

Then this is the progress which you call dialectic?

True.

But the release of the prisoners from chains, and their translation from the shadows to the images and to the light, and the ascent from the underground den to the sun, while their eyes are weak and they are unable to look on animals and plants and the light of the sun, but are able to look upon the divine images[4] in the water and the shadows of true existence (not shadows of images cast by a light of fire, which is likewise only the image of the sun)—this power of raising the highest principle in the soul to the contemplation of that which is best in existence, as in the figure, of the most luminous of the senses to the sight of that which is brightest in the visible world—this power is given, as I was saying, by all that study and pursuit of the arts which has been described.

I agree in what you are saying, he replied, which may be hard to believe, yet, from another point of view, is harder still to deny. But whether proven or not, let us assume all this, which may be the theme of many another discussion; and now proceed at once from the prelude or preamble to the chief strain or law, and describe that in like manner. Say, then, what is the nature and what are the divisions of dialectic, and what are the paths that lead thither; for these paths will also lead to our final rest.

Dear Glaucon, I said, you will not be able to follow me here, 533 though I would do my best, and you should behold not an image only but the absolute truth, according to my notion. I cannot indeed be confident that this is the exact truth, but that something like this is the truth I am confident.

Certainly, he replied.

And further, I must tell you that the power of dialectic alone can reveal this, and only to one who is a disciple of the previous sciences.

Of that too, he said, you may be confident.

And no one, I said, will argue that there is any other process or way of comprehending all true existence; for the arts in general are referable to the wants or opinions of men, or are cultivated for the sake of production and construction, or for the care of

---

4 Omitting ἐνταῦθα δὲ πρὸς φαντάσματα.

such productions and constructions; and as to the mathematical
arts which, as we were saying, have some apprehension of true
being—geometry and the like—they only dream about being,
but never can they behold the waking reality so long as they leave
the hypotheses which they use undisturbed, and are unable to
give an account of them. For when a man knows not his own
first principle, and when the conclusion and intermediate steps
are also constructed out of he knows not what, how can he imagine that such an arbitrary agreement will ever become science?

Impossible, he said.

Then dialectic, and dialectic alone, goes to a principle, and
is the only science which does away hypotheses in order to establish them; the eye of the soul, which is literally buried in some
outlandish slough, is by her taught to look upwards; and she uses as
handmaids, in the work of conversion, the sciences which we have
been discussing. Custom terms them sciences, but they ought to
have some other name, implying greater clearness than opinion
and less clearness than science: and this, in our previous sketch,
was called understanding. But there is no use in our disputing
about names when we have realities of such importance to
consider.

No, he said; any name will do which expresses the thought
clearly.

At any rate, we are satisfied, as before, to have four divisions;
two for intellect and two for opinion, and to call the first division science, the second understanding, the third belief, and the
fourth knowledge of shadows: opinion being concerned with
534 generation, and intellect with true being; and then to make a
proportion—

As being : generation : : pure intellect : opinion.
As science : belief : : understanding : knowledge of shadows.

But let us leave the further distribution and division of the objects
of opinion and of intellect, which will be a long enquiry, many
times longer than this has been.

As far as I understand, he said, I agree.

And do you also agree, I said, in describing the dialectician as
one who has a conception of the essence of each thing? And may
he who is unable to acquire and impart this conception, in what-

ever degree he fails, in that degree also be said to fail in intelligence? Will you admit that?

Yes, he said; how can I deny that?

And you would say the same of the conception of the good? Until a person is able to abstract and define the idea of good, and unless he can run the gauntlet of all objections, and is ready to disprove them, not by appeals to opinion, but to true existence, never faltering at any step of the argument—unless he can do all this, you would say that he knows neither absolute good nor any other good; he apprehends only a shadow, which is given by opinion and not by knowledge;—dreaming and slumbering in this life, before he is well awake, here he arrives at the world below, and finally has his quietus?

All that I should most certainly say.

And surely you would not have the children of your ideal State, whom you are nurturing and educating—if the ideal ever becomes a reality—you would not allow the future rulers to be like posts[5], having no reason in them, and yet to be set in authority over the highest matters?

Certainly not.

Then you will enact that they shall have such an education as will enable them to attain the greatest skill in asking and answering questions?

Yes, he said, I will, with your help.

Dialectic, then, as you will agree, is the coping-stone of the sciences, and is placed over them; no other can be placed higher: the nature of knowledge can go no further?

I agree, he said.

But to whom are we to assign these studies, and in what way 535 are they to be assigned?—that is a question which remains to be considered.

Yes, plainly.

You remember, I said, how the rulers were chosen before?

Certainly, he said.

The same natures must still be chosen, and the preference again given to the surest and the bravest, and, if possible, to the fairest; and, having noble and manly tempers, they should also have the natural gifts which accord with their education.

---

[5] γραμμάς, literally lines, probably the starting-point of a race-course.

And what are they?

Such gifts as keenness and ready powers of acquisition; for the mind more often faints from the severity of study than from the severity of gymnastics: the toil is more entirely the mind's own, and is not shared with the body.

Very true, he replied.

Further, he of whom we are in search should have a good memory, and be an unwearied, solid man who is a lover of labour in any line, or he will never be able to undergo the double toil and trouble of body and mind.

Certainly, he said; a man must have some natural gifts.

The mistake at present is, I said, that those who study philosophy have no vocation, and this, as I was before saying, is the reason why she has fallen into disrepute: her true sons should study her and not bastards.

How do you mean?

In the first place, her votary should not have a lame or one-legged industry—I mean, that he should not be half industrious and half idle: as, for example, when a man is a lover of gymnastic and hunting, and all other bodily exercises, but a hater rather than a lover of the labour of learning or hearing or enquiring. Or a man may be lame in another way, and the love of labour may take an opposite form.

That is quite true, he said.

And as to truth, I said, is not a soul to be deemed halt and lame who hates voluntary falsehood and is extremely indignant at himself and others when they tell lies, and yet receives involuntary falsehood, and does not mind wallowing like a swinish beast in the mire of ignorance, and has no shame at being detected?

Most certainly, he said.

536 And, again, as to temperance and courage and magnanimity, and every other virtue, should they not observe the ways of the true son and of the bastard? for wherever States and individuals have no eye for these sort of qualities, they unconsciously make a friend or perhaps a ruler of one who is in a figure a lame man or a bastard, from a defect in some one of these qualities.

That is very true, he said.

All these things, then, will have to be carefully considered, and

B b 2

those whom we introduce to this vast system of education and training must be sound in limb and mind, and then justice herself will have nothing to say against us, and we shall be the saviours of the State; but, if our pupils are men of another stamp, the reverse will happen, and we shall pour a still greater flood of ridicule on philosophy.

That would be discreditable.

Yes, I said, that is quite true; and yet, perhaps, in thus turning jest into earnest I am equally ridiculous.

In what respect?

I had forgotten, I said, that we were not in earnest, and spoke with too much excitement. For when I saw philosophy trampled under foot of men I could not help feeling a sort of indignation at the authors of her disgrace: and my anger made me vehement.

Indeed; I did not observe that you were more vehement than was right.

But I felt that I was. And now let me remind you that, although in our former selection we chose old men, that will not do in this. Solon was under a delusion when he said that a man as he is growing older may learn many things—for he can no more learn than he can run; youth is the time of toil.

That is certainly true.

And, therefore, calculation and geometry and all the other elements of instruction, which are a preparation for dialectic, should be presented to the mind in childhood; not, however, under any notion of forcing them.

Why not?

Because a freeman ought to be a freeman in the acquisition of knowledge. Bodily exercise, when compulsory, does no harm; but knowledge which is acquired under compulsion has no hold on the mind.

Very true, he said.

Then, my good friend, I said, do not use compulsion, but let early education be a sort of amusement; that will better enable 537 you to find out the natural bent.

There is reason in that, he said.

Do you remember our saying that the children, too, must be taken to see the battle on horseback; and if there were no danger they might be led close up and, like young hounds, have a taste of blood given them?

Yes, I remember.

Now that may be practised, I said, in other things—labours, lessons, dangers—and he who appears to be most ready ought to be enrolled in a select number.

At what age?

At the age when the necessary gymnastics are over: the period whether of two or three years which passes in this sort of training is useless for any other purpose; for sleep and exercise are unpropitious to learning; and the trial of who is first in gymnastic exercises is one of the most important tests to which they are subjected.

Certainly, he replied.

After that time those who are selected from the class of twenty years old will be promoted to higher honour, and the sciences which they learned without any order in their early education will now be brought together, and they will be able to see the correlation of them to one another and to true being.

Yes, he said, that is the only kind of knowledge which is everlasting.

Yes, I said; and the capacity for such knowledge is the great criterion of dialectical talent: the speculative or comprehensive mind is always the dialectical.

I agree in that, he said.

These, I said, are the points which you must consider; and those who have most of this comprehension, and who are most steadfast in their learning, and in their military, and generally in their public duties, when they arrive at the age of thirty will have to be chosen by you out of the select class, and elevated to higher honour; and you will have to prove them by the help of dialectic, in order to learn which of them is able to give up the use of sight and other senses, and in company with truth to attain absolute being. And here, my friend, great caution is required.

Why great caution?

Do you not remark, I said, how great the evil is which dialectic has introduced?

What is that? he said.

The lawlessness of which the professors of the art are full.

That is true, he said.

Do you think that there is anything unnatural in their case? or shall I ask you to make allowance for them?

What sort of allowance?

I want you, I said, by way of parallel, to imagine a supposititious son who is brought up in great wealth; he is one of a large and numerous family, and has many flatterers. When grown up he 538 learns that his alleged are not his real parents; but who the real ones are he is unable to discover. Can you tell me how he will be likely to behave towards his flatterers and his supposed parents, first of all during the period when he was ignorant of the false relation, and then again when he knew? Or would you like to hear my suspicion?

Very much.

I suspect, then, that while he was ignorant of the truth he would be likely to honour his father and his mother and his supposed relations more than the flatterers; he would be less willing to see them in want, or to do any violence to them, or say anything evil of them, and in important matters less willing to disobey them.

That might be expected.

But when he has made the discovery, I should imagine that he would diminish his honour and regard for them, and would become more devoted to the flatterers; their influence over him would greatly increase; he would now live after their ways, and openly associate with them, and, unless he were of an unusually good disposition, he would think no more of his parents or other supposed friends.

Well, that is extremely probable. But how is the image applicable to the disciples of philosophy?

In this way: you know that there are certain principles about justice and good, which were taught us in childhood, and under their parental authority we have been brought up, obeying and honouring them.

That is true.

And there are also opposite maxims and habits of pleasure which flatter and attract our soul, but they do not influence those who have any sense of right, and who continue to honour the maxims of their fathers and obey them.

True.

Now, when a man is in this state, and the questioning spirit asks what is fair or honourable, and he answers as the law directs, and then arguments come and refute the word of the legislator, and he is driven into believing that nothing is fair any more than foul, or just and good any more than the opposite, and the same of all his time-honoured notions, do you think that he will still honour and obey them?

That is impossible.

539 And when he ceases to think them honourable and natural as heretofore, and he fails to discover the true, can he be expected to pursue any life other than that which flatters his desires?

He cannot.

And from being an observer of the law he is converted into a lawless person?

Unquestionably.

Now all this is very natural in those who study philosophy in this manner, and also, as I was just now saying, most excusable.

Yes, he said, and, as I may add, pitiable.

Therefore, that your feelings may not be moved to pity about our thirty-years-old citizens, every care must be taken in introducing them to dialectic.

Certainly.

They must not be allowed to taste the dear delight too early; that is one thing specially to be avoided; for young men, as you may have observed, when they first get the taste in their mouths, argue for amusement, and are always contradicting and refuting others in imitation of those who refute them; they are like puppy-dogs, who delight to tear and pull at all who come near them.

Yes, he said, that is their great delight.

And when they have made many conquests and received defeats at the hands of many, they violently and speedily get into a way of not believing anything that they believed before, and hence, not only they, but philosophy generally, has a bad name with the rest of the world.

That is very true, he said.

But when a man begins to get older, he will no longer be guilty of that sort of insanity; he will follow the example of the dialectician who is seeking for truth, and not of the eristic, who is contradicting for the sake of amusement; and the greater moderation of his character will increase and not diminish the honour of the pursuit.

Very true, he said.

And did we not make special provision for this, when we said that the natures of those to whom philosophy was to be imparted were to be orderly and steadfast, not, as now, any chance aspirant or intruder?

Very true, he said.

Suppose, I said, that the study of philosophy be continued diligently and earnestly and exclusively for twice the number of years which were passed in bodily exercise—will that be enough?

Would you say six or four years? he asked.

Suppose five years to be the time fixed, I replied; after that they must be sent down into the den and compelled to hold any military or other office which young men are qualified to hold: in this way they will get their experience of life, and there will be an opportunity of trying whether, when they are drawn all manner of ways by temptation, they will stand firm or stir at all.

And how long is this stage of their lives to last? 540

Fifteen years, I answered; and when they have reached fifty years of age, then let those who still survive and have distinguished themselves in every deed and in all knowledge come at last to their consummation: the time has now arrived at which they must raise the eye of the soul to the universal light which lightens all things, and behold the absolute good; for that is the pattern according to which they are to order the State and the lives of individuals, and the remainder of their own lives also, making philosophy their chief pursuit; but, when their turn comes, also toiling at politics and ruling for the public good, not as if they were doing some great thing, but of necessity; and when they have brought up others like them and left them in their place to be governors of the State, then they will depart to the Islands of the Blest and dwell there; and the city will give them public memorials and sacrifices and honour them, if the Pythian oracle consent, as demigods, and at any rate as blessed and divine.

You are a statuary, Socrates, and have made our governors perfect in beauty.

Yes, I said, Glaucon, and our governesses too; for you must

not suppose that what I have been saying applies to men only and not to women as far as their natures can go.

There you are right, he said, if, as we described, they are to have all things in common with the men.

Well, I said, and you would agree (would you not?) that what has been said about the State and the government is not a mere dream, and although difficult not impossible, but only possible in the way that has been supposed; that is to say, when the true philosopher kings, one or more of them, are born in a State, despising the honours of this present world which they deem mean and worthless, above all esteeming right and the honour that springs from right, and regarding justice as the greatest and most necessary of all things, whose ministers they are, and whose principles will be extended by them when they set in order their own city?

How will they do that? he said.

They will begin by sending out into the country all the inhabitants of the city who are more than ten years old, and will take possession of their children, who will be unaffected by the habits of their parents; they will then train them in their own habits and laws, that is to say, in those which we have given them: and in this way the State and constitution of which we were speaking will soonest and most easily succeed, and the nation which has such a constitution will be most benefited.

Yes, that will be the best way. And I think, Socrates, that you have very well described the way in which such a constitution might come into being.

And have we not said enough of the State, and of the man who corresponds to the State, for there is no difficulty in seeing how we shall describe him?

There is no difficulty, he replied, and I say with you, enough.

BOOK VIII.

AND SO, Glaucon, we have arrived at the conclusion that in 543
the perfect State wives and children are to be in common; and
education and the arts of war and peace are also to be common,
and the best philosophers and the bravest warriors are to be their
kings?

That, replied Glaucon, is acknowledged.

Yes, I said; and we have further acknowledged that the governors, when appointed themselves, would take their soldiers and
place them in houses such as we were describing; nor would
any one say that anything which he had was his own—their
houses were to be common; and as for their property, you remember about that?

Yes, I remember that no one was to have any of the ordinary
possessions of mankind; they were to be a sort of warrior
athletes and guardians, receiving from the other citizens, in lieu
of annual payment, only their maintenance, and they were to take
care of themselves and of the whole State.

True, I said; and now that this division of our work is concluded, let us find the point at which we digressed, that we may
return into the old path.

There is no difficulty in doing that, he replied; you appeared
then, as now, to have finished the description of the State; and
you said that such a State was good, and the man was good who
answered to the State, although you had more excellent things to
relate both of State and man. And you said further, that if this 544
was the true form, then the others were false; and of the false forms,
you said, as I remember, that there were four principal ones, and
that the defects of them, and of the individuals corresponding to
them, were worth examining: when we had seen them all, and
finally agreed as to who was the best and who was the worst
of them, we might consider, as you said, whether the best was

not also the happiest, and the worst the most miserable. And when I asked you what the four forms of government were of which you spoke, then Polemarchus and Adeimantus put in their word; and you began again, and have found your way to the point at which we have now arrived.

Your recollection, I said, is most exact.

Then, like a wrestler, he replied, you must put yourself again in the same position; and let me ask the same questions, and do give me the same answer which you were about to give me then.

Yes, if I can, I will, I said.

I shall particularly wish to hear what were the four constitutions of which you were speaking.

That, I said, is easily answered: the four governments of which I spoke, so far as they have distinct names, are, first, the Cretan and Spartan, which are generally applauded: next, there is oligarchy; this is not equally approved, and is a form of government which has many evils: thirdly, democracy, which naturally follows oligarchy, although different: and lastly comes tyranny, great and famous, which is different from them all, and is the fourth and worst disorder of a State. I do not know of any other constitution which can be said to have a distinct form, but there are lordships and principalities which are bought and sold, and some other intermediate forms of government; and these nondescripts are found among barbarians oftener than among Hellenes.

Yes, he replied, there are said to be many curious forms of government among them.

Do you know, I said, that governments vary as the characters of men vary, and that there must be as many of the one as there are of the other? Or perhaps you suppose that States are made of 'oak and rock,' and not out of the human natures which are in them, and which turn the scale and draw other things after them?

Nay, he said, the States are as the men are; they do but grow out of human characters.

Then if the constitutions of States are five, the disposition of individual minds will also be five?

Certainly.

Him who answers to aristocracy, and whom we rightly call 545 just and good, we have already described; and now we have to describe the inferior sort of natures, being the contentious and ambitious, who answer to the Spartan polity; also the oligarchical, democratical, and tyrannical man. Let us place the most just by the side of the most unjust, and then we shall be able to compare the relative happiness or unhappiness of pure justice and pure injustice: this will complete the enquiry. And then we shall know whether we are to pursue injustice, as Thrasymachus advises, or justice, as the present argument counsels.

Certainly, he replied, that will be the way.

Suppose, then, following our old plan, which we adopted as being clearer, of taking the State first and then proceeding to the individual, we begin with the government of honour (for I know of no name for such a government other than timocracy, or perhaps timarchy); and then we will view the like character in the individual; and, after that, consider oligarchy and the oligarchical man; and then again we will turn our attention to democracy and the democratical man; and lastly, we will go and view the city of tyranny, and there take a look into the tyrant's soul, and try to arrive at the final decision.

That way of viewing and judging of the matter will be very rational.

First, then, I said, let us enquire how timocracy (or the government of honour) arises out of aristocracy (or the government of the best). Clearly, all political changes originate in divisions of the actual governing power; for a government which is united, however small, cannot be moved.

That is true, he said.

In what way, then, will our city be moved, and in what manner will the two classes of auxiliaries and rulers disagree among themselves or with one another? Shall we, after the manner of Homer, pray the muses to tell us 'how strife was first kindled?' Shall we imagine them, in tragic style, pretending to be in earnest, playing with us as with children in solemn words?

How would they address us?

After this manner:—A city which is thus constituted can hardly 546 be shaken; but, seeing that everything which has a beginning has also an end, even this constitution will in time perish and come to dissolution. And this is the dissolution:—In plants that grow on the earth, as well as in animals that move on the earth's surface, fertility and sterility of soul and body occur when the circles are completed, in short-lived existences passing over a short space, in long-lived ones over a long space. But, to the knowledge of human fecundity and sterility all the wisdom and education of your rulers will not attain; the laws which regulate them will not be discovered by an intelligence which is alloyed with sense, but will escape them, and they will bring children into the world when they have no business. Now that which is of divine birth has a period which is contained in a perfect number (i. e. a cyclical number, such as 6, which is equal to the sum of its divisors 1, 2, 3, so that when the circle or time represented by 6 is completed, the lesser times or rotations represented by 1, 2, 3 are also completed), but that which is of human birth is contained in a number in which first (i. e. declining from the perfect cycle) increments by involution and evolution giving three intervals and four terms of approximating and differentiating and increasing and waning numbers make all agreeable and commensurable[1]. The base of these (3) with a third added (4) when joined with a figure of five (20) and raised to the third power furnishes two harmonies; [2]the first a square which is a hundred times as great ($400 = 4 \times 100$), and the other a figure having one side equal to the former, which, taken one way, is equilateral, but also oblong, consisting of a hundred numbers squared upon rational diameters of a square (i. e. in which fractions are omitted), the side of which is five ($7 \times 7 = 49 \times 100 = 4900$), each of them being less by one (than the perfect square which includes the fractions sc. 50) or less by two perfect squares of irrational diameters (of a square the side of which is five $= 50 + 50 = 100$); and a hundred cubes of three ($27 \times 100 = 2700 + 4900 + 400 = 8000$). Now this number represents a geometrical figure which has control over the good and evil of births. For when our guardians are ignorant of the right seasons, and unite bride and bridegroom out of due time, the children will not be happy or goodly. And though the best of them will be appointed by their predecessors, still they will be unworthy to hold their fathers' places, and when they come into power as guardians, they will soon be found to fail in taking care of us, the Muses, first by undervaluing music, and secondly

[1] Perhaps 3, 9, 27, 81; or $1 + 2 + 4 + 8 + 8 + 4 + 2 + 1 = 30$.
[2] Or the first a square which is $100 \times 100 = 10,000$. The whole number will then be $17500 = $ a square of 100, and an oblong of 100 by 75.

gymnastic; and hence our young men will be less cultivated.
In the succeeding generation rulers will be appointed who have
none of the qualities of guardians. In order to put to the test
the metal of your different races, which, like Hesiod's, are of
gold and silver and brass and iron, iron will be mingled with 547
silver, and brass with gold, and hence there will arise inequality
and irregularity, which always and in all places are causes of
enmity and war. Such is the origin of strife, wherever arising;
and this is the answer of the Muses to us.

Yes, he said, and we may assume that they answer truly.

Why, yes, I said, of course they answer truly; the Muses cannot
do otherwise.

And what do the Muses say next?

When strife arose, then the two races were drawn different ways:
the iron and brass fell to acquiring money and land and houses
and gold and silver; but the gold and silver races, having the
true riches in their own nature, inclined towards virtue and the
ancient order of things. There was a battle between them,
and at last they agreed to assign their land and houses to the
possession of individuals; and they enslaved their friends and
maintainers, whom they had formerly protected in the condition
of freemen, and made of them subjects and servants; while they
themselves were occupied with war and the watching of them.

That, he replied, will probably be the origin of the change.

And the new government which thus arises will be of a form
intermediate between oligarchy and aristocracy.

Very true.

And now, after the change has been made, what will be their
way of life? Clearly, the new State, being in a mean between
oligarchy and the perfect State, will partly follow one and partly
the other, and will also have some peculiarities.

That is true, he said.

In the honour given to rulers, in the abstinence of the warrior
class from agriculture, handicrafts, and other trades, in the institution of common meals, attention to gymnastics and military
training—in all these the citizen will resemble the perfect State.

True.

But in the fear of admitting philosophers to power, because
their philosophy is no longer simple and earnest, but made up of

mixed elements; and in turning from them to passionate and simpler characters, who are by nature fitted for war rather than
548 peace; and in the value which they set upon military stratagems and contrivances, and in their everlasting wars—this State will be for the most part peculiar.

Yes.

Yes, I said; and men of this stamp will be covetous of money, like those who live in oligarchies; they will have a fierce secret longing after gold and silver, which they will hoard in dark places, having magazines and treasures of their own for the deposit and concealment of them; also castles which are just nests for their eggs, and in which they will spend large sums on their wives, or on any others whom they please.

That is most true, he said.

And they are miserly because they have no means of openly acquiring the money which they prize; they will spend that which is another man's in their lust; stealing their pleasures and running away like children from the law their father: they have been schooled not by gentle influences but by force; for they have no thought of the true muse of reason and philosophy, and gymnastic is preferred by them to music.

Undoubtedly, he said, the form of government which you describe is a mixture of good and evil.

Why, there is a mixture, I said; but one thing, and one thing only, is predominantly seen,—the spirit of contention and ambition; and these are due to the prevalence of the passionate or spiritual element.

Assuredly, he said.

Such is the origin and such the character of this State, of which the outline only has been given; the more perfect execution of the sketch was not required, because the outline is enough to show the type of the most perfectly just and unjust; and to go through all the States and all the characters of men, leaving none of them out, would be an interminable labour.

Very true, he replied.

Who answers to this form of government—how did he come into being, and what is he like?

I think, said Adeimantus, that in the spirit of contention which characterizes him, he is not unlike our friend Glaucon.

Perhaps, I said, he may be like him in that one point; but there are other respects in which he is very different.

In what respects?

He should have more of self-assertion and be somewhat less favoured by the Muses, yet not other than a lover of the Muses; and he should be a good listener, but not a speaker. A man of 549 this sort may be imagined to be rough with slaves, not like the educated man, who is too proud for that; and he will also be courteous to freemen, and remarkably obedient to authority; he is a lover of power and a lover of honour; claiming to be a ruler, not because he is a speaker, or on any ground of that sort, but because he is a soldier, and, as a soldier, has performed feats of arms;—he is also a lover of gymnastic exercises and of the chase.

Yes, he said, that is the character of timocracy.

Such an one will despise riches only when he is young; but as he gets older he will be more and more attracted to them, because he has a piece of the avaricious nature in him, and is not single-minded towards virtue, having lost his best guardian.

Who is that? said Adeimantus.

Philosophy, I said, tempered with music, who comes and takes up her abode in a man through life, and is the only saviour of his virtue.

Good, he said.

Such, I said, is the timocratical youth, and he is like the timo-cratical State.

Exactly.

His origin is as follows:—He is often the son of a brave father, who dwells in an ill-governed city, the honours and offices of which he declines, and will not go to law, but is ready to waive his rights in order that he may escape trouble.

And how does the son come into being?

The character of the son begins to develope when he hears his mother grumbling at her husband for not having a seat in the government, the consequence of which is that she loses prece-dence among other women. Further, when she sees her husband not very eager about money, and instead of battling and railing in the law courts or assembly, taking everything of that sort quietly; and when she observes that his thoughts always centre in himself, while he treats her with very considerable indifference, she is annoyed at all this, and says to her son that his father is only half a man and far too easy-going: not to mention other similar complaints which women love to utter.

Yes, said Adeimantus, they give us plenty of them, and in their own characteristic style.

And you know, I said, that the old servants of the family, who are supposed to be attached, talk privately in the same strain to the sons; and if they see any one who owes money to their father, or is wronging him in any way, and he fails to prosecute them, they tell the youth that when he grows up he must retaliate upon 550 his injurers, and be more of a man than his father. He has only to walk abroad and he hears and sees the same sort of thing: those who do their own business in the city are called simple, and held in no esteem, while the busy-bodies are honoured and applauded. The result is that the young man, hearing and seeing all these things—hearing, too, the words of his father, and having a nearer view of his way of life, and making comparisons of him and others—is drawn opposite ways: while his father is watering and nourishing the rational principle in his soul, the others are encouraging the passionate and appetitive; and he being not originally of a bad nature, but having kept bad company, is brought by their joint influence to a middle point, and gives up the kingdom which is within him to the middle principle of contentiousness and passion, and becomes proud and ambitious.

You seem to me to have described his origin perfectly.

Then we have now, I said, the second form of government and the second type of character?

We have.

Next, let us look at another man who, as Aeschylus says, is set over against another State; or rather, as our plan requires, begin with the State.

By all means.

I believe that oligarchy follows next in order.

And what manner of government do you term oligarchy?

A government resting on a valuation of property, in which the rich have power and the poor are deprived of power.

I understand, he replied.

Shall I describe how the change from timocracy to oligarchy arises?

Yes.

Well, I said, no eyes are required in order to see how that comes about.

How?

That private hoard of theirs is the source of the evil; the accumulation of gold ruins timocracy: they invent some extravagance which is in open contravention of the law, but neither they nor their wives care about this.

That might be expected.

And then one seeing another prepares to rival him, and thus the whole body of the citizens acquires a similar character.

Likely enough.

After that they get on in trade, and the more they think of this the less they think of virtue; for when riches and virtue are placed together in the scales of the balance, the one always rises as the other falls.

True.

And in proportion as riches and rich men are honoured in the State, virtue and the virtuous are dishonoured. 55

Clearly.

And what is honoured is cultivated, and that which has no honour is neglected.

That is the case.

And so at last, instead of loving contention and glory, men become lovers of trade and money, and they honour and reverence the rich man, and make a ruler of him, and dishonour the poor man.

Certainly.

Then they proceed to make a law which fixes a sum of money as the qualification of citizenship; the money fixed is more or less as the oligarchy is more or less exclusive; and they forbid any one whose property is below the amount fixed to share in the government: these changes in the constitution they effect by force of arms, if intimidation has not already done the work.

Very true.

And this, speaking generally, is the way in which oligarchy is established.

Yes, he said; but what are the characteristics of this form of government, and what are the supposed defects?

First of all, I said, consider the nature of the qualification. Just think what would happen if the pilots were to be chosen according to their property, and a poor man refused permission to steer, even though he were a better pilot?

You mean that they would shipwreck?

Yes; and is not this true of the government of anything[3]?

Yes, that is what I should imagine.

And would you say this of a city also, or do you make an exception in favour of a city?

Nay, he said, the case of a city is still stronger, in proportion as the rule of a city is greater and more difficult.

This, then, will be the first great defect of oligarchy?

Clearly.

And here is another defect which is quite as bad.

What defect?

The inevitable division; such a State is not one, but two States, the one of poor men, the other of rich men, who are living on the same spot and ever conspiring against one another.

Yes, that is equally bad.

Another discreditable feature is the impossibility of carrying on any war, because if they arm and use the multitude they are more afraid of them than of the enemy: that is unavoidable. If they do not use them, then, in the hour of battle, they appear oligarchs indeed, few to fight and few to rule: and at the same time their fondness for money makes them unwilling to pay taxes.

That is not creditable.

And what do you say of our former charge that, under such a constitution, the same persons are busy at many things, and are husbandmen, tradesmen, warriors, all in one? Does that seem well?

Anything but well.

There is another evil which is, perhaps, the greatest of all, and to which this State first begins to be liable.

What is the evil?

The evil is that a man may sell all that he has, and another may possess his property, yet after the sale he may dwell in the city of which he is no longer a part, being neither trader, nor artisan, nor horseman, nor hoplite, but only poor and helpless.

552

---

[3] Omitting ἤ τινος.

C C 2

Yes, that begins in this State.

An oligarchy offers no security against this; for oligarchies have both the extremes of great wealth and utter poverty.

True.

But think again: what sort of a gentleman is this? In his wealthy days, while he was spending his money, was he a whit more good to the State for the purposes of which we were just now speaking? Or did he only seem to be a member of the ruling body, being really no more a ruler than he was a subject, but just a spendthrift?

As you say, he seemed to be a ruler, but was only a spendthrift.

May we not say that this is the drone in the house who is like the drone in the honeycomb, and that the one is the plague of the city as the other is of the hive?

Just so, Socrates.

And God has made the flying drones, Adeimantus, all without stings, whereas of the walking drones he has made some without stings and others with dreadful stings: of the stingless class are those who in their old age end by dying paupers; of the stingers come all the criminal class, as they are termed.

Most true, he said.

Clearly then, whenever you see paupers in a State, somewhere in that neighbourhood there are hidden away thieves and cut-purses and robbers of temples, and other malefactors.

That is clear.

Well, I said, and in oligarchical States do you not find paupers?

Yes, he said; nearly everybody is a pauper who is not a ruler.

And may we be so bold as to suppose that there are also many criminals to be found in them, rogues who have stings, and whom the authorities are careful to restrain by force?

Certainly, we may be so bold.

The existence of such persons is to be attributed to want of education, ill-training, and an evil constitution of the State?

True.

Such, then, is the form and such are the evils of oligarchy; and there may be other evils.

That is pretty much the truth.

Then now oligarchy, or the form of government in which the 553 rulers are elected for their wealth, may be regarded as dismissed.

Let us next proceed to consider the nature and origin of the individual who answers to the State.

Yes, by all means.

Is not this the manner of the change from the timocratical to the oligarchical? Suppose the representative of timocracy to have a son: at first he begins by emulating his father and walking in his footsteps, but presently he sees him strike all in a moment on a sunken reef, which is the State, and he and all that he has are lost; he may have been a general or some other high officer who is brought to trial under a prejudice raised by informers, and either put to death, or exiled, or deprived of the privileges of a citizen, and all his property taken from him.

That is very likely to happen.

And the son has seen and known all this—he is a ruined man, and his fear has taught him to knock ambition and passion head-foremost from his bosom's throne: humbled by poverty he takes to money-making and by mean and small savings and doings gets a fortune together. Is not this man likely to seat the concupiscent and covetous elements on that vacant throne? They will play the great king within him, and he will array them with tiara and collar and scimitar.

Likely! Yes, he replied.

And when he has made the reasoning and passionate faculties sit on the ground obediently on either side, and taught them to know their place, he compels the one to think only of the method by which lesser sums may be converted into larger ones, and schools the other into the worship and admiration of riches and rich men; no ambition will he tolerate except the ambition of getting rich and the means which lead to this.

Of all conversions, he said, there is none so speedy or so sure as when the ambitious youth changes into the avaricious one.

And the avaricious, I said, is the oligarchical youth?

Yes, he said; at any rate the individual out of whom he came is like the State out of which oligarchy came.

Let us then consider whether there is any likeness between them.

554 Very good.

First, then, they resemble one another in the value which they set upon wealth?

Certainly.

Also in their penurious, laborious character; the individual only satisfies his necessary appetites, and confines his expenditure to them; his other desires he subdues, under the idea that there is no use in them?

True.

He is a shabby fellow, I said, who saves something out of everything and makes a purse for himself; and this is the sort of man whom the vulgar applaud. Is he not like the State which he represents?

That would be my view of him, he replied; at any rate, money is highly valued by him as well as by the State.

Why, he is not a man of cultivation, I said.

I imagine not, he said; had he been educated he would never have made a blind god director of his chorus, or given him chief honour[4].

Excellent! I said. Yet consider this: Will there not be found in him, owing to his want of cultivation, dronelike desires as of pauper and rogue, which are forcibly kept down by his general habit of life?

True.

Do you know where you will have to look if you want to discover his rogueries?

Where must I look?

Let him be the guardian of an orphan, or have some other great opportunity of acting dishonestly, and then he will show that, in sustaining the reputation of uprightness which attaches to him in his dealings generally, he coerces his other bad passions by an effort of virtue; not that he convinces them of evil, or exerts over them the gentle influence of reason, but he acts upon them by necessity and fear, and because he trembles for his possessions.

That is clear.

Yes, indeed, I said, my dear friend, you will find that the natural desires of the drone commonly exist in him all the same, whenever he has the spending of another's goods.

No mistake about that.

---

[4] Reading καὶ ἐτίμα μάλιστα. Εὖ, ἦν δ᾽ ἐγώ, according to Schneider's emendation.

This sort of man, then, will be at war with himself; he will be two men, and not one; but, in general, his better desires will be found to prevail over his inferior ones.

True.

For these reasons such an one will be more decent than many are; yet the true virtue of a unanimous and harmonious soul will be far out of his reach.

That I believe.

555 And surely, in his private capacity, the miser will be an ignoble competitor in a State for any prize of victory, or other object of honourable ambition; he is too much afraid of awakening his expensive appetites and inviting them to help and join in the struggle; in true oligarchical fashion he fights with a small part only of his resources, and the result commonly is that he loses the prize and saves his money.

Very true.

Can we any longer doubt, then, that the miser and money-maker answers to the oligarchical State?

Certainly not.

Next comes democracy and the democratical man; the origin and nature of them we have still to learn, that we may compare the individual and the State, and so pronounce upon them.

That, he said, is our method.

Well, I said, is not this the way in which the change from oligarchy into democracy arises?—they are insatiable of wealth which they propose to themselves as their end; and the rulers, who are aware that their own power rests upon property, refuse to curtail by law the extravagance of the spendthrift youth because they will gain by their ruin; they lend them money and buy them out of their land and grow in wealth and honour?

Exactly.

There can be no doubt that in a State you cannot have in the citizens the love of wealth and the spirit of moderation; one or the other will have to be disregarded.

That is tolerably clear.

And in oligarchical States, from carelessness and the indulgence of their extravagance, men of good family have often been reduced to beggary?

Yes, often.

And still they remain in the city; there they are, and they have stings and arms, and some of them owe money, some are no longer citizens: a third class are in both predicaments, and they hate and conspire against those who have got their property, and anybody else, and are eager for revolution.

That is true.

On the other hand, the men of business, stooping as they walk, and pretending never so much as to see those whom they have already ruined, insert the sting—that is, their money—into anybody else who is not on his guard against them, and recover the parent or principal sum many times over multiplied into a family of children: this is the way in which they make drone and pauper to abound in the State.

Yes, he said, there are plenty of them, that is certain. 556

The evil is like a fire which is blazing up and which they will not extinguish either by placing restrictions on the disposition of property or—

What is the other solution of the difficulty?

One which is about as good, and has the advantage of compelling the citizens to look to their characters :—Let there be an ordinance that every one shall enter into voluntary contracts at his own risk, and there will be less of this scandalous money-making, and the evils of which we were speaking will be greatly lessened in the State.

Yes, they will be greatly lessened.

At present the governors, induced by the motives which I have named, treat their subjects badly; while they and their adherents, especially the young men of the governing class, lead a life of luxury and idleness both of body and mind; they do nothing, and are incapable of holding out against pleasure and pain.

Very true.

They care only for making money, and are as indifferent as the pauper to the cultivation of virtue.

Yes, quite indifferent.

Now in this state of things the rulers and their subjects come in one another's way, whether on a journey or some other occasion of meeting, or on a pilgrimage or march as fellow-soldiers or fellow-sailors; they observe each other in the moment of danger (and where danger is there is no fear that the poor will be despised by the rich), and very likely the wiry sunburnt poor man may be placed in battle at the side of a wealthy one who has never spoilt his complexion, and has plenty of superfluous flesh—when he sees such an one puffing and at his wits'-end, can he avoid drawing the conclusion that men of this sort are only rich because no one has the courage to despoil them? And when they meet in private will they not be saying to one another that our 'warriors are nothing worth?'

Yes, he said, I am quite aware that this is their way of talking.

And, as where a body is weak the addition of a touch from without may bring on illness, and sometimes even when there is no external provocation a commotion may arise within, in the same way where there is weakness in the State there is also likely to be illness, the occasion of which may be very slight, one party introducing their democratical, the other their oligarchical allies, and the State may fall sick, and be at war with herself and in a state of distraction, even when there is no 557 external cause?

Yes, surely.

And then democracy comes into being after the poor have conquered their opponents, slaughtering some and banishing some, while to the remainder they give an equal share of freedom and power; and this is the form of government in which the magistrates are commonly elected by lot.

Yes, he said, that is the nature of democracy, whether established by arms or by fear, and the withdrawal of the opposite party.

And now what is their manner of life, and what sort of a government is this? for as the government is such will be the man.

Clearly, he said.

In the first place, are they not free? and the city is full of freedom and frankness—there a man may do as he likes.

Yes, that is often said, he replied.

And where this freedom is, there every man is clearly able to order his life as he pleases?

Clearly.

Then in this kind of State there will be the greatest variety of human natures?

There will.

This, then, is likely to be the fairest of States and may be compared to an embroidered robe which is spangled with flowers; and being in like manner spangled with the manners and characters of mankind will appear to be the fairest of them all. And just as women and children think variety charming, so there are many men who will deem this the fairest of States.

Yes.

Yes, I said, my noble Sir, and a good place in which to go and look for a government.

Why?

Because of the liberty which reigns there: they have a complete assortment of constitutions; and if a man has a mind to establish a State, as we are doing, he must go to a democracy as he would go to a bazaar, where they sell them, and pick out one that suits him; then, when he has made his choice, he may lay the foundation of his State.

He will be sure, he said, to have patterns enough.

And there being no necessity, I said, for you to govern in this State, even if you have the capacity, or to be governed unless you like, or to go to war when the others go to war, or to be at peace when others are at peace, unless you are disposed—there being no necessity also because some law forbids you to hold office or be a dicast, that you should not hold office or be a dicast, if you have a mind yourself—is not that a way of life which for the 558 moment is supremely delightful?

Yes, for the moment, that is true.

And is not the calmness of those[5] against whom sentence has been given often quite charming? Under a government of this sort there are men who, when they have been condemned to death or exile, stay where they are and walk about the world; the gentleman parades like a hero, as though nobody saw or cared.

Yes, he replied, I have often remarked that.

Yes, I said; and the forgiving spirit of democracy, and the 'don't care' about trifles, and the disregard which she shows of all the fine principles which we were solemnly affirming at the foundation of the city—as when we said that, except in the case of some rare natures, never will there be a good man who from

[5] Or, 'their good nature about those.'

his early youth has not made things of beauty an amusement and also a study—how grandly does she trample all that under foot, never giving a thought to the pursuits which make a statesman, and is satisfied to honour a man who says that he is the people's friend.

Yes, he said, that is glorious.

These and other kindred characteristics are proper to democracy, which is a charming form of government, full of variety and diversity, and dispensing equality to equals and unequals alike.

That, he said, is sufficiently well known.

Consider now, I said, what manner of man the individual is, or rather consider, as in the case of the State, how he is created.

Very good, he said.

Is not this the way—he is the son of the miserly and oligarchical father who has trained him in his own habits?

Exactly.

And, like his father, he keeps under the pleasures which are of the spending and not of the getting sort, being those which are called by us unnecessary. The argument will be clearer if we here distinguish which are the necessary and which are the unnecessary pleasures.

I should like to do that.

Necessary pleasures are those of which we cannot get rid, and which benefit us when they are satisfied; both kinds are rightly called necessary, because our nature is necessarily attracted to them.

559   True.

And therefore we are not wrong in calling them necessary?

We are not.

Again, as to the desires which a man may get rid of, if he makes that his object when young, the presence of which, moreover, does no good, and in some cases the reverse of good—shall we not be right in saying that all these are unnecessary?

Yes, certainly.

Suppose we select an example of either kind, in order that we may have a general notion of them?

Very good.

Will not the desire of eating, that is, of simple food and condiments, as far as they are required for health and strength, be of the necessary class?

That is what I should suppose.

The pleasure of eating is necessary in two ways—first as beneficial, and also as needed for the support of life?

Yes.

But the condiments are only necessary as being good for health?

Certainly.

And the desire which goes beyond this of viands of a less simple kind, which might generally be got rid of, if controlled and trained in youth, and is hurtful to the body and hurtful to the soul in the pursuit of wisdom and virtue, may be rightly called unnecessary?

Very right.

May we not say that these spend and the other desires make money, because they are of use with a view to production?

Certainly.

And of the pleasures of love, and all other pleasures, the same holds good?

True.

And the drone of which we were speaking meant him who was surfeited in pleasures and desires of this sort, and was governed by the unnecessary desires, whereas he who was governed by the necessary was miserly and oligarchical?

Very true, he said.

Again, I said, let us see how the democratical man grows out of the oligarchical: the following, as I suspect, is commonly the process.

What?

When a young man who has been brought up as we were just now describing, in a vulgar and miserly way, has tasted drones' honey and has come to associate with fierce and cunning natures who are able to provide for him all sorts of refinements and varieties of pleasure—then, as you may imagine, the change will begin of the oligarchical principle within him into the democratical.

That, he said, is the inevitable result.

And as in the city like was helping like, and the change was effected by an alliance from without assisting one division of the

citizens, so the young man also changes by a class of desires from
without assisting a class of those within, that which is akin and
alike again helping that which is akin and alike.

Certainly.

And if there be any ally which aids the oligarchical side,
560 whether the influence of friends or kindred, advising or rebuking
him, then there arises a faction and an opposite faction, and the
result is a civil war.

Certainly.

And there are times when the democratical principle gives way
to the oligarchical, and some of his desires die, and others are
banished; a spirit of reverence enters into the young man's soul
and order is restored.

Yes, he said, that sometimes happens.

And then, again, after the old desires have been driven out
fresh ones spring up, which are like them; they have never
known a parent's discipline, and this makes them fierce and
numerous.

Yes, he said, that often occurs.

They draw him to his old associates, and holding secret intercourse with him, breed and muster in him?

Very true.

At length they seize upon the citadel of the young man's soul,
which they perceive to be void of all fair accomplishments and
pursuits and of every true word, which are the best guardians and
sentinels in the minds of men dear to the gods.

None better.

False and boastful words and conceits grow up instead of them,
and take the same position in him?

Yes, he said; indeed they do.

And so the young man returns into the country of the lotus-
eaters, and takes up his abode there in the face of all men; and
if any help be sent by his friends to the oligarchical part of him,
the Messieurs Vain Conceit shut the gate of the king's fastness;
they will not allow the new ally to pass. And if ambassadors,
venerable for their age, come and parley, they refuse to listen to
them; there is a battle and they win: then modesty, which they call
silliness, is ignominiously thrust into exile by them. They affirm
temperance to be unmanliness, and her also they contemptuously

eject; and they pretend that moderation and orderly expenditure
are vulgarity and meanness; and, with a company of vain appetites
at their heels, they drive them beyond the border.

Yes, with right good will.

And when they have made a sweep of the soul of him who is
now in their power, and is being initiated by them in great
mysteries, the next thing is to bring back to their house insolence and anarchy and waste and impudence in bright array,
having garlands on their heads, with a great company, while they
hymn their praises and call them by sweet names; insolence they 561
term breeding, and anarchy liberty, and waste magnificence, and
impudence courage. In this way the young man passes out of
his original nature, which was trained in the school of necessity,
into the freedom and libertinism of useless and unnecessary
pleasures.

Yes, he said, that is obviously the way.

When the change has been made he lives on, spending his
money and labour and time on unnecessary pleasures quite as
much as on necessary ones; but if he be fortunate, and is not too
much intoxicated with passion, when he gets older, after the
tumult of freedom has mostly passed away—supposing that he
then re-admits into the city some part of the exiled virtues, and
does not wholly give himself up to their successors—in that case
he balances his pleasures and lives in a sort of equilibrium,
putting the government of himself into the hands of the one that
offers and wins the turn; and when he has had enough of that,
then into the hands of another, and is very impartial in his
encouragement of them all.

Very true, he said.

Neither does he receive or admit into the fortress any true
word of advice; if any one says to him that some pleasures are
the satisfactions of good and noble desires, and others of evil
desires, and that he ought to use and honour some and curtail
and reduce others—whenever this is repeated to him he shakes
his head and says that they are all alike, and that one is as honourable as another.

Why, yes, he said; that is the sort of man and that is his way
of behaving.

Yes, I said, he lives through the day indulging the appetite of the hour; and sometimes he is lapped in drink and strains of the flute; then he is for total abstinence, and tries to get thin; then, again, he is at gymnastics; sometimes idling and neglecting everything, then once more living the life of a philosopher; often he is at politics, and starts to his feet and says and does anything that may turn up; and, if he is emulous of any one who is a warrior, off he is in that direction, or of men of business, once more in that. His life has neither order nor law; and this is the way of him—this he terms joy and freedom and happiness.

Yes, he said, there is liberty, equality, and fraternity enough in him.

Yes, I said; he may be described as

> ' A man so various that he seems to be
> Not one, but all mankind's epitome.'

He is, like the State, a rare being, and has many forms. And many a man and many a woman will emulate him, and many a constitution and many an example of life is contained in him.

That is true.

562 Let him then be set over against democracy; he may truly be called the democratic man.

Let that be his place, he said.

And now comes the most beautiful of all, man and State alike, tyranny and the tyrant; these we have to consider.

Quite true, he said.

Say then, my friend, how does tyranny arise—out of democracy of course?

Clearly.

And does not tyranny spring from democracy in the same way as democracy from oligarchy—I mean, after a sort?

How is that?

The good which oligarchy proposed was excess of wealth; in this oligarchy originated. Am I not right?

Yes.

And the insatiable desire of wealth and the neglect of all other things for the sake of money-getting, was also the ruin of oligarchy?

True.

And democracy has a notion of good, the insatiable desire of which also brought her to an end?

What notion of good?

Freedom, I replied; that, as people often say, is best in a democracy—and, therefore, in a democracy only will the freeman of nature deign to dwell.

Why, said he, that is very often said.

And, I was going to observe, that the insatiable desire of this and the neglect of other things, introduces the change in democracy, which occasions a demand for tyranny.

How is that?

When a democracy which is thirsting for freedom has evil cup-bearers presiding over the feast, and has drunk too deeply of the strong wine of freedom, then, unless her rulers are very amenable and give a plentiful draught, she calls them to account and punishes them, and says that they are cursed oligarchs.

Yes, he replied, that is a very common thing.

Yes, I said; and loyal citizens are insulted by her as lovers of slavery and men of naught; she would have subjects who are like rulers, and rulers who are like subjects: these are men after her own heart, whom she praises and honours both in private and public. Now, in such a State, can liberty have any limit?

Certainly not.

Nay, I said, the anarchy grows and finds a way into private houses, and ends by getting among the animals and infecting them.

How do you mean?

I mean that the father gets accustomed to descend to the level of his sons and to fear them, and the son to be on a level with his father, he having no shame or fear of either of his parents; and this is his freedom, and the metic is equal with the citizen and the citizen with the metic, and the stranger on a level with either. 563

Yes, he said, that is true.

That is true, I said; and, moreover, little things of this sort happen: the master fears and flatters his scholars, and the scholars despise their masters and tutors; and, in general, young and old are alike, and the young man is on a level with the old, and is ready to compete with him in word or deed; and old men condescend to the young and are full of pleasantry and gaiety; they do not like to be thought morose and authoritative, and therefore they imitate the young.

Quite true, he said.

The last extreme of popular liberty is when the slave bought with money, whether male or female, is just as free as his or her purchaser; nor must I forget to tell of the liberty and equality of the two sexes in relation to each other.

Why not, he said, as Aeschylus remarks, utter the word which rises to our lips?

Yes, I replied; that is what I am now doing; and I must say that no one who does not know would believe, how much greater is the liberty which animals who are under the dominion of men have in a democracy than in any other State: for truly, the she-dogs, as the proverb says, are as good as their she-mistresses, and the horses and asses come to have a way of marching along with all the rights and dignities of freemen; and they will run at any body whom they meet in the street if he does not get out of their way: and all things are just ready to burst with liberty.

You tell me, he said, my own dream; for that which you describe often happens to me when I am taking a country walk.

And above all, I said, and as the result of all, see how sensitive the citizens become; they chafe impatiently at the least touch of authority, and at length, as you know, they cease to care even for the laws, written or unwritten; for they will have no one over them.

Yes, he said, that I know quite well.

And this, my friend, I said, is the fair and glorious beginning out of which springs tyranny.

Glorious indeed, he said. But what is the next step?

The ruin of oligarchy is the ruin of democracy; the same disorder intensified by liberty dominates over democracy, the truth being that the excessive increase of anything often causes a
564 reaction in the opposite direction; and this is the case not only in the seasons and in vegetable and animal forms, but above all in forms of government.

That is very likely.

For excess of liberty, whether in States or individuals, seems only to pass into excess of slavery.

Yes, that is the natural order.

Then tyranny naturally arises out of democracy, and the most aggravated form of tyranny and slavery out of the most extreme form of liberty.

Yes, he said, there is reason in all that.

That, however, was not, as I believe, your question—you rather desired to know what is that disorder which is generated alike in oligarchy and democracy, and enslaves both?

True, he replied.

Well, I said, I meant to refer to the class of idle spendthrifts, of whom the more courageous are the leaders and the more timid the followers, the same whom we were comparing to drones, some stingless, and others having stings.

A very just comparison, he said.

These two classes are the plagues of every city in which they are generated, being what phlegm and bile are to the body. And the good physician and lawgiver of the State ought, like the wise bee-master, to keep them at a distance and prevent, if possible, their ever coming in; and if they have anyhow found a way in, then he should have them and their cells cut out as speedily as possible.

Yes, indeed, he said, that he should.

Then, in order that we may see more clearly what we are doing, let us imagine democracy to be divided into three classes, which also exist in fact; for liberty creates drones quite as much in the democratic as in the oligarchical State.

That is true.

But in the democracy they are more intensified.

How is that?

The reason is, that in the oligarchical State, as they are disqualified and driven from power, they cannot train or gather strength; whereas in a democracy they are almost the entire ruling power, and the keener sort speak and act, while the rest sit buzzing about the bema and will not suffer a word to be said on the other side; and hence there is hardly anything in these States which is not their doing.

Very true, he said.

Then there is another class which is divided from the multitude.

What is that?

The richest class, which in a nation of traders is generally the most orderly.

That may be assumed.

They are the most squeezable persons and yield the largest amount of honey to the drones.

Why, he said, there is little to be squeezed out of people who have little.

And this is called the wealthy class, and the drones feed upon them.

565   That is pretty much the case, he said.

There is also a third class, consisting of working men, who are not politicians, and have little to live upon. And this, when assembled, is the largest and most powerful class in a democracy.

Why, that is true, he said; but then the multitude is seldom willing to meet unless they get a little honey.

And do they not share? I said. Do not their leaders take the estates of the rich, and give to the people as much of them as they can, consistently with keeping the greater part themselves?

Why, yes, he said, to that extent the people do share.

And the persons whose property is taken from them are compelled to defend themselves as they best can?

Of course.

And then, although they may have no desire of change, the others charge them with plotting against the State and being friends of oligarchy?

True.

And the end is that when they see the people, not of their own accord, but through ignorance, and because they are deceived by slanderers, seeking to do them wrong, then at last they are forced to become oligarchs in reality, and this is occasioned by the stings of the drones goading them?

Exactly.

Then come impeachments and judgments and trials of one another.

True.

The people have always some one as a champion whom they nurse into greatness.

Yes, that is their way.

And this is the very root from which a tyrant springs; when he first appears above ground he is a protector.

Yes, that is quite clear.

How then does a protector begin to change into a tyrant?

Clearly when he does what the man is said to do in the tale of the Arcadian temple of Lycaean Zeus.

What tale?

The tale is that he who has tasted the entrails of a single human victim minced up with the entrails of other victims is destined to become a wolf. Did you never hear that?

O yes.

And the protector of the people is like him; having a mob entirely at his disposal, he is not restrained from shedding the blood of kinsmen; by the favourite method of false accusation he brings them into court and murders them, making the life of man to disappear, and with unholy tongue and lips tasting the blood of kindred; some he kills and others he banishes, at the same time proclaiming abolition of debts and partition of lands: and after this, what can be his destiny but either to perish at the hands of his enemies, or from being a man to become a wolf— 566 that is, 'a tyrant?'

That is inevitable.

This, I said, is he who begins to make a party against the rich.

The same.

And then he is driven out and comes back, in spite of his enemies, a tyrant full made.

That is clear.

And if they are unable to drive him out, or get him condemned to death by public opinion, they form the design of putting him out of the way secretly.

Yes, he said, that is the usual plan.

Then comes the famous request of a body-guard, which is made by all those who have got thus far in their career, 'Let not the people's friend,' as they say, 'be lost to them.'

Exactly.

This the people readily grant; all their fears are for him— they have no fear for themselves.

Very true.

And when a man who is wealthy and is also accused of being an enemy of the people sees this, then, my friend, as the oracle said to Croesus,

'By pebbly Hermas' shore he flees and rests not, and is not ashamed to be a coward.'

And quite right too, said he, for, if he were ashamed, he would never be ashamed again.

Yes, I said, and he who is caught is put to death.

Inevitably.

And he, the protector of whom we spake, is not fallen in his might, but himself the overthrower of many, is to be seen standing up in the chariot of State with the reins in his hand, no longer protector, but tyrant absolute.

No doubt, he said.

And now let us tell of the happiness of the man, and also of the State, in which this sort of creature is generated.

Yes, he said, let us tell of that.

At first, in the early days of his power, he smiles upon every one and salutes every one;—he to be called a tyrant, who is making promises in public and also in private! liberating debtors, and distributing land to the people and to his followers, and wanting to be kind and good to every one.

That is the regular thing.

But when he has got rid of foreign enemies, and is reconciled with some of them and has destroyed others, and there is nothing to fear from them, then he is always stirring up some 567 war or other, in order that the people may require a leader.

Yes, that may be expected of him.

Has he not also another object, which is that they may be impoverished by payment of taxes, and thus compelled to devote themselves to their daily wants and therefore less likely to plot against him?

Clearly.

Yes, and if he suspects any of them of having notions of freedom, and of being disloyal to him, he has a good pretext for destroying them by giving them up to the enemy; and for all these reasons the tyrant is always compelled to be getting up a war.

That is inevitable.

Now he begins to grow unpopular.

That is the necessary result.

Then some of those who joined in setting him up, and who are in power—that is to say, the most courageous of them— speak their minds to him and to one another, and cast in his teeth the things which are being done.

Yes, that is to be expected.

And the tyrant, if he means to rule, must get rid of them; he cannot stop while he has a friend or an enemy who is good for anything.

That is plain.

And therefore he must use his eyes and see who is valiant, who is high-minded, who is wise, who wealthy; happy man, he is the enemy of them all, and must seek occasion against them whether he will or no, until he has made a purgation of the State.

Yes, he said, and a rare purgation.

Yes, I said, not the sort of purgation which the physicians make of the body; for they take away the worse and leave the better part, but he does the opposite.

I suppose that he cannot help himself, he replied.

What a blessed alternative, I said, to be compelled to dwell only with the many bad, and hated by them, or not to live at all.

Yes, that is the alternative.

And the more detestable he is in his actions the more satellites and the greater devotion in them will he require?

Certainly.

And who are the devoted band, and where will he procure them?

They will flock to him, he said, of their own accord, if he pays them.

By the dog! I said, you are again introducing drones out of other lands and of every sort.

Yes, he said, that I am.

But will he not desire to get them on the spot?

How do you mean?

He will emancipate the slaves and enrol them in his body-guard?

To be sure, he said, and he will be able to trust them best of all.

What a blessed fellow, I said, must this tyrant be; when he has put to death the others he has only these for his trusted friends.

568

Yes, he said, and they are his friends.

Yes, I said, and these are the new citizens whom he has called into existence, who admire him and live with him, while the good hate and avoid him.

Of course.

Verily, then, tragedy is a wise thing and Euripides a great tragedian.

Why do you say that?

Why, because he is the author of that rare saying,

'Tyrants are wise by living with the wise;'

and he clearly meant to say that they are the wise with whom the tyrant lives.

Yes, he said, and he also praises tyranny as godlike; this and many other things of the same kind are said by him and the other poets.

And therefore, I said, the tragic poets in their wisdom will forgive us and others who have a similar form of government, if we object to having them in our State, because they are the eulogists of tyranny.

Yes, he said, those who have the wit will doubtless forgive us.

Yes, I said, and they go about to other cities and attract mobs; and have voices fair and loud and persuasive, and draw the cities over to tyrannies and democracies.

Very true.

Moreover, they are paid for this and receive honour—the greatest honour from tyrants, and the next greatest from democracies; but the higher they ascend our constitution hill, the more their reputation fails, and seems unable from shortness of breath to proceed further.

True.

But we are digressing. Let us therefore return and enquire how the tyrant will maintain that fair and numerous and various and ever-changing army of his.

If, he said, there are sacred treasures in the city, he will spend them as far as they go; that is obvious. And he will then be able to diminish the taxes which he would otherwise have to impose.

And when these fail?

Why, clearly, he said, then he and his boon companions, whether male or female, will be maintained out of his father's estate.

I see your meaning, I said. You mean that the people who begat him will maintain him and his companions?

Yes, he said; he cannot get on without that.

But what if the people go into a passion, and aver that a grown-up son ought not to be supported by his father, but that the father should be supported by the son? He did not bring his 569 son into the world and establish him in order that when he was grown up he himself might serve his own servants, and maintain him and his rabble of slaves and companions; but that, having such a protector, he might be emancipated from the government of the rich and aristocratic, as they are termed. And now, here is this son of his, bidding him and his companions pack, just as a father might drive out of his house a riotous son and his party of revellers.

In the end, he said, the parent will be certain to discover what a monster he has been fostering in his bosom; and, when he wants to drive him out, he will find that he is weak and his son strong.

Why, you do not mean to say that the tyrant will use violence? What! beat his father if he resists?

Yes, he will; and he will begin by taking away his arms.

Then he is a parricide, and a cruel unnatural son to an aged parent whom he ought to cherish; and this is real tyranny, about which there is no mistake: as the saying is, the people who would avoid the slavery of freemen, which is smoke and appearance, has fallen under the tyranny of slaves, which is fire. Thus liberty, getting out of all order and reason, passes into the harshest and bitterest form of slavery.

Yes, he said, that is true.

Very well, I said; and may we not say that we have discussed enough the nature of tyranny, and the manner of the transition from democracy to tyranny?

Yes, quite enough, he said.

BOOK IX.

LAST of all comes the tyrannical man; about whom we have once more to ask how is he formed out of the democratical? and how does he live, in happiness or in misery?

Yes, he said, he is the only one remaining.

There is, however, I said, a previous question which I should like to consider.

What is that?

I do not think that we have adequately determined the nature and number of the appetites, and until this is accomplished the enquiry will always be perplexed.

Well, but you may supply the omission.

Very true, I said; and observe the point which I want to understand. Certain of the unnecessary pleasures and appetites are deemed to be unlawful; every man appears to have them, only in some persons they are controlled by the laws and by reason, and the better desires prevail over them, and either they are wholly banished or are few and weak; while in the case of others they are stronger, and there are more of them.

Which appetites do you mean?

I mean those which are awake when the reasoning and taming and ruling power is asleep; the wild beast in our nature, gorged with meat or drink, starts up and walks about naked, and surfeits after his manner, and there is no conceivable folly or crime, however shameless or unnatural—not excepting incest or parricide, or the eating of forbidden food—of which such a nature may not be guilty.

That is most true, he said.

But when a man's pulse is healthy and temperate, and he goes to sleep cool and rational, after having supped on a feast of reason and speculation, and come to a knowledge of himself; having

indulged appetites neither too much nor too little, but just enough
to lay them to sleep, and prevent them and their enjoyments and
pains from interfering with the higher principle—leaving that 572
in the solitude of pure abstraction, free to contemplate and
aspire to the knowledge of the unknown, whether in past, present,
or future: when, again, before going to sleep he has allayed the
passionate element, if he has a quarrel against any one—I say,
when, after pacifying the two irrational principles, he rouses up
the third or rational element before he takes his rest, then, as
you know, he attains truth most nearly, and is least likely to
be the sport of fanciful and lawless visions.

In that opinion I entirely agree.

In saying this I have been running into a digression; but the
point which I desire to note is that in all of us, even in good
men, there is such a latent wild-beast nature, which peers out
in sleep. Pray, consider whether I am right, and you agree with
me in this view.

Yes, I agree.

Remember then the character which we assigned to the democratic man. He was supposed from his youth upwards to have
been trained under a miserly parent, and to have encouraged the
saving appetites, and discountenanced the lighter and more ornamental ones?

True.

And then he got into the company of a more refined, licentious
sort of people, and he took to wantonness, and began to have a
dislike of his father's narrow ways. At last, being a better man
than his corruptors, he came to a mean, and led a life, not of
lawless and slavish passion, but of regular and successive indulgence. That was our view of the way in which the democrat
was generated out of the oligarch?

Yes, he said; and that is still our view.

And now, I said, years will have passed away, and you must
imagine this man, such as he is, to have a son, who is brought
up in his father's principles; and then further imagine the same
thing to happen to the son which has already happened to the
father—he is seduced into a perfectly lawless life, which is termed
perfect liberty; and his father and friends take part with his
moderate desires, while others assist the opposite ones. At

length, these dire magicians and tyrant-makers begin to fear that they will be unable to hold the youth, and then they con trive to implant in him a master passion, to be lord over his 573 idle and spendthrift desires—like a monster drone having wings. That is the only image which will depict him and his lusts.

Yes, he said, that is the best, the only image of him.

And while the other lusts amid clouds of incense and perfumes and garlands and wines, and all the dissoluteness of social life are buzzing around him and flattering him to the utmost, there is implanted in him the sting of desire, and then this lord of the soul is in a frenzy—madness is the captain of the guard—and if he discerns in his soul any opinions or appetites which may be regarded as good, and which have any sense of shame remaining, he puts an end to them, and casts them forth until he has purged away temperance and brought in madness to the full.

Yes, he said, that is the way in which the tyrannical man is generated.

And is not this the reason why of old love has been called a tyrant?

Yes, perhaps.

Further, I said, has not a drunken man also the spirit of a tyrant?

True.

And you know that a man who is deranged and not right in his mind, will fancy that he is able to rule, not only over men, but also over the gods?

True.

And the tyrannical man comes into being just at that point when either under the influence of nature, or habit, or both, he becomes drunken, lustful, passionate?

Exactly.

Such is the man and such is his origin. And next, how does he live?

That, as people facetiously say, you may as well tell me.

I imagine, I said, as the next step in his progress, that there will be feasts and carousals and revellings, and courtezans, and all that sort of thing; love is the lord of the house within him, who orders all the concerns of the soul.

That is certain.

Yes; and every day and every night desires grow up many and formidable, and their demands are many.

They are indeed, he said.

His revenues, if he has any, are soon spent.

True.

Then he borrows money, and his estate is taken from him.

Of course.

When he has nothing left, must not his desires, crowding in the nest like young ravens, be crying aloud for food; he, goaded on by them, and especially by love himself on whom they dance attendance, is at his wits' end to discover whom he can defraud or 574 despoil of his property, in order that he may gratify them?

Yes, that is sure to be the case.

He must have money, and no matter how, if he is to escape horrid pangs and pains.

He must.

And as in himself there was a succession of pleasures, and the new got the better of the old and took away their rights, so he being younger will claim to have more than his father and his mother, and if he has spent his own property, he will take a slice out of theirs.

No doubt of that.

And if his parents will not suffer this, then he will try to cheat and deceive them.

Very true.

And if. he cannot, then he will plunder and force them.

Yes, probably.

And if the old man and the old woman hold out against him, will he be very careful of doing anything which is tyrannical?

Nay, he said, I should not feel at all comfortable about his parents.

But, O heavens! Adeimantus, on account of some new-fangled love of a harlot, who is anything but a necessary connection, can you believe that he would strike the mother who is his ancient friend and necessary to his very existence, and would place her under the authority of the other, when she is brought under the same roof with her; or that, under like circumstances, he would do the same to his withered old father, first and most indispensable of friends, for the sake of some blooming love of a youth who is the reverse of indispensable?

Yes, indeed, he said; I believe that he would.

Truly, then, I said, a tyrannical son is a blessing to his father and mother.

Yes, indeed, he replied.

He first takes their property, and when that fails, and pleasures are beginning to swarm in the hive of his soul, then he breaks into a house, or steals the garments of some nightly wayfarer, and the next thing is that he lifts a temple; and while all this is going on, the old opinions about good and evil which he had when a child, and which were thought by him to be[1] right, are overthrown by those others which have just been emancipated, and are now the guard and associates of love, being those which in former days, when he was a partisan of democracy and subject to the laws and to his father, were only let loose in the dreams of sleep. But now that he is under the tyranny of love, he becomes always and in waking reality what he was then very rarely and in a dream only; he will commit the foulest murder, or eat forbidden food, 575 or be guilty of any other horrid act. Love is his tyrant, and lives lordly in him, and being himself a king emancipated from all control, leads him on—like man like State—into the performance of reckless deeds in order to maintain himself and his rabble, which evil communications have brought in from without, or which he himself has allowed to break loose within him by reason of a similar character in himself. Is not this a picture of his way of life?

Yes, indeed, he said.

And if there are only a few of them, and the rest of the people are well disposed, they go away and become the body-guard or mercenary soldiers of some other tyrant who may probably want them for a war; and if there is no war, they stay at home and do mischief in the city.

What sort of mischief?

For example, they are the thieves, burglars, cut-purses, footpads, robbers of temples, man-stealers of the community, and if they are able to speak they play the part of informers, and bear false witness, and take bribes.

---

[1] Reading τὰς δικαίας ποιουμένας.

And these, he replied, are not very small evils, even if the perpetrators of them are a few in number.

Yes, I said; but small and great are comparative terms, and all these things, in the misery and evil which they inflict upon a State, do not come within a thousand miles of the tyrant; the people are fools, and this class and their followers grow numerous and are aware of their numbers, and they take him who has most of the tyrant in his soul, and make him their leader.

Yes, he said, that is natural; for he will be the most tyrannically disposed.

If the people yield, well and good; but if they resist him, as he began by beating his own father and mother, so now, if he has the power, he beats his dear old fatherland and motherland, as the Cretans say, and brings in his young retainers to be their rulers and masters. And this is the end of his passions and desires.

Exactly.

Even in early days and before they get power, this is the way of them; they associate only with their own flatterers or ready tools; or, if they want anything from anybody, they themselves are equally ready to fall down before them; there is no attitude into which they will not throw themselves, but when 576 they have gained their point they know them no more.

Yes, truly.

They are always either the masters or servants and never the friends of anybody; the tyrant never tastes of true freedom or true friendship.

Certainly not.

And may we not call such men treacherous?

No question.

Also they are utterly unjust, if we were right in our notion of justice?

Yes, he said, and in that we were perfectly right.

Let us then sum up in a word, I said, the character of the worst man: he is the waking reality of what we dreamed.

Most true.

And this is he who being most of a tyrant by nature bears rule, and the longer he lives the more of a tyrant he becomes.

That is certain, said Glaucon, taking his turn to answer.

And will not he who has been shown to be the wickedest,

be also the most miserable? and he most of all and longest of all who has tyrannized longest and most, and is most of a tyrant—although this may not be the opinion of men in general?

Yes, he said, that is inevitable.

And must not the tyrannical man be like the tyrannical State, and the democratical man like the democratical State; and the same of the others?

Certainly.

And as State is to State in virtue and happiness, man is to man?

To be sure.

Then comparing the former city which was under a king and the city which was under a tyrant, how do they stand as to virtue?

They are the opposite extremes, he said, for one is the very best and the other is the very worst.

There can be no mistake, I said, as to which is which, and therefore I will at once enquire whether you would arrive at a similar decision about their relative happiness and misery. And here we must not allow ourselves to be panic-stricken at the apparition of the tyrant, who is only a unit and may perhaps have a few retainers about him; but let us go as we ought and view the whole city and look all around, and then we will give our opinion.

A fair invitation, he replied; and I see, as every one must, that a tyranny is the wretchedest form of government, and monarchy the happiest.

And may I not fairly ask in like manner to have a judge of the
577 men whose mind can enter into and see through human nature; he must not be a child who looks at the outside and is dazzled at the pompous aspect which tyranny assumes to the beholder, but let him be one who has a clear insight. May I suppose that the judgment is given in the hearing of us all by one who is able to judge, and has dwelt in the same place with him, and been present at his daily life and known him in his family, in which he is seen stripped of his tragedy attire, and again in the hour of public danger; he shall tell us about the happiness and misery of the tyrant when compared with other men?

That again, he said, is a very fair proposal.

Let us now assume this able and experienced judge to be ourselves, and then we shall have some one who will answer our enquiries.

By all means.

Let me ask you not to forget the parallel of the individual and the State; bearing this in mind, and glancing in turn from one to the other of them, will you tell me their respective conditions?

In what points? he asked.

Beginning with the State, I replied, would you say that a city which is governed by a tyrant is free or enslaved?

Nothing, he said, can be more completely enslaved.

And yet, as you see, there are masters and there are freemen in such a State?

Yes, he said, I see that there are—a few; but the people as a whole (speaking generally) and the best of them are disgracefully and miserably enslaved.

Then if the man is like the State, I said, must not the same hold of the man? his soul is full of meanness and serfdom—the best elements in him are enslaved; and there is a small ruling part, which is also the worst and maddest.

That is inevitable.

And would you say that the soul of such an one is the soul of a freeman or of a slave?

He has the soul of a slave, in my judgment.

And the State which is enslaved under a tyrant is very far from acting voluntarily?

Very far, indeed.

And also the soul which is under a tyrant (I am speaking of the soul taken as a whole) is very far from doing as she desires; there is a gadfly which goads her, and she is full of trouble and remorse?

Certainly.

And is the city which is under a tyrant rich or poor?

Poor.

And the tyrannical soul must be always poor and insatiable? 578

True.

And must not such a State and such a man be always full of fear?

Yes, indeed.

Is there any State in which you will find more of lamentation and sorrow and groaning and pain?

Certainly not.

And is there any man in whom you will find more misery of the same kind than in the tyrannical man, who is in a fury of passions and desires?

Impossible.

Reflecting then upon these and similar evils, you held the tyrannical State to be the most miserable of States?

And I was right, he said.

Certainly, I said. And when you see the same evils in the tyrannical man, what do you say of him?

I say that he is by far the most miserable of all men.

There, I said, I think that you are wrong.

How is that? he said.

I do not think that he has as yet reached the utmost extreme of misery.

Then who is more miserable?

One of whom I am about to speak.

Who is that?

He who is of a tyrannical nature, and instead of leading a private life is cursed with the further misfortune of being a public tyrant.

I should conjecture from the previous remarks that you are right.

Yes, I said; but in this high argument of good and evil you should not conjecture only—you should have a certainty.

That is very true, he said.

Let me then offer you an illustration, which may, I think, have an application to this subject.

What is your illustration?

The case of rich individuals in cities who possess many slaves: from them you may form an idea of the tyrant's State, for they both have slaves; the only difference is that he has more slaves.

Yes, that is the difference.

You know that they live securely and have no fear of their servants?

What should they fear?

Nothing. But do you observe the reason of this?

Yes; the reason is, that the whole city is leagued together for the protection of each individual.

That is quite true, I said. But imagine that one of these owners is carried off by a god into the wilderness, where there are no freemen to help him—he and his household, and he is the master say of about fifty slaves—will he not be in an agony of apprehension lest he and his wife and children should be put to death by his slaves?

Yes, he said, he will be in the utmost alarm.   579

Will he not be compelled to flatter divers of his slaves, and make many promises to them of freedom and other things, much against his will?—he will become the servant of his servants.

Yes, he said, that will be the only way of saving his life.

And suppose that the same god who carries him off puts him down among neighbours who will not allow a man to be the master of another, and, if they catch him, are ready to inflict capital punishment upon him?

Then his case will be even worse, he said, when he is surrounded and watched by enemies.

And is not this the sort of prison in which the tyrant will be bound?—he being by nature such as we have described, is full of all sorts of fears and lusts. His soul is dainty and greedy, and yet he only, of all men, is never allowed to go on a journey, or to see the things which other freemen desire to see, but he lives in his hole like a woman hidden in the house, and is jealous of any other citizen who goes into foreign parts and sees anything of interest.

Very true, he said.

Such being his evil condition, am I not right in saying that the tyrannical man, ill-governed in his own person, whom you just now described as the most miserable of all, will be yet more miserable in a public station, when, instead of leading a private life, he is constrained by fortune to be a tyrant? He has to be master of others when he is not master of himself: he is like a diseased or paralytic man who is compelled to pass his life, not in retirement, but fighting and combating with other men.

Yes, he said, that is very true, and the similitude is most exact.

Is not his case utterly miserable? and does not the actual tyrant lead a worse life than him whom you determined to be worst?

Certainly.

He who is the real tyrant, whatever men may think, is the real slave, and is obliged to practise the greatest adulation and servility, and to be the flatterer of the vilest of mankind. He has desires which he is utterly unable to satisfy, and has more wants than any one, and is truly poor, if you know how to inspect the whole soul of him: all his life long he is beset with fear and is full of convulsions and distractions, even as the State which he 580 resembles; and surely the resemblance holds?

True, he said.

Moreover, as we were saying, he grows worse from having power: he becomes of necessity more jealous, more faithless, more unjust, more friendless, more impious; he entertains and nurtures every evil sentiment, and the consequence is that he is supremely miserable, and thus he makes everybody else equally miserable.

No man of any sense will dispute that.

Come then, I said, and as the universal arbiter gives sentence in the games, do you also decide who in your opinion is first in the scale of happiness, and who second, and in what order the others follow: there are five of them in all—they are the royal, timocratical, oligarchical, democratical, tyrannical.

The judgment will be easily given, he replied; they shall be choruses entering on the stage, and I will decide the place of each of them by the criterion of virtue and vice, happiness and misery.

Need we hire a herald, or shall I proclaim the result—that the son of the best (Ariston) is of opinion that the best and justest man is also the happiest, and that this is he who is the most royal master of himself; and that the worst and most unjust man is also the most miserable, and that this is he who is the greatest tyrant of himself and of his State?

Make the proclamation, he said.

And shall I proclaim further, 'whether seen or unseen by gods and men'?

Yes, he said, you had better add that.

Then this, I said, will be the first proof; and there is another, which may also have some weight.

What is that?

The second proof is derived from the nature of the soul: seeing that the individual soul, like the State, has been divided by us into three principles, the division may furnish a new demonstration.

Of what nature?

There are three pleasures which correspond to the three principles, and also three desires and governing powers.

How do you mean? he said.

There is one principle with which a man learns, another with which he is angry; the third, having many forms, has no single name, but is termed appetitive, from the extraordinary strength and vehemence of the pleasures of eating and drinking and the other sensual appetites; also money loving, because these sort of desires can only be gratified by the help of money.

That is true, he said.

581

If we were to say that the loves and pleasures of this third part of the soul were concerned with gain, we should then be able to fall back on a single class; and might truly describe this part of the soul as loving gain or money.

Yes, I should say that.

Again, is not the passionate element wholly set on ruling and conquering and getting fame?

True.

Suppose we call that contentious or ambitious—would the term be suitable?

Extremely suitable.

On the other hand, every one sees that the principle of knowledge is wholly directed to the truth, and cares less than any of the others for gain or fame?

Far less.

'True lover of wisdom,' 'lover of knowledge,' are titles which are rightly applicable to that part of the soul?

Certainly.

One principle prevails in the souls of one class of men, another in others, just as may happen?

Yes.

Then we may assume that there are three classes of men—lovers of wisdom, lovers of ambition, lovers of gain?

Exactly.

And there are three kinds of pleasures, which are their several objects?

Very true.

Now, if you examine the three classes, and ask of them in turn which of their lives is pleasantest, each of them will be found praising his own and depreciating that of others: the money-maker will contrast the vanity of honour or of learning with the solid advantages of gold and silver?

True, he said.

And the lover of honour—what will be his opinion? Will he not think that the pleasure of riches is vulgar, while the pleasure of learning, which has no meed of honour, he regards as all smoke and nonsense?

True, he said.

But may we not suppose, I said, that philosophy estimates other pleasures as nothing in comparison with the pleasure of knowing the truth[2], and in that abiding, ever learning, in the pursuit of truth, not far indeed from the heaven of pleasure? The other pleasures the philosopher disparages by calling them necessary, meaning that if there were no necessity for them, he would not have them.

There ought to be no doubt about that, he replied.

Since, then, the pleasures of each class and the life of each are in dispute, and the question is not which life is more or less 32 honourable, or better or worse, but which is the more pleasant or painless—how shall we know?

I cannot tell, he said.

Well, but what ought to be the criterion? Is any better than experience and wisdom and reason?

There cannot be a better, he said.

Then, I said, reflect. Of the three individuals, which has the greatest experience of all the pleasures which we enumerated? Has the lover of gain greater experience of the pleasure of knowledge derived from learning the nature of the truth than the philosopher has of the pleasure of gain?

The philosopher, he replied, has greatly the advantage; for he has always known the taste of the other pleasures from his youth upwards: but the lover of gain in all his experience has

---

[2] Or taking τῆς ἡδονῆς οὐ πάνυ πόρρω after νομίζειν, 'to go but a short way in pleasure;' i. e. to be shallow pleasures only in comparison.

not of necessity tasted—or, I should rather say, could hardly have tasted by any process of learning the nature of things—the sweetness of intellectual pleasures.

Then the lover of wisdom has a great advantage over the lover of gain, for he has a double experience?

Very great indeed.

Again, has the philosopher greater experience of the pleasures of honour, or the lover of honour of the pleasures of knowledge?

Nay, he said, they are all honoured in proportion as they attain their object; for the rich man and the brave man and the wise man alike have their crowd of worshippers, and as they all receive honour they all have experience of the pleasures of honour, but the delight which is to be found in the knowledge of true being is known to the philosopher only.

His experience, then, will enable him to judge better than any one?

Far better.

And he is the only one who has wisdom as well as experience?

Certainly.

The very faculty which is the instrument of judgment is not possessed by the covetous or avaricious man, but only by the philosopher?

What faculty?

Reason, which, as we were saying, ought to have the decision.

Yes.

And reasoning is peculiarly his instrument?

Certainly.

If wealth and gain were the criterion, then what the lover of gain praised and blamed would surely be truest?

Assuredly.

Or if honour or victory or courage, in that case the ambitious or contentious would decide best?

Clearly.

But since experience and wisdom and reason are the judges, the inference of course is, that the truest pleasures are those which are approved by the lover of wisdom and reason.   And so we arrive at the result, that the pleasure of the intelligent part of the soul 583 is the pleasantest of the three, and that he in whom this is the ruling principle has the pleasantest life?

Unquestionably, he said, the wise man has the fullest right to approve of his own life.

And what does the judge affirm to be the life which is next, and the pleasure which is next?

Clearly that of the soldier and lover of honour; that is nearer to himself than that of the trader.

Last comes the lover of gain.

Very true, he said.

Twice, then, has the just man overthrown the unjust; and now comes the third trial, which is sacred to the Olympic saviour Zeus: a sage whispers in my ear that no pleasure except that of the wise is quite true and pure—all others are a shadow only; and this will surely prove the greatest and most decisive of falls?

Yes, the greatest; but will you explain how this is?

If you will answer, I will think, I said, while you are answering. Put your questions.

Say, then, is not pleasure opposed to pain?

True.

And there is a neutral state which is neither pleasure nor pain?

There is.

A state which is intermediate, and a sort of repose of the soul about either—that is what you mean?

Yes.

You remember what people say when they are sick?

What do they say?

That after all nothing is pleasanter than health. But then they never knew that this was the greatest of pleasures until they were ill.

Yes, I remember, he said.

And when persons are suffering from acute pain you must have heard them say that there is nothing pleasanter than to get rid of their pain?

I have.

And there are many other cases of suffering in which the mere rest and cessation of pain, and not any positive enjoyment, is extolled by them as the greatest pleasure?

Yes, he said, at the time, rest is pleasant and delightful to them.

Again, when pleasure ceases, that sort of rest will not be pleasant but painful?

Doubtless, he said.

Then the intermediate state of rest will be pleasure and will also be pain?

That is assumed.

But can that which is neither become both?

I should say not.

And both pleasure and pain are motions in the soul, are they not?

Yes.

But that which is neither was just now shown to be rest and 584 not motion, and in a mean between them?

Yes.

How, then, can we be right in saying that the absence of pain is pleasure, or that the absence of pleasure is pain?

Impossible.

Then this is an appearance only and not a reality; that is to say, the rest is pleasure at the moment and in comparison of what is painful, and painful in comparison of what is pleasant; but all these representations, when tried by the test of true pleasure, are unsound and a species of imposition?

That is the inference.

Look at the other class of pleasures which have no antecedent pains and you will no longer suppose, as you perhaps may at present, that pleasure is only the cessation of pain, or pain of pleasure.

What pleasures, he said, and where shall I find them?

There are many of them: take as an example the pleasures of smell, which are very great and have no antecedent pains; they come in a moment, and when they depart leave no pain behind them.

Most true, he said.

Let us not, then, be induced to believe that pure pleasure is the cessation of pain, or pain of pleasure.

No.

Still, the more numerous and violent pleasures which reach the soul through the body are generally of this sort—they are reliefs of pain.

That is true.

And is not this also true of the anticipations of pleasure and pain which precede them and are followed by them?

Yes.

Shall I give you an illustration of them?

Let me hear.

You would allow, I said, that there is in nature an upper and lower and middle region?

I admit that.

And if a person were to go from the lower to the middle region, would he not imagine that he is going up; and he who is standing in the middle and sees whence he has come, would imagine that he is already in the upper region? for he has never seen the true upper world.

To be sure, he said; how can he think otherwise?

But if he were taken back again he would imagine that he was descending, and that would be true?

No doubt.

All that would arise out of his ignorance of the true upper and middle and lower regions?

Yes.

Then can you wonder that persons who are inexperienced in the truth, as they have wrong ideas about many other things, should have wrong ideas about pleasure and pain and the intermediate; so that when drawn towards the painful they are really 585 pained and know the truth, but when drawn away from pain to the neutral or intermediate state, they firmly believe that they have reached the goal of satiety and pleasure; they, not knowing pleasure, err in comparing pain with the absence of pain, which is like comparing black with grey instead of white— can you wonder, I say, at this?

No, indeed; I should be much more disposed to wonder at the opposite.

Look at the matter thus:—Hunger, thirst, and the like, are inanitions of the bodily state?

Yes.

And ignorance and folly are inanitions of the soul?

True.

And food and wisdom are the corresponding satisfactions of either?

Certainly.

And is the satisfaction truer of that which has less, or of that which has more existence?

Clearly, of that which has more.

Which classes of things are they which, in your judgment, have a greater share in pure existence—those of which food and drink and condiments and all kinds of sustenance are examples, or the class which contains true opinion and mind and, in general, all virtue? Put the question in this way:—Which has a more real being—that which is concerned with the invariable, the immortal, and the true, and is found in the invariable, immortal, true; or that which is concerned with the variable and mortal, and is found in the variable and mortal?

Far more excellent, he replied, is that which is concerned with the invariable.

And does the essence of the invariable partake of knowledge as well as of essential being, and in the same degree?

Yes, of knowledge in the same degree.

And of truth in the same degree?

Yes.

And, conversely, that which has less of truth will also have less of essence?

Necessarily.

Then, in general, those qualities which are in the service of the body have less of truth and being than those which are in the service of the soul?

Far less.

And the body has actually less of truth and reality than the soul?

Yes.

That which is filled with more real existence, and actually has a more real existence, is more really filled than that which is filled with less real existence and is less real?

Of course.

And if there be a pleasure in being filled with that which agrees with nature, that which is more really filled with more real being will have more real and true joy and pleasure; whereas that which participates in less real being will be less truly and surely satisfied, and will participate in a less true and real pleasure?

That is not to be doubted.

586   Those then who know not wisdom and virtue, and are always busy with gluttony and sensuality, go down and up again as far as the mean; and in this space they move at random throughout life, but they never pass into the true upper world; thither they neither look, nor do they ever find their way, neither are they truly filled with true being, nor do they taste of true and abiding pleasure. Like brute animals, with their eyes down and bodies bent to the earth or leaning on the dining-table, they fatten and feed and breed, and, in their excessive love of these delights, they kick and butt at one another with horns and hoofs which are made of iron; and they kill one another by reason of their insatiable lust. For they fill themselves with that which is not substantial, and the part of themselves which they fill is also unsubstantial and incontinent.

Verily, Socrates, said Glaucon, you describe the life of the many like an oracle.

Their pleasures are mixed with pains. How can they be otherwise? For they are mere images and shadows of the true, and are coloured only by contrast, and this way of looking at them doubly exaggerates them, and implants in the minds of fools insane desires of them; and they are fought about as Stesichorus says that the Greeks fought about the shadow of Helen at Troy in ignorance of the truth.

Yes, inevitably, he said; that is the way.

And must not the like happen with the spirited or passionate element of the soul? Will not the passionate man be in the like case, if he carries his passion into act, either because he is envious and ambitious, or violent and contentious, or angry and discontented and is seeking to attain honour and victory and the satisfaction of his anger without reason or sense?

Yes, he said, the same will happen with the spirited element also.

Then may we not confidently assert that the lovers of money and honour, when they seek their pleasures under the guidance and in the company of reason, and pursue after and win the pleasures which wisdom shows them, will also have the truest pleasures in the highest degree which is attainable to them, inasmuch as they follow truth; and they will also have those which are natural to them, if that which is best to each one is also most natural to him?

Yes, certainly; the best is the most natural.

Then, when the whole soul follows the philosophical principle, and there is no division, the several parts each of them do their own business, and are just, and each of them enjoy their own best 587 and truest pleasures?

Exactly.

But when either of the other principles prevails, it fails in attaining its own pleasure, and compels the others to pursue after a shadow of pleasure which is not theirs?

True.

And the greater the interval which separates them from philosophy and reason, the more strange and illusive will be the pleasure?

Yes.

And that is farthest from reason which is at the greatest distance from law and order?

Clearly.

And the lustful and tyrannical desires are at the greatest distance?

Yes.

And the royal and orderly desires are nearest?

Yes.

Then the tyrant will live most unpleasantly, and the king most pleasantly?

Yes.

Would you know the measure of the interval between them?

If you will tell me.

There appear to be three pleasures, one genuine and two spurious: now the transgression of the tyrant reaches a point beyond the spurious; he has run away from the region of law and reason, and taken up his abode with certain slave pleasures which are his satellites, and the measure of his inferiority can only be expressed in a figure.

How is that? he said.

I assume, I said, that the tyrant is in the third place from the oligarch, as the democrat was in the middle?

Yes.

And if there is truth in what has preceded, he will be wedded to an image of pleasure which is thrice removed as to truth from the pleasure of the oligarch.

He will.

And the oligarch is third from the royal; for we count as one royal and aristocratical?

Yes, he is third.

Then the tyrant is removed from true pleasure by the space of a number which is three times three [3 × 3=9]?

That is manifest.

The shadow then [3] (or diminishing reflection) of tyrannical pleasure, will be a superficial figure, which is determined by the number of length [that is, a square of three, the number which is called the number of length being 9]?

Exactly.

And if we consider this line [of nine] which represents the interval between the tyrannical and true pleasure, in reference to the square and third increment, there is no difficulty in seeing how vast the interval of distance becomes.

Yes; the arithmetician will easily do the sum.

And if a person, instead of going from the tyrant to the king, inverts the order, and tells the measure of the interval which separates the king from the tyrant in truth of pleasure, he will find him, when the multiplication is completed, living 729 times 588 more pleasantly, and the tyrant more painfully by this same interval.

What a wonderful calculation! And how enormous is the interval which separates the just from the unjust in regard to pleasure and pain!

Yet a true calculation, I said, and a number which nearly concerns human life, if human life is concerned with days and nights and months and years [4].

Yes, he said, human life is certainly concerned with them.

Then if the good and just man be thus superior in pleasure to the evil and unjust, his superiority will be infinitely greater in propriety of life and in beauty and virtue?

Immeasurably greater, indeed, he said.

---

[3] The square number suggests a figure which is called a shadow.

[4] 729 *nearly* equals the number of days and nights in the year.

Well, I said, and now we have arrived at this point I may resume the beginning of the argument, which arose out of some one saying that injustice was a gain to the perfectly unjust who was reputed to be just. Was not that said?

Yes, that was said.

Come then, I said, and now that we have determined the power and quality of justice and injustice, let us have a word with him.

What shall we say to him?

Let us make an image of the soul, that he may have his own words presented before his eyes.

What sort of an image?

An ideal image of the soul, like the creations of ancient mythology, such as the Chimera or Scylla or Cerberus, or any other in which two or more different natures are said to grow into one.

There are said to have been such unions.

Then do you now model the form of a multitudinous, polycephalous beast, having a ring of heads of all manner of beasts, tame and wild, which he is able to generate and metamorphose at will.

That, he said, implies marvellous powers in the artist; but, as language is more pliable than wax or similar substances, I have done as you say.

Suppose now that you make a second form as of a lion, and a third of a man, the second smaller than the first, and the third smaller than the second.

That, he said, is an easier task; and I have made them as you say.

Then now join them, and let the three grow into one.

That has been accomplished.

Now fashion the outside into a single image, as of a man, so that he who is not able to look within, and sees only the outer hull or vessel, may believe the beast to be a single human creature.

That is completed, he said.

And now let us say to him who maintains the profitableness of justice and the unprofitableness of injustice, that his doctrine amounts to this: he is asserting that his interest is to feast and strengthen the lion and the lion-like qualities and to starve and 589 weaken the man; who in consequence of this is at the mercy of either of the other two, and he is not to attempt to familiarize or harmonize them with one another: he ought rather to suffer them to fight and bite and devour one another.

Certainly, he said; that is what the approver of injustice says.

To him the supporter of justice makes answer that he ought rather to aim in all he says and does at strengthening the man within him, in order that he may be able to govern the many-headed monster. Like a good husbandman he should be watching and tending the gentle shoots, and preventing the wild ones from growing; making a treaty with the lion-heart, and uniting the several parts with one another and with themselves.

Yes, he said, that is quite what the maintainer of justice will say.

And in every point of view, whether of pleasure, honour, or advantage, the approver of justice is right and speaks the truth, and the disapprover is wrong and false, and ignorant?

Yes, truly.

Come, now, and let us reason with the unjust, who is not intentionally in error. 'Sweet Sir,' we will say to him, 'what think you of the noble and ignoble? Is not the noble that which subjects the beast to the man, or rather to the god in man; and the ignoble that which subjects the man to the beast?' He can hardly avoid admitting this—can he now?

Not if he has any regard for my opinion.

But, if he admit this, we may ask him another question: How would a man profit if he received gold and silver on the condition that he was to enslave the noblest part of him to the worst? Who can imagine that a man who sold his son or daughter into slavery for money, especially if he sold them into the hands of fierce and evil men, would be the gainer, however large might be the sum which he received? And will any one say that he is not 590 a miserable caitiff who sells his own divine being to that which is most atheistical and detestable, and has no pity? Eriphyle took the necklace as the price of her husband's life, but he is taking a bribe in order to compass a worse ruin.

Yes, said Glaucon, far worse, I will answer for him.

Is not intemperance censured, I said, because in this condition that huge multiform monster is allowed to be too much at large?

Clearly.

And pride and sullenness are blamed as occasioning the growth and increase of the lion and serpent element out of proportion?

Yes.

And luxury and softness are blamed, because they relax and weaken this same element, and make a man a coward?

Very true.

And is not a man reproached for flattery and meanness who subordinates the spirited animal to the unruly monster, and, for the sake of money, of which he can never have enough, habituates him in the days of his youth to be trampled in the mud, and from being a lion to become a monkey?

True, he said.

And why are vulgarity and handicraft arts a reproach? Only because they imply a natural weakness of the higher principle, and the individual is unable to control the creatures within him, but has to court them, and his only study is how to flatter them?

That appears to be true.

And, therefore, that he may be under the same rule as the best, we say that he ought to be the servant of the best; not, as Thrasymachus supposed, to the injury of him who served, but because every one had better be ruled by divine wisdom dwelling within him; or, if that be impossible, then by an external authority, in order that we may be all, as far as possible, under the same government?

True, he said.

And this is clearly seen to be the intention of the law, which is the ally of the whole city; and is seen also in the authority which is exerted over children, and the refusal to allow them to be free until the time when, as in a State, we have given them a constitution, and by cultivation of the higher element have 591 established in their hearts a watchman and ruler like our own, and when this is done they may go their ways.

Yes, he said, that is a further proof.

In what point of view, then, and on what ground shall a man be profited by injustice or intemperance or other baseness, even though he acquire money or power?

There is no ground on which this can be maintained.

What shall he profit, if his injustice be undetected? for he who is undetected only gets worse, whereas he who is detected and punished has the brutal part of his nature silenced and humanized; the gentler element in him is liberated, and his whole soul is perfected and ennobled by the acquirement of justice and temperance and wisdom, more than the body ever is by receiving gifts of beauty, strength and health, in proportion as the soul is more honourable than the body.

Certainly, he said.

The man of understanding will concentrate himself on this as the work of life. And in the first place, he will honour studies which impress these qualities on his soul, and will disregard others?

Clearly, he said.

In the next place, he will keep under his body, and so far will he be from yielding to brutal and irrational pleasures, that he will regard even health as quite a secondary matter; his first object will be not that he may be fair or strong or well, unless he is likely thereby to gain temperance, but he will be always desirous of preserving the harmony of the body for the sake of the concord of the soul?

Certainly, he replied, that he will, if he has true music in him.

And there is a principle of order and harmony in the acquisition of wealth; this also he will observe, and will not allow himself to be dazzled by the opinion of the world and heap up riches to his own infinite harm?

I think not, he said.

He will look at the city which is within him and take care to avoid any change of his own institutions, such as might arise either from abundance or from want; and he will duly regulate his acquisition and expense, in so far as he is able?

Very true.

592 And, for the same reason, he will accept such honours as he deems likely to make him a better man; but those which are likely to disorder his constitution, whether private or public honours, he will avoid?

Then, if this be his chief care, he will not be a politician?

By the dog of Egypt, he will! in the city which is his own, though in his native country perhaps not, unless some providential accident should occur.

I understand; you speak of that city of which we are the founders, and which exists in idea only; for I do not think that there is such an one anywhere on earth?

In heaven, I replied, there is laid up a pattern of such a city, and he who desires may behold this, and beholding, govern himself accordingly. But whether there really is or ever will be such an one is of no importance to him; for he will act according to the laws of that city and of no other?

True, he said.

BOOK X.

595   Of the many excellences which I perceive in the order of
our State, there is none which upon reflection pleases me better
than the rule about poetry.

What rule?

The rule about rejecting imitative poetry, which certainly
ought not to be received; as I see far more clearly now that the
parts of the soul have been distinguished.

What do you mean by that?

Speaking in confidence, for I should not like to have my words
repeated to the tragedians and the rest of the imitative tribe—
but I do not mind saying to you that all poetical imitations are
a sort of outrage on the understanding of the hearers, and that
the only cure of this is the knowledge of their true nature.

Explain the purport of your remark.

Well, I will tell you: although I have always from my earliest
youth had an awe and love of Homer, which even now makes
the words falter on my lips, for he is the great captain and
teacher of all that goodly band of Tragic writers; but a man
is not to be reverenced before the truth, and therefore I will
speak out.

Very good, he said.

Listen to me then, or rather, answer me.

Put your question.

Can you tell me what imitation is? for I really do not know.

A likely thing, then, that I shall know.

596   Why not? even supposing that you were dull, may not the duller
eye often see a thing sooner than the keener?

That is true, he said; but in your presence I should not have
the courage to speak, even if I had anything to say. Will you
examine for yourself?

Well then, shall we begin as usual by bringing a number of individuals which have a common name under one form or idea? that has been our usual plan—do you understand me?

I do.

Let us take any instance; there are beds and tables in the world and many of them, are there not?

Yes.

But there are only two ideas or forms of them—one the idea of a bed, the other of a table.

True.

And the maker of either of them makes a bed or he makes a table for our use, in accordance with the idea—that is our way of speaking in this and similar instances—but he does not make the ideas themselves.

Certainly not.

And there is another artist,—I should like to know what you would say of him.

Who is he?

One who is the maker of all the works of all other workmen.

What an extraordinary man!

Wait a little, and there will be more reason for your saying that. For this is he who makes not only vessels of every kind, but plants and animals, himself and all other things—the earth and heaven, and the things which are in heaven, or under the earth; he makes the gods also.

He must be a rare master of his art.

Oh! you are unbelieving, are you? Do you mean that there is no such maker or creator, or that in one sense there might be a maker of all these things but not in another? Do you not see that there is a way in which you could make them yourself?

What is this way?

An easy way enough; or rather, there are many ways in which the feat might be accomplished, none quicker than that of turning a mirror round and round, and catching the sun and the heavens, and the earth and yourself, and other animals and plants, and all the other creations of art as well as nature, in the mirror.

Yes, he said, but that is an appearance only.

Very good, I said, you are coming to the point now; and the painter, as I conceive, is just a creator of this sort, is he not?

That is true.

But then I suppose you will say that what he creates is untrue. And yet there is a sense in which the painter also creates a bed?

Yes, he said, but not a real bed.

597 And what of the maker of the bed? were you not saying that he does not make the idea which, according to our view, is the essence of the bed, but only a particular bed?

Yes, I did say that.

Then if he does not make that which exists he cannot make true existence, but only some semblance of existence; and if any one were to say that the work of the maker of the bed, or of any other workman, has real existence, he could hardly be supposed to be speaking the truth.

At any rate, he replied, philosophers would say that he was not speaking the truth.

Can we wonder, then, that there is an indistinctness about his work too, when compared with truth?

No indeed.

Suppose that we enquire into the nature of this imitator as seen in the examples given?

If you please.

Well then, here are three beds; one is natural, which, as I think that we may say, is made by God,—no one else can be the maker?

No.

There is another which is the work of the carpenter?

Yes.

And the work of the painter is a third?

Yes.

Beds, then, are of three kinds, and there are three artists who superintend them: God, the maker of the bed, and the painter?

Yes, there are three of them.

God, whether from choice or from necessity, made one bed and one only; two or more such ideal beds, neither ever have been or ever will be made by God.

Why is that?

Because even if he had made but two, still a third would appear behind them in which the idea of both of them would be contained, and that would be the ideal bed and not the two others.

Very true, he said.

God knew this, and He desired to be the real maker of a real bed, not a particular maker of a particular bed, and therefore in nature He created one bed only.

Yes, that may be assumed.

Shall we, then, speak of Him as the natural author or maker of the bed?

Yes, he replied; as His nature is so should His name be, and His nature is that He is the creator of this and of all other things.

And what shall we say of the carpenter—is not he also the maker of the bed?

Yes.

But would you call the painter a creator and maker?

Certainly not.

Yet if he is not the maker what is he in relation to the bed?

I think, he said, that we may fairly designate him as the imitator of that which the others make.

Good, I said; then you call him an imitator who is third in the descent from nature?

Certainly, he said.

And the tragic poet is an imitator, and therefore, like all other imitators, he is thrice removed from the king and from the truth?

That appears to be the case.

Then about the imitator we are agreed. And now about the 598 painter, I would like to know whether he imitates that which originally exists in nature, or only the creations of artists?

The latter.

As they are or as they appear? you have still to determine this.

What do you mean?

I mean, that you may look at a bed from different points of view, obliquely or directly or from any other point of view, and the bed will appear different, but there is no difference in reality. And this is true of all things.

Yes, he said, they differ, but only in appearance.

Now let me ask you another question: Which is the art of painting—an imitation of things as they are, or as they appear—of appearance or of reality?

Of appearance.

Then the imitator, I said, is a long way off the truth, and can do all things because he lightly touches on a small part of them, and that part an image. For example: a painter will paint a cobbler, carpenter, or any other artist, though he knows nothing of their arts; and, if he is a good artist, he may deceive children or simple persons, when he shows them his picture of a carpenter from a distance, and they will fancy that they are looking at a real carpenter.

Certainly.

And whenever any one informs us that he has found a man who knows all the arts, and all things else that everybody knows, and every single thing, with a higher degree of accuracy than any other man—whoever tells us this, I think that we can only imagine him to be a simple creature who is likely to have been deceived by some wizard or actor whom he met, and whom he thought all knowing, because he himself was unable to analyse the nature of knowledge and ignorance and imitation.

That is very true, he said.

Or again; when we hear persons saying that the tragedians, and Homer, who is at their head, know all the arts and all things human, virtue as well as vice, and divine things too, for that the good poet must know what he is talking about, and that he who has not this knowledge can never be a poet, we ought to consider whether in this also there is not a similar illusion. Perhaps they

599 may have been deceived by imitators, and may never have considered when they saw their works that these were but imitations thrice removed from the truth, and could easily be made without any knowledge of the truth, because they are appearances only and not real substances? Or, after all, they may be in the right, and poets do really know the things about which they seem to the many to speak well?

Yes, that is a matter which has to be considered.

Now do you suppose that if a person were able to make the original as well as the image, he would devote himself to the image-making branch? Would he allow this to be the ruling principle of his life, when he could do so much better?

I should say not.

The real artist who knew what he was imitating would be

interested in realities and not in imitations; and would leave
as memorials of himself works many and fair; and, instead of
being the author of encomiums, he would prefer to be the theme
of them.

Yes, he said, that would bring him much greater honour and
profit.

Then I think that we must put a question to Homer; not about
medicine, or any of the arts to which his poems only incidentally
refer; we are not going to ask him, or any other poet, whether he
has cured patients like Asclepius, or left behind him a school of
medicine such as were the Asclepiads, or whether he only talks
about medicine at second-hand, but we have a right to know
respecting war, military tactics, politics, education, which are the
chiefest and noblest subjects of his poems, and we may fairly ask
him about them. 'Friend Homer,' then, we say, 'if you are only
in the second remove from truth and excellence, and not in the
third—not an image maker or imitator—and if you are able to
discern what pursuits make men better or worse in private or
public life, tell us what State was ever better governed by your
help? The good order of Lacedaemon is due to Lycurgus, and
many other cities great and small have been similarly benefited by
others; but who says that you have been a good legislator to them
and have done them any good? Italy and Sicily can tell of
Charondas, and there is Solon who is renowned among us; but
what city has anything to say about you?' Is there any city which
he might name?

I think not, said Glaucon; not even the Homeridae themselves
pretend that he was a legislator.

Well, but is there any war which was carried on by him, or 600
aided by his counsels, when he was alive?

There is not.

Or is there any invention[1] of his applicable to the arts, or to
human life, such as Thales the Milesian, or Anacharsis the
Scythian, and other ingenious men have made, which is attributed to him?

There is nothing at all of the kind.

But, if Homer never did any public service, was he privately a
guide or teacher of any? Had he in his lifetime friends and

---

[1] Omitting εἰς.

associates who loved him, and handed down to posterity an
Homeric way of life, such as that which Pythagoras invented and
his followers continue, who are still called after his name, and
seem to have a certain distinction above other men?

Neither is there anything of this kind recorded of him. For
surely, Socrates, Creophÿlus, the companion of Homer, that child
of flesh, whose name always makes us laugh, might be more justly
ridiculed for his want of education, if, as is said, Homer was
greatly neglected by him and others in his own day when he was
alive?

Yes, I replied, that is the tradition. But can you imagine,
Glaucon, that if Homer had really been able to educate and
improve mankind, if he had possessed knowledge and not been a
mere imitator—can you imagine, I say, that he would not have had
many followers, and been honoured and loved by them? Protagoras of Abdera, and Prodicus of Ceos, and a host of others, have
only to suggest to their contemporaries that they will never be
able to manage either their own house or their State unless they are
made by them presidents of education; and for this wisdom of
theirs they are so much beloved that their companions all but carry
them about on their heads. And are we to believe that the contemporaries of Homer, or again, of Hesiod, would have allowed
either of them to beg their way as rhapsodists, if they had really
been able to improve mankind? Would they not have been as
unwilling to part with them as with gold, and have compelled
them to stay at home with them? Or, if the master would not stay,
then the disciples would have followed him about whithersoever
he went, until they had got education enough?

Yes, Socrates, that, I think, is quite true.

Then must we not infer that all the poets, beginning with
Homer, are only imitators; they copy images of virtue and the
601 like, but the truth they never reach? The poet is like a painter
who, as has already been observed, will make a likeness of a
cobbler though he understands nothing of cobbling; and this is
good enough for those who know no more than he does, and judge
only by colours and figures. Also, the poet lays on certain colours
of each of the arts in the shape of nouns and verbs, himself understanding their nature only enough to imitate; and other people,
who are as ignorant as he is and judge only from his words,

imagine that if he speaks of cobbling in metre and harmony and rhythm, or of military tactics, or of anything else, he speaks very well—such is the sweet influence which melody and rhythm have naturally. And I think that you must know, for you have often seen the quality of poetical compositions when stripped of the colours which music puts upon them, and only recited?

Yes, he said.

They are like faces which were never really beautiful, but only blooming; and now the bloom of youth has passed away from them?

Exactly.

Here is another point: The imitator or maker of the image knows nothing of true existence, he knows appearances only. Am I not right?

Yes.

Then let us have a clear understanding, and not be satisfied with half an explanation.

Proceed.

Of the painter we say that he will paint reins, and he will paint a bridle?

Yes.

And the worker in leather and brass will make them. But does the painter know the right form of the bridle and reins? Nay, this can hardly be said even of the maker; only the horseman who knows how to use them—he knows their right form.

Most true.

And may we not say the same of all things?

What?

That there are three arts which are concerned with all things: one that uses, another that makes, a third that imitates them?

Yes.

The excellence or beauty or truth of each structure, animate or inanimate, and of each action of man, has reference to the use of them, either natural or artificial?

True.

Then the user of them must have the greatest experience of them, and he must intimate to the maker the good or bad qualities which develope themselves in use; for example, the flute-player will tell the flute-maker which of his flutes answer in playing; he will tell him how he ought to make them, and the other will attend to him?

Of course.

The one knows and therefore speaks about the goodness and badness of flutes, and the other believes and obeys him?

True.

The vessel is the same, but about the good and bad qualities of the vessel the maker will only attain belief; and this he will gain from him who knows, by talking to him and hearing what he has 602 to say, whereas the user will have knowledge?

True.

But will the imitator have knowledge, or opinion only? Will he know from use whether or no his drawing is straight or beautiful? or will he have right opinion only, and be compelled to depend on others who have knowledge, and from whom he takes his orders?

Neither.

Then he will no more have true opinion than he will have knowledge about the goodness or badness of that which he imitates?

I suppose not.

Then the imitative artist will be in a brilliant state of intelligence about his own creations?

Nay, rather the reverse.

And yet he will go on imitating good and evil, of which he has no knowledge, and will therefore only imitate the appearance which good and evil wear to the ignorant and to the vulgar?

That will be all.

And so we may fairly conclude that the imitator has no knowledge worth mentioning. Imitation is only a kind of play or sport, and the tragic and epic poets are imitators in the highest degree?

Very true.

Come, then, and answer this: Is not imitation concerned with that which is thrice removed from truth?

Certainly.

And what is the faculty in man to which imitation is addressed?

What do you mean?

I will explain my meaning: The body which is large when seen near, appears small when seen at a distance?

True.

And the same objects appear straight when looked at out of the water, and crooked when in the water; and the convex becomes concave, owing to the illusion about colours to which the sight is liable. There is no end to this sort of confusion in the mind; and there is a similar deception about painting in light and shade, and juggling, and other ingenious devices, which have quite a magical power of imposing upon our weakness.

True.

And the arts of measuring and numbering and weighing come to the rescue of the human understanding—that is the beauty of them—and the apparent greater or less, or more or heavier, no longer reign in us, but give way before calculation and measure and weight?

Most true.

And this, surely, must be the work of the calculating and rational principle in the soul?

Yes, surely.

And this is the principle which measures and certifies that some things are equal, or that some are greater or less than others, and then there is an apparent contradiction?

True.

But were we not saying that such a contradiction is impossible — the same cannot have contrary opinions at the same time about 603 the same?

Yes, and that is true.

Then that which has an opinion contrary to measure is not the same with that which has an opinion in accordance with measure?

True.

But that which trusts to measure and calculation is the best part of the soul?

Certainly.

And that which is opposed to them is one of the inferior principles of the soul?

No doubt.

That was the conclusion at which I wanted to arrive when I said that painting or drawing and imitation in general is remote from truth, and is the companion and friend and associate of a principle which is remote from reason, and has no true or healthy aim.

Exactly.

The imitative art is an inferior who marries an inferior, and has inferior offspring.

Very true.

And is this confined to the sight only, or applicable to the hearing also, in reference to what is termed poetry?

Probably the same holds of poetry.

But do not rely, I said, on the analogy of painting; let us further examine and see whether the faculty with which poetical imitation is concerned is good or bad. Now imitation imitates the action of man, either voluntary or involuntary, in which there is expectation of a bad or good event, and present experience of pleasure or pain. Is there anything more?

No, there is nothing else.

But in all this is the man at unity with himself—or rather, as in the instance of sight there was confusion and opposition, so here also is there not strife and inconsistency in human actions? Though I need hardly raise this question again, for, if I am not mistaken, all this has been already admitted by us; the soul has been acknowledged to be full of endless oppositions of this sort occurring at the same moment?

And we were right in admitting that, he said.

Yes, I said, in that we were right; but there was an omission which must now be supplied.

What was that?

Were we not saying that a good man, when he loses his son or anything else which is most dear to him, will bear the loss with more equanimity than another?

Yes.

But we never thought of adding, that although he will sorrow, for he cannot help this, he will moderate his sorrow—will he not?

Yes, he said, he will.

604 And now tell me: will he be more likely to struggle and hold out against his sorrow when he is seen by his equals, or when he is by himself alone in a desert?

He will be more likely to hold out when he is in company.

But when he is left alone he will not mind saying or doing many things which he would be ashamed of any one hearing or seeing?

True.

There is a principle of law and reason in him which bids him resist, while passion urges him to indulge his sorrow?

True.

But when a man is drawn in two opposite directions, to and from the same object, this, as we affirm, necessarily implies two distinct principles in him?

Certainly.

One of them is obedient to the law?

How do you mean?

The law would say that to be patient under suffering is best, and that we should not give way to impatience, as there is no knowing whether such things are good or evil; and nothing is gained by impatience; also, because no human thing is of serious importance, and grief stands in the way of that which at the moment is most required.

What is that? he asked.

Good counsel, I said, which, as at a game of dice, takes the measures which reason prescribes, according to the number of the dice; and will not allow us, like children who have had a fall, to be keeping hold of the part struck and wasting time in setting up a howl, when we should be accustoming the soul forthwith to apply a remedy, raising up that which is sickly and fallen, banishing the cry of sorrow by a real cure.

Yes, he said, that is the best way of meeting the attacks of fortune.

Yes, I said; and the higher principle is ready to follow this suggestion of reason.

Clearly.

And the other principle which inclines us to recollection of our troubles and to lamentation, and can never have enough of them, we may call irrational, indolent, and cowardly?

Indeed, we may.

And does not the latter—I mean the rebellious principle—furnish a great variety of materials for imitation? Whereas the wise and calm temperament, being always nearly equable, is not easy to imitate or to appreciate when imitated, especially at a theatre in which all sorts of men are gathered together. For the feeling which is represented is one to which they are strangers.

Certainly.

605 Then the imitative poet is not by nature made, nor his art intended, to affect or please the rational principle in the soul, if his object is to be popular; but he will prefer the passionate and fitful temper, which is easily imitated?

That is evident.

And now we may fairly take him and set him up by the side of the painter, for he is like him in two ways: first, inasmuch as his creations have an inferior degree of truth—in this, I say, he is like him; and he is also like him in being concerned with an inferior part of the soul; and therefore we shall be right in not receiving him in a well-ordered State, because he awakens and nourishes and strengthens the feelings and impairs the reason. As in a city we cannot allow the evil to have authority and the good to be put out of the way, even so in the city which is within us we refuse to allow the imitative poet to create an evil constitution indulging the irrational nature which has no discernment of greater and less, and thinks the same thing at one time great and at another small; or to manufacture images which are very far removed from the truth.

Very true.

But we have not yet brought forward the heaviest count in our accusation—the power which poetry has of harming even the good (and there are very few who are not harmed), which is surely an awful thing?

Yes, certainly, if that is the effect.

Hear and judge: the best of us, as I conceive, when we listen to a passage of Homer, or one of the tragedians in which he represents some pitiful hero who is drawling out his sorrows in a long oration, or possibly singing, and smiting his breast—the best of us, I say, as you know, delight in giving way to sympathy, and are in raptures at the excellence of the poet who stirs our feelings most.

Yes, of course.

But when any sorrow happens to ourselves, then you know that we pride ourselves on the opposite quality of quietness and endurance; this is the manly part, and that which then enraptured us is now deemed to be the part of a woman.

I know, he said.

Now can we be right in praising that in another which a man would abominate and be ashamed of in his own person?

No, he said, that is certainly not reasonable.

Yes, I said, but quite reasonable from a certain point of view. 606

What point of view?

If you consider, I said, that there is in us a natural feeling which is just hungering after sorrow and weeping, and desiring to be indulged, and that this feeling, which is kept under control in our own calamities, is the same which is satisfied and delighted by the poets:—the better nature in each of us, not having been sufficiently trained by reason or habit, is taken unawares because the sorrow is another's; and the spectator fancies that there can be no disgrace to himself in praising and pitying any one who comes telling him what a good man he is, and making unseasonable lamentations—he thinks that the pleasure is a gain which he must not lose by the rejection of the poem. For the reflection is not often made that from the evil of others the fruit of evil is reaped by ourselves, or that the feeling of pity which has been nursed, and has acquired strength at the sight of the misfortunes of others, will come out in our own misfortunes, and cannot easily be controlled.

That is a very true remark.

And does not the same hold also of the ridiculous? There are jests which you would be ashamed to make yourself, and yet on the comic stage, or again in private, when you hear them, you are greatly amused by them, instead of being disgusted at their unseemliness;—the case of compassion recurs; there is a principle within which is disposed to raise a laugh, and this was once kept in order by you because you were afraid of being thought a buffoon, but is now let loose again and encouraged by the theatre, and you are often unconsciously betrayed into playing the comic poet in your own person.

Quite true, he said.

And the same may be said of lust and anger and all the other affections, of desire and pain and pleasure which are held to be inseparable from every action—in all of them poetry feeds and waters the passions instead of withering and starving them; she lets them rule instead of ruling them as they ought to be ruled, with a view to the happiness and virtue of mankind.

I cannot deny that.

Therefore, Glaucon, I said, whenever you meet with any of the eulogists of Homer declaring that he has been the educator of Hellas, and that he is profitable for the management and administration of human things, and that you should take him up and read
607 him and regulate your whole life according to him, we may love and honour the intentions of these excellent people, as far as their light extends; and we are ready to acknowledge that Homer is the greatest of poets and first of tragedy writers; but we must remain firm in our conviction that hymns to the gods and praises of famous men are the only poetry which ought to be admitted into our State. For if you go beyond this and allow the honeyed muse to enter, either in epic or lyric verse, not law and reason, which by the consent of all is ever to be deemed the best, but pleasure and pain will be the rulers in our State.

That is most true, he said.

Let this then be the explanation which we give of our reasons for expelling poetry, that we have only followed the course of the argument; and let us also make an apology to her, that she may not charge us with any harshness or want of politeness. We will tell her, 'that there is an ancient quarrel between philosophy and poetry;' of which there are many proofs, such as the saying of 'the yelping hound howling at her lord,' or of one 'mighty in the vain talk of fools,' and 'the mob of sages circumventing Zeus,' and the 'subtle thinkers who are beggars after all;' and there are ten thousand other signs of ancient enmity between them. Notwithstanding this, let us assure our sweet friend, and the sister arts of imitation, that if she will only prove her title to existence in a well-ordered State we shall be delighted to receive her, knowing that we ourselves also are very susceptible of her charms; but we may not on that account betray the truth. I dare say, Glaucon, that you are as much charmed by her as I am, especially when you see her in the garb of Homer?

Yes, indeed, I am greatly charmed.

Shall I propose, then, that she be allowed to return from exile, on this condition—that she is to make a defence of herself in lyrical or some other metre?

Certainly.

And I think that we may grant a further privilege to those of her defenders who are lovers of poetry and yet not poets; they shall be allowed to speak in prose on her behalf: let them show not only that she is pleasant but also useful to States and to human life and we will gladly listen, for if this can be proved we shall surely be the gainers, that is to say, if there is a use in poetry as well as a delight?

Certainly, he said, we shall be the gainers.

If her defence fails, then, my dear friend, though much against our will we must give her up, after the manner of lovers who abstain when they think that their love is not good for them; for we too are inspired by that love of poetry which the education of 608 noble States has implanted in us, and therefore we would have her appear at her best and truest; but so long as she is unable to make good her defence, even though our ears may listen, our souls will be charmed against her by repeating this discourse of ours, and into the childish love which the many have of her we shall take care not to fall again, for we see that poetry being such as she is, is not to be pursued in earnest or regarded seriously as attaining to the truth; and he who listens to her will be on his guard against her seductions, fearing for the safety of the city which is within him, and he will attend to our words.

Yes, he said, I quite agree with you.

Yes, I said, my dear Glaucon, for great is the issue at stake, greater than appears, whether a man is to be good or bad. Neither under the influence of honour or money or power, aye, or under the excitement of poetry, ought he to fail in the observance of justice and virtue.

I agree, he said; and I think that any one would agree who heard the argument.

And yet, I said, no mention has been made of the greatest prizes and rewards of virtue.

If, he said, there are others greater than these they must be of an inconceivable greatness.

Why, I said, what was ever great in a short time? The whole period of three-score years and ten is surely but a little thing in comparison with eternity?

Say rather 'nothing,' he replied.

And should an immortal being seriously think of this little space rather than of the whole?

Yes, he said, I think that he should. But what do you mean?

Are you not aware, I said, that the soul is immortal and imperishable?

He looked at me in astonishment, and said: No, indeed; you do not mean to say that you are able to prove that?

Yes, I said, I ought to be able, and you too, for there is no difficulty.

I do not see that, he said; and I should like to hear this argument of which you make no difficulty.

Listen then, I said.

I am attending, he said.

You speak of good and of evil?

Yes, he replied.

Would you agree that the corrupting and destroying element is the evil, and the saving and improving element the good?

609 Yes, he said.

And you admit that everything has a good and also an evil; as ophthalmia is the evil of the eyes and disease of the whole body; as mildew is of corn, and rot of timber, or rust of iron and steel: in everything, or almost everything, I say that there is an inherent evil and disease?

Yes, he said.

And anything which is infected by any of these evils is made evil, and at last wholly dissolves and dies?

True.

The vice and evil which is inherent in each is the destruction of each; and if this does not destroy them there is nothing else that will, for good certainly will not destroy them, nor again, that which is neither good nor evil.

That is impossible.

If, then, we find any nature which having this inherent corruption cannot be dissolved or destroyed, we may be certain that of such a nature there is no destruction?

That may be assumed, he said.

Well, I said, and is there no evil which corrupts the soul?

Yes, he said, there are all the evils of which we were speaking: unrighteousness, intemperance, cowardice, ignorance.

But do any of these dissolve or destroy her?—and here do not let us fall into the error of supposing that the unjust and foolish, when they are detected, perish through their injustice, which is an

evil of the soul. Take the analogy of the body : The evil of the
body is a disease which wastes and reduces and annihilates the
body; and all the things of which we were just now speaking come
to annihilation through their own inherent evil clinging to them
and destroying them. Is not this true?

Yes, he said.

Now consider the soul in the same way. Do the injustice and
other evil that there are in the soul waste and consume the soul?
Do they, by inhering in her and clinging to her at last, bring her
to death, and separate her from the body?

Nay, he said, that is not at all the case.

And yet, I said, there is something unreasonable in supposing
that anything can perish from without through external affection
of evil, which could not be destroyed from within by any internal
corruption?

Yes, that is unreasonable, he said.

Consider, I said, Glaucon, that even the badness of food,
whether staleness, decomposition, or any other kind of badness,
when confined to the actual food, is not supposed to destroy the
body; although, if the corruption of food communicates corruption
to the body, then we say that the body also suffers from internal 610
corruption or disease and perishes; but that the body, being one
thing, can be destroyed by the badness of food, which is another thing,
without any internal infection—that will never be admitted by us?

Very true.

And, on the same principle, unless some bodily evil can produce
an evil of the soul, we must not suppose that the soul, which is one
thing, can be dissolved by any external evil which belongs to another?

Yes, he said, there is reason in that.

Either, then, let us refute this argument, or, while this argument
of ours remains unrefuted, let us never say that fever, or any other
disease, or the knife put to the throat, or even the cutting up of
the whole body into the minutest pieces, can destroy the soul,
until the soul also is proved to become more unholy or unrighteous
in consequence of these things being done to the body; but that
the soul, or anything else which is not destroyed by an internal
evil, can be destroyed by an external one, is not to be supposed.

No one, he replied, will ever show that the souls of men become more unjust in consequence of death; that is certain.

And if some one who would rather not admit the immortality of the soul boldly denies this, and says that the dying do really become more evil and unrighteous, then, if the speaker is right, I suppose that injustice, like disease, must be assumed to be fatal to the unjust, and that those who take this disorder die by the natural inherent power of destruction which evil has, and which kills them sooner or later in quite another way from that in which, at present, the wicked receive death at the hands of others as the penaltyof their deeds?

Nay, he said, then after all injustice, if fatal to the unjust, will not be so very terrible to him, for he will be delivered from evil. But I rather suspect that this is not the truth, and that injustice which murders others keeps the murderer alive—aye, and unsleeping too; so far is she from bringing death where she has taken up her abode.

True, I said; if the inherent natural vice or evil of the soul is unable to kill or destroy her, hardly will that which is appointed to be the destruction of the body destroy a soul or anything other than the body.

Yes, he said, that can hardly be.

611 But the soul which cannot be destroyed by evil, whether inherent or external, must exist for ever, and, if existing for ever, must be immortal?

That is certain.

That is the argument, I said; and, if the argument holds, then the souls must always be the same, for if none be destroyed they will not diminish in number. Neither will they increase, for the increase of the immortal natures must come from something mortal, and all things would thus end in immortality.

Very true.

But reason cannot admit this any more than we can admit that in the truth of nature the soul, in herself, is full of variety and difference and dissimilarity.

What do you mean? he said

The soul, I said, being immortal, as is now clear, and also compounded of many elements, must be the fairest of compositions?

Yes, indeed, he said.

Her immortality may be proven by the previous argument and by other arguments; and you should also see her original nature, not as we now behold her, marred by communion with the body and other miseries, but you should look upon her with the eye of reason, pure as at birth, and then her beauty would be discovered, and in her image justice would be more clearly seen, and injustice, and all the things which we have described. But now, although we have spoken the truth concerning her as she appears at present, we must remember that we have seen her only in a condition which may be compared to that of the sea-god Glaucus, whose original image can hardly be discerned because his natural members are broken off and crushed and in many ways damaged by the waves, and incrustations have grown over them of seaweed and shells and stones, so that he is liker to some sea-monster than to his natural form. And the soul is in a similar condition, disfigured by ten thousand ills. But not there, Glaucon, not there must we look.

Where then ?

At her love of wisdom. Let us see whom she affects, and what converse she seeks in virtue of her near kindred with the immortal and eternal and divine ; also how different she would become if wholly following this superior principle, and borne by a divine impulse out of the ocean in which she now is, and disengaged from the stones and shells and things of earth and rock which in wild variety grow around her because she feeds upon earth, and is 612 crusted over by the good things of this life as they are termed : then you would see her as she is, and know whether she have one form only or many, or what her nature is. Of her form and affections in this present life I have said enough.

True, he said.

Thus, I said, have we followed out the argument[2], putting aside the rewards and glories of justice, such as you were saying that Homer and Hesiod introduced ; and justice in her own nature has been shown to be best for the soul in her nature : let her do what is just, whether she have the ring of Gyges or not, and, besides the ring of Gyges, the helmet of Hades.

That is very true.

And now, Glaucon, there will be no harm in further enumerating how many and how great are the rewards which justice and the other virtues procure to the soul from gods and men, both in life and after death.

[2] Reading ἀπελυσάμεθα.

Certainly, he said.

Will you repay me, then, what you borrowed in the argument?

What was that?

I granted that the just man should appear unjust and the unjust just: for you were of opinion that even if the true state of the case could not possibly escape the eyes of gods and men, still this ought to be admitted for the sake of the argument, in order that pure justice might be weighed against pure injustice. Do you not remember?

You would have reason to complain of me if I had forgotten.

Then, as the cause is decided, I demand on behalf of justice that the glory which she receives from gods and men be also allowed to her by you; having been shown to have reality, and not to deceive those who truly possess her, she may also have appearance restored to her, and thus obtain the other crown of victory which is hers also.

The demand, he said, is just.

In the first place, I said—and this is the first point which you will have to give back—the nature both of just and unjust is truly known to the gods?

I am willing to restore that.

And if they are both known to them, one must be the friend and the other the enemy of the gods, as we admitted at first?

True.

613 And the friend of the gods may be supposed to receive from them every good, excepting only such evil as is the necessary consequence of former sins?

Certainly.

Then this must be our notion of the just man, that even when he is in poverty or sickness, or any other seeming misfortune, all things will in the end work together for good to him in life and death: for the gods have a care of any one whose desire is to become just and to be like God, as far as man can attain his likeness, by the pursuit of virtue?

Yes, he said; if he is like God he will surely not be neglected by him.

And of the unjust may not the opposite be assumed?

Certainly.

Such, then, is the prize of victory which the gods give the just?

Yes, he said, that is my belief.

And what do they receive of men? Look at things as they really are and you will see that the clever unjust are in the case of runners, who run well from the starting-place to the goal, but not back again from the goal: they start off at a great pace, but in the end only look foolish, slinking away with their ears draggling on their shoulders, and without a crown; but the true runner comes to the finish and receives the prize and is crowned. And this is the way with the just; he who endures to the end of every action and occasion of his entire life has a good report and carries off the prize which men bestow.

True.

And now you must allow me to repeat the blessings which you attributed to the fortunate unjust. I shall say of the just as you were saying of the unjust, that as they grow older, if that is their desire, they become rulers in their own city; they marry whom they like and give in marriage to whomsoever they like; all that you said of the others I now say of these. And, on the other hand, I say of the unjust that the greater number, even though they escape in their youth, are found out at last and look foolish at the end of their course, and when they come to be old and miserable are flouted alike by stranger and citizen; they are beaten and then come those things unfit for ears polite, as you truly term them; they will be racked and burned, as you were saying: I shall ask you to suppose that you have heard all that. Will you allow me to assume thus much?

Certainly, he said, for what you say is true.

These, then, are the prizes and rewards and gifts which are 614 bestowed upon the just by gods and men in this present life, in addition to those other good things which justice of herself gives.

Yes, he said; and they are fair and lasting.

And yet, I said, all these things are as nothing either in number or greatness in comparison with those other recompenses which await both just and unjust after death, which are more and greater far. And you ought to hear them, and then both of them will have received the perfect meed of words due to them.

Speak, he said; there are few things which I would more gladly hear.

Well, I said, I will tell you a tale; not one of the tales which Odysseus tells to Alcinous, yet this too is a tale of a brave man, Er the son of Armenius, a Pamphylian by birth. He was slain in battle, and ten days afterwards, when the bodies of the dead were brought in already in a state of corruption, he was brought in with them undecayed, and carried home to be buried. And on the twelfth day, as he was lying on the funeral pile, he returned to life and told them what he had seen in the other world. He said that when his soul departed he went on a journey with a great company, and that they came to a mysterious place at which there were two chasms in the earth; they were near together and over against them were two other chasms in the heaven above. In the intermediate space there were judges seated, who bade the just, after they had judged them, ascend by the heavenly way on the right hand, having the signs of the judgment bound on their foreheads; and in like manner the unjust were commanded by them to descend by the lower way on the left hand; these also had the symbols of their deeds fastened on their backs. He drew near, and they told him that he was to be the messenger of the other world to men, and they bade him hear and see all that was to be heard and seen in that place. Then he beheld and saw on one side the souls departing at either chasm of heaven and earth when sentence had been given on them; and at the two other openings other souls, some ascending out of the earth dusty and worn with travel, some descending out of heaven clean and bright. And always, on their arrival, they seemed as if they had come from a long journey, and they went out into the meadow with joy and there encamped as at a festival, and those who knew one another embraced and conversed, the souls which came from earth curiously enquiring about the things of heaven, and the souls which came from heaven of the things of earth. And they told one another of what had happened by the way, some weeping and sorrowing at the remembrance of the things which they had endured and seen in their journey beneath the earth (now the journey lasted a thousand years), while others were describing heavenly blessings and visions of inconceivable beauty. There is not time, Glaucon, to tell all; but the sum was this:—He said that for every wrong which they had done to any one they suffered tenfold; the thousand years answering to the hundred years which are reckoned as the life of man. If, for example, there were any who had committed murders, or had betrayed or enslaved cities or armies, or been guilty of any other evil behaviour, for each and all of these they received punishment ten times over, and the rewards of beneficence and justice and holiness were in the same proportion. Not to repeat what he had to say concerning young children dying almost as soon as they were born; of piety and impiety to gods and parents, and of murderers, there were retributions yet greater which he narrated. He mentioned that he was present when one of the spirits asked another, 'Where is Ardiaeus the Great?' (Now this Ardiaeus was the tyrant of some city of Pamphylia, who had murdered his aged father and his elder brother, and had committed many other abominable crimes, and he lived a thousand years before the time of Er.) The answer was: 'He comes not hither, and will never come.' And, 'indeed,' he said, 'this was one of the terrible sights which was witnessed by us. For we were approaching the mouth of the cave, and, having seen all, were about to re-ascend, when of a sudden Ardiaeus appeared and several others, most of whom were tyrants; and there were also besides the tyrants private individuals who had been great criminals; they were just at the mouth, being, as they fancied, about to return into the upper world, but the opening, instead of receiving them, gave a roar, as was the case when any incurable or unpunished sinner tried to ascend; and then wild men of fiery aspect, who knew the meaning of the sound, came up and seized and carried off several of them, and Ardiaeus and 616 others they bound head and foot and hand, and threw them down and flayed them with scourges, and dragged them along the road at the side, carding them on thorns like wool, and declaring to the pilgrims as they passed what were their crimes, and that they were being taken away to be cast into hell[3]. And of all the terrors of the place there was no terror like this of hearing the voice; and when there was silence they ascended with joy.' These were the penalties and retributions, and there were blessings as great.

Now when the spirits that were in the meadow had tarried seven days, on the eighth they were obliged to proceed on their

---

[3] Reading καὶ ὅτι.

journey, and on the fourth day from that time they came to a place where they looked down from above upon a line of light, like a column extending right through the whole heaven and earth, in colour not unlike the rainbow, only brighter and purer; another day's journey brought them to the place, and there, in the midst of the light, they saw reaching from heaven the extremities of the chains of it: for this light is the belt of heaven, and holds together the circle of the universe, like the undergirders of a trireme. And from the extremities of the chains is extended the spindle of Necessity, on which all the revolutions turn. The shaft and hook of this spindle are made of steel, and the whorl is made partly of steel and also partly of other materials. Now the whorl is in form like the whorl used on earth; and you are to suppose, as he described, that there is one large hollow whorl which is scooped out, and into this is fitted another lesser one, and another, and another, and four others, making eight in all, like boxes which fit into one another; their edges are turned upwards, and all together form one continuous whorl. This is pierced by the spindle, which is driven home through the centre of the eighth. The first and outermost whorl has the rim broadest, and the seven inner whorls narrow, in the following proportions—the sixth is next to the first in size, the fourth next to the sixth; then comes the eighth; the seventh is fifth, the fifth is sixth, the third is seventh, last and eighth comes the second. The largest [or fixed stars] is spangled, and the seventh [or sun] is brightest; the eighth [or moon] coloured by 617 the reflected light of the seventh; the second and fifth [Mercury and Saturn] are like one another, and of a yellower colour than the preceding; the third [Venus] has the whitest light; the fourth [Mars] is reddish; the sixth [Jupiter] is in whiteness second. Now the whole spindle has the same motion; but, as the whole revolves in one direction, the seven inner circles move slowly in the other, and of these the swiftest is the eighth; next in swiftness are the seventh, sixth, and fifth, which move together; third in swiftness appeared to them to move in reversed orbit the fourth; the third appeared fourth, and the second fifth. The spindle turns on the knees of Necessity; and on the upper surface of each circle is a siren, who goes round with them, hymning a single sound and note. The eight together form one harmony; and round about, at equal intervals, there is another band, three in number, each sitting upon her throne : these are the Fates, daughters of Necessity, who are clothed in white raiment and have garlands upon their heads, Lachesis and Clotho and Atropos, who accompany with their voices the harmony of the sirens—Lachesis singing of the past, Clotho of the present, Atropos of the future; Clotho now and then assisting with a touch of her right hand the motion of the outer circle or whorl of the spindle, and Atropos with her left hand touching and guiding the inner ones, and Lachesis laying hold of either in turn, first with one hand and then with the other.

Now when the spirits arrived, their duty was to go to Lachesis; but first a prophet came and arranged them in order; then he took from the knees of Lachesis lots and samples of lives, and going up to a high place, spoke as follows: 'Hear the word of Lachesis, the daughter of Necessity. Mortal souls, behold a new cycle of mortal life. Your genius will not choose you, but you will choose your genius; and let him who draws the first lot have the first choice of life, which shall be his destiny. Virtue is free, and as a man honours or dishonours her he will have more or less of her; the chooser is answerable—God is justified.' When the Interpreter had thus spoken he cast the lots among them, and each one took up the lot which fell near him, all but Er himself (he 618 was not allowed), and each as he took his lot perceived the number which he had drawn. Then the Interpreter placed on the ground before them the samples of lives; and there were many more lives than the souls present, and there were all sorts of lives—of every animal and every condition of man. And there were tyrannies among them, some continuing while the tyrant lived, others which broke off in the middle and came to an end in poverty and exile and beggary; and there were lives of famous men, some who were famous for their form and beauty as well as for their strength and success in games, or, again, for their birth and the qualities of their ancestors; and some who were the reverse of famous for the opposite qualities. And of women likewise; there was not, how-ever, any definite character among them, because the soul must of necessity choose another life, and become other. But there were many elements mingling with one another, and also with elements of wealth and poverty, and disease and health; and there were mean states also. And this, my dear Glaucon, is the great danger of man; and therefore the utmost care should be taken. Let each one of us leave every other kind of knowledge and seek and follow one thing only, if peradventure he may be able to learn and find who there is who can and will teach him to distinguish the life of good and evil, and to choose always and everywhere the better life as far as possible. He should consider the bearing of all these things which have been mentioned severally and collectively upon a virtuous life; he should know what the effect of beauty is when compounded with poverty or wealth in a particular soul, and what are the good and evil consequences of noble and humble birth, of private and public station, of strength and weakness, of cleverness and dullness, and of all the natural and acquired gifts of the soul, and study the composition of them; then he will look at the nature of the soul, and from the consideration of all this he will determine which is the better and which is the worse life, and at last he will choose, giving the name of evil to the life which will make his soul more unjust, and good to the life which will make his soul more just; all else he will disregard. For this, as we have seen, is the best choice both for this life and after death.

619 Such an iron sense of truth and right must a man take with him into the world below, that there too he may be undazzled by the desire of wealth or the other allurements of evil, lest, coming upon tyrannies and similar villanies, he do irremediable wrongs to others and suffer yet worse himself; but let him know how to choose the mean and avoid the extremes on either side, as far as in him lies, not only in this life but in all that which is to come. For this is the way of happiness.

And this was what the Interpreter said at the time, as the messenger from the other world reported him to have spoken: 'Even for the last comer, if he chooses wisely and will live diligently, there is appointed a happy and not undesirable existence. Let not the first be careless in his choice, and let not the last despair.' As he spoke these words he who had the first choice drew near and at once chose the greatest tyranny; his mind, having been darkened by folly and sensuality, he did not well consider, and therefore did not see at first that he was fated, among other evils, to devour his own children. But, when he came to himself and saw what was in the lot, he began to beat his breast and lament over his choice, forgetting the proclamation of the

Interpreter; for, instead of blaming himself as the author of his calamity, he accused chance and the gods, and everything rather than himself.   Now he was one of those who came from heaven, and in a former life had dwelt in a well-ordered State, but his virtue was a matter of habit only, and he had no philosophy. And this was more often the fortune of those who came from heaven, because they had no experience of life; whereas, in general, the dwellers upon earth, who had seen and known trouble, were not in a hurry to choose.   And owing to this inexperience of theirs, and also because the lot was a chance, many of the souls exchanged a good destiny for an evil or an evil for a good.   For if a man had always from the first dedicated himself to sound philosophy, and had been moderately fortunate in the number of the lot, he might, as the messenger reported, be happy in this life, and also his passage to another life and return to this, instead of being rugged and underground, would be smooth and heavenly.   Most curious, he said, was the spectacle of the election—sad and laughable and strange; the souls generally choosing according to their 620 condition in a previous life.   There he saw the soul that was once Orpheus choosing the life of a swan out of enmity to the race of women, hating to be born of a woman because they had been his murderers; he saw also the soul of Thamyris choosing the life of a nightingale; birds, on the other hand, like the swan and other musicians, choosing to be men.   The soul which obtained the twentieth[4] lot chose the life of a lion, and this was the soul of Ajax the son of Telamon, who would not be a man, remembering the injustice which was done him in the judgment of the arms.   The next was Agamemnon, who took the life of an eagle, because, like Ajax, he hated human nature on account of his sufferings.   About the middle was the lot of Atalanta; she, seeing the great fame of an athlete, was unable to resist the temptation; and after her there came the soul of Epeus the son of Panopeus passing into the nature of a woman cunning in the arts; and far away among the last who chose, the soul of the jester Thersites was putting on the form of a monkey.   There came also the soul of Odysseus having yet to make a choice, and his lot happened to be the last of them all.   Now the recollection of former toils had disenchanted him of ambition, and he went about

4 Reading εἰκοστήν.

for a considerable time in search of the life of a private man who had nothing to do; he had some difficulty in finding this, which was lying about and had been neglected by everybody else; and when he saw it, he said that he would have done the same had he been first instead of last, and that he was delighted at his choice. And not only did men pass into animals, but I must also mention that there were animals tame and wild who changed into one another and into corresponding human natures, the good into the gentle and the evil into the savage, in all sorts of combinations. All the souls had now chosen their lives, and they went in the order of their choice to Lachesis, who sent with them the genius whom they had severally chosen, to be the guardian of their lives and the fulfiller of the choice; this genius led the soul first to Clotho, and drew them within the revolution of the spindle impelled by her hand, thus ratifying the destiny of each; and then, when they were fastened, carried them to Atropos, who spun the threads and made them irreversible; whence without turning round they

621 passed beneath the throne of Necessity; and when they had all passed, they marched on in a scorching heat to the plain of Forgetfulness, which was a barren waste destitute of trees and verdure; and then towards evening they encamped by the river of Negligence, the water of which no vessel can hold; of this they were all obliged to drink a certain quantity, and those who were not saved by wisdom drank more than was necessary; and those who drank forgot all things. Now after they had gone to rest, about the middle of the night there was a thunderstorm and earthquake, and then in an instant they were driven all manner of ways like stars shooting to their birth. He himself was hindered from drinking the water. But in what manner or by what means he returned to the body he could not say; only, in the morning awaking suddenly, he saw himself lying on the pyre.

And thus, Glaucon, the tale has been saved and has not perished, and may be our salvation if we are obedient to the word spoken; and we shall pass safely over the river of Forgetfulness and our soul will not be defiled. Wherefore my counsel is, that we hold fast to the heavenly way and follow after justice and virtue always, considering that the soul is immortal and able to endure every sort of good and every sort of evil. Thus shall we live dear to one another and to the gods, both while remaining here and when, like conquerors in the games who go round to gather gifts, we receive our reward. And it shall be well with us both in this life and in the pilgrimage of a thousand years which we have been reciting.

TIMAEUS.

INTRODUCTION.

OF all the writings of Plato the Timaeus is the most obscure and
repulsive to the modern reader, and has nevertheless had the greatest
influence over the ancient and mediaeval world. The obscurity arises
in the infancy of physical science, out of the confusion of theological,
mathematical, and physiological notions, out of the desire to conceive
the whole of nature without any adequate knowledge of the parts,
and from a greater perception of similarities which lie on the surface
than of differences which are hidden from view. To bring sense under
the control of reason; to find some way through the labyrinth or chaos
of appearances, either the highway of mathematics, or more devious
paths suggested by the analogy of man with the world, and of the
world with man; to see that all things have a cause and are tending
towards an end—this is the spirit of the ancient physical philosopher.
But we neither appreciate the conditions of knowledge to which he
was subjected, nor have the ideas which fastened upon his imagination
the same hold upon us. For he is hovering between matter and mind;
he is under the dominion of abstractions; his impressions are taken
almost at random from the outside of nature; he sees the light, but
not the objects which are revealed by the light; and he brings into
juxtaposition things which to us appear wide as the poles asunder, because he finds nothing between them. He passes abruptly from persons
to ideas and numbers, and from ideas and numbers to persons; he
confuses subject and object, first and final causes, and is dreaming of
geometrical figures lost in a flux of sense. And an effort of mind
is required on our parts in order to understand his double language;
or appreciate the twilight character of this knowledge, and the genius

H h 2

of ancient philosophers, which under such conditions seems by a divine power in many instances to have anticipated the truth.

The influence which the Timaeus has exercised upon posterity is partly due to a misunderstanding. In the supposed depths of this dialogue the Neo-Platonists found hidden meanings and connections with the Jewish and Christian Scriptures, and out of them they elicited doctrines quite at variance with the spirit of Plato. Believing that he was inspired by the Holy Ghost, or had received his wisdom from Moses, they seemed to find in his writings the Christian Trinity, the Word, the Church, the creation of the world in a Jewish sense, as they really found the personality of God or mind, and the immortality of the soul. All religions and philosophies met and mingled in the schools of Alexandria, and the Neo-Platonists had a method of interpretation which could elicit any meaning out of any words. They were really incapable of distinguishing between the opinions of one philosopher and another, or between the serious thoughts of Plato and his passing fancies. They were absorbed in his theology, and under the dominion of his name, while that which was truly great and truly characteristic of him, his effort to realize and connect abstractions, was not understood by them at all. And yet the genius of Plato and Greek philosophy reacted upon the East, and a Greek element of thought and language overlaid the deeper and more pervading spirit of Orientalism.

There is no danger of the modern commentators on the Timaeus falling into the absurdities of the Neo-Platonists. In the present day we are well aware that an ancient philosopher is to be interpreted from himself, and by the contemporary history of thought. We know that mysticism is not criticism. The fancies of the Neo-Platonists are only interesting to us because they exhibit a phase of the human mind which prevailed widely in the first centuries of the Christian era, and is not wholly extinct in our own day. But they have nothing to do with the interpretation of Plato, and in spirit they are opposed to him. They are the feeble expression of an age which has lost the power not only of creating great works, but even of understanding them. They are the spurious birth of a marriage between philosophy and tradition, between Hellas and the East—εἰκὸς γεννᾶν νόθα καὶ φαῦλα (Rep. VI. 496). Whereas the so-called mysticism of Plato is purely Greek, arising out of his imperfect knowledge and high aspirations, and is the growth of an age in which philosophy is not wholly separated from poetry and mythology.

A greater danger with modern interpreters of Plato is the tendency to regard the Timaeus as the centre of his system. We do not know how Plato would have arranged his own dialogues, or whether the thought of arranging any of them, besides the two 'Trilogies' which he has expressly connected, was ever present to his mind. But, if he had arranged them, there are many indications that this is not the place which he would have assigned to the Timaeus. We observe, first of all, that the dialogue is put into the mouth of a Pythagorean philosopher, and not of Socrates. And this is required by dramatic propriety; for the investigation of nature was expressly renounced by Socrates in the Phaedo. Nor does Plato himself attribute any importance to his guesses at science. He is not at all absorbed by them, as he is by the *idea* of good. He is modest and hesitating, and confesses that his words partake of the uncertainty of the subject. Again, the dialogue is primarily concerned with the animal creation, including under this term the heavenly bodies, and with man only as one among the animals. But we can hardly suppose that Plato would have preferred the study of nature to man, or that he would have deemed the formation of the world and the human frame to have the same interest which he ascribes to the mystery of being and not being, or to the great political problems which he discusses in the Republic and the Laws. There are no speculations on physics in the other dialogues of Plato, and he himself regards the consideration of them as a rational pastime only. He is beginning to feel the need of further divisions of knowledge; and is becoming aware that besides dialectic, mathematics, and the arts, there is another field which has been hitherto unexplored by him. But he has not as yet defined this intermediate territory which lies somewhere between medicine and mathematics, and he would have felt that there was as great an impiety in ranking theories of physics first in the order of knowledge, as in placing the body before the soul.

Thus we are led by Plato himself to regard the Timaeus, not as the centre or inmost shrine of the edifice, but as a detached building in a different style, framed, not after the Socratic, but after some Pythagorean model. As in the Cratylus and Parmenides, we are uncertain whether Plato is expressing his own opinions, or appropriating and perhaps improving the philosophical speculations of others. In all three dialogues he is exerting his dramatic and imitative power; in the Cratylus mingling a satirical and humorous purpose with true principles of language; in the Parmenides overthrowing Megarianism by a sort of ultra-Megarianism, which discovers contradictions in the one as great as those which have been previously shown to exist in the ideas. There is a similar uncertainty about the Timaeus; while in the first part of the dialogue Plato is filled with a Pythagorean contemplation of the heavens, in the latter part he treats in a bald and superficial manner of the functions and diseases of the human frame, which he vainly attempts to connect with his astronomical theories.

If we allow for the difference of subject, and for some growth in Plato's own mind, the discrepancy between this and the other dialogues will not appear to be great. The relation of the ideas to God or of God to the world was differently conceived by him at different times of his life. In all his later dialogues we observe a tendency in him to personify mind or God, and he therefore naturally inclines to view creation as the work of design. The creator is like a human artist who frames in his mind a plan which he executes by the help of his servants. Thus the language of philosophy which speaks of first and second causes is crossed by another sort of phraseology: 'God made the world because he was good, and the demons ministered to him.' The Timaeus is cast in a more theological and less philosophical mould than the other dialogues, but the same general spirit is apparent; there is the same dualism or opposition between the ideal and actual—the soul is prior to the body, the intelligible and unseen to the visible and corporeal. There is the same distinction between knowledge and opinion which occurs in the Theaetetus and Republic, the same enmity to the poets, the same combination of music and gymnastics. The doctrine of transmigration is still held by him as in the Phaedrus; and the soul has a view of the heavens in a prior state of being. The ideas also remain, but they have become types in nature, forms of men, animals, birds, fishes. And the attribution of evil to physical causes accords with the doctrine which he maintains in the Laws respecting the involuntariness of vice.

The style and plan of the Timaeus differ greatly from that of any other of the Platonic dialogues. The language is weighty, abrupt, and in some passages sublime. But Plato has not the same mastery over his instrument which he exhibits in the Phaedrus or Symposium. Nothing can exceed the beauty or art of the introduction, in which he is using words after his accustomed manner. But in the rest of the dialogue the power of language seems to fail him. He could write in one style, but not in another, and the Greek language had not as yet been fashioned by any poet or philosopher to describe physical phenomena. The early physiologists had generally written in verse; Democritus and Anaxagoras never attained to a connected or periodic style. And hence we find the same sort of clumsiness in the Timaeus of Plato which characterizes the philosophical poem of Lucretius. There is a want of flow and often a defect of rhythm; the connection is frequently obscure, and there is a greater use of apposition and more of repetition than occurs elsewhere in Plato. His employment of the particles is sometimes unmeaning; and he places sentences side by side, leaving the relation between them to be inferred. The narrative portion of the Timaeus retains several characteristics of the first Greek prose composition; for the great master of language was speaking on a theme with which he was imperfectly acquainted, and had no words to express his meaning. The rugged grandeur of the opening passage of the speech of Timaeus (Tim. 28-31) may be compared with the more harmonious beauty of a similar passage in the Phaedrus (p. 245).

To the same cause we may attribute the want of plan. Plato had not that command of his materials which would have enabled him to produce a perfect work of art. And he warns his reader, that as is the nature of the subject so will the style be—as his knowledge is fragmentary and unconnected, his style partakes of the same character. His speculations about the Eternal, his theories of creation, his mathematical anticipations, are supplemented by desultory remarks on the one immortal and the two mortal souls of man, on the functions of the bodily organs in health and disease, on sight, hearing, smell, taste, and touch. He soars into the heavens, and then, as if his wings were suddenly clipped, he walks ungracefully and with difficulty upon the earth. The greatest things in the world, and the least things in man, are brought within the compass of a short treatise. But the intermediate links are missing, and we cannot be surprised that there should be a want of unity in a work which embraces astronomy, theology, physiology, and natural philosophy in a few pages.

It is not easy to determine how Plato's cosmos may be presented to the reader in a clearer and shorter form; or how we may supply a thread of connection to his ideas without giving greater consistency to them than they possessed in his mind, or adding on consequences to which he would have been a stranger. For he has glimpses of the truth, but no comprehensive or perfect vision. There are isolated expressions which have a wonderful depth and power; but we are not justified in assuming that they are the keynotes of the whole, or had any greater significance to his mind than remarks which to us appear trivial; they were, perhaps, truer than he knew. With a view to the illustration of the Timaeus I propose to divide this Introduction into sections, of which the first will contain an outline of the dialogue: (2) I shall consider the aspects of nature which presented themselves to Plato and his age: (3) the theology and physics of the Timaeus, including the soul of the world, the conception of time and space, and the composition of the elements: (4) in the fourth section I shall consider the Platonic astronomy, and the position of the earth. There will remain, (5) the psychology, (6) the physiology of Plato, and (7) his analysis of the senses to be briefly commented upon; (8) lastly, we may examine in what points Plato approaches or anticipates the discoveries of modern science.

§ I.

Socrates begins the Timaeus with a summary of the Republic. He touches on the composition of the State, and the double nature of the guardians, on the community of property and of women and children. But he makes no mention of the second education, or of the government of philosophers.

And now he desires that the ideal State should be realized in life and action; he would like to see how she behaved in some great struggle. But he is incapable of inventing such a narrative himself, and he is afraid that the poets are equally incapable; for, although he has nothing to say against them, he remarks that they are a tribe of imitators, who can only describe what they have seen. And he fears that the Sophists, who are plentifully supplied with graces of speech, in their erratic way of life having never had a city or house of their own, are as ignorant of statesmanship as they are of philosophy. And therefore to you I turn, Timaeus, citizen of Locris, who are at once a philosopher and a statesman, and to you, Critias, whom all Athenians know to be similarly accomplished, and to Hermocrates, who is also fitted by nature and education to share in our discourse. *Her.* 'We will do our best, and have been already preparing; for on our way home, Critias asked my opinion about a certain ancient tradition, which he was thinking of reciting:—I wish, Critias, that you would repeat the tale to Socrates.' 'I will, if Timaeus approves.' 'I approve.' Listen then, Socrates, to a tale of Solon, which he narrated to Dropidas my great grandfather, who told me. In this tale are recorded ancient famous actions of the Athenian people, and one special one, which I will rehearse in honour of you and of the goddess. This ancient history was told me by an ancient man, for Critias was ninety years old at that time, I being not more than ten. The occasion was the festival of the Apaturia or registration of youth, at which our parents gave prizes for recitation. Some poems of Solon were recited by the boys. They had not at that time gone out of fashion, and the recital of them led some one to say, perhaps in compliment to Critias, that Solon was not only the wisest of men but also the best of poets. The old man brightened at hearing the praises of his friend, and said: Had Solon only had the leisure which was required to complete the great poem which he brought with him from Egypt he would have been as distinguished as Homer and Hesiod. 'And what was the subject of the poem?' said the person who addressed him. The subject was a very noble one, descriptive of the most famous action in which the Athenian people were ever engaged. But the memory of their exploits has passed away owing to the lapse of time and the extinction of the actors. 'Tell us,' said the other, 'the whole story, and where Solon heard the story.' He replied—There is at the head of the Egyptian Delta, where the river Nile divides, a city and district called Sais; the city was the birthplace of King Amasis, and is under the protection of the goddess Neith or Athene. The citizens have a friendly feeling towards the Athenians, believing themselves to be related to them. Hither came Solon, and was received with honour; and here he first learnt, by conversing with the Egyptian priests, how ignorant he and his countrymen were of antiquity. Perceiving this, and with the view of eliciting their stores, he told them the tales of Phoroneus and Niobe, and also of Deucalion and Pyrrha, and he endeavoured to count the generations which had since passed. Thereupon an aged priest said to him, O Solon, Solon, you Hellenes are ever young, and there is no old man who is an Hellene. 'What do you mean?' said he. 'In mind,' replied the priest, 'I mean to say that you are children; there is no opinion or tradition of knowledge among you which is white with age; and I will tell you the reason of this. Like the rest of mankind you have suffered from convulsions of nature, which are chiefly brought about by the two great agencies of fire and water. The latter is symbolized in the Hellenic tale of young Phaethon who drove his father's horses the wrong way, and having burnt up the earth was himself burnt up by a thunderbolt. For there occurs from time to time a derangement of the heavenly bodies, and then the earth is destroyed by fire. At such times, and when fire is the agent, those who dwell by rivers are safer than those who dwell upon high and dry places, who in their turn are safer when the danger is from water. Now the Nile is our saviour from fire, and rising only from below never does any harm to us by water; whereas the inhabitants of other cities and countries are swept by the rivers into the sea. The memorials which your own and other nations have once had of the famous actions of mankind perish in the waters at certain periods; and the rude survivors in the mountains begin again, knowing nothing of the world before the flood. But in Egypt the traditions of our own and other lands are by us registered for ever in our temples. The genealogies which you have recited to us out of your own annals, Solon, are a mere children's story. For in the first place, you remember one deluge only, and there were many of them, and you know nothing of that fairest and noblest race of which you are a seed or remnant. The memory of them was lost, because there was no written voice among you, for in the days before the flood Athens was the greatest and best of cities and did the noblest deeds and had the best constitution of any under the face of heaven.' Solon marvelled, and desired to be informed of the particulars. 'You are welcome to hear them,' said the priest, 'both for your own sake and for that of the city, and above all for the sake of the goddess who is the common foundress of both our cities. Nine thousand years have elapsed since she founded yours, and eight thousand since she founded ours, as our annals record. Many laws exist among us which are the counterpart of yours as they were in the olden time. I will briefly describe them to you, and you shall read the account of them at your leisure in the sacred registers. In the first place, there was a caste of priests among the ancient Athenians, and another of artisans; also castes of shepherds, hunters, and husbandmen, and lastly of warriors, who, like the warriors of Egypt, were separated from the rest, carrying shields and spears; a custom which the goddess first taught you, and then the Asiatics, and we among Asiatics first received from her. Observe again, what care the law took in the pursuit of wisdom, searching out the deep things of the world, and applying them to the use of man. The spot of earth which the goddess chose had the best of climates, and produced the wisest men; in no other was she herself, the philosopher and warrior goddess, so likely to have votaries. And there you dwelt as became the children of the gods, excelling all men in virtue, and many famous actions are recorded of you. The most famous of them all was the overthrow of the island of Atlantis. This was a continent lying over against the Pillars of Heracles, in extent greater than Libya and Asia put together, and was the passage to other islands and to another continent of which the Mediterranean sea was only the harbour; and within the Pillars the empire of Atlantis reached to Egypt and Tyrrhenia. This mighty power was arrayed against Egypt and Hellas and all the countries bordering on the Mediterranean. Then did your city bravely, and won renown over the whole earth. For at the peril of her own existence, and when the other Hellenes had deserted her, she repelled the invader, and of her own accord gave liberty to all the nations within the Pillars. A little while afterwards there was a great earthquake and your warrior race all sank into the earth; and the great island of Atlantis also disappeared in the sea. This is the explanation of the shallows which are found in that part of the Atlantic ocean.'

Such was the tale, Socrates, which Critias heard from Solon; and I noticed when listening to you yesterday, how close the resemblance was between your city and citizens and the ancient Athenian State. But I would not speak at the time, because I wanted to refresh my memory. I had heard the old man when I was a child, and though I could not remember the whole of our yesterday's discourse, I was able to recall every word of this, which is branded into my mind; and I am prepared, Socrates, to rehearse to you the entire narrative. The imaginary State which you were describing may be identified with the reality of Solon, and our antediluvian ancestors may be your citizens. 'That is excellent, Critias, and very appropriate to a Panathenaic festival; the truth of the story is a great advantage.'

'Then now let me explain to you the order of our entertainment; first, Timaeus, who is a natural philosopher, will speak of the origin of the world, going down to the creation of man, and then I shall receive the men whom he has created, and some of whom will have been educated by you, and introduce them to you as the lost Athenian citizens of whom the Egyptian record spoke. As the law of Solon prescribes, we will bring them into court and judge them ourselves.' I see, replied Socrates, that I shall be well entertained; and do you, Timaeus, offer up a prayer and begin:

Tim. All men who have any right feeling at the beginning of any enterprise call upon the gods; and he who is about to speak of the origin of the universe has a special need of their aid. May my words be acceptable to them, and may I speak in the manner which will be most intelligible to you and will best express my meaning.

First, I must distinguish between endless being which has no becoming and is apprehended by reason and reflection, and endless becoming which has no being, and is conceived by opinion with the help of sense. All that becomes and is created is the work of a cause, and that is fair which the artificer makes after an eternal pattern, but that which is fashioned after a created pattern is not fair. Is the world then created or uncreated? that is the first question. Created, I reply, being visible and tangible and having a body, and therefore sensible; and if sensible, then created; and if created, made by a cause, and the cause is the father of all, who had in view an eternal archetype. For to imagine that the archetype was created would be blasphemy, seeing that the world is the noblest of creations, and God is the best of causes. And the world being thus created according to the eternal pattern is the copy of something; and we may assume that words and ideas are akin to the matter of which they speak. The unchanging or intelligible has permanent forms of expression, the created image likely or probable ones; essence being to generation as truth is to belief. And in the variety of opinions which have arisen about God and the nature of the world we must be content to take probability for our guide, considering that I who am the speaker, and you who are the judges are only men, and to probability we may attain but no further.

Soc. Excellent, Timaeus, I like your manner of approaching the subject—proceed.

Tim. Why did the Creator make the world? He was good, and desired that all things should be like himself. Wherefore he set in order the visible world, which he found in disorder. Now he who is the best could only create the fairest, and reflecting that of visible things the intelligent is superior to the unintelligent, he put intelligence in soul and soul in body, and framed the universe to be the best and fairest work in the order of nature, and the world became a living soul through the providence of God.

In the likeness of what animal was the world made? That is the third question. The form of the animal was a whole, and contained all intelligible beings, and the visible animal, made after the pattern of this, included all visible creatures.

Were there many heavens or one only? That is the fourth question. One only, having no other. For if there had been more than one they would have been the parts of a third which would have been the true pattern of the world, and therefore there is, and will ever be, one only begotten and created heaven. Now that which is created is of necessity corporeal and visible and tangible, and because visible lighted by fire, and because tangible therefore solid and made of earth. But two terms must be united by a third, which is a mean between them, and had the earth been a surface only, three would have sufficed, but four terms are required in the construction of a solid. And as the world was to be solid, between the elements of fire and earth God placed two other elements of air and water, and arranged them in a continuous proportion,

fire : air : : water : earth,

and so put together a visible heaven, which he made palpable to sight and touch, having harmony and friendship in the union of the four elements. Each of the elements was taken into the universe whole and entire; for he considered that the animal should be perfect, and that he should be one, leaving no remnants out of which another animal could be created, and that he should be free from age and disease, which might be produced by external violence. And as he was to contain all, he was himself made in the all-containing form of a sphere, round as from a lathe and every way equidistant from the centre, as was natural and suitable to him. He was finished and smooth, having neither eyes, ears, nor hands; for there was nothing without him which he could see or hear, and he had no need to carry food to his mouth,

or breathe the outer air, and he did not require hands, for there was
nothing without him of which he could take hold. All that he did
was within him; and he moved in a circle, which was the most
intellectual of motions, but the other six motions were wanting to him;
wherefore the universe had no feet or legs.

And so the thought of God made a God in the image of a perfect
body, having intercourse with himself and needing no other, but in
every part harmonious and self-contained and truly blessed. The soul
was first made by him—the elder to rule the younger; not in the order
in which our wayward fancy has led us to describe them, but the soul
first and afterwards the body. God took of the unchangeable and
indivisible essence and also of the divisible and corporeal, and out of
the two he made a third nature, which was in a mean between them
and partook of the same and the other, the intractable nature of the
other being compressed into the same. He then began to divide
into portions the mass which he had compounded, in the ratios of
1, 2, 3, 4, 9, 8, 27, and proceeded to fill up the double and triple
intervals

$$\left[\ \overline{1},\ \tfrac{4}{3},\ \overline{\tfrac{3}{2}},\ \overline{2},\ \tfrac{8}{3},\ 3,\ \overline{4},\ \tfrac{16}{3},\ 6,\ \overline{8}\ \right]$$

$$\left[\ \overline{1},\ \tfrac{3}{2},\ \overline{2},\ 3,\ \tfrac{9}{2},\ 6,\ \overline{9},\ \tfrac{27}{2},\ 18,\ \overline{27}\ \right]$$

in which double series of numbers are two kinds of means; the one
exceeds and is exceeded by equal parts of the extremes, e. g. 3, 4, 6;
the other kind of mean is one which is equidistant from the extremes—
2, 4, 6. In the former intervals he introduced ratios of thirds, 3 : 2;
of fourths, 4 : 3; of ninths, 9 : 8; and the interval of a fourth he filled
up with a ninth, leaving a remnant which is in the ratio of 256 : 243.
The entire compound was divided by him lengthways into two parts,
which he joined together at the centre like the figure **X**, and bent them
into an inner and outer circle, cutting one another at a point over
against the point of contact. The outer circle was named by him the
sphere of the same—the inner the sphere of the other or diverse, and the
one revolved horizontally to the right, the other obliquely to the left.
To the sphere of the same which was undivided he gave dominion,
but the sphere of the other or manifold was distributed into seven orbits,
having intervals in ratios of twos and threes, three of either sort, and
he bade them move in opposite directions to one another—three of

them, the Sun, Mercury, Venus, with equal swiftness, and the remaining four—the Moon, Saturn, Mars, Jupiter, with unequal swiftness to the three and to one another, but all in due course.

When the Creator had made the body in the interior of the soul he united them, and the soul interfused everywhere from the centre to the circumference of heaven began a divine life of everlasting motion. The body of heaven is visible, but the soul is invisible, and partakes of reason and harmony, and is the best of creations, being made by the best. And being composed of the same, the other, and the essence, these three, and also, divided and bound in harmonical proportion, and moving in the circle of herself—the soul when touching anything which has essence, whether divided or undivided, is stirred to utter the sameness or diversity of things, and to tell how and when and where individuals are affected or related, whether in the world of change or of essence. When reason is in the neighbourhood of sense, and the circle of the other or manifold is also moving truly, then arise true opinions and beliefs; when reason is in the sphere of thought, and the circle of the same runs smoothly, then intelligence is perfected.

When the Father who begat the world saw the image which he had made of the Eternal Gods moving and living, he rejoiced; and he resolved, as the archetype was eternal, to make the creature eternal as far as this was possible. Wherefore he made an image of eternity which is time, having an uniform motion according to number, parted into months and days and years, and also having greater divisions of past, present, and future. These apply only to generation in time, and have no meaning in relation to the eternal nature, which ever is and never will be, for the unchangeable is never older or younger, and when we say the past is past, the future is future, we are speaking of generation, and not of true being. These are the forms of time which imitate eternity and move in a circle measured by number.

Thus was time made in the image of the eternal nature and together with the heavens, in order that if they were dissolved time might perish with them. And God made the sun and moon and five other wanderers, as they are called, seven in all, and to each of them he gave a body moving in an orbit, being one of the seven into which the circle of the other was divided. The moon moved in the orbit which was nearest to the earth, the sun in that next, the morning star and Mercury in the course opposite to the sun, but with equal swiftness, which is the reason why they overtake and are overtaken by one another. All these bodies became living creatures, and learnt their appointed tasks, and began to move, the nearer more swiftly, the remoter more slowly, according to the oblique movement of the other, which was controlled by the movement of the same. And as the movement of the other was in an opposite direction, that appeared fastest which was slowest, and that which overtook others appeared to be overtaken by them. And God lighted a fire in the second orbit which is called the sun, to give light over the whole heaven, and to teach intelligent beings that knowledge of number which is derived from the revolution of the same. Thus arose day and night, which are the periods of the most intelligent nature; a month was created by the revolution of the moon, a year by that of the sun. Other periods of wonderful length and complexity are not observed by men in general, although there is a cycle or perfect year at the completion of which they all meet and coincide. For the stars in their revolutions imitate the eternal nature.

Thus far the universal animal was made in the divine image, but the other animals were not as yet included in him. And God created them according to the patterns or species of them which existed in the divine image. There are four of them, one of gods, another of birds, a third of fishes, and a fourth of animals. The gods were made in the form of a circle, which is the most perfect figure, and the figure of the universe. They were created chiefly of fire, that they might be bright, and were made to know and follow the best, and to be the glory of the heavens. Two kinds of motion were assigned to them—first, the revolution on the same and around the same, in peaceful unchanging thought of the same; and to this was added a forward motion which was under the control of the same. And for this reason the fixed stars were created, being divine and eternal animals, revolving on the same spot, and the wandering stars, which also revolve, were created after their likeness. The earth, which is our nurse, compacted (or circling) round the pole which passes through the universe, he made to be the guardian and artificer of night and day, first and eldest of gods that are in the interior heaven. Vain would be the labour of telling about all the figures of them, moving as in dance, and their conjunctions and oppositions, and when and where and behind what other stars they appear or disappear and give signs of the future terrible to man—to tell of all this without looking up at the heavens would be labour in vain.

The knowledge of the other gods is beyond us, and we can only accept the traditions of the ancients, who were the children of the gods, as they said, and they must surely have known their own ancestors. Although they give no proof they seem to be speaking of matters familiar to them, and we must believe them as the law requires. They tell us that Oceanus and Tethys were the children of earth and heaven; Phorcys, Cronos, and Rhea are in the next generation, and are followed by Zeus and Herè, whose brothers and children are known to everybody.

When all of them, both those who show themselves in the sky, and those who retire from view, had come into being, the Creator addressed them thus—'Gods, and sons of gods, my works, if I will, are indissoluble. That which is bound may be loosed, but only an evil being would loose that which is harmonious and happy. And although you are not immortal you shall not die, for I will hold you together. Hear me, then:—Three tribes have still to be created, and if created by me they might become like gods. Do ye therefore make them, as I have made you; I will implant in them the seed of immortality, and you shall weave together the mortal and immortal, and provide food for them, and receive them again in death.' Thus he spake, and poured the remains of the elements which he had been mingling into the cup in which he had made the soul of the universe. They were no longer pure as before, but diluted; and when he had completed the mixture he distributed souls equal in number to the stars; but, first, placing them as in a chariot, he showed them the nature of the universe, and told them of their future birth and equal human lot. They were to be sown in the vessels of their appointed times, that hereafter they might bring forth man the most religious of the animals, having two forms, a superior and inferior. The souls were implanted in bodies, and when objects approached or receded from them, there would arise in them, he said, sensation of some kind; secondly, love, which is a mixture of pleasure and pain; thirdly, fear and anger, and the opposite affections: and if they conquered these they would live righteously, but if they were conquered by them, unrighteously. He who lived well would return to the habitation of his star, and would there have a blessed existence; but, if he lived ill, he

would pass into the nature of a woman, and if he did not then alter
his ways, into the likeness of some animal, until he returned to the
courses of the like and the same, and the reason which was in him
reasserted her sway over the elements of fire, air, earth, water, which
had engrossed her, and he regained his first and better nature. Having
given this law to his creatures that he might be guiltless of their future
evil, he sowed them, some in the earth, some in the moon, and some
in the other vessels of time; and he ordered the younger gods to
frame human bodies for them and to make the necessary additions to
them, and to avert from them all but self-inflicted evil.

Meanwhile he remained in his own nature, and his children fulfilled his commands. Receiving from him the immortal principle, they
borrowed portions of earth, air, fire, water, hereafter to be returned,
which they fastened together, not with the adamantine bonds which
bound themselves, but by little invisible pegs, making the body one,
subject to influx and efflux, and containing the courses of the soul.
These swelling and surging as in a river moved irregularly in all the
six possible ways, forwards, backwards, right, left, up and down. But
violent as were the internal and alimentary fluids, the tide became still
more violent when the body came into contact with the flaming fire,
or the solid earth, or the gliding waters; the motions produced by
these impulses pass through the body to the soul and are called
sensations. They accompany the ever-flowing current, and shake the
courses of the soul, binding fast the principle of the same and confounding and entangling the harmonical intervals and the mean terms
which connect them—these are greatly affected by them, though they
cannot be wholly dissolved except by the creator. You may imagine a
motion of the body in which the head is knocking against the ground,
and the legs striking out in the air, and the top is bottom and the left
right. This is what happens when the motions of the soul come into
contact with any external thing; they say the same or the other in a
manner which is the very opposite of the truth, and they become false
and foolish, and have no guiding principle in them. And when external
impressions enter into them, though they are really conquered, they
seem to conquer.

By reason of these affections the soul is at first without sense, but
as time goes on the stream of nutriment abates, and the courses of
the soul have a regular motion which apprehends the same and the

other and gives the use of reason. The soul of him who has education is whole and perfect and escapes the worst disease, but, if education be neglected, he walks lamely through life and returns good for nothing to the world below. This, however, is an after-stage—at present, we are only concerned with the creation of the body and soul.

The two divine courses were encased by the gods in a sphere which is called the head, and is the god and lord of us. And to this they gave the body to be a vehicle, and the members to be instruments, having the power of flexion and extension. This was the origin of legs and arms. In the next place, the gods gave a forward motion to the human body, because the front part of man was the more honourable and had authority. In this front part they inserted organs to minister in all things to the providence of the soul. They first contrived the eyes, into which they conveyed the gentle light of everyday life, making the fire which is within us to flow pure through the pupil of the eye and meet the light of day. When the light of the eye is surrounded by the light of day then like falls upon like, and there is a union of them formed in any direction in which the visual ray strikes upon the light coming from an object. And as like is affected by like, whatever touches or is touched by this stream of vision is diffused over the whole body and finds a way into the soul. But when the visual ray goes forth into the darkness, then like falls upon unlike—the eye no longer sees, and we go to sleep. The fire, or light which is kept in, equalizes the inward motions, and there is rest accompanied by few dreams; only when the greater motions remain they engender in us corresponding visions of the night. And now we shall be able to understand the nature of reflections in mirrors. The fires from within and from without meet about the smooth and bright surface of the mirror; and when they meet in a manner contrary to the usual mode of meeting, the objects seen in them are inverted in various ways, according to the form and position of the mirrors.

These are the second causes which God used as his ministers in fashioning the world. They are thought by many to be the prime causes, but this is not true; for they are destitute of mind and reason, and the lover of mind will not allow that there are any prime causes other than the rational and invisible ones—these he investigates first, and afterwards those which are visible and are moved by others, and work by chance and without order. Of the second or concurrent causes of sight I have already spoken, and I will now speak of the higher purpose of God in giving us eyes. Sight is the source of the greatest benefits to us; for if our eyes had never seen the sun, stars, and heavens, the very words which we are using would not have been uttered. The sight of them and their revolutions has given us the knowledge of number and time, and the power of enquiry, and we have derived philosophy from them, which is the great blessing of human life; not to speak of the lesser benefits which even the vulgar can appreciate. God gave us the faculty of sight that we might behold the order of the heavens and create a corresponding order in our own erring minds. To the like end the gifts of speech and hearing were bestowed upon us; not for the sake of irrational pleasure, but in order that we might harmonize the courses of the soul by sympathy with the harmony of sound, and reconcile man to himself, and cure him of his irregular and graceless ways.

Thus far we have spoken of the works of mind; and there are other works done from necessity, which we must now place beside them; for the creation is made up of both, mind persuading necessity as far as possible to work out good. Before the heavens there existed the elements of fire, air, water, earth, which we may suppose men to know, though no one has explained their nature, and we erroneously maintain them to be the letters of the whole, although they cannot reasonably be compared to the syllables or first compounds. I am not now speaking of the first principles of things, because I cannot discover them by our present mode of enquiry. And I will begin anew, seeking by the grace of God to attain probability, above all at the beginning of my discourse.

In our former discussion I made two kinds of matter—the unchanging or invisible, and the visible or changing. These were sufficient for my purpose at the time; but now a third kind of being is required, which I shall call the receptacle or nurse of generation. There is a difficulty in arriving at an exact notion of this third kind, because the four elements themselves are of inexact natures and easily pass into one another, and are too transient to be detained by any one name; wherefore we are compelled to speak, not of water or fire, but of natures such as water or fire. They may be compared to golden images which are always changing their forms. Somebody asks what they are?—the safest answer is that they are gold. In like manner there is a universal nature from which all things are made, and which is like none of them; but they enter into and pass out of her, and are made after patterns of the true in a wonderful and inexplicable manner. The containing principle may be likened to a mother, the source or spring to a father, the intermediate nature to a child; and we may also remark that the matter which receives every variety of form must originally be formless, like the inodorous liquids which are prepared to receive scents, or the smooth and soft materials on which figures are impressed. In the same way the original or material substance is neither earth nor fire nor air nor water, but is an invisible and formless being which receives all things, and in an incomprehensible manner attains to a portion of the intelligible. But we may say, speaking generally, that fire is the element which burns, water that which is moist, and the like.

Let me ask a question in which a great principle is involved: Is there an essence of fire and the other elements, or are there only fires visible to sense, and is the rest a mere name? I answer in a word: If mind is one thing and true opinion another, then there are self-existent essences; but if mind is the same as opinion, then the visible and corporeal is the reality. But they are not the same, and they have a different origin and nature. The one comes to us by instruction, the other by persuasion; the one is rational, the other is irrational; the one is moveable by persuasion, the other immoveable; the one is possessed by every man, the other by the gods and by very few men. And we must acknowledge that as there are two kinds of knowledge, so there are two kinds of being corresponding to them; the one invisible and uncreated, which is seen by intelligence only; the other created, which is apprehended by opinion and sense, and is always becoming in place and vanishing out of place. There is also a third nature—that of space, which is indestructible, and is perceived by a kind of spurious reason without the help of sense. This is presented to us in a dreamy manner, and yet has a kind of necessity, for we say that all things must be in some place. But these, although they are the waking realities of nature, are seen by us in a dream only, and therefore we are unable to describe them. For they are the images of other things and exist only in others, and true reason assures us that while two things are different they cannot inhere in one another, so as to be one and two at the same time.

To sum up, being and generation and space, these three, existed before the heavens, and the nurse or vessel of generation, moistened by water and inflamed by fire, took the forms of air and earth, and all the various shapes which are taken by them. When the vessel was shaken, the elements were divided, like grain which is winnowed by fans, the close and heavy particles settling in one place, the light and airy ones in another. At first all things were without reason or measure, but when the world began to get into order, the four elements, which in their original state had only certain faint traces of themselves, came together and were fashioned by form and number. In this, as in every other part of creation, I suppose God to have made things, as far as was possible, fair and good, out of other things which were not fair and good.

And now I will explain to you the generation of the world by a method with which your education will have made you familiar. Fire, air, earth, and water are bodies and therefore solids, and solids are made up of planes, and the plane rectilinear figure is made up of rectangular triangles. They are originally of two kinds, one kind having the opposite sides equal, the other unequal. These we may fairly assume to be the original elements of fire and the other bodies; what principles are prior to these God only knows, and he of men whom God loves. Next, we must determine what are the four most beautiful figures which are unlike one another and capable of resolution into one another. Of the two kinds of triangles the equal-sided has one form only, the unequal-sided has an infinite variety of forms; and there is none more beautiful than that which forms the half of an equilateral triangle. Let us then choose two triangles; one, the triangle which has equal sides, the other having a longer side of which the square is three times as great as the square of the lesser side; and affirm that, out of these, fire and the other elements have been constructed.

I was wrong in imagining that all the four elements were generated from one another. For they are really generated, three of them from the triangle which has the sides unequal, the fourth from the triangle which has equal sides; and the three can be resolved into one another, but not the fourth. So much for their passage into one another: I must now speak of their combinations. Beginning with the triangle of which the hypothenuse is twice the lesser side, out of this the three first regular solids are formed—first, the equilateral pyramid or tetrahedron; secondly, the octahedron; thirdly, the icosahedron; and from the isosceles triangle is formed the cube; and there is a fifth figure which is made out of twelve pentagons, the dodecahedron—this God also employed in the construction of the universe.

Let us now assign the geometrical forms to their respective elements. The cube is the most stable of them because resting on a quadrangular plane surface, and the equal-sided triangle is more stable than the unequal. To the earth then, which is the most stable of bodies and the most easily modelled of them, may be assigned the form of a cube; to fire the form of a pyramid, and the remaining forms to the other elements; to air the octahedron, and to water the icosahedron, according to their degrees of lightness or heaviness or power or want of power of penetration. The single particles of any of the elements are not seen by reason of their smallness; they only become visible when collected. The ratios of their motions, numbers, and other properties, are ordered by the gods, who harmonized them as far as necessity allowed them.

The probable result of all this is as follows:—Earth, when dissolved by the more penetrating element of fire, whether acting immediately or through the medium of air and water, is dispersed but not changed. Water, when divided by fire or air, becomes one part fire, and two parts air. The volume of air divided becomes a double volume of fire. On the other hand, when condensed, two volumes of fire make a volume of air; and two and a half parts of air make water. Any element which is fastened upon by fire is cut by the sharpness of the triangles, and at length, coalescing with the fire, is at rest; for similars are not affected by similars, but inferiors are conquered by their superiors, and only cease from their tendency to extinction when they combine with them. When two kinds of bodies quarrel with one another, then the tendency to decomposition continues until the smaller either escape to their kindred element or become one with their conquerors. And this tendency in bodies to condense or escape is the source of motion. For where there is motion there must be a mover, and where there is a mover there must be something to move. These cannot be in equipoise, and therefore motion is the want of equipoise. But then why, when things are divided after their kinds, do they not cease from motion? The answer is, that the circular motion of all things compresses them, and as 'nature abhors a vacuum,' the finer and more subtle elements of fire and air are thrust into the larger interstices of the heavier, and all the elements are on their way up and down everywhere into their own places. Hence there is a principle of inequality, and therefore of motion, pervading all nature.

In the next place, we may observe that there are different kinds of fire—(1) flame, (2) light that burns not, (3) the red heat of the embers of fire. And there are varieties of air, as for example, the pure aether, the opaque mist, and other nameless forms which are caused by the inequalities of the triangles. Water, again, is of two kinds, liquid and fusile. The liquid is composed of small and unequal particles, the fusile is composed of larger and more equal particles and is more solid, but nevertheless melts at the approach of fire, and then is poured upon the earth. When the substance cools, the fire passes into the air, which is displaced, and forces together the liquid mass into the place quitted by the fire. This process is called cooling and congealment. Of the fusile kinds the fairest and heaviest is gold; this is hardened by filtration through rock, and is of a bright yellow colour. The hard and black matrix of gold is called adamant. There is another kind called brass (?), which is harder and yet lighter because the interstices are larger than gold. This is mingled with a fine and small portion of earth which comes out in the form of rust. These are a few of the conjectures which philosophy forms, when, leaving the eternal nature, she turns for innocent recreation to consider the truths of generation only.

To proceed: the water which is mingled with fire is called liquid because it rolls upon the earth, and soft, because its bases give way. This becomes more equable when separated from fire and air, and is compressed into hail or ice, or the looser forms of hoar frost or snow. There are other waters which are called juices and are distilled through plants, first, wine, which warms the soul as well as the body; secondly, the oily nature which glistens; thirdly, honey, which diffuses sweetness and spreads to the passages of the mouth; fourthly, there is opium (?), which is frothy and has a burning quality and dissolves flesh. Of the kinds of earth, that which is filtered through water passes into stone; the water which is expelled rises into the air—this in turn presses upon the mass of earth, and the earth, compressed into an indissoluble union with the remaining water, becomes rock. The rock which is made up of equal particles is fair and transparent, but the reverse when of unequal. Earth is converted into pottery when the moisture is suddenly drawn away; or if the moisture remains, the earth which has been fused by fire, when cooled, turns into a stone of a black colour. When the earth is finer and of a briny nature then a half-solid body is formed, soluble in water,—either nitre or salt. The strong compounds of earth and water are not soluble by water, but only by fire; the weaker either by fire or air. Earth, when not thus consolidated, is dissolved by water; when consolidated, by fire only. The cohesion of water, when strong, is dissolved by fire only; when weak, either by air or fire, the former entering the interstices, the latter penetrating even to the triangles. Air when strongly condensed is indissoluble by any power which does not penetrate to the triangles, and even when not strongly condensed is only resolved by fire. Dense substances which are compounded of earth and water are unaffected by water while the water occupies the interstices, but begin to liquefy when fire enters into the interstices of the water. They are of two kinds; some of them having less water, and some less earth.

I have now to consider the origin of flesh and of the mortal soul; and this is connected with the perceptions of sense. In order that I may proceed regularly I will begin by speaking of the affections which equally concern body and soul.

What makes fire burn? The fineness of the sides, the sharpness of the angles, the smallness of the particles, the quickness of the motion. Moreover, the pyramid is the original figure of fire, and is more cutting than any other figure. The feeling of cold is produced by the larger particles in the body trying to eject the smaller ones which they only compress, and therefore equalize and coagulate. Shivering is caused by the conflict of things naturally at war which are brought together. That is hard to which the flesh yields, and soft which yields to the flesh. The yielding matter is that which has the slenderest base, whereas that which has a rectangular base is the most compact and repellent. Light and heavy are wrongly explained with reference to a lower and higher in place. ·For in the universe, which is a sphere, there is no opposition of above or below, and that which is to us above would be below to a man standing at the antipodes. The effort to detach any element from its like is the real cause of heaviness or of lightness. If you draw the earth into the dissimilar air, the particles of earth cling to their native element, and you more easily detach a small portion than a large. There would be the same difficulty in drawing down any of the upper elements to the lower. The smooth and the rough are severally explained by the union of evenness with compactness, and of hardness with inequality.

The cause of pleasure and pain is the most important enquiry which remains. According to our general doctrine of sensation the body which is easily moved and communicates motion, at last reaches the mind, but a body which is not easily moved and does not diffuse motion has no effect upon the patient. The ordinary affection is not accompanied by pleasure or pain, but a violent impression, if contrary to nature, causes pain, or if congenial to nature, pleasure. The impressions of sight are an example of the ordinary affections which are unattended either with pleasure or pain, because they are not violent or sudden. The replenishments of the body, on the other hand, cause pleasure, and cuttings and burnings have the opposite effect.

These are the general affections of the body: I will now proceed to the particular ones. The affections of the tongue appear to be caused, like most others, by composition and division, but they have more of roughness or smoothness than is found in others. Earthy particles, entering into the small veins about the tongue, when rough are astringent, or if not so rough, like potash and soda, they are only harsh and abstergent, and are termed bitter. Purgatives of a weaker sort are called salt and are rather agreeable. Light and inflammatory bodies, which are soluble in the mouth and get up into the head, are termed pungent. But when these are refined by putrefaction and enter the narrow veins, and meet the earthy or airy elements, two kinds of globules are formed—one of earthy and impure liquid, which boils and ferments, the other of pure and transparent water, which are called bubbles; of all these affections the cause is termed acid. When, on the other hand, the composition of the deliquescent particles is congenial to the tongue, and disposes the parts according to their nature, this remedial power in them is called sweet.

Smells are not divided into kinds; all of them are transitional, and arise out of the decomposition of one element into another, for the simple air or water is without smell. They are mists or smoke, thinner than water and thicker than air: and hence in drawing in the breath, when there is an obstruction, the air passes, but there is no smell. They have no names, but are distinguished as pleasant and unpleasant, and their influence extends over the whole region from the head to the navel.

Hearing is the effect of a stroke which is transmitted through the ears by means of the air, brains, and blood to the soul, beginning at the head and extending to the liver. The sound which moves swiftly is acute; that which moves slowly is grave; that which is uniform is smooth, and the opposite is harsh. Loudness depends on the quantity of the sound. Of the harmony of sounds I will hereafter speak.

Colours are a flame which emanates from all bodies, having particles corresponding to the sense of sight. Some of the particles are less and some greater, and some are equal to the parts of the sight. The equal particles are transparent, the larger contract, and the lesser dilate the sight; white is produced by the dilatation, black by the contraction, of the particles of sight. There is also a swifter motion of another sort of fire which forces a way into the passages of the eyes, and elicits from them a union of fire and water which we call tears. The fires from without and within meet and are extinguished in the tear-drop, and all sorts of colours are generated in the mixture. This affection is termed by us dazzling, and is produced by a flash. There is yet another sort of fire which mingles with the moisture of the eye without flashing, and produces a colour like blood—to this we give the name of red. Again, the bright element mingling with the red and white produces a colour which we call auburn. The law of proportion, however, in which the several colours are formed, cannot be determined scientifically or even probably. Red, when mingled with black and white, gives a purple hue, which becomes umber when the colours are burnt and a greater portion of black is added. Flame-colour is a mixture of auburn and dun; dun of white and black; pale yellow of white and auburn. White and light meeting, and falling upon a full black, become dark blue; dark blue mingling with white becomes a light blue; the union of flame-colour and black makes leek-green. There is no difficulty in seeing how other colours are probably composed. But he who should attempt to test the truth of this in fact, would forget the difference of the human and divine nature. God only is able to compound and resolve substances; such experiments are impossible to man.

These are the elements of necessity which the Creator received in the world of generation when he made the all-sufficient and perfect creature, using the secondary causes as his ministers, but himself fashioning the good in all things. For there are two sorts of causes, the one divine, the other necessary; and we should seek to discover the divine first, and afterwards the necessary, because without them the higher cannot be attained by us.

Having now before us the causes out of which the rest of our discourse is to be framed, let us go back to the point at which we began, and add a fair ending to our tale. As I said at first, all things were originally a chaos in which there was no order, and nothing had any kind or name. The elements of this chaos were arranged by the Creator, and out of them he made the world. Of the divine he himself was the author, but committed to his offspring the creation of the mortal. They in imitation of him received from him the immortal soul, and made the body to be a vehicle of the soul, and constructed within another soul which was mortal, and subject to terrible affections— pleasure, the inciter of evil; pain, which deters from good; rashness and fear, foolish counsellors; anger implacable; hope deceived by sense, and by all-daring love. These they mingled according to necessary laws and framed man. But, fearing to pollute the divine element, they gave the mortal soul a separate habitation in the breast, parted off from the head by a narrow isthmus. And as in a house the women are divided from the men, the cavity of the thorax or breast-plate was further divided into two parts, a higher and a lower. The higher of the two, which is the seat of courage and anger, is in the neighbourhood of the head and assists the reason in restraining the desires. For the heart is the house of guard in which all the veins meet, and through them reason sends her commands to the extremity of her kingdom. When the passions are in revolt, or danger approaches from without, then the heart beats and swells; and the creating powers, knowing this, implanted in the body the soft and bloodless substance of the lung, having a porous and springy nature like a sponge, and receiving and cooling the heated streams, and they cut the passages of the trachea which lead to the lung.

The desire of the soul for meat and drink was placed by them between the midriff and the navel—there to dwell imprisoned like a wild beast, out of the way of the council chamber, and not allowed to interfere with the good of the whole. For the Creator knew that the belly would not listen to reason, and was under the power of idols and fancies. Wherefore God framed the liver to connect with the lower nature, contriving that it should be compact, and bright, and sweet, and also bitter, and smooth, in order that the power of thought which originates in the mind might there be reflected, terrifying the belly with the elements of bitterness and gall, and the suffusion of bilious colours when the liver is contracted, and causing pain and misery by twisting and dislocating the lobe and other vessels. And the converse happens when some gentle inspiration coming from intelligence mirrors the opposite fancies, giving rest and sweetness and freedom, and at night, moderation and peace accompanied with prophetic insight, when reason and sense are asleep. For the authors of our being, in obedience to their Father's will and in order to make men as good as they could, gave them prophecy, which never acts when men are awake or in health; but when they are under the influence of some disorder or enthusiasm then gives intimations which are interpreted by others who are called prophets, but should rather be called interpreters of prophecy; these after death become unintelligible. The spleen which is situated in the neighbourhood, on the left-hand side, keeps the liver bright and clear like a mirror, and the evacuations of the liver are received into the hollows of the spleen, which for a time waxes with impurity, and after the body is purged returns to a natural size.

The truth concerning the soul can only be established by the word of God. Still, we may venture to assert what is probable both concerning soul and body.

The creative powers were aware of our tendency to excess. And so when they made the belly to be a receptacle for food, in order that men might not perish by disease, they formed the convolutions of the intestines, in this way retarding the passage of food through the body, lest mankind should be absorbed in eating and drinking, and the whole race become impervious to divine philosophy.

The creation of bones and flesh was on this wise. The root of mortal life is the marrow which binds together body and soul, and the marrow is made out of the triangles of the first formation specially adapted to produce all the four elements. These God took and mingled them in due proportion, making as many kinds of marrow as there were hereafter to be kinds of souls. The receptacle of the divine seed he made round, and called that portion of the marrow brain, intending that the vessel containing this substance should be the head. The remaining part he divided into long and round figures, and from these as from anchors, casting the bonds of the whole soul, he proceeded to make the rest of the body, first forming for them a covering of bones. The bone was formed by sifting pure smooth earth and wetting it with marrow. It was then thrust alternately into fire and water, and thus rendered insoluble by either. Of bone he made a globe which he placed around the brain, leaving a narrow opening, and around the marrow of the neck and back he formed the vertebrae like hinges which extended from the head through the whole of the trunk. And as the bone was brittle and liable to mortify and destroy the marrow by too great rigidity and susceptibility to heat and cold, he contrived sinews and flesh—the first to give united motion and flexibility, the second to guard against heat and cold, and to be a protection against falls, containing a moisture which in summer exudes in the form of dew, and in winter is a defence against cold. Having this in view, the Creator mingled earth with fire and water and put them together, making a ferment of acid and salt which he mingled with them, forming a pulpy flesh. But the sinews he made of an unfermented mixture of bone and flesh, giving them a mean nature between the two, and a yellow colour. Hence they were more glutinous than flesh, but softer than bone. The bones which have most of the living soul within them he covered with the thinnest film of flesh, those which have least he lodged deeper. At the joints he diminished the flesh in order not to impede the flexure of the limbs, and also to avoid their clogging the perceptions of the mind. About the thighs and arms, which have no sense because the soul of the marrow does not reach them, and about the inner bones for the same reason, he laid the flesh thicker. For where the flesh is thicker there is less feeling, except in certain parts which the Creator has made solely of flesh, as for example, the tongue. Had the combination of solid bone and thick flesh been consistent with acute perceptions, the Creator would have given man a sinewy and fleshy head, and then he would have lived twice as long. But our creators were of opinion that a shorter life which was better was preferable to a longer which was worse, and therefore they covered the head with thin bone, and placed the sinews at the extremities of the neck, and fastened the cheeks to them below the face. And they framed the mouth, having teeth and tongue and lips, with a view to the necessary and the good, for food is a necessity, and the river of speech is the best of rivers. Still, the head could not be left a bare globe of bones on account of the extremes of heat and cold, nor be allowed to become dull and senseless by the overgrowth of flesh. Wherefore it was covered by a peel or skin which met and grew by the help of the cerebral humour. The sutures of the head were watered and closed up by the moisture, which sprang up within, and the diversity of them was caused by the struggle of the food against the courses of the soul. The skin was pierced by fire, and out of the punctures came forth a moisture, part liquid and part of a skinny nature, which was hardened by the pressure of the external cold and became hair. And God gave the head of man hair to be a shade in summer and shelter in winter, but not to interfere with his perceptions. The union of sinews, skin, and bone in the structure of the finger, and the nails which are found in many creatures, were formed by the creators with a view to the future when, as they knew, women and other animals would be framed out of us.

The gods also mingled natures akin to that of man with other forms and perceptions. These are the trees and plants, which were originally wild and have been adapted by cultivation to our use. They partake of that third kind of life which is seated between the midriff and the navel, and is altogether passive and incapable of motion and reflection.

When the creators had furnished all these natures for our sustenance, they cut channels through our bodies to water them like a garden. Two were cut down the back, along the back bone, where the skin and flesh meet, one on the right and the other on the left, and between them flowed the marrow of generation. In the next place, they divided the veins about the head and interlaced them about each other in order that they might form an additional link between the head and the body, and that the sensations from both sides might be diffused throughout the body. In the third place, they contrived the passage of liquids, which may be explained in this way:—Finer bodies contain coarser, but not the coarser the finer, and the belly is capable of containing food, but not fire and air. God therefore formed a network of fire and air to irrigate the veins, having two passages or openings, one of which he made with two heads, and stretched cords reaching from both the openings to the extremity of the network. The inner parts of the net were made by him of fire, the openings and the hollow of air. One of the openings he made to pass into the mouth; this he divided into two, one part descending by the air-pipes into the lungs, the other by the side of the air-pipes into the belly. The first opening he divided into two parts, and both of these he made to communicate with the channels of the nose, that the mouth when closed might still be fed with air. The other hollow of the network he caused to flow around the hollows of the body, making the entire receptacle which was composed of air to flow into and out of the passages of the network, the tissue of the lung finding a way into and out of the pores of the body, and the rays of fire following them. These, as we affirm, are the phenomena of respiration. And all this process took place in order that the body might be watered and cooled and nourished, and the meat and drink digested and liquefied and carried into the veins.

The causes of respiration have now to be considered. The exhalation of the breath displaces the external air, and at the same time leaves a vacuum into which through the pores the air which is displaced enters as with the regularity of a wheel. The explanation of this may be supposed to be as follows: Every animal has within him a fountain of fire, which has been compared by us to a net of fire extended through the centre of the body, and having an outer envelopment of air. The fire seeks the place of fire, and in doing so finds a way in through the body or out at the nostrils, accordingly as the body is either hot or cold. When the body is hotter the particles of fire find their way out, when cooler the hot element finds a way in, and thus by action and reaction, inspiration and expiration are produced.

The phenomena of medical cupping-glasses and of swallowing, and the hurling of bodies, are to be explained on a similar principle ; as also sounds, which are sometimes discordant on account of the inequality of them, and again, harmonious by reason of equality. The slower sounds reaching the swifter, when they begin to pause, by degrees assimilate with them: whence arises a pleasure which even the unwise feel, and which to the wise becomes a higher sort of delight, being an imitation of divine harmony in mortal motions. Streams flow, lightnings play, amber and the magnet attract, not by reason of attraction, but because 'nature abhors a vacuum.'

I will now return to the phenomena of respiration. The fire minces the food and in the process of respiration fills the veins out of the belly by drawing from thence the divided portions of food, and thus the streams of food are diffused through the body. The fruits or grass which are our daily food acquire all sorts of colours when newly cut, but the colour of red or fire predominates, and hence the liquid which we call blood is red, being the nurturing principle of the body whence all parts are watered and the empty places filled.

The process of repletion and depletion is produced by the attraction of like to like, after the manner of the universal motion. The elements are always entering into the body which is akin to them, and causing us to consume away: the particles of blood, too, to which the body is a sort of heaven, are attracted towards their kindred nature. When more is taken away than flows in, then we decay; and when less, we grow and increase.

The young of every animal have the triangles closely locked together, and yet the entire frame is soft and delicate, as if made of marrow and nurtured on milk. These triangles are sharper than those which enter the body from without in the shape of food, and therefore they cut them up. But as life advances, the triangles which enclose the marrow wear out and are no longer able to assimilate their food; and at length getting unfixed they unloose the bonds of the soul, which is released and flies away. And so man without pain, and even with pleasure, passes away in the course of nature.

Hence we may learn the causes of diseases. They are occasioned by the disarrangement of the elements out of which the body is framed; and they arise in a variety of ways. The dry may become moist, the light heavy, the hot cold, and any addition or subtraction or undue proportion may produce an estrangement and perturbation of nature. This is the origin of many of them, but the worst of all owe their severity to the following causes: there is a natural order in the human frame according to which the flesh and sinews are made of blood; the sinews out of the fibres which are akin to them, and the blood out of the congealed substance which is formed out of the fibres. The glutinous matter which comes away from the sinews and the flesh, not only binds the flesh to the bones, but nourishes the marrow, being composed of the smoothest and oiliest of the triangles which alone find their way through the solid bone; and when these processes take place in regular order the body is in health. But when the wasting flesh returns into the veins there is discoloured blood as well as air in the veins, having acid and salt qualities from which are generated all sorts of phlegm and bile. All things go the wrong way and cease to give nourishment to the body, no longer preserving the natural order of the courses, but at war with themselves and destructive of the constitution of the body. The oldest part of the flesh which refuses to

assimilate blackens from long burning, and from being corroded grows
bitter, and as the bitter element refines away, becomes acid; and when
tinged with blood the bitter substance has a red colour, or when
mixed with black the hue of grass; or again, has an auburn colour,
when the new flesh is melted by the internal flame. To all which
phenomena some physician or philosopher who was able to see the
one in many has given the name of bile. Now there are various kinds
of bile which have names answering to their colours. Lymph is of two
kinds: first, the whey of blood, which is gentle; secondly, that which
is produced by dark and bitter bile mingled under the influence of heat
with any salt substance; thirdly, there is the white phlegm, which is
a wasting of young and tender flesh when accompanied by air encased
in moisture, which emits little invisible bubbles having the appearance
of foam. The water of tears and perspiration and other similar bodies
is also the watery part of fresh phlegm. All these humours arise when
the blood is replenished by irregular ways and not by food or drink,
and they are the sources of disease. The danger, however, is not so
great when the foundation remains, for then there is a possibility of
recovery. But when the bond which unites the flesh and bones is
diseased, and the blood which is made out of the fibres and sinews
separates from them, and from being oily and smooth and glutinous
becomes rough and salt and dry, then the substance which is detached
crumbles away under the flesh and sinews, and the fleshy part leaves the
sinews bare and full of brine, and the flesh gets back again into the
circulation of the blood. There are other and worse diseases which
precede this; as when the bone through the density of the flesh does
not receive sufficient air, and becomes stagnant and gangrened, and
the bone passes into the food, and the food into the flesh, and the flesh
returns again into the blood. Worst of all and most fatal is the disease
of the marrow, by which the whole course of the body is reversed.
There is a third class of diseases which are produced, some by wind
and some by phlegm and some by bile. When the lung, which is the
steward of the air, is obstructed by rheums, and in one part no air, and
in another too much, enters in, then the parts which are unrefreshed by the
air corrode, and other parts are distorted by the excess of air; and in this
manner painful diseases are produced. The most painful are generated
when the wind gets about the sinews, and especially when the pressure
is upon the great sinews of the shoulder—these are termed tetanus.

The cure of them is difficult, and they generally end in fevers. The white phlegm—though dangerous if kept in, by reason of the air bubbles—is not equally dangerous, because capable of relief, and only variegates the body, generating divers kinds of leprosies. When phlegm mingling with black bile only disturbs the courses of the head in sleep, there is not so much danger, but when assailing those who are awake, then the attack is far more dangerous, and is called epilepsy or the sacred disease. An acid and salt phlegm is the source of catarrh, and is called by various names, according to the places into which the phlegm finds a way.

Inflammations originate in bile, which is sometimes relieved and finds an exit in boils and swellings, but when detained, and above all when mingled with pure blood, generates many inflammatory disorders, disturbing the order of the fibres which are scattered about in the blood in order to maintain the balance of rare and dense. The manner in which this is effected may be seen if any one presses the fibres together after death; for the blood flows out, and the fibres, left to themselves, congeal. The fibres are the cause of bile, which is only stale blood, and from being flesh is decomposed, and coming in little by little, warm and moist, is congealed by the fibres and produces internal cold and shuddering. But when it enters with more of a flood it reaches the spinal marrow, and then the cables of the ship are cut and the soul is set free from the body. When on the other hand the body, though wasted, still holds out, then the bile is expelled, like an exile from an insurgent state, causing diarrhœas and dysenteries and similar disorders. The body which is diseased from the effects of fire is in a continual fever; when air is the agent, the fever is quotidian; when water, the fever intermits a day; when earth, which is the most sluggish of agents, the fever intermits three days and is with difficulty shaken off.

Of mental disorders there are two sorts, one madness, the other ignorance, and they may be justly attributed to disease. Excessive pleasures or pains are one of the greatest diseases, and literally take away the power of sense. When the seed about the spinal marrow is too fruitful or productive, the body has too great pleasures and pains; and during a great part of his life a man is more or less mad. He is often thought bad, but this is a mistake; for the truth is that the intemperance of lust is produced by the flux of a single element in the moist and relaxed state of the bones. And this is true of vice in general, which is commonly regarded as disgraceful, whereas all vice is really involuntary and arises from a bad habit of the body and evil education. In like manner the soul is often made vicious by the influence of pain; the briny phlegm and other bitter and bilious humours wander over the body and find no exit, but are compressed within, and blend with the motions of the soul, and are carried to the three places of the soul, creating infinite varieties of trouble and melancholy, of tempers rash and cowardly, and also of forgetfulness and stupidity. When men are in this evil plight of body, and evil forms of government and evil discourses are superadded, and there is no education to save them—all men turn to evil, through these two causes, but of neither of them are they really the authors. For the planters are to blame rather than the plants, the educators and not the educated. Still, we should endeavour to attain virtue and avoid vice; but this is a part of another subject.

Enough of disease—I have now to speak of the means by which the mind and body are to be preserved, a higher theme than the other. The good is the beautiful, and the beautiful is the symmetrical, and there is no greater or fairer symmetry than that of body and soul, as the contrary is the greatest of deformities. A leg or an arm too long or too short is at once ugly and unserviceable, and the same disproportion is discernible in the relation of soul and body. For the soul may 'o'erinform the tenement of clay,' and so produce diseases and convulsions. The violence of controversy, or the earnestness of enquiry, will often generate rheums and fevers which are not understood, or assigned to their true cause by the professors of medicine. And in like manner the body may be too much for the soul, obscuring the rational, and quickening the animal desires. The only security is to preserve the balance of the two, and to this end the mathematician or philosopher must practise gymnastics, and the gymnast must practise music, and allow the movements of the soul to inform the body. And as the whole body should be treated in relation to the whole soul, so are the parts of the body to be treated in relation to each other. For the body is liable to be heated and cooled by the elements which enter in, and again is dried up and moistened by external things, and is therefore injured, if given up to motion when at rest. But on the other hand, the use of exercise, as in the world, so also in the human body, restores harmony and divides the hostile powers from one another. The best exercise is the spontaneous motion of the body, as in gymnastics, because most akin to the motion of the mind; not so good is the motion of which the source is in another, as in sailing or riding; least good when the body is at rest and the motion is in the parts only, which is a species of motion produced by physic. This should only be resorted to by men of sense in extreme cases; lesser diseases are not to be educated by medicine. For every disease is akin to the living being and has an appointed term, just as life has, which depends on the form of the triangles, and cannot be protracted when the triangles are worn out. And he who, instead of accepting his destiny, endeavours to prolong his life by medicine is likely to multiply and magnify his diseases. Regimen and not medicine is the true cure, when a man has time at his disposal.

Enough of the nature of man and of the body, and of rational education, and of self education. The subject is a great one and cannot be adequately treated as an appendage to any other. To sum up all in a word: there are three kinds of souls located within us, and any one of them, if remaining inactive, becomes very weak; if exercised, very strong. Wherefore we should train and exercise the three parts of the soul.

But there is also a divinity within us whom God has lodged in our heads, to raise us, like plants which are not of earthly origin, from earth to our kindred which is in heaven; for the head is the root in which the generation of the soul began, and on which the whole body hangs. He who is intent upon the gratification of his desires, has all his ideas of mortal birth, and is himself in the truest sense mortal. But he who seeks after knowledge and exercises the divine part of himself in godly and immortal thoughts, attains to truth and immortality, as far as is possible to man, and also to happiness, while he is training up within him the divine principle and indwelling power of order. There is only one way in which one person can benefit another; and that is by assigning to him his proper nurture and motion. To the motions of the soul answer the motions of the universe, and by the study of these the individual is restored to his original nature.

Thus we have finished the discussion of the universe, which was to be brought down to the creation of man. Completeness seems to require that something should be briefly said about other animals: first of women, who are probably degenerate or effeminate men. And when they degenerated, the gods implanted in men the desire of union with them, distributing in the two sexes the living being in the following manner:—The passage for liquid they connected with the living principle of the spinal marrow, which the man has a desire to emit into the fruitful womb of the woman; this is like a fertile field in which the seed is quickened and matured, and at last brought to light. When this desire is unsatisfied the man is overmastered by the power of the generative organs, and the woman is subjected to disorders from the obstruction of the passages of the breath, until the two meet and pluck the fruit of the tree.

The race of birds was created out of innocent, light-minded men, who thought to pursue the study of the heavens by sight; these were transformed into birds, and grew feathers instead of hair. The race of animals were men who had no philosophy, and never looked up to heaven or used the courses of the head, but followed only the influences of the heart. Naturally they turned to their kindred earth, and put their forelegs to the ground, and had their heads crushed into strange oblong forms. Some of them have four feet, and some of them more than four feet; the latter, who are the more senseless, drawing closer to their native element; the most senseless of all have no limbs and trail their whole body on the ground. The fourth kind are the inhabitants of the waters; these are made out of the most senseless and ignorant and impure of men, whom God placed in the uttermost parts of the world in return for their utter ignorance, and caused them to respire water instead of the finer elements of air. These are the laws by which animals pass into one another, according to their degrees of knowledge and ignorance.

And so the world received animals, mortal and immortal, and was fulfilled with them, and became a visible God, as they also were visible, made in the image of the Creator, being the one perfect only-begotten heaven.

§ 2.

Nature in the aspect which she presented to a Greek philosopher of the fourth century before Christ is not easily reproduced to modern eyes. The associations of mythology and poetry have to be added, and the unconscious influence of science has to be subtracted, before we can behold the heavens or the earth as they appeared to the Greek.

The philosopher himself was a child and also a man—a child in the range of his attainments, but also a great intelligence having an insight into nature, and often anticipations of the truth. He was full of original thoughts, and yet liable to be imposed upon by the most obvious fallacies. He occasionally confused numbers with ideas, and atoms with numbers; his *a priori* notions were out of all proportion to his experience. He was ready to explain the phenomena of the heavens by the most trivial analogies of earth. The experiments which nature worked for him he sometimes accepted, but he never tried experiments for himself which would either prove or disprove his theories. His knowledge was unequal; while in some branches, such as medicine and astronomy, he had made considerable proficiency, there were others, such as chemistry, of which the very names were unknown to him. He was the natural enemy of mythology, and yet mythological ideas still retained their hold over him. He was endeavouring to form a conception of principles, but these principles or ideas were regarded by him as real powers or entities, to which the world had been subjected. He was always tending to argue from what was near to what was remote, from what was known to what was unknown, from man to the universe, and back again from the universe to man. While he was arranging the world, he was arranging the forms of thought in his own mind; and the light from within and the light from without often helped to cross and confuse one another. He might be compared to a builder engaged in some great design, who was obliged to dig with his hands because he was unprovided with the commonest tools.

The Hesiodic and Orphic cosmogonies were a phase of thought intermediate between mythology and philosophy and had a great influence on the beginnings of physical science. They made men think of the world as a whole; they carried the mind back into the infinity of past time; they suggested the first observation of the effects of fire and water on the earth's surface. To the ancient physics they stood much in the same relation which geology does to modern science. The mind of the Greek was not confined to a period of four or six thousand years; he was able to speculate freely on the effects of infinite ages in the production of physical phenomena. He could imagine cities which had existed time out of mind, laws or forms of art and music which had lasted, 'not in word only but in very truth,' for ten thousand years; he was aware that natural phenomena like the Delta of the Nile might have slowly accumulated in myriads of years. But he seems to have supposed that the course of events was recurring rather than progressive. To this he was probably led by the lateness of Greek history, when compared with the primeval antiquity of Egypt.

The ancient philosophers found in mythology many ideas which, whether originally derived from nature or not, were easily transferred to her—such, for example, as love or hate, corresponding to attraction or repulsion; or the conception of necessity allied both to the regularity and irregularity of nature; or of justice, symbolizing the law of compensation; or of the Fates and Furies, typifying the fixed order or the extraordinary convulsions of nature. Their own interpretations of Homer and the poets were supposed by them to be the original meaning. Musing in themselves, they were relieved at being able to utter the thoughts of their hearts in figures of speech which to them were not figures, and were already consecrated by tradition. Hesiod and the Orphic poets moved in a region of half-personification in which the meaning or principle appeared through the person. In their vaster conceptions of Chaos, Erebus, Aether, Night, and the like, the first rude attempts at generalization are dimly seen.

Under the influence of such ideas, perhaps also deriving from the traditions of their own or of other nations scraps of medicine and astronomy, men came to the observation of nature. The Greek looked upon the blue circle of the heavens and conceived that all things were one; the tumult of sense abated, and the mind found repose in the thought which former generations had been striving to realize. The first expression of this was some element, rarefied by degrees into a pure abstraction, and purged from any tincture of sense. Soon an inner world of ideas began to be created, more absorbing, more overpowering, more abiding than the brightest of visible objects, which to the eye of the philosopher looking inward, seemed to pale before them, retaining only a faint and precarious existence. At the same time, the minds of men parted into the two great divisions of those who saw only a principle of motion, and of those who saw only a principle of rest, in nature and in themselves; there were born Heracliteans or Eleatics, as there have been in later ages, born Aristotelians or Platonists. Like some philosophers in modern times, who are accused of making a theory first and finding their facts afterwards, the advocates of either opinion never thought of applying either to themselves or to their adversaries the criterion of fact. They were mastered by their ideas and not masters of them. Like the Heraclitean fanatics whom Plato has described in the Theaetetus, they were incapable of giving a reason of the faith that was in them, and had all the animosities of a religious sect. Yet, doubtless, there was some first impression derived from external nature, which, as in mythology, so also in philosophy, worked upon the minds of the first thinkers. Though incapable of induction or generalization in the modern sense, they caught an inspiration from the external world. The most general facts or appearances of nature, the circle of the universe, the nutritive power of water, the air which is the breath of life, the destructive force of fire, the seeming regularity of the greater part of nature and the irregularity of a remnant, the solid earth and the impalpable aether, were always present to them.

The great source of error and also the beginning of truth to them was reasoning from analogy; they could see resemblances, but not differences; and they were incapable of distinguishing illustration from argument. Analogy in modern times only points the way, and is immediately verified by experiment. The dreams and visions, which pass through the philosopher's mind, of resemblances between different classes of substances, or between the animal and vegetable world, are put into the refiner's fire, and the dross and other elements which adhere to them are purged away. But the contemporary of Plato and Socrates was incapable of resisting the power of any analogy which occurred to him, and was drawn into any consequences which seemed to follow. He had no methods of difference or of concomitant variations, by the use of which he could distinguish the accidental from the essential. He could not isolate phenomena, and he was helpless against the influence of any word which had an equivocal or double sense.

Yet without this crude use of analogy the ancient physical philosopher would have stood still; he could not have made even 'one guess among many' without comparison. The course of natural phenomena would have passed unheeded before his eyes, like fair sights or musical sounds before the eyes and ears of an animal. Even the fetichism of the savage is the beginning of reasoning; the assumption of the most fanciful of causes indicates a higher mental state than the absence of all enquiry about them. The tendency to argue from the higher to the lower, from man to the world, has led to many errors, but has also had an elevating influence on philosophy. The conception of the world as a whole, a person, an animal, has been the source of hasty generalizations; yet this general grasp of nature led also to a spirit of comprehensiveness in early philosophy, which has not increased, but rather diminished, as the fields of knowledge have become more divided. The modern physicist confines himself to one or perhaps two branches of science. But he comparatively seldom rises above his own department, and often falls under the narrowing influence which any single branch, when pursued to the exclusion of every other, has over the mind. Language, too, exercised a spell over the beginnings of physical philosophy, leading to error and sometimes to truth; for many thoughts were suggested by the double meanings of words, and the accidental distinctions of words often caused the ancients to make corresponding differences in things. 'If they are the same, why have they different names; or if they are different, why have they the same name?'—is an argument not easily answered in the infancy of knowledge. The modern philosopher has always been taught the lesson which he still imperfectly learns, that he must disengage himself from the influence of words. Nor are there wanting in Plato, who was himself too often the victim of them, many admonitions that we should regard not words but things. But upon the whole, the ancients, though not entirely dominated by them, were much more subject to the influence of words than the moderns. They had no clear divisions of colours or substances; even the four elements were undefined; the fields of knowledge were not as yet parted off. They were bringing order out of disorder, having a small grain of experience mingled in a confused heap of *a priori* notions. And yet, probably, their first impressions, the illusions and mirages of their fancy, created a greater intellectual activity and made a nearer approach to the truth than any patient investigation of isolated facts, for which the time had not yet come.

There was one more illusion to which the ancient philosophers were subject, and against which Plato in his later dialogues seems to be struggling—the tendency to mere abstractions; not perceiving that pure abstraction is only negation, they thought that the greater the abstraction the greater the truth. Behind any pair of ideas a new idea which comprehended them began at once to appear. Two are truer than three, one than two. The words 'being,' or 'unity,' or 'essence,' or '.good,' became sacred to them. They did not see that they had a word only, and in one sense the most unmeaning of words. They did not understand that the content of notions is in inverse proportion to their universality—the element which is the most widely diffused is also the thinnest; or, in the language of the common logic, the greater the extension the less the comprehension. But this vacant idea of a whole without parts, of a subject without predicates, a rest without motion, has been also the most fruitful of all ideas. It is the beginning of *a priori* thought, and indeed of thinking at all. Men were led to conceive it, not by a love of hasty generalization, but by a divine instinct, a dialectical enthusiasm, in which the human faculties seemed to yearn for enlargement. We know that 'being' is the verb of existence, the copula, the most general symbol of relation, the first and most meagre of abstractions; but, to some of the ancient philosophers, this little word appeared to attain divine proportions and to comprehend all truth. Being or essence, and similar words, represented to them a supreme or divine being, in which they thought that they found the containing principle of the universe. In a few years the human mind was peopled with abstractions; a new world was called into existence to give law and order to the old. But between them there was still a gulph, and no one could pass from one to the other.

Number and figure were the greatest instruments of thought which were possessed by the Greek philosopher; having the same power over the mind which was exerted by abstract ideas, they were also capable of practical application. Many curious and, to the early thinker, mystical properties of them came to light when they were compared with one another. They admitted of infinite multiplication and construction; in Pythagorean triangles or in proportions of $1 : 2 : 4 : 8$ and $1 : 3 : 9 : 27$, or compounds of them, the laws of the world seemed to be more than half revealed. They were not like being or essence, mere vacant abstractions, but admitted of progress and growth, while at the same time they confirmed a higher sentiment of the mind, that there was order in the universe. There was a real sympathy between the world within and the world without. The numbers and figures which were present to the mind's eye became visible to the eye of sense; the laws of nature were mathematical; the other properties of objects seemed to reappear only in the light of number. An instrument of such power and elasticity could not fail to be 'a most gracious assistance' to the first feeble efforts of human intelligence.

There was another reason why numbers had so great an influence over the minds of early thinkers — they were verified by experience. Every use of them, even the most trivial, assured men of their truth; they were everywhere to be found, in the least things and the greatest alike. One, two, three, counted on the fingers were a 'trivial matter,' a little instrument out of which to create a world; but from these and by the help of these all our knowledge of nature has been developed. They were the measure of all things, and seemed to give law to all things; nature was rescued from chaos and confusion by their power; the notes of music, the motions of the stars, the forms of atoms, the recurrence and evolutions of days, months, years, the military divisions of an army, the civil divisions of a state, seemed to afford a 'present witness' of them: what would have become of man or of the world if deprived of number? The mystery of number and the mystery of music were akin. There was a music or rhythm of harmonious motion everywhere; and to the real connection which existed between music and number, a fanciful or imaginary relation was superadded.

Two points strike us in the use which the ancient philosophers made of number. First, they applied to external nature the relations of them which they found in their own minds; and where nature seemed to be at variance with number, as for example in the case of fractions, they protested against her (Rep. VII. 525). Having long meditated on the properties of $1 : 2 : 4 : 8$, or $1 : 3 : 9 : 27$, or of 3, 4, 5, they were disposed to find in them the secret of the universe. Secondly, they applied number and figure equally to those parts of physics, such as astronomy or mechanics, in which the modern philosopher expects to find them, and to those in which he would never think of looking for them, as for example, physiology. For the sciences were not yet divided, and there was nothing really irrational in arguing that the same laws which regulated the heavenly bodies were partially applied to the erring limbs or brain of man. Astrology was the form which the lively fancy of ancient thinkers almost necessarily gave to astronomy. The observation that the lower principle, e. g. mechanics, is always seen in the higher, e. g. in the phenomena of life, further tended to perplex them. Plato's doctrine of the same and the other ruling the courses of the heavens and of the human body is not a mere vagary, but is a natural result of the state of knowledge and thought at which he had arrived.

When in modern times we look up at the heavens, a certain amount of scientific truth imperceptibly blends, even with the cursory glance of an unscientific person. He knows that the earth is revolving round the sun, and not the sun around the earth. He does not imagine the earth to be the centre of the universe, and he has some conception of chemistry and the cognate sciences. A very different aspect of nature would have been present to the mind of the early Greek philosopher. He would have beheld the earth a surface only, not mirrored, however faintly, in the glass of science, but indissolubly connected with some theory of one, two, or more elements. He would see the world pervaded by number and figure, animated by a principle of motion, immanent in a principle of rest. He would try to construct the world on a quantitative principle, seeming to find in endless combinations of geometrical figures a sufficient account of the variety of phenomena. To these *a priori* speculations he would add a rude conception of matter and his own immediate experience of the supposed causes of health and disease. His cosmos would necessarily be imperfect and unequal, being the first attempt to impress form and order on the primaeval chaos of human knowledge.

§ 3.

Plato's account of the soul is partly mythical or figurative, and partly literal. Not that either he or we can draw a line between them, or say, 'This is poetry, this is philosophy;' for the transition from the one to the other is imperceptible. There is a further difficulty in explaining this part of the Timaeus—the natural order of thought is inverted. We begin with the most abstract, and proceed from the abstract to the concrete, although at p. 34 (cp. 53 D) Plato acknowledges that this order cannot always be maintained. But the abstract is unmeaning to us until brought into relation with man and nature. That which is spoken of first is really last, and is on the uttermost verge of human knowledge. And yet the priority of this abstract God, and the world which he is imagined to have created, gives a kind of awe to them. As in other systems of theology and philosophy, that of which we know least has the greatest interest to us.

There is no use in attempting to define or explain the first God in the Platonic system, who has sometimes been thought to answer to God the Father; or the first world or eternal soul, in whom the Fathers of the Church seemed to recognize 'the firstborn of every creature.' Nor need we discuss how far Plato agrees in the later Jewish conception of creation, according to which God made the world out of nothing. For the original conception of matter having no qualities is really a negation, and might as well be represented by nothing. If we said that God took of the same and the other, of the divided and undivided, of the finite and infinite, of the positive and negative, and made the world, we should find expressions in the Timaeus which would justify all these aspects of creation : So various are the forms in which Plato describes the works which no tongue can utter—his language, as he himself says, partaking of his own uncertainty about the things of which he is speaking.

Yet we may remark in passing, that the Platonic compared with the Jewish description of the process of creation has less of freedom or spontaneity. The Creator in Plato, however far removed from us into a distant heaven, is still subject to a remnant of necessity which he cannot wholly overcome. The reason appears to be that Plato is more sensible than the Hebrew prophet of the existence of evil, which he seeks as far as possible to put away from God. And he can only accomplish this by committing the lesser works of creation to inferior powers.

Nor can we attach any intelligible meaning to his words when he speaks of the visible, being in the image of the invisible. For how can that which is divided be like that which is undivided? or that which is changing be the copy of that which is unchanging? All the old difficulties about the ideas come back upon us in a slightly altered form. We can imagine two worlds, one of which is the mere double of the other, or one of which is the vanishing ideal of the other; but we cannot imagine an intellectual world which has no qualities—'a thing in itself'— a point which has no parts or magnitude, which is nowhere, and nothing. This cannot be the archetype according to which God made the world, and is in reality, whether in Plato or Kant, a mere negative residuum of human thought.

There is another aspect of the same difficulty which appears to have no satisfactory solution. In what relation does the archetype stand to the Creator himself? For the idea or pattern of the world is not the thought of God, but a separate, self-existent nature, of which creation is the copy. We can only reply, (1) that to the mind of Plato the distinction between the subject and the object as yet hardly existed; (2) that he supposes the process of creation to take place in accordance with his own theory of ideas; and as we cannot give an intelligible account of the one, neither can we of the other. He means (3) to say that the creation of the world is not a material process of working with legs and arms, but ideal and intellectual; according to his own fine expression, 'the thought of God made God.' He means (4) to draw an absolute distinction between the invisible and unchangeable which is the place of mind or being, and the world of sense or becoming which is visible and changing.

There are some other questions which we might ask and which can receive no answer, or at least only an answer of the same kind as the preceding. How can matter be conceived to exist without form? Or, how could there have been motion in the chaos when as yet time was not? Or, how did chaos come into existence, if not by the will of the Creator? Or, how could the Creator have taken portions of an indivisible same? Or, how could space have been eternal when time is only created? Or, how could the surfaces of geometrical figures have formed solids? We must reply again that we cannot follow Plato in all his inconsistencies, but that the gaps of thought are probably more apparent to us than to him. He would, perhaps, have said that 'the first things are known only to God and to him of men whom God loves.' And we may say that only by an effort of metaphysical imagination can we hope to understand Plato from his own point of view; we must not ask for consistency.

The soul of the world may be conceived as the personification of the numbers and figures in which the heavenly bodies move. Imagine these as in a Pythagorean dream, stripped of qualitative difference and reduced to mathematical abstractions. They are what Plato calls the principle of the same, and may be compared with the modern conception of laws of nature. They are in space, but not in time, and they are the makers of time. They are represented as constantly thinking of the same; for thought in the view of Plato is equivalent to truth or law, and is not inseparably bound up with a human consciousness. To this principle of the same is opposed the principle of the other—the principle of irregularity and disorder, of necessity and chance, which is only partially impressed by mathematical laws and figures. (We may observe by the way, that the principle of the other, which is the principle of plurality and variation in the Timaeus, has nothing in common with the

'other' of the Sophist, which is the principle of determination.) The
element of the same dominates to a certain extent over the other—the
fixed stars keep the 'wanderers' of the inner circle in their courses, and
a similar principle of fixedness or order appears to regulate the bodily
constitution of man. But there still remains a rebellious seed of evil
derived from the original chaos, which is the source of disorder in
the world, and of vice and disease in man.

Before they are immersed in matter the same and the other are
blended in a third nature which Plato terms the essence. The compound thus obtained is divided by the Creator into certain proportions
which he comprehended in a uniform motion around a centre in two
circles, of which the outer contained the fixed, the inner the wandering
stars. Thus the essence became the soul of the world, diffused everywhere from the centre to the circumference. To this God gave a body,
consisting at first of fire and earth, and afterwards receiving an addition
of air and water; because solid bodies, like the world, are always connected by two middle terms and not by one. The world was made
in the form of a globe, and all the elements, both material and im-
material, were exhausted in the work of creation.

The proportions in which the soul is divided answer to a series of
numbers 1, 2, 3, 4, 9, 8, 27, composed of the two Pythagorean progressions 1, 2, 4, 8 and 1, 3, 9, 27. This series, of which the intervals are
afterwards filled up, probably represents (1) the diatonic scale according
to Plato; (2) the order and distances of the heavenly bodies; and
(3) may possibly contain an allusion to the music of the spheres, which
has been already referred to in the myth at the end of the Republic.
The meaning of the words that 'solid bodies are always connected by
two middle terms' has been much disputed. The most received explanation is that of Martin, who supposes that Plato is only speaking
of surfaces and solids made up of prime numbers (i. e. of numbers not
made up of two factors, or only measurable by unity). The product
of two such numbers represents a surface, of three a solid. The
squares of numbers which are primes (e. g. 2^2, $3^2 = 4$, 9), have always
a single mean proportional (e. g. 4 and 9 have the single mean 6),
whereas cubes which are primes (e. g. 3^3 and 5^3) have always two
mean proportionals, e. g. 27 : 45 : 75 : 125. But to this explanation
of Martin's we may object, (1) that Plato nowhere says that his proportion is to be limited to prime numbers; (2) that the limitation of

surfaces to squares is also wanting; (3) that the figures and the ratios afterwards assigned to the elements do not correspond to the proportions between solid numbers which are thus obtained; (4) that Plato's doctrine of a mean is supposed by him to apply not only to surfaces and solids, but to any powers whatever; and he must have known, if Martin's explanation be correct, that there was no single mean between two cubes. What Plato chiefly intends to express is that a solid requires a stronger bond than a surface; and that the double bond which is given by a proportion of four terms is stronger than the single bond of three terms. The vagueness of his language does not allow us to determine whether anything more than this was intended by him.

Leaving the further explanation of these details, which the reader will find discussed at length in Boeckh and Martin, we may return to the main argument: Why did God make the world? Like man, He must have a purpose; and his purpose is the diffusion of that goodness or good which He himself is. The term 'goodness' is not to be understood in this passage as meaning benevolence or love, in the Christian sense of the term, but rather law, order, harmony, like the idea of good in the Republic. The ancient mythologers, and even the Hebrew prophets, had spoken of the jealousy of God; and the Greek had imagined that there was a Nemesis attending always the prosperity of mortals. But Plato delights to think of God as the author of order in his works, who, like a father, lives over again in his children, and can never have too much of good or friendship among his creatures. Only, as there is a certain remnant of evil inherent in matter which he cannot get rid of, he detaches himself from them and leaves them to themselves, that he may be guiltless of their faults and sufferings.

Between the ideal and the sensible Plato interposes the two natures of time and space. Time is conceived by him to be only the shadow or image of eternity, which ever is and never has been or will be, but is described in a figure only as past or future. This is one of the great thoughts of early philosophy, which are still as difficult to our minds as they were to the early thinkers; or perhaps more difficult, because we more distinctly see the consequences which are involved in such an hypothesis. All the objections which may be urged against Kant's doctrine of the ideality of space and time at once press upon us. If time is unreal, then all which is contained in time is unreal—the succession of human thoughts as well as the flux of sensations; there is no connecting link between φαινόμενα and ὄντα. Yet, on the other hand, we are conscious that knowledge is independent of time, that truth is not a thing of yesterday or to-morrow, but an 'eternal now.' To the 'spectator of all time and all existence' the universe remains at rest. The truths of geometry and arithmetic in all their combinations are always the same. The generations of men, like the leaves of the forest, come and go, but the mathematical laws by which the world is governed remain, and seem as if they could never change. The ever-present image of space is transferred to time—succession is conceived as extension. (We may remark that Plato has done away with the above and below in space, as he has done away with the past and future in time.) The course of time, unless regularly marked by divisions of number, partakes of the indefiniteness of the Heraclitean flux. By such reflections we may conceive the Greek to have attained the metaphysical conception of eternity, which to the Hebrew was gained by meditation on the Divine Being. No one saw that this objective was really a subjective, and involved the subjectivity of all knowledge. 'Non in tempore sed cum tempore finxit Deus mundum,' says St. Augustine, repeating a thought derived from the Timaeus, but apparently unconscious of the results to which his doctrine would have led.

The conception of space is scarcely distinguishable from what Plato terms the 'containing vessel or nurse of generation.' Reflecting on the simplest kinds of external objects, which to the ancients were the four elements, Plato was led to a more general notion of a kind out of which they were all fashioned. Thus seems to have arisen the first dim perception of ὕλη or matter, which has played so great a part in the metaphysical philosophy of Aristotle and his followers. Akin to this, for we can hardly distinguish between such extreme abstractions, is space, which Plato, perhaps inconsistently, regards as eternal. He seems, indeed, more willing to admit of the unreality of time than of the unreality of space; because, as he says, we have a notion that all things must necessarily exist in space. Yet he admits that our knowledge of space is of a dreamy kind, and is attained by a spurious reason without the help of sense. (Cp. the hypotheses and images of Rep. VI. 511.) That two things can be two in a real sense and one in an equally real, though not the same, sense, is a truth to which Plato has not as yet attained. In his attempt to conceive of space and matter we must remember that the two abstract ideas of weight and extension, which are familiar to us, had never passed before his mind.

Thus far God, working according to an eternal pattern, out of his goodness has created the same, the other, and the essence (compare the three principles of the Philebus—the finite, the infinite, and the union of the two), and out of them has formed the outer circle of the fixed stars and the inner circle of the planets, divided according to certain musical intervals; he has also created time, the moving image of eternity, and space, existing by a sort of necessity and hardly distinguishable from matter. The matter out of which the world is formed is not absolutely void, but retains in the chaos certain germs or traces of the elements. These Plato, like Empedocles, supposed to be four in number—fire, air, earth, and water. They were at first mixed together, and in the process of creation parted company from each other, the more volatile elements of fire and air propelling water and earth. They are so far from being elements or letters in the higher sense that they are not even syllables or first compounds. The real elements are the simplest forms of triangles; for all solids are terminated by surfaces, and all surfaces are resolvable into triangles. These are of two kinds: the rectangular scalene, which is the half of an equilateral triangle and has the hypothenuse double the lesser side — this from the greater regularity of its proportions is conceived by Plato to be the most beautiful of scalene triangles, and is therefore chiefly employed in the creation of the world, having, moreover, an infinite variety of forms. There is also the rectangular isosceles triangle, which has one form only, and is less adapted for construction.

Out of these triangles Plato proceeds to generate the four first of the five regular solids, perhaps forgetting that he is only constructing surfaces which have no solidity. The first solid is a regular pyramid, of which the base and sides are formed by four equilateral or twenty-four scalene triangles. The second solid is composed of the same triangles, which unite as eight equilateral triangles, and make one solid angle out of four plane angles—six of these angles form a regular octahedron. The third solid is a regular icosahedron, having twenty triangular equilateral bases, and therefore 120 rectangular scalene triangles. The fourth regular solid, or cube, is formed by the combination of four isosceles triangles into one square and of six squares into a cube. The fifth regular solid, or dodecahedron, cannot be formed by a combination of either kind of triangle, but each of its faces may be regarded as composed of thirty triangles of another kind. Probably Plato notices this as the only remaining regular polyhedron, which from its approximation to a globe, and possibly because, as Plutarch remarks, it is composed of $12 \times 30 = 360$ scalene triangles (Platon. Quaest. 5), representing thus the signs and degrees of the Zodiac, as well as the months and days of the year, God may be said to have 'used in the delineation of the universe.' According to Plato the earth was composed of cubes, the air of regular octahedrons, the water of regular icosahedrons, the fire of regular pyramids. The stability of the three last increases with the number of figures.

The elements are supposed to pass into one another. We must remember that these transformations are not the transformations of real solids, but of imaginary geometrical figures; in other words, we are composing and decomposing the faces and not the forms of the triangles. Yet perhaps Plato may regard them as only the forms which are impressed on pre-existent matter. It is remarkable that he should speak of each of these solids as a possible world in itself, though upon the whole he inclines to the opinion that they are one. To suppose that these forms are infinite, as Democritus had said, would be, as he satirically observes, 'the mark of a very indefinite mind.'

The twenty triangular faces of an icosahedron form the faces or sides of two regular octahedrons and of a regular pyramid $(20 = 8 \times 2 + 4)$; and therefore, according to Plato, a particle of water when decomposed is supposed to give two particles of air and one of fire. So because an octahedron gives the sides of two pyramids $(8 = 4 \times 2)$, a particle of air is resolved into two particles of fire.

The transformation is effected by the superior power or number of the conquering elements. The manner of the change is (1) a separation of portions of the elements from the mass in which they are collected; (2) a resolution of them into their own original triangles; and (3) a reunion of them in new forms. The finer natures are those which have the fewest bases, and being the most cutting have the advantage in any disturbances of matter; they force their way in, but are sometimes crushed by the weight or hardness of the surrounding element. Plato himself proposes the question, why does motion continue at all when the elements are settled in their places? The answer is, that although the world has been reduced to order by the Creator, the circular motion still retains a condensing power, and thrusts three of the elements into each other and into the fourth. Changes can only be effected by the greater number or power of dissimilars; when there is assimilation there is rest. Fire, air, water have a decomposing effect on all the four, but earth has no similar power over them. No single particle of the elements is visible, but only the aggregates of them are seen. The different subordinate species which are formed out of them depend upon the sizes of the original triangles. The obvious physical phenomena from which Plato has gathered his views of the relations of the elements seem to be the effect of fire upon air, water, and earth, and of water upon earth. The particles are supposed by him to be in a perpetual process of circulation caused by inequality. This process of circulation does not admit of a vacuum. Yet he appears to be inconsistent with himself. For in some of his remarks, e. g. in his strange account of the phenomena of respiration, he supposes air to be incompressible, as water really is, while in other places he supposes air to be condensed. And even the most penetrating element, fire, like all the rest, is composed of angles, and therefore cannot find a way into other geometrical figures without leaving a void, however small.

Of the phenomena of light and heavy he speaks afterwards, when treating of sensation, but they may be more conveniently considered by us in this place. They are not, he says, to be explained by 'above' and 'below,' which in the universal globe have no existence, but by the attraction of similars towards the great masses of similar substances; fire to fire, air to air, earth to earth. Plato's doctrine of attraction implies not only (1) the attraction of smaller bodies to larger ones, but (2) of similar elements to one another. Had he stopped at the first he would have arrived, though, perhaps, without any further result or any sense of the greatness of the discovery, at the modern doctrine of gravitation. He does not observe that water has an equal tendency towards both water and earth. So easily did the most obvious facts which were inconsistent with his theories escape him.

The general physical doctrines of the Timaeus may be summed up as follows: (1) Plato supposes the greater masses of the elements to

have been settled in their places at the creation : (2) the four elements
are formed of rectangular triangles variously combined into regular solid
figures : (3) three of them, fire, air, and water, admit of transformation
into one another; the fourth, earth, cannot be similarly transformed :
(4) different sizes of the same triangles form the lesser species of each
element : (5) there is an attraction of the lesser to the greater, and of like
to like.   Like Empedocles, Plato divides the earth from the other
elements; with the atomists, he attributes the differences of substances
to differences in the forms of atoms.   But he does not explain the
process by which geometrical surfaces become solids ; and he characteristically ridicules Democritus for not seeing that the good and the
true ' are of the nature of the finite.'

§ 4.

The astronomy of Plato is based on the two principles of the same
and the other, which God combined in the creation of the world.   The
soul which is compounded of the same, the other, and the essence, is
diffused from the centre to the circumference of the heavens.   We speak
indeed of a soul of the universe; but more truly regarded, the universe of the Timaeus is a soul, governed by mind, and holding in solution a residuum of matter, which the author of the world is unable to
expel, and of which Plato cannot tell us the origin.   The creation,
in Plato's sense, is really the creation of order in the world; and the
first step in giving order is the division of the heavens into an inner
and outer circle of the same and the other, of the indivisible and
divisible, answering to the spheres of the fixed stars and of the planets,
all together moving around the earth, which is their centre.   To us
there is a difficulty in apprehending how that which is indivisible can
be divided by the courses of the fixed stars, or how that which is
at rest can also be in motion.   The whole description is so ideal and
imaginative, that we can hardly venture to attribute to many of Plato's
words in the Timaeus any more meaning than to his mythical account
of the heavens in the Republic and in the Phaedrus.   The stars are
also gods, and the original habitations of the souls of men, from which
they come and to which they will hereafter return.   In attributing to
them only the most perfect motion—that which is on the same spot
or circling around the same—he might perhaps have said that to ' the

spectator of all existence and all time,' to borrow once more his own grand expression, or viewed, in the language of Spinoza, 'sub specie aeternitatis,' they were still at rest, but appeared to move in order to teach men the periods of time. Although absolutely in motion, they are relatively at rest; or we may conceive of them as resting, while the space in which they are contained, or the whole *anima mundi* revolves.

A different motion is ascribed to the planets and to the fixed stars. The universe revolves around a centre once in twenty-four hours, but the orbits of the fixed stars take a different direction from those of the planets—the first moving in a circle from left to right, the second diagonally from right to left; or, in other words, the first move in the path of the equator, the second in the path of the ecliptic. The motion of the second is controlled by the first, and hence the oblique line in which they are supposed to move becomes a spiral. The motion of the same is said to be undivided, whereas the inner motion is split into six portions or intervals containing seven unequal orbits—three in ratios of two, and three in ratios of three:—the Sun, Mercury, Venus moving in one direction with equal swiftness; the remaining four, Moon, Saturn, Mars, Jupiter, with equal swiftness to the former three and to one another. Thus arises the following progression:— Moon 1, Sun 2, Venus 3, Mercury 4, Mars 8, Jupiter 9, Saturn 27. This series of numbers is the compound of the two Pythagorean ratios, having the same intervals as the mixture which was originally divided in forming the soul of the world.

Plato was struck by the phenomenon of Mercury, Venus, and the Sun appearing to overtake and be overtaken by one another. The true reason of this, namely, that they lie within the circle of the earth's orbit, was unknown to him, and the reason which he gives—that they move in opposite directions to the four other planets—is far from explaining the appearance of them in the heavens. All the planets, including the sun, are carried round in the daily motion of the circle of the fixed stars, and their oblique motion gives the explanation of the different lengths of the sun's course in different parts of the world. The fixed stars have two movements—a movement on the same spot around an axis, which Plato calls the movement of thought about the same; as well as the forward movement in their orbit which is common to the whole circle.

The revolution of the world around the earth, which is accomplished in a single day and night, is described as being the most perfect. Yet Plato also speaks of an 'annus magnus' or cyclical year, in which periods wonderful for their complexity are found to coincide in a perfect number, i.e. a number which equals the sum of its factors. This, although not literally contradictory, is in spirit irreconcileable with the perfect revolution of twenty-four hours. The same remark may be applied to the complexity of the appearances and occultations of the planets, which, if the fixed stars are supposed to be moving around the centre once in twenty-four hours, must be confined to the effects produced by the seven planets. The truth is that Plato seems to confuse the actual observation of the heavens with his desire to find in them mathematical perfection. The same spirit is carried yet further by him in the Laws, in which he refuses to allow the planets or wandering stars to be called by this name, and the common opinion about them is deemed blasphemy.

We have now to consider the much discussed question of the rotation or immobility of the earth. Plato's doctrine on this subject is contained in the following words:—'The earth which is our nurse compacted (or circling) around the pole which is extended through the universe, he made to be the guardian and artificer of night and day, first and eldest of gods that are in the interior of heaven.' There is an unfortunate doubt (1) in this passage about the meaning of the Greek word which is translated 'compacted' or 'circling,' and is equally capable of either sense. A doubt (2) may also be raised as to whether the words 'artificer of day and night' are consistent with the mere passive causation of them, produced by the immobility of the earth in the midst of the circling universe. We must admit, further, (3) that Aristotle attributed to Plato the doctrine of the rotation of the earth. Yet the reasons which may be urged on the opposite side of the argument are far stronger. For, firstly, if the earth goes round with the outer heaven and the planets, including among them the sun, in twenty-four hours, there is no possibility of accounting for the alternation of day and night, or for any movement of the heavens; for the equal motion of the earth and heavens would have the effect of absolute immobility. Nor, secondly, can we suppose with Mr. Grote, that Plato has fallen unawares into this enormous contradiction; for though he was ignorant of many things which are familiar to us, and often confused in his ideas where we have become clear, we have no right to attribute to him a childish want of reasoning about very simple facts, or an inability to understand the necessary deductions from geometrical figures or movements. Of the causes of day and night the pre-Socratic philosophers, and especially the Pythagoreans, gave various accounts, and therefore the question can hardly be imagined to have escaped him. Thirdly, Mr. Grote supposes, not that ἰλλομένην means 'circling,' or that this is the sense in which Aristotle understood the word, but that the rotation of the earth is necessarily implied in its adherence to the cosmical axis. But (a) if Plato did not see that the rotation of the earth on its axis and of the heavens around the earth in equal times was inconsistent with the alternation of day and night, neither need we suppose that he would have seen the immobility of the earth to be inconsistent with the rotation of the axis. And (β) what proof is there that the axis of the world revolves at all? (γ) The comparison of the two passages quoted by Mr. Grote (see p. 19 of his pamphlet on 'The Rotation of the Earth') from Aristotle De Coelo (c. 13, ἔνιοι—γέγραπται, and c. 14, ἡμεῖς—μέσον) clearly shows, although this is a matter of minor importance, that Aristotle, as Proclus and Simplicius supposed, understood ἴλλεσθαι in the Timaeus to mean circling or revolving. For the second passage, in which motion on an axis is expressly mentioned, refers to the first, but this would be unmeaning unless ἴλλεσθαι in the first passage meant rotation on an axis. (4) The immobility of the earth is more in accordance with Plato's other writings than the opposite hypothesis. For in the Phaedo the earth is described as the centre of the world, and is not said to be in motion. In the Republic the pilgrims appear to be looking out from the earth upon the motions of the heavenly bodies; in, the Phaedrus, Hestia, who remains immovable in the house of Zeus while the other gods go in procession, is probably the symbol of the earth, who is here called the first and eldest of the gods. These passages are not conclusive, but then, again, the silence of Plato in them is more favourable to the doctrine of the immobility of the earth than to the opposite. If he had meant to say that the earth revolves on her axis, he would probably have expressed this in distinct words, and have explained the relation of her movements to those of the other heavenly bodies. (5) The meaning of the words ' artificer of day and night' is literally true according to Plato's view. For the alternation of day and night is not produced by the motion of the heavens alone, or by the immobility of the earth alone, but by both together; and that which has the inherent force or energy to remain at rest when all other bodies are moving, may be truly said to act, equally with them. (6) We should not lay too much stress on Aristotle having adopted the other interpretation of the words, although Alexander of Aphrodisias thinks that he could not have been ignorant either of the doctrine of Plato or of the sense which he intended to give to the word ἰλλομένην. For the citations of Plato in Aristotle are frequently misinterpreted by him; and he seems hardly ever to have had in his mind the connection in which they occur. In this instance the allusion is very slight, and there is no reason to suppose that the diurnal revolution of the heavens was present to his mind. Hence we need not attribute to him the error from which we are defending Plato.

§ 5.

The soul of the world is framed on the analogy of the soul of man, and many traces of anthropomorphism blend with Plato's highest flights of idealism. The heavenly bodies are endowed with thought, the principle of the same is the true law of the human mind as well as of the fixed stars. The soul of man is made out of the remains of the cup which contained the same, the other, and the essence; these remains, however, are diluted to the third degree; or, speaking still in a figure, there are dregs of necessity which are mingled with them. The human soul, like the cosmical, is framed before the body, as the mind is before the soul of either—this is the order of the divine work—and the finer parts of the body, which are more akin to the soul, such as the spinal marrow, are prior to the bones and flesh. The brain, which is the vessel of the soul, is (nearly) in the form of a globe, which is the image of the gods and the figure of the fixed stars and of the universe.

There is, however, an inconsistency in Plato's manner of conceiving the soul of man; he cannot get rid of the element of necessity which is allowed to enter. He does not, like Kant, attempt to vindicate for men a freedom out of space and time; but he acknowledges him to be subject to the influence of external causes, and leaves hardly any place for freedom of the will. The lusts of men are caused by their bodily constitution, though they may be increased by bad education and bad laws, which implies that they may be decreased by good education and good laws. He appears to have an inkling of the truth that to the higher nature of man evil is involuntary. Still, in the Timaeus, as well as in the Laws, he regards vices and crimes as simply involuntary; they are diseases analogous to the diseases of the body, and arising out of the same causes. If we draw together the opposite poles of Plato's system, we find that, like Spinoza, he combines idealism with fatalism.

The soul of man is divided by him into three parts, answering roughly to the charioteer and steeds of the Phaedrus, and to the λόγος, θυμός, and ἐπιθυμία of the Republic and Nicomachean Ethics. First, there is the immortal part which is seated in the brain, and is alone divine, and akin to the soul of the universe. Secondly, there is the higher mortal soul which, though liable to perturbations of her own, takes the side of reason against the lower appetites. The seat of this is the heart, in which courage, anger, and all the nobler affections are supposed to reside. There is also a third or appetitive soul, which receives the commands of the immortal part, not immediately but mediately, through the higher mortal nature, which reflects in the liver the admonitions and threats of the reason.

The liver is imagined by Plato to be a smooth and bright substance, having a store of sweetness and also of bitterness, which reason freely uses in the execution of her mandates. In this region, as ancient superstition told, were to be found intimations of the future. But Plato is careful to observe that this knowledge is only given in a measure to the inferior parts of man, and then requires to be interpreted by the superior. Reason, and not enthusiasm, is the true guide of man; he is only inspired when he is demented by some distemper or possession. The ancient saying, 'that only a man in his senses can judge of his own actions,' is approved by modern philosophy too. The same irony which appears in Plato's remark, 'that the men of old time must surely have known the gods who were their ancestors, and we must believe them as the law requires,' is also manifest in his account of divination.

The appetitive soul is seated in the belly, and there imprisoned like a wild beast, far away from the council chamber, as Plato graphically calls the head, in order that the animal passions may not interfere with the deliberations of reason. Though the soul is independent of the body, yet we cannot help seeing that Plato has really modelled the soul on the body—this threefold division in fact springing from the head and heart and belly. The human soul differs from the soul of the world in this respect, that she is enveloped and finds her expression in matter, whereas the soul of the world is the element in which matter moves. The breath of man is within him, but the air or aether of heaven is the element which surrounds him and all things.

Pleasure and pain are attributed in the Timaeus to the suddenness of our sensations—the first being a sudden restoration, the second a sudden violation, of nature (cp. Philebus). The sensations become conscious to us when they are exceptional. Sight is not attended either by pleasure or pain, but hunger and the appeasing of hunger are pleasant and painful because they are extraordinary.

§ 6.

I shall not attempt to connect the physiological speculations of Plato either with ancient or modern medicine. What light I can throw on them will be derived from the comparison of them with his general system.

There is no principle so apparent in the physics of the Timaeus, or in ancient physics generally, as that of continuity. The world is conceived of as a whole, and the elements are formed into and out of one another; the infinite substances and processes are hardly known or noticed. And so the human body is conceived of as a whole, and the different substances of which, to a superficial observer, it appears to be composed—the blood, flesh, sinews, and bone—like the elements of which they are formed, are supposed to pass into one another in regular order, while the infinite complexity of the human frame remains unobserved. And the source of diseases is the inversion of this order— when the natural proportions of the four elements are disturbed, and the secondary substances which are formed out of them, namely, blood, flesh, sinews, bone, are generated in an inverse order.

Plato found heat and air within the human frame, and the blood circulating in every part. He assumes, in language almost unintelligible to us, that an inner network of fire, having openings and an exterior envelopment of air, commencing at the passages of the throat, encased a great part of the human frame. This case, or network, of fire is a figure or fancy, under which Plato describes the internal heat of the body, and which he made the containing vessel of some of the organs, because fire was composed of the finest particles, and was therefore impenetrable by the other elements. The entire net has two lesser nets or openings, one leading to the stomach, the other to the lungs; and the latter is forked or divided at the upper end into the passages which lead to the nostrils and to the mouth.

Of the anatomy and functions of the body he was almost entirely ignorant; he knew nothing of the uses of the nerves in conveying motion and sensation, which he attributes to the veins; he was also ignorant of the distinction between veins and arteries; the spinal marrow he conceived to be the seed of generation; he had absolutely no idea of the phenomena of respiration, which he attributes to a law of equalization in nature, the air which is breathed out displacing other air which finds a way in through the pores; he was wholly unacquainted with the process of digestion. Except the general divisions into the spleen, the liver, the belly, and the lungs, and the obvious distinctions of flesh, bones, and the limbs of the body, we find nothing that reminds us of anatomical facts. But we find much which is derived from his theory of the universe, and transferred to man. The microcosm of the human frame is the lesser image of the macrocosm. The same equipoise is to be maintained in both; the animal is a 'sort of heaven' to the particles of the blood which circulate in it. Childhood is the chaos or first turbid flux of sense prior to the establishment of order; the intervals of time which may be observed in some intermittent fevers correspond to the intervals of the elements. The human frame, like the universe, is formed out of triangles, the very finest sort of all being those which are used in making the spinal marrow; and the process of digestion is carried on by the superior sharpness of the triangles of the substances of the human body to the substances which are introduced into it in the shape of food. The freshest and acutest forms of triangles are those that are found in children, but they become more obtuse with advancing years; and when they finally wear out and fall to pieces, old age and death supervene.

As in the Republic, Plato is still the enemy of the purgative treatment of physicians, which, except in extreme cases, no man of sense will ever adopt. For, as he adds, perhaps with an insight into the truth, 'every disease is akin to the nature of the living being and is only irritated by stimulants.' He is of opinion that nature should be left to herself, and is inclined to think that physicians are in vain. As in the Charmides he tells us that the body cannot be cured without the soul, so in the Timaeus he strongly asserts the sympathy of soul and body, any defect of which is the occasion of the greatest discord and disproportion. We cannot deny that his conception of the human body falls under the condemnation which Hippocrates, or some one writing in his spirit ('On Ancient Medicine'), has passed upon hypothetical medicine; and yet, amid all his extravagance, he is not deserted by a true tact.

§ 7.

In Plato's explanation of sensation we are struck by the fact that he has not the same distinct conception of organs of sense which is familiar to ourselves. The senses are not instruments, but rather passages, through which external objects strike upon the mind. The eye is the aperture through which the stream of vision passes, the ear is the aperture through which the vibrations of sound pass. But that the complex structure of the eye or the ear is in any sense the cause of sight and hearing he seems hardly to be aware.

The process of sight is the most complicated, and consists of three elements—the light which is supposed to reside within the eye, the light of the sun, and the light emitted from external objects. When the light of the eye meets the light of the sun, and both together meet the light issuing from an external object, this is the simple act of sight. When the particles of light which proceed from the object are exactly equal to the particles of the visual ray which meet them from within, then the body is transparent. If they are larger and dilate the visual ray which mingles with them, a white colour is produced by them; if they are smaller, a black. Other phenomena are produced by the variety and motion of light. A sudden flash of fire at once elicits light and moisture from the eye. A more subdued light of fire, which touches the surface and mingles with the moisture of the eye, produces a red colour. Out of these elements all other colours are supposed to be derived. All of them are combinations of light and fire with white and black. Plato himself tells us that he does not know in what proportions they combine, and he is of opinion that such knowledge is granted to the gods only. To have seen the affinity of them to each other and their connection with light, is not a bad basis for a theory of colours. We must remember that they

were not distinctly defined to his, as they are to our eyes; he saw
them, not as they are divided in the prism, or artificially manufactured
for the painter's use, but as they exist in nature, blended and confused
with one another.

We can hardly agree with him when he tells us that smells do not
admit of kinds. He seems to think that no definite qualities can attach
to bodies which are in a state of transition or evaporation; but he
makes the subtle observation that smells must be denser than air,
though thinner than water. The proof of this is that air can percolate
without any accompanying smell.

The affections peculiar to the tongue are of various kinds, and, like
many other affections, arise out of composition and division. Some
of them are produced by astringent, others by abstergent substances,
stronger or weaker, acting upon the testing instruments of the tongue,
and producing a more or less disagreeable sensation, while other
particles congenial to the tongue harmonize them, according to their
nature. The instruments of taste reach to the heart. Plato has a
lively sense of the manner in which sensation and motion are com-
municated from one part of the body to the other, though he confuses
the affections with the organs. In like manner hearing is a blow
which passes through the ear and ends in the region of the liver,
being transmitted by means of the air, the brains, and the blood to
the soul. The swifter sound is acute, the sound which moves slowly
is grave. A great body of sound is loud, the opposite is low. Discord
is produced by the swifter and slower motions of two sounds, and
is converted into harmony when the swifter motions begin to pause
and are overtaken by the slower.

The general phenomena of sensation are partly internal, but the
more violent are caused by conflict with external objects. Proceeding
by a method of superficial observation, Plato remarks that the more
sensitive parts of the human frame are those which are least covered
by flesh, as is the case with the head and the elbows. Man, if his
head had been covered with a thicker pulp of flesh, might have been
a longer lived animal than he is, but could not have had as quick
perceptions. On the other hand, the tongue is one of the most sensitive
of organs; but then this is made, not to be a covering to the bones
which contain the marrow or source of life, but with an express purpose,
and in a separate mass.

§ 8.

We have now to consider how far in any of these speculations Plato approximated to the discoveries of modern science. The modern physical philosopher is apt to dwell exclusively on the absurdities of ancient physical science, on the hap-hazard fancies and *a priori* assumptions of the ancient physical teacher, on his ignorance and regardlessness of facts. He hardly allows to his notions the merit of being 'the dead men's bones' out of which he has himself risen to a higher knowledge. According to the view taken in these volumes, the general notions were necessary to the discovery of the particular facts, the metaphysical to the physical. Before men could observe the world, they must be able to conceive the world.

To do justice to the subject, we should consider the physical philosophy of the ancients as a whole; we should remember, (1) that the nebular theory was the received belief of the early physicists; (2) that the developement of animals out of frogs who came to land, and of man out of the animals, was held by Anaximenes in the sixth century before Christ; (3) that even by Philolaus and the early Pythagoreans, the earth was held to be a body like the other stars revolving in space; they thought (4) that there was a sex in plants as well as in animals; (5) that musical notes depended on the relative length or tension of the strings from which they were emitted, and were measured by ratios of number; (6) that mathematical laws pervaded the world, and even qualitative differences were supposed to have their origin in number; (7) the annihilation of matter was denied by several of them, and held to be a transformation only. For, although one of these discoveries might have been supposed to be a happy guess, we can hardly attribute them all to mere coincidences.

Such reflections, although they cannot be dwelt upon at length in this place, lead us to take a favourable view of the speculations of the Timaeus. We have to consider not how much Plato actually knew, but how far he has contributed to the general ideas of physics, or supplied the notions, which, whether true or false, have stimulated the minds of thoughtful men in the path of discovery. Some of them may seem old-fashioned, and may nevertheless have had a great influence in promoting system and assisting enquiry, while in others of them we hear the latest word of physical or metaphysical philosophy. There is also a third class, in which Plato falls short of the truths of modern science, though he can hardly be said to be wholly unacquainted with them. (1) To the first class belong the teleological theory of creation. Whether all things in the world can be explained as the result of natural laws, or whether we must not admit of tendencies and marks of design also, has been a question much disputed of late years. And if all things are the result of natural forces, we must admit that there are many more things in heaven and earth 'than our philosophy dreams of,' which are as well expressed under the image of mind or design as under any other. At any rate, the language of Plato has been the language of natural theology down to our own time, nor can any description of the world wholly dispense with it. The notion of first and second or co-operative causes, which originally appears in the Timaeus, has also survived to our own day, and has been a great peace-maker between theology and science. Plato also approaches very near to our doctrine of the primary and secondary qualities of matter, p. 22. (2) Another popular notion which is found in the Timaeus, is the feebleness of the human intellect—'God knows the original qualities of things; man can only hope to attain to probability.' We speak in almost the same words of human intelligence, but not in the same manner of the uncertainty of our knowledge of nature. The reason is that this is assured to us by experiment, and is not contrasted with the certainty of ideal or mathematical knowledge. We are conscious that mathematics are the great interpreter of nature; the ancient philosopher was only half conscious of this. While he saw one part of nature in harmony with mathematical laws, there was another part which seemed to him to have no law, and to be a mere residuum of an original chaos.

But, secondly, besides popular notions, we seem to find also in the Timaeus, some true and some new conceptions of physical science. First, the doctrine of equipoise. Plato affirms, almost in so many words, that nature abhors a vacuum. Wherever there is a void the elements are pushing and thrusting one another until equality is restored. We must remember that these ideas were not derived from any definite experiment, but were the original reflections of man, fresh from the first observation of nature. The latest word of modern philosophy is continuity and development, but to Plato this is the beginning and foundation of science; there is nothing that he is so strongly persuaded of as that the world is one, and that all the various existences which are contained in it are only the transformations of the same soul of the world acting on the same matter. He would have readily admitted that out of the protoplasm all things were formed by the gradual process of creation; but he would have insisted that mind and intelligence—not meaning by this, however, a conscious mind or person—was prior to them, and could alone have created them. Lastly, there remain two points in which he seems to touch great discoveries of modern times—the law of gravitation, and the circulation of the blood. (1) The law of gravitation, according to Plato, is a law, not only of the attraction of lesser bodies- to larger ones, but of similar bodies to similar, having a magnetic power as well as a principle of gravitation. He observed that the earth, the water, and the air, had settled down to their places, and he imagined the fire or exterior aether to have a place beyond the air. When air and fire seemed to go upwards and solid bodies to go downwards, they were seeking their native elements. He did not remark that his own explanation did not suit all phenomena; and the simpler explanation, which assigns to bodies degrees of heaviness and lightness proportioned to the mass and distance of the bodies which attract them, never occurred to him. Yet the affinities of similar substances have some effect upon the composition of the world, and of this Plato may be thought to have had an anticipation. He may be described as confusing the attraction of gravitation with the attraction of cohesion. (2) Plato is perfectly aware—and he could hardly be ignorant—that blood is a fluid in constant motion. He also knew that blood is partly a solid substance consisting of several elements, which as he might have observed in the use of 'cupping-glasses' decompose and die, when no longer in motion. But the specific discovery that the blood flows out on one side of the heart through the arteries and returns through the veins on the other, which is commonly called the circulation of the blood, was absolutely unknown to him.

ERRATA IN THE TIMAEUS.

p. 568, l. 22, *for* 'shoulders' *read* 'arms'

p. 571, l. 23. According to Galen's Commentary on the Timaeus, p. 18 (Fragments du Commentaire sur le Timée par le Ch. D'Aremberg), with which Dr. Greenhill has made me acquainted, τούτοις refers not to ὄχετοι but to πνεῦμα and πῦρ, the antecedents in the preceding sentence. Though the resumption of a previous antecedent is in the manner of the Timaeus, I believe that this mode of taking the words agrees better with the connection. *For* 'channels' *read* 'elements'

p. 571, l. 26, *for* 'openings' *read* 'lesser nets or openings'

p. 576, l. 10, *for* 'liquefied' l. 28, 'melted' p. 577, l. 4, 'dissolution' *read* 'decomposed' 'decomposition'—as the same word is used in all three passages.

p. 577, last line, *for* 'passage' *read* 'passages'

p. 578, l. 13, *for* 'These, from the intensive nature of the affection, are termed tetanus and recurvation.' *read* 'These are called tetanus and opisthotonus, by reason of the tension which accompanies them.'

p. 578, l. 18, *for* 'white leprosies' *read* 'leprous eruptions' *or* 'divers kinds of leprosies'

p. 584, l. 8 from bottom, *for* 'wombs and other organs' *read* 'the so-called womb or matrix'

These corrections have been suggested by remarks which Dr. Greenhill of Hastings has kindly sent me.

TIMAEUS.

PERSONS OF THE DIALOGUE.

SOCRATES.   CRITIAS.
TIMAEUS.   HERMOCRATES.

Socrates. ONE, two, three; and where, my dear Timaeus, is the fourth of those who were yesterday our guests and are to be our entertainers to-day?

Timaeus. He has been taken ill, Socrates, or he certainly would not have been absent at such a meeting as this.

Soc. Then, if he is not coming, you and the two others must supply his place.

Tim. Assuredly we will do all that we can; having been handsomely entertained by you yesterday, we who remain ought gladly to entertain you in return.

Soc. Do you remember how many points there were of which I told you that we must speak?

Tim. We remember some of them, and you will be able to remind us of what we may have forgotten: or rather, if we are not troubling you, will you briefly recapitulate the whole, and then we shall be more certain?

Soc. I was enquiring yesterday how and of what citizens the best State would be composed;—that was the main purpose of what I was saying.

Tim. I am sure, Socrates, that your words were very much to our mind.

Soc. Do you remember the part about the husbandmen and the artisans; and how we began by separating them from the class of defenders of the State?

Tim. Yes.

Soc. And when we had given to each one that single employment and particular art which were suited to his nature, we spoke of those who were intended to be our warriors, and said that they were to be guardians of the city against the attacks of enemies internal as well as external, and to have no other employment; with gentleness they were to judge their subjects, of whom they were by nature friends, but when they came in the way of their enemies in battle they were to be fierce with them. Steph. 18

Tim. Exactly.

Soc. We said, if I am not mistaken, that the guardians should be gifted with a passionate and also with a philosophical temper, and that this would be the true way of making them gentle to their friends and fierce to their enemies.

Tim. Certainly.

Soc. And what did we say of their education? Were they not to be trained in gymnastic, and music, and all other sorts of knowledge which were proper for them?

Tim. Very true.

Soc. Thus trained, our citizens were not to think of gold and silver, or any other possession as their own private property; they were to be hired troops, receiving pay for keeping guard from those who were protected by them—the pay was to be no more than would suffice for men of simple life; and they were to have their expenses in common, and to live together in the continual practice of virtue, which was to be their sole pursuit.

Tim. That also was said.

Soc. Neither did we forget the women, of whom we said, that their natures should be made as nearly as possible like those of men, and that they should share with them in their military pursuits and in their general way of life.

Tim. That, again, was as you describe.

Soc. And what was said about the procreation of children? That was too singular to be easily forgotten, for the proposal was that all wives and children should be in common; and we devised means that no one should ever be able to know his own child, but that all should imagine themselves to be of one family, and should regard as brothers and sisters those who were within a certain limit of age; and those who were of an elder generation they were to regard as parents and grandparents, and those who were of a younger generation as children and grandchildren.

Tim. Yes, indeed, there is no difficulty in remembering that.

Soc. And do you also remember how, with a view of having as far as we could the best breed, we said that the chief magistrates, male and female, were to contrive secretly, by the use of certain lots, so to arrange the nuptial meeting, that the bad of either sex and the good of either sex should pair with their like, and there was to be no quarrelling on this account, for they were to imagine that the union was a mere chance, and was to be attributed to the lot?

Tim. I remember.

Soc. And you remember how we said that the children of the
19 good parents were to be educated, and the children of bad parents secretly dispersed among the other citizens, and when they began to grow up the rulers were to be on the look out, and to bring up from below in their turn those who were worthy, and those among themselves who were unworthy were to take the places of those who came up?

Tim. True.

Soc. Then have I now given you a complete summary of our yesterday's discussion? Or is there anything, dear Timaeus, that has been omitted?

Tim. No, Socrates, those were precisely the heads of the discussion.

Soc. Then let me now proceed to tell you my own feeling about the State which we have described. I might compare myself to a person who, on beholding beautiful animals either created by the painter's art, or really alive but at rest, is seized with a desire of beholding them in motion or engaged in some struggle or conflict to which their forms appear suited. This is my feeling about the State which we have described: there are conflicts which all cities undergo, and I should like to hear some one tell of our own city carrying on a struggle against her neighbours, and how she went out to war in a fitting manner, and when at war showed a result answerable to her training and education, both in her modes of action and fashions of speech, when dealing with other cities. Now I, Critias, and Hermocrates, am conscious that I myself should never be able to set forth the city and her citizens in proper terms of praise, and I am not surprised at my own incapacity; to

me the wonder is rather that the poets present as well as past are
no better—not that I mean to depreciate them, but every one can
see that they are a tribe of imitators, and will imitate best and
most easily that in which they have been brought up; whereas that
which is beyond the range of a man's education can hardly be
imitated by him in action, and with still more difficulty in speech.
I am aware that the Sophists have plenty of brave words and fair
devices, but I am afraid that being only wanderers from one city
to another, and having never had homes of their own to manage,
they may err in their ideas of philosophers and statesmen, and may
fail to know what they do and say in their dealings with mankind
on all the various occasions of peace and war.   And thus people of
your class are the only ones remaining who are fitted by nature and
education to take part at once in politics and philosophy.   Here
is Timaeus, of Locris in Italy, a city which has excellent laws, and 20
who is himself in wealth and rank the equal of any of his fellow-
citizens; he has held the most important and honourable offices in
his own State, and, as I believe, has scaled the heights of philosophy ; and here is Critias, whom every Athenian knows to be well
acquainted with the things of which we are speaking; and as to
Hermocrates, I am assured by many witnesses that he is by nature
and education well suited to philosophical enquiries.   And therefore yesterday when I saw that you wanted me to discuss the
formation of the State I readily complied, being very well aware,
that, if you only would, none were better qualified to carry the discussion further, and that when you had engaged our city in a
suitable war, you of all men living could best exhibit her playing
her part in that situation.   Having now completed my task, I in
return impose this other task upon you.   There was an agreement
that you were to entertain me as I have entertained you.   Here
am I in festive array, and no man can be more ready for the promised banquet.

Her. And we too, Socrates, as Timaeus says, willdo our ut -
most; there would be no excuse for our refusal to comply.   As
soon as we arrived yesterday at the guest-chamber of Critias, with
whom we are staying, or rather on our way thither, we talked the
subject over, and he told us an ancient tradition, which I wish,
Critias, that you would repeat to Socrates, and then he will be able
to judge whether it fulfils his requirements.

Crit. That I will, if Timaeus, who is our partner, approves.

Tim. I approve.

Crit. Then listen, Socrates, to a strange tale which is, however, certainly true, as Solon, who was the wisest of the seven sages, declared. He was a relative and a great friend of my great-grandfather, Dropidas, as he himself says in several of his poems; and Dropidas told Critias, my grandfather, who remembered and told us:—That there were of old great and marvellous actions of the Athenians, which have passed into oblivion through time and the destruction of the human race, and one in particular, which was the greatest of them all, the recital of which will be a suitable testimony of our gratitude to you, and also a hymn of praise true and worthy of the goddess, which may be sung by us at the festival in her honour.

Soc. Very good. And what is this ancient famous action of which Critias spoke not as a mere legend, but as a veritable action of the Athenian state, which Solon recounted?

Crit. I will tell an old-world story which I heard from an aged man; for Critias was, as he said, at that time nearly ninety years of age, and I was about ten years of age. Now the day was that day of the Apaturia which is called the registration of youth, at which, according to custom, our parents gave prizes for recitations, and the poems of several poets were recited by us boys, and many of us sang the poems of Solon, which were new at the time. One of our tribe, either because this was his real opinion, or because he thought that he would please Critias, said that in his judgment Solon was not only the wisest of men, but also the noblest of poets. The old man, as I very well remember, brightened up at this and said, smiling: Yes, Amynander, if Solon had only, like other poets, made poetry the business of his life, and had completed the tale which he brought with him from Egypt, and had not been compelled, by reason of the factions and troubles which he found stirring in this country when he came home, to attend to other matters, in my opinion he would have been as famous as Homer or Hesiod, or any poet.

And what was the poem about, Critias? said the person who addressed him.

About the greatest action which the Athenians ever did, and which ought to have been the most famous, but which, through the lapse of time and the destruction of the actors, has not come down to us.

Tell us, said the other, the whole story, and how and from whom Solon heard this veritable tradition.

He replied:—At the head of the Egyptian Delta, where the river Nile divides, there is a certain district which is called the district of Sais, and the great city of the district is also called Sais, and is the city from which Amasis the king was sprung. And the citizens have a deity who is their foundress; she is called in the Egyptian tongue Neith, and is asserted by them to be the same whom the Hellenes called Athene. Now the citizens of this city are great lovers of the Athenians, and say that they are in some way related to them. Thither came Solon, who was received by them with great honour; and he asked the priests, who were most skilful in such matters, about antiquity, and made the discovery that neither he nor any other Hellene knew anything worth mentioning about the times of old. On one occasion, when he was drawing them on to speak of antiquity, he began to tell about the most ancient things in our part of the world—about Phoroneus, who is called 'the first,' and about Niobe; and after the Deluge, to tell of the lives of Deucalion and Pyrrha; and he traced the genealogy of their descendants, and attempted to reckon how many years old were the events of which he was speaking, and to give the dates. Thereupon, one of the priests, who was of a very great age, said: O Solon, Solon, you Hellenes are but children, and there is never an old man who is an Hellene. Solon hearing this, said, What do you mean? I mean to say, he replied, that in mind you are all young; there is no old opinion handed down among you by ancient tradition; nor any science which is hoary with age. And I will tell you the reason of this. There have been, and will be again, many destructions of mankind arising out of many causes; the greatest have been brought about by the agencies of fire and water, and other lesser ones by innumerable other causes. There is a story, which even you have preserved, that once upon a time Phaëthon, the son of Helios, having yoked the steeds in his father's chariot, because he was not able to drive them in the path of his father, burnt up all that was upon the earth, and was himself destroyed by a thunderbolt. Now, this has the form of a myth, but really signifies a declination of the bodies moving around the earth and in the heavens, and a great conflagration of things upon the earth recurring at long intervals of time; when this happens, those who live upon the mountains and in dry and lofty places are more liable to destructions than those who dwell by rivers or on the seashore. And from this calamity the Nile, who is our never-failing saviour, saves and delivers us. When, on the other hand, the gods purge the earth with a deluge of water, among you, herdsmen and shepherds on the mountains are the survivors, whereas those of you who live in cities are carried by the rivers into the sea. But in this country, neither at that time nor at any other, does the water come from above on the fields, having always a tendency to come up from below, for which reason the things preserved here are said to be the oldest. The fact is, that wherever the extremity of winter frost or of summer sun does not prevent, the human race is always increasing at times, and at other times

23 diminishing in numbers. And whatever happened either in your country or in ours, or in any other region of which we are informed—if any action which is noble or great or in any other way remarkable has taken place, all that has been written down of old, and is preserved in our temples; whereas you and other nations are just being provided with letters and the other things which States require; and then, at the usual period, the stream from heaven descends like a pestilence, and leaves only those of you who are destitute of letters and education; and thus you have to begin all over again as children, and know nothing of what happened in ancient times, either among us or among yourselves. As for those genealogies of yours which you have recounted to us, Solon, they are no better than the tales of children; for in the first place you remember one deluge only, whereas there were many of them; and in the next place, you do not know that there dwelt in your land the fairest and nobiest race of men which ever lived, of whom you and your whole city are but a seed or remnant. And this was unknown to you, because for many generations the survivors of that destruction died and made no sign. For there was a time, Solon, before the great deluge of all, when the city which now is Athens, was first in war and was pre-eminent for the excellence of her laws, and is said to have performed the noblest deeds and to have had the fairest constitution of any of which tradition tells, under the face of heaven. Solon marvelled at this, and earnestly requested the priest to inform him exactly and in order about these former citizens. You are welcome to hear

about them, Solon, said the priest, both for your own sake and for that of the city, and above all, for the sake of the goddess who is the common patron and protector and educator of both our cities. She founded your city a thousand years before ours, receiving from the Earth and Hephaestus the seed of your race, and then she founded ours, the constitution of which is set down in our sacred registers as 8000 years old. As touching the citizens of 9000 years ago, I will briefly inform you of their laws and of the noblest of their actions; and the exact particulars of the whole we will hereafter go through at our leisure in the sacred registers 24 themselves. If you compare these very laws with your own you will find that many of ours are the counterpart of yours as they were in the olden time. In the first place, there is the caste of priests, which is separated from all the others; next there are the artificers, who exercise their several crafts by themselves and without admixture of any other, and also there is the class of shepherds and that of hunters[1], as well as that of husbandmen; and you will observe, too, that the warriors in Egypt are separated from all the other classes, and are commanded by the law only to engage in war; moreover, the weapons with which they are equipped are shields and spears, and this the goddess taught first among you, and then in Asiatic countries, and we among the Asiatics first adopted. Then as to wisdom, do you observe what care the law took from the very first, searching out and comprehending the whole order of things down to prophecy and medicine (the latter with a view to health); and out of these divine elements drawing what was needful for human life, and adding every sort of knowledge which was connected with them. All this order and arrangement the goddess first imparted to you when establishing your city; and she chose the spot of earth in which you were born, because she saw that the happy temperament of the seasons in that land would produce the wisest of men. Wherefore the goddess who was a lover both of war and of wisdom, selected and first of all settled that spot which was the most likely to produce men likest herself. And there you dwelt, having such laws as these and still better ones, and excelled all mankind in all virtue as became the children and disciples of the gods.

---

[1] Reading τὸ τῶν θηρευτῶν.

Many great and wonderful deeds are recorded of your State in our histories. But one of them exceeds all the rest in greatness and valour. For these histories tell of a mighty power which was aggressing wantonly against the whole of Europe and Asia, and to which your city put an end. This power came forth out of the Atlantic Ocean, for in those days the Atlantic was navigable; and there was an island situated in front of the straits which you call the columns of Heracles; the island was larger than Libya and Asia put together, and was the way to other islands, and from the 25 islands you might pass to the whole of the opposite continent which surrounded the true ocean; for this sea which is within the Straits of Heracles is only a harbour, having a narrow entrance, but that other is a real sea, and the surrounding land may be most truly called a continent. Now in this island of Atlantis there was a great and wonderful empire which had rule over the whole island and several others, as well as over parts of the continent, and, besides these, they subjected the parts of Libya within the columns of Heracles as far as Egypt, and of Europe as far as Tyrrhenia. The vast power thus gathered into one, endeavoured to subdue at one blow our country and yours and the whole of the land which was within the straits; and then, Solon, your country shone forth, in the excellence of her virtue and strength, among all mankind; for she was first in courage and military skill, and was the leader of the Hellenes. And when the rest fell off from her, being compelled to stand alone, after having undergone the very extremity of danger, she defeated and triumphed over the invaders, and preserved from slavery those who were not yet subjected, and freely liberated all the others who dwell within the limits of Heracles. But afterwards there occurred violent earthquakes and floods; and in a single day and night of rain all your warlike men in a body sank into the earth, and the island of Atlantis in like manner disappeared, and was sunk beneath the sea. And that is the reason why the sea in those parts is impassable and impenetrable, because there is such a quantity of shallow mud in the way; and this was caused by the subsidence of the island.

I have told you shortly, Socrates, the tradition which the aged Critias heard from Solon. And when you were speaking yesterday about your city and citizens, this very tale which I am telling you came into my mind, and I could not help remarking how, by some coincidence not to be explained, you agreed in almost every particular with the account of Solon; but I did not like to speak at 26 the moment. For as a long time had elapsed, I had forgotten too much, and I thought that I had better first of all run over the narrative in my own mind and then I would speak. And for this reason I readily assented to your request yesterday, considering that I was pretty well furnished with a theme such as the audience would approve, and to find this is in all such cases the chief difficulty.

And therefore, as Hermocrates has told you, on my way home yesterday I imparted my recollections to my friends in order to refresh my memory, and during the night I thought about the words and have nearly recovered them all. Truly, as is often said, the lessons which we have learned as children make a wonderful impression on our memories, for I am not sure that I could remember all that I heard yesterday, but I should be much surprised if I forgot any of these things which I have heard very long ago. I listened to the old man telling them, when a child, with great interest at the time; he was very ready to teach me, and I asked him about them a great many times, so that they were branded into my mind in ineffaceable letters. As soon as the day broke I began to repeat them to my companions, that they as well as myself might have a material of discourse. And now, Socrates, I am ready to tell you the whole tale of which this is the introduction. I will give you not only the general heads, but the details exactly as I heard them. And as to the city and citizens, which you yesterday described to us in fiction, let us transfer them to the world of reality; this shall be our city, and we will suppose that the citizens whom you imagined, were our veritable ancestors—the same of whom the priest was telling; they will perfectly agree, and there will be no inconsistency in saying that the citizens of your republic are these ancient Athenians. Let us distribute the discussion amongst us, and all endeavour as far as we can to carry out your instructions. Consider then, Socrates, if this narrative is suited to the purpose, or whether we should seek for some other instead.

Soc. And what other, Critias, can we find that will be better than this which is natural and suitable to the festival of the goddess; and has the very great advantage of being a fact and not a fiction? How or where shall we find others if we abandon

this? There are none to be had, and therefore you must tell the
27 tale, and good luck to you; and I in return for my yesterday's discourse will now rest and be a listener.

Crit. Let me proceed to explain to you, Socrates, the order in which we have arranged our entertainment. The intention is that Timaeus, who is the most of an astronomer amongst us, and has made a special study of the nature of the universe, should speak first, beginning with the generation of the world and going down to the creation of man; next, I am to receive the citizens of whom he is the imaginary parent, and some of whom will have profited by the excellent education which you have given them; and then, in conformity with the law of Solon, we will bring the heroes of his tale into court and judge them ourselves, as if they were those very Athenians whom the sacred Egyptian record has recovered from oblivion, and we shall thenceforward be entitled to speak of them as Athenians and fellow-citizens.

Soc. I see that I shall receive in my turn a perfect and noble feast of reason. And now, Timaeus, you I suppose are to follow, first offering up a prayer to the gods as is customary.

Tim. All men, Socrates, who have any degree of right feeling do this at the beginning of every enterprise great or small—they always call upon the gods. And we, too, who are going to discourse of the nature of the universe, whether created or uncreated, if we be not altogether out of our wits, must invoke and pray the gods and goddesses that we may say all things in a manner pleasing to them and consistent with ourselves. Let this, then, be our invocation to the gods, to which I add an exhortation to myself that I may set forth this high argument in the manner which will be most intelligible to you, and will most accord with my own intent.

First, if I am not mistaken, we must determine, What is that which always is and has no becoming; and what is that which is always becoming and has never any being. That which is apprehended by reflection and reason always is, and is the same; that, on the other hand, which is conceived by opinion with the help of sensation and without reason, is in a process of becoming and perishing, but never really is. Now everything that becomes or is created must of necessity be created by some cause, for nothing can be created without a cause. That of which the artificer looks always

to the same and unchangeable, and of which he works out the form
and nature after an unchangeable pattern, must of necessity be
made fair and perfect; but that of which the artificer looks to the
created only, and fashions after a created pattern, is not fair or
perfect. Was the heaven then or the world,—whether called by
this or any other more appropriate name—the question which I
am going to ask has to be asked about the beginning of everything
—was the world, I say, always in existence and without beginning? or created and having a beginning? Created, I reply, being
visible and tangible and having a body, and therefore sensible;
and all sensible things which are apprehended by opinion and
sense are in process of creation and created. Now that which is
created must of necessity be created by a cause. But how can we
find out the father and maker of all this universe? Or when we
have found him how shall we be able to speak of him to all men?
And there is still another question to be asked about him, Which
of the patterns had the artificer in view when he made the world,
the pattern which is unchangeable, or that which is created? If
the world be indeed fair and the artificer good, then, as is plain,
he must have looked to that which is eternal. But if what I may 29
not venture to say is true, then he looked to the created pattern.
Every one will see that he must have looked to the eternal, for
the world is the fairest of creations and He is the best of causes.
And being of such a nature the world has been framed by him
with a view to that which is apprehended by reason and mind
and is unchangeable, and if this be admitted must of necessity
be the copy of something. Now that the beginning of everything should be according to nature is a great matter. Let us
then assume about the copy and original that the words are
akin to the matter which they describe, and that when they
relate to the lasting and permanent and intelligible, they ought
to be lasting and unfailing, and as far as is in the nature of
words irrefutable and immovable, and nothing less than this.
But the words which are the expression of the imitation of the
eternal things, which is an image only, need only be likely and
analogous to the former words. What essence is to generation, that, truth is to belief. If then, Socrates, amid the many
opinions about the gods and the generation of the universe, we
are not able to give notions that are in every way exact and

consistent with one another, do not wonder at that. If only we adduce probabilities as likely as any others, that ought to be enough for us, when we remember that I who am the speaker, and you who are the judges are only mortal men, and we ought to accept the tale which is probable and not enquire further.

Soc. Excellent, Timaeus, your words shall be taken as you mean them. We have heard your prelude with the greatest pleasure, and now beg you to proceed to the strain which follows.

Tim. Let me tell you then, why the creator of the world generated and created this universe. He was good, and no goodness can ever have any jealousy of anything. And being free from jealousy, he desired that all things should be as like himself as possible. This is the true beginning of creation and of the world, 30 which we shall do well in receiving on the testimony of wise men: God desired that all things should be good and nothing bad as far as this could be accomplished. Wherefore also finding the whole visible sphere not at rest, but moving in an irregular and disorderly manner, out of disorder he brought order, considering that this was far better than the other. Now he who is the best neither creates nor ever has created anything but the fairest, and reflecting upon the visible works of nature, he found that no unintelligent creature taken as a whole was fairer than the intelligent taken as a whole; and that intelligence could not exist in anything which was devoid of soul. For these reasons he put intelligence in soul, and soul in body, and framed the universe to be the best and fairest work in the order of nature. And therefore using the language of probability, we may say that the world became a living soul and truly rational through the providence of God.

This being supposed, let us next proceed to consider the further question, in the likeness of what animal did the Creator make the world? Certainly we cannot suppose that the form was like that of beings which exist in parts only; for nothing can be beautiful that is like any imperfect thing; but we may regard the world as the very likeness of that of which all other animals, both individually and as tribes are portions. For the pattern of the universe contains in itself all intelligible beings, just as this world contains us and all other visible creatures. For the Deity intending to make this world like the fairest and most perfect of intelligible beings, framed one visible animal comprehending within all other

animals of a kindred nature.   Are we right in saying that there is 31
one heaven, or shall we rather say that they are many and infinite?
There is one, if the created heaven is to accord with the pattern.
For that which includes all other intelligible creatures cannot have
a second or companion; in that case there would be need of
another living being which would include those two, and of which
they would be parts, and the likeness would be more truly said to
resemble not those two, but that other which included them.   In
order then that the world might be like the perfect animal in
unity, he who made the worlds made them not two or infinite in
number; but there is and ever will be one only-begotten and
created heaven.

Now that which is created is of necessity corporeal, and also
visible and tangible.   And nothing is visible when there is no
fire, or tangible which is not solid, and nothing is solid without
earth.   Wherefore also, God in the beginning of creation made
the body of the universe to consist of fire and earth.   But two
things cannot be held together without a third; they must have
some bond of union.   And the fairest bond is that which most
completely fuses and is fused into the things that are bound;
and proportion is best adapted to effect such a fusion.   For
whenever in three numbers, whether solids or of any other power,
there is a mean, and the mean is to the last term what the first 32
term is to the mean; and again, when the mean is to the first
term as the last term is to the mean, then the mean becoming
first and last, and the first and last both becoming means, all
things will of necessity come to be the same, and being the same
with one another will all be one.   If now the universal frame
had been created a surface only and had no depth, one mean
would have sufficed to bind together itself and the other terms;
but now, as the world must be solid, and solid bodies are always
compacted not by one mean but by two, God placed water and
air in the mean between fire and earth, and made them to have
the same proportions as far as was possible (as fire is to air so is
air to water, and as air is to water so is water to earth), and thus
he bound and put together a visible and palpable heaven.   And
for these reasons, and out of these elements, which are in number
four, the body of the world was created in the harmony of proportion, and therefore having the spirit of friendship; and being

at unity with itself, was indissoluble by the hand of any other than the framer.

Now the creation took up the whole of each of the four elements; for the Creator compounded the world out of all the fire and all the water and all the air and all the earth, leaving no part of any of them nor any power of them outside. He intended, in the first place, that the whole animal should be perfect, as far as possible, and that the parts of which he was formed should

33 be perfect; and that he should be one, leaving no remnants out of which another such world might be created: and, also, that he should be free from old age and unaffected by disease. And, considering that hot and cold and other powerful forces which unite bodies are apt to surround and attack them from without when they are unprepared, and by bringing diseases and old age upon them, make them to dissolve and die—for this cause and on these grounds, he fabricated the world whole and of whole elements, perfect and not liable to old age and disease. And he gave to the world the figure which was suitable and also natural. But, to the animal which was to comprehend all animals, that figure was suitable which comprehends within itself all other figures. Wherefore also he made the world in the form of a globe, round as from a lathe, in every direction equally distant from the centre to the extremes, the most perfect and the most like itself of all figures; for he considered that the like is infinitely fairer than the unlike. This he finished all round, and made the outside quite smooth for many reasons; in the first place, because eyes would have been of no use to him when there was nothing remaining without him, or which could be seen; and there would have been no use in ears when there was nothing to be heard; nor was there any surrounding atmosphere to be breathed; nor would there have been any use of implements by the help of which he might receive his food or get rid of what he had already digested; for there was nothing which went from him or came to him, seeing that there was nothing beside him. And he himself provided his nutriment to himself through his own decay, and all that he did or suffered was done in himself and by himself, according to art. For the Creator conceived that a being which was self-sufficient would be far more excellent than one that lacked anything; and, as he had no need to take anything or defend himself against any one, he had no need of hands,

and the Creator did not think necessary to furnish him with them
when he did not want them: nor had he any need of feet, nor
of the whole apparatus of walking; but he assigned to him the 34
motion appropriate to his spherical form, being that of all the
seven which is most appropriate to mind and intelligence, and
so he made him move in the same manner and on the same spot,
going round in a circle turning within himself. All the other
six motions he took away from him, and made him incapable of
being affected by them. And as this circular movement required
no feet, he made the universe without feet or legs.

Such was the whole scheme of the eternal God about the god
that was to be, to whom he for all these reasons gave a body,
smooth, even, and in every direction equi-distant from a centre,
entire and perfect, and formed out of perfect bodies. And in
the centre he put the soul, which he diffused through the whole,
and also spread over all the body round about; and he made one
solitary and only heaven a circle moving in a circle, having
such excellence as to be able to hold converse with itself, and
needing no other friendship or acquaintance. Having these purposes in view he created the world to be a blessed god.

Now God did not make the soul after the body, although we
have spoken of them in this order; for when he put them together
he would never have allowed that the elder should serve the
younger, but this is what we say at random, because we ourselves too are very largely affected by chance. Whereas he made
the soul in origin and excellence prior to and older than the
body, to be the ruler and mistress, of whom the body was to be
the subject. And the soul he made out of the following elements
and on this manner:—he took of the unchangeable and indivisible 35
essence, and also of the divisible and corporeal which is generated,
and he made a third sort of intermediate essence out of them
both, partaking of the nature of the same and of the other, and
thus he compounded a nature which was in a mean between the
indivisible and the divisible and corporeal. These three elements
he took and mingled them all in one form, compressing the
reluctant and unsociable nature of the other into the same. And
when he had mixed them with the essence and out of all the three
made one, he again divided this whole into as many portions as
was fitting, each of them containing an admixture of the same

and of the other and of the essence. And he began to divide
on this wise :—first of all, he took away one part of the whole,
and then he separated

$$[\ 1,\ 2,\ 3,\ 4,\ 9,\ 8,\ 27,\ ]$$

a second part which was double the first, and then he took away
a third part which was half as much again as the second and
three times as much again as the first, and then he took a fourth
part which was twice as much as the second, and a fifth part which
was three times as much as the third, and a sixth part which was
eight times as much as the first, and a seventh part which was
twenty-seven times the first. After this he filled up the double
36 and triple intervals [i. e. 1, 2, 4, 8, and 1, 3, 9, 27], cutting off
portions from the whole and placing them between the intervals,
so that in each interval there were two kinds of means—

$$[\ \overline{1},\ \tfrac{4}{3},\ \tfrac{3}{2},\ \overline{2},\ \tfrac{8}{3},\ 3,\ \overline{4},\ \tfrac{16}{3},\ 6,\ \overline{8},\ ]$$
$$[\ \overline{1},\ \tfrac{3}{2},\ 2,\ \overline{3},\ \tfrac{9}{2},\ 6,\ \overline{9},\ \tfrac{27}{2},\ 18,\ \overline{27},\ ]$$

the one exceeding and exceeded by equal parts of the respective
extremes [as for example 1, $\tfrac{4}{3}$, 2, in which the mean $\tfrac{4}{3}$ is one-
third more than 1 and one-third less than 2], the other being
that kind of mean which exceeds and is exceeded by an equal
number. Where there are intervals of $\tfrac{3}{2}$ and of $\tfrac{4}{3}$ and of $\tfrac{9}{8}$,
made by the connecting terms in the former intervals, he
filled up all the intervals of $\tfrac{4}{3}$ with the intervals of $\tfrac{9}{8}$, leaving
a part of each, of which the interval was in the ratio of 256 to
243 [2]. And thus the whole mixture out of which he cut these
portions was all exhausted by him. This entire compound he
divided lengthways into two parts, which he joined to one
another at the centre like the figure of a X, and bent them into
a circular form, connecting them with themselves and each other
at the point opposite to that of contact; and, comprehending them
in an uniform motion on the same spot around a centre, he made
the one the outer and the other the inner circle. Now the

[2] E. g. 243 : 256 :: $\frac{81}{64}$: $\frac{4}{3}$ :: $\frac{243}{128}$: 2 :: $\frac{81}{32}$: $\frac{8}{3}$ :: $\frac{243}{64}$: 4 :: $\frac{81}{16}$: $\frac{16}{3}$ :: $\frac{242}{32}$: 8. (MARTIN.)

motion of the outer circle he called the motion of the same,
and the motion of the inner circle the motion of the other. The
motion of the same he made to proceed round by the side to
the right, and the motion of the other diagonally to the left.
And he gave dominion to the motion of the same and the like,
for that he left single and undivided; but the inner motion he
split into six portions and made seven unequal orbits, having their
intervals in ratios of two and three, three of each, and bade their
orbits move in a direction opposite to one another; and three
[Sun, Mercury, Venus] he made to move with equal swiftness,
and the remaining four [Moon, Saturn, Mars, Jupiter] to move
with unequal swiftness to the three and to one another, but all
in due course.

Now when the Creator had framed the soul according to his
will, he formed within the mind the corporeal universe, and
brought them together, and united them centre to centre. The
soul, interfused everywhere from the centre to the circumference
of heaven, of which she is the external envelopment, herself
turning in herself, began a divine beginning of never-ceasing
and rational life enduring throughout all time. The body of
heaven is visible, but the soul invisible, and partakes of reason 37
and harmony, and being made by the best of intelligible and everlasting beings, is the best of things created. And as, being composed of the nature of the same and of the other and of the essence,
these three, and divided and bound together in proportion, and
revolving in the circle of herself, the soul, when touching anything
which has essence, whether dispersed in parts or undivided, is
stirred throughout her being to declare the sameness and diversity
of things, and as to what and in what way and how and when
individuals are related or affected, both in the world of generation
and in the world of immutable being. And when reason, which
works with equal truth both in the circle of the other and of the
same, — in the sphere of the self-moved in voiceless silence
moving,—when reason, I say, is in the neighbourhood of sense,
and the circle of the other also moving truly[3] imparts the intimations of sense to the whole soul, then arise fixed and true
opinions and beliefs. But when reason is in the sphere of the rational, and the circle of the same moving smoothly indicates this,

[3] Reading αὐτό.

then intelligence and knowledge are of necessity perfected. And if any one affirms that in which these are found to be other than the soul, he will say the very opposite of the truth.

When the father and creator saw the image that he had made of the eternal gods moving and living, he was delighted, and in his joy determined to make his work still more like the pattern; and as the pattern was an eternal creature, he sought to make the universe the same as far as might be. Now the nature of the intelligible being is eternal, and to bestow eternity on the creature was wholly impossible. But he resolved to make a moving image of eternity, and as he set in order the heaven he made this eternal image having a motion according to number, while eternity rested in unity; and this is what we call time. For there were no days and nights and months and years before the heaven was created, but when he created the heaven he created them also. All these are the parts of time, and the past and future are created species of time, which we unconsciously but wrongly transfer to the eternal essence; for we say indeed that he was, he is, he will be, 38 but the truth is that 'he is' alone truly expresses him, and that 'was' and 'will be' are only to be spoken of generation in time, for they are motions, but that which is immovably the same cannot become older or younger by time, nor ever did or has become, or hereafter will be, older, nor is subject at all to any of those states of generation which attach to the movements of sensible things. These are the forms of time when imitating eternity and moving in a circle measured by number. Moreover, when we say that what has become has become, and what is becoming is becoming, and that what will become will become, and that what is not is not, —all these are inaccurate modes of expression. But perhaps this is not the place in which we should discuss minutely these matters.

Time, then, was created with the heaven, in order that being produced together they might be dissolved together, if ever there was to be any dissolution of them; and was framed after the pattern of the eternal nature, that it might, as far as possible, resemble it, for that pattern exists throughout all ages, and the created heaven has been, and is, and will be in all time. Such was the mind and thought of God in the creation of time. And in order to accomplish this creation, he made the sun and moon and five other stars, which are called the planets, to distinguish and preserve the numbers of time, and when God made the bodies of these several stars he gave them orbits in the circle of the other. There were seven orbits, as the stars were seven; first, there was the moon in the orbit nearest the earth, and then the sun in the next nearest orbit beyond the earth, and the morning star and the star sacred to Hermes, which revolve in their orbits as swiftly as the sun, but with an opposite principle of motion, which is the reason why the sun and Hermes and Lucifer meet or overtake, and are met or overtaken by each other. To enumerate the places which he assigned to the other stars, and the reasons of them, if they were all to be counted, though a secondary matter, would give more trouble than the primary ones. These things at some future time, when we are at leisure, may have the consideration which they deserve, but not at present.

Now, when all the stars which were needed to make time had attained a motion suitable to them, and their bodies fastened by vital chains, had come into being as living creatures, and learnt their appointed task according to the motions of the other, which is oblique, and passes through and is overruled by the motions of the same, they revolved, some in a larger and some in a lesser 39 orbit,—those which have the lesser orbit revolving faster, and those which have the larger moving more slowly. But in the movement of the same, those which revolved fastest appeared to overtake and be overtaken by those which moved slower; for all the orbits of the same moved in a spiral, because they went two ways in opposite directions, and hence that which receded most slowly from the sphere of the same, which was the swiftest, appeared to follow it most nearly. That there might be some visible measure of their relative swiftness and slowness as they proceeded in their eight courses, God lighted a fire, which we now call the sun, in the second of these orbits, that it might give light to the whole of heaven, and that the animals, who were by nature fitted, might participate in number; this was the lesson which they were to learn from the revolutions of the same and the like. Thus, then, and by these means the night and the day were created, being the period of the one most intelligent revolution. And the month was created when the moon had completed her orbit and overtaken the sun, and the year when the sun had completed his own orbit. The periods of the other stars have not

been understood by men in general, but only by a few, and they
have no name for them, and do not estimate their comparative
length by the aid of number, and hence they are hardly aware that
their wanderings, which are infinite in number and admirable for
their variety, make up time. And yet there is no difficulty in
seeing that the perfect number of time completes the perfect year
when all the eight revolutions, having their relative degrees of
swiftness, are accomplished together and again meet at their
original point of departure, measured by the circle of the same
moving equally. Thus, and to this end, came into existence such
of the stars as moved and returned through the heaven, in order
that the created heaven might be as like as possible to the perfect
and intelligible animal, and imitate the eternal nature.

Until the creation of time, all things had been made in the
likeness of that which was their pattern, but in so far as the
universe did not as yet include within itself all animals, there
was a difference. This defect the creator supplied by fashioning
them after the nature of the pattern. And as the mind perceives
ideas or species of a certain nature and number in the ideal
animal, he thought that this created world ought to have them of a
like nature and number. There are four such; one of them is the
40 heavenly race of the gods; another, the race of birds moving in the
air; the third, the watery species; and the fourth, the pedestrian
and land animals. Of the divine, he made the greater part out of
fire, that they might be the brightest and fairest to the sight, and
he made them after the likeness of the universe in the form of a
circle, and gave them to know and follow the best, distributing
them over the whole circumference of the heaven, which was to
be a true cosmos or glory spangled with them. And he bestowed
on each of them two motions; first, the motion in the same,
because they ever continue thinking about the same things, and
also a forward motion, in that they are controlled by the revolution of the same and the like; but the other five motions were
wanting in them: and thus each of them was the best possible. And for this reason also the fixed stars were created, being
divine and eternal animals, ever-abiding and revolving after the
same manner and on the same spot; and the other stars which
revolve and also wander, as has been already described, were
created after their likeness. The earth, which is our nurse,

compacted (or *circling*) around the pole which is extended through the universe, he made to be the guardian and artificer of night and day, first and eldest of gods that are in the interior of heaven. Vain would be the labour of telling about all the figures of them moving as in a dance, and their meetings with one another, and the return of their orbits on themselves, and their approximations, and to say which of them in their conjunctions meet, and which of them are in opposition, and how they get behind and before one another, and at what times they are severally eclipsed to our sight and again reappear, sending terrors and intimations of things about to happen to those who can calculate them—to attempt to tell of all this without looking at the models of them would be labour in vain. Let what we have said about the nature of the created and visible gods be deemed sufficient and have an end.

To tell of other divinities, and to know their origin, is beyond us, and we must accept the traditions of the men of old time who affirm themselves to be the offspring of the gods, and they must surely have known the truth about their own ancestors. How can we doubt the word of the children of the gods? Although they give no probable or certain proofs, still, as they declare that they are speaking of family traditions, we must believe them in obedience to the law. In this manner, then, according to them, the genealogy of these gods is to be received and narrated:—

Oceanus and Tethys were the children of Earth and Heaven, and from these sprang Phorcys and Cronos and Rhea, and many more with them; and from Cronos and Rhea sprang Zeus and Here, and all those whom we know as their brethren, and others 41 who were their children.

Now, when all of them, both those who visibly appear in their revolutions as well as those other gods who are of a more retiring nature, had come into being, the creator of the universe spoke as follows:—Gods and sons of gods who are my works, and of whom I am the artificer and father, my creations are indissoluble, if so I will. All that is bound may be dissolved, but only an evil being would wish to dissolve that which is harmonious and happy. And although being created, ye are not altogether immortal and indissoluble, ye shall certainly not be dissolved, nor be liable to the fate of death; having in my will a greater and mightier bond than those which bound you when ye were created. And, now, listen to my instructions:—Three tribes of mortal beings remain to be created,—without them the universe will be incomplete, for it will not have in it every kind of animal which a perfect world ought to have. On the other hand, if they were created and received life from me, they would be on an equality with the gods. In order then that there may be mortals, and that this universe may be truly universal, do ye, according to your natures, betake yourselves to the formation of animals, imitating the power which I showed in creating you. The divine and immortal part of them, which is the guiding principle of those who are willing to follow justice and the gods—of that divine part I will myself give you the seed and beginning. And do you then weave together the mortal and immortal, and make and beget living creatures, and give them food, and make them to grow and receive them again in death. Thus he spake, and once more and in the same manner poured the remains of the elements into the cup in which he had previously mingled the soul of the universe, no longer, however, pure as before, but diluted to the second and third degree. And when he had framed the universe he distributed souls equal in number to the stars, and assigned each soul to a star; and having placed them as in a chariot, he showed them the nature of the universe, and the decrees of destiny appointed for them, and told them that their first birth would be one and the same for all, and that no one should suffer at his hands; and that they must be sown in the vessels of the times severally adapted to them, and then there would come forth the most religious of

42 animals; and as human nature was of two kinds, the superior race would hereafter be called man. Now, as they were implanted in bodies by necessity, and objects were always approaching or receding from them, in the first place there was a necessity that they should have one natural mode of perceiving external force; in the second place, they must have love, which is a mixture of pleasure and pain; also fear and anger, and the feelings which are akin or opposite to them; if they conquered these they would live righteously, and if they were conquered by them, unrighteously. Also, he said, that he who lived well during his appointed time would return to the habitation of his star, and there have a blessed and suitable existence. But if he failed in attaining this, in the second generation he would pass into a woman, and should

he not cease from evil in that condition, he would be changed
into some brute who resembled him in his evil ways, and would
not cease from his toils and transformations until he followed the
original principle of sameness and likeness within him, and overcame, by the help of reason, the later accretions of turbulent and
irrational elements composed of fire and air and water and
earth, and returned to the form of his first and better nature.
When he had given all these laws to his creatures, that he might
be guiltless of their future evil, he sowed some of them in the
earth, and some in the moon, and some in the other stars which
are the measures of time; and when he had sown them he committed to the younger gods the fashioning of their mortal bodies,
and desired them to furnish what was still lacking to the human
soul, and make all the suitable additions, and rule and pilot
the mortal animal in the best and wisest manner that they could,
and avert all but self-inflicted evils.

When the creator had given all these commands he remained
in his own nature, and his children heard and were obedient to
their father's command, and receiving from him the immortal
principle of a mortal creature, in imitation of their own creator
they borrowed portions of fire, and earth, and water, and air from 43
the world which were hereafter to be returned—these they took
and welded together, not with the indissoluble chains by which
they were bound themselves, but with numerous pegs invisible on
account of their smallness which they welded together, forming
out of them all one body which was subject to influx and efflux,
and fastened the courses of the immortal soul in the body.　Now
these courses, detained as in a vast river, neither overcame nor
were overcome; but bore and were borne along violently, so that
the whole animal was moved and progressed, irregularly however
and irrationally, and in any direction, wandering and coursing
according to the six kinds of motion backwards and forwards, and
right and left, and up and down, and every way according to the
six directions of place.　For great as was the advancing and retiring
flood which provided nourishment, the affections produced by external contact caused still greater tumult—when the body met and
came into collision with external fire, or with the solid earth or
the gliding waters, or was caught in the whirlwind hurried along
by the air, and the motions produced by any of these impulses

were carried through the body to the soul. All such motions have consequently received the general name of 'sensations,' which they still retain. And these at the moment occasion a very great and mighty movement; they accompany the ever-flowing current, and stir and shake the courses of the soul, and altogether bind fast the course of the same with their opposing flux and hinder it from ruling and proceeding; and the nature of the other they so shake, that the three intervals which formed a progression of doubles (1, 2, 4; 8), and also of triples (1, 3, 9, 27), together with the mean terms and connecting links of the ratios of 3 : 2, and 4 : 3, and of 9 : 8, which cannot be wholly dissolved except by him who tied them together, they twist in all sorts of ways, and bend and disorder the circles as far as they can, so that they are tumbling to pieces, and move irrationally, at one time in the opposite direction, and then again obliquely, and then upside down, as you might imagine a person who is upside down and has his head leaning upon the ground and his feet up against something in the air; and when he is in such a condition, both he and the spectators fancy that the right of the other is his left, and the left right. This and the like of this is what violently moves the

44 courses when they meet with some external thing, either of the class of the same or of the other; and they speak of it as the same with something or the other of something in a manner which is the very opposite of the truth; and they become false and foolish, and there is no course or revolution in them which has a guiding or directing power; and if again any sensations enter in violently from without and drag after them the whole vessel of the soul, then though they seem to conquer they are really conquered.

And by reason of all these affections, the soul when enclosed in a mortal body is at first without sense; but when the stream of growth and nutriment flows in with diminished speed, and the courses of the soul attaining a calm go their own way and become steadier as time advances, then the revolutions of the several circles return to their natural figure, and call the same and the other by their right names, and make the possessor of them a rational being. And if these combine in him with any true nurture or education, he attains the fulness and health of the perfect man, and escapes the worst disease of all; but if he neglects

education he walks lame throughout existence in this life, and
returns imperfect and good for nothing to the world below. This,
however, is an after-stage, and our business now is to treat more
accurately of our present subject. There are previous matters
relating to the generation of the body and its members, and as to
how the soul was created, and from what causes and by what
foreknowledge of the gods, which have to be discussed; in this
enquiry we hold fast to probability—that is the path in which we
must proceed.

First, then, the gods, imitating the spherical shape of the universe, enclosed the two divine courses in a spherical body, that,
namely, which we now term the head, being the most divine part
of us and the lord of all that is in us: to this the gods who put
together the body gave all the rest to be a servant, contriving that
it should partake of every sort of motion; in order then that it
might not tumble about among the deep and high places of the
earth, but might be able to get out of the one and over the other,
they provided the body to be a vehicle and means of locomotion;
which consequently had length and was furnished with four limbs
extended and jointed; these the gods contrived as instruments of
locomotion with which it might take hold and find support, and
so be able to pass through all places, carrying on high the dwelling- 45
place of the most sacred and divine part of us. This was the
origin of legs and arms, which were therefore attached to all men;
and the gods, esteeming the front part of man as more honourable
and having more authority than the hinder part, they gave men
mostly a forward motion. Now it was necessary that man should
have his front part distinguished and unlike the rest of his body.
Wherefore also about the vessel of the head, in the first place
they put in a face in which they inserted organs to minister in all
things to the providence of the soul, and they assigned to this ante-
rior part a share of authority. And of the organs they first contrived the eyes to give light, fixing them by a cause on this wise:
they contrived that as much of fire as would not have the power of
burning, but would only give a gentle light, the light of every-day
life, should be formed into a body; and the pure fire which is
within us and akin to this they made to flow through the eyes
in a single, entire, and smooth substance, at the same time
compressing the centre of the eye so as to retain all the denser

element, and only to allow this to be sifted through pure. When therefore the light of day surrounds the stream of vision, then like falls upon like, and there is a union, and one body is formed by natural affinity according to the direction of the eyes, wherever the light that falls from within meets that which comes from an external object. And everything being affected by likeness, whatever touches and is touched by this stream of vision, their motions are diffused over the whole body, and reach the soul, producing that perception which we call sight. But when the external and kindred fire passes away in night, then the stream of vision is cut off; for going forth to the unlike element it is changed and extinguished, being no longer of one nature with the surrounding atmosphere which is now deprived of fire: and the eye no longer sees, and we go to sleep; for when the eyelids are closed, which the gods invented as the preservation of the sight, they keep in the internal fire. And the power of the fire diffuses and equalizes the inward motions; and when they are equalized there is rest, and when the rest is profound sleep comes with few dreams; but wherever the greater motions remain, whatever may be their nature and situations, they engender corresponding visions within us, and which are remembered by us when we are awake and in the external world. And now there is no longer any difficulty in understanding the creation of images in mirrors and in all smooth and bright surfaces. The fires from within and from without communicate about the smooth surface, and form one image which is variously refracted. All which phenomena necessarily arise by reason of the fire or light about the face combining with the fire or ray of light about the smooth and bright surfaces. And when the parts of the light within and the light without meet and touch in a manner contrary to the usual mode of meeting, then the right appears to be left and the left right; but the right again appears right, and the left left, when the position of one of the two concurring lights is inverted; and this happens when the smooth surface of the mirror, which is convex, repels the right stream of vision to the left side, and the left to the right[4]. Or if the mirror be turned longways, then the face appears upside down,

46

[4] He is speaking of two kinds of mirrors, first the plane, secondly the cylindrical; and the latter is supposed to be placed, first vertically, secondly horizontally.

and the upper part of the rays are driven downwards, and the lower upwards.

These are the works of the second and co-operative causes which God uses as his ministers when executing the idea of the best as far as possible. They are thought by most men not to be the second, but the prime causes of all things, which they cool and heat, and contract and dilate, and the like. But [this is not true, for] they are incapable of reason or intellect; the only being which can properly have mind is the soul, and this is invisible; whereas fire and water, and earth and air, are all of them visible bodies. Now the lover of intellect and knowledge ought to explore causes of intelligent nature first of all, and, secondly, those which are moved of others and of necessity move others. And this is what we also must do. Both kinds of causes should be considered by us, but a separation should be made of those which are endowed with mind and are the workers of things fair and good, and those which are deprived of intelligence and accomplish their several works by chance and without order. Of the second or concurrent causes of sight, which give the eyes the power which they now possess, enough has been said. I will therefore proceed to speak of the higher use and purpose for which God has given them to us. The sight in my opinion is the source 47 of the greatest benefit to us, for had the eyes never seen the stars, and the sun, and the heaven, none of the words which we have spoken about the universe would ever have been uttered. But now the sight of day and night, and the revolution of the months and years, have given us the invention of number, and a conception of time, and the power of enquiring about the nature of the whole; and from this source we have derived philosophy, than which no greater good ever was or will be given by the gods to mortal man. This, I say, is the greatest boon of sight: and of the lesser benefits why should I speak, the loss of which even the common mind would vainly bewail? Thus much let us say: that God invented and gave us sight to this end,—that we might behold the courses of intelligence in the heaven, and apply them to the courses of our own intelligence which are akin to them, the unperturbed to the perturbed; and that we, learning them and being partakers of the true computations of nature, might imitate the absolutely unerring courses of God and regulate our own vagaries. The same may be affirmed of speech and hearing; they have been given by the gods for the same ends and purposes. For speech greatly contributes to this purpose, and this is the chief use of musical sound, which is given to the hearing for the sake of harmony. And harmony, which has motions akin to the revolutions of our souls, is not regarded by him who intelligently uses the Muses as given by them with a view to irrational pleasure, which is the prevailing opinion, but with a view to the inharmonical course of the soul, and as an ally for the purpose of reducing this into harmony and agreement with itself; and rhythm was given by them for the same purpose, on account of the irregular and graceless ways which prevail among mankind generally, and to help us against them.

Thus far in what we have been saying, with small exceptions, the works of intelligence have been set forth; and now we must place by the side of them the things done from necessity—for 48 the creation is mixed, and is the result of a union of necessity and mind. Mind, the ruling power, persuaded necessity to bring the greater part of created things to perfection, and thus in the beginning, when the influence of reason got the better of necessity, the universe was created. But if a person will truly tell of the way in which this came to pass, he must include the other influence of the variable cause as well. Wherefore, we must return again and find another suitable beginning, as about the former matters, so also about these. To which end we must consider the nature of fire, and water, and air, and earth, which were prior to the generation of the heavens, and what happened before them; for no one has as yet explained their generation, but we speak of fire and the rest of them, whatever they mean, as though men knew their natures, and we maintain them to be the letters or elements of the whole, when they cannot reasonably be compared by a man of any sense even to the syllables or first compounds. And let me say thus much: I will not speak of the first principle or principles of all things, or by whatever name they are to be called, for this reason,—because it is difficult to set forth my opinion according to the mode of discussion which we are at present employing. Do not imagine, any more than I can bring myself to imagine, that I should be right in undertaking so difficult a task. I will observe the rule of probability with which I began,

and I will do my best to speak probably; and above and before
all[5] at the beginning of each and all. Once more, then, I call
upon God, at the beginning of my discourse, and beg him to be
our saviour out of a strange and unwonted enquiry, and to bring
us to probability. And now let us begin again.

This new beginning of our discussion of the universe requires a
fuller division than the former; for then we made two classes, now
a third must be added. For those two classes were sufficient for
the former discussion: one which was assumed by us to be a
pattern intelligible and always the same; and there was a second,
which was only the imitation of the pattern, generated and visible;
the third kind we did not distinguish at the time, conceiving that 49
the two would be enough. But now the argument seems to require
that we should make clear another kind, which is difficult of explanation and dimly seen. What natural power are we to attribute
to this new kind of being? Such a power as this:—that it is the
receptacle, and in a manner the nurse, of all generation. I have
said the truth; but I must give a clearer explanation, and this will
be an arduous task for many reasons, and in particular because I
must first raise questions concerning fire and the other elements, and
say what each of them is; for example, which of them is properly
called water as distinct from fire, and by what name any element
is called as distinguished from each and all of them; and to give
a certain or satisfactory proof of this is not easy. How, then,
and in what way, can we arrive at any probable conclusion in
this difficulty?

In the first place, that which we are now calling water, when
congealed becomes stone and earth, as our sight seems to show us;
and this same element, when melted and dispersed, passes into
vapour and air. Air, again, when burnt up, becomes fire; and
again fire, when condensed and extinguished, passes once more
into the form of air; and once more, air, when collected and condensed, produces cloud and vapour; and from these, when still
more compressed, comes flowing water, and from water comes
earth and stones once more; and thus generation appears to be
transmitted from one to the other in a circle. Thus, then, as the

---

[5] Or taking μᾶλλον δὲ κ.τ.λ. with the preceding words, 'but more probably;'
or laying the stress on ἀπ' ἀρχῆς, ' but above and before all, I will begin at the
beginning of each and all.'

elements never appear in the same form, how can any one have
the assurance to maintain strongly that any of them is one thing
rather than another? No one can. But much the safest plan is
to speak of them as follows:—Let us not call that which we see
to be continually changing 'fire,' but rather say, 'that some such
nature is fire;' and let us not speak of that other thing as water,
but rather say that some such nature is water; and let us not
speak of objects at all as having stability or erroneously imagine ourselves to indicate any of them by the term 'this' or
'that,' for they are too volatile to be detained in any such
expressions as this, or the nature of this, or the nature belonging to this, or any other form of language which implies
their permanence. We must not speak of them as individual
things, but rather say, of each and all of them, that there is
some such uniform principle which circulates in them; for example, of fire we should say that the general principle is of such a
nature always, and so of everything that has generation. The place
in which these principles severally grow up, and appear, and decay,
50 that alone is to be called by the name 'this' or 'that, but that
which is of a certain nature, hot or white, or their opposites, and
all that proceeds from them, are not to be so denominated. Let
me make one more attempt to explain my meaning more clearly.
Suppose a person to make all kinds of figures of gold, and never to
cease transforming out of one form into all the others;—somebody
points to one of them and asks, What is that? By far the safest
and truest answer is, That is gold; and not to speak of the triangle
or of any other figures which are formed in the gold as having real
existence, inasmuch as they are in process of change while he is
making the assertion; but if he be willing to take the general
answer, it is enough. And the same may be said of the universal
nature which receives all bodies—that must be always called the
same; for, while receiving all things, she never departs at all from
her own nature, and never in any way, or at any time, assumes a
form like that of the things which enter into it, being in fact the
natural recipient of all impressions, which is moved and fashioned
by them, and varies in appearance from time to time because of
them. Now the images of realities which enter in and go out are
modelled after their patterns in a wonderful and inexplicable manner, which shall be hereafter investigated by us. But for the

present we have only to conceive of three natures: first, that which is in process of generation; secondly, that in which the generation takes place; and thirdly, that of which the thing generated is the natural resemblance. Moreover, we may liken the receiving principle to a mother, and the source or spring to a father, and the intermediate nature to a child; and may remark further, that if the model is to take every variety of form, then the matter in which the model is fashioned, when duly prepared, must be formless, and the forms must come from without. For if the matter were like any of the supervening forms, then when any opposite or entirely different nature was impressed the representation would be a bad one, because the matter would shine through. Wherefore, that which is to receive all forms should have no form; as in making perfumes they first contrive that the liquid substance which is to receive the scent shall be as inodorous as possible. Or as those who wish to impress figures on soft substances do not allow any previous impression to remain, but make the surface as 51 even and smooth as possible. In the same way that which is to receive perpetually and through its whole extent the resemblances of eternal beings ought to be destitute of any particular form. Wherefore, the mother and receptacle of all created and visible, and in any way sensible things, is not to be termed earth, or air, or fire, or water, or any of their compounds, or any of the elements out of which they are composed, but is an invisible and formless being which receives all things and attains in an extraordinary way a portion of the intelligible, and is most incomprehensible. In saying this we shall not be far wrong; as far, however, as we can attain to a knowledge of her from the previous considerations, we may truly say that fire is that part of her nature which is inflamed, and water that which is moist, earth and air being also parts, as far as the mother substance receives the impressions of them.

Let us consider this question more precisely. Is there any self-existent fire? and are all those things of which we speak self-existent? or are only those things which we see, or in some way perceive through the bodily organs, truly existent, and no others besides them? And is all that which we call an intelligible essence nothing at all, and only a word? Here is a question which we must not leave unexamined or undetermined, or affirm too confidently that there can be no decision; neither must we interpolate in our present long discourse a digression as long, but if there be a way in which a great principle may be set forth in a few words, that will be just what we want.

Thus I state my view :—If mind and true opinion are two distinct classes, then I say that there certainly are these self-existent ideas unperceived by sense, and apprehended only by the mind; but if, as some say, true opinion differs in no respect from mind, then everything that we perceive through the body is to be considered as most real and certain. But we must affirm them to be distinct, for they have a distinct origin and are of a different nature, and the one is implanted in us by instruction, and the other by persuasion, and the one is always accompanied by true reason, and the other is without reason; the one is not to be moved by persuasion, but the other may be moved; and lastly, every man may be said to share in the one, but mind is shared only by the gods and by very few men. Wherefore, also, we must acknowledge that there is one kind of being which is always the 52 same, uncreated and indestructible, never receiving anything into itself from without, nor itself going out to any other, but invisible and imperceptible by any sense, and of which the sight is granted to intelligence only. And there is another nature of the same name with it, and like to it, perceived by sense, generated, always in motion, becoming in place and again vanishing out of place, which is apprehended by opinion and sense. And there is a third nature, which is space, and is eternal, and admits not of destruction, and provides a home for all created things, and is perceived without the help of sense, by a kind of spurious reason, and is hardly matter of belief, which we behold as in a dream, and say, that all existence must of necessity be in some place and occupy a space, and that what is neither in heaven nor in earth has no existence. These things, and others akin to these, relating to the true and waking reality of nature, we, having only this dreamlike sense of them, are unable to arouse ourselves truly to describe or to determine. For an image, not possessing that of which the image is, and existing ever as the changing shadow of some other, must for this reason be in another [i. e. in space], and in some way take hold of essence, or not be at all. But true and exact reason vindicating the nature of true being, maintains that while two things (i. e. the idea and the image) are different they cannot exist one of them in the other so as to become one and also two at the same time.

Thus have I concisely given the result of my thoughts; and my opinion is that being and space and generation, these three, in their three manners existed before the heaven; and that the nurse of generation, moistened by water and inflamed by fire, and receiving the various forms of earth and air, and experiencing all the other accidents that attach to them, took a variety of shapes; and being full of powers which were neither similar nor equally balanced, was never in any part in a state of equipoise, but swaying unevenly to and fro, was shaken by them, and by its motion again shook them, and the elements when moved were divided like the grain shaken and winnowed by fans and other instruments used in the threshing of corn, when the close and heavy particles are borne away and settle in one direction, and the loose 53 and light particles in another. In this manner the four kinds or elements were then shaken by the recipient matter which was itself moved, and like a winnowing machine separated off the elements most unlike from one another, and thrust the similar elements together. Wherefore also these had different places before the universe that was arranged out of them came into being. And at first all things were without reason and measure. But when the world began to get into order, first fire and water and earth and air, having only certain faint traces of themselves, and being altogether such as everything may be expected to be in the absence of God—this, I say, being their nature, God fashioned them by form and number. Let us always, and in all that we say, hold that God made them as far as possible the fairest and best, out of things which were not fair and good. And now I will endeavour to show you the disposition and generation of them by an unaccustomed argument, which however you will be able to follow, for the methods which I must use will be those with which your education has made you familiar.

In the first place, then, as is evident to all, fire and earth and water and air are bodies. And every sort of body possesses solidity, and every solid must necessarily be contained in planes; and the plane rectilinear figure is composed of triangles; and all triangles are originally of two kinds, both of which are made up of one right and two acute angles; one of them has at either

end of the base the half of a right angle which is divided by equal
sides, while in the other unequal parts of a right angle are
divided by unequal sides.   These, then, we assume to be the
original elements of fire and the other bodies, as we affirm, proceeding by a combination of probability with demonstration; but
the principles which are prior to these God only knows, and he
of men whom God loves.   And next we have to determine what
are the four most beautiful bodies which are unlike one another,
and yet in some instances capable of resolution into one another;
and when we have discovered this, we shall know the true origin
of earth and fire and the proportionate and intermediate elements.
And then we shall not be willing to allow that there are visible
bodies fairer than these having distinct kinds.   Wherefore we
must endeavour to join together these four forms of bodies which
excel in beauty, and be able to say that we have sufficiently
apprehended their nature.   Of the two triangles, the isosceles has
54 one form only; the scalene or unequal-sided has an infinite
number.   Of the infinite forms we must select the most beautiful,
if we are to proceed in due order.   But if any one can shew a
more beautiful form for the composition of these bodies, he shall
carry off the palm, not as an enemy, but as a friend.   Now, the
one which we maintain to be the most beautiful of all the many
figures of triangles (and we need not speak of the others) is that
of which the double forms an equilateral triangle; the reason
of this would be long to tell; he who disproves the fact and proves
that this is otherwise is entitled to a friendly victory.   Then let
us choose two triangles, out of which fire and other bodies have
been constructed, the one isosceles, the other having a longer
side the square of which is three times as great as the square of
the lesser side.

Now is the time to explain what was before obscurely said:
there was an error in imagining that all the four elements might
be generated by and into one another; this, I say, was wrong, for
there are generated from the triangles which we have taken four
kinds—three from the one which has the sides unequal; the fourth
alone is framed out of the isosceles triangle.   Hence they cannot
all be resolved into one another, or compounded into larger out
of smaller bodies, or the reverse.   But three of them can be
thus resolved and compounded, for they all spring from one, and

when the greater bodies are dissolved, many small bodies will spring up out of them and take their own proper figures; or, again, when many small bodies are distributed in triangles, a single number will unite them into one large mass of another kind. So much for their passage into one another. I have now to speak of their several kinds, and show out of what combinations of numbers each of them was formed. The first kind will be that which is smallest, and its element is that triangle which has its hypotenuse twice the lesser side. When two such triangles are joined at the diagonal, and this is repeated three times, and the triangles rest their diagonals and shorter sides on the same point as a centre, a single equilateral triangle is formed out of six triangles; and four equilateral triangles, if put together, make out of every three plane angles one solid angle [=two right angles], which is nearest to the most obtuse of plane angles; 55 and out of the combinations of these four angles arises the first solid form which distributes into equal and similar parts the whole surface. The second species of solid is formed out of the same triangles, which unite as eight equilateral triangles and form one solid angle out of four plane angles, and out of six such angles the second body is completed. And the third body is made up of 120 triangular elements, forming twelve solid angles, each of them included in five plane equilateral triangles, having altogether twenty bases, each of which is an equilateral triangle. The one element [that is, the triangle with unequal sides] having generated these figures, generates no more; but the triangle which has equal sides produces the fourth elementary figure, which is compounded of them by fours, joining their right angles in a centre, and forming one equilateral quadrangle. Six of these united form eight solid angles, each of which is made by the combination of three plane right angles; the figure of the body thus composed is a cube, having six plane quadrangular equilateral bases. There was yet a fifth combination which God used in the delineation of the universe.

Now, he who, reflecting on all this, enquires whether the worlds are to be regarded as infinite or finite, will be of opinion that the notion of their infinity is characteristic of a very indefinite and ignorant mind. There is, however, more reason in doubting whether they are to be truly regarded as one or five. My opinion is that they are one, and this I deem probable; another, regarding the question from another point of view, may be of another mind. But, leaving this enquiry, let us proceed to distribute the elementary forms, which have now been created in idea, among the four elements.

To earth, then, let us assign the cubical form; for earth is the most immoveable of the four and the most easily modelled of all bodies, and that which has the most stable bases must of necessity be of such a nature. Now, of the triangles which we mentioned at first, that which is of equal sides is by nature more stable than that which has unequal sides; and of the compound figures which are formed out of either, the plane equilateral quadrangle has a more stable and necessary basis than the equilateral triangle, both in the whole and in the parts. Wherefore, in assigning this figure to earth, we adhere to probability; and to water we assign that one of the remaining forms which is the most immoveable; and the most moveable to fire; and to air that which is intermediate between them. Also we assign the smallest body to fire, and the greatest to water, and the intermediate body to air; and, again, the acutest body to fire, and the next in acuteness to air, and the third to water. Of all these elements, that which has the fewest bases must necessarily be the most moveable and the acutest and most penetrating in every direction; and must also be the lightest as being composed of the smallest number of similar particles: and the second body has similar properties in a second degree, and the third body in the third degree. Let it be agreed, then, both according to strict reason and according to probability, that the solid form of the pyramid is the original element and seed of fire; and let us assign the second element in the order of generation to air, and the third to water. We must imagine all these to be so small that no single particle of any of the four kinds is seen by us on account of their smallness: but when many of them are collected together the aggregate is seen. And the ratios of their numbers, motions, and other properties, everywhere the God, as far as necessity consented and allowed, has exactly perfected, and harmonized them all in due proportion.

From all that we have just been saying, the most probable result is as follows:—earth, meeting with fire and dissolved

by its sharpness, is borne hither and thither, either by dissolution
in the fire itself or in the air or in the water, until its parts,
meeting together and mutually harmonizing, again become earth,
for they can never take any other form. But water, when divided
by fire or by air, on reuniting, becomes one part fire and two
parts air; and a single volume of air divided becomes two of fire.
Again, when a small body of fire is contained in a larger body of
air or water or earth, and both are moving, and the fire struggling
is overcome and decomposed, then two volumes of fire form one
volume of air; and when air is overcome and cut up into small
pieces, two and a half parts of air are condensed into one part
of water. Let us consider the matter in this way again. When
one of the other elements is fastened upon by the fire, and is 57
cut by the sharpness of its angles and sides, it coalesces with
the fire, and then ceases to be cut by them any longer. For
among bodies which are similar and uniform, none can change
or be changed by another of the same class and in the same state.
But in the process of transition, and during the conflict of the
weaker with the stronger, the dissolution continues. Again,
smaller bodies detained in larger ones, the few encompassed by
the many, which are in process of decomposition and extinction,
only cease from their tendency to extinction when they consent
to pass into the conquering nature, and fire becomes air and air
water. But if one kind of bodies goes and does battle against
bodies of another kind, the process of dissolution continues until
they are completely ejected and dissolved, and make their escape to
the kindred element, or else, being overcome and assimilated to the
conquering power, they remain and dwell with their victors, and
from being many become one. And owing to these affections, all
things are changing their place, for the motion of the receiving
principle distributes the multitude of classes into their natural
places; but those things which become unlike themselves and
like other things are hurried by the concussion into the place of
the things which they resemble.

Now all unmixed and primary bodies are produced by these
causes. As to the subordinate species which are included in the
greater kinds, they are to be attributed to the various constitutions
of the two original triangles. For these differ in magnitude, and
are larger and smaller and have as many sizes as there are

differences of species. Hence when mingled with themselves
and with one another they are infinite in their diversity, which
those who would arrive at the probable reason of nature ought
duly to study.

Unless a person comes to an understanding about the nature
and conditions of rest and motion, he will meet with many difficulties in the discussion which follows. Something has been said
of this matter already, and something more remains to be said,
which is, that motion never exists in equipoise. For to conceive
that anything can be moved without a mover is hard or indeed
impossible, and equally impossible to conceive that there can be a
mover without something that will be moved;—motion cannot
exist where these are wanting, and for these to be in equipoise is
impossible, and therefore we assign rest to equipoise and motion
to the want of equipoise; and inequality is the cause of the
nature which is wanting in equipoise. Of this inequality we
have already described the origin. But there still remains the
question, why things when divided after their kinds do not cease
from motion and transition from one into another; this we will
now proceed to explain. The revolution of the universe in which
are comprehended all natures, being circular and having a tendency to unite with itself, compresses all things and will not
allow any place to be left void Wherefore, also, fire above all
things penetrates everywhere, and air next, as being next in rarity
of the elements; and the rest in like manner penetrate according
to their degrees of rarity. For those things which are composed
of the largest particles have the largest void left in their compositions, and those which are composed of the smallest particles have
the least. And the tendency towards condensation thrusts the
smaller particles into the interstices of the larger. And thus,
when the small parts are placed side by side with the larger, and
the lesser divide the greater and the greater unite the lesser, all
the elements are borne up and down and every way towards their
own places; for the change in the size of each changes their
position in space. And these causes generate an inequality which
is always maintained, and is continually creating a perpetual
motion of the elements in all time.

In the next place we have to consider that there are divers kinds
of fire. There are, for example, first, flame; and secondly, those

emanations of flame which do not burn but only give light to the eyes; thirdly, the remains of fire, which are seen in things red-hot after the flame has been extinguished. There are similar differences in the air; of which the brightest part is called the aether, as the most turbid sort of air is called mist and darkness; and there are various other nameless kinds which are formed by the inequality of the triangles. Water, again, admits in the first place of a division into two kinds; the one liquid and the other fusile. The liquid kind is composed of the small and unequal particles of water; and moves itself and is moved by other bodies because of the inequality of the particles and the shape of the figure; whereas the fusile kind being formed of large and equal elements is more stable than the other, and is solid and compact by reason of its equability. But when fire gets in and dissolves and destroys the equability, it becomes more moveable, and when capable of motion is repelled by the neighbouring air and spread upon the earth; and this dissolution of the solid masses is called melting, and the spreading out upon the earth is called flowing. 59 When the fire goes out again it does not pass into a vacuum, but into the neighbouring air; and the air which is displaced forces together the liquid and still moveable mass into the place which was occupied by the fire, and mingles it with itself. Thus compressed the mass resumes its equability, and is again at unity with itself, because the fire which was the author of the inequality has retreated; and this departure of the fire is called cooling, and the coming together which follows upon it is termed congealment. Of all the kinds termed fusile, that which is the densest and is formed out of the finest and most equable parts is that most precious possession which is called gold, and is hardened by filtration through rock; this is unique in kind, and has a bright and yellow colour. A matrix of gold, which is so dense as to be very hard, and is blackened, is termed adamant. There is also another kind which has parts nearly like gold, and of which there are several species; this, which is denser than gold, and contains but a small and fine portion of earth, and is therefore harder, and yet because of the great interstices within is lighter, is a sort of bright and condensed fluid, and when made into a mass is called brass (?). There is an alloy of earth mingled with it, and when the two parts grow old and are disunited, this comes out in the form of what is called rust. The remaining phenomena of the same kind there will be no difficulty in reasoning out by the method of probabilities. A man may sometimes set aside the arguments about eternal things, and for recreation turn to consider the truths of generation which are probable only; thus he attains a pleasure not to be repented of, and makes for himself during his life a wise and moderate pastime. Let us continue to grant ourselves this indulgence, and recount the series of probabilities which follows next in order.

The water which is mingled with fire being of that sort which is fine and liquid, is called liquid, because of its motion and the way in which it rolls upon the earth; and soft, because its bases give way and are less stable than those of earth. This, when separated from fire and air and isolated, becomes more equable, and by their retirement is compressed into itself; and when thus compressed above the earth is called hail, and when on the earth, ice; and that which is congealed in a less degree and is only half solid, when above the earth is called snow, and when upon the earth, and condensed from dew, hoar-frost. Then, again, there are the numerous kinds of water which have been mingled with one another, and are distilled through plants which grow in the earth; and this class is called by the general name of juices or saps. The unequal admixture of these fluids creates a variety of species; most of which are nameless, but four which are of a fiery nature are clearly distinguished and have names. First, there is wine, which warms the soul as well as the body;—secondly, there is the oily nature, which is smooth and divides the light of vision, and for this reason is bright and shining and of a glistening appearance, including pitch, the juice of the castor berry, oil, and other things of a like nature; also, thirdly, there is the diffusive class, which produce sweetness extending as far as the passages of the mouth;—these are included under the general name of honey: and, lastly, there is opium (?), which differs from all other juices, and is a frothy liquid having a burning quality which dissolves the flesh.

As to the kinds of earth, that which is filtered through water passes into stone in the following manner:—the water which mixes with the earth and is broken up in the process, passes into air, and taking this form mounts into its own place. And as there is no vacuum the neighbouring air is thrust out, and this being heavy and diffused and coagulated around the mass of earth, violently compresses it and drives it into the vacant space from whence the new air had come up; and the earth when compressed by the air into an indissoluble union with water becomes rock. The fairer sort is that which is made up of equal and similar parts and is transparent; that which has the opposite qualities is inferior. But when all the watery part is suddenly drawn out by fire, a more brittle substance is formed, to which we give the name of pottery. Sometimes also the moisture may remain, and the earth which has been fused by fire becomes, when cool, a stone of a black colour. A like separation of the water may occur in substances composed of finer particles of earth, and of a briny nature, and then a half-solid body is formed, soluble in water— either nitre which is used for purifying oil and earth, or else salt, which harmonizes so well in the combinations of the palate, and is, as the law testifies, a substance dear to the gods. The compounds of earth and water are not soluble by water, but by fire only, and for this reason:—neither fire nor air melt masses of earth; this is owing to the smallness of their particles, which enables them easily to penetrate the larger interstices of earth without violence; and they leave the earth unmelted and undissolved, but the particles of water being larger force a passage and dissolve and melt the earth. Earth when not 61 thus consolidated by force is dissolved by water only; when consolidated, by nothing but fire; this is the only body which can find an entrance. The cohesion of water again when very strong is dissolved by fire only—when weaker, then either by air or fire— the former entering the interstices, and the latter penetrating even to the triangles. But nothing can dissolve air when strongly condensed, which does not reach the elements or triangles; or if not strongly condensed, then only fire can dissolve it. As to bodies composed of earth and water, while the water occupies the vacant interstices of the earth and holds them compacted together, the circumfluent particles of water finding no entrance leave the entire mass unaffected; but the particles of fire entering into the interstices of the water, do to the air as the water does to the earth, and are the sole causes of the compound body of earth and water liquefying and becoming fluid. Now these bodies are of two kinds; some of them, such as glass and the fusible sort of stones, have less water than they have earth; on the other hand, substances of the nature of wax and incense have more of water entering into their composition.

I have thus set forth the various forms and classes of bodies as they are diversified by their combinations and changes into one another, and now I must endeavour to show how the feelings are produced with which they impress us. In the first place, the bodies which I have been describing are necessarily objects of sense. But we have not yet considered the origin of flesh, or what belongs to flesh, or that part of the soul which is mortal. And these things cannot be explained without also explaining the perceptions of sense; nor can the latter be fully explained without these: and yet to explain them together is hardly possible, for which reason we must explain one first, and then proceed to the other. In order, then, that the enquiry may proceed regularly, let us begin by speaking of the affections which equally concern body and soul.

First, let us see why we say that fire is hot, reasoning from the dividing or cutting power which it exercises on our bodies. We all of us feel that fire is sharp; and we may further consider the fineness of the sides, and the sharpness of the angles, and the smallness of the particles, and the swiftness of the motion; all this makes the action of fire violent and sharp, and enables it to cut whatever it meets. And we must not forget that the 62 original figure of fire [i. e. the pyramid], more than any other form, has a dividing power which cuts our bodies into small pieces, and thus naturally produces that affection to which we give the name of heat, which is derived from this (θερμὸς, cp. θερίζω, κερματίζω). Now, the opposite of this is sufficiently manifest, yet for the sake of completeness may here be added. For in the case of moist natures which have to do with the body, the larger particles entering in and driving out the lesser, but not being able to take their places, compress the moist principle in us, which, from being unequal and disturbed, is forced by them into a state of rest and equability, and made to coagulate by pressure. Whereas things brought together contrary to nature are naturally at war, and repel one another; and to this war and convulsion the name of shivering and trembling is given; and the whole affection and the cause of the affection are both termed cold. That is called hard to which our flesh yields, and soft which yields to our flesh; and things are also termed hard and soft relatively to one another. That which yields has a small base; but that which rests on quadrangular bases is firmly posed and offers the greatest resistance, and is also that which is the most compact and therefore repellent. The nature of the light and the heavy will be best understood when examined in connection with our notions of above and below; for it is quite wrong to suppose that the universe is parted into two regions, separate from and opposite to each other, the one a lower one to which all things tend which have any bulk, and an upper one to which things only ascend against their will. For as the universe is a globe, all the extremities being equidistant from the centre are equally extremities, and the centre which is equidistant from them is equally to be regarded as the opposite of them all. Such being the nature of the world, when a person says that anything is above and below, may he not justly be charged with using an improper expression? For the centre of the world cannot be rightly called either above or below, but is the centre and nothing else; and the circumference is not the centre, and has in no one part a greater tendency to the centre than in any of the opposite parts. Indeed, when the parts are in every direction similar, how can one rightly give them names which imply opposition? For if there were any solid body in equipoise at the centre of the 63 universe, it could not be carried to any of the extremes on account of their perfect similarity; and if a person were to go round it in a circle, he would often, when standing at the antipodes, speak of the same as above and below; for, as I was saying just now, to speak of the whole which is in the form of a globe as having one part above and another below is not like a sensible man. The reason why these terms are used, and the cases in which they are ordinarily applied by us to the division of the heavens, may be elucidated by the following supposition:—If a person were to stand in that part of the universe which is the appointed place of fire, and where there is the great mass of fire to which fiery bodies gather—if, I say, he were to ascend thither, and, having the power to do this, were to abstract particles of fire and put them in scales and weigh them, and then, raising the balance, were to draw the fire by force towards the uncongenial element of the air, it would be very evident that the smaller mass would yield more readily than the larger; for when two things are simultaneously raised by one and the same power, the smaller body must necessarily yield to the superior power with less reluctance than the larger; and the larger body is called heavy and said to tend downwards, and the smaller body is called light and said to tend upwards. And we may detect ourselves who are upon the earth doing precisely the same thing. For we often separate earthy natures, and sometimes we draw the earth itself into the uncongenial element of air by force and contrary to nature, both tending to cling to their native element. But that which is smaller yields to the impulse given by us towards the dissimilar elements more easily than the larger; and the former we call light and the place towards which it is impelled we call above, and the contrary state and place we call heavy and below respectively. These must necessarily differ from one another, because the principal masses of the different elements hold opposite positions; for that which is light in the one place is opposed to that which is light in the other, and the heavy to the heavy, and that which is below to that which is below, and that which is above to that which is above; and in their various states of being and becoming they will all be found to be contrary and transverse and in every way diverse in relation to one another. And about all of them this has to be considered :–that the tendency of each towards the kindred elements makes the body which is moved heavy, and the place towards which the motion tends below, and of things which are in a contrary position the contrary is true. Such are the causes which we assign to these phenomena. As to the soft and the rough, every one who sees them will be able to explain the reason of them to another. For roughness is hardness mingled with inequality, and smoothness is produced by the joint effect of equality and density.

64   The most important of the affections which concern the whole body remains to be considered. This is the cause of pleasure and pain in the things which we have mentioned, and in all other things which are perceived by sense through the parts of the body, and have pleasures and pains consequent upon them. Let us imagine the causes of every affection, whether of sense or not,

to be of the following nature, remembering that we have already
distinguished between the nature which moves and that which is
immoveable; for this is the direction in which we must hunt
the prey which we mean to take. A body which is easily moved
on receiving any slight impression communicates this to the parts
affected, and these to other parts in an ever widening circle, until
at last reaching the principle of mind they announce the power
of the agent. But a body of the opposite kind, being at rest, and
having no circular motion, is alone affected, and does not move
any of the neighbouring parts; and thus the parts not distributing
their first impression to other parts, having no effect of motion
on the whole animal, produce no effect on the patient. This
is true of the bones and hair and other more earthy parts of the
human body; whereas what was said above relates mainly to
sight and hearing, because they have in them the greatest force
of fire and air. Now, we must conceive of pleasure and pain
in this way. An impression produced in us contrary to nature
and violent, if sudden, is painful; and, again, the sudden return
to nature is pleasant, and that which is gentle and gradual is
imperceptible and *vice versa*. The affection which is easily produced is most readily perceived, and not accompanied by pleasure
or pain; as, for example, the affections of sight itself, which has
been already said to be in the day-time a body in close union
with us; for in the use of sight cuttings and burnings and other
affections do not produce pain, nor, again, is there pleasure when
the sight returns to its natural state; but the strongest and
clearest perceptions are produced in as far as the sense is affected
and in proportion as the sight itself meets objects; for there is
no such thing as violence either in the composition or division
of sight. But bodies which are formed of larger particles yield to
the agent only with a struggle; and then they impart their motions
to the whole and cause pleasure and pain—pain when alienated
from their natural conditions, and pleasure when restored to
them. Things which experience gradual withdrawings and emp- 65
tyings of their nature, and great and sudden replenishments, fail
to perceive the emptying, and do perceive the replenishment;
these occasion no pain, but the greatest pleasure to the mortal
part of the human soul, as is manifest in the case of perfumes.
But things which are changed all of a sudden, and only gradually

and with difficulty return to their own nature, have all the opposite effects, as is evident in the case of burnings and cuttings of the body.

Thus have we discussed the general affections of the whole body, and the names of the agents which produce them. And now I will endeavour to speak of the affections of particular parts, and the causes and agents of them, as far as I am able. In the first place let us add what was omitted when we were speaking of juices, concerning the affections peculiar to the tongue. These, like most of the other affections, appear to be caused by certain compositions and divisions, but they have also more of roughness and smoothness than is found in other affections; for whenever earthy particles enter into the small veins which are the testing instruments of the tongue, reaching to the heart, and fall upon the moist, delicate portions of flesh—when by the process of melting they contract and dry up the little veins, they are astringent if they are rougher, but if not so rough then only harsh. Those of them which are of an abstergent nature, and wash the parts about the tongue, if they do this in excess, and take up into themselves and consume away a part of its nature, like potash and soda, are all termed bitter. Those, again, which are of a weaker sort, and which purge only moderately, are called salt, and have no bitterness or roughness, but are regarded rather as agreeable. Bodies which share in and are softened by the heat of the mouth, and which are inflamed, and again in turn inflame that which heats them, and whose lightness is such that they are carried upwards to the sensations of the head, and cut all that comes in their way, by reason of these qualities in them, are all termed pungent. But 66 when these same particles, refined away by putrefaction, enter into the narrow veins, and there meet the earthy and airy particles, and set them whirling, and while they are in a whirl cause them to interpenetrate with one another and form new hollows exterior to the particles which enter—as happens with the hollow drop surrounding the air, which is sometimes mixed with earth and sometimes pure, in the latter case forming hollow watery vessels of air of a circular shape, pure and transparent, which are called bubbles, while those composed of the earthy liquid which is in a state of general agitation and rising, are called boiling or fermentation;—of all these affections the cause is termed acid.

And there is the opposite affection arising from an opposite cause, when the composition of the particles which enter dissolved in liquid is congenial to the tongue, and smoothes and oils over the roughness, and relaxes the parts which are unnaturally contracted, and contracts the parts which are relaxed, and disposes them all according to their nature; that sort of remedy of violent affections is pleasant and agreeable to every man, and has the name sweet. Enough of this.

As to the faculty of smell, that does not admit of kinds; for all smells are but half-formed substances, and no element is so proportioned as to have any smell. The veins about the nose are too narrow to admit the various kinds of earth and water, and too wide to admit those of fire and air; and for this reason no one ever smells any of them, but smells always proceed from bodies that are damp, or putrefying, or liquefying, or smoking, and are perceptible only in the intermediate state, when water is changing into air and air into water, and all of them are either smoke or mist. That which is passing out of air into water is mist, and that which is passing from water into air is smoke; and hence all smells are thinner than water and thicker than air. The proof of this is, that when there is any obstruction to the respiration, and a man draws in his breath by force, then no smell filters through, but the air only without the smell penetrates; and this is the reason why there are only two varieties of them, because they are not com-67 posed of many simple elements, and they have no name, but are distinguished as painful and pleasant, the one irritating and disturbing the whole cavity which is situated between the head and the navel, the other having a soothing influence, and restoring this same region to an agreeable and natural condition.

And now we have to speak of hearing, which is a third kind of sense, and of the causes in which this affection originates. We may assume speech to be a blow which passes through the ears, and is transmitted by means of the air, the brain, and the blood, to the soul, and that hearing is the motion of this blow, which begins in the head and ends in the region of the liver; and the sound which moves swiftly is acute, and the sound which moves slowly is grave, and that which is uniform is equable and smooth, and the reverse is harsh. A great body of sound is loud, and the opposite is low. Respecting the harmony of sounds I must hereafter speak.

There is a fourth class of sensible things, comprehending many varieties, which have now to be distinguished. They are called by the general name of colours, and are a flame which emanates from all bodies, and has particles corresponding to the sense of sight. I have spoken already, in what has preceded, of the causes of the generation of sight, and this will be a natural and suitable place in which to give some account of colour.

Of the particles coming from other bodies which fall upon the sight, some are less and some are greater, and some are equal to the parts of the sight itself. Those which are equal are imperceptible, or transparent, as they are called by us, whereas the larger contract, the smaller dilate the sight, having a power akin to that of hot and cold bodies on the flesh, or of astringent bodies on the tongue, or of those heating bodies which are termed pungent by us. White and black, although they are found in another class of objects, and for this reason are imagined to be different, are affections of the same kind. Wherefore, we ought to term that white which dilates the visual ray, and the opposite of this black. There is also a swifter motion and impact of another sort of fire which dilates the ray of sight and reaches the eyes, forcing a way
68 through their passages and melting them, and eliciting from them a union of fire and water which we call tears, being itself an opposite fire which comes to them from without—the one flashes forth like lightning, and the other finds a way in and is extinguished in the tear-drop, and all sorts of colours are generated in the mixture. This affection we term dazzling, and that which produces it is called bright and flashing. There is another sort of fire which is intermediate, and which reaches and mingles with the moisture of the eye without flashing; and in this, the fire mingling with the ray of the tear-drop produces a colour like blood, to which we give the name of red. A bright hue mingled with red and white gives the colour called auburn (ξανθόν). The law of proportion, however, in which the several colours are formed, even if a man knew he would be foolish if he attempted to tell, as he could not give any necessary reason, nor even any tolerable or probable account of them. Again, red, when mingled with black and white, gives a purple hue, which becomes umber (ὄρφνινον) when the colours are burnt as well as mingled and the black is more thoroughly mixed with them. Flame colour

(πυρρὸν) is produced by a union of auburn and dun (φαιὸν), and dun by an admixture of black and white; pale yellow (ὠχρὸν) by an admixture of white and auburn. White and light meeting, and falling upon a full black, become dark blue (κυανοῦν), and when dark blue mingles with white, a light blue (γλαυκὸν) colour is formed, as leek green (πράσιον) is formed also out of the union of flame colour and black. There will be no difficulty in seeing how other colours are to be mingled and assimilated in accordance with probability. He, however, who should attempt to test the truth of them in fact, would forget the difference of the human and divine nature. For God only has the knowledge and also the power which are able to combine many things into one and again dissolve the one into many. But no man either is or ever will be able to accomplish either of these operations.

These are the elements, thus of necessity then subsisting, which the creator of the fairest and best received in the world of generation, when he made the self-sufficing and most perfect God, using the secondary causes as his ministers in the creation of these things, but himself fashioning the good in all his creations. Wherefore we may distinguish two sorts of causes, the one divine and the other necessary, and may seek for the divine in all things, as far as our nature admits, for the sake of the blessed life; but the 69 necessary kind only for the sake of the divine, considering that without them and when isolated from them, these higher things for which we look cannot be apprehended or received or in any way attained by us.

Seeing, then, that we have now before us the various classes of causes which are the material out of which the remainder of our discourse is to be framed, just as wood is the material of the carpenter, let us recur rapidly to the point at which we began, and then let us endeavour to add on a suitable beginning and ending to our tale.

As I said then at first, when all things were in disorder God created in each thing, both in reference to itself and to other things, certain harmonies in such degree and manner as they are capable of having proportion and harmony. For in those days nothing had any order except by accident; nor did any of the things which now have names deserve to be named at all—as, for example, fire, water, and the rest of the elements. All these the creator first arranged, and out of them he constructed the universe, which was a single animal comprehending all other animals, mortal and immortal, in itself. Now of the divine, he himself was the creator, but committed to his offspring the creation of the mortal. And they, imitating him, received from him the immortal principle of the soul; and around this they fashioned a mortal body, and made the whole body to be a vehicle of the soul, and constructed within, a soul of another nature which was mortal, subject to terrible and irresistible affections, first of all, pleasure, the greatest incitement of evil; then pain, which deters from good; also rashness and fear, foolish counsellors, anger implacable, and hope easily deceived by sense without reason and by all-daring love;—these they mingled together according to necessary laws, and framed man. Wherefore, fearing to pollute the divine any more than is necessary, they separated the mortal nature and gave that a habitation in another part of the body, placing the neck between them to be the isthmus and boundary line, which they constructed between the head and the breast, that they might be kept distinct. And in the breast, and in what is termed the thorax or breastplate of man, they encased the mortal soul, and as one part of this was superior and the other inferior

70 they divided the cavity of the thorax into two parts, as the women's and men's apartments are divided in houses; and placed the midriff to be a wall of partition between them. That part of the inferior soul which is endowed with courage and spirit and loves contention they settled nearer the head, in the interval between the midriff and the neck, in order that it might be under the control of reason and might join with it in forcing and restraining the desires when they are no longer willing of their own accord to obey the command of reason issuing from the citadel.

The heart, which is at once the source[3] of the veins and the fountain of the blood which is in rapid circulation through all the limbs, they placed in the guard-house, that when the spirit was roused at the instigation of reason making proclamation of any wrong assailing them from without or being perpetrated by the desires from within, quickly the whole power of feeling in the body, perceiving these commands and threats, might obey and follow through every turn and alley, and thus allow the principle

[3] Or reading αμμα, the knot.

of the best to have the command in all of them.   But as the gods foreknew that the palpitation of the heart, in the expectation of danger or in the excitement of anger, was caused by fire, and that this led to the swellings of passion, they formed and implanted the lung as a sort of aid to it.   Now this was, in the first place, soft and bloodless, and also had within hollows like the pores of a sponge, in order that, receiving the breath and the drink and cooling them, it might give the power of respiration and alleviate the heat.   Wherefore also they cut the passages of the trachea which lead to the lung, and placed the lung about the heart as a soft spring, that, when anger was rife in it, the heart, beating against the yielding body, might be refreshed and alleviated, and might thus become more ready to accompany passion in the service of reason.

The part of the soul which desires meats and drinks and such things as the bodily frame needs, they placed between the midriff and the navel, contriving in all this region a sort of manger for the food of the body; and there they bound the desires down as a wild animal which was chained up with man, and must be nourished if man was to exist.   In order that this lower creature might be always feeding at the manger, and have his dwelling as far as possible from the council chamber, making as little noise and disturbance as possible, and permitting the best part to advise quietly for the good of the whole, they appointed for him this place.   And knowing that this principle in man would not listen 71 to reason, and even if attaining to some degree of perception would never naturally care for any arguments, and was liable to be led away by phantoms and visions of the night and also by day, God, considering this, framed the liver, to connect with the lower nature and to dwell there, contriving that it should be compact and smooth, and bright and sweet, and also bitter, in order that the power of thought, which originates in the mind, might be reflected as in a mirror which receives and gives back images to the sight. And this power, being akin to the bitter part of the liver, by the help of that inspires terror, and comes threatening and invading, and suddenly mingling with the entire liver produces colours like bile, and contracts every part and makes it wrinkled and rough; or, on the other hand, twisting out of their right place and contracting the lobe and receptacles and gates, or again, closing and shutting them up—in these and other ways creates pain and disgust. And the converse happens when some gentle inspiration of the understanding pictures images of an opposite character, and allays the bile and bitterness by not stirring them, and refuses to touch the nature opposed to itself, but by making use of the natural sweetness of the liver, straightens all things and makes them to be right and smooth and free, and makes the portion of the soul which resides about the liver happy and joyful, having in the night a time of peace and moderation, and the power of divination in sleep when it no longer participates in sense and reason. For the authors of our being, remembering the command of their father when he bade them make the human race as good as they could, thus ordered our inferior parts in order that they too might obtain a measure of truth, and in the liver placed their oracle, which is a sufficient proof that God has given the art of divination to the foolishness of man. For no man, when in his senses, attains prophetic truth and inspiration; but when he receives the inspired word either his intelligence is enthralled by sleep, or he is demented by some distemper or possession. And he who would understand what he remembers to have been said, 72 whether in dream or when he was awake, by the prophetic and enthusiastic nature, or what he has seen, must recover his senses; and then he will be able to explain rationally what all such words and apparitions mean, and what indications they afford to this man or that, of past, present, or future good and evil. But, while he continues demented, he cannot judge of the visions which he sees or the words which he utters; the ancient saying is very true that 'only a man in his senses can act or judge about himself and his own affairs.' And for this reason it is customary to appoint diviners or interpreters as discerners of the oracles of the gods. Some persons call them prophets; they do not know that they are only repeaters of dark sayings and visions, and are not to be called prophets at all, but only interpreters of prophecy.

Such is the nature and position of the liver, which is intended to give prophetic intimations. During the life of each individual these intimations are plainer, but after his death the liver becomes blind, and delivers oracles too obscure to be intelligible. The spleen is situated in the neighbourhood on the left-hand side, and is constructed with a view of keeping the liver bright and pure, like a sponge, always ready prepared and at hand to clean the mirror. And hence, when any impurities arise by reason of disorders of the body affecting the liver, the loose nature of the spleen, which is composed of a hollow and bloodless tissue, receives them all and purges them away, and when filled with the unclean matter, becomes enlarged and diseased, but, again, when the body is purged, settles down into the same place as before, and is humble.

Concerning the soul, as to which part is mortal and which divine, and where they exist, and what are their conditions, and why they are separated, the truth can only be established, as has been said, by the word of God; still, we may venture to assume that what has been said by us is probable, and will be rendered more probable by investigation. Let us affirm this.

The creation of the body comes next, and this we may investigate in a similar manner. And it appears to be very meet that the body should be framed on the following principles:—

The authors of our race were aware that we should be intemperate in eating and drinking, and take a good deal more than was necessary or proper, by reason of gluttony. In order then that disease might not quickly destroy us, and lest our mortal race should perish and fail of fulfilling its end—intending to provide 73 against this, the gods made a receptacle for the superfluous meat and drink, which is called the lower belly, and formed the convolution of the bowels, so that the food might be prevented from passing quickly through and compel the body to require more food, thus producing insatiable gluttony, and making the whole race an enemy to philosophy and music, and rebellious against the divinest element within us.

The bones and flesh, and other similar parts of us, were made as follows. The first principle of all of them was the generation of the marrow. For the bonds of life which unite the soul with the body are made fast there, and they are the root and foundation of the human race. The marrow itself is created out of other elements: God took such of the triangles as were of the first formation, straight and smooth, and specially adapted by their perfection to produce fire and water, and air and earth—these, I say, he separated from their kinds, and mingling them in due proportions with one another, made the marrow out of them to be a universal seed

of the whole race of mankind; and after that he planted and
enclosed in this the various kinds of souls, and in the original
distribution gave the marrow as many and various forms as there
were hereafter to be kinds of souls. That which, like a field, was
to receive the divine seed, he made round every way, and called
that portion of the marrow, brain, intending that, when an animal
is perfected, the vessel containing this substance should be the
head; but as touching the remaining and mortal part of the soul
—that which was intended to contain this—he divided into round
and long figures, and he called them all by the name 'marrow,'
and from these, as from anchors, casting the bonds of the whole
soul, he proceeded to fashion around them the entire framework
of our body, constructing for the marrow, first of all, a complete
covering of bones.

The bones were composed by him in the following manner.
Having sifted pure and smooth earth he kneaded it and wetted it
with marrow, and after that he put it into the fire and then into
the water, and once more into the fire and again into the water
in this way by frequent transfers from one to the other he made
it insoluble by either. With this bone he fashioned, as in a lathe,
74 a globe made of bone, which he placed around the brain, and in
this globe he left a narrow opening; and around the marrow of
the neck and back he formed the vertebrae like hinges, beginning
at the head and extending through the whole of the trunk. Thus
he preserved the entire seed, which he enclosed in a case like
stone, inserting joints, and using in them the intermediate nature
of the other, in order to obtain motion and flexion. Then again,
considering that the bone would be too brittle and inflexible, and
when inflamed and again cooled would soon mortify and destroy the
seed within—having this in view, he contrived the sinews and the
flesh, that so binding all the members together by the sinews,
which admitted of being stretched and relaxed about the vertebrae, he might thus make the body capable of flexion and extension, while the flesh would serve as a protection against the
summer heat and against the winter cold, and also against falls,
like articles made of felt, softly and easily yielding to external
bodies, and containing in itself a warm moisture which in summer
exudes in the form of dew, and imparts to the body a natural
coolness; and again in winter by the help of its own fire forms a

very tolerable defence against external and surrounding cold. The
great moulder and creator considering this, mingled earth with fire
and water and put them together, making a ferment of acid and
salt which he mingled with them and formed a soft and pulpy
flesh ; and as for the sinews, he made them of an unfermented
mixture of bone and flesh, attempered so as to be in a mean, and
gave them a yellow colour, and hence the sinews have a firmer
and more glutinous nature than flesh, but a softer and moister
nature than the bones. With these God covered the bones and
marrow, which he bound together with sinews, and then enshrouded
them all in an upper covering of flesh. The more living and
sensitive of the bones he enclosed in the smallest film of flesh,
and those which had the least life he enclosed in the most solid
flesh. So again on the joints of the bones, where reason indicated
that no more was required, he placed only a small quantity of flesh,
that it might not interfere with the flexion of our bodies and make
them uneasy because difficult to move ; and also that they might
not by being crowded and pressed and matted in one another, lose
the power of sensation by reason of their hardness, and make the
parts which have to do with the mind dull of remembering and
hearing. Wherefore also the thighs and the legs and the loins, 75
and the bones of the shoulders and the forearms and other parts
which have no joints, and the inner bones, which on account of
the rarity of the soul in the marrow are destitute of reason—all
these are filled up with flesh ; but such as have feeling are in
general less fleshy, except where the creator has made some part
solely of flesh ; as, for example, the tongue, in order to give sensation. But generally this is not the case. For the combination
of solid bone and much flesh with acute perceptions, is contrary to
the laws of the composite nature. More than any other part the
framework of the head would have had them, if they could have
co-existed, and the human race, having a strong and fleshy and
sinewy head, would have had a life twice and many times as long,
and also more healthy and free from pain. But our creators
considering whether they should make a long-lived race which was
worse, or a short-lived race which was better, came to the conclusion that the preference should be given by every one to a shorter
span of life which was better, rather than to a longer one which
was worse ; and therefore they covered the head which has no

flexure with thin bone, but not with flesh and sinews; and thus the head was added, having more wisdom and sensation than the rest of the body, but also being in every man far weaker. And for a like reason God placed the sinews at the extremity of the head, in a circle round the neck, and glued them together and fastened the cheeks to them at the extremity underneath the face, and other sinews he dispersed throughout the body, fastening limb to limb. The framers of our being framed the mouth, as now, having teeth and tongue and lips, with a view to the necessary and the good, contriving the way in for necessary purposes, the way out for the best purposes; for that is necessary which enters in and gives food to the body; but the river of speech which goes out of a man and ministers to the intelligence is the fairest and noblest of all streams. Still the head could neither be left a bare frame of bones, on account of the extremes of heat and cold in the different seasons, nor be allowed to be wholly covered, and so become dull and senseless by an overgrowth of flesh. The fleshy 76 nature was not therefore wholly dried up, but a large sort of peel was parted off and remained over, which is now called the skin. This met and grew by the help of the cerebral humour, and became the circular envelopment of the head. And the moisture springing up from beneath the sutures watered and closed them at the top, fastening them into a knot; the diversity of the sutures was caused by the power of the courses of the soul and of the food, and the more these struggled against one another the greater the diversity became, and grew less if the struggle diminished. This skin the divine power pierced all round with fire, and out of the punctures which were thus made the moisture issued forth, part liquid and hot which came away pure, and a mixed part which was composed of the same material as the skin, but was driven upwards and outwards, and extended to a great length, having a fineness equal to the punctures, and being too slow to find an exit, and thrust back by the external air, taking a condensed form, settled underneath the skin. And owing to these affections the hair sprang up in the skin, being of a skinny and stringy nature, but harder and closer through the pressure of the cold, by which each hair separated from the skin is compressed and cooled. In this manner the creator formed our head all hairy, making use of the causes which I have mentioned, and reflecting also that instead of flesh the part about the brain needed the hair to be a light covering or guard, which would give shade in summer and shelter in winter, and at the same time would not impede our quickness of perception. From the combination of sinew, skin, and bone, in the structure of the finger, there arises a triple compound which, when dried up, takes the form of one hard skin partaking of all three natures, and was fabricated by these second causes, but designed by the principal mind or cause with an eye to the future. For those who formed us well knew that women and other animals would some day be framed out of men, and they further knew that many animals would require the use of nails for many purposes ; wherefore also they stamped in men at their first creation the form of nails. From this cause and for these reasons they fashioned skin, hair, and nails at the extremities of the limbs.

And now that all the parts and members of the mortal animal 77 had come together, and their life of necessity consisted of fire and spirit, and was liable therefore to melt away and perish from exhaustion, the gods contrived the following remedy for this : they mingled a nature akin to that of man with other forms and per-ceptions, and thus created another kind of living being. These are the trees and plants and seeds, which by cultivation are now adapted to our use ; anciently there were only the wild kinds, which are older than the cultivated. For everything that partakes of life may be truly called a living being, and this of which we are now speaking partakes of the third nature of the soul, which is said to be seated between the midriff and the navel, and has no part in opinion or reason or mind, but only perception of plea-sure and pain and the desires which accompany them. For this nature is always in a passive state, and revolving in and about itself, repelling the motion from without and using its own, and not gifted originally with the power of seeing or reflecting on its own concerns. Wherefore it lives and is a living being, but is fixed and rooted in the same spot, having no power of self-motion.

Now, after the superior powers had created all these natures to be food for us who are of the inferior nature, they cut various channels through our bodies, as in a garden, watering them as with a perennial stream. In the first place, they cut two secret channels or veins down the back where the skin and the flesh join,

corresponding severally to the right and left side of the body.
These they placed along the backbone, so as to receive between
them the marrow of generation, the growth of which might be
thus promoted, and that the descending flood supplied thence to
other parts might equalize the irrigation. In the next place, they
divided the veins about the head, and, interlacing them, they sent
them in opposite directions; those coming from the right side
they sent to the left of the body, and those from the left they
turned towards the right, that they as well as the skin might
bind the head to the body, inasmuch as the head was not enclosed
at the top by the sinews, and also that the sensations from both
sides might be distributed over the whole body. And next, they
ordered the course of liquids in a manner which I will describe,
and which we shall more readily understand if we begin by
78 admitting that all things which are composed of lesser parts
retain the greater, but the greater cannot retain the lesser. Now,
of all natures fire has the smallest parts, and therefore penetrates
through earth and water and air and their compounds, nor can
anything hold it; and this is true also of the belly, which is able
to retain meats and drinks that have passed into it, but is not
able to retain air and fire, which consist of smaller particles than
those of which it is composed.

These channels, therefore, God employed for the sake of distributing moisture from the belly into the veins, weaving together
a network of fire and air like basket nets, at the entrance of which
he made two openings, the one of which he further formed with
two branches, and from the openings he extended a sort of cord
reaching all round to the extremity of the network. All the inner
parts of the network he made of fire, but the openings and the
cavity he made of air. The network he took and spread over
the newly-formed animal in the following manner:—he let one
of the openings pass into the mouth; this opening was twofold,
and he let one part of it descend by the air-pipes into the lungs,
the other by the side of the air-pipes into the belly. The other
opening he divided into two parts, both of which he made to
communicate with the channels of the nose, so that when there
was no way through the mouth the streams of the mouth were
replenished from the nostril. But the other cavity of the network
he placed around so much of the body as was hollow, and the

entire receptacle which was composed of air he made to flow into the passages of the network, which then flowed back; the tissue of the lung found a way in and out of the pores of the body, and the rays of fire which were interlaced followed the passage of the air either way; this continuing as long as the mortal being holds together. These, as we affirm, are the phenomena which the imposer of names called respiration and expiration. And all this process of cause and effect took place in order that the body might be watered and cooled, and thus have nourishment and life; for when the respiration is going in and out, and the fire, which follows at the same time, is moving to and fro, and, entering through the belly, reaches the meat and drink, it liquefies them, and, dividing them into small portions and guiding them through the passages where it goes, draws them as from a fountain into 79 the channels or veins, and makes the stream of the veins flow through the body as through a conduit.

Let us further consider the phenomena of respiration, and enquire what are the real causes of it. They are as follows. Seeing that there is no such thing as a vacuum into which any of those things which are moved can enter, and the breath is carried from us into the external air, the next point is, as will be clear to every one, that it does not go into a vacant space, but pushes its neighbour out of its place, and that which is thrust out again thrusts out its neighbour; and in this way of necessity everything at last comes round to that place from whence the breath came forth, and enters in there, and follows with the breath, and fills up the place; and this goes on like the circular motion of a wheel, because there can be no such thing as a vacuum. Wherefore also the breast and the lungs, which emit the breath, are again filled up by the air which surrounds the body and which enters in through the pores of the flesh and comes round in a circle; and, again, the air which is sent away and passes out through the body forces the breath within to find a way round through the passage of the mouth and the nostrils. Now, the origin of this may be supposed to be as follows. Every animal has his inward parts about the blood and the veins as warm as possible; he has within him a fountain of fire, which we compare to the texture of a net of fire extended through the centre of the body, while the outer parts are composed of air. Now, we must admit that heat naturally proceeds outward to its own place and to its kindred element; and as there are two exits for the heat, the one through the body outwards, and the other through the mouth and nostrils, when it moves towards the one, it drives round the other, and that which is driven round falls into the fire and is warmed, and that which goes forth is cooled. But when the condition of the heat changes, and the particles at the other exit grow warmer, the hotter air inclining in that direction and carried towards its native element fire, pushes round the other; and thus, by action and reaction, there being this circular agitation and alternation produced by the two—by this double cause, I say, inspiration and expiration are produced.

80 The phenomena of medical cupping-glasses and of the swallowing of drink and of the hurling of bodies, whether discharged in the air or moving along the ground, are to be explained on a similar principle; as also the nature of sounds, whether swift or slow, sharp or flat, which are sometimes discordant on account of the inequality of the motion which they excite in us, and then again harmonical on account of their equality; for the slower sounds reach the motions of the antecedent swifter sounds when these begin to pause and come to an equality, and after a while overtake and propel them. When they overtake them they do not introduce another or discordant motion, but they make the slower motion by degrees correspond with the swifter; and when the motion leaves off, they assimilate them and cause a single mixed expression to be produced from sharp and flat, whence arises a pleasure which even the unwise feel, and which to the wise becomes a higher sort of delight, as being an imitation of divine harmony in mortal motions. Moreover, as to the motions of water, the thunderbolt, and the marvels that are observed about the attraction of amber and the Heraclean stones,—in none of these cases is there any attraction; but, as there is no vacuum, these substances thrust one another round and round, all severally passing and succeeding to their own places by composition and dissolution. Such will appear to the reasonable investigator to be the causes whose united influence produces these wonders.

I have spoken of the nature and causes of respiration, in which our discourse originated. As I before said, the fire divides the food and rises within in company with the breath; in the process of respiration filling the veins out of the belly by drawing from thence the divided portions of the food, by which means the streams of food are diffused through the whole body in all animals. The fruits or grass, which are of a kindred nature, and which God planted to be our daily food, when newly cut, acquire all sorts of colours by reason of their admixture; but the red colour for the most part predominates, being a nature made by the cutting power of fire leaving a stain in moisture; and hence the liquid which circulates in the body has such a colour as we have described, which we call blood, being the nurturing principle of the flesh and of the whole body, whence all parts are watered 81 and the empty places filled.

Now the process of repletion and depletion is effected after the manner of the universal motion of all things, which is due to the tendency of kindred natures towards one another. For the external elements which surround us are always causing us to consume away, and distributing and sending away like to like; the particles of blood, too, which are divided and contained within the frame of the animal, which is a sort of world to them, are compelled to imitate the motion of the universe. Each, therefore, of the divided parts within us, being carried to its kindred nature, replenishes the void. When more is taken away than flows in, then we decay, and when less, we grow and increase.

The young of every animal has the triangles new, and may be compared to the keel of a vessel which is just off the stocks; they are locked closely together and yet the entire frame is soft and delicate, as if freshly formed of marrow and nurtured on milk. Those triangles, therefore, which come in from without and are contained in the bodily frame, from which are formed meats and drinks, being older and weaker than its own triangles, the frame of the body gets the better of them and cuts them up with the new triangles, and the animal grows and is nourished by the assimilation of particles. But when the root of the triangles is relaxed by having undergone many conflicts with many things in the course of time, they are no longer able to cut or assimilate the food which enters into them, but are easily subverted by the new bodies which come in from without. In this way the whole animal is overcome and decays, and this state of things is called old age.

But at last, when the bonds of the triangles which enclose the marrow no longer hold, and get unfixed by the toil of which I spoke, they unfix also the bonds of the soul, and she, being released, in the order of nature joyfully flies away. For that which is not in the order of nature is painful, but that which takes place according to nature is pleasant. And thus, too, death, if caused by disease or produced by wounds, is painful and difficult; but that sort of death which comes of old age and fulfils the debt of nature is the least painful of deaths, and is accompanied with pleasure rather than with pain.

Now, every one can see whence diseases arise. There are four natures out of which the body is compacted—earth and fire and water and air, and the unnatural excess and defect of these, or the change of any one of them from their own natural place into another, or, again, the assumption on the part of these diverse natures of fire and the like of that which is not suitable to them, or anything of that sort, produces diseases and disorders; for each being produced or changed in a manner contrary to nature, the elements which were previously cool grow warm, and those which were dry become moist, and the light become heavy, and the heavy light; all sorts of changes occur. For we affirm that only the same, in the same and like manner and proportion added or subtracted to or from the same, will allow the body to remain in the same state, whole and sound, and that, whatever is taken away or added in violation of these rules causes all manner of changes and infinite diseases and disorders. But as there are secondary compositions which are according to nature, he who will understand diseases may also have another or second notion of them. For whereas the marrow and the bone and the flesh and the sinews are composed of these elements, as the blood is likewise composed of them but in a different degree, the greater number of them are caused in the way which I have already mentioned; but the worst of all owe their severity to the following causes. When the generation of them proceeds in an order contrary to nature, then the elements are destroyed. For the natural order is that the flesh and sinews are made of blood, the sinews out of the fibres to which they are akin, and the flesh out of the congealed substance which is formed by separation from the fibres. And the glutinous and rich

matter which comes away from the sinews and the flesh not only
binds the flesh to the bones, but nourishes and imparts growth
to the bone itself which surrounds the marrow, and by reason of
the solidity of the bones, that which is filtered through is the
purest and the smoothest and the oiliest sort of the triangles
which drops like dew from the bones and waters the marrow.
And when these are the conditions, health usually ensues; when
the conditions are of an opposite nature, disease. For when the
flesh becomes liquefied and sends back the wasting substance into
the veins, then there is a great deal of blood of different kinds
as well as of air in the veins, having various degrees of colour
and bitterness: and also from its acid and salt qualities it
generates all sorts of bile and lymph and phlegm. For all things
go the wrong way and are corrupted, and first of all destroy the
blood, and then ceasing to give nourishment to the body are 83
carried along the veins in all sorts of ways, no longer preserving
the order of their natural courses, but at war with themselves,
because they have no enjoyment of themselves, and are hostile to
the abiding constitution of the body, which they destroy and waste.
The oldest part of the flesh which wastes away, refusing to assimilate, grows black from long burning, and from being corroded in
every direction becomes bitter, and is injurious to every part of
the body which is not yet corrupted. And then instead of bitterness the black part assumes an acidity from the bitter element
refining away; or, again, the bitter substance being tinged with
blood has a redder colour; or, when mixed with black, has the[4]
hue of grass; and once again, an auburn colour is mingled with
the bitter matter when the new flesh is melted by the fire which
surrounds the internal flame;—to all which some physician, or some
philosopher, who had the power of seeing many dissimilar things
and recognising in them one nature common to them all and
deserving of a name, has assigned the common name of bile. But
the kinds of bile have also their peculiar names corresponding to
their several colours. As for lymph, that sort which is the whey of
blood is gentle, but that which is produced by dark and bitter bile
is of a fierce nature when mingled by the power of heat with any
salt substance, and is then called acid phlegm. Again, the dissolution
of new and tender flesh which is accompanied by air when inflated

[4] Reading χλοῶδες.

and encased in liquid producing bubbles which separately are invisible owing to their small size, but when collected together are of a bulk which is visible, and have a white colour arising out of the generation of foam—all this dissolution of tender flesh when intermingled with air is termed by us white phlegm. And the whey or sediment of phlegm when just formed is sweat and tears, and includes the various secretions which arise daily out of the purgation of the body. Now all these become the instruments of disease when the blood is not replenished according to nature by meats and drinks but gains bulk from contraries in violation of the laws of nature. When the several parts of the flesh are separated by disease, if the foundation remains, the trouble 84 is only half as great, and recovery is still possible; but when that which binds the flesh to the bones is diseased, and the blood, which is made out of the fibres and sinews, separates from them, and no longer gives nourishment to the bone, or is a bond of union to flesh and bone, and from being oily and smooth and glutinous becomes rough and salt and dry, owing to bad regimen, then the substance which is detached, crumbles away under the flesh and the sinews, and separates from the bone, and the fleshy parts fall away from their foundation and leave the sinews bare and full of brine, and the flesh again gets into the circulation of the blood and makes the previously-mentioned disorders still greater. And if these bodily affections be severe, still worse are those which precede them; as when the bone itself, by reason of the density of the flesh, does not receive sufficient air, but becomes stagnant and hot and gangrened and receives no nutriment, and the natural process is inverted, and the bone crumbling passes into the food, and the food into the flesh, and the flesh again falling into the blood causes maladies yet more violent than those already mentioned. But the worst of all is when the marrow is diseased, either from excess or defect; and this is the cause of the very greatest and most fatal disorders in which the whole course of the body is reversed. There is a third class of diseases which may be conceived of as arising in three ways, and are produced sometimes by wind, and sometimes by phlegm, and sometimes by bile. When the lung, which is to the body the steward of the air, is obstructed by rheums and has the passage stopped up, having no egress in one part, while in another part too much air enters in, then the parts which are unrefreshed by the air corrode, while in other parts the excess of wind forcing its way through the veins distorts them and consumes the body at the centre, and is there shut in. and holds fast the midriff; thus numberless painful diseases are produced, accompanied by copious sweats. And oftentimes when the flesh is dissolved in the interior of the body, wind, generated within and unable to get out, is the source of quite as much pain as the air coming in from without; but the greatest pain is when the wind gets about the sinews and the veins connected with them, and swells them up, especially when the pressure is upon the great sinews of the shoulder and twists back the ligaments that fasten them. These, from the intensive nature of the affection, are termed tetanus and recurvation. The cure of them is difficult, and they generally end in fevers. The white phlegm, though 85 dangerous when detained within by reason of the air-bubbles, yet being capable of relief by expiration, is less severe, and only discolours the body, generating white leprosies and similar diseases. When the phlegm is mingled with black bile and dispersed about the courses of the head, which are the divinest part of us, and disturbs them in sleep, the attack is not so severe; but when assailing those who are awake it is hard to be got rid of, and, being an affection of a sacred part, is most justly called sacred. An acid and salt phlegm, again, is the source of all those diseases which are of a catarrhal nature, but, because the places into which they flow are of various kinds, they have all sorts of names.

Inflammations of the body come from burnings and inflamings, and all of them originate in bile. When bile finds a means of discharge, it boils up and sends forth all sorts of tumours; but when kept down within, it generates many inflammatory diseases, above all when mingled with pure blood; as it then disturbs the order of the fibres which are scattered about in the blood and are designed to maintain the balance of rare and dense, in order that the blood may not by reason of heat perspire through the pores of the body, nor again become too dense and thus find a difficulty in circulating through the veins. The just temperament of these things is preserved by the fibres according to the appointment of nature; and if any one collects them together when the blood is dead and

congealed, then the blood that remains in them flows out, and
thus left to themselves they also soon congeal with the surrounding cold. Such is the power which the fibres have of acting upon
the blood; and from them arises bile, which is only stale blood,
and from being flesh is liquefied again, and at the first influx
comes in little by little warm and moist, and is congealed by the
power of the fibres; and if congealed and extinguished by force
produces internal cold and shuddering. But when it enters with
more of a flood and overcomes the fibres by its heat, and makes
them boil and bubble in a disorderly manner, if it have power
enough completely to get the better, it passes into the marrow and
burns up and unmoors what may be termed the cables of the ship,
and frees the soul; but when there is not so much, and the body
though wasted still holds out, it is either mastered and banished
from the whole body, or is thrust through the veins into the lower
or upper belly, and is driven out of the body like an exile out of
86 an insurgent state, and causes diarrhoeas and dysenteries, and all
sorts of similar disorders. When the constitution is disordered by
excess of fire, then the heat and fever are constant; when air is
the cause, then the fever is quotidian; when water, which is a
more sluggish element than either fire or air, then the fever
intermits a day; when earth is the cause, which is the most
sluggish of the four, and is only purged away in a four-fold period,
the result is a quartan fever, which can only with difficulty be
shaken off.

Such is the course of the diseases of the body; and the disorders
of the soul which originate in the body are as follows. The disorder of the mind will be acknowledged to be folly; but there are
two kinds of folly—one, madness, and the other ignorance; and
whatever affection gives rise to either of them may be called
disease. Excessive pains and pleasures are justly to be regarded
as the greatest diseases of the soul, for a man who is in great joy
or in great pain, in his irrational eagerness to attain the one and
to avoid the other, is not truly able to see or to hear anything;
but he is mad, and is at the time quite incapable of any participation in reason. For he who has the seed about the spinal
marrow too fruitful and prolific, like a tree overladen with fruit,
has many throes, and also obtains many pleasures in his desires
and their gratifications, and is for the most part of his life mad,

because his pleasures and pains are so very great; his soul is rendered foolish and disordered by his body; and he is regarded not as one diseased, but as one who is voluntarily bad, which is a bad mistake. For the truth is that the intemperance of love for the most part grows into a disease of the soul by reason of the moist and fluid state of one element, and this arises out of the loose consistency of the bones. And in general, all that which is termed the intemperance of pleasure is unjustly charged upon those who do wrong, as if they did wrong voluntarily. For no man is voluntarily bad; but the bad become bad by reason of an ill disposition of the body and bad education: every man finds these things to be an evil and a mischief; and in like manner the soul is often vicious through the bodily influences of pain. For where the sharp and briny phlegm and other bitter and bilious humours wander over the body, and find no exit or escape, but are compressed within and mingle their own vapours with the motions of the soul, and are blended with them, they produce an infinite variety of diseases 87 in all sorts of degrees, and being carried to the three places of the soul on which any of them may severally chance to alight, they create infinite varieties of trouble and melancholy, of tempers rash and cowardly, and also of forgetfulness and stupidity. Further, when men's bodies are thus ill made, and evil forms of government are superadded—when in states evil discourses are uttered in private as well as in public, and when from youth upward no sort of instruction is given which may heal these ills, here is another source of evil; and these are the two ways in which all of us who are bad become bad, through two things which are wholly out of our power. And for this the planters are to blame rather than the plants, the educators rather than the educated. Still we should endeavour as far as we can by education, and studies, and learning, to avoid vice and attain virtue; this, however, is part of another subject.

There is a corresponding enquiry concerning the modes in which the mind and the body are to be treated, and by what means they are preserved, on which I may and ought to enter; for it is more our duty to speak of the good than of the evil. Everything that is good is fair, and the fair is not without measure, and the animal who is fair may be supposed to have measure. Now we perceive lesser symmetries and comprehend them, but about the highest and greatest we have no understanding; for with a view to health and disease, and virtue and vice, there is no symmetry or want of symmetry greater than that of the soul to the body; and this we do not perceive, or ever reflect that when a weaker or lesser frame is the vehicle of a great and mighty soul, or conversely, when they are united in the opposite way, then the whole animal is not fair, for it is defective in the most important of all symmetries; but the fair mind in the fair body will be the fairest and loveliest of all sights to him who has the seeing eye. Just as a body which has a leg too long, or some other disproportion, is an unpleasant sight, and also, when undergoing toil, has many sufferings, and makes violent efforts, and often stumbles through awkwardness, and is the cause of infinite evil to its own self—in like manner we should conceive of the double nature which we call the living being; and when in this compound there is an impassioned soul more powerful than the body, 88 that soul, I say, convulses and disorders the whole inner nature of man; and when too eager in the pursuit of knowledge, causes wasting; or again, when teaching or disputing in private or in public, and strifes and controversies arise, inflames and dissolves the composite frame of man and introduces rheums; and the nature of this is not understood by most professors of medicine, who ascribe the phenomenon to the opposite of the real cause. And once more, when a body large and too much for the soul is united to a small and weak intelligence, seeing that there are two desires natural to man,—one of food for the sake of the body, and one of wisdom for the sake of the diviner part of us —then, I say, the motions of the stronger principle, getting the better and increasing their own power, but making the soul dull, and stupid, and forgetful, engender ignorance, which is the greatest of diseases. There is one protection against both:—that we should not move the body without the soul or the soul without the body, and thus they will aid one another, and be healthy and well balanced. And therefore the mathematician or any one else who devotes himself to some intellectual pursuit, must allow his body to have motion also, and practise gymnastic; and he who would train the limbs of the body, should impart to them the motions of the soul, and should practise music and all philosophy, if he would be called truly fair and truly good. And in like manner should the parts be treated, and the principle of the whole similarly applied to them; for as the body is heated and also cooled within by the elements which enter in, and is again dried up and moistened by external things, and experiences these and the like affections from both kinds of motions, the result is that the body if given up to motion when in a state of quiescence is overmastered and destroyed; but if any one, in imitation of that which we call the foster-mother and nurse of the universe, will not allow the body to be at rest, but is always producing motions and shakings, which constantly react upon the natural motions both within and without, and by shaking moderately the affections and parts which wander about the body, brings them into order and affinity with one another according to the theory of the universe which we were maintaining, he will not allow enemy placed by the side of enemy to create wars and disorders in the body, but he will place friend by the side of friend, producing health.   Now of all motions that is the best which is produced in a thing by itself, for it is most 89 akin to the motion of the intelligent and the motion of the universe; but that motion which is caused by others is not so good, and worst of all is that which moves the parts of the body, when prostrate and at rest, in parts only and by external means; wherefore also that is the best of the purifications and adjustments of the body which is effected by gymnastic; next is that which is effected by carrying the body, as in sailing or any other mode of conveyance which is not fatiguing; the third sort of motion may be of use in a case of extreme necessity, but in any other will be adopted by no man of sense: I mean the purgative treatment of physicians; for diseases which are not attended by great dangers should not be irritated by purgatives, for every form of disease is in a manner akin to the living being—for the combination out of which they were formed has an appointed term of life and of existence.   And the whole race and every animal has his appointed natural time, apart from violent casualties; for the triangles are originally framed with power to live for a certain time, beyond which no man can prolong his life.   And this holds also of the nature of diseases, for if any one regardless of their appointed time would destroy nature by purgatives, he only increases and multiplies them.   Wherefore we ought always to manage them by regimen, as far as a man can spare the time,

and not provoke a disagreeable enemy by medical treatment. Let
this much be said of the general nature of man, and of the body
which is a part of him, and of the manner in which a man may
govern himself and be governed best, and live most according to
reason: and we must begin by providing that the governing principle shall be the fairest and best possible for the purpose of
government. But to discuss such a subject accurately would be
a sufficiently long business of itself. As a mere supplement or
sequel of what has preceded, it may be summed up as follows.
As I have often said, that there are three kinds of soul located
within us, each of them having their own proper motions—so I
must now say in the fewest words possible, that the one part,
if remaining inactive and ceasing from the natural motion,
must necessarily become very weak, but when trained and exercised then very strong. Wherefore we should take care that
90 the three parts of the soul are exercised in proportion to one
another.

Concerning the highest part of the human soul, we should consider that God gave this as a genius to each one, which was to
dwell at the extremity of the body, and to raise us like plants,
not of an earthly but of a heavenly growth, from earth to our
kindred which is in heaven. And this is most true; for the divine
power suspended the head and root of us from that place where the
generation of the soul first began, and thus made erect the whole
body. He, therefore, who is always occupied with the cravings
of desire and ambition, and is eagerly striving after them, must
have all his opinions mortal, and, as far as man can be, must
be all of him mortal, because he has cherished his mortal part.
But he who has been earnest in the love of knowledge and
true wisdom, and has been trained to think that these are the
immortal and divine things of a man, if he attain truth, must
of necessity, as far as human nature is capable of attaining
immortality, be all immortal, as he is ever serving the divine
power; and having the genius residing in him in the most perfect order, he must be pre-eminently happy. Now there is
only one way in which one being can serve another, and this
is by giving him his proper nourishment and motion. And the
motions which are akin to the divine principle within us are
the thoughts and revolutions of the universe. These each man

should follow, and correct those corrupted courses of the head
which are concerned with generation, and by learning the harmonies and revolutions of the whole, should assimilate the per-
ceiver to the thing perceived, according to his original nature, and
by thus assimilating them, attain that final perfection of life,
which the gods set before mankind as best, both for the present
and the future.

Thus the discussion of the universe which, according to our
original proposition, was to reach to the origin of man, seems to
have an end. A brief mention may be made of the generation of
other animals, but there is no need to dwell upon them at length;
this would seem to be the best mode of attaining a due proportion.
On the subject of animals, then, the following remarks may be
offered. Of the men who came into the world, those who are
cowards or have led unjust lives may be fairly supposed to change
into the nature of women in the second generation. Wherefore
also at the time when this took place the gods created in us the
desire of generation, contriving in man one animated substance, 91
and in woman another, which they formed respectively in the
following manner. The passage for the drink by which liquids
pass through the lung under the kidneys and into the bladder, and
which receives and emits them by the pressure of the breath, was
so fashioned as to penetrate also into the body of the marrow,
which passes from the head along the neck and through the back,
and which in our previous discussion we have named the seed.
And the seed having life, and becoming endowed with respiration,
produces, in that part in which it respires, a lively desire of emis-
sion, and thus creates in us the love of procreation. Wherefore also
in men the organ of generation becoming rebellious and masterful,
like an animal disobedient to reason, seeks, by the raging of the
appetites, to gain absolute sway; and the same is the case with
the wombs and other organs of women; the animal within them is
desirous of procreating children, and when remaining without fruit
long beyond its proper time, gets discontented and angry, and
wandering in every direction through the body, closes up the passages of the breath, and, by obstructing respiration, drives them
into the utmost difficulty, causing all varieties of disease, until at
length the desire and love of the man and the woman, as it were
producing and plucking the fruit from the tree, cause the emis-

sion of seed into the womb, as into a field, in which they sow animals unseen by reason of their smallness and formless; these they again separate and mature them within, and after that, bring them out into the light, and thus perfect the generation of animals.

Thus were created women and the female sex in general. But the race of birds was created out of innocent light-minded men who, although their thoughts were directed towards heaven, imagined, in their simplicity, that the clearest demonstration of the things above was to be obtained by sight; these were transformed into birds, and they grew feathers instead of hair. The race of wild pedestrian animals again came from those who had no philosophy in all their thoughts, and never considered at all about the nature of the heavens, because they had ceased to use the courses of the head, and followed the guidance of those parts of the soul which surround the breast. In consequence of these habits of theirs they had their forelegs and heads trailing upon the earth to which they were akin; and they had also the crowns of their heads oblong, and in all sorts of curious shapes, in which the courses of the 92 soul were compressed by reason of disuse. And this was the reason why quadrupeds and polypods were created: God gave the more senseless of them the more support that they might be more attracted to the earth. And the most foolish of them, who trailed their bodies entirely upon the ground and have no longer any need of feet, he made without feet to crawl upon the earth. The fourth class were the inhabitants of the water: these were made out of the most entirely ignorant and senseless beings, whom the transformers did not think any longer worthy of pure respiration, because they possessed a soul which was made impure by all sorts of transgression; and instead of allowing them to respire the subtle and pure element of air, they thrust them into the water and gave them a deep and muddy medium of respiration; and hence arose the race of fishes and oysters, and other aquatic animals, which have received the most remote habitations as a punishment of their extreme ignorance. These are the laws by which animals pass into one another, both now and ever changing as they lose or gain wisdom and folly.

And now we may say that our discourse about the nature

of the universe has come to an end. The world has received animals, mortal and immortal, and is fulfilled with them, and has become a visible animal comprehending the visible—the sensible God who is the image of the intelligible, greatest, best, fairest, and most perfect—the one only-begotten universe.

CRITIAS.

INTRODUCTION.

THE Critias is a fragment which breaks off in the middle of a sentence. It was designed to be the second part of a trilogy, which, like the other great Platonic trilogy of the Sophist, Statesman, Philosopher, was never completed. Timaeus had brought down the origin of the world to the creation of man, and the dawn of history was now to succeed the philosophy of nature. The Critias is also connected with the Republic. Plato, as he has already told us, intended to represent the ideal state engaged in a patriotic conflict. This mythical conflict is prophetic or symbolical of the struggle of Athens and Persia, perhaps in some degree also of the wars of the Greeks and Carthaginians, in the same way that the Persian is prefigured by the Trojan war to the mind of Herodotus; or as the narrative of the first part of the Aeneid foreshadows the wars of Carthage and Rome. The small number of the primitive Athenian citizens (20,000), 'which is about their present number,' is evidently designed to contrast with the myriads and barbaric array of the Atlantic hosts. The passing remark in the Timaeus (25 C) that Athens was left alone in the struggle, in which she conquered and became the liberator of Greece, is also an allusion to the later history. Hence we may safely conclude that the entire narrative is due to the imagination of Plato, who would easily invent 'Egyptians or anything else' (Phaedrus), and who has used the name of Solon (of whose poem there is no trace in antiquity) and the tradition of the Egyptian priests to give verisimilitude to his story. To the Greek such a tale, like that of the earth-born men, would have seemed perfectly accordant with the character of his mythology, and not more marvellous than the wonders of the East narrated by Herodotus and others. The fiction has exercised a great influence over the imagination of later ages. As many attempts have been made to find the great island, as to discover the country of the lost tribes. Without regard to the description of Plato,

and without a suspicion that the whole narrative is a fabrication, interpreters have looked for the spot in every part of the globe, America,
Palestine, Arabia Felix, Ceylon, Sardinia, Sweden.   The story had also
an effect on the early navigators of the sixteenth century.

Timaeus concludes with a prayer that his words may be acceptable to
the God whom he has revealed, and Critias, whose turn follows, begs that
a larger measure of indulgence may be conceded to him, because he has
to speak of the men whom we know and not of the gods whom we do
not know.   Socrates readily grants this indulgence to him, and anticipating that Hermocrates will make a similar request, is ready to grant
the same indulgence to him.

Critias returns to his story, professing only to repeat what Solon was
told by the priests.   The war of which he was about to speak had
occurred 9000 years ago. (This is slightly inconsistent with the Timaeus,
which gives the same date for the foundation of the city Tim. 23 E.;
the mistake may indicate that the Critias was not written until some time
afterwards.)   One of the combatants was the city of Athens, the other
was the great island of Atlantis.   Critias proposes (after the manner of
Herodotus and others) to give an account of the various tribes of
Greeks and barbarians who took part in the war, as they successively
appear on the scene.   But first of all he will speak of the antediluvian
Athens, and then of the island of Atlantis.

In the beginning the gods agreed to divide the earth by lot in a
friendly manner, and when they had made the allotment (comp. Polit.)
they settled their several countries, and were the shepherds of mankind, whom they governed by persuasion, which is the helm of the
soul, and not by blows like other shepherds.   Hephaestus and Athene,
brother and sister deities, in mind and art united, obtained as their lot
the land of Athens, a land suited to the growth of virtue and wisdom;
and there they settled a brave race of children of the soil, in whom they
implanted a spirit of law and order.   The names of some of them remain,
although the memory of their deeds has passed away, for there were
many deluges, and the remnant who survived in the mountains lost the
art of writing, and during many generations were wholly devoted to
acquiring the means of life.

But the Egyptian priests had preserved the actions as well as the
names of the kings before Theseus, such as Erechtheus and Erichthonius,

and of women in like manner. And the armed image of the goddess which was dedicated by the ancient Athenians is an evidence to other ages that men and women had in those days, as they ought always to have, common virtues and pursuits. There were various classes of citizens, including handicraftsmen and husbandmen and a superior class of warriors who dwelt alone, and were educated, and had all things in common like your guardians. The country in those days extended southwards to the Isthmus and inland as far as the heights of Parnes and Cithaeron, but a single night of excessive rain washed away the earth and left the rock bare. The traces of this catastrophe are still discernible in the form of the shore, which is a lofty cliff, and goes down sheer into the deep sea. The soil was then and still is in some places the most fertile in the world and abounded in rich plains and pastures. And the inhabitants of this fair land were endowed with intelligence and love of beauty.

The Acropolis of the ancient Athens extended to the Ilissus and Eridanus, and included the Lycabettus and Pnyx on the opposite side, having a level surface and deep soil. The side of the hill was inhabited by the craftsmen and husbandmen; and the warriors dwelt by themselves on the summit, around the temples of Hephaestus and Athene, in an enclosure which was like the garden of a single house. In winter they retired into houses on the north of the hill, in which they held their syssitia. These were modest dwellings, which they bequeathed to their children and grandchildren. On the south side they had gardens and gymnasia and places for their summer syssitia, and in the midst of the Acropolis was a fountain, which gave an abundant supply of cool water in winter as well as in summer; of this there are still some traces. They were careful to preserve the number of fighting men at 20,000, which is about the present number, and so they passed their lives as guardians of the citizens. They were a just and famous race, celebrated for their beauty and virtue all over Europe and Asia.

And now I will speak to you of their adversaries, but first I ought to explain that the Greek names were translated by Solon from the Egyptian; he wrote them down and left them with my grandfather in a writing which I still possess. In the division of the earth Poseidon obtained as his portion the island of Atlantis, and there he begat children whose mother was a mortal. In the centre of the island towards the sea there was a very fair and fertile plain, and about fifty stadia from the centre there was a narrow mountain in which dwelt a man named Evenor and his wife Leucippe and their daughter Cleito of whom Poseidon became enamoured. He to secure his love enclosed the mountain with rings or zones at equal distances, two of land and three of sea, which his divine power readily enabled him to excavate, and, as there was no shipping in those days, no man could get into the place. To the interior island he conveyed under the earth springs of water hot and cold, and supplied the land with all things needed for the life of man. Here he begat a race with five pairs of twins, of whom he made the eldest, Atlas, the king of the centre island, while to his twin brother, Eumelus or Gadeirus as he was called in the national language, he assigned that part of the country which was nearest the Straits. The other brothers he made chiefs of the adjacent islands. His own kingdom extended as far as Egypt and Tyrrhenia, and he had a fair posterity, and abundance of treasures, derived from mines of gold and silver and orichalcum, and there was abundance of wood, and herds of elephants, and pastures for animals of all kinds, and fragrant herbs, and grasses, and trees bearing fruit. These they used, and employed themselves in constructing their temples, and palaces, and harbours, and docks, in the following manner:—First, they bridged over the zones of sea, and made a way to the royal palace which they built in the sacred island. This ancient palace was ornamented by successive generations; and they dug a canal which passed through the zones of land from the island to the sea. The zones of earth were surrounded by stone walls of divers colours, black and white and red, which they sometimes intermingled for the sake of ornament; the outermost wall was coated with brass, the second with tin, and the third, which was the wall of the citadel, flashed with the red light of orichalcum. In the interior of the citadel was a holy temple, dedicated to Cleito and Poseidon, and surrounded by an enclosure of gold, and there was Poseidon's own temple, which was covered with silver, and the pinnacles with gold. The roof was of ivory, adorned with gold and silver and orichalcum, and the rest of the interior lined with orichalcum. In the centre was the god standing in a chariot drawn by six winged horses, and touching the roof with his head; around him were the hundred Nereids, riding on dolphins. Outside the temple were placed golden statues of all the ten kings and their wives, and other offerings; there was an altar too, and temples, and palaces, corresponding to the greatness of the kingdom.

Also there were fountains of hot and cold water, and trees, and suitable buildings surrounding them, and there were baths both of the king and of private individuals, and separate baths for men and for women, and also for cattle. The water from the baths was carried to the grove of Poseidon, and from thence by aqueducts over the bridges to the outer circle. And there were temples in the zones, and in the larger of the two there was a racecourse for horses, which ran all round the island. The guards were distributed in the zones according to the trust reposed in them; the most trusted of them were stationed in the citadel. The table-land which surrounded the city extended three thousand stadia in one direction and two thousand in another. The docks were full of triremes and naval stores. The citadel was surrounded by a wall, and was densely crowded with dwellings, and the canal resounded with the din of human voices.

The plain around the city was highly cultivated and sheltered from the north by mountains; it was encompassed by a foss of a hundred feet in depth and a stadium in breadth, and ten thousand stadia in length. The foss received the streams which came down from the mountains, as well as the canals of the interior, and found a way to the sea. The entire country was divided into sixty-thousand lots, each of which was a square of ten stadia; and the owner of a lot was bound to furnish the sixth part of a war-chariot, two horses, and an attendant and charioteer, a light chariot without a seat, two hoplites, two archers, two slingers, three stone-shooters, three javelin-men, and four sailors, to make up the complement of twelve hundred ships.

Each of the ten kings was absolute in his own city and island. The relations of the different governments to one another were determined by the injunctions of Poseidon, which had been inscribed by the first men on a column of orichalcum in the temple of Poseidon, at which the people were gathered together and held a festival every fifth and every sixth year. Around the temple ranged the bulls of Poseidon, whom the ten kings offered in sacrifice, shedding the blood of the victim over the inscription, and vowing not to transgress the laws of their father Poseidon. When night came, they put on azure robes and gave judgment against offenders. The most important of their laws related to their dealings with one another. They were not to take up arms against one another, and were to come to the rescue if any of their brethren were attacked. They were to deliberate in common, and the king was not to have the power of life and death over his kinsmen, unless he had the assent of the majority.

For many generations, as tradition tells, the people of Atlantis were obedient to the laws, and practised gentleness and wisdom in their intercourse with one another.   They knew that they could only have the true use of riches by not caring about them.   But gradually the divine portion of their souls became diluted with too much of the mortal admixture, and they began to degenerate, though to the outward eye they appeared glorious as ever at the very time when they were filled with all iniquity. The all-seeing Zeus, wanting to punish them, held a council of the gods, and when he had called them together, he spoke as follows:—

No one knew better than Plato how to invent 'a noble lie.'   Observe (1) the innocent declaration of Socrates, that the truth of the story is a great advantage: (2) the manner in which traditional names and indications of geography are intermingled ('Why, here be truths!'): (3) the extreme minuteness with which the numbers are given, as in the Old Epic poetry: (4) the ingenious reason assigned for the Greek names occurring in the Egyptian tale: (5) the remark that the armed statue of Athene indicated the common warrior life of men and women: (6) the particularity with which the last deluge before that of Deucalion is affirmed to have been the great destruction: (7) the confession that the depth of the ditch, made by the hand of man, was not to be believed, and 'yet he could only repeat what he had heard;' while the triple zones of water in the midst of the country are attributed with greater appearance of probability to the supernatural power of the god: (8) the traditional rivalry of Poseidon and Athene, and the creation of the first inhabitants out of the soil.   Plato here, as elsewhere, ingeniously gives the impression that he is telling the truth which mythology had corrupted.

In contrasting the small Greek state numbering about twenty thousand inhabitants with the barbaric greatness of the island of Atlantis, Plato had evidently intended to show that such a state, though 'consisting of only a thousand citizens,' was invincible when matched with the hosts of Xerxes.   Even in a great empire there might be a degree of virtue and justice, such as the Greeks believed to have existed under the sway of the first Persian kings.   But all such empires were liable to degenerate, and soon incurred the anger of the gods.   Their Oriental wealth, and splendour of gold and silver, and variety of colours, seemed also to be at variance with the simplicity of Greek notions. In the island of Atlantis, Plato is describing a sort of Babylonian or Egyptian city, to which he opposes the frugal life of the true Hellenic citizen. It is remarkable that in his brief sketch of them, he idealizes the husbandmen ' who are lovers of honour and true husbandmen,' as well as the warriors, who are his sole concern in the Republic; and that though he speaks of the common pursuits of men and women, he says nothing of the community of wives and children.

It is singular that Plato should have prefixed the most detested of Athenian names to this dialogue, and even more singular that he should have put into the mouth of Socrates a panegyric on him. Yet we know that his character was accounted infamous by Xenophon, and that the mere acquaintance with him was made a subject of accusation against Socrates. We can only infer that in this, and perhaps in some other cases, Plato's characters have no reference to the actual facts. The desire to do honour to his own family, and the connection with Solon, may have suggested the introduction of his name. Why the Critias was never completed, whether from accident, or from advancing age, or from a sense of the artistic difficulty of the design, cannot be determined.

CRITIAS.

PERSONS OF THE DIALOGUE.

CRITIAS.   TIMAEUS.
HERMOCRATES.   SOCRATES.

Timaeus. How thankful I am, Socrates, that I have arrived at last, and, like a weary traveller after a long journey, may now be at rest! And I pray the being who always was of old, and has now been by me declared, to receive and preserve my words, in so far as they have been spoken truly and acceptably to him; and if unintentionally I have said anything wrong, I pray that he will impose upon me a fitting retribution, and the proper retribution of him who errs is to set him in the right way. Wishing, then, that for the future I may speak truly concerning the generation of the gods, I pray them to give me knowledge, which of all medicines is the most perfect and best.—That is my prayer. And now I deliver the argument into the hands of Critias, according to our agreement.

Critias. And I, Timaeus, accept the trust, and as you at first said that you were going to speak of high matters, and begged that some allowance might be extended to you, I must request the same or a greater allowance for what I am about to say. And although I very well know that I am making an ambitious and a somewhat rude request, I must not be deterred by that. For will any man of sense deny that you have spoken well? I can only attempt to show that my theme is more difficult, and claims more indulgence than yours; and I shall argue that to seem to speak well of the gods to men is far easier than to speak well of mortals to one another: for the inexperience and utter ignorance of his hearers about such matters is a great assistance to him who has to speak of them, and we know how ignorant we are concerning the gods. But I should like to make my meaning clearer, if you will follow me. All that we are any of us saying can only be imitation and assimilation. For if we consider how the works of the painter represent bodies divine and heavenly, and the different degrees of gratification with which the eye of the spectator receives them, we shall see that we are satisfied with the artist who is able in any degree to imitate the earth and its mountains, and the rivers, and the woods, and the universe, and the things that are and move therein, and further, that knowing nothing precise about such matters, we do not examine or analyse the painting; all that is required is a sort of indistinct and deceptive mode of shadowing them forth. But when a person endeavours to paint the human form we are quick at finding out defects, and our familiar knowledge makes us severe judges of any one who does not render every point of similarity; and this is also true of discourse; we are satisfied with a picture of divine and heavenly things which has very little likeness to them; but we are more precise in our criticism of mortal and human things. Wherefore if at the moment of speaking we cannot suitably express what we mean, you must excuse us, considering that to form approved likenesses of human things is the reverse of easy. This is what I want to 108 suggest to you, and at the same time to beg, Socrates, that I may have not less, but more indulgence conceded to me in what I am about to say. Which favour, if I am right in asking, I hope that you will be ready to grant.

Socrates. Certainly, Critias, we will grant that, and we will grant the same by anticipation to Hermocrates, who has to speak third; for I have no doubt that when his turn comes a little while hence, he will make the same request which you have made. In order, then, that he may provide himself with a fresh beginning, and not be compelled to say the same things over again, let him understand that the indulgence is already extended by anticipation to him. And now, friend Critias, I will announce to you the judgment of the theatre. They are of opinion that the last performer was wonderfully successful, and that you will need a great deal of indulgence if you are to rival him.

Hermocrates. The warning, Socrates, which you have addressed to him, I must also regard as applying to myself. But remember, Critias, that faint heart never yet raised a trophy; you must go and attack the argument like a man. First invoke Apollo and the Muses, and then let us hear you sing the praises of your ancient citizens.

Crit. Friend Hermocrates, you who are stationed last and have another in front of you, have not lost heart as yet; whether you are right or not, you will soon know; meanwhile I accept your exhortations and encouragements. But in addition to the gods whom you have mentioned, I would specially invoke Mnemosyne; for all the important part of what I have to tell is dependent on her favour, and if I can recollect and recite enough of what was said by the priests and brought hither by Solon, I doubt not that I shall satisfy the requirements of this theatre. To that task then I will at once address myself.

Let me begin by observing first of all, that nine thousand was the sum of years which had elapsed since the war which was said to have taken place between all those who dwelt outside the pillars of Heracles and those who dwelt within them; this war I am now to describe. Of the combatants on the one side, the city of Athens was reported to have been the ruler and to have directed the contest; the combatants on the other side were led by the kings of the islands of Atlantis, which, as I was saying, once had an extent greater than that of Libya and Asia; and when afterwards sunk by an earthquake, became an impassable barrier of mud to voyagers
109 sailing from hence to the ocean. The progress of the history will unfold the various tribes of barbarians and Hellenes which then existed, as they successively appear on the scene; but I must begin by describing first of all the Athenians, as they were in that day, and their enemies who fought with them; and I shall have to tell of the power and form of government of both of them. Let us give the precedence to Athens:

In former ages, the gods had the whole earth distributed among them by allotment; there was no quarrelling; and you cannot suppose that the gods did not know what was proper for each of them to have; or, knowing this, that they would seek to procure for themselves by contention that which more properly belonged to others. Each of them obtained righteously by lot what they wanted, and peopled their own districts; and when they had peopled them they tended us human beings who belonged to them

as shepherds tend their flocks, excepting only that they did not use
blows or bodily force, as the manner of shepherds is, but governed
us like pilots from the stern of a vessel, which is an easy way of
guiding animals, by the rudder of persuasion, taking hold of our
souls according to their own pleasure;—thus did they guide all
mortal creatures.   Now different gods had their inheritance in
different places which they set in order.   Hephaestus and Athene,
who were brother and sister, and sprang from the same father,
having a common nature, and being united also in the love of philosophy and of art, both obtained as their allotted region this land,
which was naturally adapted for wisdom and virtue; and there
they implanted brave children of the soil, and put into their minds
the order of government; their names are preserved, but their
actions have disappeared by reason of the destruction of those who
had the tradition, and the lapse of ages.   For the survivors of each
destruction, as I have already said, dwelt in the mountains; they
were ignorant of the art of writing, and had heard only the names
of the chiefs of the land, and a very little about their actions.   The
names they gave to their children out of affection, but of the virtues and laws of those who preceded them, they knew only by
obscure traditions; and as they themselves and their children were
for many generations in want of the necessaries of life, they directed
their attention to the supply of their wants, and of that they discoursed, to the neglect of events that had happened in times long
passed; for mythology and the enquiry into antiquity are intro- 110
duced into cities when they have leisure, and when they see the
necessaries of life already beginning to be provided, but not before.
And this is the reason why the names of the ancients have been
preserved to us without their deeds.   This I infer because Solon
said that the priests in their narrative of that war mentioned most
of the names which are recorded prior to the time of Theseus,
such as Cecrops, and Erechtheus, and Erichthonius, and Erysichthon,
and the names of the women in like manner.   Moreover, the
figure and image of the goddess show that at that time military
pursuits were common to men and women, and that in accordance
with that custom they dedicated the armed image of the goddess
as a testimony that all animals, male and female, which consort
together, have a virtue proper to each class, which they are all able
to pursue in common.

Now the country was inhabited in those days by various classes of citizens;—there were artizans, and there were husbandmen, and there was a warrior class originally set apart by divine men; these dwelt by themselves, and had all things suitable for nurture and education; neither had any of them anything of their own, but they regarded all things as common property; nor did they require to receive of the other citizens anything more than their necessary food. And they practised all the pursuits which we yesterday described as those of our imaginary guardians. Also about the country the Egyptian priests said what is not only probable but also true, that the boundaries were fixed by the Isthmus, and that in the other direction they extended as far as the heights of Cithaeron and Parnes; the boundary line came down towards the plain, having the district of Oropus on the right, and the river Asopus on the left, as the limit towards the sea. The land was the best in the world, and for this reason was able in those days to support a vast army, raised from the surrounding people. And a great proof of this fertility is, that the part which still remains may compare with any in the world for the variety and excellence of its fruits and the suitableness of its pastures to every sort of
III animal; and besides beauty the land had also plenty. How am I to prove this? and of what remnant of the land then in existence may this be truly said? I would have you observe the present aspect of the country, which is only a promontory extending far into the sea away from the rest of the continent, and the surrounding basin of the sea is everywhere deep in the neighbourhood of the shore. Many great deluges have taken place during the nine thousand years, for that is the number of years which have elapsed since the time of which I am speaking; and in all the ages and changes of things, there has never been any settlement of the earth flowing down from the mountains as in other places, which is worth speaking of; it has always been carried round in a circle and disappeared in the depths below. The consequence is, that in comparison of what then was, there are remaining in small islets only the bones of the wasted body, as they may be called; all the richer and softer parts of the soil having fallen away, and the mere skeleton of the country being left. But in former days, and in the primitive state of the country, what are now mountains were only regarded as hills; and the plains, as they are now termed, of Phelleus were

full of rich earth, and there was abundance of wood in the mountains. Of this last the traces still remain, for there are some of the
mountains which now only afford sustenance to bees, whereas not
long ago there were still remaining roofs cut from the trees growing
there, which were of a size sufficient to cover the largest houses;
and there were many other high trees, bearing fruit and abundance
of food for cattle. Moreover, the land enjoyed rain from heaven
year by year, not, as now, losing the water which flows off the
earth into the sea, but having an abundance in all places, and
receiving and treasuring up in the close clay soil the water which
drained from the heights, and letting this off into the hollows,
providing everywhere abundant streams of fountains and rivers;
and there may still be observed indications of them in ancient
sacred places, where there are fountains; and this proves the
truth of what I am saying.

Such was the natural state of the country, which was cultivated,
as we may well believe, by true husbandmen, who were lovers of
honour, and of a noble nature, and did the work of husbandmen,
and had a soil the best in the world, and abundance of water, and
in the heaven above an excellently tempered climate. Now the
city in those days was arranged on this wise; in the first place the
Acropolis was not as now. For the fact is that a single night of 112
excessive rain washed away the earth and laid bare the rock; at
the same time there were earthquakes, and then occurred the third
extraordinary inundation, which immediately preceded the great
destruction of Deucalion. But in primitive times the hill of the
Acropolis extended to the Eridanus and Ilissus, and included the
Pnyx and the Lycabettus as a boundary on the opposite side to
the Pnyx, and was all well covered with soil, and level at the top,
except in one or two places. Outside the Acropolis and on the
sides of the hill there dwelt artizans, and such of the husbandmen
as were tilling the ground near; at the summit the warrior class
dwelt by themselves around the temples of Athene and Hephaestus,
living as in the garden of one house, and surrounded by one enclosure. On the north side they had common houses, and had prepared for themselves winter places for common meals, and had all
the buildings which they needed for the public use, and also
temples, but unadorned with gold and silver, for these were not in
use among them; they took a middle course between meanness

and extravagance, and built moderate houses in which they and their children's children grew old, and handed them down to others who were like themselves, always the same. And in summer-time they gave up their gardens and gymnasia and common tables and used the southern quarter of the Acropolis for such purposes. Where the Acropolis now is there was a single fountain, which was extinguished by the earthquake, and has left only a few small streams which still exist, but in those days the fountain gave an abundant supply of water, which was of equal temperature in summer and winter. This was the fashion in which they lived, being the guardians of their own citizens and the leaders of the Hellenes, who were their willing followers. And they took care to preserve the same number of men and women for military service, which was to continue through all time, and still is,—that is to say, about twenty thousand. Such were the ancient Athenians, and after this manner they righteously administered their own land and the rest of Hellas; they were renowned all over Europe and Asia for the beauty of their persons and for the many virtues of their souls, and were more famous than any of their contemporaries. And next, if I have not forgotten what I heard when I was a child, I will impart to you the character and origin of their adversaries. For friends should not keep their stories to themselves, but have them in common.

13 Yet, before proceeding further in the narrative, I ought to warn you, that you must not be surprised if you should hear Hellenic names given to foreigners. I will tell you the reason of this: Solon, who was intending to use the tale for his poem, made an investigation into the meaning of the names, and found that the early Egyptians in writing them down had translated them into their own language, and he recovered the meaning of the several names and re-translated them, and copied them out again in our language. My great grandfather, Dropidas, had the original writing, which is still in my possession, and was carefully studied by me when I was a child. Therefore if you hear names such as are used in this country, you must not be surprised, for I have told you the reason of them. The tale, which was of great length, began as follows:—

I have before remarked in speaking of the allotments of the gods, that they distributed the whole earth into portions differing

in extent, and made themselves temples and sacrifices. And Poseidon, receiving for his lot the island of Atlantis, begat children by
a mortal woman, and settled them in a part of the island, which I
will proceed to describe. On the side towards the sea and in the
centre of the whole island, there was a plain which is said to have
been the fairest of all plains and very fertile. Near the plain
again, and also in the centre of the island at a distance of about
fifty stadia, there was a mountain not very high on any side. In
this mountain there dwelt one of the earth-born primeval men of
that country, whose name was Evenor, and he had a wife named
Leucippe, and they had an only daughter who was called Cleito. The
maiden was growing up to womanhood, when her father and mother
died; Poseidon fell in love with her and had intercourse with her,
and breaking the ground, inclosed the hill in which she dwelt all
round, making alternate zones of sea and land larger and smaller,
encircling one another; there were two of land and three of water,
which he turned as with a lathe, out of the centre of the island,
equidistant every way, so that no man could get to the island, for
ships and voyages were not as yet heard of. He himself, as he
was a god, found no difficulty in making special arrangements for
the centre island, bringing two streams of water under the earth,
which he caused to ascend as springs, one of warm water and the
other of cold, and making every variety of food to spring up abundantly in the earth. He also begat and brought up five pairs of
male children, dividing the island of Atlantis into ten portions;
he gave to the first-born of the eldest pair his mother's dwelling 114
and the surrounding allotment, which was the largest and best, and
made him king over the rest; the others he made princes, and
gave them rule over many men, and a large territory. And he
named them all; the eldest, who was the king, he named Atlas,
and from him the whole island and the ocean received the name
of Atlantic. To his twin brother, who was born after him, and
obtained as his lot the extremity of the island towards the pillars
of Heracles, as far as the country which is still called the region of
Gades in that part of the world, he gave the name which in the
Hellenic language is Eumelus, in the language of the country
which is named after him, Gadeirus. Of the second pair of twins
he called one Ampheres, and the other Evaemon. To the third
pair of twins he gave the name Mneseus to the elder, and

Autochthon to the one who followed him. Of the fourth pair of twins he called the elder Elasippus, and the younger Mestor. And of the fifth pair he gave to the elder the name of Azaes, and to the younger that of Diaprepes. All these and their descendants were the inhabitants and rulers of divers islands in the open sea; and also, as has been already said, they held sway in the other direction over the country within the pillars as far as Egypt and Tyrrhenia. Now Atlas had a numerous and honourable family, and his eldest branch always retained the kingdom, which the eldest son handed on to his eldest for many generations; and they had such an amount of wealth as was never before possessed by kings and potentates, and is not likely ever to be again, and they were furnished with everything which they could have, both in the city and country. For because of the greatness of their empire many things were brought to them from foreign countries, and the island itself provided much of what was required by them for the uses of life. In the first place, they dug out of the earth whatever was to be found there, mineral as well as metal, and that which is now only a name and was then something more than a name, orichalcum, was dug out of the earth in many parts of the island, and with the exception of gold was esteemed the most precious of metals among the men of those days. There was an abundance of wood for carpenter's work, and sufficient maintenance for tame and wild animals. Moreover, there were a great number of ele-
115 phants in the island, and there was provision for animals of every kind, both for those which live in lakes and marshes and rivers, and also for those which live in mountains and on plains, and therefore for the animal which is the largest and most voracious of them. Also whatever fragrant things there are in the earth, whether roots, or herbage, or woods, or distilling drops of flowers or fruits, grew and thrived in that land; and again, the cultivated fruit of the earth, both the dry edible fruit and other species of food, which we call by the general name of legumes, and the fruits having a hard rind, affording drinks and meats and ointments, and good store of chestnuts and the like, which may be used to play with, and are fruits which spoil with keeping, and the pleasant kinds of dessert, which console us after dinner, when we are full and tired of eating—all these that sacred island lying beneath the sun, brought forth fair and wondrous in infinite abundance. All

these things they received from the earth, and they employed
themselves in constructing their temples and palaces and harbours
and docks; and they arranged the whole country in the following
manner:—

First of all they bridged over the zones of sea which surrounded
the ancient metropolis, and made a passage into and out of the
royal palace; and then they began to build the palace in the
habitation of the god and of their ancestors. This they continued
to ornament in successive generations, every king surpassing
the one who came before him to the utmost of his power, until
they made the building a marvel to behold for size and for beauty.
And beginning from the sea they dug a canal of three hundred feet
in width and one hundred feet in depth, and fifty stadia in length,
which they carried through to the outermost zone, making a passage from the sea up to this, which became a harbour, and leaving
an opening sufficient to enable the largest vessels to find ingress.
Moreover, they divided the zones of land which parted the zones of
sea, constructing bridges of such a width as would leave a passage
for a single trireme to pass out of one into another, and roofed
them over; and there was a way underneath for the ships; for the
banks of the zones were raised considerably above the water.
Now the largest of the zones into which a passage was cut from
the sea was three stadia in breadth, and the zone of land which
came next of equal breadth; but the next two, as well the zone
of water as of land, were two stadia, and the one which surrounded
the central island was a stadium only in width. The island in 116
which the palace was situated had a diameter of five stadia. This
and the zones and the bridge, which was the sixth part of a
stadium in width, they surrounded by a stone wall, on either side
placing towers, and gates on the bridges where the sea passed in.
The stone which was used in the work they quarried from underneath the centre island, and from underneath the zones, on the
outer as well as the inner side. One kind of stone was white,
another black, and a third red, and as they quarried, they at the
same time hollowed out docks double within, having roofs formed
out of the native rock. Some of their buildings were simple,
but in others they put together different stones which they intermingled for the sake of ornament, to be a natural source of
delight. The entire circuit of the wall, which went round the

outermost one, they covered with a coating of brass, and the circuit of the next wall they coated with tin, and the third, which encompassed the citadel, flashed with the red light of orichalcum. The palaces in the interior of the citadel were constructed on this wise:—In the centre was a holy temple dedicated to Cleito and Poseidon, which remained inaccessible, and was surrounded by an enclosure of gold; this was the spot in which they originally begat the race of the ten princes, and thither they annually brought the fruits of the earth in their season from all the ten portions, and performed sacrifices to each of them. Here, too, was Poseidon's own temple of a stadium in length, and half a stadium in width, and of a proportionate height, having a sort of barbaric splendour. All the outside of the temple, with the exception of the pinnacles, they covered with silver, and the pinnacles with gold. In the interior of the temple the roof was of ivory, adorned everywhere with gold and silver and orichalcum; all the other parts of the walls and pillars and floor they lined with orichalcum. In the temple they placed statues of gold—there was the god himself standing in a chariot—the charioteer of six winged horses—and of such a size that he touched the roof of the buildings with his head; around him there were a hundred Nereids riding on dolphins, for such was thought to be the number of them in that day. There were also in the interior of the temple other images which had been dedicated by private individuals. And around the temple on the outside were placed statues of gold of all the ten kings and of their wives, and there were many other great offerings both of kings and of private individuals, coming both from the city itself and the foreign cities over which they held sway. There was an altar too, which in size and workmanship corresponded to the rest of the work, and there were palaces, in like manner, which answered to the greatness of the kingdom, and the glory of the temple.

In the next place, they used fountains both of cold and hot springs; these were very abundant, and both kinds [1] wonderfully adapted to use by reason of the sweetness and excellence of their waters. They constructed buildings about them and planted suitable trees; also cisterns, some open to the heaven, others which

---

[1] Reading ἑκατέρου πρὸς τὴν χρῆσιν.

they roofed over, to be used in winter as warm baths; there were the king's baths, and the baths of private persons, which were kept apart; also separate baths for women, and others again for horses and cattle, and to each of them they gave as much adornment as was suitable for them. The water which ran off they carried, some to the grove of Poseidon, where were growing all manner of trees of wonderful height and beauty, owing to the excellence of the soil; the remainder was conveyed by aqueducts which passed over the bridges to the outer circles; and there were many temples built and dedicated to many gods; also gardens and places of exercise, some for men, and some set apart for horses, in both of the two islands formed by the zones; and in the centre of the larger of the two there was a race-course of a stadium in width, and in length allowed to extend all round the island, for horses to race in. Also there were guard-houses at intervals for the body-guard, the more trusted of whom had their duties appointed to them in the lesser zone, which was nearer the Acropolis; while the most trusted of all had houses given them within the citadel, and about the persons of the kings. The docks were full of tri-remes and naval stores, and all things were quite ready for use. Enough of the plan of the royal palace. Crossing the outer har-bours, which were three in number, you would come to a wall which began at the sea and went all round: this was everywhere distant fifty stadia from the largest zone and harbour, and enclosed the whole, meeting at the mouth of the channel towards the sea. The entire area was densely crowded with habitations; and the canal and the largest of the harbours were full of vessels and merchants coming from all parts, who, from their numbers, kept up a multitudinous sound of human voices and din of all sorts night and day.

I have repeated his descriptions of the city and the parts about the ancient palace nearly as he gave them, and now I must endea-vour to describe the nature and arrangement of the rest of the 118 country. The whole country was described as being very lofty and precipitous on the side of the sea, but the country immediately about and surrounding the city was a level plain, itself surrounded by mountains which descended towards the sea; it was smooth and even, but of an oblong shape, extending in one direction three thousand stadia, and going up the country from the sea, through the centre of the island, two thousand stadia; the whole region of the island lies towards the south, and is sheltered from the north. The surrounding mountains he celebrated for their number and size and beauty, in which they exceeded all that are now to be seen anywhere; having in them also many wealthy inhabited villages, and rivers, and lakes, and meadows supplying food enough for every animal, wild or tame, and wood of various sorts, abundant for every kind of work.

I will now describe the plain, which had been cultivated during many ages by many generations of kings. It was rectangular, and for the most part straight and oblong; and what it wanted of the straight line followed the line of the circular ditch. The depth, and width, and length of this ditch were incredible, and gave the impression that such a work, in addition to so many other works, could hardly have been wrought by the hand of man. But I must say what I have heard. It was excavated to the depth of a hundred feet, and its breadth was a stadium everywhere; it was carried round the whole of the plain, and was ten thousand stadia in length. It received the streams which came down from the mountains, and winding round the plain and touching the city at various points, was there let off into the sea. From above, likewise, straight canals of a hundred feet in width were cut in the plain, and again let off into the ditch towards the sea: these canals were at intervals of an hundred stadia, and by them they brought down the wood from the mountains to the city, and conveyed the fruits of the earth in ships, cutting transverse passages from one canal into another, and to the city. Twice in the year they gathered the fruits of the earth—in winter having the benefit of the rains, and in summer introducing the water of the canals.

As to the population, each of the lots in the plain had an appointed chief of men who were fit for military service, and the 119 size of the lot was to be a square of ten stadia each way, and the total number of all the lots was sixty thousand. And of the inhabitants of the mountains and of the rest of the country there was also a vast multitude having leaders, to whom they were assigned according to their dwellings and villages. The leader was required to furnish for the war the sixth portion of a war-chariot, so as to make up a total of ten thousand chariots; also two horses and riders upon them, and a light chariot without a seat, accompanied by a fighting man on foot carrying a small shield, and having a charioteer mounted to guide the horses; also, he was bound to furnish two heavy armed, two archers, two slingers, three stone-shooters, and three javelin-men, who were skirmishers, and four sailors to make up the complement of twelve hundred ships. Such was the order of war in the royal city—that of the other nine governments was different in each of them, and would be wearisome to narrate.

As to offices and honours, the following was the arrangement from the first. Each of the ten kings in his own division and in his own city had the absolute control of the citizens, and in many cases, of the laws, punishing and slaying whomsoever he would. Now the relations of their governments to one another were regulated by the injunctions of Poseidon as the law had handed them down. These were inscribed by the first men on a column of orichalcum, which was situated in the middle of the island, at the temple of Poseidon, whither the people were gathered together every fifth and sixth years alternately, thus giving equal honour to the odd and to the even number. And when they were gathered together they consulted about public affairs, and enquired if any one had transgressed in anything, and passed judgment on him accordingly, and before they passed judgment they gave their pledges to one another on this wise:—There were bulls who had the range of the temple of Poseidon; and the ten who were left alone in the temple, after they had offered prayers to the gods that they might take the sacrifices which were acceptable to them, hunted the bulls, without weapons, but with staves and nooses; and the bull which they caught they led up to the column; the victim was then struck on the head by them and slain over the sacred inscription. Now on the column, besides the law, there was inscribed an oath invoking mighty curses on the disobedient. When therefore, after offering sacrifice according to their customs, they had burnt the limbs of the bull, they mingled a cup and cast in a clot 120 of blood for each of them; the rest of the victim they took to the fire, after having made a purification of the column all round. Then they drew from the cup in golden vessels, and pouring a libation on the fire, they swore that they would judge according to the laws on the column, and would punish any one who had previously transgressed, and that for the future they would not, if they could help, transgress any of the inscriptions, and would not command or obey any ruler who commanded them, to act otherwise than according to the laws of their father Poseidon. This was the prayer which each of them offered up for himself and for his family, at the same time drinking and dedicating the vessel in the temple of the god, and after spending some necessary time at supper, when darkness came on, and the fire about the sacrifice was cool, all of them put on most beautiful azure robes, and, sitting on the ground, at night, near the embers of the sacrifices on which they had sworn, and extinguishing all the fire about the temple, they received and gave judgment, if any of them had any accusation to bring against any one; and when they had given judgment, at daybreak they wrote down their sentences on a golden tablet, and deposited them as memorials with their robes.

There were many special laws which the several kings had inscribed about the temples, but the most important was the following: That they were not to take up arms against one another, and they were all to come to the rescue if any one in any city attempted to overthrow the royal house; like their ancestors, they were to deliberate in common about war and other matters, giving the supremacy to the family of Atlas. And the king was not to have the power of life and death over any of his kinsmen unless he had the assent of the majority of the ten kings.

Such was the vast power which the god settled in the lost island of Atlantis; and this he afterwards directed against our land on the following pretext, as traditions tell: For many generations, as long as the divine nature lasted in them, they were obedient to the laws, and well-affectioned towards the gods, who were their kinsmen; for they possessed true and in every way great spirits, practising gentleness and wisdom in the various chances of life, and in their intercourse with one another. They despised everything but virtue, not caring for their present state of life, and thinking lightly of the possession of gold and other property, which seemed only a burden to them; neither were they intoxicated by luxury; nor did wealth deprive them of their self-control; but they were sober, and saw clearly that all these goods are increased by virtuous friendship with one another, and that by excessive zeal for them, and honour of them, the good of them is lost and friendship perishes with them. By such reflections and by the continuance in them of a divine nature, all that which we have described waxed and increased in them; but when this divine portion began to fade away in them, and became diluted too often and with too much of the mortal admixture, and the human nature got the upper hand, then they, being unable to bear their fortune, became unseemly, and to him who had an eye to see, they began to appear base, and had lost the fairest of their precious gifts; but to those who had no eye to see the true happiness, they still appeared glorious and blessed at the very time when they were filled with unrighteous avarice and power. Zeus, the god of gods, who rules with law, and is able to see into such things, perceiving that an honourable race was in a most wretched state, and wanting to inflict punishment on them, that they might be chastened and improve, collected all the gods into his most holy habitation, which being placed in the centre of the world, sees all things that partake of generation. And when he had called them together, he spake as follows :—

LaVergne, TN USA
19 November 2010
205507LV00003B/3/P